THE LANDSCAPE TRILOGY

~

THE AUTOBIOGRAPHY OF

L.T.C. ROLT

INTRODUCTION BY SONIA ROLT

SUTTON PUBLISHING

Landscape with Machines first published in 1971
First published by Sutton Publishing Limited in 1984

Landscape with Canals first published in 1977
First published by Sutton Publishing Limited in 1984

Landscape with Figures first published in 1992 by
Sutton Publishing Limited

This combined edition first published in 2001 by
Sutton Publishing Limited

This paperback edition first published in 2005 by
Sutton Publishing Limited · Phoenix Mill
Thrupp · Stroud · Gloucestershire · GL5 2BU

British Library Cataloguing in Publication Data
A catalogue record for this book is available from the
British Library

ISBN 0 7509 4139 1

Printed and bound in Great Britain by
J.H. Haynes & Co. Ltd, Sparkford.

List of Plates

Picture Acknowledgements

Thanks are due to the following for granting reproduction permission: Mrs Barbara Curwen, pls 6 and 7; the Montagu Motor Museum (W.J. Brunell Collection), pl. 9; James Brymer, pl. 10; Eric de Maré, pl. 11; the *Illustrated London News*, pl. 12; the Estate of Angela Rolt, pls 13 and 14; John Snell, pl. 17; P.B. Whitehouse, pl. 18; John Adams, pl. 19; *Autocar*, pl. 20; Michael Charity, pl. 26. The rest of the plates are from the author's collection.

Foreword

I wonder how Polonius would have described L.T.C.
Rolt's *The Landscape Trilogy* had he been called upon to
introduce it to the court at Elsinore?

> 'The best commentator in the land, either for
> history, biography, technology; poetical, poetical-
> practical, visionary-poetical, romantic-historical-
> technical-pastoral . . .'

Maybe. For though there are professional writers with an
interest in engineering, as well as qualified engineers with a
gift for putting pen to paper, literary engineering cognoscenti
who are also elegant philosophers are actually pretty rare. In
his autobiography, the questing, energetic Tom Rolt accepts
that Man, uniquely equipped to understand the mechanism
of the world, has also the power to tinker with the works,
with possibly disastrous consequences. While tirelessly
campaigning for the retention of a particular building, the
preservation of a piece of machinery, or the salvation of a
particular craft skill, he never loses sight of the possibility that
our well-meaning labour might just result in a serious offence
to the natural environment.

I never actually met Tom (I feel, through having known
Sonia, his widow, for some years, that I might be allowed to
call him Tom) although I only just missed sight of him when
as a schoolboy enthusiast I visited the then practically
inoperative Talyllyn Railway in west Wales, just as he was
leading a small group of pioneers to rescue the 140-year-old
line and establish it as the very first railway in Britain to be

run by a preservation society as a going concern. The success of the experiment spread among enthusiasts like wildfire, of course; today there are nearly sixty such undertakings dotted around the United Kingdom.

In his first book, *Narrow Boat*, Tom Rolt introduced to us his fascination with the British canal system and the floating home upon which, later in *The Landscape Trilogy*, he explores its waters, charts the growth of the Inland Waterways Association, and gives us a preview of the vast programme of canal restoration and development that has now assumed the status of a significant tourist industry. A major renaissance, due very largely to the author of this thoughtful, entertaining, surprising and often hazardous adventure story.

Timothy West
March 2005

Introduction to
The Landscape Trilogy

Old or new readers of the books of L.T.C. (Tom) Rolt might want to know how a series of autobiographical volumes would finally achieve, in this one combined edition, the status of a single life.

Tom, my husband, lived to see the first book, *Landscape with Machines*, published in 1971 by Longman, the publishing house to which he gave his chief loyalty. It was praised, and he knew that it had given pleasure, not only to many of those who wrote to say that he had shown them an unusual life of its time and class – aspects of which echoed their own – and of a kind which had not previously been expressed.

More to the point, and more markedly than many of his books, it was to be for himself. It was his intention to write on, to complete the story of his life. He was sixty. He had mentioned, not perhaps intimations of death, but intimations of it being the time to do it. With deference to the high claim and assumptions of all autobiographical writing he had wanted to put his own order upon the backward look.

It was not too soon. His friend Felix Kelly, the artist, had brought to him recently as a present a delightful small painting evocative of memories such as were being aroused of those earliest days of apprenticeship in agricultural engineering in the Vale of Evesham. Here a dream procession of the great steam-ploughing engines with mud-caked wheels in majesty clanks, grinds and smokes its way over the brow. It was used as the cover image for that first volume and seems perfect for both Tom and the book.

Alas, those intimations. In the spring of 1972 indications that his physical life was to present an ordeal meant that the second volume was tackled, after some recovery, under pressure to complete it.

The book, which was named *Landscape with Canals*, covers a happy and sad period which had started with his marriage and the boat *Cressy* and high and romantic hopes. It included the story of the publication of *Narrow Boat* and of all the early efforts and campaigning, the start of the great movement which ensures we have a canal system today, a canal system whose present policies and ideals now are to a large extent the outcome of that early vision. In the end the campaigning ate up Tom's first marriage and the author felt it would eat up the writer, and it all came to an end.

Another Felix Kelly picture had been painted for an early 1970s exhibition. It was inspired by all this, the boat *Cressy* and Tom's enthusiasm and involvement in another subject – narrow gauge railways, and the Talyllyn Railway in particular, which Tom was instrumental with others in saving – and it became the cover for the second book.

He wrote on, more or less until his life ended in early May 1974, when at last the winter was over and the swifts came again. Chapter succeeded chapter, the episodes of his life, the subjects and things that he loved, giving them form. Finally he summed up, having heard he was to go soon. It seemed best to let this manuscript rest, this episodic narrative, so personal an effort to roll up a life to a whole.

It was nearly two decades later that a particular publisher, an admirer, a fan, a persistent pursuer, coaxed me to allow him to read the text. I was persuaded then to allow the questions to be answered, that it would not diminish what had gone before and was a fitting conclusion to the story. We changed the manuscript title, 'Gifts of Gradual Time', to *Landscape with Figures* to make it unmistakably a linked trilogy. A venial sin, I hope. Felix Kelly's painting of the Steam Fair was kindly lent, to create a cover.

Now in, and on, a single volume. Tom had said to a friend 'I have had a happy life'. The diversity of that life, with its pleasures and pains, its loves and enthusiasms, amused and amusing, and above all its noble effort to make sense of its experiences, lies within these pages.

SONIA ROLT
Stanley Pontlarge, 2001

Landscape
with Machines

Contents

Foreword

This autobiography is intended to reflect the two sides of my own nature and the varied interests that have stemmed from them. They have often been at war with each other and have seldom achieved more than an uneasy truce. For this reason I have never found myself a particularly easy person to live with; I ask myself too many awkward questions.

That small minority who care for such things have for years been fighting to save something of the beauties of England and the English Tradition from the barbarity and philistinism of science and technology. Whose side am I on? There has never been any doubt in my mind, but I fear that, in this conflict which reflects the conflict within myself, I must seem to both sides an equivocal figure like that egregious vicar of Bray.

The battle is the more tragic because the gulf of non-understanding between the two sides seems to be so unbridgeable. For this reason, this book may fall with a dull thud in the no-man's-land between the two opposing forces. I wonder ruefully whether it should not be printed in two colours or two contrasting type faces, thus enabling each side to skip the part they prefer to ignore. but that would be to admit defeat in a desperate situation. For where there is no mutual understanding there can be no hope of remedy.

L. T. C. R.

Of dying man
His living mind
By writing deeds
His Children find.

*Inscription over a cottage doorway
at Welcombe, North Devon*

Part I

Chapter 1

Poverty, Powder and Gold

No one with any sense of place could fail to be aware that Chester is a Roman city. To stand on the red rampart of its walls and look south-westward over the great defensive loop of the Dee towards the blue mountains of Wales on the far horizon is to comprehend the reason for the city's foundation as a legionary fortress. Chester, like its counterpart Caerleon-upon-Usk at the opposite end of the Welsh Border, was a stronghold of Imperial Rome, designed to impose the Pax Romana on the turbulent mountain country of the Celt. It was in this ancient city that I was born and it was on the Welsh March between Chester and Caerleon that the most impressionable years of my childhood were spent.

My birthplace, and my home for the first four years of my life, was a house in Eaton Road in what was then the respectable outer suburban fringe of the city, poised between extremes of wealth and poverty. Eaton Road follows part of the line of a Roman highway. Heading due south, this passes through the village of Eccleston and by Eaton Hall, then the seat of the Duke of Westminster, a vast, pretentious Victorian pile by Alfred Waterhouse whose demolition even the most enthusiastic devotee of nineteenth-century architecture could scarcely lament. Northwards, the road went through the parish of Handbridge, falling steeply towards the old sandstone bridge over the Dee, and thence entered the city by the south gate. On the right of the road as it stooped towards the bridge there was then a malodorous huddle of slum property which I suspect had once housed a colony of Dee fisherfolk but had since become notorious for its squalor. The crumbling brick cottages, leaning crazily against one another as though for mutual support, appeared in imminent danger of plunging down the steep slope towards the river in a torrent of rotten brick and shattered slates.

When pushing me in my pram towards the city, my nurse

3

always hurried past this squalid rookery with averted eyes, clinging to the opposite side of the road. Sometimes, if the odour of poverty was particularly strong, she would spit upon the pavement and enjoin me urgently to do likewise. 'Spit! Spit!', she would hiss at me. I realise now that this strange ritual was a survival of those pre-Pasteur Victorian days when the frightful epidemics of cholera and typhus were attributed to what was politely called 'the miasma'. Spitting was not a superstitious warding off of the evil eye, but a practical precaution to prevent one swallowing the supposedly deadly stench. Another precaution of my nurse's which I remember was the spreading of sheets of newspaper on the seats of railway carriages before one sat down.

On one occasion when we were scuttling past Handbridge, I recall seeing two middle-aged women fighting viciously on the pavement opposite before an audience of rough looking men who lounged in cottage doorways, jeering and egging them on. Their work-worn, dirty hands were hooked like a hawk's talons as they clawed at each other's eyes or tore at the ragged curtains of greying hair that hung loose over their faces. Not surprisingly, this scene of primitive violence was indelibly imprinted on my infant mind.

Other random recollections emerge from the dark glass of these earliest years. One is of a journey by motorcycle combination with my father and mother—quite a venturesome one it must have been in those days—to take luncheon with my great-uncles and aunt, brothers and sister to my paternal grandmother 'Grannie Garnett'. Four bachelor brothers, they lived together in a great square house of blackened stone known as Wyreside Hall in the Lancashire Pennines above Garstang with their spinster sister 'Aunt Louis' to preside over the household. One of them was a director of the London and North Western Railway and wore his director's gold pass on his watch chain. And a most potent talisman it was, for at his bidding even the lordliest West Coast Scotch express would stop at the little wayside station of Bay Horse to pick him up. But their lives at Wyreside seem to have been mainly devoted to shooting on the moors and fishing the waters of the Wyre.

Of that awesome family luncheon party I remember only one thing: the footmen who waited at table. With their powdered wigs, velvet breeches, white stockings and buckled shoes, they were far more attractive to my childish eye than my great-uncles and aunt of whom I have not the slightest recollection. I discovered much later, however, that they formed my only tenuous family link with engineering history, for their father, Henry Garnett, had been the financial partner of the celebrated James Nasmyth, inventor of the steam hammer, in his famous engineering business at the Bridgewater Foundry, Patricroft. Nasmyth referred to him as: 'my excellent friend Henry Garnett, Esq., of Wyre Side, near Lancaster. He had been my sleeping partner or "Co." for nearly twenty years, and the most perfect harmony always existed between us.'[1] It was in memory of this happy association that one of my great-uncles was christened Frank Nasmyth.

But I think my earliest recollection of all was of the silver half-sovereign case that my father habitually wore on one end of his watch chain. He would draw it from his waistcoat pocket, press the catch which released the spring lid, and hold it out for my investigation. As my questing forefinger slid out one of the little golden coins, another would move up to replace it, impelled by the action of the spring beneath. It seemed to me a magic box, ever brim-full with an inexhaustible fount of gold.

These three recollections, of ragged women fighting in the street, of powdered footmen and gold coins, preserved by chance from these my earliest years in the rag-bag of the mind, seem now to be strangely apposite, typifying for me the world into which I was born in February 1910, a world destined so soon to vanish utterly away. That a social conscience was already astir was something I only learned later from the history books. From those about me I accepted such evidences of the extremes of wealth and poverty as something inevitable like sunlight or storm. They were part of the unalterable common lot of man; the outward manifestations of innate inequality.

Of the grown-ups among whom I moved, I saw and remember little of my mother's family. They were not very thick upon the ground anyway. For my maternal grandmother was an orphan who had married at an early age an obscure elderly gentleman named Clarke of Cogshall Hall near Comberbatch where my mother Jemima and her only sister, my aunt Augusta, were born in quick succession. After achieving this remarkable feat— he was over seventy years of age at the time—Mr Clarke understandably passed away. This frustrated the optimistic hopes of my grandmother's guardian who, it is said, had made the match in the expectation that she would provide an heir for

---

[1] James Nasmyth, *Autobiography*, pp. 371-2 f.

Cogshall. Long before I was born, my grandmother had taken as her second husband a dubious clergyman of good family named Timperley, of Hintlesham in Norfolk. He had objected strenuously but unavailingly to my father's marriage to his step-daughter, the reason being, as my father subsequently discovered, that the reverend gentleman had been cheerfully making away with the handsome dowry left to my mother by the munificent Mr Clarke.

Not surprisingly, therefore, with the exception of my aunt Augusta, my mother's family did not figure largely in my life. With the Rolts, however, it was quite otherwise for there was a positive legion of Rolt uncles and aunts. The two favourite pastimes of my grandfather, Thomas Francis Rolt, who died nine years before I was born, appear to have been hunting and procreation. He and his elder brother Henry, always known in my family as 'Uncle Hen.', were the only sons of Sir John Rolt, a mysteriously elusive Anglo-Irish figure of whom I gave some account in an earlier book.[1] My grandfather moved from house to house about the English Shires, sampling the pleasures of different hunting countries, accompanied by a string of hunters, a lengthening string of children and his long-suffering wife. Apparently, his brother, who was in holy orders, frequently upbraided him for what he considered the wanton extravagance of this way of life. He pointed out that his private means, supplemented only by the half-pay he received from his regiment (the Coldstream Guards), was not adequate to support both his horses and his family. Though this was patently true, it had no moderating influence whatsoever upon my grandfather. Judging from the indifferent education that my father received and his very meagre patrimony, the horses consumed the lion's share of the family fortunes.

It seems my grandfather had a particular fondness for the Heythrop country, for no less than six of his family of twelve, including my father, were born at Stow-on-the-Wold, between the years 1865 and 1874, in a house that stands back from the central square and is now a hotel. An earlier sojourn in Worcestershire proved far less successful, for the house the Rolts took in the village of Cropthorne was so heavily haunted that they were compelled to leave after only one child had been born there. Almost every night the family was awakened by the sound of heavy footfalls tramping up the stairs and through the cor-

[1] *Green and Silver*, 1949, p. 23.

ridors. This recurrent perambulation invariably ended with two resounding thumps from the attic, suggesting that the visitor had violently flung off a pair of heavy boots. My grandfather, who was no coward, lay in wait for the visitor, armed to the teeth, but although the footsteps passed him by, nothing could be seen. An untitled water-coloured drawing in one of my grandfather's numerous sketch books purports to show this haunted house, but I have not succeeded in identifying it on the ground. No doubt it was pulled down.

At a time when the more avant-garde were already using cameras, my grandfather preferred his pencil and water-colours. The many sketch books of his now in my possession are the equivalent of the family photograph album and contain portraits, hunting scenes and landscapes. The latter predominate to show that he travelled widely in Europe, Algeria and Morocco. One of these water-colour sketches appeals to me particularly. It was made early in his married life when he was living at Tor Grove, Plymouth, and it shows Brunel's great bridge over the Tamar under construction.

If the Edwardian world into which I was born appears as remote and fantastic as some half-remembered dream, the Rolt uncles and aunts with which my grandfather so liberally endowed me seem in recollection to belong to an extinct species. Their like does not exist today, certainly not in my experience. Perhaps this is just as well. An old nobleman once remarked to me sadly in 1947 that 'Today I am a hawk pursued by sparrows' and I fear that those Rolts would have found the modern world equally hostile—and not without justice. For some inexplicable reason, no blue-blooded aristocrats could have been more intensely proud of their ancestry and this gave them a sublime self-assurance which today would be regarded as intolerable. Each was enviably certain of the rightness of his own views on any subject, but as these opinions were seldom shared by brothers or sisters, when two or more Rolts were gathered together, loud voiced and animated arguments invariably developed. Such disputes were conducted in a strange dialect (gairl for girl, larndry for laundry, etc.) which had little in common with the so-called upper class accent of today and seems to have died out with their generation. Whereas my aunts all possessed unusually deep voices, curiously enough, those of my uncles were light and high-pitched. This trait was particularly marked in my uncle Wilfred who spoke in a high falsetto and was nicknamed 'Squeaker' in consequence. With his extremely long and narrow

7

face, I always looked upon Wilfred as a kind of caricature of a Rolt uncle in whom all the family characteristics were exaggerated. In old age he became so absent-minded that he frequently forgot where he had parked his car and used to invoke the aid of the police to help him to find it.

Serene self-confidence allied to the conviction that they knew best not infrequently involved my uncles and aunts in incidents which, even at that time, caused some consternation. Of these one example will suffice. On an occasion when my aunt Dorothy, a keen animal lover, was travelling by rail, her train drew up at a large station where she espied an unfortunate nanny goat, with a label round its neck, tethered to an awning column. Observing that this goat was in obvious discomfort, its udder swollen with milk which was dripping from its teats, she let down her compartment window with a bang and, leaning out, called in a loud clear voice which drew many passengers to the train windows: 'Porter! Can't you see that that goat needs milking? Attend to it at once!' Seeing that the porter only gazed at her in mute bewilderment, she threw open the carriage door, strode across the platform, hitched up her long skirts and, squatting down upon her haunches, proceeded to milk the goat, oblivious alike to her wondering audience and to the discomfiture of the guard, who stood by, fiddling nervously with his whistle, while little rivulets of milk flowed down the platform. Not until my aunt's errand of mercy was completed and she had regained her compartment could the train proceed on its way.

The surprising thing is that such imperious behaviour was not the product of great wealth. Thanks to my grandfather's profligacy, his children were left as poor as church mice. At the same time he took no steps to ensure that they could earn their livings in any gainful occupation. They were brought up to be ladies and gentlemen but were denied the means to be independent. That they were thus so severely handicapped can only have been due to that absurd Victorian snobbery that to be 'in trade' was unworthy of a gentleman. This attitude was wholly illogical since it would be difficult to find a Victorian gentleman without a tradesman or a business tycoon somewhere in his family tree. This was certainly true of the Rolts. Their ancestor Sir Thomas Rolt (d. 1722) of Sacomb Park, High Sheriff of Hertfordshire and 'President of India', whose portrait, wearing an extraordinary eastern costume, was painted by Reynolds, was certainly a successful, and probably unscrupulous, tycoon. But subsequent Rolt generations seem to have done little more than erode the fortune he amassed. As a start, they lost a packet when the South Sea Bubble burst.

Thus, although I liked and admired my Rolt uncles, I can now see that, lacking both money and training, they all led fairly unsatisfactory and frustrating lives. It is true that my uncle Vivian became quite a successful artist in water-colour and a member of the so-called 'Sussex School', a county in which he eventually settled; also that my uncle Harry, in the face of strong family disapproval, became an actor, appearing on the London stage under the name of Henry Bayntun though not with any conspicuous success. Uncle Harry's curious ability to consume the smoke of an entire cigarette and later to exhale it slowly through his ears was a source of considerable wonderment to me. He liked to perform the second part of this trick in the non-smoking compartments of trains to the consternation of his fellow passengers.

It was apparently in order for a gentleman to stoop to trade provided he was safely out of sight abroad, for both my uncles Neville and Wilfred became tea planters in Ceylon. But my favourite uncle Algernon was probably the most successful in the worldly sense. Somehow, I know not how, he obtained the job of tutor to the heir of the Maharajah of Cooch Behar, schooling him to the manners of an English gentleman. A strikingly handsome man, my uncle must have been well paid by the maharajah for he subsequently retired to London where he led a life of slightly raffish bachelordom as a man-about-town. I remember as a boy being taken by him on a visit to his first cousin Bernard Rolt who was a bird of somewhat similar feather and a close and devoted friend of Dame Nellie Melba. He is said to have been the only man who could cope with her tantrums with complete equanimity. In 1929 Bernard published a single novel, *Kings Bardon*, which I suspect, like many first novels, was partly autobiographical.

As for my father, Lionel, he went foot-loose about the world, gaining much varied experience but little profit. After working on an Australian cattle ranch and an indigo plantation in India, his last exploit was to set out on the famous 'Trail of '98' to the Yukon Territory. I have a faded photograph of him beside the shore of Great Slave Lake looking like a character in an early Western film, heavily bearded, guns in holsters at hip. I have two of those revolvers still, a ·38 Colt automatic and non-automatic Smith and Wesson of the same calibre. The ensuing sad story is related in the pages of his faded journal. Finding no gold and betrayed by his companions, he was left practically penniless in that bitter country but managed to make his way to Herschel Island. Here he was able to pick up a whaler on which he worked his passage back to civilisation and so home to his widowed mother who was by then living at Holly Bank, Christleton, near Chester. Five years later he married at the age of 39 and after another five years, in February 1910, I, his only child, was born.

Meanwhile my uncle Harry had left the stage and bought himself a house near Hay, Welsh Hay, or Hay-on-Wye as it is now called. Here he devoted the remainder of his life to the growing of roses, a hobby of which he was passionately fond. He sent us such glowing accounts of that country and of the fishing on the Wye that my father asked him to look for a suitable house in the district for us. Such a house was eventually found and, on the eve of the outbreak of war in August 1914, when I was four years old, we moved from Chester to the southern marches of Wales.

Chapter 2

Kilvert's Country

An important literary event occurred in July 1938 when the *Diary* of Francis Kilvert was published. As most people now know, from 1865 to 1872 Kilvert was curate at Clyro, a Radnorshire village just across the Wye from Hay. As a result of the acclaim with which this *Diary* was rightly received, Kilvert has become a minor literary celebrity and there is even a Kilvert Society whose members make an annual pilgrimage to what is now often referred to as Kilvert's Country. Naturally, when we moved into the Hay district in the fateful summer of 1914 this was all in the future and, so far as I know, we never even heard the name of Kilvert mentioned. Although this simple, kindly man was evidently beloved in his parish, his short life would have ended in oblivion had he not shyly recorded, with no thought of publication, his great love for the people and the landscape of this part of the Welsh Border.

Kilvert was neither the first nor the last man to be influenced by the powerful magic of this mountain country. I know that in my early boyhood its beauty and wildness was capable of inducing in me a strange feeling of intense exaltation that was part awed reverence and part terror. It could make my spine tingle and the hair on my head stand up. It was from such experiences and not from the teachings of any organised religion that there has stemmed my conviction that there is a God beyond human conceptions of good and evil. The reverse of this medal is that I believe these same experiences to be the source of my lifelong interest in supernatural evil. When, much later in life, I discovered the great mystical writings of the Silurist Henry Vaughan and his contemporary Thomas Traherne, I realised with shock of wonderment that they had been similarly influenced by the same landscape. And when, at about the same time, I read those short stories of Arthur Machen, *The Novel of the Black Seal,*

11

The Great God Pan, The Shining Pyramid and *The White People*,
I knew that he, born at Caerleon, had experienced its darker side.
Yet Machen also has expressed his belief 'that man is made a
mystery for mysteries and visions, for the realisation in his
consciousness of ineffable bliss, for a great joy that transmutes
the whole world, for a joy that surpasses all joys and overcomes
all sorrows'.

Although there are several references to Wordsworth in his
Diary, Kilvert never mentions Henry Vaughan, while Machen
was still unborn. As for Traherne, the seventeenth-century
incumbent of the nearby parish of Credenhill, he, like Kilvert
himself, enjoys a posthumous fame, for his greatest work, *The
Centuries of Meditations*, was only discovered by chance in 1895,
sixteen years after Kilvert's untimely death at Bredwardine. Yet
a single terse and otherwise inexplicable sentence: 'An angel
satyr walks these hills', which suddenly appears in his *Diary*
between mundane trivialities under the date 20 June 1871
reveals that Kilvert, too, was of this company. But whereas the
ordinary mortal cannot exist for very long on the mystical plane
that Vaughan and Traherne inhabit, the great merit of Kilvert's
Diary is that it is a faithful reflection of life itself in its rapid
shifts from pathos to bathos, from the sublime to the ridiculous
and from prose of visionary quality to homespun detail or
country gossip. It is for this reason and also because no other
book has the power to evoke such vivid memories of my childhood that his *Diary* has become one of my favourite bedside
books.

In 1914, so little had changed in the district during the forty-
four years that had passed since Kilvert wrote, that his world
became my world, and by this I mean not only the landscape
but the way of life of the folk who peopled it. The men and
women I remember, riding their sure-footed ponies down from
their lonely mountain farms to crowd the little streets of Hay
on market days, were still such people as Kilvert knew and
described so affectionately. Many of the local landowners and
middle-class families bore the same names as they did in his day,
and in summer they still joined forces in communal walks and
pinics such as he describes. I took part in many of these neigh-
bourly excursions. Even today, the district has changed less than
anywhere else I know outside western Ireland.

Kilvert's *Diary* has its darker side. Reading it, one cannot but
be aware that the writer was always acutely conscious of life's
transience. It could scarcely have been otherwise when it fell

to the lot of that sentimental and susceptible curate to read the burial service over many of those rosy country girls about whose charms he waxed so eloquent. Like so many early faded flowers, he would watch them sicken and die. Tuberculosis was then the arch enemy of youth and in 1914 the disease was still rife in the district, particularly in the mountain farms. Tombstones in the local churchyards reveal that the people either succumbed to this scourge before they were thirty or they lived to a ripe old age.

Kilvert's characteristic Victorian reticence and inhibition, not to say prurience, on the subject of sex was offset by a realistic attitude towards death which we now find morbid. We do so because our way of thinking on these subjects has turned topsy-turvy since Kilvert's day. Obsessively frank about sexual matters, we are extremely reticent about death as though trying to pretend it does not exist. This is misguided. So far from being morbid, a constant awareness that 'all flesh is grass' makes us appreciate the beauty of the world and the potential riches of life the more keenly. Kilvert's *Diary* is a proof of this. His love of natural beauty and his zest for the small, homely pleasures of life would not shine so brightly from his pages were it not for an awareness of life's brevity which he makes his readers share.

I learnt to appreciate this myself during my years at Hay, for I was then a sickly small boy who occasioned his parents considerable anxiety. I suffered from recurrent bouts of bronchitis which confined me to bed with a 'low fever' for weeks on end each winter. It was feared I had fallen a victim to the prevalent disease and there was dark whispered talk about a suspected 'patch' on my lungs. But my blood seemed to respond like sap to the lengthening days. Spring spelled convalescence and summer full health. Consequently I savoured these far off spring and summer days so intensely that memories of them now seem ineffably sweet.

I should like to be able to say that my home during these years was some romantic old house in the mountains, but the truth is far more prosaic. The architecture of every small town along the Welsh Marches reveals the fact that there was a sudden increase in their moneyed population in late Victorian or early Edwardian times bringing a brief period of prosperity. The more wealthy of these immigrants emparked land and built themselves considerable mansions, but the majority were content with neat detached villas surrounded by large gardens. This influx was reflected in the towns by the building of new shops, hotels and public buildings: market halls, town halls and clock towers. By contrast with the bleak and characterless cubes of today, many of these buildings have now acquired a certain period charm, but in 1914 we regarded them as hideously over ornate. No book that I have read about the Welsh Border even mentions this social phenomenon. I suspect the reason for it was that the belated coming of railways to the Marches made such small towns suddenly accessible. At a time when it was becoming more difficult and more expensive to lead the life of a country gentleman, railways opened up a new territory where property was cheap, where there was no shortage of domestic servants and where good fishing and rough shooting could be had for the asking. These were certainly the considerations that drew, first my uncle Harry and then my father to Hay.

In the scattered parish of Cusop, lying a little to the south of Hay, a small housing estate had been built at the turn of the century which was known locally as 'the Forty Acres'. The houses, which an agent would describe as 'desirable detached residences standing in own grounds' were served by a rectangle of narrow road that enclosed a single green field. This central field has since been built upon and there are other examples of what the planners call 'judicious infilling', but in 1914 there were, at most, a dozen houses and my father acquired one of the more retired of these. It was called 'Radnor View'. Instead of facing the central field as most of the others did, it stood apart at the furthest corner of the estate at the end of a short drive fringed by pine trees that have long since been cut down. These trees became so many eyries for me, the ladder-like set of their branches a positive invitation to climb them. My knees would be sticky and scented by the clear resinous gum their trunks exuded and as I lay in bed I could hear their branches, heavy-laden with dark pine needles, soughing on windy nights with a sound like the sea. In winter those branches would bow to the ground beneath their burden of snow.

These trees made a somewhat gloomy approach to what was a not unattractive house. From the end of the drive one could see its front porch of green-painted wood framed in an arc of dark trees. But the house was set at such an angle to the drive that its plain sash windows looked out across a tennis lawn and over the little town in the valley below to the gentle slope of Radnor, a mosaic of fields and copses that rose behind the village of Clyro beyond the Wye. Unlike the 'Sea Views' of so many coastal resorts, at least the house was honestly named. Beyond the house, the drive led to a small coach-house and stable with a

hayloft above which fronted a paddock intended to furnish the
necessary winter fuel supply for the horse transport. This stable was
a singularly ugly building of cream-painted corrugated iron with
green doors and windows. But at a time when the motor-car was
beginning to oust the horse-drawn carriage for private transport,
it must have been one of the latest buildings of its kind. In our
time the only appropriate occupant of the stable was Meg, a
diminutive Shetland pony which my parents bought for me in a
misguided moment. She proved to be a vicious little brute with
the habits of biting her rider in the leg, or crushing his foot against
any convenient wall or tree. This effectually put me off riding
for good and all. I have ever since preferred wheels to hooves.

My father, who at one time had been a keen amateur racing
cyclist, greatly favoured two wheels (or at the most three) to
four and throughout the war years the coach-house at Radnor
View housed the two motorcycles he had brought with him from
Chester: a 2¾ h.p. solo A.J.S. for personal transport, and a huge
unwieldy Williamson combination for family use. This last was
a somewhat rare breed. It was powered by a flat twin water-
cooled Douglas engine and had radiators mounted beside the
front forks as on a Scott. In my recollection it was not particularly reliable and as a family we never motored very far afield.
I cannot think what had prompted my father to buy it, as he was
a devotee of A.J.S. motorcycles, maintaining that they were the
finest machines in the world.

The house had a red-tiled roof and walls of rough-dressed
local old red sandstone with brick quoins. At the front, these
walls were practically invisible under a dense tangle of white
flowering clematis and ivy. If one looks at old photograph
albums it is surprising how many houses were densely clothed
in creepers at this time. It cannot have been good for the
masonry, making it impossible to see when it needed repointing,
while many unwelcome insect visitors found their way in through
the windows. These included earwigs of which I had a positive
horror, having been told by nurse that they were liable to crawl
into my ears and drive me mad.

As one entered the front door, my mother's drawing-room
lay to the right while on the left was my father's smoking-room.
This had a high fender topped by a padded leather seat surrounding the fireplace. On walls and shelves were numerous
memorials of his roving life: an Australian boomerang and nulla-
nulla of aborigine origin and a long stock-whip to remind him
of his days 'down under'; a silver trophy won when playing polo

for the Behar Light Horse in India; a length of whalebone, and the broken head of a harpoon recalling his empty-handed return from the Yukon expedition; a pelican's head mounted on a wooden shield from heaven knows where. A mahogany glass-fronted gun case housed his revolvers (one fitted with a long saloon barrel), a ·22 Winchester repeating rifle and a magnificent pair of shot guns—16-bore Holland and Holland Royals. My father was a deadly shot who spurned a 12-bore as though it had been a blunderbuss. Shooting with the smaller 16s he could hold his own with any man. Much later, after my father's death, I became a sufficiently good shot myself to be able to appreciate the superb quality and balance of these guns, but since I could not use them in the manner my father had, I regretfully decided to sell them at a time when I was particularly hard-up. I should have got a great deal more for them had they been 12-bores.

Sometimes, to entertain his small son and to prove to himself that he still had the knack, my father would take his stock-whip down from its hook and out on to the tennis lawn. There, while I watched him goggle-eyed from a safe distance, he would whirl the long whip faster and faster about his head until it made a loud whistling noise. Then, with a quick flick of the wrist, the spinning circle would suddenly become a straight line and the lash would crack with a noise like a gun shot.

At the back of the house facing south were the dining-room, the kitchen and the servants' quarters where dwelt a housemaid and my beloved Welsh nurse, Mary Gwynne. The dining-room had a pair of French windows opening on to a small lawn, sunny and sheltered, where we frequently sat out in basket chairs in summer. A grass path flanked by herbaceous borders led away from this lawn and from it one could look across green fields to the foothills of the Black Mountains: wooded Mouse Castle to the left, Cusop Hill, with a solitary white cottage halfway down its steep slope, directly opposite and, away to the right beyond the deep cleft of Cusop Dingle, the hill oddly named the Haynault which had a curious crest of outcropping rocks. Of these three hills, only the first was a true outlier; the other two were merely the steep faces of a high, wide moorland which we called the plateau, a great windy, unenclosed and curlew-haunted sheepwalk of close, springy turf and bracken which served as a plinth for those two northern gables of the Black Mountain ridges, Pen y Beacon (or Hay Bluff) and Rhiw Wen.

Although the Black Mountains are in reality of no great height, nowhere substantially exceeding 2,000 ft, they appear to be far higher and wilder. There are two reasons for this. First, their most prominent escarpments face north and east and are therefore nearly always in shadow. Hence they appear to loom over the rich red fields, the pastures and orchards of Herefordshire as darkly menacing as a thunder cloud. Secondly, they have a perfection of outline and symmetry that is incomparably grand. So majestic are the curves by which their projecting bluffs stoop towards the plain below that one is reminded of a succession of great waves, petrified upon the instant of breaking.

Seen from beyond the Wye, from Clyro or from the Radnor Hills beyond, these mountains with their outer rampart of foothills compose what I always consider to be one of the finest landscapes in all Britain. It was a scene that continually drew Kilvert's eye while he was at Clyro. He gives one particularly fine description of a stormy late afternoon in March 1870 when, as he watched, the clouds that had veiled the mountains from sight all day suddenly lifted and dissolved to reveal the whole range glistening with snow in the light of a setting sun. 'One's first involuntary thought in the presence of these magnificent sights,' he wrote, 'is to lift up the heart to God and humbly thank Him for having made the earth so beautiful . . . I could have cried with the excitement of the overwhelming spectacle . . . it seemed to me as if one might never see such a sight again.'

From our much closer vantage at Cusop we were denied such splendours. With the exception of one portion of the high shoulder of Pen y Beacon which appeared in the cleft of Cusop Dingle, the mountains lay hidden behind their foothills. But at least it was that much easier to explore their high solitudes and somehow I was always conscious of their presence.

Gradually, I came to know this country intimately. My first walks were necessarily confined to the more immediate neighbourhood, but as I slowly gained stature and strength I was able to range further afield. From what my father subsequently told me, my birth had been a traumatic experience for my mother. Consequently, it was some time after I was born before she could be persuaded even to look at me. In the meantime, I would have died but for my father's affection and the care of my nurses. Hence it was upon the latter, and in particular my Welsh nurse, Mary Gwynne, that my affections were at first centred. It was she who accompanied me on my first walks at Cusop. Initially these were part walk, part pram ride and they almost invariably took us along the narrow road that closely followed the Dulas Brook up Cusop Dingle. Perhaps I should explain

that 'dingle' means a deep and narrow valley, the equivalent of
the Welsh 'cwm'. Like other local terms such as 'glat', meaning
a stile or any other form of climbable gap in a hedge, 'dingle'
became a part of my growing vocabulary. No matter how many
times I went that way, I never grew tired of Cusop Dingle,
for the flowers in the cottage gardens beside the road and the
changing foliage of the many and varied trees that overhung the
brook ensured that on no two occasions did it look the same. But
above all I loved the Dulas Brook. It fell down its narrow valley
in a succession of small waterfalls, shadowed pools and boulder-
strewn stickles. It was spanned by many narrow wooden foot-
bridges by which the people from the cottages and farms on
the opposite bank gained access to the road. I loved to stand on
these bridges, gazing down into dark pools, flecked with moving
patterns of gold by the sunlight that filtered through the hazels
overhead, looking for trout. I would spot them sinuously
breasting the clear water with the lazy motion of trailing water
weeds, swayed by the current. There were birds, too, to look
for; wagtails and white-throated dippers bobbing on the boulders
in mid-stream, shy ring-ouzels, and occasionally the azure flash
of a kingfisher flying fast and low over the water.

At such times the brook seemed half asleep, its voice sunk to
a murmur as soothing as the hum of bees. But after a heavy
storm on the mountains where it had its source the Dulas
would become suddenly and violently awake and this I found
terribly exciting. A great torrent of tawny water would come
rushing down, filling the whole valley with its thunder. Tree
branches were varnished by the spray that rose from the larger
falls like drifting steam and, on the surface of the pools, gobbets
of foam spun giddily in the eddies. When such sudden spates
subsided as quickly as they had come there were always changes
to look for; here a tree had been undermined and had fallen
across the stream, there a miniature landslide of red earth had
altered the shape of a familiar pool.

When I was recovering from my recurrent bouts of bronchitis
in the spring, Mary used to push me up the Dingle in an old Bath
chair which I steered by the long handle that controlled the
single pivoting front wheel. On such occasions I would persuade
Mary to let me coast down on the return journey. Good-
naturedly, though somewhat rashly, she would consent to this
practice, allowing me to disappear rapidly out of her sight.
Although the gradient was nowhere steep, it was almost continuous, the road rough and the elderly vehicle quite unsuited

to such speeds, having a high centre of gravity and no form of brake. Why it did not overturn I do not know, but, as there was no risk of meeting wheeled traffic, I was able to pick the best line through the corners. When I had eventually rolled to rest I would wait for the faithful Mary to appear, somewhat flushed and breathless, brushing her brown hair out of her eyes.

That the Dingle road was rough is not strictly a true statement. One stretch of about 150 yards on the lower and more frequented portion had been given a tarred surface by the wealthy owners of a neighbouring house, partly to silence the iron-tyred wheels of passing carts and partly to prevent white road dust from blowing over their garden. It was then the only road of its kind for many miles around and although it was apt to become disconcertingly soft and sticky in hot weather, I used to regard with wonderment its smooth and dustless surface.

Later, when my mother realised that I was approaching the age of rationality and was fully in control of my bodily functions, she began to take the place of Mary as my companion on these walks. Sometimes my father would accompany us, but usually he was too preoccupied in shooting or fishing. In this way we established a normal relationship and she began to usurp my father's place in my affections. In retrospect, this seems a little unfair, but it was simply a reversal of the normal shift in the proportion of affection a boy feels for his parents as he grows up.

These walks with my mother took us further and further afield; to the tree-crowned mound and vallum of Mouse Castle, to the top of Cusop Hill and finally to 'the plateau' and the Black Mountains beyond. In order to reach the latter we had to walk up Cusop Dingle to the point where the metalled road ended, turn right-handed, cross the Dulas by a footbridge, and then climb steeply by a rough track, now a completely overgrown watercourse, to a farm called New Forest. It was by this farm that we gained a track that led up to the high plateau past the little lonely shepherd's holding that we knew as Cock-a-Lofty.[1] Although it entailed a considerable climb, it cannot have been much more than three miles from our house to the plateau and we often went up in late summer to pick whinberries or the rarer cranberries. But the occasion I remember most vividly must have been in early spring. All was fresh green below, but when we had climbed to Cock-a-Lofty it was to be rewarded with a sight such as had ravished Kilvert so many years before. For

[1] Many of these local names are corruptions of Welsh words.

under a sky of cloudless blue all the wide plateau and the slopes beyond were white with new-fallen snow and lay glittering in the sunshine, the folds on the flanks of the mountains shadowed to an unbelievable shade of deepest blue. I remember sliding over the black surface of a small, frozen tarn.

The track that we struck at New Forest Farm on these occasions led down to Hay in one direction and in the other it climbed ever higher up the side of Pen y Beacon until it finally curved out of sight between the two peaks to cross the high saddle between them by the Gospel Pass. This is known in Welsh as Bwlch yr Efengel, the Pass of the Evangelists, because, it is said, the Apostles Peter and Paul once crossed it on their mission to bring the gospel of Christ to the Silures. The summit of this pass was too far for my small legs and I used often to wonder what undiscovered country lay beyond those gables of the mountains until, on one memorable summer's day, I saw it for the first time.

My mother's mother, 'Grannie Timperley', was staying with us and, as a special treat, my father had hired an open two-horse wagonette to take us over the pass. A large wicker picnic hamper was stowed on board and we all set off on a perfect morning in June. When we reached the plateau, the clink of hooves and the grinding of the steel-shod wheels fell silent on the smooth close-bitten turf of the track so that one could hear the creaking of the harness as the two horses toiled steadily upward along the flank of Pen y Beacon. As we climbed ever higher, a breath-taking view unfolded over the valley of the middle Wye to Radnor Forest and the mountains of Wales beyond. But when we eventually turned left-handed and passed quickly through the narrow defile of the Gospel Pass, we turned our backs upon this familiar country and I found myself translated into a landscape much smaller in scale but in my eyes far more fascinating because it appeared so lonely, so secret and so strange. This was my first glimpse of the Vale of Ewyas, that deep and rich valley that the Black Mountains harbour in their heart. The child is always captivated by the miniature, and, after the broad prospect, suddenly to come upon this small and exquisite landscape that the mountains guarded so jealously was an experience I never forgot.

The head of the valley into which we had come was wild and treeless, its steep slopes furrowed by a fan of converging streams, but I could see below the first small green fields with a glimpse of distant trees beyond and as we slowly descended towards the valley floor we soon left the open mountain for a narrow high-banked lane where arching hazels made a tunnel of green shade. And so we came to the lost hamlet of Capel-y-ffyn with its tiny church and Baptist chapel. Here we turned aside to visit the Monastery, scene of that ill-starred attempt by Joseph Leycester Lyne, self-styled 'Father Ignatius', to found a community of Anglican Benedictine monks. Though tenantless, the Monastery buildings still appeared externally to be in good order, for Father Ignatius had died only some ten years before. The high roof of the choir—the only portion of the great church he planned that was actually built—still looked sound and secure, though eventually its vaulting would fall, covering the tomb of Ignatius, who lies buried beneath the central aisle, under tons of masonry. Beside this church, we saw the monastery bell, 'Big Bernard', still hanging within its wooden framework; how it was ever got up the narrow valley road is still a mystery to me. We saw, too, the white marble statue of Our Lady standing incongruous and ghostly in the corner of a field below the Monastery, marking the spot where she is alleged to have appeared to the brothers. This happening is commonly attributed to wishful thinking. Maybe so, but I will only say that if ever it is vouchsafed to man to see visions, then it would be in such a place as this valley whose very air seemed to a child to be numinous and charged with magic. That one of the remote mountain holdings nearby is called the Vision Farm is nothing to do with nineteenth-century mysticism but recalls some far older tradition.

I thought the Monastery, on the dark side of the valley and surrounded by gloomy pines, a sad, depressing place and was glad when we were rumbling on our way again along the narrow winding lane down the valley. The sun shone down out of a clear sky; there were wild strawberries and foxgloves growing in the hedge banks and through gateways in the hazels there were occasional glimpses of meadows carpeted with wild flowers; the creamy froth of meadowsweet; the purple spires of orchis. The further we went, the stronger sounded the voice of the stream below the lane, the taller and richer grew the trees until at length we turned aside and came to our destination—the ruined Priory of Llanthony, or 'The Abbey' as it is called in the valley. Here the picnic basket was unpacked and we lunched on the green turf beside the columns of the ruined nave.

No building in Britain has so majestical a setting as Llanthony. The valley hereabouts is at its widest and most luxuriant. Like some gigantic outflung lion's paw, the high, bracken-furred wall of Hatterall Hill encloses its richness in a majestic protective arc terminating in a steep fall. Its slopes were thickly sewn with sheep and in that breathless summer stillness the sound of their distant bleating mingled with the singing of birds in the valley below. Everything seemed to conspire to charm my five senses. Nor was this first childish impression in any way delusive. For since this first ever-memorable visit I have returned to the Vale of Ewyas countless times at all stages of my life and have seen it in every kind of weather and seasonal mood. Yet its beauty has never failed to equal my expectation; in fact and in recollection it was to prove an unfailing source of spiritual solace to me from that day to this.

It was after this first visit to Llanthony that I began to take part in those communal, Kilvert-like walks and picnic parties to which I have already referred. Among those who joined us on these outings were our neighbours, Major Herbert Armstrong and his wife, who lived in a large and ugly house of yellow brick called Mayfield on the road down to Hay. He was a solicitor though he usually wore his uniform and had what was called a 'military bearing'. He had singularly piercing blue eyes and used to read the lessons in Cusop church. I stood rather in awe of him. Little did we realise then that in the dapper Major we were harbouring a dangerous viper with poisoned fangs in our peaceful country nest. But of this, more later.

A much more likeable companion on these picnics was Thomas Southwick, a retired inspector of schools, a mild, scholarly and kindly man with a grey beard and pince-nez. My father took to him although the two men were quite dissimilar in character. He used to stroll down the road on summer evenings for a quiet game of bowls with my father on our tennis lawn. I used to listen to the click of the woods and the soothing murmur of male voices as I lay in bed. Thomas Southwick became my tutor and each morning I trotted up the road through the Forty Acres to take my lessons in his study. He was an inspired teacher who taught me more than I ever learned subsequently at school.

I remember sitting at my mid-morning lesson in Mr Southwick's study when the steam hooter at the sawmills near Hay Station suddenly and unexpectedly blared. Why was it sounding so loud and so long at such a time? Thomas Southwick leaned back in his chair and sighed: 'Well, it's over at last,' he said. The date was 11th November 1918 and the Armistice had just been declared.

Later, when I came to realise fully the terrible carnage and

agony of the Great War and that these years had been a time of
the breaking of nations, it used to make me feel guilty to think
how little the even tenor of our lives had been affected by it. I
remember only my father, who was too old to serve, shaking his
head over the headlines in the newspaper and the dark green
blinds which we put up as a precaution against air raids, although
no Zeppelin ever came within a hundred miles of Hay. Thanks
to my father's proficiency with rod and gun, plus the produce of
a large vegetable garden, we hardly felt the effects of food
rationing. Our larder was always kept well supplied with fish
and game in season. I recall sitting on the bank of the Wye and
watching my father, within two hours, take three salmon, none
of them under 15 lb, from the Wyecliff pool just above Hay.
But, although he was an expert salmon fisherman, he much preferred trout fishing as calling for the greater skill and when my
uncle Neville came to stay they would go off on trout fishing
expeditions, fishing the Kentchurch Court water on the Monnow
or, latterly, the Usk at Brecon. It was a disappointment to my
father that I never took up fishing; I think I reacted against his
total commitment to the sport.

Although there were—and still are—grouse on the Black
Mountains, the population was never very great and as the
'Twelfth' came round my father's 'Royals' would be carefully
dismantled and packed in their fitted travelling case ready for his
annual pilgrimage to Scotland. There he would join a wealthy
shooting friend named Holmes who each year rented Methven
Castle in Perthshire. Highly coloured postcards of purple moors
briefly reporting the 'bag' would arrive together with several
brace of grouse to festoon our larder. Lack of refrigeration never
worried my father who liked his game high. He used to maintain that grouse should hang until maggots appeared on the
flags below. At other seasons my father found plenty of rough
shooting locally. In Norfolk jacket, breeches, puttees and
shooting boots, with a capacious shooting bag on his back and a
cartridge belt round his waist, he would set off for a day's
shooting, gun under arm and cocker spaniel trotting at heel.
His cockers 'Don' and 'Flora' successively inhabited a kennel
behind the stable and were not permitted to cross the threshold
of the house. He never returned from these expeditions without
at least a brace of pheasants or partridges, depending on the
season.

We salted down farm butter in a great earthenware crock and
my father bought two small piglets to fatten for the table. This,

his only venture in livestock keeping, was only partially successful. For one of the pigs somehow contrived to fall into our compost pit where it proceeded to gorge itself on decaying lawn mowings until it practically burst and the local vet had to be called to put it out of its misery. Such misfortunes my father would dismiss with a sigh and a shrug as an example of what he termed the 'Rolt luck'. In fact this luck, or rather ill-luck, was really due to the fact that the Rolt ability to excel in any form of field sport was matched by an almost total incapacity to deal efficiently with anything which had to do with the practical business of living.

The seasons also brought the fruits of the field: wild strawberries in profusion on the high hedge banks at midsummer; mushrooms in quantity from the old pastures; whinberries from the mountains and, of course, blackberries. Gathering hazel-nuts was a favourite pastime of mine on autumn walks in the deep lanes. When I brought the nuts home I used to pack them into tins and then bury them in the earth of the garden, like a squirrel, digging them up at Christmas. I used to think they tasted better that way.

From the boundary hedge of our small paddock, one looked across a couple of meadows to a farm beneath the slopes of Mouse Castle. This farm, which I used to call 'Lididiway' (it was really Lidiart-y-Wain), was unusually large for this district of small farms. It was of very ancient origin. There were traces of a moat and ranges of barns, bartons and stables all of local old red sandstone with walls of massive thickness. Local people used to say that they had originally been built to keep out the wolves. Whether this was true or no, it was like a farm in a story book, a mixed farm of the traditional kind with arable fields under oats, wheat and roots and with green pastures heavily stocked with red Hereford bullocks, milking cows and, of course, the ubiquitous sheep. At the farm there were pigs in the styes and a great stable full of horses, for everything was done by horse-power. Ducks and geese swam in the large pond which was part of the old moat, while the farmyard was full of scratching chickens, turkeys strutting among them with an air of affronted dignity.

I became friendly with the son of this farmer (I cannot now recall his name), a boy of about my own age, and used often to slip away across the fields to join him. Wet or fine, that farm with its great barns was a wonderful place for boys. On one occasion we succeeded in mounting and riding a couple of rams.

I returned home reeking with the smell of their oily fleeces to the consternation of my mother and Mary. In the cart shed was every kind of horse-drawn vehicle from light gigs and traps to great four-wheeled Herefordshire harvest wagons whose massive wheels were not tyred but shod with a double row of iron strakes. There was also a type of two-wheeled harvest cart which we called a gambo.[1]

We used to help at haysel and harvest, pitching until the load grew too high for our small arms, or setting the corn sheaves in stook. And we loved to ride back to the farm, sprawled on top of the loaded wains, their loads brushing the hazels as they lumbered down the narrow lanes. I remember—it must have been at the height of the U-boat blockade in 1917, I think—that I first saw a Fordson tractor at plough on this farm. I little thought then that this was the thin end of a very large wedge that would drive the horse from the farm altogether within my lifetime, leaving gaily painted wagons and harness bright with polished ornament to rot and to tarnish.

Apart from my friend the farmer's boy, I knew few local children for I was, and still am, an unsociable animal and I always disliked children's parties. Occasions of this sort were reserved for Christmas when we invariably went to Chester to stay with my aunt Augusta and her doctor husband. Our neighbours may have thought me a lonely child, but solitary would have been a better word for I was never consciously lonely. Nor do I recall reading much as lonely children are apt to do. For although Thomas Southwick had given me an excellent grounding in the first two of the three Rs, I never felt the need to escape into imaginary worlds conjured up by other minds. Of my first four years in Chester I retained only a few shadowy memories like a random collection of faded snapshots. It was this little world of the Welsh Border that I discovered for myself and made peculiarly my own. When, years later, I first read that famous meditation of Thomas Traherne which begins: 'The corn was orient and immortal wheat, which never should be reaped, nor was ever sown', I knew it to be a superbly articu-

[1] The true gambo, however, originated in Radnorshire where it was designed for use in steeply sloping fields. This Radnorshire gambo was part cart part sledge with a pair of massive fore-wheels and a pair of large bosses behind to act as runners. It would be drawn uphill on its wheels and come down on its runners with the wheels locked.

late expression of all that I had felt as a child. It is said that the child is father to the man; certainly this 'first Light which shined in my infancy' affected me profoundly for the rest of my life. It was something which I learned to set my course by.

But I could not live in paradise forever, or, as my nurse would say tritely when I was reluctant to come to bed on a summer evening: 'All good things have got to come to an end, Master Tom.' I had to go to school; I had to learn, as Traherne puts it, 'the dirty devices of this world'.

Chapter 3

Holidays and Schooldays

If I saw any cars in the Hay neighbourhood during the First
World War I do not remember them. There must have been a few,
though doubtless their use was severely restricted by the petrol
shortage. It was an entirely horse-drawn world that I recall;
indeed most of the minor roads in the district were too rough
and too steep for the cars of those days. In most country districts, the local doctor was usually the first to adopt the motor-
car for obvious reasons, but our doctor, Tom Hinks, habitually
rode on his rounds wearing a hacking jacket, cord breeches and
leggings of polished leather. On the rare occasions when we went
away as a family we hired an ancient four-wheeled 'growler'
from Hay to convey us to the station, luggage piled upon its
roof and straw on the floor.

We had no gas or electric light. Our cook/housemaid tended
a voracious coal range and lighting was by wick paraffin lamps
with bead-fringed shades of pleated silk. There were no tele-
phones in Cusop and I doubt if there were any in Hay either,
certainly I never saw one. Sometimes on clear nights the sky
over the mountains would glow a faint but angry red. I was told
that this was the reflection of the iron furnaces of industrial
South Wales, Ebbw Vale, or Dowlais, but this information held
no meaning for me. For there was no industry in Hay apart from
the steam sawmills and the local railway was the only evidence
that an Industrial Revolution had ever come about.

With my unprofessional and non-technical family background, brought up as I was in such a completely rural environment, it has always been a wonder to me that I should have
begun so soon to take a keen interest in all things mechanical.
I wanted to become an engineer, mysteriously acquiring this
sense of vocation in that pre-industrial world whose natural
beauty, simplicity and order influenced me so deeply. That by

making this inexplicable choice I was sowing the seeds of future inner conflict I then had no inkling.

I think it must have been *Katie* that first seduced me into the world of machines. Built in 1890 and long since scrapped, *Katie* was a tiny four-wheeled steam locomotive which worked over the three miles of fifteen-inch gauge line that had been laid out and equipped by Sir Percival Heywood for the Duke of Westminster. It linked Eaton Hall with exchange sidings at Balderton station on the Great Western Shrewsbury–Chester line. I cannot remember exactly when it was, perhaps it was on a visit to Eaton Park with my nurse before we moved from Chester, but the first sight of this diminutive engine puffing energetically along between the trees of the park was enough. I became a railway enthusiast from that moment.

Hay station was not a very rewarding place for a railway-minded small boy, for no great expresses thundered through it. Like the small town it served, its atmosphere of somnolent calm was but rarely disturbed. Trains were few, and for most of the day there was no louder sound to be heard than the cool voice of the Wye flowing over rock-shelving rapids just behind the up platform. The station was served by two single track branches, the Hereford, Hay and Brecon line of the Midland Railway and the Great Western's Golden Valley branch from Pontrilas. Both were relics of wildly optimistic territorial ambitions that had remained completely unfulfilled. The Hereford, Hay and Brecon had originally been a creation of that inveterate Welsh railway promoter and contractor Thomas Savin of Oswestry, whose policy it was to promote and to build railways in the expectation that one or other of the great companies would subsequently acquire them. In this case the line had been amalgamated with the Midland in the teeth of the bitterest opposition from the Great Western. By the exercise of running powers, the Midland Company had rosy visions of its acquisition forming part of a new through route between its own system and the industrial riches of South Wales. But the dream of train loads of Northamptonshire iron ore rumbling through Hay en route for Ebbw Vale was never realised and the line had remained a remote and isolated backwater of the Midland system. When I knew it the train service—and indeed the trains themselves—can have changed very little since Kilvert's day. He was, as his diary reveals, a frequent passenger, often using the railway for surprisingly short journeys such as that between Hay and Whitney-on-Wye, the next station up the line. One would think it might have been quicker to walk. Little 0-4-4 passenger tank engines drew trains that, even by the standards of 1916, were archaic. There were a few clerestory-roofed, gas-lit six-wheeled coaches, but these were exceptional; usually the trains were made up of four-wheelers with pot lamps in their elliptical roofs. There was no steam heating. Footwarmers covered in brilliantly hideous scarlet and green carpeting were slid into the compartments on winter mornings.

Although the first sod of the Golden Valley Railway was cut with no little pomp and ceremony at Peterchurch in 1876, three years before Kilvert's death at Bredwardine, it was not completed until thirteen years later after a protracted struggle to overcome difficulties that were financial rather than physical, for it was not a difficult line to build. A prospectus announcing an issue of debentures in 1888 was accompanied by a map which was a masterpiece of mendacious cartography. It showed the nineteen miles of this remote rural railway between Pontrilas and Hay (together with a projected extension down the Monnow valley to Monmouth which was never built) as a vital link in a new direct through route between Bristol and Liverpool. What the map did not reveal was that this 'direct' route was not only longer than those already existing but that it consisted almost entirely of heavily graded and sharply curved single line along the Welsh Border and that in order to make such a journey a through train would have to make more than one reversal.

The line was eventually opened from Pontrilas to Hay in 1889 and struggled along in the face of mounting financial difficulties until 1898 when it closed down only to be rescued and re-opened in 1901 by the Great Western Railway Company to which it was sold for a fraction of its cost. Despite such distinguished ownership, however, the Golden Valley remained the most bucolic and dilatory of rural branch lines. To a small boy it formed an unflattering first introduction to a great railway company which was later to win my devoted allegiance. Trains on the Midland line might be archaic but at least they kept reasonable time whereas on the Golden Valley time seemed to be of no account at all. Although an intermediate passing loop had originally been provided at the half-way station at Dorstone, it was never used as such, traffic being conducted on the 'one engine only in steam' principle. This single locomotive used to work three mixed trains of passengers and goods daily in each direction. These performed desultory shunting operations at intermediate stations, dropping empties and picking up truckloads of cattle or timber. The conveyance of passengers was of secondary importance. I remember one frustrating occasion when my mother and I went to Hay station intending to take the afternoon train to Pontrilas. As we stood on the platform we could see our train, the little green tank engine with the single coach attached, performing seemingly interminable shunting operations in Hay goods yard, its every movement punctuated by a prolonged pause. At each sign of animation our hopes rose; now, surely, the train was coming to pick us up. But alas, although we waited until long after departure time, it never did so until, much to my disappointment, we were compelled to abandon our proposed excursion.

Although they had been comparatively lately built, no doubt the coming of these railways was something of a nine days' wonder, for in such remote country there must have been many who had never seen a railway train before. Yet by the time I knew them, these byways of the steel rail with their leisurely train services, their sleepy stations bright with flowers and staffed by stolid slow-moving countrymen, had become an accepted part of the country scene. They taught me nothing of that distant Industrial Revolution which had brought them to birth. To me, as I lay in bed of an evening, the distant cry of a Midland whistle as the last train from Hereford ran up the Wye valley seemed as natural a sound as the hoot of an owl from the fir trees outside my window. It was on our occasional visits to Chester that I formed my first clear impressions of that larger world of which our local railways were the only evidence.

Each year we went to Chester to spend Christmas with my mother's only sister, her doctor husband and their two young daughters. I cannot recall the precise date when this custom began, and as it continued for some years, recurring visits cannot now be separated in memory but have left a composite impression. My uncle, Dr George Taylor, lived in a large, rambling house called Grey Friars. It was very old, but had been rebuilt and encased in brickwork in Georgian times. For an impressionable small boy there could have been few more romantic houses, and certainly no more romantic city, in which to spend Christmas. After the simplicities of Hay, the brightly lit shop fronts in the old streets and rows seemed so many glittering Aladdin's caves filled with rich treasure.

One grocer's shop especially fascinated me. This was in an ancient building and its counters, laden at Christmas time with glittering crystallised fruits, candied peel and other magical wares, occupied the length of a long, narrow, stone-vaulted crypt-like hall below street level. A complex system of miniature aerial railways connected each counter to the cashier's office right at the back of the shop. If change was required, the shop assistant would place your money in a round wooden canister, screw it on to the two-wheeled traveller that ran on the wire, and pull the handle of the cord that sent it whizzing away down the length of the shop. In due course it would come singing back along the wire with the change, reaching its terminus with a satisfying *clunk*. I was fascinated by this device and could have played with it for hours. Sometimes a kindly assistant would allow me to be held up so that I might pull the cord.

But one recollection stands out in memory above all. It is of walking back to Grey Friars through the snow after a Christmas Eve carol service at the cathedral. Our way took us down Watergate Street. This was a narrow cobbled road flanked by even narrower pavements and shadowed by the over-sailing timbered gables of the houses. Because both street and pavements were thickly carpeted by new-fallen snow, we climbed the stone steps to the shelter of the row. Unlike the more frequented rows with their gay shop fronts, Watergate Row was a dim, mysterious place after dark, lit only by infrequent flickering gas lamps. It was inhabited—as it doubtless had been since the Middle Ages—by small craftsmen, coopers, tinsmiths and the like. The windows of their workshops were shuttered now, though some showed chinks of light and there were sounds of unknown activity within. Occasionally the mouth of a narrow alley, dark as midnight and leading who knows where, opened up between them. Perhaps it was the tunes of the already familiar carols which I had just heard sung in the candle-lit choir of the cathedral, the anticipations of Christmas and the contrasting whiteness of the snow outside that combined to induce a receptive mood in which my recollection of this dim tunnel of Watergate Row was registered and stored away in some most profound level of conscious memory. I could not have said why this was so. For a child's apprehensions spring from some mysterious source—racial memory perhaps—which becomes harder to tap as the years pass. The adult must needs rationalise and formulate what the child grasped intuitively. Attempting to formulate at this distance of time I would say that what I perceived then was an embodiment of the continuing life of an ancient city, labyrinthine, dark, mysterious yet not sinister but intensely human. I think I was born just in time, for which of our modern cities, I wonder, could make such an impression upon a child?

My recollections of Grey Friars House are a random mixture of ancient and modern. There was electric light, dim carbon filament bulbs glowing redly in the long corridors. They were operated by switches with covers of fluted brass. There was that magical instrument the telephone, hidden away in a little forbidden room, the size of a downstairs lavatory, next door to my uncle's consulting room. The inside of the bowl of the w.c. was decorated in blue willow pattern and discreetly concealed beneath the lid of a built-in chest of polished mahogany. A second smaller lid opened to disclose a pull-up flushing handle. The bath, with its big brass taps, was of enormous proportions and similarly encased in mahogany, like an outsized coffin. Its interior felt somewhat rough to the bare behind. It occupied one end of a large, cold and otherwise empty room with a polished wooden floor. This seemed to me an ideal place in which to discharge a small cannon which I had rashly been given as a Christmas present. Having stuffed the barrel to the mouth with black powder, it went off with a tremendously satisfying report, filling the room with smoke. Unfortunately, though successful, this experiment spread instant alarm and despondency through the entire household; they became convinced that the antiquated heating system had exploded and I fell into dire disgrace.

Grey Friars was a large warren of a house with the traditional baize doors on both floors which sealed off the servants' quarters and back stairs. Every room, even the bathroom, seemed to have two doors and this feature, combined with mysterious corridors and many dark corners, made an ideal setting for hide-and-seek and other Christmas games. The house was held on good authority to be haunted by an apparition in a habit (presumably a Grey Friar) which frequented the back stairs. On the occasion of one Christmas visit when foundations for two new buttresses, one on either side of the front door, were being dug, a number of human bones were unearthed. Some held that this betokened the Friary graveyard, others an old plague pit.[1] My two young cousins and I made off with a skull

---

[1] Chester suffered a terrible visitation of the plague in the seventeenth century. 'God's Providence House' in Watergate Street was so named because it is said to have been the only house to escape.

and placed it at the head of the back stairs, arguing with childish logic that the ghost would be sure to come and claim it. We took special precautions to ensure that the slightest movement of the skull could be detected and were keenly disappointed next morning to find that, apart from disconcerting the female domestic staff, the result of our ghost-baiting experiment had been completely negative.

The house stood on the western walls of the city. The big bay window of the long first floor drawing-room and the smaller barred window of the children's nursery looked out over the walls on to the Roodee, a great level expanse of green on which agricultural shows and the annual Chester Cup race meeting were held. This was bounded on the south-west by the river Dee and on the north-west by the railway which crossed the Roodee on a long viaduct of squat brick arches terminating in a steel girder bridge over the river. Although distant, I could hear from the nursery the hollow booming sound that the trains made as they passed from the viaduct on to the bridge. Here there was plenty of traffic for me to watch, for the bridge carried four tracks, two of them the Great Western Shrewsbury–Chester line over which I travelled on my visits to Chester from Hay, and the other two the London and North Western main line to Holyhead. The two diverged at Saltney Junction, just out of sight beyond the bridge. I would watch the trains through binoculars from the nursery window, the gleaming black locomotives of the North Western contrasting with the more familiar green ones of the Great Western. Sometimes I would see strange coaches with salmon pink upper panels. These, I learned, were London and South Western stock, working over Great Western metals on through trains between Chester and the South Coast. Hankering for a closer look, my favourite walk was across the Roodee to the footway beside the railway bridge. On the further side of the river, this footway ascended to the road bridge above by a flight of wooden steps which provided an ideal vantage point. Later, as I grew more independent, I used frequently to take a tram to Chester General station and haunt its platforms by the hour. It was here, armed with a new No. 2 Brownie box camera, that I took my first successful photograph —of a shining North Western 'Precursor' standing in a bay platform at the head of a train for Manchester.

For Chester Northgate station I had little time, I chiefly remember it for the remarkable notice over the gentlemen's lavatory which read:

CHESHIRE LINES.

NOTICE.

These closets are intended for the convenience of passengers only, workmen, cabmen, fishporters and idlers are not permitted to use them.   BY ORDER.

But I thought the Cheshire Lines trains poor things compared with the great expresses whose arrival and departure at the General Station I watched with awed admiration. Best of all were the Euston–Holyhead expresses of the North Western which were usually double-headed, a 'Precedent' piloting a 'GeorgeV' or a 'Precursor'. I found their arrival more thrilling than their departure. As the two locomotives came drifting into the great station with steam shut off and their long train snaking behind them, their coupling rods rang with a continuous reverberation, like a tintinnabulation of tenor bells, that re-echoed from the station roof. I can hear this sound still and it will forever be associated in my mind with the locomotives of the London and North Western Railway. In fact, it may have been a symptom of technical imperfection but to a small boy it was a brave and thrilling sound; the proud voice of power, proclaiming sonorously: 'I have travelled fast and far; make way, here I come!'

After the railway, my second greatest enjoyment on these visits to Chester was to be allowed to accompany my uncle on his professional rounds. They were the first journeys by car that I can recall. My uncle owned two Daimlers. One was a mud-coloured open two-seater with what seemed to me brass head-lamps of enormous size flanking its brass finned radiator. This car, which was of pre-war origin, he drove himself. For his rounds he used a 20 h.p. six-cylinder Daimler of later date. An enclosed drive landaulette in battleship grey with black head and nickel-plated radiator and lamps, it was always driven by his faithful chauffeur Ellis who lived in a cottage over the garage in a nearby mews where my uncle kept his cars. On these expeditions I sat in front on the black leather seat beside Ellis while behind the glass division my uncle reclined in solitary state amid Bedford cord and polished wood panelling. With his keen dark eyes and hawk-like nose, my uncle George would have looked perfect in the part of Sherlock Holmes. He always wore high, white stand-up collars that came close up under his chin and jaw and looked to me extremely uncomfortable. This somewhat formidable appearance was misleading for he was the mildest and kindest of men. This made him a very good doctor for, in a G.P., personality and humanity matter more than medicine. He was a capable but extremely cautious driver. Even on the uncluttered roads of those days he would never exceed 30 m.p.h. and would slow down and sound his bulb horn at even the most minor side turning. His chauffeur Ellis was, needless to say, a very proficient driver who found his master's excessive caution somewhat irksome. Sometimes if the round had been long and had taken us far afield, Ellis would obviously be anxious to get home for, no matter how late his return, his first act was always to leather down the car ready for the morning. With a sly sidelong glance at me he would let the car very gradually gather speed above the permitted limit of 30 m.p.h. But although my uncle was unable to see the speedometer from where he was sitting, this ruse was never successful. Sooner rather than later, he would lean forward and tap peremptorily on the glass division with his stethoscope whereupon Ellis, with a sigh of resignation, would return to the regulation speed.

On these trips with my uncle I became familiar with the countryside around Chester, but although this was far less built-up than it is today it never appealed to me. Whether it was due to the influence that the Black Mountains had upon me during the impressionable years of my childhood or to some deeper, primitive instinct I do not know, but I have never felt happy or at home in flat country. I must have hills or mountains about me. Some people have the same sense of mysterious affinity for the sea which maybe springs from a similarly ancient source, but though I can appreciate the beauties of the sea, I am aware that this is a conscious, aesthetic appreciation very different from that strange exaltation that I can only call a sudden awareness of the numinous, of the recognition of some profound reality behind appearances, that certain mountain country is capable of awakening within me. Even on these comparatively brief visits to Chester, enjoyable though they were and rich with fresh and exciting experiences, I used to miss my mountains and suffer occasional twinges of home-sickness. But whenever the weather was clear the far peak of Moel Fammau, sometimes blue, sometimes white with snow, became visible to the south-west from the window of the nursery. I found the sight of it reassuring. The mountains, after all, were not far away. It would remind me that the ancient reason for the city's existence was to keep the mountain people in check; its walls still watched Wales and

I would imagine myself some hawk-eyed Roman legionary, pacing the parapet below the window.

Chester's link with Wales was emphasised in my mind by the fact that my uncle owned a country house there to which his family would annually migrate for long periods during the summer months accompanied by their numerous animals, dogs and cats, goats and donkeys. My aunt's excessive fondness for animals was shared by her younger daughter, Rosalind, but by no one else. Like the goats, the domestic dogs and cats smelled abominably. They were grossly overfed, they moulted all over the chairs and carpets and were never house-trained so that one was always made unpleasantly aware of their existence. My aunt's misplaced affection would never permit them to be 'put down' so that they seemed to me to be in a perpetual state of advanced decrepitude that was at once painful and obscene. My father used to regard these wretched creatures with ill-concealed disfavour, muttering that the only proper place for a dog was in a kennel, but my uncle George bore his burden with saint-like resignation. It must have been a considerable expense to transport this seedy menagerie annually to Wales, but he paid up gladly as it ensured him at least a few weeks' peace from pets. For he would remain in solitary state at Grey Friars looking after his practice and make only brief visits to see his family, driving himself in the two-seater Daimler. On one occasion my aunt had the happy notion of transporting her goats to Wales in the back of the big Daimler, but this proved too much for the patience of the faithful chauffeur Ellis who threatened to give notice if the car upon which he lavished so much loving care was ever again used as a cattle truck.

When my uncle George finally retired to a small manor house in Hertfordshire, he found himself accompanied by a strange and gruesome assortment of live and dead stock. The former included two donkeys, bought for my cousins when they were small girls but now so senile that they could scarcely walk. A series of soap boxes filled with ashes contained the remains of pets that had passed on. The annual summer pilgrimage to Wales still continued. A motor horse box was hired to convey thither the two superannuated donkeys. My uncle and aunt followed by car accompanied by the latest pet dog. They habitually broke their journey at Bridgnorth, and as dogs were not permitted in the hotel where my uncle slept, my aunt remained all night in the car.

The house in Wales was called Plas-y-Garth. It could be described as a large *cottage ornée* of white-painted woodwork and walls of pink-washed pebbledash and it stood high on the steep south-facing slope of the Ceiriog valley in Denbighshire overlooking the slate roofs of the village of Glynceiriog. It was approached from this village by a lane which was then far too rough, narrow and steep to be passable by any car, a fact which considerably magnified the difficulties of the Taylor family's annual migration. In front of the house a high retaining wall of unbonded slate had been built in order to form a broad level terrace. In my recollection, this was the most pleasant and memorable feature of Plas-y-Garth. It included a deep embrasure built as though for a cannon and large enough to admit a table and garden seat, in which one could have al fresco meals while enjoying magnificent views, eastwards down the valley towards Chirk, westwards through the narrower defile that led to Llanarmon. The front door of Plas-y-Garth opened on to this terrace, but the hill slope was so steep that the back door was on the first floor and gave on to a lane, terraced along the hillside. Whoever had built the house had omitted to include any plumbing or the essential mod. cons. that go with it. This deficiency had been partially overcome at some later date by means of a structure of quite extraordinary eccentricity and ugliness. This consisted of a bathroom perched on wooden stilts on the opposite side of the back lane, the whole crazy edifice being clad in sheets of corrugated iron. This remarkable bathroom was reached from the top floor of the house by a kind of covered bridge of sighs of similar construction spanning the lane. I cannot recall that I ever took a bath at Plas-y-Garth. This is scarcely surprising for naturally each winter the plumbing was put out of action by frost and even in summer the most furious stoking would only produce tepid water from so remote a bath tap. If the bath was unusable, the w.c. was non-existent. Instead, a reeking earth privy, known to the family as the Fairy Glen, lurked in the midst of a dense laurel shrubbery at the eastern end of the terrace. It was cleared so infrequently and stank so dreadfully that a stay at Plas-y-Garth usually left me acutely constipated.

On my occasional visits to this house, the greatest source of attraction for me was undoubtedly the narrow-gauge Glyn Valley Tramway which linked Glynceiriog with the Great Western station at Chirk. As our train from Hereford drew in to Chirk station, I would look out eagerly for the rake of box-like four-wheeled coaches, a long tail of empty granite or slate wagons coupled in the rear, and the little tramway-type locomotive, *Sir Theodore*, *Dennis* or *Glyn*, at its head, standing at the parallel platform waiting to take us up the valley. Some of the coaches were open above the waistline and others closed, both with two compartments and the latter sharing a single pot lamp in the roof. Soon we would set off, swaying and rattling down a steep gradient through thick woods to the floor of the valley at Pontfaen where the line crossed the road which it then accompanied all the way to Glynceiriog.

On the hillside above the village was the Wynne Slate Quarry which was connected to the railway by a rope-worked incline. From the foot of this, loaded slate trains in charge of brakesmen were worked by gravity over a short mineral spur that crossed the village street on its way to join the main line. The Wynne Quarry was of the underground type and the manager, Mr Roper, once allowed us to visit it. This was a great thrill. Crouched in empty slate wagons hauled by a tiny, cabless steam locomotive, we travelled through what seemed to be miles of dark and mysterious underground caverns. However, the most important traffic on the Glyn Valley Tramway was not slate but granite road stone from the Hendre Quarry, situated two miles above Glynceiriog in the direction of Llanarmon. Passenger trains terminated at Glynceiriog, so the line beyond was a mineral extension only. It did not follow the road but was a reserved track and thus, to my eyes, a true railway. From the station platform it could be seen curving enticingly away out of sight up the narrow valley.

On my last visit to Plas-y-Garth from Gloucestershire in 1922 I had an experience even more exciting than the underground journey through the slate quarries. By dint of hanging around looking wistfully expectant while a driver topped up his tank at the station water column preparatory to taking a train of empties up to Hendre, I achieved my first ride on a locomotive footplate. With a jerk of his head and a terse 'Come on up then', the overalled king of the footplate condescended to let me share his throne. I was speechless with gratitude and wonderment. The locomotive was not one of the original tram engines but a later acquisition, one of the five hundred 4-6-0 side tank engines built by the Baldwin Locomotive Company of Philadelphia for service on the Western Front. After the war she had been bought by the G.V.T. and after re-gauging and other modifications, went into service in 1921. Unlike the older engines she was not given a name but was simply referred to in the valley as 'the Baldwin'. My chief impressions were of great heat, tremendous mechanical commotion (she had very small driving wheels) and of a ride so rough that it seemed incredible that we managed to stay on the rails. Later, I learned that these engines were notoriously rough riders. The load which we brought back from the Hendre Quarry that day represented only a minute fraction of the many thousands of tons of roadstone that were carried over the railway during its lifetime. In this fashion the G.V.T. literally paved the way for its own death. It was finally closed down in 1935 and today its surviving traces are so slender that only the initiated would guess that there had ever been a railway up the Ceiriog Valley.

Just after the war, my father skidded and crashed when returning home from Hereford on his A.J.S. Although he was unhurt apart from a few bruises, he evidently decided that the time had come to take to four wheels and the two motorcycles were sold. There could not have been a worse time to buy a car. Prices were inflated and manufacturers had long waiting lists. My father fancied a Calthorpe but because he could obtain no promise of early delivery, he finally bought the only new car that was then readily available, an Overland 'four', a black four-seater tourer which was Willys Overland's reply to the ubiquitous Model T Ford that it in many ways resembled. Though reasonably reliable, it was a very dreary car even by the standards of 1920, so as it cost my father nearly £500 by the time he had bought the various essential 'extras' like the headlamps and the horn, it was not a good buy. However, it did make us more mobile and I remember going off in the Overland for a summer holiday at St David's in Pembrokeshire. Although that part of Pembrokeshire is relatively flat, its narrow roads had numerous steep little pitches on them and I recall seeing the English light cars of the period failing on these hills and being compelled to tackle them in reverse. At least our Overland would go up anything in bottom gear, albeit slowly. It is the only time I can remember feeling snobbish about that car.

That holiday in Pembrokeshire was a bright spot in what was for me the blackest of black years. For, having reached the age of ten, my parents decided it was time I went to school and at the end of May 1920 I was sent to the Junior School of Cheltenham College as a boarder for the summer term. I think Cheltenham was chosen for its family associations, for although my father had not been there, a number of his brothers were old Cheltonians, and my uncle Vivian's son John was already in the senior school. I suppose that Cheltenham Junior School was no worse than other preparatory schools of the period and probably a great deal better than some, but to me, who had never been away from home by myself before, that first term was a traumatic experience. The school was an ugly barrack of red brick with the school playing field on one side and on the other a bleak expanse of asphalt surrounded by a high brick wall like some prison yard. Except on Sundays when we attended the College chapel in the morning and went for a walk in charge of a master in the afternoon, we were never allowed out, so that playing field and yard were the limits of our world. To one side of the playing field there was a small ornamental lake with an island linked by an ornamental bridge to a circumferential path. Even this was out of bounds. Occasionally some venturesome boy would be 'dared' by his fellows to run round this lake and over the bridge, but the strictest watch was maintained at all times and he was usually caught and beaten by the headmaster.

Most of the boys slept in two large dormitories divided into individual cubicles by partitions of varnished pitch-pine, their tops bristling with nails to discourage climbers. Bare, unpolished board floors could send long splinters into unwary feet. The narrow window of my cubicle in the upper dormitory overlooked the school yard and from its high vantage I could see over its wall into the garden of a large private house in the Grecian style which has since become part of the college. There was a wide expanse of smooth green lawn shaded by a great cedar tree and on hot summer evenings when I was unable to sleep I would see a small group of fortunate strangers reclining in basket chairs under the cedar. The sight reminded me of my father and my old tutor playing bowls on the tennis lawn at home, part of another world that now seemed infinitely far away. No banished Adam recalling lost Eden could have felt more desolate.

From late-coming and uneasy sleep I was awakened to face another day's purgatory by the school porter, Nash, a lugubrious and taciturn individual with a black walrus moustache who clumped along the corridor between the cubicles in his heavy boots clanging a large hand-bell. The first ritual of the day was a wash in cold water poured from a ewer into a tin washbasin. In my case this was usually perfunctory, consisting of creating enough lather to cloud the water suitably. This was particularly the case in winter when I often had to break the ice in my ewer, for the dormitories, though insufferably hot in summer, became bitterly cold in winter. Hot baths were taken only once a week by rota, but even this rare luxury was marred

by another horrible ritual designed to ensure that every boy's
bowels were kept open. With great jugs of senna tea, the matron
and assistant matron stood guard before the upper and lower
dormitories and each boy, as he returned from the bath, was
given an enamelled tin mug filled with the disgusting stuff. The
ruse for evading this was always to approach the hazard in
couples. Then, while one boy engaged the matron's attention,
either by a beguiling display of false charm or by detailing dire
imaginary symptoms ('I think I've got spots on my chest,
Matron') the other would covertly pour the contents of his mug
into his sponge. With expertise and a sufficiently large sponge,
most of the senna tea could be absorbed in this way, the sponge
being subsequently wrung out of one's cubicle window.

What astonished me was the fact that most of the boys
appeared to be quite resigned to such a way of life, while some
seemed to find it positively enjoyable. To me, school was a
prison which excluded me from all the wonder, beauty and
excitement of the world outside its walls and when I contemplated the long vista of school terms lying ahead of me I
despaired; it was as though I had been sentenced to penal servitude for life. It seemed incredible that my elders and betters, the
masters, could have created such a barbarous little world and
should appear to be so satisfied with it. It seemed to have been
planned on the assumption that small boys were so many beasts
who, if every waking minute of work or play were not ordered,
dragooned and disciplined, would run riot and commit fearful
crimes. I did not realise that the majority of my masters took
school life for granted because they had known no other. They
seemed to have none of that mature and kindly wisdom that had
made my old tutor such a good teacher and consequently I
learned nothing from them, or if I did I speedily forgot it.

Even if school life had been more civilised I believe it would
still have been anathema to me. For I was a solitary boy who
hated any form of hearty, communal life. Days so organised that
I was never allowed a moment to myself were an endless tor-
ment. The only time I was alone was in my cubicle at night.
There I would lie, open-eyed in the darkness, thinking by the
hour of my lost freedom, of Cusop Dingle, of the Black Mountains and Llanthony. For most people home-sickness is merely a
figure of speech, but for me that first term it became a physical
illness. Utterly miserable, I pined so intensely that I became
feverish and had to be moved into the sick bay. Since I revealed
no obvious physical symptoms, the school doctor could not

Chapter 4

Gloucestershire

It must have been towards the end of my summer holidays in 1920 that 'The Misfortune' occurred and it was a little ironical that my favourite uncle Algy should have been the agent of it. Urbane and charming as ever, he came down from London bearing bad tidings. I overheard raised Rolt voices arguing at length in my father's smoking room and later noticed that my mother had been in tears. I subsequently learned that, on my uncle's advice, my father had invested a sizeable slice of his meagre capital in a company which had just failed. My mother was extremely angry with both of them, perhaps unjustifiably; angry with my father for allowing himself to be led astray and with my uncle for leading him. My father was more resigned, attributing the loss to the inscrutable workings of fate; the 'Rolt luck' had struck again.

The drastic economies that became necessary as a result of this misfortune led to a number of changes, the most important of which was the decision to sell the house at Cusop and move to some smaller house, nearer to civilisation in England, which could be run without staff. My parents determined to look for such a house in the vicinity of Cheltenham, not because they intended to economise to the extent of making me a day boy, but because they had taken a fancy to the town and to the Cotswold country around it.

After a protracted search, they finally settled upon a house in the tiny hamlet of Stanley Pontlarge on the lower slopes of the north Cotswold scarp, eight miles from Cheltenham and three from Winchcombe. Known as 'the Cottage', in fact it consisted of two roomy attached cottages of Cotswold stone which had been converted into one house immediately after the war to the order of an elderly maiden lady who had not lived long to enjoy it. The two cottages were of widely different dates, the one being late eighteenth century and the other of great antiquity— fourteenth century if not earlier. My mother purchased this house, which included a large garden and an orchard, paying for it out of her dowry, or rather as much of it as had remained to her following the depredations of her step-father. Although comparatively near Cheltenham, the house stood in what was then deep country, reached by narrow, dusty, single-track white roads between high hedgerows. Apparently other members of my family thought my parents mad to bury themselves in such a remote place and considered that they had paid far too high a price for the property.

Our house at Cusop was sold to a young solicitor named Martin, who had recently put up his plate in Hay and who promptly changed its name from 'Radnor View' to 'Bredon'. Meanwhile our neighbour Mrs Armstrong at 'Mayfield' had become so seriously ill that she had to be removed to a nursing home in Gloucester. Almost the last social engagement that my mother fulfilled before we left the district was to attend a tea-party at Mayfield given by Mrs Armstrong to celebrate her remarkably rapid recovery and return. The congratulations of the local ladies on this occasion proved sadly premature, however, for their hostess shortly afterwards suffered a sudden relapse and died in a matter of days. The full significance of these events, however, was not revealed until later.

We moved to Gloucestershire in the spring of 1921. Although I soon learned to appreciate this country, particularly its incomparable stone buildings, it remained always very much a second love. It was the Welsh Border that had my heart. Even the spacious stone-walled uplands of Cotswold seemed tame to me when I compared them with the wildness and grandeur of the Black Mountains. From our new house a rough trackway led to the top of Stanley Mount, a promontory of the Cotswold edge. On clear evenings from his high vantage point I could see the Black Mountains on the skyline to the west, a high wall looming dark as a damson against the sunset over the nearer folds of the foothills. At least they were not so very far away. There were also other consolations. The ancient stone house fired my imagination in a way that the Edwardian villa we had left could never do. I used to speculate about the many forgotten generations who must have been born, lived and died in the house: what clothes they had worn, what they cooked and ate and how they spent their working lives. The more I learned of English history the more incredible did it seem that, since the Middle Ages, my new home had survived such an immensity of change practically unaltered. On what strange, wild landscape had its windows first looked? They may not even have been glazed then, for some of their stone sills still bore the squared mortice holes for the uprights of their original iron grilles. It gave me a strange sense of satisfaction to follow with my fingers the chamfer of an oak beam or the concave curve of a stone mullion and to think of the men who had fashioned them with adze and chisel at least five centuries ago.

Looking back, I believe that this house, in a different but related way, influenced me as profoundly as the landscape of the Welsh Border had earlier done. That country had revealed to me the heart-stopping beauty and permanence of the natural world. Now, the old house not only quickened my appreciation of craftsmanship, but taught me how man can make a positive and enduring contribution to the beauty of this world. Its builders had been primitive and unlettered men, yet by fashioning wood and local stone in such a manner that their work would stand long after their bones had become dust upon the wind, they had made, so it seemed to me, a magnificent affirmation of faith. I knew that all finite things must have an end, yet in this way I learned to value only those works of art or craftsmanship whose maker had endowed them with a mysterious quality of timelessness, as though they had contributed to them something of their own spirit and by that gift had transcended their mortality. Because only such things possessed for me an intrinsic value and so were truly life-enhancing, it was through this that I came to see the tragic paradox of the world in which I grew up. This was that in a society that worshipped material progress, all material things of man's creation were becoming increasingly ephemeral and therefore intrinsically valueless; ingenious certainly but, to paraphrase Traherne, 'an innumerable company of objects, rude, vulgar and worthless things'.

Besides the house itself, another source of great satisfaction to me was that it stood beside the Honeybourne–Cheltenham line of the Great Western Railway. This was then a comparatively new line, having been built as part of a determined effort made in the early years of this century to dispose of the jibe that the letters G.W.R. stood for Great Way Round. Opened throughout in August 1906, it provided the company with a new through route between Birmingham, South Wales, Bristol, and the West of England. Following the foot of the hills, the new railway passed our house in a shallow cutting, slicing diagonally through what had been a rectangular orchard with the effect that the orchard we acquired consisted of a long tapering triangle, its longest side separated from the bank of the cutting by a railway fence of posts and wire.

I made myself a comfortable wooden seat in the fork of one of the old apple trees overlooking the line and here I would sit, especially on Saturdays during the summer holidays when traffic was particularly heavy, watching the trains go by. There was a regular service of fast trains between Cardiff or Bristol and the Midlands which were then invariably hauled by locomotives of the 'Atbara' or 'Flower' classes—inside cylinder 4-4-0s with outside frames and taper boilers. But there was one train I used to look out for with particular eagerness, a through express (later to be called The Cornishman) which ran once a day in each direction between Wolverhampton and Penzance. This was invariably hauled by a locomotive of the 'County' class, a heavier and more powerful four-coupled engine with outside cylinders. I invested this train with all that romance of far journeys which we normally associate with an ocean-going steamship, for I had never been to Cornwall and Penzance seemed as foreign and remote as Pernambuco.

At first, most of the engines were in their war-time livery of unlined green, but soon they blossomed out in all their pre-war finery of elaborate lining, brass-beaded splashers and gleaming copper-capped chimneys. The trains they drew also changed as the crimson lake livery adopted for coaching stock in 1912 reverted to the familiar 'chocolate and cream' which I thought a tremendous improvement. At summer holiday week-ends, traffic to and from the west of England became so heavy that sometimes the Penzance express had to be run in as many as four parts. Hence my interest, for such traffic brought many unfamiliar locomotives to the line. Sometimes these would include a locomotive of the 'City' class that then carried a legendary aura of fame because, as I knew, one of them, *City of Truro* was said to have reached a speed of 100 m.p.h. down Wellington bank in Somerset.

One of the steps my father took as a result of the financial misfortune was to sell the Overland. This was wise for it had a voracious appetite for petrol and gave singularly little in return. He decided we must have a smaller and more economical car and purchased a new Belsize-Bradshaw, a small open two-seater with a single dickey seat to which I used to be relegated. I do not know what considerations governed this choice, but it proved singularly unfortunate. The car was an optimistic and unsuccessful bid on the part of the Belsize Company to conquer the British light car market with what was really a refined cyclecar. It was propelled by a 90° twin-cylinder oil-cooled engine designed by Granville Bradshaw which was a beautiful piece of engineering and, when running, was as smooth and silent as any four-cylinder engine of the day. Unfortunately, however, my father, who was by now advancing in years, could never succeed in starting it and this, as can be imagined, proved to be a very serious disadvantage. It was not helped by the fact that the car had no self-starter. For reasons of economy he had neglected to purchase this 'extra' in the first place, but why he did not subsequently do so is a question I cannot answer. Perhaps it was merely a stubborn refusal to admit defeat.

Stanley Pontlarge is situated upon a hill, a circumstance that has proved its value throughout my lifetime's association with peculiar and often temperamental motor-cars, but never more so than in the case of my father and his Belsize. By starting it down this hill, at least we were able to set out in the car, but once we stopped it on level ground our minds would be haunted by nagging doubt as to whether it could ever be induced to start again. I remember one such embarrassing occasion when we had stopped it outside the Lygon Arms at Broadway while we had tea. We sat in the car trying to look unconcerned, while my father applied himself to the starting handle with concentrated but unavailing fury. A succession of kindly but slightly patronising chauffeurs took pity on him ('Let me have a go, sir') and were each in turn reduced to a state of breathless apoplexy. Finally they pushed us off down the road and when, by this agency, the engine fired, the small crowd that had gathered gave us an encouraging cheer. I found such scenes most humiliating. Their cause was that the 90° angle of the twin-cylinders does not agree with the armature positions of maximum polarity on a normal magneto. This faces the mechanic with a choice of evils: either two indifferent sparks or one powerful one and one extremely weak. Presumably our car had been given the first of these two settings. I did not discover this until some years later, while it was completely beyond my father's comprehension.

From this it will be understood why normally we only used the Belsize for long journeys such as our annual Christmas visits to Chester and relied on public transport or bicycles for shopping expeditions to Cheltenham or other local outings. There were no 'buses in those days, so public transport meant the service of 'push-and-pull' local trains that served all stations and halts between Cheltenham (St James) and Honeybourne. We boarded these at Gretton Halt, a typical Great Western halt with its wooden platforms and pagoda-like shelters situated a quarter of a mile away. We were very dependent on the railway's reliable and comfortable service, a state of affairs that continued for many years. We even had our *Morning Post* delivered by rail from the bookstall at Cheltenham St James, bearing a G.W.R. newspaper stamp. The guard of the 8 a.m. 'local' was officially supposed to leave it in the up side shelter at Gretton Halt but, to save us the trouble of going to collect it, whenever the weather was fine he threw it out of the window opposite a platelayers' hut by our orchard. It would then be retrieved by a friendly lengthman who stuck it in the railings by the house.

I shall always remember one early excursion by rail to Cheltenham with my mother because, when we had boarded the train at St James to return, she opened the local evening newspaper she had just bought at the bookstall and read the astounding news that our erstwhile neighbour, Major Armstrong, had been arrested and charged with the murder of his wife. Soon we learned the whole fantastic and terrible story. When Martin, the young solicitor who had bought our old house, started practice in Hay, Armstrong had determined to rid himself of this unwelcome competitor by poisoning him with arsenic. His opening gambit was to send Martin an anonymous present of a box of chocolates through the post. This failed because neither Martin nor his wife liked chocolates, but when they subsequently handed them round at a bridge party, their guests became seriously ill. His suspicions aroused, Martin then sent the remaining chocolates to the Public Analyst who discovered that each contained arsenic which had been injected through a minute hole in the base. Martin then remembered that the box had been addressed to his house under its new name although he had only just made the change and no one outside the immediate district had been notified of it. This convinced him that the poisoner must be someone living locally.

Meanwhile, finding that his chocolates had failed to have the desired effect, Armstrong began repeatedly pressing Martin to take tea with him. Although Martin had taken a hearty dislike to the man, Armstrong was so persistent that he could no longer with good manners refuse a business colleague. So he reluctantly accepted. That night Martin was taken so seriously ill that had he not possessed a remarkably strong constitution he would have died. As he was recovering, he recalled a curious little incident at that tea party. There had been a plate of buttered scones on the table. 'Have a scone?' Armstrong had asked and, without waiting for his answer, had remarked 'Excuse fingers' as he selected one and placed it on his guest's plate.

Undaunted by this second failure, Armstrong renewed his invitations but, not unnaturally, after his previous experience, his prospective victim stolidly refused, having secretly informed Scotland Yard of the suspicious circumstances. The two plain clothes detectives who visited Hay, ostensibly travelling in cheap watches, were not only interested in Martin. In the light of his experience they were concerned to investigate the circumstances of Mrs Armstrong's sudden death. When her body was secretly exhumed in Cusop churchyard there was scarcely any need for an autopsy for even the soil around the coffin was impregnated with arsenic. Armstrong had been slowly poisoning her so that it was no wonder she made so remarkable a recovery when she was removed to a nursing home beyond his reach. No wonder, either, that the celebratory party the unfortunate woman gave on her return proved to be the last nail in her coffin where her husband was concerned. He felt that things had dragged on far too long and speedily administered the final, fatal dose.

Following these ghoulish proceedings, people recalled that the last two representatives of a respectable old firm of family solicitors in Hay named Cheese had died suddenly in recent years shortly after Armstrong had set up in business. Whether they should also be exhumed was seriously considered, but in the event this was not necessary. After a long and sensational trial in which Armstrong pleaded that the arsenic found in envelopes in his desk (each envelope containing a fatal dose) was purchased from the local chemist for the purpose of killing the dandelions on his lawn, he was sentenced to death and hanged. For many years afterwards his effigy stood in the Chamber of Horrors at Madame Tussaud, but as memories of his crime faded the sight of the little erect figure with the bright blue eyes failed to produce any *frisson* and it was either put into store or melted down.

After their first astonishment and shock, my parents' feeling was one of relief that we had left Hay when we did, because otherwise they might have been called as witnesses at the trial.

I think this unlikely because if Martin had not bought our old house, Armstrong might never have attempted his life, or at least not in such a bungling way, and the murder would still be unsuspected.

At this distance of time it is difficult to recall the precise effect that the revelation of these sensational events had upon me. I think my reaction was then, as it is now, one of sheer incredulity. I found it very hard to believe that in such a peaceful little community these things could actually have happened. I made a mental effort to recall the Major Armstrong I had known, striding over the hills or reading the lessons in Cusop church, in order to discover whether, in retrospect, there was anything sinister about him. For some reason the occasion I found I could recall most vividly was of watching him wind up the carbide container of the acetylene gas lighting plant which he had in-stalled in an outhouse at Mayfield. This container, as I remem-ber it, was suspended by wire cables and was actuated by some clockwork mechanism which allowed it to sink slowly into a tank of water. I could hear the clicking of the pawl on its ratchet as Armstrong wound it up. Perhaps it was some association between the white powder of the spent carbide and arsenic that made this gas generator seem in recollection a sinister infernal machine and the building which housed it a Bluebeard's chamber. But there was never any doubt in my mind that, despite the fact that he murdered 'in cold blood', Armstrong was as mad as a hatter. His story is like some monstrous black comedy. No sane man would go about his fell business in so naïve and ridiculous a manner. His conviction and execution led me in later life to question the validity of the McNaghten rules and the whole concept of capital punishment.

It is difficult nowadays to appreciate what the sudden loss of domestic help meant to my parents' generation. For my mother it was undoubtedly the consequence of 'The Misfortune' which she found the hardest to bear. Being house-proud, she took to housework happily enough while gardening was the consuming passion of her life. But she always insisted that she hated cooking although she became quite proficient at it, using a reeking paraffin cooker in the scullery in preference to the large kitchen range which was soon ousted in favour of an independent boiler. However, like some shameful secret, she was always at pains to conceal the fact that we now had no staff. Consequently friends or neighbours were seldom or never entertained and even the visits of members of the family became rarer. Mrs Peart, a dear old countrywoman, tiny and bird-like, used to arrive from time to time on an ancient bicycle to 'do the rough' for my mother. Her husband, old 'Lisha Peart, was the local pig-killer and terrier man for the hunt and they lived in a cottage at the top of Prescott Hill nearby. On the very rare occasions when we had a visitor to luncheon, Mrs Peart would be summoned to wait at table, tricked out in housemaid's uniform, and in this way honour was saved.

The move to Gloucestershire coincided with, or may have helped to bring about, a marked change in my mother's standards of taste. Edwardian furniture which we had hitherto taken for granted now suddenly looked incongruous in its new surroundings. Over the years it was gradually replaced by antiques purchased with shrewd judgement by my mother. All the bric-à-brac of the Edwardian drawing-room, precarious occasional tables, brass 'hearth furniture', art nouveau vases, family photographs and weak water-colours on wide mounts in gilt frames, was consigned to oblivion in the attic along with (I suspect to his secret regret) my father's trophies: the silver cups, the whale bone and the pelican's head. Even his gun case was relegated to an inconspicuous position under the stairs. The two ugly modern grates with glazed tiles which had been installed in the hall and drawing-room as part of the recent 'restoration' were ripped out. Patterned wallpaper was taboo and we now lived in almost monastic simplicity surrounded by white or cream washed walls and an almost complete lack of colour and ornament apart from chintz curtains and bowls of flowers. No greater contrast to our two previous homes could be imagined.

The only part of this transformation I have lived to regret was that every piece of interior woodwork, ancient or modern, was stained almost black according to the mistaken notion of the time that all old houses must be 'black and white'. Only the massive roof timbers of the older of the two wings were spared this treatment and retained the lovely pale colour of ancient seasoned oak. The whole of the first floor had once been open to this roof, forming a single great hall, originally reached by a tallet or outside staircase.[1] But the first floor had been ceiled off and partitioned

---

[1] Early references to a court house at Stanley Pontlarge have led me to suspect that this may have been the hall in which the manorial courts were held. The manor was originally given by William the Conqueror to one of his kinsmen, Robert de Pont l'Arch—hence the name.

in the seventeenth century leaving a large, chapel-like attic above which became my particular domain.

To recall this part of Gloucestershire as I knew it as a boy in the 1920s is a somewhat melancholy exercise, so great have been the changes that have come about since, not all of them for the better. Rural life in the neighbourhood has changed more profoundly in my lifetime than at any other period since this ancient house was built, the enclosures not excepted. When I was a boy, an old Gloucestershire yeoman farmer named Mr Bowl ran the neighbouring Manor Farm on traditional mixed farming lines little different from those I had known at Cusop. I can see him now as he walked down the lane, leading his sheep, crook in hand and wearing a magnificent smock, richly embroidered over the chest. The farm tractor had not then reached Stanley Pontlarge and there was a large stable of horses at the Manor Farm. The fields surrounding the farm and on the hill slopes above were all permanent pastures grazed by cattle and sheep and by a large herd of cows which filled the stalls of the long cow byre at milking time. Each morning, the bulk of the milk was despatched in brightly polished churns on a horse-drawn milk float to Winchcombe station and one of my pleasures during the holidays was to accompany the farmer's son on this errand and give him a hand with the churns. In the fresh air of sunlit summer mornings it was delightful to jog along between the green hedgerows, the iron tyres of the float rumbling over the white, dusty road. Some of the milk would be kept back for local consumption and I would go to the dairy, presided over by the farmer's daughter, Florence, to fetch our daily jug of milk. Here on slate slabs the milk stood in great flat pans so that the cream would rise to the surface to be skimmed off. Those who buy their cream in cartons will never know the richness and flavour of such cream as that.

The farm's arable fields were all on the light Cotswold brash on the top of the hill and at harvest time the heavy-laden wagons would come swaying slowly down the rough track to the big stone barn. When this barn was full, the sheaves were built into symmetrical and beautifully thatched ricks in the adjacent rick-yard. Then, on some misty autumn morning, came the thrill of the threshing. A traction engine belonging to the Winchcombe Steam Ploughing Company, brass lagging bands a-twinkle, would come panting heavily up the lane past our house towing threshing drum and straw elevator and 'set up' in the rickyard. For the next few days we would hear the drone of the drum, its note rising and falling as the sheaves were fed in, while a column of steam and smoke rose over the roof of the barn.

In the orchard beyond the barn a stone-walled dam had been built to impound a small stream that came off the hill. Below this dam was a washpool where, each year at the end of May, the ritual of washing farmer Bowl's sheep flock took place. Here I would watch the men who, standing on the parapet of the pool, wielded their long dipping-hooks deftly to guide the floundering sheep and ensure that each was properly immersed. Such men were highly skilled in innumerable farming tasks and could as readily repair one of the dry-stone walls that surrounded the arable fields on the uplands as they could lay a hedge in the vale below. Yet they received little in return. One farm labourer I remember named Gregory kept a wife and nine children on 26s a week. He and his family lived in a small stone shepherd's cottage halfway up the hill which was inaccessible except on foot.

This particular district midway between hill and vale was noted for its cider, for it was said that the heavy clay land that extends to the knees of the hills hereabouts grew particularly good cider fruit. Although the drink was always referred to as cider, it was the practice to use more pears than apples in its making and many varieties of pear were grown, each of which imparted a particular flavour and quality to the cider. These pear trees grow to great size and when white with blossom in spring put on a beauty that would have ravished the eye of Samuel Palmer. There are still three such trees in our orchard and a few years ago I asked an old farmer whether he could identify them. 'Them's Malvern 'ills,' he said. 'We used 'em to make sweet cider for the ladies and them's Bucks, we used 'em to make a man's drink, sharp and strong.' But when I was a boy there used to be another tree in our orchard, now long vanished, which bore pears of a bright red colour. Like many another species, its precise use is probably now lost to memory. Such fruit is useless for any other purpose. I remember my mother, attracted by their appetising colour, attempting without success to stew those red pears. The fruit remained obstinately wooden and tasteless.

Every farm along the lower slopes of the hills not only had its cider orchard but a great stone mill for pulping the fruit which was turned by a horse. There was—and still is—the circular stone trough and roller of such a mill in our orchard; it had not been used since time out of mind though other mills of similar type still worked at neighbouring farms. There was also a local public 'cider house' which had its own orchard and mill.

Old farmer Bowl at the Manor Farm was a connoisseur of cider. He used to leave the fruit heaped up in an old farm wagon until it was rotten before making his cider and transferring the liquor to the great wooden casks in his cellar. The result was of superb quality, richly flavoured and bland but deceptively potent. It was totally different from that sharp rough cider known as scrumpy that removes the varnish from one's teeth and from that gaseous liquid in bottles that now bears the name. In later years after I had left school, whenever I returned on a visit to my parents I habitually spent an evening yarning with this old farmer. It was a ritual to which I always looked forward. His first action after greeting me was to draw a jug of cider from his cellar which we drank from china mugs seated one on either side of the wood fire. The mellow liquor, the warmth and the scent of the glowing logs and the placid voice of the old man as he spoke of country matters past or present in his rich Gloucestershire dialect had upon me an effect that was positively euphoric. I used to feel delicious but indescribable sensations crawling up my spine into the base of my neck and all the anxieties of life would seem of no account. I have since found that, even without such aids as a wood fire and alcohol, the talk of certain wise old people, usually countrymen or craftsmen, can have a similarly therapeutic effect upon me.

While most of the nearby villages depended on outside stand-pipes, at Stanley Pontlarge we did have piped water. It flowed—and still flows—by gravity from a spring on the hillside into roof storage tanks. But we had no electric light or telephone and I have to confess that it was I who first introduced the wire-scape to Stanley Pontlarge. As a result of a judicious swop at school I became the proud owner of a crystal wireless receiving set. This latest marvel of science consisted of a little box of stained and varnished deal with a couple of coils, one fixed and one movable, sprouting from its side. In the centre of its black vulcanite top was mounted the little glass cylinder containing the crystal and the slender corkscrew of the 'cat's-whisker', clamped in the adjusting arm. Also two terminals to which one attached the headphones. I bore this magical piece of apparatus home in triumph. My mother looked at the box as though it contained a poisonous snake and banished it to the attic forth-with. My father, however, was more co-operative and inquisi-tive. He rigged up a long aerial for me, slinging it from the roof to a branch of a nearby pear tree, bringing the lead-in through an attic window and fixing up an earth lead. Triumph! When all the connections had been made, the coils adjusted and the crystal delicately probed with the cat's-whisker, the distant voice of 2LO spoke clearly through the headphones. Despite this success, however, my mother's prejudice was not lightly overcome and for many months the wireless set was confined to the attic. My father used to go furtively aloft sometimes to listen to the news.

My mother never permitted the set in our drawing-room, but by a very gradual process of compromise she came, first to tolerate it and finally even to listen to it. The set was eventually brought down to one of the window sills in the hall where it was concealed behind a curtain. Finally, my father constructed a terminal board to which two pairs of headphones could be attached. By unwinding from the board a long length of flex, it could be conveyed into the drawing room where my parents would 'listen in', seated one on either side of the fire. Since they rarely liked the same programme, headphones had their advantages. This arrangement had a serious drawback, however. More often than not, no sooner was my father settled in his chair with his pipe going well than a heavy goods train would pass by and its vibration shake the cat's-whisker off the sensitive spot in the crystal. Then, muttering curses under his breath, he would have to get up from his chair and go out, paraffin lamp in hand and trailing terminal board and flex, into the dark hall to adjust the set. Nevertheless, despite such snags, this device survived until after my father's death in 1941 although by that time reception was hardly satisfactory due to the unselectivity of a crystal set in an ether becoming increasingly crowded. Often it would produce a positive babel of sound as it received at least three stations at equal strength with the Post Office transatlantic telephone beam from Hillmorton thrown in for good measure. When, in its later days, I picked up the headphones expecting to hear the news and listened instead to two voices negotiating the sale of a dog across the Atlantic, I wondered if we could boast the last crystal set still in regular use in England.

One of these listening-in sessions was more alarmingly interrupted than by a passing train. There was suddenly a loud report in the drawing-room. In the same instant a small round hole appeared in the ceiling above my father's head and his lap was filled with shreds of smouldering tobacco. It transpired that a round of ·22 ammunition which he was carrying in his pocket (he had been potting starlings on the roof with the Winchester) had found its way into his tobacco pouch and from thence inadvertently into his pipe.

Dramatic incidents of this kind rarely disturbed the even tenor of life at Stanley Pontlarge. Compared with life today it seems remarkably static and uneventful. My parents occupied themselves with gardening during the day and usually retired to bed at ten o'clock. Visitors were extremely rare and this unvarying domestic routine would be punctuated only by the weekly shopping expedition to Cheltenham and, during term time, by fetching me from school after morning chapel on Sundays for a few hours. In such a level plain a few experiences stand out like mountains, the highest peak being when my father took me to see the Wembley Exhibition. It was my first visit to London and we stayed at Berners Hotel. I remember gazing in awe at the *Flying Scotsman* and *Caerphilly Castle* in the Palace of Engineering; also at the ingenious 'Never-stop Railway' through the Exhibition grounds in which the cars were 'threaded' on a screw of varying pitch revolving between the rails so that they slowed to a crawl at the station platforms. But there was such an indigestible plethora of 'serious' exhibits that I soon tired of it and confess that I spent much of my time and most of my father's money ecstatically riding on the Giant Switchback, the Great Racer and the Scenic Railway in the amusement park. In the evenings my father took me to see *The Green Goddess* at the St James's Theatre, with George Arliss in Western clothes and turban playing the smooth and sinister rajah, and to 'Maskelyne's Theatre of Mysteries' at St George's Hall. I think all subsequent generations of children have been the poorer for the passing of Maskelyne's. It was, in both senses of the word, a magical entertainment with which no pantomine could compare and it held me completely enthralled.

In the autumn of 1925 my father made another of his rare trips to London to visit the Motor Show at Olympia. I do not know whether he went with the serious intention of buying another car to replace the recalcitrant Belsize—I suspect not—but he was so attracted by a Model TE sports four-seater displayed on the Alvis stand that he bought it on the spot. It was a fairly expensive car at that time and a somewhat surprising choice for an elderly man to make. What my mother thought of his extravagance I do not know. It was my father's last financial fling but, unlike previous ones, it proved a good investment. For throughout the remaining sixteen years of his life, the Alvis was an unfailing source of pleasure and pride to him. Though he was quite unmechanically minded, the car never let him down on the road and never needed any major repairs. And because it is still in my possession I have every reason to endorse the wisdom of his choice.

Such longevity is the more surprising because, although for a man of his age my father was a fast and spirited driver, he never succeeded in mastering the art of changing gear on a 'crash' gearbox. Unable to equate engine speed to road speed, he always changed down to third by pushing the lever straight through with a sickening crunch most horrible to the mechanical ear. His other besetting fault was his impatience. After following a slower vehicle for some distance along a winding road he would invariably become exasperated and, shouting 'Why can't the dam' feller get a move on?' above the high-pitched whine of the gears, storm past in third quite regardless of any lack of visibility ahead. This manœuvre caused even the most unimaginative of passengers to shut his eyes and offer up a silent prayer. It is unlikely that either my father or his Alvis could have survived for long under modern traffic conditions. One trip beside him, never to be repeated, was enough to convince my ultracautious uncle George that he was a serious menace. But, miraculously, he never had an accident of any kind and the recurring appearance of the Alvis outside the College chapel on Sunday mornings to take me out 'on invite' raised my stock considerably. I became an insufferable little car snob.

Over my school life at this period it were best to draw a kindly veil. Although, like every other schoolboy, I was assured that school days would give me the best time of my life, in fact my experience was the precise opposite. I have yet to meet a man who subscribes to this 'best years of your life' myth, while autobiographers of my generation agree in anathematising their school days so roundly and at such length that for me to join their chorus would be tedious. Suffice it to say that I duly passed from the Junior House into the Military and Engineering side of Cheltenham College where I fondly hoped I would learn something about engineering. I was soon disappointed. I was not an academic type, but by some fluke I did so well in Common Entrance that I passed straight in to the fourth form in the college where I remained floundering ever after like some stranded fish. I made only two friends at college. Dissimilar in character and united only in our intense dislike of 'corps', compulsory games, school meals and petty rules, customs and conventions, we were looked upon as a thoroughly disreputable trio, entirely lacking the 'college spirit'. In such a closed community I felt completely cut off from the outside world and by the end of 1925, this frustrating situation had become quite intolerable. It was the more intolerable because I was now old enough to realise that my parents could scarcely afford to pay my school fees. That they should have to make such a financial sacrifice to enable me to waste my precious time when all I wanted to do was to get out into the world struck me as an absurd situation. So I asked my father if he would take me away from school at the end of the spring term and, somewhat to my surprise, he agreed to do so.

When my father gave notice of his intention, he and I were bidden to the presence of the headmaster as though we were two errant pupils. That interview was frigid and extremely brief. We found the head seated behind the large desk in his study, elbows on the desk top and fingertips together in a stern judicial pose. 'I suppose you realise, Mr Rolt,' he intoned gravely, 'that by taking this step you are ruining your son's career.' My father was not in the least overawed. 'I think that is a matter for me to judge,' he replied smoothly and, taking me by the arm, we walked out together. I felt like cheering and clapping my father on the back so great was my sense of relief and my joy in the prospect of an early end to a prison sentence that had seemed interminable. Seven long wasted years would soon be ended. At last I could begin living and learning in a much larger school.

It was one of the red-letter days of my life when, in April 1926 at the age of sixteen, I finally turned my back on school. Nor have I ever had cause to regret this precipitate step. I suppose that by taking it I was the 1920s equivalent of today's so-called 'drop-outs'. But there was a difference. For whereas they depend on doles from an 'establishment' they affect to despise, my great ambition was to be dependent on no one but myself. It is true that during the five years of my apprenticeship my parents had to contribute towards my board and lodging but, knowing their straitened circumstances, my aim from the start was to earn my own living as soon as might be. It was going to be a much more difficult goal to achieve than I bargained for, so dark were the economic clouds that would soon gather.

Part II

Chapter 5

Steam at Pitchill

Apart from that one tenuous link with James Nasmyth, my family had no connections whatever with engineering so, at this critical time, my parents and I turned for help and advice to my uncle—as I called him—Kyrle Willans, who had married my mother's great friend and my godmother, Hero Taylor, sister to my uncle George. Because no man had a greater influence upon the course of my life for several years to come than Kyrle Willans, some account of the family background and career of this most remarkable man will not be out of place at this point.

He was the son of Peter Willans, a brilliantly inventive mechanical engineer whose most famous invention was the central valve steam engine, a vertical, fully enclosed high speed unit which, in association with his friend Colonel R. E. B. Crompton, was developed for electricity generation. Willans engines of this type were employed in many of the early power stations before the advent of the steam turbine. With his partner, Mark Robinson, Peter Willans built his engines and small steam craft at the Ferry Works, Thames Ditton. Later, he removed to Rugby to a factory which is still referred to locally as the Willans Works. It was at Rugby that Peter Willans died prematurely in May 1892 as a result of a fall from a trap.

While he was at Thames Ditton, Peter Willans owned a demonstration steam launch which he fitted with one of his early engines and named *Black Angel*. About the year 1879, he made a voyage of 1,000 miles through the inland waterways in *Black Angel* from the Thames to Ripon and back. This fact is not without significance, for Kyrle Willans inherited his father's interest in inland waterways and, in turn, communicated it to me. He also inherited from his father and passed on to me views on the value of practical engineering training and experience which would be considered deplorably old-fashioned and heretical today. While it is true that British engineering has suffered in the past from too great a reliance on practice to the exclusion of theory, I wonder sometimes whether the pendulum has not now swung too far the other way. 'A pinch of practice is worth a pound of theory' was one of my uncle's favourite maxims and he would refer to 'that curse of all works, the designer without workshop experience', quoting one of his famous father's trenchant remarks: 'Any fool can tighten a nut with a pencil'. He was a brilliant mechanical engineer with much of his father's inventive talent. He was also an uncompromising individualist with no respect at all for the upper hierarchies of commerce or for the sanctities of the boardroom. Hating pomposity and pretension, he had a delightfully sardonic sense of humour which made him a past-master in the art of deflating self-esteem. When he was in a mellow mood there could be no more delightful companion, but he was self-opinionated to a degree and extremely touchy. Quick to take offence, often where none was intended, he would suddenly become inexplicably morose. He was a short, thick-set man with a square face, a firm humorous mouth downturned at the corners and a massive jaw. I found him at once endearing and formidable and admired him enormously.

With such a character it is not surprising that Kyrle Willans was regarded askance as something of a stormy petrel by an engineering world which, to an increasing extent, was becoming dominated by the board room, the accountant and the theorist. He could seldom disguise his contempt for 'white collar men' who had no experience on the shop floor yet who sought to interfere in practical engineering matters. Consequently, for all his undoubted engineering genius, he pursued a roving career from job to job, never attaining the high position that his talent merited. I do not think he would have been happy if he had, for such a position would almost certainly have cut him off from those practical engineering activities which he loved. Owing to his peripatetic existence I would not care to count accurately the number of different houses he and his family occupied. This was hard on my godmother, 'aunt Hero' who, like my mother, was passionately fond of gardening. No sooner had she got a garden established to her liking than her husband would decide to move on and she had to begin all over again, often in a totally different part of England. Yet she never complained for she was one of the kindest and best of women whose memory I cherish with deep affection.

While I was still at school, Kyrle Willans held the post of chief engineer with a small firm of general engineers named Blackwells in Northampton and the Willans family had moved into a roomy old house of golden Northamptonshire limestone known as The Grange in the attractive village of Milton Melzor between Northampton and Blisworth. During my holidays, my mother and I paid more than one visit there, travelling from our nearest Midland Railway station at Beckford through Evesham to Broom Junction and thence via the Stratford-on-Avon and Midland Junction Railway[1] to Blisworth. At that time my uncle Kyrle was using a 1906 6 h.p. single-cylinder Rover to commute between his house and the works at Northampton, a choice of vehicle which, even in 1924, was considered a trifle eccentric since it possessed neither hood nor windscreen. It was a brilliant summer's day with a sky of cloudless blue when my uncle first invited me to accompany him to the works in the Rover. I was therefore somewhat surprised when he attired himself for so short a journey in a seaman's oilskin and sou'-wester. It was a precaution which I thought excessive, but I soon discovered the reason for it. Ascending the hill on the approach to Northampton in bottom gear, the Rover began to boil so violently that we were liberally sprayed with hot water and so enveloped in steam that it became difficult to see the road ahead. That was the first car I ever drove. In low gear and on full lock, I remember circulating proudly round and round the yard at the back of the house at Milton.

For works transport, Blackwells used an even more remarkable vehicle, a White steam lorry of indeterminate date. Outwardly, this resembled a solid-tyred petrol-engined lorry of the period, but its bonnet concealed a vertical steam engine which was supplied from a flash boiler under the seat of the cab, its 'radiator' being a condenser. On one occasion my cousin Bill Willans and I were allowed to accompany the driver of this vehicle on his rounds. I think that the paraffin burner which fired the flash boiler must have been more than usually temperamental, for the cab would sometimes fill with choking fumes and I was alarmed by the tongues of flame which occasionally

[1] The S.M.J. was rudely christened the Slow, Mouldy & Jolting. Tedious it may have been, yet I have the happiest memories of these slow journeys by this unfrequented railway byway that wandered across the breadth of the midland shires. Like most cross-country lines, it is now no more than a memory.

licked out in unexpected places. One of our ports of call was a local celluloid factory where, not unnaturally, the strictest fire precautions were enforced. Here the appearance of the White, exuding smoke and flame, occasioned considerable alarm and we were unceremoniously shooed away.

One of Blackwells' regular jobs was the repair of industrial steam locomotives from the local ironstone quarry railways. My uncle, a steam man born and bred, deplored the inefficiency of the orthodox steam locomotive for such slow-moving applications, arguing that a steam engine which could be geared down to the wheels would be far more efficient because it could be kept turning at an economic speed, avoiding unnecessary heat losses accompanied by condensation of the steam in the cylinders. When a small Manning Wardle four-coupled saddle tank locomotive named *Ancoats*, from the Isham Quarries between Kettering and Wellingborough, came into the works for repair and it was found that she needed a new boiler, my uncle, with the permission of the quarry company, was able to try out his theory. An old Sentinel steam waggon was purchased second-hand, its engine and boiler removed and mounted in the frames of *Ancoats*. The engine drove on to one axle by roller chain and a second similar chain was used to couple the two axles together. On my first visit to Blackwells, I saw this conversion in progress on the shop floor and on a subsequent visit I was able to ride the footplate of *Ancoats* when she made her first trial run over the Isham Quarry line.

So successful did *Ancoats* prove that the Sentinel Waggon Works at Shrewsbury decided to take up the manufacture of geared steam locomotives. Engine and boiler units of greater power and capacity than those used in the road vehicle were designed for the new locomotives and my uncle was appointed to take charge of a Sentinel locomotive sales office in Chester. This entailed a move from Northamptonshire and at the time I left school the Willans family were installed in a house called Deebank in the village of Farndon. This was situated on the upstream side of Farndon bridge, looking out from a high bank across the Dee which here forms the border between Cheshire and Flintshire. From the house one could see the weekly Sunday pilgrimage of thirsty Welshmen crossing the bridge from 'dry' Wales into 'wet' Cheshire. I visited Deebank on my first motorcycle, a 2¼ h.p. B.S.A., at the time of the General Strike.

With such exciting experiences during my holidays it can be imagined how eagerly I looked forward to the day when I would no longer be a passive spectator of the engineering activities of others but would be able to put on a suit of overalls and get down to the job myself. My uncle Kyrle recommended my parents to send me as a pupil for two years to his friends, the brothers Douglas, Leslie and Ernest Bomford, farmers and agricultural engineers of Pitchill, near Evesham. This was only fifteen miles away from Stanley Pontlarge, so I should be able to come home for week-ends on my motorcycle. I began my new life at Pitchill on 29th May 1926.

Pitchill is on the fringe of the Vale of Evesham near the Worcestershire–Warwickshire border and the Bomfords had been farming there for three generations. Their grandfather, Benjamin Bomford, had been a pioneer in the district of steam cultivation and there are old photographs extant showing his first set of steam cable engines—curious Savory machines with rope drum encircling the boiler barrel. Their father had been a great friend of Sir Oliver Lodge who frequently came to stay at the former's home at Bevington Hall. On one of these occasions Sir Oliver determined to try the effect of high tension, low amperage current on the growth of strawberry plants and with his friend's enthusiastic collaboration a trial plot in one of the strawberry fields was strung with a cat's-cradle of wires supported on poles. Such strange goings-on were not popular with the farm labourers whose hoes were apt to make contact with the wires with electrifying results. But apparently the strawberry plants benefited, though not to an economic extent. With the same pioneer spirit as their forebears, the three Bomford brothers not only ran a very large farm, part of it devoted to growing fruit, but also maintained a sizeable engineering workshop beside the farm at Pitchill. This, besides dealing with home farm machinery, repaired and serviced the five sets of steam cable ploughing tackle with which they undertook contract cultivation and ploughing all over the Evesham vale. Four of these sets consisted of Fowler compounds, while the fifth was a pair of compound MacLarens. A sixth set of very old single-cylinder Fowlers was kept for use on the home farm. In addition there was a Ransome traction engine and threshing drum which went out on contract and also did work on the farm. Finally, there was an old Sentinel steam waggon which did farm road haulage and a Marshall steam portable engine which was used to drive the workshop machinery. My uncle was right in thinking that working in this small shop would be a good introduction to steam engineering.

For a young apprentice straight from school it is far better that his initiation should be in a small jobbing engineering workshop of this kind rather than in some large works. Not only does he get more personal attention, but there is a much greater variety of work. Almost every day some new job comes along with its own special problems to test his aptitude, his initiative and his manual dexterity whereas, in a large production shop he is often given some menial, unskilled task to perform which may last for weeks or even months. This may be good discipline but it is a waste of his precious training time because it does not teach him his craft.

Besides myself, there were only seven on the regular strength of the Pitchill shop. They were Percy Lester, the working foreman, Will Salisbury and Alan Bloxham, fitters and machinists, a blacksmith whose name I do not remember, Ernest Cole the carpenter, Joe Bailey, an ex-steam-plough driver, and a little shop boy, younger than myself, named George Leonard. Joe Bailey finished his steam-ploughing career when he lost his forearm in the motion of his engine. He was now the shop labourer and looked after the portable engine which supplied the power. With the exception of Percy Lester, whose home was in Redditch and who came to work on a motorcycle, all were local countrymen. Humorous, wise and gentle men, they taught me much, not only about their crafts but about human nature and country ways. While the memory of many men with whom I have been associated subsequently has faded, after more than forty years I find I can recall them most clearly to mind, see their faces, their characteristic expressions and gestures, and even hear their voices.

When a set of ploughing tackle which had been out on contract work returned to its base at Pitchill for attention and overhaul, its living van would be parked in the yard and the men in charge of it then helped with the maintenance work. This meant that there were usually more than seven of us working in the shop. Because they came and went, I do not recall these 'outside' men so clearly. I remember Archie Ellison, a small, lean, gnome-like man who was in charge of the big MacLarens and Will Robbins who drove the Sentinel steam waggon and, occasionally, one of the steam ploughing engines used on the farm. Will Robbins was a tall, lugubrious man of about sixty with the expression of a sad spaniel. He wore a heavy black moustache which completely concealed his mouth so that I do not know if he ever smiled. I assumed so from the occasional twinkle that lit

his steady blues eyes. But of the steam plough drivers the man I
remember best of all was old Bill Smith. Over seventy years of
age, he no longer went out on contract work but was in charge
of the two old Fowler engines which were used on the farm. He
therefore spent much more of his time in the shop than did the
other drivers. Bill Smith was a rural character of a kind rarely
to be met today. His notions of personal hygiene were minimal.
He habitually wore a very battered and faded trilby hat, wisps
of sparse white hair straying beneath its brim. Because he never
wore overalls and apparently never changed his clothes he presented an appearance so filthy and so tattered that it verged
upon the indecent. The humorous wrinkles that fanned from the
corner of his eyes were deeply ingrained with dirt. Not surprisingly, he smelt, but fortunately this stench was usually
overlaid by the reek of his incredibly strong shag tobacco. He
rolled this between his grimy paws before stuffing it in an old
briar pipe from which the vulcanite mouthpiece had long since
broken off. Consequently, it was so short that the edge of the
bowl touched the tip of his nose. He appeared to subsist entirely
on thick slices of cold boiled bacon wedged between great hunks
of bread. This he washed down with noisy gulps from a bottle
of home-made parsnip wine of great potency. One hot noon day,
Ernest Cole the carpenter incautiously accepted a swig from
Bill Smith's proffered bottle, tottered back to his shop and was
discovered later that afternoon stretched out insensible upon
his bench. Yet Bill habitually drank a pint of the stuff at each
lunchtime sitting and appeared to suffer no ill effects. Since he
often ate his lunch with hands plastered in white lead after making
a new joint for a steam pipe or inspection cover, he was apparently
impervious alike to poison, strong drink or strong tobacco. Yet
he was an engaging old man with a salty wit, experienced and
wise in the ways of steam.

I lived in the farmhouse at Pitchill with Ernest Bomford, who
was unmarried, and we were looked after by a middle-aged
married couple. In one room of this large early Victorian house
was the farm office. Ernest Bomford ran the farm and had
nothing to do with the engineering side of the business which
was the sole concern of his eldest brother Douglas who lived
with his wife Betty at nearby Bevington Hall. Except in their
voices, the two brothers were quite unlike each other. Ernest,
nicknamed by his brothers 'Herx', was a massive sandy-haired,
red-faced man, always very friendly and jovial towards me.

Douglas Bomford, on the other hand, was tall, slim and dark.

He walked with the aid of a stick as the result of a wound in the leg which he had received during the war when he was also badly gassed. Many years later I came to know Douglas very well as an equal and found in him, until his recent death in 1969, a most charming and delightful friend. But at this time I stood very much in awe of him. He was never so forthcoming towards me as his brother Ernest, seeming to be stern and withdrawn, never allowing me to forget that he was the boss and I his pupil, although he always treated me with scrupulous fairness. If he seemed to me moody it was, I think, because his leg frequently pained him and he suffered ill health as a result of the gassing. Like my uncle Kyrle, he was a 'natural' mechanical engineer with considerable power of invention and the ability to solve a tricky mechanical problem on the spot with a quick sketch on the back of an old envelope. Indeed the two men, though quite unlike physically, temperamentally had much in common and I soon understood the reason for their friendship.

There was a fourth and youngest brother, Dick, who resembled Ernest in appearance and whom I saw but rarely as he became a doctor and was at this time studying for his degree in London. Of the four brothers, my favourite then was Leslie. Next in age to Douglas, he was like him physically and also shared his engineering bent. I found in him, young as I was, the friend I was later to find in Douglas and we got along famously.

Leslie owned a Stanley steam car, a 1921 four-seater tourer which, unlike the earlier pre-war models, was fitted with a condenser. The Stanley's two-cylinder engine was mounted horizontally to the rear of the chassis and was in unit with the back-axle which it drove through fixed reduction gears. There was a vertical, multitubular boiler under the bonnet fired by a petrol/paraffin burner which worked on the same principle as a blowlamp, the petrol pilot burner heating the vaporiser of the main paraffin burner which resembled a greatly enlarged gas ring. From the moment of lighting the pilot burner, it took about fifteen minutes to raise a full head of steam at 600 lbs. p.s.i. In the heyday of the Stanley car in America when petrol there was very cheap, it was the practice of owners to leave the pilot burner alight all night in the garage to ensure a quick start next morning. But by 1926 steam cars of any make had become extremely rare in England and they resembled the more orthodox cars of the day so closely that if the pilot burner was left on there were apt to be embarrassing misunderstandings. Thus on one occasion Leslie Bomford parked the Stanley in Birmingham and returned to find an apprehensive crowd watching it from a safe distance, convinced that it was about to burst into flames or explode. Someone had glimpsed a flicker of flame from the pilot burner, had mistaken for smoke the wisp of steam that was drifting through the bonnet louvres and had prudently sent for the fire brigade. Leslie had some difficulty in convincing these men that their services were not required.

In my spare time in the evenings I helped Leslie overhaul the Stanley in the workshop. By the time I had explored the intricacies of the automatic fuel and water controls, I had learned that a steam car is by no means the delightfully simple affair that most people suppose it to be. When the work was done I was rewarded for my help with a trial run in the car for some miles along the road towards Redditch. At a time when such ordinary cars as I had experienced made a lot of mechanical commotion, particularly in the indirect gears, the complete silence of the Stanley, its feeling of effortless power and surging acceleration, made a profound impression upon me so that I became an enthusiastic devotee of the steam car from that moment. In fact, as I learned later, with this model Stanley it was impossible to maintain a speed much in excess of 40 m.p.h. without losing steam pressure, although, by driving judiciously, one could keep power in reserve for hill-climbing or for short bursts of speed.

I was sorry when, not long after I came to Pitchill, Leslie Bomford and his steam car removed themselves to Shrewsbury. Through the agency of my uncle Kyrle, he had obtained a post at the Sentinel Waggon Works. My uncle was himself now stationed at Shrewsbury, having removed his family yet again to a house at Dovaston on the Welsh Border some miles to the west of the town.

Work in the Pitchill shop began at seven o'clock, though I had a half-hour break at 9 a.m. when I returned to the farmhouse for breakfast. Then work continued until 5 p.m. with an hour's break for lunch at one o'clock. Throughout the summer months this timetable was pleasant enough, but on dark, frosty mornings in winter with only a quick cup of tea to warm my belly the first two hours were an ordeal. The only heat in the shops came from the blacksmith's hearth, and a malodorous acetylene gas plant, which lurked in a small shed at the back of the shop, provided the only light from bat's wing burners. The big steam ploughing engines stood side by side in a large open-sided shed in front of the workshops and to work on them in the first pallid dawnlight of a winter morning was the coldest job I have ever known. Their metal was so cold that one's fingers stuck to it.

Here, slowly and very painfully, I began to learn the rudiments of the engineer's craft: how to use a hammer and chisel; how to file a surface truly flat; how to scrape and fit a bearing brass; how to strike for the blacksmith (a welcome job on a cold day) and how to turn a screw with an odd number of threads to the inch in a lathe. When chiselling I at first had my eye fixed nervously on the chisel head while I tapped it ineffectually with the hammer, holding its shaft only about four inches below the head. This provoked amused cries of 'hit it, don't kiss it!' until, at the price of bruised and bloody knuckles, I learned to swing a hammer properly, keeping my eye on the cutting edge of the chisel the while. Moreover, because I happened to be ambidextrous, I found I could do this equally well with the hammer held in either hand. This can be a great advantage when working in a confined space. 'Didn't know you was amphibious' remarked one of my workmates admiringly on one occasion. Others, less polite, used to call me 'keg-handed'.

We had no powered hand tools, so any work on an engine or farm implement that could not be removed to the machine shop had to be done slowly and laboriously by muscle power. Many an hour I spent and many a blister I raised on my palms in the infinitely tedious task of drilling large holes in steel or iron with a ratchet drill using, not twist drills, but the old hand-forged and hardened spear-pointed drill bits. Any new rivets or stays had to be closed by hand, one man wielding a riveting hammer and the other 'holding up'. When any old rivets had to be removed, their heads were cut off by means of a chisel bar and sledge hammer. The one job I really disliked was holding the chisel bar while my mate belted it with a sledge, knowing that if I lost my nerve and failed to hold the bar true and steady he would strike it a glancing blow or miss it altogether and probably break my arm. As in the case of hammer and chisel, the golden rule was to keep one's eye on the cutting end of the bar and try to forget about the striker.

Whenever there was work to be done inside a boiler or a water tank, plates to be scaled or new rivets to be held up, the task was allotted to me or to the shop boy, George Leonard, because we were the only ones slim enough to crawl through the man-holes. The boiler man-holes on the Fowler compounds were very awkwardly placed on the top of the barrel between the two sets of motion. It was easy enough to get in by simply lowering oneself down, but it was extremely difficult to get out again and more than once I got stuck. At such times the rule that one must never panic was not so easy to observe in practice.

One valuable lesson I learnt during my two years at Pitchill was that many routine jobs were by no means so simple and unskilled as they appeared to be. It was the judgement and economy of effort born of long practice with which they were performed that made them appear deceptively simple. For example, one-armed Joe Bailey's job of looking after the shop portable engine seemed as simple as stoking some domestic boiler. Joe never hurried. Occasionally he would casually throw on a shovelful of coal or, as casually, close the feed-pump by-pass cock to supply the boiler with water. And all day long the steam pressure never varied by more than 5 lb. while the water gauge showed constant half glass. Yet when I was asked to deputise for him I seemed to be constantly rushing out to fiddle with the fire or the water pump while steam and water gauges fluctuated wildly. There seemed always to be either too much steam and too little water or vice versa.

It was exactly the same with the mill. This was housed in one of the substantial brick barns on the opposite side of the yard from the shop and it was used once or twice a week to grind cattle meal. It was powered by an old Tangye hot bulb horizontal oil engine. Alan Bloxham normally took charge of the running of this mill and whenever I passed by he appeared to be casually propping up the mill doorway, enjoying the morning sunshine and puffing at his pipe, his old trilby hat pulled down over his eyes and his dirty blue overalls dusted with flour. What a pleasant, easy job I used to think until one day Alan was called away to some urgent job and I was told to deputise for him. It was simple, he said. There were only three things I had to do. First, to ensure that the wooden hoppers on the topmost floor of the mill were kept filled with grain, for to deny millstones their grain is like running an engine short of oil. Secondly, to remove the sacks from their hooks under the flour shoots when they were full, replacing them by empty ones and tying their necks with binder twine. Thirdly, to prevent the hot bulb of the engine from becoming either too hot or too cold. He showed me the small pipe and cock which achieved this temperature regulation by feeding a drip of water to the hot bulb. Ideally, he explained, it should be kept just below red heat.

There was to be no basking in the sunshine for me. No sooner had Alan, having delivered his simple-sounding instructions, strolled away, than I became the slave of the mill, a kind of demented sorcerer's apprentice. I hurried panting up to the top floor to see to the hoppers and by the time I had humped in more sacks of grain and clattered pell-mell down the wooden stairs, one of the flour sacks was overflowing and the hot bulb of the engine was glowing an ominous cherry red. Later, when I had for the second time gone aloft to feed the insatiable hoppers, I heard the engine change its steady beat and the chattering voice of the damsels that fed the grain into the centre of the runner stones became less insistent. I flew down the stairs, realising that I had now turned on too much water to the hot bulb and that it was becoming too cold in consequence. But somehow I managed to keep the mill running until Alan returned, but never was I more glad to see him. 'Well, how d'ye get on, Tom?' he asked. 'Oh, all right,' I replied casually, but he eyed me quizzically and I am afraid my red and sweating face must have betrayed me.

It was Alan Bloxham who first taught me to drive, or rather patiently allowed me to teach myself. This was on the 10 cwt. Model T Ford truck which was used for servicing ploughing engines in the field or on other outside maintenance jobs. There must be many people of my generation who learned to drive on the famous Model T because it was an ideal vehicle for the purpose. Having epicyclic gears that called for no skill, the learner could concentrate all his attention on the control of the vehicle and on acquiring road sense without having to worry about that bane of the learner-driver, the crash gearbox. Having thus graduated on the Model T, my father soon allowed me to take the wheel of his 12/50 Alvis. I then found that, having already mastered the feel of driving a car, the art of changing gear was very easily acquired.

My experience at Pitchill was by no means confined to the workshop. An old cherry orchard nearby had got past bearing and to old Bill Smith was assigned the task of grubbing it up— in other words uprooting the trees, using one of the old single-cylinder Fowler ploughing engines. One of my first outside jobs was to be sent along as his mate on this exploit. My job was simple. I had to wrap a chain sling round a tree bole, hitch the hook on the end of the engine's steel rope on to this chain and then stand back. Old Bill would first of all nudge his regulator, open a crack to take up the slack and then open it fully. One of two things happened, either the tree came crashing down or the engine, after giving one powerful snort, stuck on dead centre. In the latter event, old Bill, who always moved with the country-man's slow deliberation, would ponder the situation for a few moments, removing that foul stub of a pipe from his mouth and spitting a thin yellow stream over the side of his engine. Then sometimes he would try another pull, but more usually he would screw down the knurled brass nut on the top of the Salter safety valve. He would then adopt the classic steam-plough driver's stance, left foot up on the raised side of his footplate, left arm resting casually on bent knee while his right hand grasped the regulator. In this attitude he appeared to fall into profound meditation while steam pressure in the ancient boiler mounted far above its prescribed limit. Meanwhile my instinct for self-preservation was such that I took cover behind a tree bole at what I considered a safe distance. But no disaster occur-red and the trees all came up. I still think it was something of a miracle that Bill Smith was not blown sky high, for when the boiler of his engine was given a hydraulic test a few months later, the crown of the firebox dropped three-eighths of an inch. However, the boiler inspector was in a mellow mood and passed it. As was usual before he inspected the older engines, he had been liberally entertained at the Queen's Head during the lunch hour.

It is incredible what an old boiler will stand without failure. Once Will Salisbury and I were sent to Worcester to retube an elderly portable engine which was supplying process steam at 25 lbs. pressure for sterilising in an ice-cream factory. As we drew the old tubes they literally fell apart in our hands. Only the scale appeared to have been holding them together.

Sometimes I would be despatched on my motorcycle with a message or a small spare part for one of the steam ploughing sets that was working out on contract somewhere in the Evesham vale. I seldom had difficulty in finding them. Usually a column of steam and smoke rising above the hedgerows betrayed their presence, but if not I would stop my motorcycle and listen for the labouring beat of an engine or the unmistakable ring of the drum gearing which carried surprisingly far over the fields. Similarly, when a set was due back at Pitchill, we invariably heard it coming a mile away. As a complete set of ploughing tackle consisted of two engines, a Fowler balanced plough with two sets of five or six plough bodies, a massive cultivator, a four-wheeled living van and a water cart, it made an impressive cavalcade on the road. Perched aloft on the footplate or at the steering wheel you felt like a lord of creation for the great engines towered above all other traffic and every head would turn as they rumbled majestically through a village. Moving a set from place to place was not always easy. Although they bore a small brass plate on their smoke boxes inscribed '14T' this was a brazen lie for in fact they weighed far more than this, though exactly how much was a dark secret that no one seemed willing to divulge. Certain bridges had to be avoided. Evesham was out of bounds for this reason as the railway bridge on the only approach to the town from Pitchill, though it still stands today, was judged incapable of taking their weight. Some roads also had to be avoided because the old plough drivers knew that there was no convenient stream or pool beside them where the engines could stop to suck up water through their armoured hoses. In hot summer weather, the engines could move on the road only in the early hours of the morning. Otherwise the diagonal strakes on their driving wheels would pick up long strips of hot tarmac from the road to leave a nicely corrugated surface behind them which made the local road surveyor tear his hair.

My first experience of steering one of these steam jugger-nauts was terrifying. I was deputed to steer one on the old farm engines across the fields, her driver being Will Robbins. Unlike all later machines, which have irreversible worm-and-wheel steering gear, the mechanism on these old engines consisted of a vertical steering column, mounted on the side of the tank and bunker just aft of the nearside rear wheel, which operated chain and rod connections to the swivelling front axle through straight gears. The steersman stood on a little metal platform, perilously outrigged from the bunker side, grasping the huge horizontal iron steering wheel. No sooner had I assumed this precarious perch, feeling like a small monkey on the top of a very tall stick, than Will Robbins, perhaps with malicious aforethought, set off full tilt at about 3 m.p.h., driving the engine diagonally across an old pasture of deep ridge and furrow. As we lumbered over this uneven ground the front axle swung to and fro sending the steering wheel spinning uncontrollably first one way and then the other. It nearly broke my wrist and flung me off the steering platform. It was only then that I grasped the significance of the gadget on the steering column immediately below the wheel. It was a primitive form of steering damper consisting of a disc encircled by a brake band which could be tightened by a hand-screw. Under such conditions the correct thing to do was to tighten up the damper as much as possible and then leave the wheel severely alone until it became essential to alter course.

On many occasions I worked on the steam ploughing tackle in the fields, riding the plough or the cultivator, and so eventually graduated to driving the engines. These stood one at either end of the field, drawing the implement back and forth between them, the idle engine moving an implement's width along the headland while the other was pulling until the whole field had been covered. Two men rode the plough, the ploughman behind the metal wheel on its long horizontal column, guiding it along the furrow, and his mate perched on a little tip-up seat right at the tail of the plough frame. The plough was balanced like a seesaw about its central axle. When it reached the end of the furrow, its crew jumped off their seats, tipping the plough to bring the other set of plough bodies into action, and swinging it into its new position as the other engine began slowly to pull. Then both jumped on again, the mate hinging down his seat at the plough tail, hitching the trailing rope over the hook beneath it. I can only compare the unique sensation of riding a steam plough to that of sailing a ship through the earth. Under good conditions, the taut rope ahead drew the plough along at a surprising speed and as it tore through the ground with a hissing sound the brown earth billowed away from the gleaming steel mouldboards like water from the prow of a ship. It was all very exhilarating and I used to revel in the sensation of silent but irresistible power, mingled with slight misgiving as to what might happen if the steel rope broke. Would it come snaking back and cut my head off? I have never heard tell of such an accident although ropes occasionally broke harmlessly, in which case the ploughmen would splice them in the field.

The cultivator was a totally different implement from the plough. Its massive tines were set in a triangular frame mounted on three wheels, the third pivoting in a turntable and controlled by the steering wheel. This turntable also carried a Vee-shaped double drawbar to which both engine ropes were attached, one pulling while the other trailed along the side of the frame. At the end of the field, when the rope that had been trailing took the pull its effect was to swing the drawbar and the front wheel round. By means of a chain connection and linkage, this movement also lifted the whole frame of the cultivator, thus raising the tines clear of the ground. It was retained in this position by a toothed sector and pawl, the latter being part of a lever which could be pulled to drop the cultivator frame again when the turn had been completed. When turning the cultivator in this way, the engineman had to pull very slowly otherwise the implement would tilt alarmingly. The old steam plough drivers could judge to a nicety how far to make it tip without actually turning over and this was their favourite trick whenever there was a new man on the cultivator. As the tyro jumped from his seat and ran for his life (as I did when the trick was played on me) they would shake with laughter.

A good set of steam tackle could get over the ground as fast or faster than a modern tractor plough, but the snag was the great width of the headlands which were left. These amounted to the width of an engine plus half the length of the implement. Consequently when the field had been covered, the tackle had to be twice repositioned to plough or cultivate the headlands. In a small or irregularly shaped field, the speed of steam tackle was nullified by this time-consuming process of finishing off. This is why the use of steam tackle survived longest in the large flat fields of East Anglia. It was also expensive in labour, for in addition to the four men who worked the tackle, a fifth was needed to haul water and coal to the engines. While the ploughing contractor supplied a water cart, his farmer customer usually supplied a horse and man to draw it.

Another disadvantage was the great weight of the engines. When the ground was soggy 'spuds' had to be attached by bolts to the rims of the driving wheels to provide extra grip, as if the big wheels began to slip an engine very soon dug itself in. Each of these spuds must have weighed at least a quarter of a hundredweight. Of T section with one end bent over to clasp the rim of the wheel, when not in use they were hung on a bar surrounding the water tank. Putting them on was a heavy and tedious job, but taking them off again on leaving a field for the hard road when spuds, bolts and wheels were plastered in slimy mud was one of the most unpleasant tasks I have ever had to perform. By the time it was done we looked like so many mudlarks, as filthy as the wheels themselves.

One day, while waiting its turn to pick up water from a pond at Norton, near Worcester, one of the big Fowlers slowly subsided sideways into a deep ditch as the bank at the side of the road gave way under her weight. She finally assumed such an alarming angle that her driver hurriedly drew the fire in case the firebox crown sheet sustained damage. It took us two days of hard labour before, with aid of a pull from the rope of her sister engine, she finally got back on to the hard road. Fortunately, relaying had recently been done on the Worcester–Paddington line which was close by, so we were able to use many old railway sleepers. These were laid in the ditch to form, first a firm foundation for our bottle jacks, and later a platform for the wheels. But before any of this work could start part of the hedge and bank had to be dug away.

Another of my outside experiences was to serve as fireman to Will Robbins on the Sentinel steam waggon. I do not know the exact date of this vehicle except that it was an early model made before the 'Super Sentinel' was introduced. Unlike the latter, it had no windscreen but was open to the elements above the simple semi-circular apron which surrounded the vertical boiler in the front of the cab. Firing a Sentinel called for no skill whatever. One simply shovelled coal from the bunker at the back of the cab and poured it down a vertical shoot in the centre of the boiler on to the circular firegrate beneath, relying upon the vibration of the vehicle to distribute the fire evenly over the grate. When running at from 15 to 20 m.p.h. on solid tyres, this vibration had to be experienced to be believed. The designer of the Sentinel had evidently assumed that the driver's mate would be a moron, for he had placed the injector and the control valve of the alternative water pump on the driver's side of the boiler. For some reason best known to himself, Will Robbins preferred to use the injector. To get this instrument to pick up cleanly as we rattled and jolted along called for the nice and patient adjustment of the steam and water controls, a proceeding I used to find very alarming as it completely diverted Will's attention from the wheel and from the road ahead. I could not have grabbed the wheel had an accident appeared imminent because it was out of reach from where I sat. There were some disconcerting moments, too, when the safety valve suddenly blew off. Although a pipe was provided which, in theory, conducted the steam above the cab roof, in practice we were instantly enveloped in an impenetrable fog.

Although the Sentinel boiler was so unscientifically fired, it was distinctly choosy about the type of fuel it consumed. Given anything but the best Welsh steam coal it was not only a shy steamer, but it became a very fair imitation of a travelling volcano, vomiting smoke and red hot cinders to the confusion of any motorist following behind. Every ten miles or so the water would need replenishing, using the steam water-lifter to draw supplies through a hose from a convenient roadside stream or pond. Like the steam plough drivers, Will Robbins carried in his mind a map of local watering points and knew which roads had to be avoided because they were waterless.

We carried a variety of loads in the Sentinel. For example, we spent two hot summer days discharging a truckload of shoddy at Salford Priors station. Shoddy is a waste product from the Yorkshire woollen mills, then widely used in the Evesham district as a fertiliser. It was brown in colour, of a flock-like consistency, acrid smelling and extremely dusty. As, hour after hour, we shovelled the stuff, the choking dust filled our lungs and stuck to our sweating faces. But when I complained to Will he merely remarked dourly that I should thank my lucky stars it was shoddy and not blood. Dried blood from slaughter-houses was another favoured fertiliser at this time and, according to Will, smelt worse than the shoddy, besides being more difficult to handle.

On another occasion we carried a load of strawberries in wooden tubs to a jam factory in Evesham. I have always thought there is a lot of truth in the old saying that we must all eat a peck of dirt before we die, believing that too great a concern for sterilisation must inevitably lower the body's natural resistance to infection. Nevertheless, this experience put me off strawberry jam for a long time afterwards. To begin with, by the time they reached the factory, the strawberries in our tubs were reduced to a glutinous mass of purple porridge. As the Sentinel rolled into the factory yard I saw a number of women working amid the great open-topped pans in which the jam was boiling. This boiling shed was open at the sides and buzzing with eager wasps and flies. An old labourer with a wooden barrow and shovel was keeping the women supplied with sugar from a large bin at the opposite side of the yard as though it had been coal. In fact, I strongly suspected he used the same barrow and shovel to bring coal to the boiler house.

The Bomfords grew a considerable acreage of strawberries at Pitchill at this time so that I came to know something of the usages and hazards of the soft fruit trade. Each strawberry season a tatterdemalion horde from the Black Country would descend like starlings on the farm to pick the fruit. Although the Black Country was little more than thirty miles away from Pitchill it might have been on a different continent so far as the local countrymen were concerned. They habitually referred to these foreign invaders as 'the Dudleys' and regarded them with suspicion as an alien and primitive race, wild, dirty and of very questionable habits. They were certainly verminous. To house

them, the lofts of two large barns on the farm had been converted
into dormitories. I went into one of these barns shortly after it
had been occupied and noticed a strange phenomenon. There appeared to be a slight mist hanging over a patch of the barn floor
immediately below the vertical ladder and opening that led to
the loft above. On closer approach I saw that this effect was
produced by millions of hopping fleas. The ground was literally
sizzling with them. Small wonder that cleaning up and fumiga-
ting these lofts after the Dudleys' annual visit was considered
the most unenviable job on the farm. The man who benefited
most from their visits was the landlord of the Queen's Head, but
even to him they must have been a doubtful blessing, for each
night around closing time his pub became the centre of rowdy,
drunken scenes such as we associate with the old railway navvy
gangs. Police frequently had to be called in to restore order and
the landlord's regular customers wisely stayed at home.

The harvesting of the strawberry crop was always peculiarly
subject to the vagaries of the weather. Picking into chip baskets
for dessert would be in full swing when a sudden heavy shower
of thundery rain, falling on dry ground, might cover the fruit
with grit and enforce an immediate switch to picking into tubs
for jam. This was a disaster for grower and picker alike, the
former because jam fruit commanded a much lower price, the
latter because picking into tubs earned proportionately less per
pound. Our trip to the jam factory with the Sentinel had followed
a disaster of this kind.

That old Sentinel waggon eventually suffered a spectacular
mechanical disintegration. The classic Sentinel two-cylinder
poppet valve engine was slung horizontally under the chassis
driving the rear axle by means of sprockets and a single large
roller chain. The chain sprocket on the axle incorporated the
differential unit, four large pins fitting between its teeth acting
as journals for the four star-wheels. Will Robbins was trundling
happily through the village of Salford Priors one day with a 5
ton load of bricks on board when one of these four pins broke.
As the sprocket revolved, the broken pin slid out until it came
into violent contact with the lower portion of the driving chain,
forcing it downwards into the road. The old waggon had never
stopped so suddenly in its life; it literally took root in the road
and even the phlegmatic Will Robbins was shaken. When he
clambered down from his cab and peered underneath a scene of
ruin met his eyes. Above a large, tell-tale pool of oil the stout
cast iron crankcase was broken and the driving end of the crank-

shaft had been torn out of the engine. A secondhand engine was acquired to replace the wrecked unit and the waggon eventually took to the road again.

Despite such vicissitudes, the Sentinel was undoubtedly the best and the most popular of commercial steam road vehicles and just as my uncle Kyrle had been encouraged to fit a Sentinel engine and boiler into a locomotive, so now, inspired by his example, Leslie and Douglas Bomford began to consider similar agricultural applications. The fruit of Leslie's work at Shrewsbury was the Sentinel 'Rhino'. A wheeled tractor for direct cultivation designed for colonial use, it was fitted with the larger boiler and engine which had been developed for the locomotive. Later, a crawler version of this tractor was produced. The prototype Rhino with Leslie in charge came down to Pitchill for field trials, towing a cable set cultivator. I did not have anything directly to do with this tractor although I remember being very impressed by its performance.

Meanwhile we had built in the shop at Pitchill a cable ploughing engine to Douglas Bomford's design using, as my uncle had done in the case of *Ancoats*, the engine and boiler out of a secondhand Sentinel waggon. At the age of sixteen I felt very proud to be intimately concerned with the construction and subsequent field trials of this new and novel machine. It consisted of a marriage of Sentinel and Fowler components, the only new item being a simple frame constructed from 'I' section girders. The Sentinel boiler was mounted at the extreme rear end of this new chassis, next came the Sentinel engine lying horizontally with the footplate beside it and the coal bunker on top of it, then a Fowler rope drum mounted vertically between the frame members and finally, at the front end, a Sentinel water tank. The four wheels were off an old Fowler ploughing engine. The engine drove by a short roller chain a cross-shaft arranged directly beneath it from which the drive was taken via countershaft gears to the rear wheels and by gears to the rope drum, these alternative final drives being engaged by sliding dog clutches operated by a lever on the footplate. The rope from the drum passed round a large diameter Vee pulley beneath the boiler, then forward to a second pulley mounted amidships from which it emerged in the orthodox manner midway between front and rear wheels. The Fowler ploughing engine has an ingenious mechanism below the drum which causes the rope guide pulleys to move up and down across the face of the drum as it rotates in order to ensure accurate coiling of the rope.

With the drum placed vertically it became impossible to use this Fowler 'coiling gear', as it was called. Douglas Bomford cudgelled his brains needlessly over this problem because we found in practice that with this arrangement of pulleys the rope coiled itself automatically and perfectly on the drum.

Although this unorthodox ploughing engine was hardly a thing of beauty it performed very satisfactorily and I cannot recall any teething troubles. But it was not capable of doing the work of a Fowler engine, as I very soon discovered when I drove it on its first serious field trial. The job was to plough a large, flat stubble field close to Pitchill. My opposite number was Bill Smith with one of the farm pair of Fowlers and it was soon obvious that he was not going to allow any quarter to this new-fangled machine and its youthful driver. When the Sentinel was pulling the plough its engine turned over at a speed so much in excess of normal that the feed pump could not be used and I had to rely entirely on the one small Penberthy injector to feed the boiler. So great was the vibration that this injector could not be worked so long as the engine was pulling and it was such a long pull that the situation became very fraught. A chronic fault of the Sentinel boiler, particularly the early model, was that it tended to lift the water, in other words, when the regulator was opened, water went out with the steam and the water gauge showed a falsely high level. I had to start each pull with the boiler three-quarters full which aggravated this trouble, for each time I opened my regulator the level in the gauge glass rose until it disappeared into the top fitting and I was deluged by the water that shot out of the chimney. Conversely, by the time I had finished the pull there would only be about half an inch of water still showing in the glass and the moment I closed the regulator this would sink out of sight. This was the most anxious moment, for I was terrified that I would 'run the plug',[1] the most ignominious mishap that can befall any engineman. I could not get that injector on quickly enough, at the same time putting the blower on to urge the fire because such a copious draught of cold water inevitably brought the steam pressure down.

In this steam raising department I was also in trouble. On the advice of the Sentinel Waggon Works we had fitted to this boiler

[1] A lead-filled plug inserted in the crown sheet of a firebox which melts, putting out the fire, if the water is low and no longer covers the firebox crown.

a new design of firegrate which was slightly conical in shape, thus encouraging the coal that was fed down the chute to distribute itself evenly. The theory had been that when the engine was standing and pulling the plough rope there would be insufficient vibration to spread the fire over a flat grate of the kind used on the waggon. In fact, of course, there was more than enough vibration with the effect that all the coal immediately ran to the perimeter of the grate, leaving a large hole in the middle. Through this hole the fierce draught drew quantities of cold air. Not only did this seriously impair steam raising but, in its free passage through the grate, the air made a penetrating humming sound which could be heard half a mile away, thus advertising to the knowledgeable the fact that I had a hole in my fire, a shame-making circumstance for any conscientious fireman.

Meanwhile, from the clouds of smoke and steam erupting from the Fowler at the opposite end of the field it was clear that Bill Smith was not prepared to show me any mercy. He would whip that plough across so that, in no time at all it seemed, it was my turn to pull again. Such an unequal contest could have only one ending and the plough was soon at a standstill while I 'waited for steam' to the accompaniment of derisive toots on the Fowler whistle.

It was obvious from this experiment that, compared with a Fowler, the Sentinel ploughing engine was underpowered, but its performance and economy were sufficiently promising to justify building a sister engine. This was not completed until after I had left Pitchill. Finally, both engines were rebuilt with larger engines and boilers and fitted with special, lighter, round-spoked wheels of welded construction. In this form they gave good service on contract work until some time in the 1930s when the firm gave up cable ploughing engines in favour of Fowler Gyrotillers propelled by oil engines.

The field where this first experiment took place was also the scene of my only venture on horseback. I was with a set of ploughing tackle there one day when Douglas Bomford rode up on his bay mare Tina. He became so deeply involved in some technical problem that he eventually turned to me and said: 'Tom, take my horse back to Pitchill'. After my childhood's experience with Meg, my Shetland pony, I regarded all members of the species with the gravest suspicion. If I had been ordered into a cage with a tiger I could hardly have been more apprehensive as I began dutifully leading Tina away by the bridle. Before me stretched the wide field of stubble and the long straight drive up to Pitchill, while the mare followed me in so docile a fashion that, as I plodded on, I began to feel a cowardly fool. I imagined Douglas and the other men regarding with contempt the fact that that I continued to walk when I could ride. So, greatly daring, I hoisted myself clumsily and with difficulty into the saddle while the mare stood perfectly still. Once aloft, I did not dare to trot but allowed Tina to walk sedately home. Arrived at Pitchill, I swung myself down from the saddle and led her into a loose-box, chewing an imaginary straw and feeling a thoroughly horsey fellow. The point of this story is that I was totally unaware of the fact that Tina was a very mettlesome creature who would allow no one but Douglas to ride her. She could invariably unseat the most experienced horsemen who attempted to do so. I can only conclude that she sensed a complete tyro and took pity on him. This incident appealed strongly to Douglas's sense of humour, but it was many years before he shared the joke with me.

While I was at Pitchill, Douglas Bomford, like many another inventive engineer before and since, became afflicted by the desire to make an infinitely variable speed gear. Like the alchemist's dream of turning base metal into gold, the pursuit of this ideal form of transmission, like the perpetual motion machine, can become an obsession. The test bed for these experiments was a basic wooden chassis powered by a Villiers two-stroke engine and carried on motorcycle wheels. This was kept in a corner of the shop and periodically dusted off and wheeled out of retirement to try out some fresh idea such as a rubber ring moving between tapering wooden rollers. The last experiment in which I participated consisted in using an adaptation of the classic Stephenson's link valve motion. The engine oscillated the vertical link while the equivalent of the valve rod on a steam engine actuated the pawl of a ratchet-and-pawl on the back axle. This meant that 'mid-gear' position became neutral and 'full-gear' top speed, the pawl taking several teeth of the ratchet at each bite. The results of a single test run down the Pitchill drive were not encouraging. A maximum speed of about 6 m.p.h. was achieved for I remember that I and its other anxious attendants had to walk very fast to keep up, but owing to the intermittent torque produced by the prodding of the pawl, progress was by fits and starts. Meanwhile, the engine roared, the transmission became a blur of fast moving rods like some demented knitting machine and the vibration was appalling. Not surprisingly, the little chassis was wheeled back into its dark corner from which it did not emerge again in my time.

Those two years I spent at Pitchill are fragrant in memory. They were also rich in experience and so more useful to me than the previous six I had spent at school. For not only did they give me a valuable grounding in the rudiments of the engineer's craft but they also taught me much about farming, about country ways and country men. In that small country workshop, engineering seemed to have been grafted on to the older country crafts of blacksmith, wheelwright and carpenter and to have grown naturally out of these ancient roots. The steam plough drivers regarded their elephantine charges with the same affection and pride that the old waggoners had felt for their horses. They groomed them with oily waste and polished their brass lagging bands till they shone. It was easy to understand and to share this pathetic fallacy, for those engines indeed resembled lovable elephants, slow moving and ponderous yet proud and powerful, warm and mysteriously alive when fire was in their bellies and steam was simmering or when they sucked up water through their armoured trunks to quench their thirst. Small wonder that their drivers habitually referred to them as 'her' or 'she'. It is a strange paradox that as machines grow more complex and able to usurp more human functions, this pathetic fallacy becomes much more difficult to sustain. No one, so far as I know, refers to a computer as 'she'.

I learned to admire and respect my workmates for their versatility in tackling the practical problems of some new job almost every day and for the calm, unhurried, dryly humorous way these countrymen set about such tasks. In trying to emulate them I was introduced to the kind of freemasonry that exists between all men who share the discipline of exacting manual work. It was through this freemasonry that I so soon found myself on terms of such easy and understanding friendship with these men, some of whom, in the words of Edmund Blunden, 'scarce could read or hold a quill'. For an unsociable boy who, at school, had found it impossible to come to terms with my masters or with boys of my own age and upbringing, I think this was the most valuable lesson of all.

Chapter 6

Stoke-on-Trent

On 11th June 1928, at the age of eighteen, I began a three years' premium apprenticeship at the California Works of Kerr, Stuart and Co. Ltd, Locomotive Engineers, of Stoke-on-Trent, finding lodgings for myself in a small terrace house, No. 439, London Road, Stoke. Under the terms of my apprenticeship indenture, the premium of £100 which my parents had paid would be returned to them at the end of three years, always assuming I behaved myself and worked diligently. The firm also undertook to pay me the princely weekly wage of 10s. for the first year, 15s. for the second and £1 for the final year. This, the first money I had ever earned, was my pocket money, my parents paying the 30s. a week for my lodgings.

So far I had spent my life in a country setting and it was a rural world that I had come to know and to love. If I had occasionally visited or travelled through industrial areas, I had had but fleeting glimpses of them from the outside which left only the most superficial impressions. Now, however, I experienced life in an industrial city from the inside which was quite a different matter. My reactions to this new environment were complex. I felt oppressed by the all-pervading dirt and squalor of the endless cobbled street lined by terrace houses of soot-blackened brick; by the smouldering waste tips, pit mounds and heaps of furnace slag. This sombre man-made landscape in which even the occasional tree or patch of grass was soiled with soot and struggled to survive was overlaid by a perpetual pall of smoke. Although Arnold Bennett's Five Towns (the locals always pointed out that the author was wrong in forgetting Fenton and that there should have been six) had then only recently combined to form the City of Stoke-on-Trent, the name had no reality; signposts in all the country round pointed simply to 'The Potteries' and one was never allowed to forget that the making of pottery was the district's chief preoccupation. All the wares it produced were then fired with coal in bottle ovens.[1] The whole area was peppered with their characteristic shapes; they would appear in serried ranks, like a row of gigantic ninepins, above the rooftops of the terrace houses. And because each oven, when it was being fired up, belched dense black smoke, the effect on the atmosphere and on all surrounding objects below may be imagined. Yet, because this smoke was the outward and visible sign of prosperity, the people of the Potteries were proud of it. Little general stores on street corners sold shiny picture postcards showing typical 'smokescapes' of Hanley, Burslem or Tunstall. But, living in such sulphurous surroundings I thought of my childhood under the clear skies of the Welsh Border and felt like some fallen angel recalling lost paradise.

But there were compensations. In contrast to the mild-mannered countrymen I had hitherto known, the people of the Potteries at first seemed coarse and hard; they spoke in a broad, harsh dialect; their wit was sharper and liberally salted with profanities and obscene four-letter words. But I soon discovered that this rough exterior was only an outer shell which they had grown to protect them from the buffets of a pitiless environment. In reality they were the most genuine, friendly and kindly people I have ever known. Honest and forthright themselves, the only thing they cordially detested was the lack of such qualities in others. They could detect the false pride and affectation of social climbers infallibly and deal with it unmercifully. They would refer contemptuously to the inhabitants of the smug suburbs on the fringes of the city as 'Them as wears plus fours and only 'as porridge for breakfast'. One of my fellow apprentices was the son of a wealthy local man in the pottery trade who had sent him to a public school. Unfortunately he could never forget the superior notions he had thereby acquired and was incapable of mixing unselfconsciously with his workmates. Whenever he walked through the shops he would be greeted by a ringing of hammers on metal and men would call after him in exaggerated mimicry of a public school accent: 'Good morning, Charles, and how are we getting on today?' Charles always struck me as a sad and lonely figure. I had my two years at Pitchill to thank for the fact that I escaped his fate, partly because my new workmates realised that I had already learned the rudiments of my

[1] For some reason they were always called ovens locally. Only those used to fire enamels were referred to as kilns.

trade and respected me accordingly, and partly because I knew that in any workshop there is only one true entitlement to superiority and that is to excel in one's craft. I can only feel humble in the presence of a man who is doing his job superlatively well and in 1928, there was no lack of such craftsmen at the California Works.

I used often to reflect how I should feel if I knew I was condemned to spend the rest of my days in this sombre environment beneath a smoke-filled sky, my life monotonously ruled by the daily summons of a steam hooter, braying into the raw dark of winter mornings, until I became too old and worn out to work any more. I shrank from such a prospect and this made me admire all the more the courage and the good-humoured stoicism of my companions. As I worked beside them, I soon realised that what made their lives tolerable was, above all, their satisfaction in their skill. That skill was a precious thing which had taken years to acquire and which no one could take away—or so I thought then.

Although the industrial scene of man-made desolation appalled me, at the same time it had an intensely dramatic quality which I found fascinating. Evening after evening I spent exploring the Five Towns, travelling by bus, on foot or on my motorcycle. Because they are situated in a hilly region near the headwaters of the Trent, the townscape of the Potteries was made the more dramatic. A street would suddenly fall away or end in a rickety fence on the edge of some steep bank to reveal an unexpected vista of bottle ovens, tall chimneys, pit-head gears and smouldering spoil banks as arid and desolate as moon mountains. My favourite viewpoint of all was on the heights of Basford which commanded the district of Etruria in the valley below and the slopes of Hanley opposite. To the right, ranged beside the Trent and Mersey Canal, was the most famous pottery of all—Josiah Wedgwood's Etruria. Its ovens still smoked then, for Wedgwood's new pottery at Barlaston with its electric kilns was still in the future. To the left, the canal snaked away to lose itself amidst a medley of mountainous tips, railway lines, blast furnaces and rolling mills that was the Shelton Iron and Steel Company or, as the locals always called it 'Shelton Bar'.[1] This prospect was spectacular at any time but never more so than at night when

---

[1] H. G. Wells made this works the scene of his horrifying short story *The Cone*.

the fume that rose from the valley beneath my feet made the streetlights of Hanley that climbed the slope opposite appear like stars glimpsed through cloud wrack. Under the arc-lights of Shelton Bar, dark shunting engines moved like shuttles over a web of gleaming rails with a recurrent clashing of buffers. At such a time the steel works made a very fair representation of the mouth of hell in some medieval Last Judgement. The works seemed to be perpetually shrouded in a cloud of smoke and steam which fumed or jetted upward from innumerable chimneys and pipes, a cloud reddened here and there by reflected furnace light. Occasionally a shunting locomotive would labour up to the top of one of the tips pushing before it a ladle of molten slag. When it reached the summit, for a few moments the tip would resemble a volcano in eruption as the molten stream coursed downwards, its vivid glare lighting up the night sky. At last I was seeing the source of that glow that I had glimpsed beyond my mountains as a child. The sight was accompanied by an appropriate cacophony of confused sounds: the crash of a sudden torrent of coke falling from the hoppers of the coking plant; the thunder of the rolling mills.

I found this fierce and violent drama of the steel works at night so hypnotically fascinating that I visited it repeatedly, viewing the spectacle from every angle; from the top of the towering tips, seamed with veins of fire and hot beneath my feet; from the towpath of the steaming canal which afforded me a glimpse into the rolling mill where huge white-hot billets of steel were flattened like pastry under a rolling pin. So this was the heart of the matter; this was what the Industrial Revolution was all about. It was a lesson I had never been taught at school. When first seen, this prospect made as profound an impression upon me as had that first childish glimpse of the Vale of Ewyas, though for a very different reason. If that prospect had seemed like paradise, this was pandemonium. It excited me, yet at the same time it filled me with a strange sense of apocalyptic foreboding. But if anyone had asked me then the source of this disquiet I should have been at a loss to explain it.

No. 439 London Road where I lodged was a step above the meanest of the terraced houses. It boasted a bay window in front and was set back from the pavement to the extent of a yard's width of blackened earth enclosed by cast-iron railings. Nevertheless, these pretensions to respectability were merely a façade offered to the main street. From the alley at the back, the house, with its narrow yard, outside lavatory, coal store and drooping clothes line, resembled a thousand others. Inside, its rooms were very small and cramped, the staircase narrow and vertiginously steep. So it did give me a very fair first-hand experience of how the average inhabitant of the district lived.

We always used the back door which opened into a tiny kitchen/scullery built on to the back of the house. This gave into the back room proper which was a general living and dining room for six days of the week. It contained table and chairs, an old Victorian horsehair-stuffed chaise longue covered in shiny black leathercloth under its single window that looked down the backyard and a tuneless upright piano against the opposite wall. These bulky objects left little space to move around. On either side of the black mock-marble mantelshelf were two large cast ornaments, also black. These depicted rearing horses whose classically draped attendants struggled to control them with reins made of brass wire. Between them stood a black clock with a brass face, which rarely kept time, and two prized pieces of Wedgwood 'black basalt' ware. As the walls were covered with densely patterned wall paper and the window admitted little light, the general effect was sombre in the extreme. Nor was it much better after dark by the light of a single pendant gas mantle with glass globe. Even this light was intermittent because it was the invariable custom to feed only one coin at a time into the penny-in-the-slot meter on the assumption, I can only suppose, that otherwise you would not get your money's worth. Whenever the light dimmed, my landlady would be heard calling frantically from the back-kitchen: 'Anyone got a penny for the gas?' and as the meter was inconveniently situated in a diminutive cellar reached by a flight of steep and narrow steps littered with extraneous objects, this cry would be followed by a prolonged period of confusion before light was restored.

In the front of the house and behind the bay window was that holy of holies, the front room which was occupied only on Sundays when I was usually out of the house. On weekdays it struck dank and chilly, its carpet-patterned linoleum smelling strongly of floor polish. It was also dark, for the lace curtains over the bay window were kept three parts drawn and the space between them almost filled by a luxuriant aspidistra in a large pot of livid green and yellow standing on a precarious bamboo table. China Alsatian dogs or cherry boys had not yet usurped the traditional aspidistra's pride of place at No. 439.

My bedroom was directly above this front room. I had imported a large and comfortable basket chair which converted it into a bed-sitter except in winter when it became much too cold. My mother had made me a present of a brocade dressing gown of which I was very proud and on spring or summer evenings I would don this resplendent garment, put a contemporary jazz record on my portable gramophone ('O where is Sahara, far across the western sea') and loll in the basket chair smoking a cheap Turkish cigarette in a long holder. The prospect from my window, however, made my fancied resemblance to Noel Coward completely incongruous. It looked across the road to the black, rubbish-strewn waters of the disused Newcastle-under-Lyme branch of the Trent and Mersey Canal. Beyond this was the high, blank boundary wall of the Michelin Tyre Works, then the only large new factory to be established in Stoke for many years.

My landlord at No. 439 was William Rock, a carter at a local pottery, a slight, lean man with a face drawn into lines of perpetual tiredness. I can see him now seated in the back kitchen in his collarless shirt sleeves, elbows on the table, one hand supporting his head while in the other he held a Woodbine between his middle fingers, his thumb flicking the ash from its glowing end which was cupped within his palm. He would often sit like this by the hour and I used to wonder what, if anything, he was thinking about. His wife was a brisk Shropshire countrywoman who had been 'in service' in her youth and fancied herself superior on this account. Her ideas of refinement sometimes took peculiar form. Thus on Saturdays when I was changing for the week-end she would call up the stairs: 'D'you want yer clean linings, Mr Tom?' I could not at first conceive what she meant by this until I realised that she could not bring herself to say 'vest and pants' or even 'underclothes' out loud.

For most of the time, I was their only lodger, but there was a third small bedroom in the house which was occasionally occupied by short term lodgers of whom I only recall two. One was a young man who worked as a clerk. He had sleek black hair which he brushed back and oiled copiously. He wore cheap, flashy suits and vivid ties and fancied himself as a ladykiller. He even prevailed on Mrs Rock to allow him to use her sacred front room and its sofa for his frequent dalliances. I cordially disliked him. The other lodger I remember was a much more endearing character. He was a massive, muscled

man of middle age, beginning to run to seed. A racy con-
versationalist, he worked for 'the Tarmac', breaking up furnace
slag for road metal. He had a fine set of false teeth of which
he was so proud that he would never eat with them. Before
each meal he took them out, laid them reverently on the table
beside him, and then champed away heartily with his bare
gums, his nose and chin almost meeting like a pair of pincers.

Each weekday morning I got up in time to eat a hurried
breakfast and reach the works before the steam hooter sounded
at eight o'clock. Usually, I walked to work, but if I was late
I took my motorcycle from the backyard. In summer, I found
this routine easy enough but cold dark mornings in winter were
a different matter and I had the utmost difficulty in dragging
myself out of bed. To overcome this I converted an old alarm
clock so that when it went off its clapper closed a contact and
rang a battery operated electric bell close beside my ear. This
continued to ring so that I had to get out of bed to break the
contact. During the works lunch hour I just had time to return
to No. 439 for my main meal of the day, though it had to be
rather a hurried affair. In the evening there was a high tea and
if I subsequently went off on one of my exploratory rambles
or to the cinema there was usually cocoa and biscuits for me
when I got back.

Many of the cinemas in the Potteries in those days were
converted theatres or music halls. The local name of the 'Blood
Tub', by which the Hippodrome at Stoke was universally
known, recalled the many turgid melodramas that had been
played on its boards. Despite their conversion, such theatres
had remained substantially unchanged, and for a young man
with a girl on his arm and the money to spare the great thing
to do was to take a box and thus ensure undisturbed privacy.
This assumed a preoccupation with matters other than the
film, for the penalty for this dearly bought privilege was that,
owing to the extreme angle of vision, all the characters on the
screen appeared to be preternaturally elongated. At this time
the screen was still silent and it was while I was in the Potteries
that it at last found a voice, albeit a somewhat unnatural and
unpredictable one at first. There were then two sound systems,
sound-on-film, which eventually triumphed, and sound-on-disc
where the sound was produced by long-playing records that
were apt to get out of synchronisation. A cinema in Hanley
was equipped with the latter system and I remember how
the audience rocked with mirth when, in a tender scene, a

beautiful Hollywood blonde suddenly began to speak in a rich baritone.

At this point I should explain how I came to be translated from a small workshop in the Vale of Evesham into what was to me an alien and, in some ways, hostile urban environment. Once again it was through the agency of my uncle, Kyrle Willans. His work on Sentinel locomotives had made him very conscious of the shortcomings of the Sentinel boiler, faults of which I, too, had become well aware through my experience with the Sentinel ploughing engine at Pitchill. He was a great admirer of the work of Loftus Perkins, the pioneer of ultra high-pressure steam, and he conceived the idea of a high pressure water tube boiler on Perkins' principles for a geared steam locomotive which would have a large grate area, a very large heating surface and thus steam freely on any fuel with the lightest of draughts. At about the same time, although he was a dedicated steam man, he became attracted to the idea of using one of the new high-speed oil engines, which were then just coming on to the scene, as an alternative power unit for an industrial locomotive. Failing to interest the Sentinel Waggon Works in these new ideas, he decided to try the nearest locomotive builders with the result that he joined Kerr Stuart and Co. as what would now be called their chief development engineer and was presently joined there by Leslie Bomford. At the time I arrived in Stoke and for many months after that, my uncle lodged in a cottage at Trentham during the week, trundling off each week-end in his Model T Ford sedan to rejoin his family at Dovaston House in Shropshire.

The firm of Kerr Stuart was originally founded in Glasgow in 1881 as factors of locomotives and railway equipment. In 1892, however, the firm decided to launch out as manufacturers and bought out one of their sub-contractors, Messrs Hartley, Arnoux and Fanning, general engineers catering especially for the pottery trade, of California Works, Stoke-on-Trent. The original works of brick and slate with iron-framed windows still survived as the offices and machine shop, but between the years 1894 and 1912 a whole series of large new shops had been built to house the Erecting Shop, the Tool Room with canteen over, the Foundry, Heavy Forge, Boiler Shop and Wagon Shop and finally the Joinery and Paint Shop. From the office entrance in Whieldon Road the works extended for over a quarter of a mile along a narrow site bounded on one side by the main line of the old North Staffordshire Railway and on the other by the Trent and Mersey Canal. When working at full pressure, this plant could employ over a thousand men and at the time I came to Stoke, Kerr Stuart had recently completed an order for fifty standard 0–6–0 goods locomotives of Midland design for the L.M.S. Railway.

As soon as I joined the firm I was handed a brass disc with a hole at the top and a number stamped below. This was my 'check'. Each morning as I came to work I handed it in through the window of the small 'check office' by the main gates to be hung on an appropriately numbered pin on the large blackboard within. During the morning, the gatekeeper's assistant, the 'check boy', would return these discs to their owners. I was first set to work in the Wagon Shop assembling bogies for a series of eight-wheeled wagon underframes which were destined for an Indian railway. This was in the northern end of a huge steel-framed building divided by columns into three equal bays. Two of these were floored with railway sleepers laid edge to edge and were shared by the Wagon Shop and Boiler Shop. The third bay on the east side housed the heavy forge at its northern end followed, at the Boiler Shop end, by hydraulic presses and rolls for shaping boiler plates. Overhead, high under the roof trusses, electric cranes moaned and rumbled to and fro emitting occasional vivid arcs of blue fire from their conductor wires. From where I worked, the view of the far end of this shop appeared indistinct in the shimmer of heat rising from the coke-fired riveting hearths of the boiler makers. Men seemed to be everywhere and their diverse and purposeful activity filled the whole building with a torrent of urgent sound. Pneumatic hammers closed stays and rivets with a deafening clamour like sudden bursts of machine-gun fire; tall steam hammers pounded and every now and again a heavy hot stamping press opposite my place of work rose creaking, hung poised for a moment, and then plummeted downwards with a crash that shook the ground under my feet. After the quiet of the little workshop at Pitchill it was like Bedlam and at first I found it bewildering and a little alarming. But I soon became used to it, which was just as well because I worked for six months or more in that building, progressing first to the Boiler Shop and then to the Forge.

The universal friendliness, kindness and helpfulness that was shown to me by the men soon made me feel at home. My bungling efforts sometimes provoked them to ridicule or coarse jokes, but never to anger. For my part, so much did I admire their skill that I felt secretly flattered by the fact that such men could accept me as an equal. For one lesson I speedily learned was the prodigious amount of human skill that went into the building of a steam locomotive. Despite the formidable array of powerful machinery, steam, hydraulic and pneumatic, there was never any doubt in this shop as to which was the servant and which the master. Sometimes the skill involved was obvious to the merest onlooker, but sometimes it was not until you tried for yourself. For example, I thought the drivers of the overhead travelling cranes had the cushiest jobs in the shop, sitting comfortably in their little cabins aloof from the turmoil on the floor below. I had to scale a vertical steel ladder, clamber into one of these cabins and take over the crane controls to discover that the job was not so pleasant and simple as I had thought and that the lives of the men below often depended on the crane driver's skill and judgement. It was by no means easy to see from this high vantage point whether the crane hook was directly above the point of balance of some heavy and awkwardly shaped load. If it was not, the load would swing dangerously when it was lifted, perhaps knocking a man down or crushing him against a column. Nor was it easy to check that such a load had been correctly and safely slung or to ensure that it did not swing when it was traversed. Yet in the hands of these men flexible chains and steel cables seemed to become rigid, such was the effortless precision with which they lifted their unwieldy loads aloft, moved them swiftly along and across the shop, both traverses working simultaneously, and then lowered them in the exact spot required. I also discovered that the atmosphere under the roof in which the crane driver had to work was often scarcely breathable. They certainly earned their frequent billy cans of sweet tea which the shop boys delivered by hanging them on the crane hooks. Needless to say, they never spilled a drop.

The making of a locomotive boiler began in the oil-fired furnaces where the plates were heated. Every now and again one of these furnaces would yawn like the mouth of hell as its counterbalanced door was lifted so that a red hot plate could be grappled with long tongs and drawn forth over rollers to the bending rolls or on to the table of the big hydraulic press. In times past, the flanges that had to be turned on tube plates, back plate and throat plate (so that the boiler barrel

and the side plates of the inner and outer fireboxes could be
united to them by riveted joints) were formed by men with
sledge hammers beating them over blocks. Now, however,
the red hot plates were squeezed between massive cast-iron
formers, male and female, held in the jaws of the press. The
most dramatic of these operations on the press was the making
of a throat plate. This must have a flange formed in one direction
to receive the firebox wrapper plate and a second, smaller,
circular flange formed in the opposite direction in the centre
of the plate to receive the barrel. For the latter purpose a pilot
hole was cut in the flat plate before it was heated. In the shaping
of these throat plates, speed was of the essence because two
operations had to be performed while the plate was still red
hot. In an inferno of heat, glare and smoke, each man in the
gang had to move with the well rehearsed speed and precision
of a ballet dancer, the men manœuvring the almost white hot
plate precisely into position under the press while the charge
hand stood tensely watchful behind the row of levers that
controlled it. When he judged its position correct he signalled
with one hand to the men to lower their tongs and stand back,
while with the other he pulled the lever which raised the platform
of the press to form the outer flange and to hold the glowing
plate firmly between the two blocks. Then at the bidding of
a second lever the centre ram of the press rose and forced a
third, dome-shaped block through the central hole in the plate,
thus forming the second flange. It was a spectacular demonstration of skilled manual team work and of hydraulic power.

In one corner of the Boiler Shop there was a huge hydraulic
Equally impressive was the sight of three strikers swinging
their seven-pound sledge hammers in perfect rhythm, the master
smith keeping the time with his hammer, as they scarf welded
the white hot ends of a foundation ring. This ring would form
the bottom of the water space between the inner and outer
fireboxes. Rectangular in shape and formed of steel bar up
to four inches square in section, it was forged in two halves
and then welded together.

In one corner of the Boiler Shop there was a huge hydraulic
gap riveter, its bulk partly sunk in a pit. The function of this
machine was to rivet the seams of boiler barrels which were
lowered between its jaws by crane. Unlike its pneumatic
counterparts, it made no noise, squeezing down the hot rivets
into neat heads by sheer silent power. By contrast, the supreme
noise maker in the whole works was a device known as 'Happy
Sam'. This was shaped like a gigantic horseshoe. Two pneu-

matic hammers could be firmly housed in its opposed ends. When hung from a crane it was lowered over an upturned firebox and used to pean the heads of the many screwed stays that passed through the water space to unite the inner and outer fireboxes. Because these stays, unlike rivets, were hammered cold and the boiler acted as a sound-box, the noise of Happy Sam in full cry was almost intolerable and the men claimed that his devilish chatter could be heard two miles away. The noise in that boiler shop certainly left me slightly deaf for the rest of my life. Nor was there any question, in this shop at any rate, of boiler makers whispering to each other and lip reading as is frequently alleged. We communicated by bawling into each other's ears at close range.

My spell in the Forge provided me with another example of craftsmanship in the highly skilled team work of the steam hammer gangs. I soon learnt that the making of a heavy forging called for perfect co-ordination between the master smith, who was in charge of the operation, his hammer driver who stood behind the hammer and worked the steam valve handle which caused the hammer to strike a hard or a soft blow, and the men who, clinging to long chain-supported tongs, manipulated the glowing billet on the anvil as the smith directed. One mistake on the part of any of them might cause the hammer to strike a false blow, springing the tongs like the arm of a Roman catapult, perhaps with lethal results. Yet I never saw a single accident of this kind occur.

A typical hammer smith was a heavily built man who wore his collarless shirt open to the midriff. His fleshy, pallid face was seamed with dirt-encrusted wrinkles. The working of each heat would leave him pouring with sweat and he would mop his face and neck on a filthy piece of coarse towelling. Long experience in his craft had given him powers of judgement that seemed almost uncanny. After a quick glance at the forging drawing of a cranked axle, a coupling or connecting rod, he would potter out into the steel yard to choose a suitable billet, followed by a labourer trundling a lifting bogie. Whereas all other men in the works carried a two-foot steel rule tucked in the rule pocket of their overalls, for some reason that I never discovered, the smith's rule was invariably of brass and usually the scale and figures on it had long since worn away. In the yard he would wave this rule as cursorily as a wand over likely billets, finally striking one with it to indicate to the labourer that he had made his choice. It measured, shall we say, a foot square by two feet long and when he had forged it into a connecting rod some six feet long there would be only a small fraction of waste metal to spare.

The smith was dwarfed by his great hammer. It towered above him like some crouching prehistoric monster. Yet for all their size and brute strength, steam-hammers are surprisingly tetchy things and he tended it as meticulously as every true craftsman cares for his tools. On cold winter mornings steam was turned on to the hammer and it was slowly warmed through to rid it of the water that condensed in the cold cylinder. The great hammer head or 'tup', as it was called, was gently lowered on to the anvil and warmed by surrounding it with pieces of red hot scrap metal. I thought this ritual an unnecessary and time-wasting precaution until I saw the piston rod of a hammer—a shaft of solid steel seven inches in diameter—shear off just above the tup as cleanly as if it had been cut with a knife. Then I learned what fatigue and frost between them could do to metal.

I was thankful that I served my stint in the Forge during the dark months of the year, for in summer the heat there became almost intolerable to anyone unused to it. With a big oil-fired furnace roaring away beside each of the eight hammers and the drop-stamp, this was inevitable. Also in the Forge was a large Thomson water-tube boiler for supplying steam to the hammers and also to the steam operated hydraulic pumps which raised an accumulator that stood just outside the building beside the tall chimney stack. It was the boilerman's job to summon us to work and send us home by sounding the steam hooter that projected through the roof above this boiler. Most of the pottery works called their workers by steam sirens similar to those used on the old steam roundabouts. Each morning these would break into a frenzy of excited whoops to which Kerr Stuarts added a deep, mournful and slightly hoarse ground bass, like the voice of a liner lost in a fog.

From the Forge I moved into the Machine Shop. Whereas the plant in the more recently built shops was contemporary with the buildings and was thus comparatively modern in the 1920s, the Machine Shop was already outdated. Not only was it housed in part of the original factory, but I suspect that many of the machine tools dated from the nineteenth century and had been taken over with the building. The shop would have seemed low roofed and dark even without the line shafting and the forest of flapping belts with which it was cluttered.

Such was the reputation of the Forge and Foundry that they secured a lot of sub-contract work which helped to tide them over periods when locomotives orders fell slack. But the Machine Shop was nothing to be proud of. Modern tungsten-carbide tipped tools were still in the future, but some of the machines still used the old carbon steel tools which were already archaic. I remember being sent to the tool smith in the Forge to get them tempered. However, the machines, though slow, were adequate for their purpose, for tolerance on the machined parts of locomotives were generous by modern standards because they assumed a great deal of skilled hand fitting. Nevertheless, like many another apprentice before me, I perpetrated the occasional 'waster'. The time-honoured procedure then was to conceal the spoiled part beneath one's overalls and consign it to the waters of the Trent and Mersey Canal. I used to wonder just how many guilty secrets would be revealed if ever that particular pound were drained. I now suspect that foremen and staff must have turned a blind eye to this practice for, on espying a young apprentice heading across the yard for the canal, they must surely have pondered on the reason why he had acquired a pot belly or a stiff leg, depending on the dimensions of the object concealed.

The Foundry was situated at low level directly alongside the canal, a convenient arrangement because it enabled the tall cupolas to be charged with coke, pig-iron and scrap at yard level. I never worked there, but I welcomed any excuse to walk through it, particularly in the late afternoon when the sand-moulds were being filled with molten metal so that the castings would have a chance to cool down overnight. For if a casting is broken out of its mould too soon it becomes chilled, making its metal hard and difficult to machine. The larger the casting the longer it must remain in the sand. The Foundry was the quietest place in the works, for here there were no noisy machines but only men, moving silently over the floor of soft black sand or stooping or kneeling beside their mould-boxes, working with the rapt concentration of a child making a sand castle. Although his hands were black, a skilled moulder used them with the precision and deftness of a surgeon. He would ease a wooden pattern from the sand with extreme care and then make good any slight damage that the edges of the fragile mould might have sustained, using little gleaming tools which the sand had burnished.

But at casting time, when the draught roared in the bellies

of the cupolas, the Foundry became a highly dramatic place. Wielding his long pricker like a lance, the furnaceman broke through the bung of fireclay that had stopped the mouth of the tapping hole and amid a dazzle of sizzling sparks a stream of white hot metal would gush out into the waiting ladle. He had a new clay bung formed ready on the end of a rod so that he could stop the flow when the ladle was full. The biggest and most complicated casting produced by this Foundry comprised the two cylinders and valve chests for a large inside cylinder locomotive. To cast this a huge ladle containing anything up to five tons of metal was needed. When it had been filled it was raised aloft by the overhead crane, traversed and then lowered gently into position in front of the mould, the crane driver leaning forward out of his cabin, his face lit by the glare from the ladle as the charge-hand below signalled to him with the palm of his hand. For the ladle had to be positioned very precisely so that when it was tilted the stream of metal would be directed precisely into the mouth of the mould runner. Then the pouring began, two men manning the hand-wheels that tipped the ladle, a third, armed with a long skimmer, holding back the dross that formed on the surface of the molten metal to prevent it falling into the mould and a fourth igniting the gas that issued from the mould vents while the charge-hand kept a vigilant eye on the whole operation. For, to be successful, it had to be carried out promptly and speedily but without haste and flurry. Otherwise, either the casting would be spoiled or there would be an accident. Molten metal is deadly stuff.

The Erecting Shop at Kerr Stuarts was as lofty as a cathedral. This was to enable the two Royce cranes to lift one locomotive over another if the need arose. Such an operation was impossible in the older erecting shops where locomotives were built in line ahead and if anything delayed completion of the engine at the head of the line, the rest were imprisoned. This new shop had been built alongside the original Erecting Shop of Hartley, Arnoux and Fanning, one wall of which had been demolished so that it now formed a kind of side aisle with a lower roof than the main building. In this aisle a variety of machine and hand operations were performed in the production of locomotive frames, wheels, axles, axle boxes and motion. At the time I came to the works there was no flame cutting and main frame plates were cut to shape by an incredibly laborious method. The plates, each an inch or more thick, were dealt with in batches of six, the top plate of each batch being white-washed and marked out with a scriber to indicate the exact form in which it was to be cut. This batch was then moved to the tables of a row of Archdale radial drilling machines whose operators proceeded to drill closely spaced holes all round the scribed outline. The metal between these holes was next cut through by hammer and chisel. This left an extremely ragged edge, so finally the batch was transferred to the table of a very large vertical milling machine to be milled all round.

Here also a giant lathe turned pairs of wheels and axles and tyres were shrunk on to wheels by a method very similar to that used by a village wheelwright to tyre wagon wheels. Safety screws were then fitted as a precaution although I have never heard of a tyre working loose. There was also a row of fitters' benches where a great deal of highly skilled and patient hand fitting of valve motion parts was done. I worked for a time at one of these benches with file, scraper and surface plate bedding the two halves of eccentric sheaves together. I found this a particularly tricky job because the two surfaces were not flat but stepped which meant that three faces, one of them vertical, had to bed accurately. Moreover, this had to be done so that, when drawn together by bolts, the sheave would 'pinch' on the axle and its keys, otherwise it would soon work loose when running. However, I persevered, knowing that with my next move I should achieve the summit of my ambition —to work in the Erecting Shop.

The men in the Erecting Shop were divided into gangs, each working as a team under a charge-hand. Each of these gangs was responsible for building a locomotive from the time the bare frame plates were set up until it left the shop under its own steam. I joined a gang led by Ernest Lines ('Ernie'), a splendid character, short, stocky and humorous with a lantern jaw who looked as though he liked his beer but was absolute master of his trade. It was particularly fortunate for me that at this time the shop was building six of the largest locomotives ever to be turned out by the firm. These were 4–8–0 mixed traffic engines destined for the Buenos Aires Central Railway (F.C.C.B.A.). Although of standard gauge, they were too big to travel over British metals to Birkenhead for shipment but had to be partially dismantled. Compared with the average British locomotive of the day, their cabs seemed vast and positively palatial with their sliding teak shutters, tip-up seats for the crew and flexibly mounted electric lights to illuminate steam and water gauges. These lights, and the big headlamps mounted fore and aft,[1] were supplied with current by a turbo-generator mounted on top of the firebox. Their tenders were so big that on one occasion, while waiting for some part to arrive, an erecting gang settled down in the water tank to play a quiet game of halfpenny nap by the light of tallow dips. They imagined they were secure from prying eyes until a member of a rival gang dropped a handful of smouldering cotton waste down through the tank filler and smoked them out.

There was much good-natured horse-play of this kind in the Erecting Shop, for the men were the aristocrats of their trade and management treated them indulgently. Perennial works jokes were played on simple apprentices. They would be sent to the stores to fetch a left-handed hammer or a long stand. On asking for the latter, the innocent youth would be kept waiting interminably until, on repeating his request, the grinning store-keeper replied 'You've had it'. The joke dated back at least a hundred years. Once, when a gang had got behind with their locomotive, they returned after the lunch break to find grass apparently growing luxuriantly out of the top of the funnel. 'Yockerton Hall' was their invariable reply to any query as to the whereabouts of an individual, a missing part or a tool. And to the obvious question that this provoked they would reply in mock surprise: 'What, yo' never 'eard o' Yockerton! It's where there's neither land nor water and they walk about on planks.' The exploits of a legendary driver named Gluepot were another feature of works mythology. He was so-called because he was said on one occasion to have filled his cylinder lubricator up with glue in mistake for hot cylinder oil with very surprising results. On another occasion he was alleged to have driven a train from Shrewsbury into Crewe with the shattered remains of Nantwich level crossing gates dangling from his front buffers, much to the dismay of station officials. These are typical examples of my workmates' humour.

For me it was a rich experience to work with such men on such a locomotive and to watch the monster grow in power and majesty from day to day. When the frames had been completed, the outside cylinders and smoke-box saddle could be bolted up. Next, the boiler was propelled into the shop on a bogie flat wagon by the works shunting engine and dropped into place

[1] Evidently they did a lot of tender-first running in Argentina.

on the frames. A big moment came when the locomotive was lifted bodily by both cranes and lowered gently on to its wheels. Additional hands were needed for this operation because a man had to guide each axle box between the cheeks of the horn-blocks on the frames. Then, after valve gear and connecting rods had been fitted up and set, the engine was gently pulled forwards by the works shunter until its driving wheels rested precisely on two rollers at track level near the shop doors. Now the time had come to raise steam. With the regulator opened a crack, the engine was allowed to run herself in for an hour or so. As she stood thus, driving wheels revolving slowly on the rollers, the men who had built her fussed about her like anxious midwives. Grimy hands felt the temperature of bearings and, as the cross-head swept to and fro, Ernie Lines passed a rapid finger across the oily surface of the slide bars before and behind it to ensure that its bronze slippers were bedding properly.

Only when this test had been passed satisfactorily was it time to fit the coupling rods and then give the locomotive its first run under steam. There was a multi-gauge track in the Erecting Shop, the gauges ranging from 2 ft. up to 5 ft. 6 in. Most of these ended at the first turnout of the works railway about fifty yards outside the shop, but the 3 ft. gauge and, of course, the 4 ft. 8½ in., continued to provide a long straight test track that ran beside the main railway boundary fence to a terminus in the paint shop at the far end of the works. So we could give our monster quite a respectable run and that Ernie Lines allowed me to handle her was more than ample reward for all the hard work that had gone before. It was the first time in my life that I had driven a locomotive and it gave me an indescribable thrill, when I nudged the regulator cautiously open, to hear the first deep exhaust beat and to feel the great machine suddenly come alive under my hand and begin to roll obediently forward. After we had progressed majestically to and fro for some time, I stopped her and took a photograph to record the great occasion, Ernie Lines posing proudly on the front buffer beam.

Locomotives intended for export as this one was were usually finished in flat 'shop grey', much to the disappointment of the paint shop, although the first of any new type was lined black and white solely for photographic purposes. But, about this time, one of the large and handsome tank engines which the firm had built just after the war for the Aylesbury line of the Metropolitan Railway came back to the works for a complete overhaul and when this was finished she received 'the full treatment' in the paint shop. After laborious de-scaling of the plates followed by seemingly endless coats of paint, each rubbed down by hand with bath-brick and water and after repeated varnishings, she emerged wearing that gleaming, lustrous livery such as one can now admire only in old photographs. Her side-tanks were like the surface of a mirror. Look how you would, you could not detect the slightest wave in the plate or the faintest suggestion of a countersunk rivet. I am glad that I saw her, for she was certainly the last locomotive to be painted in the traditional style at the California Works and probably one of the last in the country. By contrast, when twenty-five new six-coupled pannier tank locomotives were built later for the Great Western Railway, the poor standard of finish that was specified caused a lot of head-shaking in the Paint Shop. This was by no means the only dictate to cause dismay among the craftsmen at Kerr Stuarts, but there could be no argument for throughout the contract a Great Western resident inspector was on the prowl to ensure that all the work was carried out precisely to Swindon specification.

In this case the firm became virtually a sub-contractor to Swindon. Normally, the procedure was very different. Once the outline design and specification of a new type of locomotive for an overseas railway company had been approved in principle by the consulting engineers, the drawing office would produce the detail drawings and issue them to the foremen of the shops—boiler drawings to the foreman of the Boiler Shop and so on. These drawings were the basis of a tender and when they were issued everyone in the works knew that a new contract was in the wind because the foremen (each wearing the bowler hat which was his permanent badge of office) would be seen filing into the canteen for a meeting. From this each man would return, drawings under arm, to his own office where he would call a similar meeting of his charge-hands who, in their turn, would discuss matters with their gangs. Under this hierarchical system, each shop agreed upon its price for a particular part of the job and it was upon this basis that the final tender was submitted. Compared with other industries in Britain where the rate-fixer with his stop-watch had already made his appearance, this method was already obsolete, yet in human terms it possessed incalculable advantages not to be measured in terms of economics or business efficiency. For it made every skilled man in the works feel he was a responsible member of a team and the news that a tender had been accepted caused general jubilation in the shops.

I have set down in some detail the way steam locomotives were built at the California Works because the whole process has now become as much a thing of the past as the making of a farm wagon in George Sturt's wheelwright's shop at Farnham. The men I was privileged to work beside were craftsmen as surely as were Sturt's wheelwrights. If they erred it was on the side of conservatism. Occasionally they might adopt a stubborn 'nothing like leather' mentality. But in the main they resisted the changes that were coming about in engineering methods, not because they threatened their pay packets, but because they involved a lowering of the standards of workmanship in which they took such pride and satisfaction and so menaced the future of those traditional skills which were their only real assets. In short, they were of the species *homo faber* and it is as well to emphasise this now that all social or economic studies are based on the facile Marxist assumption that man is merely an economic animal, and all talk of craftsmanship or pride in work dismissed as merely romantic sentimentality. On the contrary, having worked beside such men I know that, although they had had little formal education, because they were craftsmen their general standards were exacting. Take away that craftsmanship and standards inevitably fall, only the weight of the pay packet counts, and man becomes indeed an economic animal.

Chapter 7

Shropshire Railways
and Canals

On week-days I found the demonic energy of the Pottery towns, all those belching chimneys and ovens, the jostling crowds and traffic—much of it still horse-drawn—in the streets, strangely exhilarating. It fascinated me in spite of myself in the same way that Milton was obviously attracted by the activities of Satan. But on Sundays the Potteries became anathema to me. For then innumerable furnace fires were banked allowing its skies to clear so that, in summer, the pitiless eye of the sun revealed with unfamiliar clarity the sordidness of the cobbled streets with their rows of terraced houses, their blackness unrelieved by any green thing. Apart from occasional figures squatting aimlessly on raddled front doorsteps, or the footfalls of some miner exercising his whippet, these streets were silent and deserted at such a time. The smell of roasting Sunday joints mingled with a stale smell of beer from street corner pubs, this last a hangover, like the pieces of vinegar stained newspaper that the wind stirred in the gutters, of previous Saturday night orgies. Now they were sleeping it off. Not until afternoon did the Potteries begin to show signs of life as buses began to churn down London Road carrying loads of young couples to their love-making amid the bracken of Trentham Park.

I found these Sundays so depressing that I could not wait to get out of the Potteries at week-ends. As soon as work was over at midday on Saturday and I had my 'dinner' at No. 439, I would change and head off into the country on my motorcycle. Fortunately, unlike some industrial areas, the Pottery towns are easy to get out of. Strung along the headwaters of the Trent, they form a long, narrow industrial belt with unspoiled country upon either side. Strangely enough, the northern side towards the Peak District where Staffordshire soon merges into Derbyshire never appealed to me and it was south-westwards into Shropshire that I usually turned, often to spend the weekend with the Willans family at their home near the Welsh Border.

Dovaston was one of those pleasant, roomy, four-square early nineteenth-century houses of stone-faced mellow brick with a low-pitched slate roof such as one finds in the countryside of Shropshire and Cheshire. It had only one snag; its water supply had to be pumped by hand, using an antiquated green-painted pump that stood outside the back door in a small cobbled yard surrounded by a low range of outbuildings. In my recollection of the various Willans' houses, water supply problems persistently dogged the family but were usually solved by my uncle with improvisations remarkable for their ingenuity and economy. Dovaston House was no exception. He had purchased an old horizontal 'hit-and-miss' petrol/paraffin engine. By means of a flat belt, this drove a cranked countershaft which actuated the pump handle by a long connecting rod. In action, this novel arrangement reminded me of one of Heath Robinson's crazy inventions. Quivering with animation and slopping water from its steaming cooling hopper, the engine coughed and wheezed, the driving belt slapped, while the old pump, finding its handle gripped by a tireless iron arm, rocked on its foundation and made loud groaning complaints. But it worked.

The house stood on rising ground and the tall windows of the drawing room commanded a magnificent view over a wide expanse of flood plain, the meeting place of rivers Vyrnwy and Severn, to the dramatic shapes of the Briedden Hills beyond. Although they were of modest height, as such outliers are apt to do, the Brieddens looked impressively steep and mountainous. In any season of the year, they caught and held the eye. In autumn they would look like some volcanic islands of the Pacific above a ghostly sea of mist. More than once when I was at Dovaston I looked out of my bedroom window on a Sunday morning to see their bold shapes mirrored in a real sea when heavy overnight rain over the Welsh mountains had caused both rivers to rise with astonishing speed, drowning all the land below. Where so lately there had been green fields, now only trees and hedgerows stood darkly out of an expanse of silver waters. In the midst of this plain lay the little village of Melverley, ancient and remote, where even the graveyard surrounding the little timbered church has to be protected lest Severn wash away its dead. 'God help Melverley!' was a saying in those parts whenever the floods were out, and at such times I would repeat it to myself, wondering the while why ever a village came to be built there. It seemed as improbable as that mythical Yockerton Hall.

Although it is forty years since I was last at Dovaston, I find that memory can still re-create in all its details that landscape as I saw it then. Such loveliness, so indelibly imprinted on the mind by the sensitive lens of youth is, I find, as great a solace and as evocative of the past as an old tune or remembered voices. But because we now treat our country, not as a paradise garden but as a squalid and neglected backyard, if the image is not to be shattered forever, it is usually wiser not to revisit the scenes of our youth.

I thought this Shropshire landscape like, and yet at the same time strangely unlike, that other country of the Herefordshire marches further to the south which I had come to know so well as a child. Despite its great natural beauty, however, I felt then—as I still feel—that there is something indefinably melancholy about western Shropshire. Instead of seeming to transcend time and lift the heart as did the country of my childhood, it seemed to speak of time passing and to evoke race memories of old, unhappy, far off things. I had not read Housman at this time, but when I did so, some of his poems seemed to me to be loaded with the burden of this profound sadness.

The contrast between Dovaston House and my dingy lodgings in Stoke-on-Trent was so extreme that I was loath to leave it. Rather than depart on Sunday evening, I preferred to rise at 6 a.m. the following day, creep out of the house and ride back to Stoke in time for work, even in the darkness and cold of a winter's morning. Once on such a morning I struck an unsuspected patch of black ice on a corner near Shrewsbury and skidded into a wet ditch with the bike on top of me. But I had become inured to spills of this kind, sorted myself out and was soon pressing on again through the darkness though my teeth were chattering with the cold.

By this time, my cousin Bill Willans, who was slightly younger than I was and had just left school at Stowe, was living at home. Acting on the same principle that had sent me to Pitchill—that a small shop makes the best primary school for a budding engineer—his father had arranged for him to work in the shops at nearby Kinnerley Junction. Kinnerley was the Swindon of that most endearing rural byway, the Shropshire and Montgomeryshire Railway. It had only received its title in this century from a remarkable character named Colonel H. F. Stephens who made it his precarious business to buy up moribund railways and attempt to re-animate them, using cast-off locomotives and rolling stock purchased cheap from other, grander railways. The S. & M.R. was thus the railway equivalent of some of the smaller and poorer South American airlines today and its shops at Kinnerley resembled a graveyard where old locomotives, like so many old elephants, came to die. The railway owed its existence to a crazy speculation of the 1860s aiming to provide a direct rail link between the Potteries and Portmadoc on the coast of North Wales, and Shropshire countrymen, who have long memories, habitually referred to it as 'the Pots'. Its main line set off boldly from Shrewsbury but petered out tamely at Llanymynech, just over the Welsh Border, as though the speculators had taken fright at the sight of the Welsh hills ahead. From Kinnerley a branch line curved away to the southward, crossing the Severn and its flood plain to end at Criggion at the foot of the Briedden Hills. Here there was a large granite quarry which employed a Sentinel locomotive and provided most of the S. & M.R.'s meagre freight traffic.

I will not describe this railway in detail, its ageing locomotives or the eccentric manner in which it was operated, because I have already done so fully in an earlier book.[1] But at least I should explain that although it could boast a stud of eight locomotives, there was seldom more than one of them which was capable of being steamed at any one time. The resourceful owner, however, had triumphantly overcome this deficiency by purchasing four old Model T Ford buses, mounting them on railway wheels and running them in pairs coupled back to back. To equip them for this new role, only the minimum of alteration was done. For example, steering wheels were retained. Perhaps they helped the driver to feel at home. They offered the maximum of discomfort ever achieved in rail travel, while on account of the clangour of their hollow steel wheels, which could be heard miles away in still weather, they were nicknamed 'the rattlers' by the locals.

[1] *Lines of Character* (Constable, 1952).

Bill had entered into the life of the railway wholeheartedly. No doubt he found the change from school as refreshing as I did. He was already playing for the village cricket team which was captained by Mr Funnel, the stationmaster at Kinnerley Junction, a red-faced portly man who always employed a runner because of his bad heart. Kinnerley was within walking distance of Dovaston House, and although Bill had worked on the railway all the week, it seemed as though he could never have enough of it. Whenever I arrived for the week-end we usually made a bee-line for the loco shed and repair shop which was situated at right angles to the station beside the Criggion Branch. Ancient locomotives in various stages of disrepair lay slumbering in the sunshine on the grassgrown tracks outside the shed. Here, for example, stood the rusting wreck of the locomotive *Hesperus*, patiently awaiting a new boiler which never seemed to come. (Curiously enough, to the amazement of all at Kinnerley, that new boiler did eventually arrive and *Hesperus* was rebuilt. As her sister engine *Pyramus* presently expired, it was not before time.) Equipment and facilities for repair were either non-existent or so primitive that even the most minor repair job entailed a major feat of improvisation. But, remembering that great engineer Frederick Lanchester's terse comment: 'Too much apparatus, not enough brains' on being shown round a modern research laboratory, it was obviously an ideal training school for Bill. To one who had come straight from the fiery tumult of the California Works, the contrast of this little quiet shop, dozing in the depths of the country, was extreme. I felt I had indeed come to the end of the line.

In the yard at Kinnerley there was kept one of those plate-layer's trolleys which two men can propel by means of a central seesaw handle connected to its cranked axle. By energetic pumping of the handle, this device was capable of quite a fair turn of speed and on fine Sundays Bill and I used to explore the railway. On more than one occasion we trundled off down the branch line towards Criggion. This crossed the Severn near Melverley by a timber bridge that looked as frail as an early American trestle viaduct and I used to marvel that it could ever withstand the weight of a locomotive. To cross this bridge was the thrilling highlight of the journey, for there was no decking, the rails being fixed to longitudinal baulks supported by cross beams. One could look down between these timbers to the swirling brown waters of the Severn below.

On another occasion we set out to cover the 4½ miles of main line between Kinnerley and Llanymynech in the scheduled running time of the passenger service, including making the regulation intermediate pauses at Wern Las halt and Maesbrook station en route. That we achieved this does not say much for the celerity of passenger trains on the S. & M.R. Breathless and pumping furiously on the handles, we swung round the curve leading into the old Cambrian station at Llanymynech, coming to rest in the bay platform exactly on time.

The Shropshire and Montgomeryshire Railway was not the only thing that attracted me to Dovaston House at this time. Inspired no doubt by memories of his father's steam launch *Black Angel*, my uncle Kyrle conceived the idea of building a roomy steam boat in which the Willans family and their friends could go for leisurely holidays on the canals. Only a few miles away from Dovaston was the Llangollen branch of the Shropshire Union Canal and also the canal line to Welshpool and Newtown (the old Montgomeryshire Canal) which joined the former at Frankton Junction. The Shropshire Union Railways and Canal Company and its associate, the Shropshire Union Canal Carrying Company, were both controlled by the London and North Western Railway which, because the canal passed through rival railway territory, traded vigorously on it, having a fleet of over two hundred boats in action as late as 1920. In the following year, however, the railway unions insisted that the boatmen and their families who manned these craft should in future only work an eight-hour day like the railwaymen. This typically obtuse egalitarian move, betraying a total ignorance of the very different working conditions on canals, could only have one result: the entire Shropshire Union fleet was disbanded and the boats either broken up or sold to local traders and small carrying concerns. In 1929, some of the latter were still trading on the western branches of the system though upon a much diminished scale. Among these by-traders were the Peate family who used their boats to carry grain from Ellesmere Port on the Mersey to their own mill beside the canal at Maesbury, fifteen miles north of Welshpool. It was from them that Kyrle Willans purchased *Cressy*. She had been built for the Shropshire Union Canal Carrying Company during the Great War in a dockyard at the northern end of Telford's great aqueduct at Pont Cysyllte.[1]

[1] She was named after a battle cruiser of the first world war.

Although they must all conform to approximately the same general dimensions (70 ft. long by 7 ft. beam), canal narrow boats vary so much in build that it is possible for the knowledgeable to spot the different types at a glance. Of these, in my opinion, the Shropshire Union boats were easily the most graceful. They were smaller and of lighter burthen (they were a plank lower in the side than other wooden boats), and, whereas most narrow boats are virtually elongated floating boxes with very bluff bows and sterns, the sides of the typical Shropshire Union hull were built with considerable sheer which led into a beautiful tapering and up-curving bow and stern. In boatman's parlance they were good swimmers. This, then, was the boat that, on my uncle's instructions, was brought from Maesbury to Mr Beech's dock beside the locks at Frankton Junction to be converted into a comfortable house-boat. So far as I know, there were then only two similar narrow boat conversions in existence. A trip over to Frankton Dock to inspect progress on *Cressy* thereafter became a regular feature of my visits to Dovaston House.

Cressy had been a horse-drawn boat and to propel her my uncle acquired a small vertical compound steam engine by Plentys of Newbury which had previously powered an Admiralty pinnace. In order to install this it was necessary to bore and otherwise modify the stern post to take a shaft and propeller and to fit a new rudder and tiller of motor boat type. Acting on one of his favourite maxims that 'there's no such thing as too big a boiler', my uncle bought a second-hand boiler out of a Yorkshire steam wagon to supply the little Plenty engine with steam. This was a T-shaped boiler of double-ended return tube type. Two short barrels terminating in smoke-boxes extended from either side of a central firebox, the chimney being directly above the firedoor. The boiler exactly fitted into *Cressy*, the two smoke boxes being just inboard of the gunwhales. This meant that sweeping the tubes on the water side of the boat was something of an acrobatic feat and after Bill had fallen backwards into the canal still clutching a tube brush, we usually swept the tubes while the boat was lying in a narrow lock.

Cressy's original living accommodation, a cabin at the stern and a smaller raised fore-cabin in the bow, were retained. The steam plant was installed in an engine room immediately ahead of the stern cabin and, apart from a small open deck just aft of the fore-cabin, the remainder of her hold was cabined over to provide extra accommodation.

When all this work had been completed, *Cressy* was floated out of Mr Beech's dock and a steam trial was held up the canal in the direction of Llangollen one Sunday afternoon. I remember thinking how wonderful it would be to steam over the tall aqueduct across the Vale of Llangollen at Pontcysyllte, but since our speed was only three miles an hour and the aqueduct was eleven miles away, this was manifestly impossible in the short time available and we had to turn *Cressy* about in the first convenient 'winding hole'. Exactly twenty years were to pass before I finally achieved this ambition by taking *Cressy* over Pontcysyllte.

It was at this juncture that the Willans family left Dovaston House and moved to an old house at Barlaston to the south of the Potteries. Selfishly, I welcomed this move for obvious reasons though I was saddened to think I would never see Dovaston again. Although the village of Barlaston was much more countrified then than it is today, the outskirts of the Potteries must have seemed to my long-suffering Aunt Hero a very poor exchange for west Shropshire. But, kindly and cheerful as ever, she appeared to take it in her stride and it is only now, as I look back, that I realise what a wrench it must have been to her to leave that beautiful house. This move led to a decision to steam *Cressy* from Frankton to a mooring on the Trent and Mersey Canal at the tail of Trentham lock where she would be only the breadth of a gently sloping meadow away from the new house. This would be her maiden voyage as a powered craft, and as we planned to complete it in two days, there was little room for mishap or mechanical failure. So to simplify the operation *Cressy* was moved, a week beforehand, from Frankton to a more convenient and accessible mooring at Ellesmere. For this momentous voyage there was to be an all male crew of four, my uncle Kyrle, my cousin Bill, a youth named Frank from Kinnerley, who had done odd jobs about the house at Dovaston, and myself. I took the Saturday morning off by special dispensation so that we could all sleep on board on the Friday night and make an early start the following morning.

As this was to be very much of a working trip, we were all in our overalls and slept in the old cabins fore and aft to avoid sullying the pristine accommodation amidships. It was the first night I had ever spent afloat and it was a short one. On that March morning of 1930 two of us got up while it was still quite dark to light up the boiler and to oil round.

Then, after a scratch breakfast washed down with mugs of scalding tea to fortify us against the cold while steam was making, we cast off and slipped away in the first faint light of dawn.

The long level pound of canal that we first traversed passes through a country strangely remote and of a mysterious beauty. It first runs close beside two of the Shropshire meres, Colemere and Blakemere, winds about for a space by Hampton Bank and Bettisfield, and then suddenly broadens into a wider and deeper channel that cuts straight across Whixall Moss, a great expanse of peat bog more reminiscent of Ireland than England. That morning dawned dry but cold and still with an overcast sky of a uniform pearly grey. My recollection is of the black interlacement of bare branches silhouetted against this colourless sky, of a thin white mist lying waist high over the dark waters. Tree-encircled and veiled in this mist, Blakemere might have been that magic lake of Arthurian legend into which Sir Bedivere had flung the sword Excalibur. In memory it has become the still and silent landscape of a dream and through it *Cressy* glided smoothly and quietly along, her little compound engine ticking over with no more noise than a well-oiled sewing machine. She did not intrude upon the landscape; she became a part of it like the canal itself. As I realised this, my consuming interest in engineering and my feeling for the natural world, which, since I had come to Stoke-on-Trent had begun disturbingly to conflict with each other, were suddenly reconciled and before we had covered many miles I had fallen head-over-heels in love with canals. This is it, I thought; this is what travel ought to be like.

We took turn and turn about, one at the tiller and one in the engine room, while the other two crew members worked the locks or snatched a bite of food. The engine continued to run perfectly, the boiler steamed freely and, as darkness fell, we tied up below Wardle Lock, Middlewich, at the junction of the Trent and Mersey Canal having covered 37 miles and worked through 23 locks. This may not sound much to anyone unacquainted with canal travelling but it was a pretty good day's journey for an inexperienced crew with an untried boat. This performance reflects, not so much on the ability of the crew as on the deterioration in the state of the canals between then and now.

Next morning we were up betimes as a long hard day's work lay ahead of us if we were to reach Barlaston by nightfall.

First we had to scale the thirty-four Cheshire Locks which lay between us and the northern end of the long summit tunnel at Harecastle. And after we had passed through that tunnel there would still be a further nine miles to go with five falling locks before we reached our destination. We had climbed the locks and reached the mouth of the tunnel when an unexpected hitch occurred. Knowledgeable heads were shaken over the height of *Cressy's* new cabinwork. The headroom in the tunnel had been greatly reduced owing to mining subsidence, we were told, and because, according to regulations, we would have to be towed through by an unstoppable electric tug, the new cabin would certainly be torn off in the process. There was only one thing to be done—bring her down in the water by loading up the fore-end with some suitable ballast. This put an end to our hopes of reaching Barlaston that evening. *Cressy* was moored up where she lay and left in charge of Frank. So ended my ever-memorable first canal voyage, for I had to be back at work in the morning. Next day, *Cressy* was loaded with bricks, off-loaded again when she had successfully passed through the tunnel, and worked down to Barlaston by the other three crew members.

On this first trip, *Cressy* had worked as a 'puffer', that is to say, steam from the engine exhausted up her funnel. This produced steam in such embarrassing volume that it was difficult to prevent the boiler blowing off and enveloping the steerer in a cloud of steam. Consequently, my uncle decided that she would steam quite adequately on natural draught, so he had a small jet condenser built to his design in the Boiler Shop at Kerr Stuarts. When this was finished, *Cressy* was steamed up to Stoke and moored beside the Foundry where the condenser and the necessary pipe-work were installed, the men thoroughly enjoying this unusual 'foreign order', as they termed it. After this, we made two week-end trips to Great Haywood and back before, in August 1930, I joined *Cressy* for the first week of a long fortnight's cruise.

We steamed down the canal to the Trent, turned up the Soar through Loughborough and Leicester, passed through the Leicester Section of the Grand Union and thence down the main line of that canal as far as Blisworth. There I and another member of the crew were replaced by others, leaving the boat to return to Barlaston by a different route. I remember that my cousin Bill and I had to bow-haul the boat through dense weed for a distance of a mile or more north of Alrewas on the

Trent and Mersey, but this was exceptional; over most of the route the going was much better than it is today. Once again, the steam plant performed perfectly, its silence was a delight and we made use of it to do much of our cooking. In the early evening my aunt Hero and my cousin Barbara, assisted by other spare members of the crew, would prepare the ingredients for a king-sized stew. These were put into a massive steam-jacketed pot which was placed on the cabin roof aft with a sack thrown over it. The engine room hand would couple it up to the boiler, turn on steam and in a short while the hungry steerer was regaled by the most delectable smell of cooking.

But there were snags to steam. It took up a lot of space; two men were needed to work the boat and although an electric bell was rigged up to act as an engine room telegraph, reaction in emergency was not always quick enough. Having rung 'full astern' the unfortunate steerer was apt to find the boat steaming towards some immovable obstruction because the engine room attendant was preoccupied in oiling the engine or coaxing the injector. Another source of friction between steerer and engineer was the smoke. Although *Cressy* ran more silently than before and steamed well enough with the condenser fitted, there was now not enough draught to lift the smoke over the steerer's head. Too preoccupied to see the canal ahead, the engineer often unwittingly chose to fire up the moment before *Cressy* dived into a long tunnel. This provoked bitter recriminations and these were echoed at the bow if the unfortunate steerer, blinded by smoke, bumped the side wall violently, disrupting cooking operations in the galley. Nor was it always easy to obtain supplies of suitable coal. I remember Bill and I sweating profusely one hot August afternoon as we humped hundredweight sacks from a neigh-bouring coalyard along the towing path at Loughborough.

After the move to Barlaston, Bill was apprenticed for a time in the maintenance shop of the North Staffordshire Coal and Iron Company, whose pits and furnaces (the latter long since gone) were situated beside the canal to the south of Kerr Stuarts. This work took him frequently below ground to repair compressed-air haulage engines and other equipment. Although this was exacting work carried out under difficult conditions, the men at Kerr Stuarts referred to the 'pit fitter' scathingly and regarded him as a figure of fun. They often referred to a hand-hammer as a pit-fitter's spanner, claiming that it was the only tool he used. But I learnt to appreciate his

work better after, at Bill's instigation, I had been down one
of the 'North Stafford' pits to the 800 yard level. The experience of our descent of the shaft in the cage came as no
surprise to me because I had been warned that when the cage
started I should feel as though I had left most of my insides
behind on the surface. The fastest express lift was nothing
to it. The surprising thing was to discover that the 800 yard
level was a level only in name. Because the North Staffordshire coal seams are extravagantly buckled and because the
miner naturally follows the seam, the main haulage-way
leading from the pit bottom to the working face resembled an
underground switchback railway. At the pit bottom I could hear
the draught whistling through chinks in the airlock doors
between the downcast and upcast shafts, yet the atmosphere
seemed stale and hot, the pit dry and dusty underfoot. As we
plodded along for what seemed an interminable distance, now
toiling up a steep ascent, now back on our heels as we faced an
equally steep descent, I became increasingly conscious of the
vast weight of earth and rock directly above my head. It was
not a pleasant feeling. Coal mines are definitely not for the
claustrophobic. No wooden props here; the tunnel was arched
with steel sections some of which had buckled under the
immense weight to such an extent that we had to stoop as
we passed beneath them. We must have walked the best part of
two miles before we reached the coal face where the compressed
air coal-cutting machines were running and I was reminded that
a miner's working day began and ended at the face.[1] I had
admired the way my workmates at Kerr Stuarts faced their
working lives, but after this experience I admired the coal
miner very much more.

Life at Stoke was very much more enjoyable now that I had
the company of Bill Willans in the evenings and at week-ends.
But there was one serious snag. His parents absolutely forbade
him to ride pillion on the 2¼ h.p. A.J.S. motorcycle which I had
bought to replace my old B.S.A. It is true that my motorcycling career had been one long chapter of accidents. I could
never manage the acetylene headlamp on my B.S.A. for one
thing. Either it went up in flames and became red-hot, or
it burnt with only a dim blue glow. It was on one of the latter

[1] The company were at this time sinking a new shaft at Hem
Heath, near Trentham, to reduce this distance, but this had not
yet come into operation.

occasions that I had run into the back of a Sentinel Wagon
at night on the road from Pitchill to Evesham with such
force that the driver noticed it and stopped to investigate.
If the top of my front forks had not made contact with the
tail of the Sentinel but had run underneath it, I might not
have survived. As it was I merely fell over on to a heap of
stones by the side of the road, dislocating my shoulder. Nevertheless, somehow or other I managed to ride the damaged
bike back to the farm. On another occasion at Pitchill I rode
straight through a barn door, making myself decidedly unpopular in the process. I had arrived in the farmyard at speed
only to find the footbrake rod had broken. Since the handbrake
was useless in such circumstances I instantly chose the barn
door as a more resilient form of energency stop than the brick
walls which offered the only alternative. Twice I had flown
over the handlebars and miraculously landed in the road on my
bottom instead of on my head, once when I collided with a
suicidal sheep on a Welsh mountain pass, and again when
someone, unknown to me, had slackened the front fork shock-
absorbers right off and I experienced a monumental steering
wobble. Only a week after I had acquired my new A.J.S. I had
set off from Stoke on a week-end visit to Gloucestershire
which ended in disaster in Wolverhampton on my return
journey. I collided violently with a Model T Ford Post
Office delivery van when, as I was about to pass, its driver
suddenly turned across my bows without making any signal.
My new machine was practically written off and all my friends
were very gloomy about the outcome. 'You'll never get anything out of the Post Office', they said. But, after much correspondence, the G.P.O. did pay for the damage in full.
Although, apart from the first one, all these were pure accidents,
I was certainly accident-prone and could scarcely blame my
uncle and aunt for their embargo, indeed in the light of events
I have reason to be grateful for it.

Faced with this transport problem, Bill concluded that if we
switched from two wheels to four, his family could not possibly
object and we agreed to purchase a car between us. Because
our means were slender we scanned the second-hand columns
of the local *Sentinel* anxiously and finally agreed to purchase
a 1922 G.N. 'Popular' model from its owner in Longton for £6.
I had envisaged that we should only use this car locally and that
for long journeys solo I would continue to use my motorcycle,
but I was so delighted with the G.N. that I soon repaid Bill his

share, sold the A.J.S., and thereafter used a car exclusively. Strange to say I never enjoyed motorcycling, never grew fond of my motorcycles but used them solely as a means to an end. Occasionally, I went to the works in the G.N., but although it was hardly a luxury vehicle I found it somewhat embarrassing. For I was the only employee to come to work in a car; all the rest came either on foot or by bicycle.

The G.N. was in the state that dealers describe tersely as 'good runner', which meant that it looked dilapidated and needed quite a lot of mechanical attention. However, some friends in Trentham to whom we had been introduced, and who had three beautiful daughters, very kindly agreed to let us use their garage. Here we worked in the evenings and at week-ends restoring and repainting the car, our work enlivened by the interest of the three graces. I suspect that Bill had a soft spot for the youngest, while I fancied myself madly in love with the eldest. It was she who had been indirectly responsible for our introduction, since she had attended the same finishing school in Paris as my cousin Rosemary. Tall, golden-haired and graceful, I thought her the most ravishing creature I had ever set eyes on. But I sadly concluded that such a rare mortal was far beyond the reach of a dirty-handed, scruffy apprentice with no prospects, an assumption that was probably correct. I imagined her father (a kindly and charming man) asking in solemn Victorian tones: 'And what are your prospects, young man?', and thereafter decided it would be wiser to nurse my passion in secret, like some medieval troubadour. Painful though it may be at the time, for a romantic, unrequited and hopeless love has certain advantages. The imagined possesses an immortal perfection not attainable in reality.

On one never-to-be-forgotten occasion, this goddess actually agreed to accompany me to a cinema in Hanley, riding on the pillion of my motorcycle. Never did I negotiate the cobbles and treacherous tramlines of Stoke with greater care. Later, since we had both received invitations to my cousin Rosemary's wedding, it was agreed that we should travel down to Gloucestershire in the G.N. to spend the week-end with my parents, going with them in my father's Alvis to the wedding in Hertfordshire. This, so far as I can recall, was the first long journey I had attempted in the G.N. I looked forward to the trip with a mixture of expectation and trepidation (what if the car should break down?) and spent hours checking and re-checking everything.

As anyone acquainted with the marque will know, a G.N. is hardly the most appropriate mode of conveyance for goddesses. The big air-cooled twin-cylinder engine creates an immense amount of mechanical commotion and enough vibration to set the whole frail chassis rocking on its springs. When the great day came at last, it poured with rain from leaden skies all the way down to Gloucestershire, causing steam to rise from the exposed cylinders. Rain leaked through the hood and blew in through the gap between hood and windscreen. It also leaked through the dickey seat lid, soaking the suitcase containing my passenger's wedding finery. Occasionally worse would befall. The G.N. hood was held up by two straps secured to vestigial hooks on the pillars of the one-piece screen. Every now and again the effect of a bad bump was to free the straps from their hooks, whereupon the hood, helped by the wind, would instantly furl itself. By the time we had stopped and re-erected it we were decidedly damp. But at least, throughout the round trip the engine kept happily hammering away and all the transmission chains stayed on. The fact that she was able to endure the rigours of such a journey without any complaint makes me wonder whether my fair passenger was quite so remote as I thought she was.

Chapter 8

The First Diesel Lorry

The period I spent at Stoke-on-Trent was, in retrospect, undoubtedly the 'time of my life'. So crowded was it with incident and experience that now, looking back, I find it almost impossible to believe that so much could have been crammed into little more than two years of my life. Those years not only taught me a great deal about engineering but a lot about life as well, much of it disquieting and thought-provoking, but all of it intensely stimulating. That the attempt to recapture the sum of this experience should occupy so large a space in this book faithfully reflects the fact that the human clock that ticks away our time within us is not regulated by the arbitrary measure of any mechanical clock or calendar. That mysterious internal clock runs much faster when we are young, making the ordered passing of days, months and years seem the slower by contrast.

While I was living through the experiences I have described in the last two chapters, my uncle's designs for new steam and diesel[1] locomotives and—more significant in the light of the future—a new diesel lorry, were taking shape at the California Works. Following my orthodox passage through the shops, I became increasingly concerned with them and found their technical novelty and the sense they gave that one was pioneering in new fields very exciting and challenging.

As has already been said, my uncle was a disciple of Loftus Perkins and the boiler he designed for the new geared steam locomotive was designed on Perkins' principles. I will not describe it in detail here except to say that it consisted entirely of machined components and was assembled and tested in the

---

[1] The term 'diesel' is not technically correct in this context, but as it is the popular usage I have used it throughout in this book.

Fitting Shop, a fact which caused some headshaking among the boiler makers and would doubtless have provoked a demarcation dispute today. For its size, the boiler had an immense grate area and heating surface. Steam could be raised to its working pressure of 300 lb. p.s.i. in fifteen minutes and, in striking contrast to the Sentinel boiler, it would steam freely with the gentlest of draughts. For example, in response to an inquiry from the West Indies as to whether the new locomotive would burn bagasse,[1] I spent an afternoon firing it on wood shavings from the joinery as it ran to and fro on the test track with a full load. It was one of the hottest and most exhausting afternoons I have ever known because I had to shovel the stuff on to the fire continuously. But it was all burnt and the locomotive steamed like a witch. In any other locomotive those shavings would have been sucked straight off the shovel to emerge unburnt out of the chimney.

In January 1929, my cousin Bill and I heard my uncle read a paper on this locomotive to the Junior Institution of Mechanical Engineers in London. Present in the audience was Colonel R. E. B. Crompton, then the doyen of engineers. He had come along out of affection for the memory of his friend and one-time associate, Peter Willans, my uncle's father. Afterwards we were introduced to him. It was the only occasion when I have met a truly great engineer and I felt very overawed and very privileged. I found it difficult to believe that he had been born when George Stephenson was still alive, he appeared so hale and hearty. In fact he still had eleven more years of life ahead of him.

My uncle's new diesel locomotive used the same design of chassis as the steam locomotive and came in three sizes fitted with MacLaren-Benz engines of two, four and six cylinders delivering 30, 60 and 90 h.p. respectively. J.A.P. engines had to be used to start the two larger engines. The first to be built was of 60 h.p. and I accompanied this locomotive when it was sent to North Wales for preliminary tests on the Welsh Highland Railway at Dinas Junction. The little 30 h.p. locomotive appeared next and in the summer of 1929 I spent a week driving the prototype on a short track on the Kerr Stuart stand at the Royal Show at Harrogate. It was fitted with a multivariable speed gear which worked magically on the stand when

[1] The waste sugar cane after the sugar has been extracted at the mill.

running light, but when the locomotive returned to the works and we put a load behind it, the gear dissolved in clouds of blue smoke from burning friction material. It was seen no more, being quickly replaced by a more conventional transmission. Last to emerge of these diesel locomotives was the 90 h.p. type of standard gauge. I spent a morning driving this engine to and fro on our works line before it was delivered to the Ravenglass and Eskdale Railway in Cumberland where it had a surprisingly long life.

But although it was the fascination of the steam locomotive that had drawn me into engineering and so to Kerr Stuarts, I must confess that it was the diesel lorry that I found in many ways the most exciting of all these new designs. I think this was because I sensed that here was a vehicle of an entirely new species. It was, after all, the first diesel lorry to be designed and built in this country and it was thrilling to feel that we were pioneering in a completely novel field. Although, like many another pioneering attempt, this one was ultimately doomed to failure, where we failed, others soon succeeded. At that time, long distance heavy road haulage could not compete seriously with railways because of the extravagant thirst of the petrol engine. The advent of the oil engine on the road revolutionised the economics of road haulage and brought about the greatest revolution in transport since the coming of the motor-car at the beginning of the century. It is ironical that I, so passionately drawn to railways and steam locomotives, should have become concerned with a vehicle and with a source of power destined so soon to supplant them, though just how soon I did not then realize.

Construction of the new lorry began during the winter of 1928-29 and by March it was ready for its first run. It was originally designed round the 60 h.p. MacLaren-Benz engine, but over the winter MacLarens had strongly recommended us to try their new six-cylinder Helios engine. At 45 h.p. it would be down on power, but a six should be smoother than a four, it was governed to 1,000 r.p.m. instead of 800 and, most important of all, it could be started by hand. Although I think we should have been warned by the fact that the German makers of the Helios engine had gone into liquidation and that the engine offered to us was part of the bankrupt stock that MacLarens had bought cheaply, we accepted their advice and the design was modified to receive the new engine. I do not doubt that MacLarens acted in good faith. It was not in their own interest to sell us a pup and the new engine certainly looked good. In those days none of us knew much about high-speed oil engines and we were all feeling our way.[1]

The prototype lorry was of the semi-forward control type with the rear portion of the engine under an internal bonnet in the cab. It was fitted with a flat platform body and the design was conventional; in fact, in the adoption of a final drive by chain to a dead axle it was already archaic. As a test vehicle, however, this arrangement had the advantage that the gear ratios could very easily be altered by fitting larger or smaller driving sprockets. It also meant that the unsprung weight of the back axle was much lower than a live one would have been. Suspension at the rear was by two transverse semi-elliptic leaf springs, mounted side by side in a special cast-steel cradle at the midpoint of the chassis. This relieved the chassis of all bending moments and the lorry rode remarkably well.

A fitter named Jack Hodgkinson and I were appointed to carry out the extensive road testing of this novel vehicle on a selection of routes, usually carrying a six-ton test load of cast iron blocks on the lorry's flat bed. I was issued with a series of elaborate log sheets on which I was to record every detail of each run. I still have my original master copies of these sheets. They are filled in in shaky pencil and some are covered with the imprints of my oily fingers, betokening trouble on the road. From these I see that our first historic run was to Lichfield and back on 18th March 1929, 69 miles in 3 hrs. 40 m., our greatest speed on the level being 29 m.p.h. The journey involved a total of 151 gear changes, each no mean undertaking as we shall see. Our eighth trip on 9th April was to Manchester and back, 79 miles, and I can remember the interest aroused when we stopped en route for lunch at a transport café. Most of the heavy haulage on the Manchester–Stafford road at that time was handled by articulated Scammels running on solid

---

[1] I did not know then, but have since learned, that Messrs Garretts of Leiston had two diesel lorries, one four- and the other six-wheeled, on the road a month or two before ours. They were fitted with MacLaren-Benz engines of 30 and 60 h.p. respectively and, from my experience, the smaller of the two must have been woefully underpowered. In any case, these were purely experimental vehicles with oil engines fitted in adapted steam wagon chassis, whereas our K.S. lorry was a production prototype.

tyres and their drivers could scarcely have displayed greater interest in our vehicle if it had been a space ship.

We very soon found out the snags of the Helios engine. True it could be started by hand, but only just on a cold morning. Two of us would wind the enormous starting handle until, when our arms were almost in a blur, at the breathless cry of 'Right', a third would throw over the decompression lever whereupon our arms would receive a frightful jerk as the engine came onto full compression. Sometimes the engine would fire, sometimes it would not and sometimes the compression would bring us up all standing with results almost as painful as a back-fire. To lighten this labour we resorted to the barbarous practice of pouring petrol into the air inlet manifold. This used to do the trick, but the engine started with such an anvil chorus of hideous clonks, that it is a wonder the cylinder heads were not blown off. I remember on one occasion when we had just performed this priming operation, Mr Jubb, a mild-mannered, bespectacled individual from the drawing office who was responsible for lorry design, clambered up into the cab and began measuring and sketching. We wound the starting handle; there was a loud report, a long tongue of flame licked out of the mouth of the inlet manifold and the cab filled with smoke. Mr Jubb tumbled out of that cab and made off down the shop like a startled rabbit.

The Helios engine had a separate injection pump for each cylinder. These pumps were made in unit with the injectors, were of the variable stroke type, and were actuated by the same camshaft as the valves. Their behaviour was erratic and not always sensible to the control of the governor. Consequently engine speed was apt to be equally erratic, in other words it 'hunted' badly and did not always respond to the throttle. If, on taking his foot off the accelerator, engine revolutions continue to mount, it can be very disconcerting for the driver, besides making gear changing extremely tricky. This was the cause of our first serious breakdown in Stone on our way back from a test trip to Lichfield. Jack accelerated in third gear, then released the clutch and accelerator and slipped the gear lever into neutral for the change to top. This he did not succeed in achieving because the engine continued to race. We used to run without the internal bonnet fitted, and it was somewhat disconcerting to sit helpless in close proximity to such a large engine while its speed built up far in excess of its permitted maximum. Suddenly, with an alarming sound of mechanical disintegration, the engine stopped abruptly. We found that one of the overhead valves had seized solid in its guide, breaking its rocker and punching a hole in a piston.

The engine was repaired after this mishap, but it was not long after, on our ninth test run, when we had covered a total of just over 400 miles, that the end came. We were ascending a hill into the little town of Tutbury when disaster struck. Something hit me a stinging blow on the ankle. Looking down, I saw that this was a large fragment of cast-iron and that the jagged end of a broken connecting rod was menacing me through the large hole it had knocked in the side of the crank-case. We managed with difficulty to remove the big-end of the broken rod and then made for home, running on five cylinders. On the way back there was another shattering noise as the sixth piston and the small end of the connecting rod, which we had tried in vain to get out, suddenly fell down on to the whirling crankshaft. But we did get home under our own power.

After this second disaster, it was decided to revert to the original plan by fitting the 60 h.p. four-cylinder MacLaren-Benz engine. At least we knew that it was reliable. Yet, in retrospect, I can see that in some ways this was a retrograde step, that of the two power units the Helios was the more promising. It was smaller, lighter and faster running and, on its day, more flexible than the other. Despite its higher power, we never obtained with the MacLaren so high an average speed. The besetting fault of the Helios was its fuel injection system and if this could have been replaced by something less wayward, all might have been well. The Bosch fuel injection system which supplied the real answer to such problems had not yet appeared, but I have often wondered whether the reliable pump fitted to the 90 h.p. MacLaren-Benz engine might not have been adapted to the Helios.

The installation of the MacLaren-Benz engine did not take long, for on 26th April we took to the road again with this new power unit. In this form, the lorry weighed no less than 12 cwt. more than it had done before. Governed to 800 r.p.m. its maximum speed was only 20 m.p.h., unless we 'put the stick out' and coasted down hills as we frequently did. There was one major difficulty; the engine could not be started by hand. As on the locomotives, a J.A.P. auxiliary engine was needed for this. Unlike the roomy cab of a locomotive, it required a lot of ingenuity to fit this bulky starting equipment into the very restricted space of the lorry cab. While Mr Jubb was mulling over this problem at his drawing board, we were instructed to carry on with the test runs, knowing that if the engine stopped while we were out on the road we would be unable to start it except by the aid of gravity or a tow. For this reason, Market Drayton and back, 36½ miles, became our regular test route. There were plenty of hills and on one of them there was situated an excellent country pub, the Mainwaring Arms at Whitmore, where we could—and did—frequently stop for lunch.

There was one extremely embarrassing moment, however, when the engine stalled in the middle of the small square in Market Drayton. It happened to be market day and the square thronged with booths and crowds. In the midst of this animated scene stood our lorry, completely immovable, causing what in those days was regarded as a major traffic block. To market traders who shouted to us to 'get on out of it' or to the law who ordered us to 'move along there' it was shame-making to admit that we had no means of starting our strange vehicle. Amid cheers, an enterprising local garage proprietor suddenly appeared on the scene with a Model T Ford breakdown truck, waving a tow rope. Since our lorry, with its test load, weighed 12½ tons, the Ford simply made groaning noises from its sorely tried transmission and entirely failed to move us. This was tantalising because, only fifty yards away at the end of the square, there was a suitable declivity. But we espied in the back of that Ford a long crow-bar and this proved to be our salvation. Now by levering with such a bar between wheel and rail you can, once you get the knack, move the heaviest locomotive. But try moving a 12½ ton lorry with pneumatic tyres along a tarmac road in the same fashion. Red-faced and sweating, cheered and jeered at by the crowd, Jack and I took turns to bar that lorry across the square. It seemed the longest fifty yards ever.

Sometimes in order to give him a break, I passed the log sheet over to Jack and took a trick at the wheel. This was the first and last time I have driven a 'heavy', and my goodness how heavy it was! Neither steering nor brakes were servo-assisted and the clutch was extremely heavy. Consequently one soon developed bulging biceps and calf muscles. Gear changing also called for considerable physical strength and was very slow and difficult, not because the engine ran erratically like the Helios, but simply because, with its massive crankshaft and flywheel revolving at not more than 800 r.p.m., it was so slow to respond to the movements of the accelerator pedal. To drive for any distance at a stretch was no mean feat of physical stamina. Once on arriving back at the works I jumped down from the driving seat and was immediately doubled up with acute cramp of the stomach muscles. I had to be massaged by the nurse in the ambulance room before I managed to stand upright.

Steering called for continual concentration, for with so wide a vehicle on the narrow roads of those days you had to keep the nearside front-wheel within a foot of the side of the road. Moreover, you could never for a moment relax, for owing to the steep camber the lorry tended to run off which meant that you were ditched, for once you had put a wheel on the grass verge, no power on earth could get it off again. I experienced this happening later when the lorry had gone into production. A driver had come over from Belfast to take delivery of a new vehicle and I had accompanied him on a trial run so that he could get used to it. From my seat at the nearside of the cab, I could see that he was heading for disaster and called out, but it was too late. We came to rest in a deep ditch at an angle of 45°. The new lorry was quite undamaged, but it took some getting out.

The most unfortunate thing I ever did while I was driving the prototype lorry was to carry away a shop awning in the narrow main street of Lichfield. I had not reckoned with the effect of a steep camber with the result that the nearside top corner of the cab connected with the wooden edge of the awning which fell in flapping ruin to the pavement. The owner of the shop was not at all pleased. Although the modern heavy diesel road vehicle is infinitely easier and less tiring to drive than was this crude forerunner, this experience has given me a lasting admiration and respect for all drivers of 'heavies'.

According to my log sheets, we had covered 756 miles in the prototype before it was decided to put the lorry into production. Fuel consumption had averaged 10 m.p.g. with a full load, and this with fuel which then cost only 4d a gallon. The driver of a comparable petrol-engined lorry would be lucky to average 6 m.p.g. with fuel costing four times as much. These were the facts on which our production hopes were based. The production lorry was an improvement on the prototype in many respects. It was substantially reduced in weight, notably by replacing iron castings by welded fabrications. The exterior details were tidied up and an imposing cast aluminium radiator was fitted in conjunction with an aluminium panelled cab and bonnet sheets. In my reports on the test runs I had repeatedly stressed the amount of black smoke produced when the lorry was working hard against the gradient, much to the annoyance of following traffic. We were unable to cure this, but on the production vehicle we mitigated the nuisance by mounting the silencer on the cab roof, the gases exhausting through a short vertical stub pipe and the exhaust pipe from the engine passing up one rear corner of the cab. I have often wondered since why this example was never subsequently followed. The J.A.P. starting engine was directly behind the main engine and between the seats. It was mounted in a rocking frame by means of which a friction wheel could engage the rim of the flywheel.

The first production model to be built went to a firm of haulage contractors in Belfast and other vehicles were sold to J. Beresford and Sons Ltd, of Tunstall, a local contractor, the Stroud Brewery, Greenall Whitley and Co., Brewers, of St Helens, and F. W. Lougher and Co., Pontalln Quarries, Bridgend, this last being fitted with an hydraulic three-way tipping body.

To put this novel vehicle into production in a locomotive works meant engaging new staff with the necessary know-how. A sales manager named Greenberg arrived on the scene and so did a production engineer named Gratrex. Greenberg was an ebullient individual of immense energy and gusto. He would talk endlessly, rocking to and fro on his feet and emphasising his points with stabbing motions made with the stem of his pipe. He fervently believed his own sales talk, a prime virtue in any salesman. He seized upon our method of transverse rear suspension with great enthusiasm although it seemed perfectly normal and logical engineering to us. He christened it 'enharmonic' springing and made great play with the word in his sales literature where it was accompanied by graphs to prove how the action of one spring was damped out by the other. Next door to the works was a pottery named Winkles which specialised in the manufacture of chamber pots and other sanitary wear. Greenberg prevailed on Winkles to allow one of our lorries to be loaded with chamber pots, roughly packed in open-sided crates without straw. He then took a photograph which appeared with the caption: 'Thanks to enharmonic springing, fragile loads can be carried in safety without special packing.' When he first arrived, there were no production vehicles for Greenberg to photograph. Nothing daunted, he had sides fitted to the flat platform of the old prototype and had it driven out on the Leek road where he photographed it against the background of a steep rock cutting. It seemed an unpromising background and we could not understand what he was driving at. But when we saw in the finished photograph our old lorry ascending a steep gradient with a vast load of rock and earth on board we understood. Who says the camera cannot lie?

When road testing came to an end, I was made assistant to the new production engineer, who had come to us from David Browns from whom we bought our gears. Gratrex was a very short, stocky man with a huge, determined, jutting jaw. He was always in a hurry and, despite his short stature, contrived to walk very fast, taking (for him) immensely long strides, his bowler hat crammed down over his ears. He was what might be called a new broom and as a result he made himself decidedly unpopular in certain quarters. He brought with him a set of Swedish Johannsen gauges which were then, like Maudslay's famous micrometer in the nineteenth century, the final arbiter of accuracy in workshop measurement. With these he was able to prove to his entire satisfaction that nearly all the jigs and gauges in the tool room stores were inaccurate. On which the outraged tool room foreman was heard to growl: 'If that Mr Gratrex doesn't watch out he'll get that chin of his put back where it ought to be.'

At sight of our machine shop, Gratrex could hardly be restrained from throwing his bowler hat on the ground and jumping on it. New machines were introduced, most notably a big Kerns boring machine for the in-line boring of the shaft bearing housings of the lorry gearbox. Parallel with the wagon and boiler shop was a very long and narrow shed with a single line of rails running through it which had once been used to assemble a large contract for wagons. This was the one feature of the works that seemed to please Gratrex. He rubbed his hands together and almost smiled, declaring it would make a good lorry assembly shop. He had it marked out into divisions where the various components and sub-assemblies could be stored and then put into their appointed places as the lorries, starting as bare chassis frames, moved down the shop on a travelling gantry. Meanwhile I worked beside Gratrex in his office, preparing, under his instructions, a huge progress chart which was hung on the wall. I then began to oversee what progress the shops were making with the lorry parts, in other words I became a 'progress chaser'.

Exciting though it would be to see the first production lorries roll out, I did not particularly care for my job with Gratrex and I was mightily relieved when, in July 1930, Jack Hodgkinson and I were ordered to load a 30 h.p. diesel locomotive on to the old prototype lorry and head north to Scarborough where I was to drive the locomotive for a fortnight at a Quarry Managers' and Road Surveyors' Exhibition. Apparently these gentry were holding a conference in Scarborough; most of them had their wives with them and, since the exhibition was mounted in a field some distance from the town, hardly any of them took the trouble to visit it, preferring the pleasures of the promenade, the pier and the bathing beach when they were not conferring together. Quite a few holiday makers found their way to our showground, however, so we decided to convert the exhibition into an impromptu fun-fair. I had at my disposal a much longer length of track than I had had at Harrogate the previous year, so I trundled to and fro with wagon loads of passengers, while the driver of the Ruston Bucyrus Excavator which formed the centre-piece of the show lifted people up in his bucket and then whirled them round and round. I don't think our respective firms would have been amused by this spectacle, but at least it gave a lot of pleasure and helped us to pass the time.

I have said that the 30 h.p. MacLaren-Benz engine could be started by hand. This could only be accomplished by the judicious movement of the decompression lever, first into the half compression position and then on to full. One morning at the showground when Jack and I were swinging the big starting handle for all we were worth, the helpful bystander who was manning the decompression lever, misunderstanding our instructions, pushed it straight through to full compression. The next instant we were both lying flat on the ground. I was quickly on my feet again, but Jack had fared much worse for the starting handle had caught him full in the chest, completely winding him. Dazed, I suddenly realised that despite this immensely powerful kick back the engine was running. I wondered how this could possibly be until I saw exhaust smoke pouring from the air filter on the inlet manifold. Believe it or not, that engine was running backwards! I helped Jack to a doctor, fearing broken ribs, but fortunately he was only badly bruised although the doctor insisted on strapping him up and told him he must take things easily for a week or so. This meant that I had to drive the lorry most of the way back to Stoke. It was a long haul, for the locomotive had been sold and on the way we had to deliver it to its new owners, Boan's Sandpit near King's Lynn.

I had never been to East Anglia before and I cannot now remember where this sandpit was except that it was in very deep country reached by narrow and winding lanes somewhere to the east of Sandringham. In these lanes we met an elderly lady in black riding a motor scooter. I remember this encounter very vividly because it was such a rarity at that time. Several makes of motor scooter had appeared just after the Great War but they died an early death and it was to be nearly thirty years before the motor scooter suddenly caught on. In this country anything seemed possible for it appeared to me incredibly remote and foreign. When we had unloaded the locomotive at the sandpit, we spent the night at a small country pub called 'The Royal Oak' and found the dialect of the locals in the bar so broad that we had difficulty in understanding more than one word in ten. No doubt they had equal difficulty in understanding us, for the influence of the B.B.C. had not yet ironed out such regional distinctions. They gave us a splendid meal, I remember, which we ate with wooden-handled steel knives and 'prongs', as they called them, with two needle-sharp points. Then we retired to our room with its double feather bed. Jack happily slept in his shirt which made me selfconscious of my pyjamas.

When we finally drove into the works yard after this long journey and the old engine gave a final 'clonk' as I swung down from the cab, I little thought that it was to be my last journey in a Kerr Stuart diesel lorry and that in a few weeks' time I should leave the familiar works for ever. For although the economic outlook was bleak and England was heading fast into the great slump, at Kerr Stuarts everything, including my own prospects, looked rosy. The new locomotives that my uncle had designed were a success, while with the lorry we were 'in on the ground floor' and there appeared to me to be a great future before it. On the conventional locomotive side, the works were busy building twenty-five pannier tank engines for the Great Western Railway with the prospect of a further twenty-five to come. Then, without any warning, out of this seemingly clear sky, the bolt fell.

I remember I was standing in the new lorry assembly shop one morning, idly glancing through the *Daily Mail*. I usually skipped the financial page, but for some reason my eye was caught by a small paragraph at the foot of a column. 'The Midland Bank Ltd,' it said, 'have petitioned for the compulsory winding up of Kerr, Stuart and Co. Ltd. of Stoke-on-Trent.' I showed it to the men in the shop but they only shook their heads in frank bewilderment. I motored out to Barlaston that evening and showed it to my uncle. 'Nonsense,' he replied reassuringly, 'the Midland Bank are not our bankers, there must be some mistake; no one has heard of anything.' But, alas, it was no mistake and what follows next reads like some Victorian melodrama.

The only member of the Kerr Stuart management who did not live in the district was the chairman of the company who was 'something in the City'. I remember him as a tall man in a pin-striped suit who used to visit the works occasionally (I suppose for board meetings) in a chauffeur-driven Rolls-Royce. I only saw him on these occasions because he used to walk very rapidly through the shops, looking neither to right nor left, on what was ostensibly a tour of inspection. It was true that the Midland were not our bankers, but they had acted as bankers for a company called Evos Sliding Doorways, Ltd which this precious chairman had floated, illegally, with Kerr Stuart's money. This company had failed and the Midland Bank had come back to us for money that no longer existed. There was to be no redress. When they broke into the chairman's private office in London, it was to find his secretary dead with a bullet through his brain and the hearth choked with burnt papers. But the chairman himself had disappeared and, so far as I know, he has never been heard of again from that day to this.

My uncle Kyrle made frantic efforts to save the works, but all to no avail. In the hope of invoking Government aid, he went to see the Labour M.P. for Stoke-on-Trent and found the titled lady who then held the seat reclining elegantly upon a sofa smoking a cigarette in a long holder. She did not appear in the least concerned and merely murmured soothing platitudes. I have never known my uncle so angry and so bitter as when he returned from that interview.

Meanwhile, back at the works we had no credit. We could not even purchase coal without cash, but somehow we had to complete our existing orders. So we tore up the sleeper floors of the shops and flung them into the furnace of the big Thomson boiler so that we could keep steam on the hammers and so keep the forge alive. But, as we completed our orders men began to drift away and machines to stop. No more thunder of steam hammers from the forge; no more noise like machine-gun fire from the boiler shop. The piston rods of the hammers or the hand controls of machines that had once gleamed brightly from constant use grew, first dull and then rusty. Finally, the shops fell silent. You could hear sparrows quarrelling under the roof trusses. So quiet was it in those long aisles that you tended to speak in a whisper as in the stillness of some cathedral.

So, in a mere matter of weeks, Kerr Stuarts died. It never came to life again. The plant was sold at auction by order of the receiver, but much of it, the hydraulic press, the heavy hammers, the hydraulic riveter, was considered not worth the labour of moving and was cut up on the spot. Today, only the foundry is still active. The rest of the shops, rusty and dilapidated, with water pouring through the roofs, are used as an untidy dump for scrap metal. So is the once trim and tidy yard. To me, who had known it in full work, the place is forever haunted by memories and lost hopes, indescribably forlorn.

Some nine months after the death of the works, I unwisely motored north to spend a week-end with my friends at Trentham. As I passed through the streets of Stoke I saw many of the men whom I had worked beside, admiring their skill and proud to think of them as my friends, leaning against the walls of street-corner pubs or crouching on the steps of terrace houses. Cheap mufflers were crossed about their throats, their faces and hands looked unnaturally white and clean and their eyes did not appear to focus on anything. There was no work for them. Somehow I could not bring myself to attract their attention, still less to stop and speak to them, for I felt ashamed. I did not visit Stoke-on-Trent again.

Chapter 9

Dursley Days

In the course of our brief and troubled passage through life we build little cocoons spun from our hopes and ambitions, familiar faces, places, habits and routines, and in these we curl up snugly, fancying ourselves warm and secure from the large, cold world outside. It sometimes happens, however, that we are suddenly and ruthlessly stripped of this protective clothing to be left naked and shivering in a world that seems to have become strange and hostile.

This is how I felt after the tragedy of Kerr Stuarts. It was an event that made a very deep impression on my youthful mind—for remember, I was still under 21. I had not believed that such things could happen, but now my career was gone, my friends scattered and there was nothing to do but to return home and try, with as much resolution as I could, to pick up the pieces and begin again. I even lost that £100 apprenticeship premium which my parents had promised me at the end of the three-year term, for there was nothing left over from the wreck.

What of the others? For my uncle Kyrle it was the bitterest blow of his career. He obtained a post with the National Gas Engine Company at Ashton-under-Lyne, sold the house at Barlaston, went into lodgings in Ashton and bought a cottage at Patterdale, in the Lake District near the head of Ullswater, for his family. This arrangement was shortlived, however. Within a year he had moved to Petters at Yeovil and the Willans family were then installed at Boleyn House, Ash near Martock in Somerset. I paid one visit to Patterdale—I remember climbing Helvellyn and, at Bill's instigation, spending an afternoon in the engine room of one of the elderly lake steamers. Later, I spent one week-end at Boleyn House, but inevitably I gradually lost touch with the Willans family. They were no longer closely linked with my life. *Cressy* was sold to a newspaper reporter named Fortune at Leicester who had just married and intended to live on her on the river Soar. But before he sold her, my uncle had removed the steam plant and installed a petrol engine in its stead.

As for Leslie Bomford, after the Kerr Stuart débâcle he decided to have done with engineering and he bought a farm in Hampshire. Nevertheless, it was he who was responsible for the next brief phase in my career. When the works closed, I still had about seven months of my five years' apprenticeship to serve. Leslie Bomford knew Robert Lister and it was agreed between them that I could complete my 'time' by a year's apprenticeship in the works of R. A. Lister and Co. Ltd of Dursley, Gloucestershire. This I began in January 1931.

Old Sir Ashton Lister had started his career as a blacksmith in the small town of Dursley and R. A. Lister and Co. was one of those country works which had expanded and flourished as the result of the enterprise of a rural craftsman. Ashton Lister had teamed up with two ingenious Swedes named Petersen and Mellerup who had invented a bicycle and a milk separator. Although when I went to Dursley there were still a few 'Dursley Petersen' bicycles around with their unusual frames and hammock seats, it was the milk separator and a sheep-shearing machine that had founded the fortunes of the firm. Later, they had begun making a range of small petrol engines for farm and general use and to these, at the time I joined the firm, a range of diesel engines and a small petrol-engined 'autotruck' had recently been added. It was to the engine assembly and test shops that I was assigned and, apart from a short spell on outside engine service, I remained there throughout my year at Dursley.

There were then five Lister brothers in the firm. Percy, a man of immense energy, personality and drive who was managing director, Robert who was in charge of auto-truck production, Frank who was in charge of buying, George, who today would be described as personnel manager, and Cecil, the youngest, who was on the sales side. I lodged at 'The Towers', a large house that old Sir Ashton had built for himself when he became affluent. Constructed of bright red brick with white painted woodwork and rising to a tower at one front corner, it was the kind of Edwardian mansion that would not have looked out of place amid the pines of Surrey or in the lower Thames Valley, but in the Cotswolds it looked utterly incongruous. Reached by a steep drive, it stood on a commanding site, looking over the saw-toothed roofs of the shops directly below to the old grey town that climbed the opposite slope. After Sir Ashton's death, his sons had turned it into a hostel for apprentices or students, many of whom were the sons of Listers' overseas agents, sent to England for a short spell of practical instruction in the works. It was also used to accommodate visitors to the works, while on week-days the Lister brothers habitually lunched there. This establishment was in the charge of a charming and vivacious widow in early middle age named Mrs Van der Gucht.

Soon after I came to the Towers, the number of resident students rose to ten and to provide extra accommodation, the rooms over the large garage were adapted and redecorated to provide two extra bedrooms and a bathroom. There I and an Australian of my own age named Malloch, who became my particular friend, took up our quarters. As we nearly all owned second-hand cars, mostly bought very cheaply, the garage below and the covered forecourt outside it housed a motley collection of vehicles. I suppose their total value then would not have amounted to more than £500 whereas today, in equivalent order, they would fetch around £10,000 at auction. There was Mrs Van der Gucht's little Standard 9 open two-seater and a larger Standard 14 with a similar body which had been purchased from a scrap merchant in Gloucester. There was a Ruston-Hornsby with four-seater body and a disappearing hood, very slow, cumbersome and lorry-like. There was a six-cylinder Belsize four-seater touring car of immense length, one of the last models to be built by that defunct firm, and a standard model Riley 'Redwing', the only car of the bunch to have front-wheel brakes. At 1922, my G.N. was the oldest car present, while my friend Malloch owned an early six-cylinder AC with two-seater drophead coupé body. We regarded the Redwing as the only sports car in the stable and undeniably the fastest, but the AC could give it a run for its money and was certainly the most silent and comfortable.

With a group of young men all of about my own age and all with more money to spend than I had, existence at the Towers was apt to be somewhat hectic and nothing could have been in greater contrast to the life I had led in Stoke-on-Trent. I look back on this period as others do to their undergraduate days—as a time when I sowed my wild oats. Most of my companions struck me as somewhat adolescent and immature in their high spirits because they had come to Listers' straight from school or university whereas I had over four years' experience at Pitchill and Stoke-on-Trent behind me. This may sound somewhat priggish and I hope that if any of these bygone companions chance to read this they will not take it amiss. I doubt if they will because I joined wholeheartedly in the fun and games and, indeed, my boon companion, the Australian Malloch, was the most ungovernable of the bunch, a kind of 'wild colonial boy'. In retrospect, I think that to be plunged into the social whirl of this little community was the best possible antidote to the recent disaster at Stoke-on-Trent. I could never forget it; it had made far too deep an impression on my mind for that and, inevitably, it made me regard life at the Towers with a certain detachment. Yet this new milieu did enable me to 'snap out of it' which is an essential preliminary to starting life over again. For the first time in my life I found myself basking in the reassuring warmth that comes from friendship with a group of people of my own age. Had I been left alone, either in lodgings or at home, to brood over past experience and lost opportunities at the age of only twenty-one I shudder to think what the result might have been.

The local 'county' of south Gloucestershire evidently regarded the Towers as a useful reservoir for eligible young men, so there was no lack of social engagements. These reintroduced me to a world which observed the customs and conventions which my public school had attempted without success to instil into me and which I now found utterly alien and unreal. It might once have been real but, like my Rolt uncles and aunts, it seemed to me to belong wholly to the past. For me life at Stoke-on-Trent represented the raw reality, not necessarily good but something I had got to come to terms with, whereas now, when I mixed with these 'county' families, I felt as if I had strayed on to a stage where some outdated comedy of manners was going on. Failing to find any point of contact or communication, I must have seemed an extremely gauche and unmannerly young man. Dancing with some elegantly groomed young woman, her almost invariable opening gambit would be: 'Do you hunt?' and on the reply 'No' the dialogue would either fail altogether or lapse into the usual flat platitudes about the state of the floor or the merits of the band. Similarly, when introduced to her parents they would invariably ask: 'Hah! Any relation to old "Totty" Rolt?' and receive a similar negative response. I had never heard of the man. I gathered that 'old Totty' had lived at Ozleworth

Park, near Wootton-under-Edge and was regarded locally as a bit of a character, but to this day I have not discovered anything more about him or whether he had any connection with my family.

To Malloch, fresh from Australia, the conventions of English 'county' society seemed totally incomprehensible and impossibly 'stuffed shirt'. I think this was the basis of our somewhat improbable friendship. He had an impish sense of humour and used to take advantage of the fact that he was a colonial from down under by doing and saying things that were considered quite outrageous. Having no such excuse, I could only envy him this freedom and enjoy its consequences with well concealed amusement. To the despair of good Mrs Van der Gucht, who considered it part of her mission in life to introduce her young men to polite society, Malloch and I often used to avoid such social obligations, pleading an engagement elsewhere. These 'engagements' usually consisted in seeking out the toughest pubs in the neighbourhood where we found the company a refreshing change after the polite society of Dursley and district. Two that I recall particularly were the Monk's Retreat at Gloucester and the Llandogo Trow at Bristol. Both are now completely reformed (and transformed), but in those days they were very tough indeed with an authentic low-life Rabelaisian quality about them. As for the customers, they were reminiscent of some of the more sordid or sinister characters in Dickens. Such an underworld has ceased to exist today. The wide-boy or the drug-taking drop-out may be just as seamy, violent or depraved but he is neither so racy, so entertaining or so picturesque. We found such company stimulating and exciting; sometimes too exciting, for liquor tended to make Malloch argumentative and quarrelsome. I had more experience of rough company but there were times, notably when two seamen drew knives one night in the Llandogo Trow, when it required all my tact to ensure a strategic withdrawal and so avoid an ugly brawl.

The Monk's Retreat in those days consisted of a crypt-like cellar with a medieval groined roof. Facing the long bar that occupied the whole of one side were a number of little alcoves each containing three bent-wood chairs and an up-ended barrel which served as a table. There was sawdust on the floor and a mechanical organ which, when fed with pennies, ground out old music-hall tunes. It would be a collector's piece today.

The proximity of Bristol's Old Theatre Royal has now

transformed the Llandogo Trow into a smart pub, which, like the theatre, has been preserved. At least they have not, like so much of old Bristol, been sacrificed to the motor car, but in 1931 both had a very different character. The theatre was then the lowest of low music halls where bad performers became cockshys for the audience and the night's performance was apt to end prematurely, as was the case on one occasion when we were present. Performers, members of the orchestra and their patrons became locked in conflict in the stalls and the police had to be called in to clear the house. As for the Llandogo Trow it was then, as I suppose it had always been, the haunt of seamen, the twentieth-century equivalent of that 'Admiral Benbow' in *Treasure Island* where the sinister Blind Pew put the black spot on Captain Flint. Its landlord in his younger days had been a professional strong man 'on the Halls'. He still looked the part, but just in case his customers contemplated any rough stuff, his photograph hung in a prominent position above the bar as a deterrent. This depicted him at the height of his glory, striking a defiant pose, crinkly hair, waxed moustachios, bulging, richly tattooed biceps, leopard skin and all.

We were returning to Dursley from Gloucester late one night in the AC after one of these excursions when I experienced my first serious car crash. But for sheer luck, it might have proved disastrous for us both. I was driving because Malloch was suffering from a suspected hernia and had been forbidden by his doctor to do so. I remember remarking that the steering felt curiously 'lumpy', but as it was dark we did not stop to investigate and, as things turned out, even if we had, an examination would have revealed nothing. Approaching a fairly fast right hand bend by Cam Mills at about 45 m.p.h., the steering suddenly locked solid. To be thus instantly reduced to utter helplessness was the most frightening sensation I have ever experienced while driving a motor-car. We went into that bend with both of us tugging fruitlessly at a completely immovable steering wheel. The AC mounted the bank on the nearside, was deflected, shot across the road and turned upside down on the inside of the corner. The folding head was up but afforded us little protection in such circumstances. Fortunately for us, however, the car came to rest bridging a deep and very wet ditch into which we both fell. By the mercy of providence neither of us was smoking for we were instantly subjected to a spray of petrol leaking from the filler of the scuttle tank which, on this model AC, protruded through the dashboard. When we had disentangled ourselves from each other and from the flapping ruins of the folding head, the seat cushions and the floorboards which had accompanied us into the ditch, we crawled out quite unhurt. Surveying the pitiful wreck in the moonlight we agreed that at such a time of night there was nothing we could do but leave it where it was and walk back to the Towers. As we tramped along the road, my clothing, particularly my flannel trousers, steadily began to disintegrate until I was scarcely decent, a happening that completely restored our sense of humour. I realised that my clothes had been soaked in acid from the battery which was cradled under the driving seat.

Such an accident, occurring in such circumstances, can bear, in most people's minds, only one interpretation so I was relieved to be able to demonstrate to a suspicious local policeman, who was on the scene when we recovered the car next morning, that the steering box really was locked up solid. As we later learned, this particularly nasty habit of early ACs is easy to cure,[1] but in this case the knowledge came too late, for although we had been unscathed, the unfortunate AC was a complete write-off. To replace it, Malloch purchased a second-hand 14/40 Vauxhall. It was my first experience of a marque with which I was later to have much to do. This 14/40 was a good reliable car once its disconcerting habit of suddenly shedding the crowns of its split-skirt pistons had been cured by fitting a set of different type.

We were in this Vauxhall one night when we were the helpless witnesses of an accident that alarmed us almost more than our own had done. It might indeed have had much more serious results had not the element of luck once again played a part. Malloch and I, with T. H. Edye, the owner of the Belsize, were taking three girls to a dance in Cheltenham one cold and frosty night in December. Incidentally, how many girls today would relish the prospect of being driven 25 miles to a dance on such a night in an open touring car, wearing evening dress? And how many young men would even dare to

[1] The steering gear was of the worm-and-wheel type and the teeth on the used arc of the worm-wheel can (as had happened in our case) become so worn that the worm rides up on them and becomes locked. At the first sign of 'lumpiness' in the steering, the wise AC owner dismantled the steering box and repositioned the worm-wheel so that an arc of unworn teeth was brought into play.

suggest such a thing? But in 1931 such rigours were still accepted as a matter of course by both sexes. Because of the threat of fog in the vale we decided to avoid the main road via Gloucester by keeping to the hills through Uley, Stroud and Painswick. Accordingly we set off, Edye and his girl friend leading in the Belsize while Malloch, myself and our two companions followed in the Vauxhall. We were travelling through thin fog and had reached a point near the village of Nympsfield where the road (then unfenced) clings to the extreme edge of the Cotswold scarp which hereabouts is extremely steep and almost cliff-like. Edye must have become confused by the mist, lost his sense of direction, applied his brakes and skidded on a patch of black ice. To our horror we saw the long white touring car swing broadside across the narrow road and then head straight for the edge of the hill, its long bonnet rearing for the plunge, its headlight beams shooting into the sky like searchlights. We expected the kind of frightful disaster such as one only sees in sensational films where a car plunges down, down, down in a series of sickening crashes, coming to rest a mangled wreck which usually bursts into flames. However, fortunately the bank beside the road was sufficiently high and the chassis of the Belsize was sufficiently long and low for it to ground firmly just before the mid-point and it came to a very abrupt halt. In spite of the ice on the road, Malloch had managed to stop the Vauxhall safely just short of the accident and we ran forward to find Edye and his passenger sitting, petrified with fright suspended in space. It was just as well they were petrified, for we found that the car was literally 'on the rock' and any precipitate move on their part might have sent it toppling over. Malloch and I hung our weight on the back of the car and instructed its occupants to clamber cautiously out and edge their way along the running boards back on to the road. The Belsize was immovable by our combined man-power, so, as we had not got a tow rope, we decided to abandon it till the morning. We all squeezed into the Vauxhall and continued, somewhat shaken, on our way to Cheltenham. Next morning the Belsize presented an extraordinary spectacle, visible from far away in the plain below, sticking up above the skyline of the edge like some new and curious landmark. We soon recovered it from this perilous position to find that, unlike the AC, it had sustained only superficial damage, mainly to running boards and their supporting brackets.

Meanwhile I was still running my G.N. in the face of much good-natured ridicule, for, in addition to certain built-in foibles, it was beginning to show increasing signs of infirmity, having obviously led a hard life before I acquired it. Owing to the fact that the carburettor was positioned above the magneto with the effect that petrol dripped directly on to the contact breaker, it had the alarming habit of catching fire at frequent intervals. For example, I was cruising happily along the Gloucester–Bristol road one Sunday after a week-end visit home when two men on a motorcycle pulled out and rode abreast of me. It became clear from their contorted faces that they were attempting to communicate something urgent, but as I could not hear a word they said above our combined mechanical uproar I merely smiled at them and waved. They began to gesticulate, pointing vigorously astern, whereupon, looking back, I observed that, like some destroyer on exercise, I was leaving behind me a long screen of thick black smoke. As soon as I took my foot off the throttle and applied the brakes, two large orange flames appeared with a *woosh* from beneath the cowlings over the cylinders. I stopped, turned off the petrol, tore off the bonnet and endeavoured to smother the flames with the hairy floor mat. As the scuttle petrol tank was mounted just behind the wooden bulkhead, the situation was a bit fraught, especially as a healthy little fire was burning inaccessibly in the oily undertray that ran the length of the car. I noticed my motorcycle friends had not stayed to help and when I looked up momentarily from my fire-fighting I saw a queue of cars standing well clear in both directions, their owners evidently waiting prudently for the big bang before venturing past. However, the situation was saved by the conductor of a passing Bristol bus who gave the blaze the *coup de grâce* with a fire-extinguisher as though such tasks were a matter of everyday routine. After melted pipe joints had solidified again and I had bound naked wires with insulation tape, I was able to continue on my way to Dursley as though nothing had happened.

Another foible of the G.N. was its tendency to drift its front wheels outwards on corners, particularly on a loose surface, due to the absence of a differential. I discovered this the hard way one day when turning into the Towers drive at speed. I bent my front axle and took a sizeable chip out of the corner of one of the imposing brick gate pillars. I have no doubt the scar remains to this day.

As time went on, the G.N. broke or shed its driving chains with increasing frequency as the teeth of the sprockets wore down. If I was lucky, these remained embedded in the thick oily mess in the undertray, but more often they fell in the road. I had a girl friend who lived with two much older spinster sisters in a cottage high on the flank of Stinchcombe Hill. As this cottage was only accessible by a very steep narrow and muddy lane ascending through beech woods, visiting her was always rather a challenge to the G.N.'s failing powers. On one occasion when I had been invited to dinner I was ascending the hill in fine style only to discover that I had lost the bottom gear chain. Not wishing to be late I decided to coast back to the bottom and try to take the hill by storm in second gear. Unfortunately, this gallant effort failed by a few tantalising yards. It was very dark under the trees and the chain was not in the undertray. I walked back down the hill, striking matches at intervals, trying to find it. In a lane freshly covered with autumn beech leaves, this was not easy. However, after much groping I eventually retrieved it. Replacing a chain on a G.N. is not the cleanest of tasks, so by the time I arrived at the cottage I was not only very late but looked as though I had come straight from the works.

By a happy coincidence, the man responsible for putting an end to such troubles was that same village policeman from Cam whom Malloch and I had found regarding the wreck of the AC so suspiciously. We had arrived on the scene that morning in the G.N., followed by a breakdown outfit from the Dursley garage, and when the law had satisfied himself that it was a pure accident, he strolled over to my car and began inspecting it with critical interest. I had begun to wonder uneasily in what way I was transgressing (was my licence out of date?) when: 'Like it?' he asked laconically. 'Yes, very much,' I replied, mightily relieved. 'I got one just like that,' he volunteered. 'Wouldn't like to buy it, I suppose?' And that was how I became the proud owner of G.N. HT5057, an identical 'Popular' model. I had to pay the policeman £8 for it which I though a hard bargain although it was obviously in much better condition than poor old EH3566 had ever been. More than this, I now had a complete car to cannibalise for spares and I drove my new car back to the Towers in triumph.

It was in this second G.N. that I paid my ill-advised weekend visit to Stoke-on-Trent. On my return journey I broke an exhaust valve in Wolverhampton and found I had no spare. In response to my distress call, a gallant rescue party from Dursley, bearing a spare valve, set out for Wolverhampton in the Riley Redwing. They stood by while I fitted that valve by the light of a street lamp in windy, deserted Wolverhampton in the small hours of the morning. Then we drove in convoy back to Dursley, arriving as dawn was breaking and it was almost time to go to work. Such are the things we do when we are young.

In November 1931, Mrs Van der Gucht and the Lister brothers agreed that, in return for the hospitality we had received from the local 'county', we should hold a supper dance at the Towers. The occasion was a riot. I was never fond of dancing and have found such occasions more boring than anything I can remember. This was the only one I thoroughly enjoyed, which is why the memory of it is still green. Mrs Van der Gucht asked us which particular girls we would like to invite as our partners and we all complied except Malloch who only smiled mysteriously, raised his eyes aloft and murmured 'Wait and see!'

The afternoon of the Saturday in question saw us all in a fever of preparation. One of our number named McClure, a very handsome and charming young man who was Mrs Van der Gucht's particular favourite (he was later to marry her) innocently inquired whether she would like him to prepare the fruit cup. Since he had a special reputation for his knowledge of alcoholic liquors she might have suspected the motive behind this thoughtful suggestion, but was so dazzled by his charm that she enthusiastically agreed. McClure thereupon shut himself in the butler's pantry surrounded by bottles like some alchemist in his cell. The result was a masterpiece, though he would never divulge the recipe. It both looked and tasted like a perfectly innocuous fruit cup, a fruit salad afloat in a red liquid which might have been equally suitable for a children's Christmas party. Such was McClure's ingenuity, however, that beneath this bland exterior lurked a liquor that was powerfully alcoholic. When mixed with other drinks, of which we had plenty available, it had a kick like a mule.

Included in the interior décor of the Towers were certain useless ornamental objects with which old Sir Ashton Lister had evidently thought it appropriate for a knight to surround himself. I could never understand why the huge hornet's nest under a glass dome which occupied a place of honour in the drawing room should ever have been looked upon as a status symbol, but the big black marble statue of a dying gladiator in the hall was obviously one. This gladiator had a hole drilled in his private parts into which a wire, soldered to a crudely shaped brass fig-leaf, was inserted. I used to weave fantasies about this statue. I would imagine Sir Ashton announcing 'I must 'ave a statue in the 'all' and then when it arrived, born aloft by a number of perspiring workmen he would observe its shameless nudity and exclaim 'That'll never do!' Then a tinsmith from the works would be sent for accompanied by a man with a hand drill. . . . At this point I used to speculate on the precise wording of their instructions and what these obedient servants had to say to each other and to their mates afterwards. Anyway, I am ashamed to confess that Malloch's and my sole contribution to the preparations was to remove and conceal that fig-leaf. We felt it would add an appropriate, symbolic saturnalian touch to the coming festivities. Mrs Van der Gucht only noticed its loss as she was greeting the guests in the hall. In between polite smiles and greetings she blushed and threw an accusing glance at me, but I feigned incomprehension and merely shrugged my shoulders.

Some time before the guests were due to arrive, Malloch had disappeared and we heard the sound of his Vauxhall departing down the drive. He had not let even me into his secret and, as he had shown no particular liking for any of the young women who lived locally, speculation was rife as to who his chosen partner would turn out to be. Most of the guests had already arrived before we heard his car returning and presently the door opened and Malloch made a dramatic entry. He was accompanied by a stunning young woman of radiant charm, perfectly groomed and beautifully dressed, whom he introduced to the assembled company as Lady Margaret Harcourt-Masters, whereupon his partner, with perfect poise treated us to a flashing smile and gracefully inclined her head. That Malloch had undoubtedly produced the belle of the ball was generally agreed, but who was she? The county wrinkled their brows, muttering to themselves pensively 'Harcourt-Masters? . . . Harcourt-Masters?' as they strove to recollect a name that surely must be familiar. The object of their curiosity gave them no clue, for although she continued to behave with perfect aplomb, she spoke very little except to Malloch with whom she danced the whole of the evening.

Meanwhile we began to observe the demoralising effect

of McClure's fruit cup on the young ladies of the county. With flushed faces and sparkling eyes, with wisps of hair escaping from their once impeccable hair-dos, they began to abandon their conventions. It was like watching a naturally beautiful figure emerging from the straight-lacing of a corset and the effect was as amusing as it was charming. Soon, only Lady Harcourt-Masters remained cool and collected. I reflected that either Malloch had warned her about the potency of the fruit cup or she must have a very much stronger head for drink than the others. Anyway, Malloch departed to drive her home well before the party ended.

The next morning, Mrs Van der Gucht noticed with dismay that the hornet's nest had unaccountably vanished from its accustomed place. In the general conviviality of the night before, no one had observed its loss. However, a young lady whose coy and mincing ways particularly irritated Malloch and myself rang up in a state of some embarrassment to say that to the astonishment of her parents and herself, a strange object had been found in the back of her car. So the hornet's nest was returned to its place and no one could explain the mystery although I think Malloch and I fell under grave, and not unjustified suspicion. Pressed to tell us about Lady Margaret Harcourt-Masters, Malloch confessed that this was a name which he had invented and that, in fact, the bearer of it was a barmaid from Cheltenham. I fear that Mrs Van der Gucht did not appreciate the joke, considering it a prank such as only an ill-mannered colonial could play, but she kept the secret. She could scarcely do otherwise without damaging her reputation as a hostess.

When I recall these Dursley days, it is the leisure side of them that predominates. For, on the whole, the work bored me and it has left few memorable impressions. There were a variety of reasons for this dissatisfaction, most of them due to the contrast between Kerr Stuarts and Listers. Inevitably, but unfairly, I tended to judge the Lister works by the engineering standards I had formed at the California Works whereas, in fact, the two were not strictly comparable. While locomotive building had been a craft industry, Listers were already beginning to apply mass-production methods to the manufacture of their standard ranges of small petrol and diesel engines. They were built by semi-skilled labour on an assembly line and altogether, throughout the Lister works, the proportion of unskilled or semi-skilled men was far higher and there was no aristocracy of highly skilled and independent craftsmen on the shop floor such as I had known at Stoke-on-Trent. In any case, in the rural Gloucestershire of 1931, there was no long tradition of engineering skill upon which Listers could draw. And because it is mastery of a craft that builds character in a man, I must confess that I found my workmates at Dursley less likeable than the men I had known at the California Works. They were more class-conscious, more inclined to judge their fellow men by appearance and material possessions than by innate ability. It was as though, in their concern for material things, they lost sight of the real man inside.

Although I was paid an apprentice's wage, because I was so nearly 'out of my time', I was regarded as a skilled man. Consequently I did not move through the shops but did only two jobs while I was at Listers. The first of these was in the Engine Assembly Shop, building up the larger type of diesel engine, an 18 h.p. twin cylinder. This was considered too big and too complex to put down the assembly line so each engine was the responsibility of an individual fitter. From this work I moved to the Test House where I was responsible for running engines on the dynamometer and correcting any faults.

Both jobs were not without interest and satisfaction, yet I found them irksome because I felt that I was in a blind alley so far as my future engineering career was concerned. It was very different from the exciting pioneer work on which I had been engaged at Stoke-on-Trent. Because I had been under the impression that Leslie Bomford had told Robert Lister something about my work on the Kerr Stuart lorry, I had gone to Dursley in the fond hope that I would be able to continue this work there. But although one prototype experimental Lister diesel lorry engine was, in fact, built while I was with the firm, I was never concerned with it and this promising project was allowed to die.

In January 1932, when I was nearly 22 years of age, I completed a year's work at Dursley. As this first anniversary passed completely without remark and I continued to work as usual for some weeks after, I decided that it was high time I did something about it. After all, for a year I had been working as a skilled employee for an apprentice's meagre wages. I had assumed that, after completing that year, some action would automatically follow and since it had not it was up to me to take the initiative. So I pointed out that I was 'out of my time' and what did 'they' intend to do? The response was immediate: 'We are sorry but we cannot offer you a job here.' This hit me like a blow in the face. The lesson of it was plain. So long as I was prepared to work for an apprentice's wage, all well and good, but so soon as I asked for a man's wage it was a very different matter. I felt that the firm had treated me unfairly at the time, but over the next three years I was to learn that this was just one of the harsh facts of life in England during the years of the great trade depression.

So I packed up my belongings, bade a sad farewell to all my friends at the Towers and headed for home in the G.N., wondering gloomily what the future held for me now. All that I had left behind me was the carcass of my first G.N. from which I had removed everything of value. Later, I received a bill from the firm for the cost of removing it to a scrap heap. Yet I felt that we were quits because, as a rather futile final act of defiance, I had again removed that fig leaf from the statue in the hall and this time buried it, like Prospero's staff, 'certain fathoms in the earth'. It was over thirty years before I next crossed the threshold of the Towers as the guest of the R. A. Lister Engineering Society. The old place looked very much the same. I glanced curiously at the dying gladiator. He was still unashamedly naked.

Part III

Chapter 10

The Journeyman

WHEN I left Dursley in the early spring of 1932 at the age of 22, there began a somewhat confused and unhappy period of my life which was to last for two years. True there were memorable moments in these years and I emerged from them wiser and richer in experience, but my life seemed to have lost the sense of direction and purpose it had while I was an apprentice. Then, I had been preparing myself for a future that seemed full of exciting .opportunities. Now, I found myself foot-loose in the England of the great trade slump in which such opportunities had ceased to exist. The skill which it had taken me five years to acquire was no longer a marketable commodity. In this situation I became a journeyman in the most literal sense of the word. It was not, however, a purposeful journey but one governed entirely by expediency. I applied hopefully for innumerable jobs, but whenever I was lucky enough to obtain one it did not last long. For, on the principle of 'last to come, first to go', the firm would hand me my cards as soon as it became necessary to lay off men. It is because of this roving existence that I was forced to lead that I find the precise chronology of my life during this period more difficult to recall than any other.

From April 1932 until August of the following year I worked for two small firms of agricultural engineers in the south of England, first I. A. Bennett of the Tractor Stores, Hungerford and then the Aldbourne Engineering Company of the Foundry at the nearby village of Aldbourne in the Wiltshire Downs. Although, after my high aspirations, it seemed rather an unsatisfactory dead end, my work at the Tractor Stores was varied and interesting. It consisted in overhauling the tractors that I. A. Bennett took in part exchange for new ones and refurbishing them for resale. Bennett had been distributor for the British Rushton tractor and although that ill-starred attempt to challenge the American monopoly of the British tractor market had failed, there were still a number of Rushtons around. The Rushton was a copy of the Fordson and its faults, which were serious, were entirely confined to those features that departed from the well-tried Fordson design. Much of our time was spent in devising modifications to overcome these defects.

Whenever Bennett had completed a part exchange deal, we would be sent out to deliver the new tractor and bring back the old one. For this purpose we used an ancient American International lorry with solid tyres, wooden wheels and totally ineffective brakes. It had, I remember, a curious final reduction gear incorporated in the rear wheel hubs. With this vehicle, descending steep hills off the chalk downs, such as that into the village of Shalbourne, was always something of a heart-in-mouth undertaking. At such times one became all too conscious of the size and weight of the tractor behind, its front wheels nudging the back of the rickety wooden cab. Having no brakes, the only thing to do was to go down very slowly in bottom gear, keeping close to the bank so as to be ready to turn into it the moment anything broke.

We also possessed a Rushton industrial tractor on solid rubber tyres which we used to tow in any tractor too large to load on the International. One such was an ancient American Overtime tractor which had to be towed in from a remote downland farm on Chute Causeway, and it was my unfortunate lot to steer this primitive monster. It belonged to days before the farm tractor had acquired a conventional form of its own, and it resembled a steam traction engine with a huge, crude horizontal petrol/paraffin motor where one would expect to see the boiler. It gave me one of the roughest and most uncomfortable rides I have ever had. Because the road was rough and the old tractor, with its steel-straked wheels, was towed faster than it had ever travelled in its life before, the vibration was appalling. Our progress sounded like a company of clog dancers performing on a tin roof and my loudest shouts were unheard by the driver of the towing tractor. Consequently, the many intimate bits and pieces which dropped off, some of them quite large, were never recovered. What remained of the Overtime when we finally reached Hungerford was optimistically dismantled and put in store for spares. But I very much doubt if those spares were ever needed.

It was in the spring of the following year that I moved to the Foundry, Aldbourne, lodging with the manager and his family in a cottage at the back of the little works. I found this much more to my taste. Though the present business was comparatively new, it had taken over a very old country engineering business that had previously been known as Loveday and Co. and no one knew precisely when a foundry had first been established on the site. Although the pay was low, I enjoyed the work enormously because of its great variety. For this was essentially a jobbing shop in which the six employees, of whom I was one, had to be maids-of-all-work, ready to tackle any job that came along, now fitting, now doing a bit of blacksmith's work at the forge or using the drilling machine or the very ancient and inaccurate lathe. Most of the fitting was on farm tractors, but occasionally there was other work to be done such as fitting a set of new beaters to the drum of a threshing machine. A threshing machine is far less crude than most agricultural machinery and, when the new beaters had been fitted, the drum, which is quite a large and massive affair and revolves at high speed, had to be most carefully and precisely balanced. Otherwise the machine would soon shake itself to pieces.

Once a week there was a casting day when we all went into the foundry to lend a hand with pouring the moulds. This was a small, low, ancient place which was screened from the village street by our larger and loftier general shop. Except for the inimitable smell and the carpet of black sand on the floor, nothing could have been less like that only other foundry I had known at Kerr Stuarts. A panting Lister engine drove by belt the blower that supplied the blast to the small cupola. The products of this foundry were simple and prosaic. Ploughshares, mostly, which we pulled out of their moulds while they were still smoking hot in order to chill them and so make them hard and wear resistant. Rings and end brackets for land rollers were also cast, for these rollers were the one new 'production' implement to be made at Aldbourne. When assembled, they were proudly painted in a bright 'implement blue'. Occasionally, to special order, we would cast a new fireback from one of two ancient patterns found on the site. It so happened that at this time my parents needed a fireback for their new open fireplace in the hall of our house at Stanley Pontlarge. So I bespoke one, helped to cast it, and then bore it home in triumph in the back of my G.N. It still stands in our hall today to remind me of the vanished village foundry where I once worked.

In the early 'thirties, few farms of the chalk downs had mains electricity or water supply and it was our job to service or repair the many small engines, some of them very old and primitive, which were then in use on local farms, generating current, pumping water or driving barn machinery. Deepening bore-holes for water, or sinking new ones, was another job the little firm undertook. This last was a fairly regular source of employment because the level of the water table below the chalk was constantly falling. Ten to one the deepening of a bore hole for one farmer would lead sooner or later to similar requests from his neighbours. When we were required to sink a new bore hole on a farm our first step was to engage the local dowser, who lived in the neighbouring village of Baydon, to come down to the farm with us to find with his divining rod the best place to bore. There is considerable scientific scepticism about water-divining, but I can only say that we regarded the services of this dowser in a completely matter-of-fact light and that his predictions always proved remarkably accurate. For this reason, it did not occur to me to question his mysterious gift and it was many years before I did so and became interested in the subject.

My work frequently took me out of the shop into the surrounding countryside. When I had repaired a tractor on a farm, I would drive it in the field for a time so as to be sure it was up to its work. It might be pulling a plough, a seed-drill, a mowing machine or a reaper-and-binder depending on the season and in this way I gained a brief practical experience of most farming operations. Like the farmer's boy in the old song, I knew what it was to plough, to sow, to reap and to mow. Often my primitive workshop would be some lonely thatched and weather-boarded barn or cart-hovel high upon the downs and reached only by a steep, deep-rutted track. In such remote places I sometimes worked all day, with only a brief break for a lunch of bread and cheese, trying to complete a repair on some piece of agricultural machinery before the light failed while the impatient downland wind rattled at the doors of the barn.

I soon came to know the Wiltshire Downs intimately from Wanborough in the north to Stanton St Bernard in the south. I naturally became very familiar with their topography, but I use the word intimate in a more subtle sense than this. For experience has taught me that it is only by working in a particular countryside that you acquire a sense of its *genius loci* or true character, something that nature and man between them have combined to create. By working in its fields and barns in every kind of weather, the nature of the chalk down-land revealed itself to me fortuitously in a way that it would not have done had I been merely a passive spectator, viewing the landscape objectively as though it were some romantic picture. To put it in another way, I learnt that, however beautiful a landscape may be aesthetically, without the sustenance of continuing life it becomes starved, dead and forlorn. Langland's 'fair field full of folk' was only made fair by the work that was going on in it, a fact which cannot be appreciated except by those who are prepared to endure the hardship, the sweat or the bitter cold, that such work may involve.

In geological terms the chalk landscape is still young. Time may have moulded its firm flesh but it has not succeeded in weathering it to the bone. It is a spacious country of lovely, youthful curves and folds, sensuous and shamelessly bare. Yet it conveyed to me a sense of the distant past more eloquently than any landscape I had encountered before. Everything about it seemed to me suggestive of remote antiquity; the clumps of trees, planted like look-outs, silhouetted on the high sky-lines; those great stones, so aptly named the grey wethers, dropped by a melting glacier to litter the floor of the dry valley it had scoured; solitary thorns, twisted by the wind; flint nodules, turned up by the plough, of more significant and suggestive forms than any abstract sculptor could conceive.

Because all human history is so brief compared with that of this youthful landscape, in ghostly standing stone, burial mound, strip field, trackway and fortification, early man had left his imperishable marks upon it everywhere. Of all the features of the chalk downland I found these traces of civilisations long forgotten the most potently evocative. The mere fact that I was working on the Downs for this brief second in their history gave me a sense of continuity, of kinship, with these my ancient predecessors.

Through my work I became acquainted with many ancient, living men of the Wiltshire downland, an experience that was equally rewarding. Whenever I think of such men it is old Mark Palmer who first springs to my mind. Not that he was in any way unique as a country character at that time, but simply because he worked beside me at the Aldbourne foundry and I therefore came to know him best. In his younger days, Mark

Palmer had worked for Wallis and Steevens, makers of traction engines and other agricultural machinery at Basingstoke, and he possessed an inexhaustible store of amusing anecdotes about that firm to which he remained passionately loyal despite the fact that he had long since returned to his native village. Whenever I heard the familiar words: 'I recollec' one time when I were wi' Wallis and Steevens . . .' I knew the moment had come to down tools, lean comfortably against bench or machine and listen. It was a far more soothing and relaxing experience than any tea break.

Old Mark was short and thickset but surprisingly nimble for his age. Despite the fact that his fingers resembled bunches of bananas, he was a first class fitter, patient, deft and precise. He habitually wore a collarless flannel shirt with sleeves rolled back above the elbow and an ancient pair of bib-and-brace overalls that had once been brown but had faded with age and many washings to the palest khaki colour. Over his long but sparse white hair he wore a shapeless trilby hat of the same neutral colour. An untidy white moustache partly concealed his upper lip and on his large, slightly bulbous nose was perched a pair of steel-rimmed spectacles through which his grey eyes twinkled mischievously. He was the gayest old man I have ever known. On a fine sunny morning, or when work was going well and he was feeling particularly pleased with life, I would catch him humming some indecipherable tune to himself, sometimes executing a few steps of a dance in time to the music in his head. That head was stored with memories, some drawn from his own lifetime, but others going back much further in time which must have been passed on by his forebears. He would tell tales of events that had happened in Aldbourne a century or more ago so vividly and racily that they seemed to become personal recollections. It was from Mark I learned that Aldbourne had once been a centre for the making of straw hats and that, at an earlier date still, church bells had been cast in the village, perhaps, who knows, in that same foundry where I now worked.

It often happens in rural England that neighbouring villages become traditional rivals, their respective inhabitants each targets for the other's wit. So it was with Aldbourne and Ramsbury, and Mark had a wealth of stories to illustrate the fabled follies of the Ramsbury men. He stoutly maintained that it was they who had tried to dredge the moon out of the village pond at Aldbourne, thus giving a local connotation to the perennial Wiltshire story of the moonrakers. It was also the Ramsbury men, of course, who 'set the pig upon the wall to hear the band play'. Whenever Mark was asked some question about the past which he was unable to answer he would pause for a moment in silent meditation before replying slowly: 'Ah! that were a long time ago afore Adam were a boy-chap.' His tales and his graphic turns of phrase were those that Shakespeare knew and which he put into the mouths of his English countrymen. It is sad that nowadays such characters are usually played for laughs, as the townsman's idea of a village idiot, by those who have never known such men as Mark Palmer.

I have always relished the company of men like Mark Palmer. When I was at Hungerford, rich memories of past voyages on *Cressy* led me to explore the Kennet and Avon canal from the towpath and in this way I soon discovered the canal pumping station at Crofton on the edge of Savernake Forest. This station contained the first early beam pumping engines I had ever seen and I marvelled alike at their workmanship and at the poetry of their motion. Needless to say, I soon made friends with the old engineman who lived in a solitary cottage beside the pump-house. I used to visit Crofton frequently on summer evenings or at week-ends to share the old man's vigil in the engine house while the massive beam nodded in the gloom under the rafters high overhead. I used to find the sounds of the engine as hypnotic as my companion's conversation: the rhythmical clicking as the highly polished detents of the valve gear alternately engaged and released; the heavy sigh of steam exhausting into the condenser beneath our feet; the sound of a great gush of water pouring into the open feeder channel each time the pump bucket came up.

This period was enlivened and made memorable for me because I acquired two more cars. In case this should convey a false impression of affluence, I hasten to add that they cost me two pounds a-piece, discounting the labour I expended on them. I found that I was using my G.N. far more now and decided, on the belt-and-braces principle, that I ought to have a second car as reserve in case of emergency. So I bought near my home a 1922 Belsize-Bradshaw. It had a big-end gone —a defect I soon remedied—but was otherwise in excellent order. In view of the chronic starting trouble that my father had experienced with this marque, it may seem a strange choice, but this one not only boasted a self-starter but also an impulse starter[1] on its magneto. These ensured that I never had any starting troubles. I drove the Belsize some thousands of miles, but although it was a nice little car for its date and never let me down on the road, it lacked the sporting character of the G.N. and consequently never endeared itself to me.

My third car I acquired purely as a 'fun machine'. It was a little 1903[2] Humber which I discovered neglected in a chicken run at the back of a pub in Winchcombe. It looked very forlorn for it was covered in chicken droppings, its tyres had perished and there was nothing left of the upholstery except the springs, but investigation showed that mechanically it was quite sound and almost complete. One of my two old school friends, Harry Rose, was at this time working at a garage in Cheltenham and he produced the lorry on which we conveyed the Humber to the shelter of a cart shed at Stanley Pontlarge where I was able to work on it whenever I was at home. I found that the simple little two-seater body was secured to the tubular chassis merely by hook-bolts so that it was an easy matter to remove it, the better to attend to the chassis. My mother helped me to renovate and re-cover the upholstery and, when it had been given a coat of the green paint, which I had adopted as my 'house colour', the little car, with its polished copper radiator, really looked quite smart to my eyes although far below the standard of today's restorations.

The Humber had a single cylinder de Dion type engine of $5\frac{1}{4}$ h.p. which ran anti-clockwise. A small leather-lined cone clutch of alarming ferocity took the drive to a gear box which gave two forward speeds and reverse, actuated by two levers mounted on the sides of the steering column. A short propeller shaft connected the gearbox to the live rear axle, this last a fairly advanced feature for the period. 'Gas', 'Air' and 'Ignition' were each separately controlled from the column which meant that there were no less than five levers working in quadrants below the single-spoked metal steering wheel. When I found the car, this entire complex steering column assembly was a mass of red rust, but nothing daunted I got to work on it with

[1] This device consists of a spring-loaded ratchet and two pawls, all incorporated in the magneto driving coupling. On starting, the pawls engage with the ratchet, the effect being to impart a vigorous 'flip' to the magneto. When running, centrifugal force held the pawls out of engagement.
[2] I believed it to be 1902 and ran it as such for three years, before it was re-dated 1903 by the Veteran Car Club.

a mixture of metal polish and bath-brick and found, to my surprise and delight, that the original nickel plating underneath was practically perfect. The rust had emerged through a few minute pin-holes in the plating and had spread until it had covered its entire surface.

I was determined to get the car ready in time to enter it in the next (November 1932) Veteran Car Run to Brighton. How I managed to achieve this or precisely how I contrived to get the car to London for the start I cannot now remember. I certainly did not drive it up, for although I had had the engine running, owing to lack of time I had never driven the car more than a few yards. So it was scarcely surprising that I suffered the inevitable fate that awaits those so foolish as to bring an untried car to the starting line.

The start of the Brighton Run in those days was from Moon's Garage in Victoria Street. In my recollection of that November morning, the garage was half-dark and filled with choking exhaust fumes. In this smoke-filled gloom there was feverish activity as heavily muffled figures busied themselves about their strange vehicles which emitted desperate panting, tuffing and wheezing noises. I was glad to be clear of this mêlée and bowling up Victoria Street through an avenue of spectators. Then past the Abbey, past the Houses of Parliament and over Westminster Bridge, the little engine panting away gamely. This was the life, I thought; Brighton, here I come! But elation and hope soon turned to despair. In Brixton the radiator began to boil and overheating brought chronic pre-ignition causing the engine to lose what little power it possessed. Obviously it would be folly—besides being cruel to the car—to attempt to reach Brighton under such circumstances so I rolled ignominiously to the kerb-side, enveloped in a cloud of steam. I must have been the first competitor to fall by the wayside.

I transported my Humber from Brixton back to the Tractor Stores at Hungerford, where I. A. Bennett kindly gave it house-room. There I very soon diagnosed the trouble. One of the few things which were detached from the car when I found it was the gear-type water pump which was bolted to a bracket on the chassis and driven by a chain from the front of the engine. This pump had been dismantled and I had to replace its gears which had worn away. It could be made to revolve in either direction depending on which side of it was made to take the drive. In this my choice had been determined, partly by logic and, decisively as I thought, by the length of the driving chain which I had discovered in the tool-box. I now tried the effect of reversing the rotation of the pump and, hey presto!, all was well. The job was simply and quickly done, but it meant shortening the chain. This remains a mystery to me to this day. The evidence of that chain suggests that the previous owner of the car, Mr Greening, an elderly Winchcombe market-gardener, had run it in its incorrect state. If that was the case I could well believe local stories that it used to take him most of the day to get over Cleeve Hill and into Cheltenham.

In my impecunious state, I had surrendered the licence on the Humber at the end of November, but during the following winter and early spring I was able to drive it on the road thanks to the kindness of I. A. Bennett who lent me his general trade plates. This practice of running on trade plates led to an amusing brush with the law.

For some reason, perhaps because most of my motoring has been done in peculiar motor cars, I have always been harassed by the law and charged with a variety of petty technical offences by men whose time would have been better employed in catching criminals. They have buzzed around me like so many pestilential blow-flies so I am emphatically not one of those who subscribe to the view that our policemen are wonderful. My first brush with them was at Dursley where I was charged and fined for having an illegible front number plate on my G.N., although it appeared perfectly legible to me.

One fine Sunday morning in March I headed out of Hungerford along the quiet Wantage road to try out the effect of some 'tuning' of the Humber's engine. Beside me in the passenger seat was a beauteous young Hungerford maiden. I was not particularly susceptible to her charms, but she had badgered me so persistently to give her a ride in 'that funny old car' that I had finally given way to her. Now you hardly expect to find a plain-clothes policeman on the Wantage road on a Sunday morning, so I did not suspect that the man in a cloth cap and a raincoat who was cycling towards us was a wolf in sheep's clothing until he jumped off his machine, signalled us peremptorily to stop and produced his police card. 'Having a nice little joy-ride, eh?' he asked with a mirthless smile and a significant glance towards my passenger. Very fortunately, I realised as soon as he said this that one of the absurd anomalies of our road traffic regulations was that one was allowed to carry passengers on general trade plates on weekdays but not on a Sunday. The situation was the more unfortunate because it would implicate the owner of the plates—my employer—rather than myself. The only thing to be done was to attempt to blind the law with science. So the following dialogue took place:

SELF: No, this isn't a joy-ride; I'm testing the car.

POLICEMAN: You don't need a passenger for that do you?

SELF: Oh yes I do; I need her to prevent the car from running backwards if it fails on a hill.

POLICEMAN: Aah! So your brakes are defective.

SELF (Indignantly): Indeed they are not; they are the external contracting band type which are designed to work effectively only in a forward direction. To prevent the car running backwards it is fitted with a sprag.

POLICEMAN (suspecting his leg is being pulled): And might I ask what that is?

SELF (pointing it out): There it is. You see it can be let down on to the road.

POLICEMAN (triumphantly): Then why don't you use it?

SELF: Because the sprag was designed for rough roads. On smooth tarmac like this it doesn't work.

POLICEMAN: All right, get along then.

Whereupon, baffled and furious at being cheated of his prey, this unpleasant customer remounted his bicycle and pedalled rapidly away. He had not been quite clever enough, for he had omitted to ask if the Humber had two independent working brakes as required by law. If he had, I should have lost the battle of wits, for the car had a second brake on the transmission.

When I moved from Hungerford to the Foundry at Aldbourne the Humber went with me and, as I had now got it running extremely well, I licensed it for the month of June. So on these long, fine summer evenings I made a number of trips to Hungerford and back to visit friends and in recollection these were the most pleasant journeys I have ever made with a veteran car. There were not the crowds or the traffic such as inevitably accompany an organised veteran car run and make it a self-conscious exhibition. On the contrary, I was using the car as it was meant to be used on a delightful country road which, though it had a smoother surface, can have changed very little since the car was made and, in those days, carried very little traffic. Chugging along at a steady 25 m.p.h. through the warm, richly scented air of those still summer evenings was a rare delight which no modern motorist can experience but which the pioneers must have known. Indeed, in one respect I was more fortunate than the pioneers for their one enemy—dust—was lacking. I was reminded of childhood journeys by horsedrawn vehicle, for one sits *on* rather than *in* a veteran car and has a view over hedgerows into fields or cottage gardens.

The quadrant of the lever controlling the Humber's two forward speeds was rightly labelled 'fast' and 'slow' for the gap between the ratios was enormous, speed in low gear being no quicker than a walking pace. The golden rule was never to attempt to change down until the engine was on the point of stalling. Conversely, once in 'slow' speed, it was useless to attempt to change up until the car was on the level or there was a strong following wind. Otherwise, by the time the engine revs had dropped sufficiently to enable 'fast' speed to be engaged, the car had rolled to a stop. Engine speed was controlled by advancing or retarding the spark, for once you had got its mixture right by carefully adjusting the 'gas' and 'air' levers, you left the primitive Longemaire carburettor severely alone. Fortunately, the eight miles of road between Aldbourne and Hungerford run mainly in the valley of the Kennet and include no hill which the Humber could not surmount in 'fast' gear so that I was able to bowl along happily without any tedious crawls.

I was returning to Aldbourne one evening at dusk after one of these visits to Hungerford, when I had a second encounter with the police, this time in the person of the local sergeant from Ramsbury. A stout, red-faced individual, I met him pedalling slowly and majestically towards me on his bicycle. He evidently decided that so curious a vehicle must be illegal, for as soon as he saw me he dismounted and signalled me to stop. I sat patiently at the wheel while he paced slowly round and round the car examining it minutely. At last, surveying the Humber from the front, the light of triumph brightened his eye and, whipping out a folding foot rule, he stooped and measured the figures of the front registration number, FH 12, which was painted on the bottom tank of the radiator. They were three-eighths of an inch too short, he solemnly informed me. A heinous offence had been committed! Out came the notebook from the breast pocket, the pencil was licked and full particulars taken. I remarked that the figures had very probably been there since 1903 when car registration was first introduced and that no one had remarked the crime before. He accepted this with dignity as a compliment to his vigilance. I was not prosecuted, but on two subsequent occasions this zealous man pedalled over to Aldbourne from Ramsbury, first to see for himself that I had enlarged the figures and a second time to administer an official caution.

I left the Humber in store at a garage in Hungerford when my job at Aldbourne died on me in August 1933 and I returned home. I could not afford to perambulate the country looking for work, so I must have spent six weeks or more hopefully writing round to likely firms and receiving monotonously discouraging replies until, in October, one of these letters bore fruit and I was offered a job at the Sentinel Waggon Works at Shrewsbury. With hope renewed, I headed the G.N. for Shrewsbury and found lodgings for myself in a pub at Battlebridge, not far from the works.

The firm was at that time making the latest and last of its famous steam waggons which was known as the S Type. This had the same basic layout as its predecessors with vertical Sentinel boiler in front and engine slung beneath the chassis amidships, but it was very much more refined. The engine was single-acting, a flat four-cylinder with poppet valves, which drove the rear wheels via a propeller shaft and live axle instead of by roller chain as on all the earlier models. The S Type was a fast waggon in its day being capable of maintaining a speed of 50 m.p.h. or more (illegally, of course) on the level.

I went to work in the Boiler Shop, fitting up the boilers for these S Type waggons and it was interesting to me to see the changes that had been made in the design of the Sentinel boiler since those days, that now seemed so long ago, when I had driven the first Sentinel ploughing engine at Pitchill. Most notably, internal baffles were now fitted in an attempt to cure its chronic water-lifting or 'priming' trouble. There was also a new and enlarged superheater element which raised the steam to a temperature that was then unusually high, so much so that a special lubricating oil had to be developed for the engine. My job was to assemble the boiler, lowering the outer casing over the firebox, and then to mount all the boiler fittings. When the job was completed I then had to test the boiler under steam at full working pressure. This was done in a testing bay at the end of the shop which was equipped with a Laidlaw-Drew oil burner.

The Sentinel Waggon Works was an exciting place at this time for a steam enthusiast like myself, for I would sometimes see with awed veneration the tall, white-haired figure of the American Abner Doble, striding across the yard or driving out of the works gate in one of his steam cars. Doble was then regarded as the ultimate champion of steam power against the all-conquering might of the internal combustion engine. He had come over to Shrewsbury, bringing two of his flash-steam cars with him, with the object of developing a similar flash-steam commercial vehicle. Of his two cars, one resembled in appearance a conventional large American saloon of the period, while the other was a very handsome coach-built two-seater coupé. I remember peering round the doorway of the works garage and watching the big coupé, moving to and fro with uncanny silence as it was manœuvred into its parking bay. How I itched to have a run in such a car! But I was merely a humble fitter and knew I had no hope.

I also used to see the one Sentinel/Doble flash-steam waggon that had then been built. This outwardly resembled a convention-al petrol or diesel lorry with semi-forward control except that its radiator—which was in fact the condenser—was abnormally large. The full roller-bearing two-cylinder compound engine was mounted in unit with the rear axle and was supplied with steam from the flash boiler at 1500 lbs per square inch and 500° C. superheat. This vehicle was employed on works transport at the time. I used to watch it entering or leaving the works and once, when it was standing in the yard, engaged its driver in conversation. He boasted to me of the number of summonses he had received for speeding. This I could well believe, for the Sentinel/Doble once made the 540-mile run from Shrewsbury to Glasgow and back with a full load in less than 24 hours, no mean performance in the days before motor-ways.

But as things turned out, this was the last brave gesture in a lost cause. Abner Doble, unfortunately, was one of those inventive geniuses who, unless they can be firmly controlled, will ruin any engineering firm. A perfectionist, he could never be persuaded to finalise any design. Despite its promise, his first waggon had certain serious defects which would have to be eliminated before it became a commercial proposition. Instead of trying to iron out these snags, Doble seemed to lose interest in the vehicle, devoting his whole attention and a great deal of the firm's money to the development of a new triple-expansion engine with inter-stage superheating. The final upshot was that the firm went into liquidation, the company being re-formed under a different title, while Abner Doble returned to America. As for the more conventional S Type Sentinel, it was driven off the English road by a new form of taxation which discriminated against the steam vehicle, although a number continued to be made for export for some years. A slackening in the demand for the S Type waggon found me out of a job again at the end of December after a mere two months at Shrewsbury. It has always seemed to me crazy that the only type of heavy road vehicle using home-produced fuel should have been driven off the road by taxation.

Back at home, a second spate of letter writing eventually landed me yet another job, this time with Thornycrofts at Basingstoke. This was unmemorable and proved equally brief with the result that by April 1934 I had returned home once more. Yet but for this brief sojourn in Basingstoke I should never have become part-owner of a garage only eight miles out of the town. But that was still in the future. For the rest of the year I lived, or rather was based, at home with my parents. It was the longest continuous spell I had spent at Stanley Pontlarge since my school holidays and I kept myself occupied by working on my G.N. and Belsize.

My Humber was still stabled in Hungerford, but I was determined to enter it again for the London to Brighton Run and this was the most memorable experience of these idle months. A friend of mine from Cheltenham, an enthusiastic Austin Seven owner named Mark Newth, very bravely offered to tow the Humber from Hungerford to London behind his early Austin Seven 'chummy'. With some difficulty (for the Austin had no chassis at the rear) we devised a suitable towbar and attachments and headed south to retrieve my car and set off for London. From my high perch on the Humber I could look down on the hood of the Austin Seven and as we drove through London the curious spectacle we presented attracted much ribaldry from taxi drivers. They found us the more mirth-provoking because, whenever traffic brought us to a halt, I would have to leap out and push in order to get us rolling again. For though it performed its onerous task gallantly, the one thing the Austin could not do was to start its tow from rest. Instead it suffered such violent clutch judder that it jumped up and down on its springs without any forward motion.

This gallant effort was not in vain, for this time the Humber ran like a watch and it was with immense satisfaction that I drove on to the Madeira Drive at Brighton well within the time limit. The Brighton road, though it seemed congested enough, was much clearer than it is today and I remember gazing enviously after Blake's racing Napier as it came hurtling past at what seemed an incredible velocity.

One of the two friends I had made at school was by this time working at a garage in Maidstone, and offered to stable the Humber there so, on the morning after the run, we set off in bright sunshine to tow the car to Maidstone. It was a hilly road over the downs from Brighton, but the little Austin struggled along bravely and so we eventually left the old car to slumber for another year with no clear idea as to how I should retrieve it.

The only employment I had during these idle months was totally unremunerative and consisted in endeavouring to sell on commission a patent tractor winch manufactured by the firm of Kennedy and Kempe Ltd to timber merchants in the Forest of Dean. Despite the fact that I staged quite an impressive demonstration of this winch in Priors Mesne Wood in the Forest, I never succeeded in selling a single one and decided ruefully that salemanship was not my strong suit.

I had been introduced to Kennedy and Kempe by Leslie Bomford whose farm was nearby. Colonel Kennedy and I. T. Kempe had been managing director and works manager respectively of the old firm of Taskers at Andover before setting up a business of their own in a disused war-time explosives factory at Longparish in Hampshire. They were both charming men and enterprising and inventive engineers, always keen on developing new ideas, so that I felt mortified by my failure to sell their patent winch. I disappointed them in another way also.

As a result of my experience with the KS lorry I had been cudgelling my brains about possible ways of reducing the amount of black smoke which the diesel engine emitted on heavy load. It seemed to me that if the amount of air drawn in to the cylinders could be varied in direct proportion to the amount of fuel injected, not only would the exhaust become clean but the engine would be more efficient. I had made a section drawing of a cylinder head incorporating a device to achieve this which I showed to Colonel Kennedy. He was keenly interested, advised me to take out a provisional patent and offered to send my drawing and a draft specification to his patent agents in

London for a report. Alas for my fond hopes! I still have a copy of that report. In it the agents wrote:

'Specification 334018 (Daimler-Benz, Stuttgart) describes the linking up of the throttle control with auxiliary pistons for varying the clearance whereby any desired variation can be obtained, this being practically the same idea as Mr Rolt's.'

The dream of 'Rolt the Great Inventor' was thus rudely shattered. The fact that I had been forestalled by a name so august as Daimler-Benz was small consolation, particularly when I obtained a copy of their patent specification and found it to be a master patent of principle with no indication of the mechanical means whereby it could be applied. So ended my only venture into the complex world of patents.

During these roving, rootless and largely fruitless years my mind was by no means solely occupied with engineering matters. During my apprenticeship I had been content to absorb experiences and in the previous chapters I have tried to describe as faithfully as possible their impact upon me although I could not have described them at the time. Now, however, my frequent, and sometimes prolonged, visits to my home in between one job and the next gave me an opportunity mentally to digest and ponder over my past with the effect that my brain began to buzz with new and disturbing thoughts and ideas.

Of all my varied experiences, that of my years at Stoke-on-Trent had by far the most lasting effect upon me. It had provided me with my first and most intimate insight into the kind of England that the Industrial Revolution had created. I had been fascinated by the vitality of this world of blackened streets, of spinning wheels, of smoke and steam and furnace flame; so much so that the memory of it did not fade but became more vivid with the passage of time. But because I could recall its every sight and sound so clearly, the contrast between it and the green England that I had known as a child became for me the more significant. The prospect that one day this new black world might grow until it had altogether overwhelmed the green world where I had found such sweet solace seemed to me too terrible to contemplate. And yet, as an engineer, was I not dedicated to such a course of destruction? I realised that this conflict between the black and the green was an internal as well as an external one and that philosophical problems were involved which were far beyond my limited intellectual range. The first thing to do, it seemed to me, was to acquire some knowledge as to how the Industrial Revolution had come about in the first place. Of this I was completely ignorant, for the history I had been taught at school was all to do with kings and politicians, with wars and with revolutions of a bloodier but much less significant kind. In this sort of history the Industrial Revolution appeared to be merely an incidental happening, although it now seemed to me the most important event in human history and one filled with potential menace. My thirst for knowledge was first quenched when I came upon an original three-volume edition of Samuel Smiles' *Lives of the Engineers* in a second-hand bookshop. I read it with avid interest. And so, for the princely sum of 7s. 6d., my self-education began. It was to become a lifelong study.

At the same time, the side of my nature that loved and remembered the world of my childhood found secret refreshment in poetry. Being made to learn dull passages of prose and poetry by rote at school by men who appeared to have no natural feeling for words had very effectively destroyed my appetite for literature. But at some time during these years, precisely how or when I cannot now remember, I discovered the poems of W. B. Yeats and the music and majesty of their language went straight to my heart. This experience encouraged me to read many other poets, ancient and modern, but while I drew much satisfaction from them, Yeats always seemed to me supreme among the moderns and I habitually kept a copy of his poems at my bedside. Later, I read his *Reveries over Childhood and Youth* and *The Trembling of the Veil*; also that strange book *A Vision*.

At this time, too, I felt a strong compulsion to express my thoughts and feelings in writing. Where this literary urge came from is as much a mystery to me as the source of my earlier determination to become an engineer, for there was no literary tradition in my family. Although in her later life my mother became a great reader, my parents read little during my childhood and there were few books in the house at Hay. So, lacking an example, I had read hardly at all, drawing imaginative sustenance from direct experience. I can recall only one book that I read with intense pleasure as a child and that was *The Secret Garden* by Frances Hodgson Burnett. My knowledge of the formal rules of grammar was almost nil, but my immediate liking for the poems of Yeats disclosed that

I had a feeling for the music of words. So I made a first and unsatisfactory attempt to express myself. This was in the form of a novel which I called *Strange Vista*. The title came from a poem called 'The Wheel'; rather a second-rate piece I now realise, but it chimed with my thought at the time.

Strange Vista was really very strange indeed and fell far short of its creator's hopes even when it had been completely re-written. The trouble was that the whole idea was hopelessly over-ambitious. It was intended to be a great saga in three parts, past, present and future, with representatives of the same two families playing the leading roles in each. The first part was set in the rural England of the mid-eighteenth century; the setting of the second was the large industrial town which had grown up on the same location. The town was modelled on Stoke-on-Trent and this part was autobiographical as most first novels tend to be. Finally, the last part portrayed the same town in the future. To read it now is a curious experience, for in many ways this town of the future with its tall buildings, its express lifts, its pedestrian subways and shopping 'precincts' has become strangely familiar. So have the manners and morals of its restless, unhappy, neurotic and sex-obsessed citizens. There is one scene where a troupe of girls dance almost naked in a night-club while two characters argue the pros and cons of a 'permissive' society. 'The rules of right and wrong are pretty elastic, they change with the years', says the apologist, to which the other replies: 'You can't go on changing your rules to suit your inclinations.' But I had over-estimated the pace of change. For reasons to do with the ages of my chief characters, I set this future scene in 1954, a date which, in 1932, seemed to a young man half a world away. Even so, in one respect this world of the future remains a Wellsian dream, for in it men had discovered a way of 'broad-casting' electric power. All forms of transport used electric propulsion, private cars being fitted with shilling-in-the-slot meters.

In my book, this hectic urban civilization ended not with a big bang, as now seems probable, but with a whimper. Its neurotic citizens all began to succumb to a sudden, acute and invariably fatal brain disease. The power stations stopped and everything ground to a halt. My hero and heroine, of course, were amongst the few survivors. They sought refuge on the Welsh Border where they proceeded to lead a life of Arcadian simplicity of the kind William Morris used to dream about, resolved to found a new civilization that would be better adapted to man's natural environment and his instinctive needs.

Naïve though it is, *Strange Vista*, painstakingly written in two large lined notebooks, does provide an accurate record of my state of mind at this time. It thus enables me to avoid the danger of attributing to my youthful persona thoughts and ideas which, in fact, he never held at the time. Such a back-projection of ideas is a falsification to which autobiographers are peculiarly subject, often quite unconsciously. During these difficult years of the great depression it did indeed seem to me that the industrial world was changing and might be sowing the seeds of its own dissolution. The writing and rewriting of *Strange Vista* in my spare time throughout this unsettled period of my life was the equivalent of keeping a secret and highly personal journal.

Chapter 11

The Phoenix

THE sporting character of my father's 12/50 Alvis was such that no sooner had he acquired it in 1925 than he became an enthusiastic follower of motor racing. From 1926 onward he regularly visited the speed hill climbs at Shelsley Walsh in Worcestershire and, as I accompanied him whenever I was free to do so, I soon became as keen as he was. Naturally, after I had acquired my first G.N. I became a devoted fan of B. H. Davenport who frequently made the fastest time of the day at Shelsley in his single-seater G.N. 'Spider'. On occasion, too, my father and I went to Brooklands in the Alvis. We saw the Grand Prix of the R.A.C. there in 1926, the first formula Grand Prix to be run on English soil.

My interest in motor racing had thus begun at the age of sixteen so I was pleased to find, when I went to Basingstoke eight years later, someone who fully shared it. We also shared the same lodgings in Worting Road. He was an apprentice at Thornycrofts named John Passini and, as motor racing was by no means our only common interest, we soon became firm friends. We both admired what we considered to be the right kind of car and consequently deplored the effect of the great depression on the British motor industry. Many firms had gone out of business, while of the survivors the majority had lost their separate identities by seeking refuge in amalgamations. These new combines sought salvation by adopting, not very successfully, American methods of mass-production. In America, the closed car had become the rule rather than the exception, a trend which had been vastly accelerated by the introduction of the pressed steel body which was cheaper, lighter and stronger than the older wooden-framed coach-built body which it replaced.

The introduction of these American methods to England from

1930 onwards brought about a rapid revolution on the English roads. Hitherto, Englishmen had taken for granted that a closed car was something expensive and heavy to be used as a 'town carriage' and that for long-distance motoring in the country one used an open touring car. My father and mother, for example, thought nothing of setting out to drive from Gloucestershire to Chester in mid-winter in the open Belsize or the Alvis and it would never occur to them to erect the hood unless it was actually snowing or raining. There is an interesting parallel to this in the early cab-less locomotives on our railways. But when the first small 'tin saloons' (as John and I used rudely to call them) came on to the market they proved so popular that within the space of a very few years the open touring car had become a rarity. Because our climate is bad and the average mortal is slothful and comfort-loving, this speedy change was understandable although, along with the hardship, a great deal of the pleasure went out of motoring in the process. It was one significant step in that process by which man has used his technology to cut himself off from his natural environment.

By 1934 it had already become clear that the previous decade was the golden age of motoring in England. Though main roads had become dustless they were then still traffic free. The term 'the joy of the open road' was still literally true and carried no cynical overtones. Compared with their pre-war predecessors, the better cars of the 'twenties had an immeasurably superior performance and reliability so that one could embark on the longest journey without the haunting fear of breakdowns. Because they were designed by engineers to be built by engineers rather than by machines, using methods which would now be considered impossibly expensive in labour and materials, such cars were valued by their owners, not as mere status symbols, but as objects of fine craftsmanship; for the way they handled and for the sensitivity of their response to driving skill. My father valued his Alvis in the same way as he valued his Holland & Holland guns. The experience of driving such a car on the roads of the past has been so evocatively described by Sir Osbert Sitwell in the third volume of his great autobiography *Left Hand, Right Hand!* that any further attempt to do so would be superfluous.

'They would sit together, the two of them,' he writes, 'the man at the wheel, the girl beside him, their hair blown back from their temples, their features sculptured by the wind, their bodies and limbs shaped and carved by it continually under their clothes, so that they enjoyed a new physical sensation, comparable to swimming; except that here the element was speed, not water. The winds—and their bodies—were warm that summer. During these drives, they acquired a whole range of physical conscious-ness, the knowledge of scents, passing one into another with an undreamt-of rapidity, the fragrance of the countless flowers on the lime trees, hung like bells of pagodas for the breeze to shake, changing into that of sweetbriar, the scent of early mornings, and of their darkness, of hills and valleys, outlined and tinged by memory; there was the awareness of speed itself, and the rapid thinking that must accompany it, a new alertness, and the typical effects, the sense, it might be, of the racing of every machine as dusk approaches, or the sudden access on a hot evening of cool waves of air under the tall trees;—all these physical impressions, so small in themselves, went to form a sum of feeling new in its kind and never before experienced. Even the wind of the winter, at this pace snatching tears from their eyes, and piercing through layers of clothes, was something their fathers had not known. The open car belonged to that day. No other generation had been able to speed into the sunset.'[1]

This passage stirs many a nostalgic memory for me, but already, by 1934, it had become clear that the open car belonged uniquely to the past. The new mass-produced saloon cars were appearing on the road in ever increasing numbers. That so far as weight distribution, road-holding and steering were concerned these first British attempts at mass production were some of the worst cars ever made is now a commonly accepted fact. The contrast with what had gone before could not have been more striking. I remember driving one early example which, with two heavy passengers in the back seats, became almost uncontrollable because the front wheels were practically off the road, a defect cured on later models by the crude expedient of shifting the engine forward over the axle.

It must have been one Sunday evening in March 1934 that I returned to Basingstoke in the Belsize after a visit home

[1] *Great Morning*, pp. 234-5.

to find John full of a marvellous pub he had discovered at Hartley Wintney, eight miles out of Basingstoke on the road to London. He had been introduced to it by a curious character named 'Soapy' Monkton, a car salesman from the Sarum Hill Garage just down the road. This pub was called 'The Phoenix' and it was kept by a tall Irishman named Tim Carson. This character had, John informed me excitedly, broken records at Brooklands driving a three-litre T.T. Vauxhall and now possessed a special racing 30/98 Vauxhall which he had built himself. As John portrayed it, the whole ambience of 'The Phoenix' sounded so congenial and inviting that I could scarcely wait to visit it so, on the very next evening, we drove out to Hartley Wintney together. That visit was the first of many during the next nine months, for it marked the beginning of an enduring and fruitful friendship between John Passini, Tim Carson and myself. Because, in Grand Prix racing, the Italian star was then in the ascendant, we styled ourselves jokingly the 'Scuderia Carsoni'.

Although John favoured the Lancia Lambda and I, naturally, the G.N. and the 12/50 Alvis, our taste in cars was very similar and we both enthusiastically shared with Tim his admiration for the 30/98 Vauxhall. The work of the Scuderia Carsoni was done in a humble wooden hut, known as 'the racing shed', at the back of the Phoenix and, so far as I can recall, its first public appearance was at Lewes Speed Trials in August where the stable's No 1 driver ran his 30/98 Special with the enthusiastic help of his two devoted assistants. The next outing that I remember was the September meeting at Shelsley Walsh. The team made the 'Falcon' at Bromyard their headquarters. Our tender car was a standard 30/98 'Velox' tourer in which I had an exhilarating drive up from Hampshire, the back loaded with large Rudge wheels of assorted sizes, feeling that now I really was playing a part in the racing game.

John and I soon discovered that our No. 1 driver displayed a remarkable optimism in matters mechanical. On my very first visit to the Phoenix, Tim had casually offered to give me a run in his Special, an offer I accepted with alacrity, thrilled at the thought of a trip in a fast car driven by a man who had actually taken records at Brooklands. We swept out of the inn yard and turned left on to the straight road to Odiham. Here one fine burst of acceleration was succeeded by dead silence. We rolled to a standstill and opened the bonnet when the cause of this abrupt quietus was immediately disclosed—the magneto had become disengaged from its drive. It was a new one which Tim had just fitted. Finding it too low for its holding down strap by an inch or more, there was a need for a distance piece and the first object that came to hand, namely a roll of insulation tape, had been pressed into service.

Sometimes the consequences of this trait could be much more alarming. On the morning of practice day, Tim roared off from Bromyard to Shelsley, leaving John and me to follow in his wake in the tender car. We were startled to see a large Rudge 'knock-off' hub nut lying in the road, and, on stopping to retrieve it, were even more alarmed to see that it undoubtedly belonged to the Carson Special. We pressed on madly, expecting to see disaster round every turn. Miraculously, however, we found Tim in the paddock, blissfully ignorant of the fact that one rear wheel lacked any means of retention. It then transpired that, unknown to us, Tim had decided to try the effect of smaller rear wheels and as these were suitable for short hubs whereas the hubs of his car were long, he had fitted an improvised packing piece between wheel and hub, thus defeating the whole principle of the Rudge detachable wheel.

On one side of the Phoenix yard, a petrol filling station stood beside the road. This consisted of an ugly corrugated iron building with four manual petrol pumps on its forecourt. It was run in a somewhat desultory fashion by a man named Baldwin, an ex-county cricketer and MCC umpire. At what precise moment during this summer of 1934 John and I determined to go into partnership and acquire this garage I cannot now recall, but it was this decision that accounted for my frequent visits to the Phoenix. We put up the capital in equal shares, this being the last substantial call I would make upon my parents' slender resources. Besides the garage, our purchase covered a range of buildings on the opposite side of the yard which had once been an old coachbuilding business. These included a large building with red-tiled roof, which had originally been a barn, a small office and a paint shop. Behind these was a cottage and a modern brick building standing in an open yard, this last being leased by a firm of car breakers named James and Salmon. Although we acquired all this property for what now seems a ridiculously small sum, its purchase left us with all too little working capital, a fact which was to handicap us seriously in the years ahead. We planned to start business in January 1935 in a far more energetic manner than our predecessor.

Meanwhile, at the beginning of October, a letter had appeared in the motoring press over the names of Colin Nicholson and Ned Lewis suggesting the formation of a 'Veteran Sports Car Club' for the owners of sports cars built before 1931. This idea naturally appealed strongly to the members of the Scuderia Carsoni and we immediately wrote to Messrs Nicholson and Lewis, inviting them to come down to the Phoenix and discuss the project. We were a little disappointed to discover that Nicholson owned an Austin Seven and Lewis a 1930 Morris Minor, which were not exactly the sort of cars we had in mind. I suspect they were equally taken aback by the array of somewhat less conventional motor cars owned by the Scuderia Carsoni. However, we thought their idea was a good one and promised our whole-hearted support. Because the Veteran Car Club somewhat naturally objected to the use of the word 'veteran' in the title of the new club it was changed to 'vintage'—at whose suggestion I do not know—and so the Vintage Sports Car Club was born. The Phoenix became the unofficial headquarters and rallying point of the V.S.C.C. until the outbreak of war in 1939. Each weekend would see a desirable collection of motor cars parked in the yard, and, because closing time always seemed to be pretty elastic in those days, convivial, and frequently hilarious parties in the bar used to continue until a late hour.

Although I have since been concerned in the birth of other clubs or societies formed for one object or another, in no organisation other than the V.S.C.C. have I found such good company or made so many lifelong friends. I have often wondered why this should be. It seems that the vintage car attracts a type of mind that is peculiarly congenial to me. It is not by any means a one-track mind, but one with an exacting appreciation for fine craftsmanship that is by no means confined to motor cars. But there is nothing solemn or portentous about this appreciation for it is combined with a keenly ironic sense of humour that is quite free from malice and is capable of laughing at itself. It is due to this detachment and light-hearted tolerance that the V.S.C.C. can organise its affairs and its events with a degree of efficiency combined with a complete absence of friction, empire-building or officiousness which, in my experience, is quite unique among voluntary associations, whatsoever their object. Despite the fact that its membership has grown eight-fold in recent years the Club still retains the character impressed upon it by that handful of people who used to foregather at the Phoenix thirty-five years ago. Of these people, two exercised an outstanding influence. One was Tim Carson, who has now been Secretary for over twenty-five years, and the other was Sam Clutton. Sam is as much of an authority on the organ, early keyboard instruments and horology as he is on the motor car. Driving down from London in the Frazer Nash he then owned, he was a frequent visitor to the Phoenix in these early days and has been my friend from that day to this. As the first Press Secretary and Editor of the Club's *Bulletin*, Sam drove his pen as forcefully as his motor cars so that it is difficult to say which activity was the greater formative influence.

In January 1935 the Phoenix Green Garage, as we called it, opened its doors for the first time under our joint ownership. John's sister had designed for us the emblem of a phoenix on a nest of flame which our successor uses to this day. Unlike our predecessor, we had resolved to go into the repair business and decided we ought to have a breakdown vehicle. I therefore purchased in Cheltenham for the princely sum of £10 a 1911 Silver Ghost Rolls Royce with a vast landaulette body and, having paid over the purchase money, drove it straight down to Hartley Wintney. I had never driven a Rolls Royce before and delighted in the meticulous precision with which all the controls operated and in the silence of the big engine under the long aluminium bonnet that extended before me to that well-known figure of the winged goddess that topped the brass radiator. This silence was the more remarkable because, when we came to overhaul the engine we found it had been sadly neglected. The sump was full of black sludge of the consistency of butter and when we removed the connecting rods, what was left of the white metal in the big-end brasses fell out in small pieces. Apparently the Silver Ghost engine was too well-mannered to complain even under maltreatment. We cut off the rear portion of the landaulette and substituted a truck body in which we mounted a breakdown crane. The front seats were retained, but for the landaulette roof we substituted a folding hood with roll-up rear portion for better visibility when towing. The result was a very handsome and impressive breakdown vehicle, though such a conversion would be thought barbarous nowadays.

One wet and windy winter night soon after we had opened for business, John and I were working late in the garage overhauling the Rolls Royce when we heard a car coming from the direction of London making the most appalling clatter. 'A job!' we cried, and rushed out into the rain. The car, an old Citroen, had drawn up opposite the petrol pumps, its engine still running and 'Two gallons, please' the driver shouted above the mechanical uproar. 'Hadn't we better see what's wrong?' we asked diffidently when we had pumped the petrol into the tank. 'You can do,' replied the driver casually, getting out of the car and looking over our shoulders as we lifted the bonnet. Through a large hole in the side of the crankcase the bright, jagged end of a broken connecting rod could be seen flailing round. 'O ho!' said the driver, 'I'd better take it a bit steady now.' Whereupon he shut the bonnet and drove off rapidly in the direction of Basingstoke, leaving us standing speechless in the road, watching the rear-light of 'the job' disappear into the darkness. This was only the first of our many odd experiences as garage proprietors.

The biggest job our old Rolls Royce ever had to tackle was to rescue a fallen comrade. This was a Silver Ghost hearse of much later date belonging to a firm of London undertakers. It was travelling to Southampton to collect a customer when, between Hartley Wintney and Hook, a front stub axle broke and it had finished up in the ditch. As originally built, this chassis, like ours, had had rear wheel brakes only, but it had subsequently been fitted with a front wheel brake conversion of a singularly crude kind. It was the ineptitude of this conversion which had undoubtedly caused the failure of the stub axle. However, we decided that this was the owners' headache so we duly wrote off to Rolls Royce for a new stub axle and the other spares which were needed. We had reckoned without Rolls Royce. We received in reply a letter to this effect:

'On referring to our records we find that this chassis has been fitted with brakes of alien manufacture. We regret, therefore, that we cannot supply any spares for this chassis until we receive a document, signed by you and by the owners, to the effect that these alien brakes have been removed.'

This imperious missive filled us with admiration, not only for the exacting standards of Rolls Royce but for the completeness and accuracy of their records. The owners could not do other than comply with this edict and we cheerfully threw the 'alien brakes' on to the scrap heap. This disabled hearse was so large that we parked it in the yard near the Phoenix, seizing the opportunity to play on Tim's superstitious fears by pretending that its empty coffin was occupied. When taking our morning drink in the bar, we would sniff ostentatiously and remark that we hoped the spares would arrive soon.

In our old range of buildings we discovered a number of relics of the coachbuilding business which had once been carried on there. In a bin in the old paint shop, for example, we found a large stock of long, cloth-covered springs which at first suggested that someone had once intended to mass-produce jack-in-the-boxes. In fact, they were carriage lamp springs, their function being to push up the candle as it burned and so keep its flame in the focus of the mirror. Another find was a pattern book of the crests and coats of arms of local families, all beautifully hand-painted, which had once been faithfully reproduced on carriage doors by craftsman coachpainters long since turned to dust. Yet a vestige of the old business still lived on in the person of Joe Attewell, a delightful, elderly rural character who still built farm trailers and repaired an occasional farm cart in the big barn. He was to prove a valuable tenant when there was any woodwork to be done and he built us a very useful car-transporting trailer complete with loading winch.

John was marrying Tim Carson's sister-in-law in the spring when the three of us planned to move into the cottage which was part of our property. For the first three months, while the cottage was being redecorated, John and I shared lodgings near Winchfield Station a little over a mile from the garage. I was driving back to the garage from Winchfield after lunch one day when my faithful G.N. met its Waterloo. Rounding a blind bend I suddenly saw directly in front of me a Jowett car heading my way at a fair speed, obviously making for the old road to Odiham that joined the main road at an oblique angle on my left. There was no time to take avoiding action and we met in violent head-on collision. Because it was a light and flimsy machine, the G.N. literally disintegrated around me and it is remarkable that I was able to step out of the ruins completely unhurt. As I did so I observed with a certain malicious satisfaction that the Jowett, which was a nearly new car, had been savaged pretty severely. Its owner lodged a very substantial claim for damages against me, but this was unsuccessful as it was clearly his liability.

This left me with the Belsize as my only means of transport and, as I considered it was hardly a suitable mount for a founder member of the V.S.C.C., I began to look around for another car. With Tim's help I succeeded in finding a 1924 12/50 Alvis two-seater sports model of the genus known as the 'duck's back' from the rude shape of its pointed tail. Although it was then only ten years old, it looked a sorry sight for it was lying in the open and had been sadly neglected, its polished aluminium body panels white with corrosion. I paid the owner ten pounds for it and we towed it back to the garage to receive proper care and treatment. I certainly got value for my money for, apart from an interval during the war years when it was laid up, I have been driving this car from that day to this and the pleasure and satisfaction it gives me has never palled. It has never been elaborately restored to better-than-new condition as is the modern fashion but is still a workaday motor-car. When I first drove this car on the road it was regarded with awe as a 'racer' by the youthful section of the public. Then for many years my appearance was greeted with shouts and whistles of derision, but now this has changed to admiration again, although not of so healthy a kind. By young and old alike the Alvis has come to be regarded as a sort of flashy status symbol. That I do not drive the car in order to make myself conspicuous or to gratify my ego but simply because I enjoy it seems to be beyond the comprehension of the modern mind.

The earliest motoring events organised by the V.S.C.C. were reliability trials. I have never been able to summon much enthusiasm for this type of event although I did accompany Tim Carson as navigator on the Club's first Chiltern Trial in January 1935. Our car was an E type 30/98 Vauxhall with an unusual wide two-seater body which John and I had recently acquired, the first of a number of similar cars to pass through our hands. With it Tim won a second-class award. In view of the prices that these wonderful cars now command, it is interesting that we subsequently advertised this car ('award winner') for £25 and, as there were no takers after some months, subsequently dropped the price to £20.

What attracted me far more were speed events and I decided to reincarnate my shattered G.N. as a single-seater sprint car. I fitted the engine with two magnetos and two carburettors. The latter dripped petrol over the hot cylinders, producing a haze of petrol vapour which caused Sam Clutton to observe in the Club *Bulletin* that it evidently assisted in carrying off heat and would probably carry off me as well. However, strange to relate, it never caught fire. Unlike the racing G.N.s which were so successful in the years between the wars with their potent 'Akela' or 'Vitesse' engines, my car still had the ordinary touring engine beneath this proliferation of magnetos and carburettors. Consequently it was never seriously competitive in the racing class in which, being a single-seater, it had to be entered. Nevertheless, it was a nice looking little car and gave me a great deal of fun. I first entered my G.N. for the second V.S.C.C. sprint meeting at Aston Clinton in Buckinghamshire in May 1936. The course here was a length of private drive, appallingly rough and pitted with potholes so that the chief skill consisted in preventing one's car from leaping off the road.

This meeting was most memorable for the first appearance, after many years' hibernation in East Anglia, of the 12-litre 1908 60 h.p. Grand Prix Itala which won the class for Edwardian cars in the hands of its discoverer, J. C. Pole. Sam Clutton immediately fell for this great car hook, line and sinker, as well he might, and agreed there and then to purchase it from John Pole. Sam has been driving it ever since with such characteristic and tireless verve that it has become the most famous car in the Club. No Vintage meeting is complete without Sam and his Itala. We used to maintain the Itala at the Phoenix Green Garage; it suffered certain derangements in its gearbox, I remember, due to a somewhat crude and elementary form of reverse gear, and we had to have some new pinions made for it. Driving the Itala on test was a motoring thrill such as I had never experienced before. Although the big engine, which entirely filled the bonnet, made a considerable mechanical commotion, once, with tensed calf muscles, you had gingerly engaged the heavy clutch and felt the engine take hold, you were rewarded with a sensation of effortless power such as no modern car, however potent, can possibly convey. As has been so truly said, in this respect 'there is no substitute for litres'. In 1968 I was privileged to drive the Itala round the full Silverstone circuit on the occasion of its 60th birthday celebrations and, after an interval of more than thirty years, experienced the same thrill.

My first memorable experience with the Itala was when Sam entered it for the Shelsley Walsh hill climb and I accompanied him thither as mechanic. It was the first occasion when a special class for Edwardian cars had been run at Shelsley and the first time Sam had driven there. We drove up in the car from the Phoenix to Shelsley, stopping the night at Worcester to inspect a small chamber organ in the cathedral. On practice day a mysterious air leak developed in the top of the rear petrol tank and, since fuel supply depended on air pressure, this was most unfortunate. However, such an emergency had evidently been anticipated by the provision in the cockpit of a connector to which a hand tyre pump could be attached. So we borrowed a pump and I accompanied Sam on both his runs, pumping madly.

That heroic figure the riding mechanic has long been extinct in motor racing. He was heroic because, while a racing driver holds his life in his own hands and is far too pre-occupied to feel any sense of fear, his helpless riding mechanic has little to do but watch what, if he has any imagination, seems a series of imminent accidents. No such passive heroism was called for on this occasion, however. As we thundered up to the esses, I was far too busily occupied with that tyre pump to worry whether we should get round or not. In fact, as I discovered then, although the Itala stands so high that its passengers get the impression that it must roll over when entering a corner at what seems an impossible speed, it is perfectly stable and corners impeccably. The car had—as it still has—an archaic low-tension ignition system. There are no sparking plugs as we know them, the spark being produced by the opening of contact points within the cylinder. These points are opened by a cam and closed by a spring. On this occasion our progress up the hill was punctuated by a series of deafening reports whenever engine revolutions approached their peak. I diagnosed that this could only be due to the return springs being too weak, thus causing the ignition points to flutter. So when we returned to the paddock and were asked by admiring spectators to explain these alarming explosions, we answered tersely: 'plug bounce',[1] a reply that sent the inquirers away completely baffled and unsure whether we were mad or whether their legs were being pulled.

Sam's father at this time owned and drove a 1910 Fafnir and it was this driver/car combination which is said to have started

---

[1] For the benefit of the layman, it is the valves of an engine that normally flutter at high speed if their return springs are too weak, a malady commonly referred to as valve bounce.

the Edwardian[1] car movement in the Vintage Club. This may have been so, but it is equally true that Sam and his Itala popularised a movement that his father began and in a very short time the Club could field an impressive array of Edwardian cars. There was Anthony Heal in the big Fiat, the Itala's closest rival, Dick Nash's 15½-litre Lorraine-Dietrich *Vieux Charles Trois* and Eric Giles's famous 1913 5-litre Bugatti *Black Bess*.

In some of these additions, John Passini and I were directly concerned. Just where we managed to acquire a 1907 Renault 'forty-five' racing car I cannot now remember, but we sold it to one Anthony Mills of Offchurch, near Leamington, agreeing to take his two cylinder 1905 Renault in part exchange. Anthony drove down to the Phoenix one Saturday in the little Renault and, on the following day, departed for Leamington in the 'forty-five', obviously well satisfied with what was surely one of the more remarkable part-exchange deals. The big Renault subsequently appeared in a number of early Vintage events.

One of our customers, an R.A.F. Squadron Leader whose name I have forgotten, owned two desirable motor cars, a DISS Delage with boat-decked body and a very unusual 3-litre Belgian S.A.V.A. of 1914. We were instrumental in selling the latter car to an early Club member named Aubrey Birks. Aubrey became a particular friend of mine who, alas, failed to survive the war. In 1939 he joined the mercantile marine and became a member of the crew of a petrol tanker which, as a result of enemy action, was subsequently lost with all hands.

One day we discovered that our car-breaking tenants Messrs James and Salmon had acquired for breaking up a 1914 Alfonso Hispano-Suiza. Nowadays it seems inconceivable that, even in the mid 1930s, such a car should come to such an end, but it would undoubtedly have perished had we not purchased it for a song. Having restored it, we sold this car for £35 to the late Forrest Lycett, famous for his exploits in his equally famous 8-litre Bentley,[2] painting the car in his special livery

---

[1] The term 'Edwardian' is not used literally by the Club but is used to define cars built prior to 1918. And since few cars were built in England after 1914, it commonly applies to cars of the pre-first war era.

[2] In 1959, Forrest, at the age of 74, achieved a speed of over 140 m.p.h. for the flying kilometre, driving his 8-litre Bentley on a road near Antwerp.

of black with cerise mudguards. Forrest won the Edwardian class in the first Club event in which he entered the Hispano, although both the driver and ourselves were somewhat dismayed when a wheel flew off the car just as it crossed the finishing line. The hubs all had right-hand threads and the security of the wheels depended on a ratchet locking device in the hub nuts; since this proved to be unreliable, it was subsequently modified.

John and I soon found that, where modern motor cars were concerned, the repair business was dreary and unrewarding work. It was also uneconomic. All routine overhauls of such cars were the subject of standard charges based on the use of special tools and equipment as issued to specialist agents and repairers for the particular make concerned. This meant that no small business, relying on skilled hand fitting with the minimum of special equipment, could hope to compete with the specialised service depot. This state of affairs is now commonplace, but it was then a new and novel situation brought about by American methods of mass-production. It meant that, with the exception of a few modern cars belonging to regular local customers, our work became increasingly concentrated on veteran and vintage cars, or on those few high quality equivalents which continued in limited production throughout the 1930s. In the latter respect we benefited from the proximity of the new R.A.F. station at Odiham, with many of its flying officers, owning such cars as Frazer Nash or Aston Martin, becoming our customers.

In addition to the Itala, we had many interesting early cars to work on and in this connection I remember particularly the 1908 single-cylinder Sizaire Naudin and the 1904 Darracq 'flying fifteen', both then owned by Kent Karslake, which were stabled with us for some time. The former was the most wilfully eccentric motor car I have ever driven. It boasted independent front suspension, but in every other respect it was archaic, even by the standards of 1908. It had a design of differential-cum-gearbox on the back-axle of so tortuous a complexity that I will not attempt to describe it. Suffice it to say that, because it always seemed to work while we had the car, we wisely let well alone. It had a quadrant gear change which meant that, assuming the lever was in the top gear position, it was necessary to go through the intermediate gears in order to get back to bottom. Engine speed was controlled by a throttle lever on the steering column which, to the confusion of the driver, constantly changed its position as he turned the steering wheel. Finally, its designers had asserted their lofty independence from the trammels of current convention by placing the clutch pedal on the right and the brake pedal on the left. So instinctive has the orthodox become, that we found that the only safe way to drive the car was with crossed legs; otherwise the wrong pedal was invariably depressed in an emergency. To invite some experienced but unsuspecting driver to try out the Sizaire Naudin provided us with an unfailing source of amusement.

By contrast with the Sizaire, the Darracq was a most advanced car for its date, indeed I regard it as quite the best medium-powered veteran I have ever driven. With a four-cylinder T head engine in a fairly light chassis, by the standards of 1904 it really was a flyer. When we received the Darracq from Kent it had been converted to magneto ignition and the original battery ignition system was out of action. We restored the latter and found that with both systems working together (there was a choice of three sparking plug positions per cylinder) the improvement in performance was quite remarkable.

There was at this time a desperate shortage of suitable—or even unsuitable—courses on which to run speed events. The course at Aston Clinton had been so appallingly rough that it was resolved to find an alternative for the next meeting in July. The country was scoured and finally we succeeded in finding a course right on our doorstep. Sir Denzil and Lady Cope, the then owners of Bramshill House, near Hartley Wintney, agreed to allow us the use of one of their drives. Because this event was held so close to home, the Scuderia Carsoni turned out in force. Tim ran his Special and I my G.N., while John entered our Rolls Royce breakdown truck in the Edwardian class. I also drove the Flying Fifteen Darracq with Aubrey Birks as passenger and the Sizaire was likewise entered.

As may be imagined, there was a record late night session at the Phoenix on the evening following this event. With the Phoenix ablaze with light at midnight and cars being tried out down the road to Odiham, often in a highly illegal condition, it may be wondered what the local police were doing. The answer is that the local constable was not a very zealous policeman in the eyes of his superiors because he made common-sense the yardstick of his conduct rather than the petty, and often absurd, letter of the law. Consequently, evil-doers were his concern, but the sharp eye he kept cocked for the malefactor would become afflicted with blindness when confronted by the technical offender. He was the only policeman I have ever liked and admired; if there were more of his like, England would be more law-abiding than it is today and the police would enjoy better co-operation from the public in their efforts to keep the peace. We kept the garage open late, particularly at week-ends, and often when he was on night duty he would stand airing his bottom before the welcome warmth of our coke stove, gossiping or taking an intelligent interest in the unusual cars that stood around while, clearly observable through the windows, the Phoenix presented an animated scene although it was long after closing time.

In the early autumn of 1935, we retrieved my Humber from its resting place at Maidstone and I entered it in the London to Brighton Run in this and in the three succeeding years. Three times the car made a trouble free run, once with Sam Clutton as my passenger, while John Passini drove Kent Karslake's Darracq. On the fourth occasion, when I was accompanied by Aubrey Birks, we had a bitter struggle against difficulties in pouring rain. One of the rear wheel hubs split, allowing the drive shaft to rotate within it, thus causing a complete cessation of forward motion. By pushing and coasting we got the car to a garage where the hub was temporarily repaired by welding. But alas, this effort was vain for near Bolney crossroads, only twelve miles from Brighton, we came to a standstill once more, this time with ominous sounds of tortured metal coming from the back-axle. When we finally got the car home and dismantled the axle, I found that the differential had disintegrated and had to have a new set of star wheels and spindles made for it. I had never had occasion to dismantle this part of the car before and was amazed by its diminutive size and fragility, the gears resembling clockwork. In theory, one was supposed to maintain the car in precisely original condition, but I made one or two common-sense modifications such as replacing the frail bicycle type ball bearings in the front wheels by plain phosphor-bronze bushes on the model of those used on my G.N.

One morning I was surprised to receive a telephone call from Dursley. It was from the brother-in-law of a girl friend of mine there and I had known him only very slightly. 'Would you like my Vauxhall?' he asked brusquely. Taken aback, I was a little hesitant, whereupon the distant voice said testily: 'I'm not trying to *sell* it to you, it's yours to take away if you want it.' So I set off for Dursley and drove my gift back to Hartley Wintney. It was a rare model known as the 25/70 having a six-cylinder engine with Burt and McCullum single sleeve valves as later fitted to some Bristol aero engines. It represented an unsuccessful attempt on the part of the English Vauxhall company to rival the smaller Rolls Royce in the medium-powered luxury car market. It was, in fact, the company's last expensive fling before it was taken over by General Motors of America. The car was fitted with a beautifully built enclosed landaulette body by Windover and was in perfect condition having had very little use. The reason its owner had decided to give it away was that, after many fruitless attempts to get the brakes to work, he had finally lost patience with it—he was an impulsive man. The car had the same type of hydraulic brakes as were fitted to the later 30/98 Vauxhalls. These brakes looked most impressive and were beautifully engineered, but when they could be made to work they did so extremely erratically, causing the car to swerve on braking, now to one side, now to the other, in a manner that was unpredictable and therefore decidedly unnerving for the driver. Although in our advertisements we boasted that the Phoenix was 'the home of the 30/98 Vauxhall', we were completely defeated by these brakes. When we overhauled a 30/98 of this type, we used to consign the entire front axle assembly to the scrap heap and fit in its stead a Delage front axle with mechanical brakes actuated by a vacuum servo motor. It has now been found that when fitted with modern synthetic seals the original brakes work perfectly. In other words the trouble was entirely due to the porosity of the leather seals which were the only type available before the war.

Unlike the 30/98s which passed through our hands, the 25/70 retained its original front axle and we relied mainly on the handbrake which actuated the shoes on the rear wheels only. We made the car a garage hack, fitting it with a draw-bar to suit a towbar or our car-carrying trailer. This may sound an unkind fate, but in extenuation it must be said that the car, though a rarity, was also something of a white elephant. Although capable of a fair turn of speed, it behaved in a ponderous fashion, its unusual engine emitting a subdued but curious sound like the whirr of a sewing machine. My most memorable experience with the 25/70 Vauxhall began with a telephone call one dark December evening. It was from one of my Vintage Club friends named John Morley. He explained that his 12/60 Alvis had broken down as he was coming down the Great North Road and he had parked it in a wayside garage. Would I drive over to his home near Welwyn, stay the night, and help him tow the Alvis home next day? It was not until I set out to drive to Welwyn in the 25/70, equipped with a tow bar, that I realised that John had not told me, and I had omitted to ask, the precise whereabouts of the car we were to rescue on the morrow. When I learned on arrival that it was at Scotch Corner, I was somewhat disconcerted, as this meant a round trip of something like 300 miles, and I was even more daunted by the prospect when we awoke next morning to find that snow had fallen, snow that became progressively deeper as we proceeded northwards. There were no prompt remedial measures such as gritting or salting in those days, so that the going was decidedly tricky, particularly in a heavy car with effective braking on the rear wheels only. But at least there was very little traffic on the move, such cars or lorries as there were seemed either to have skidded into ditches or to be stationary beside the road. However, the old 25/70 whirred along steadily and we eventually reached Scotch Corner, hitched the Alvis on the towbar, and started the long trek southwards. Approaching Stamford after darkness had fallen it started to snow again heavily. But at least I was in a closed car whereas John was steering an open sports car with no hood and without even the benefit of engine heat. I began to wonder uneasily whether the Alvis would suddenly veer off the road as a sign that its occupant had gone to sleep as people are said to do who fall into snow drifts as a preliminary to freezing to death. But every time I stopped to clear my windscreen of snow I was relieved to see him grinning broadly, looking exactly like an animated snowman. How John managed to survive that long ordeal I do not know. Incidentally he, like me, still owns the same Alvis to this day.

Another memorable experience of these years was the affair of the Captain, the beautiful damsel and the Rolls Royce. The Captain was a car dealer, but no ordinary one. Only thirty-seven miles from London and on a trunk road, we were within the orbit of London car dealers looking for country suckers. Seedy and furtive in appearance, they were so transparently dishonest that we found them rather pathetic. We used to call them the Mews Rats. The only thing the Captain

shared with this fraternity was dishonesty, though his was by
no means transparent. He dealt only in Rolls Royces and
radiated well-bred affluence and bonhomous charm. He was a
very plausible character indeed. He was greatly helped by the
fact that he had cut quite a figure at Brooklands for many
years and in this way had become acquainted with Tim Carson.
He disdained what he regarded as the lesser breeds of motor
car and whenever he was forced to accept one in part exchange
for a Rolls Royce, Tim allowed him to park it in a field behind
our garage. The Captain's taste in women was as extravagant
and exclusive as his taste in cars. Moreover, he demanded
quantity and variety as well as quality. Most week-ends
would find him at stud at his cottage near Camberley. When
planning one of these illicit week-ends he would run his eye
down the trade advertisements for second-hand Rolls Royces
in the motoring papers, pick out the most desirable car, ring
up the dealer concerned, and arrange to take it away for the
week-end 'for demonstration to a client'. His winning ways
were such that he invariably got away with this.

One Monday at noon the Captain swept on to our garage
forecourt driving a magnificent Phantom II Rolls Royce with
a young woman whose beauty and elegance matched the car.
'Dear old boy,' said he in his fruitiest voice, 'I wonder if
you would do me a tremendous favour by driving this car back
to London for me. I have another urgent appointment.' The
opportunity to drive such an opulent carriage was irresistible,
so I agreed and hopped into the back seat without more ado.
I found myself reclining in the comfort of the finest Bedford
cord and surrounded by fittings and what-nots of ivory and
silver. The car, I was given to understand, had been specially
built to the order of some eastern potentate who had never
taken delivery. Perhaps he had been deposed or assassinated.
We drove to the Captain's cottage. 'Go and get your things,
my dear', said he, whereupon he flung himself on his back in the
cockpit with his head beneath the dashboard and I realised that
he was reconnecting the speedometer drive cable. Thus the
car would not divulge the true mileage it had covered in his
hands. When he had completed this task and emerged looking
more red in the face than usual, his companion came tripping
down the path from the cottage carrying a small week-end
case. It was at this moment that I realised that I was not only
to return the car but the lady as well. He gave me the address of
a large and well-known firm of Rolls Royce agents in west

London to whom I was to deliver the car. 'But what about your friend?' I inquired. 'Oh, don't you worry about her', he replied, 'I'll fix all that.' So, somewhat mystified, I headed the Phantom II towards London.

I enjoyed that drive. John and I each drew a salary of only £3 a week from the business, so I also enjoyed the experience of masquerading for a brief hour as a rich and fortunate tycoon. I exchanged few words with my passenger beyond asking if I could drive her to her home. 'Oh no, thank you,' was her response, 'the garage will do', a reply which I found slightly disquieting. As we rolled silently to a standstill at traffic lights on the Great West Road I found myself gazing down with an air of remote disdain at the little cars drawn up beside me, receiving in return envious glances that appraised the car and the beautiful woman beside me. It was obvious that, to a world that worshipped material things, we represented the ultimate status symbol; the pipe-dream of every suburban male. Yet if these lesser mortals had only known it I was becoming increasingly apprehensive the nearer we approached our destination. If only I had been told to drop the girl off somewhere before returning the car I should not have been so worried. What would my reception be if I arrived at the agents with her sitting beside me? Surely they would realise that the Captain's 'demonstration' was completely phoney? I began to suspect that I had been had for a mug, that the 'urgent appointment' was a pure fiction and that, by using the bait of a drive on this magnificent vehicle, the Captain had lured me into facing the music instead of himself.

When we eventually drove majestically into the agent's large covered garage I thought for a moment that my worst fears were to be realised. For, on seeing our approach, a man who was standing in the garage turned about and made a hurried bee-line for the office. He is certainly going to phone for the police, I thought, but no; the same individual presently emerged bearing an enormous bouquet of flowers wrapped in cellophane. Opening the car door, he presented these to the lady with a slight bow and a beaming smile. 'With the Captain's compliments', he said. He then ushered her into a waiting taxi, summoned, of course, on instructions from the Captain, in which, with a charming smile and a wave, my fair companion instantly departed. As for me, I might not have existed. No questions were asked and I was left to make my way by public transport to Waterloo. The moral of this story was plain to me.

It was that provided you have sufficient effrontery and *savoir faire* you can get away with murder.

Shortly after this episode, the Captain suddenly disappeared to some unknown destination abroad. No sooner had he performed this vanishing trick than a gloomy business man from Birmingham arrived at the Phoenix and became even gloomier as he surveyed the tired collection of second-hand cars which represented all that the Captain had left behind him. This individual had, it transpired, been induced to invest £5,000 in the Captain's Rolls Royce business of which these cars were now the only remaining asset. He instructed Tim to sell them for what they would fetch, which was not much, and departed a sadder but wiser man.

An altogether more reputable friend of Tim's to whom I took a great liking was Clive Windsor-Richards. Clive was a great 30/98 Vauxhall exponent who owned two of these cars, a special two-seater which he frequently raced at Brooklands— I accompanied him to the Track as mechanic on one occasion— and a rare saloon model which he used regularly on the road. On several occasions Tim, Clive and I attended B.R.D.C. dinners and film shows in London, driving up in the 30/98 saloon. Clive was a fast, fearless and supremely competent driver and these expeditions used to be a little frightening at times, particularly on the Great West Road which then had no central reservation. We used to meet the rush-hour traffic pouring out of London sometimes four or five abreast. On sighting such an approaching phalanx, Clive used to curse under his breath, switch on his big headlamps and drive straight at them. I would shut my eyes at this point, but it was surprising how quickly those cars contrived to scuttle back to their own side of the central white line.

It was with Clive at the wheel that I first experienced a speed of a 100 m.p.h. on the road. This was in a special short chassis 38/250 Mercedes with what was termed the 'elephant' blower on occasion when we were lucky to get a clear road over Hartford Bridge Flats. What with the bellow of the exhaust, the scream of the supercharger and the roar of the wind over the open cock-pit, it was a stirring display of brute force, though by no means so impressive as the sensation of effortless power which one got from a big Edwardian such as the Itala. With this Mercedes, on the contrary, the sense of effort was positively demonic. Nevertheless, this was a memorable experience for although such speeds are now within the capability of quite ordinary saloon cars, in the 1930s, 100 m.p.h. was still a magical figure so far as road cars were concerned.

After one of his trips abroad, we were presented by the racing driver Charles Brackenbury with an unusual firework. Instead of the usual blue touch paper, two thin copper wires emerged from the top of it. We were instructed to position this firework under the bonnet of a car, attach one wire to a plug terminal and the other to earth, and then stand back and watch the effect. We treasured this device for some time before we decided upon a suitable candidate for the experiment. He was the proud owner of a very beautiful 4½-litre Bentley. It was painted British racing green and had little Union Jack emblems on its sides. He used to drive this car down from London at a very sedate speed wearing whiter-than-white racing overalls and white helmet with a similarly attired girl friend seated beside him. Arrived at the Phoenix, he would park the car as conspicuously as possible in front of the door, stroll into the bar and behave in what we thought an insufferably superior fashion. Such conduct, we decided, was not in the true spirit of the V.S.C.C. so, on one occasion when this individual was holding forth in the bar, John and I duly fixed our infernal device beneath the bonnet of the Bentley. We then joined the admiring throng inside who had been informed privily that some mischief was afoot. When he announced his departure, our friend was obviously flattered by the fact that everyone trooped out to see him off. He and his girl friend clambered into the cockpit. He adjusted his helmet with care, drew on his string-backed racing gloves and pressed the starter button. Immediately there was a tremendous report followed by a strange whistling sound, while thick black smoke seeped out through the bonnet louvres. This whistling noise continued for some time while the occupants of the car sat wide-eyed and petrified. Then there was a second loud bang and silence. It was some time before the owner could be persuaded to open the bonnet, such was his fear of the ruin that would be revealed. This despite the fact that no internal combustion engine could ever produce a succession of noises so farcical that it was extremely difficult to maintain an expression of suitable gravity. Our victim took the point; he abandoned his ostentatious ways and afterwards became a valued member of the club.

In 1935, accompanied by Tim Carson, I paid my first visit

to France to see the Circuit de Dieppe. The last motor race to be run on that circuit, Alfa Romeos of the Scuderia Ferrari filled the first two places in the hands of Chiron and Dreyfus. Tim and I also went to see the 1937 Donnington Grand Prix in which the German Mercedes and Auto Union racing cars competed. All who were fortunate enough to see this race agree that it was the most spectacular and thrilling motoring event ever to be organised in this country. Certainly it was an experience which I shall never forget. It was chiefly made memorable for me by the inspired driving of the winner, that legendary figure Tazio Nuvolari driving an Auto Union, a car that was comparatively strange to him and was obviously a handful. To see the Donnington course today and compare it with the racing circuits currently in use is to marvel that such powerful cars, developing over 600 h.p., could ever have raced each other on such a narrow and twisting road so beset with hazards. Modern racing cars may be faster, largely due to incomparably better handling and road holding, but the sheer power of these German monsters and the skill required to control them made a spectacle which can never be surpassed.

At this time the lack of suitable courses on which to stage speed events continued to exercise the minds of the members of the V.S.C.C. Bramshill was a 'once only' event and the next meetings were held on a flat stretch of new 'unadopted' concrete road which had been constructed to serve a new housing estate at Littlestone-on-Sea. All the courses we had so far used had been more or less flat and therefore rather dull. What the new club really needed was a speed hill climb course like Shelsley Walsh. But we could not use Shelsley because it was the exclusive preserve of the Midlands Automobile Club. In this dilemma I bethought me of the drive up to Prescott House, only a mile away from my home. Some years before, this house had been owned by an elderly couple named Royds who were friends of my parents and I had welcomed any excuse to visit them in my G.N. because motoring up their drive was such an exciting exercise. The house stood high on a hillside above the public road and its approach drive wound this way and that in order to ease the gradient for the horse carriages for which it had been designed. It included one hairpin bend so acute that it could not be negotiated on one lock and I used to get my G.N. round by sliding the tail, a process made much easier by the absence of a differential combined with a loose and dusty surface. In view of the fact that this and other corners were made completely blind by dense shrubberies, it was perhaps fortunate that the Royds owned no car and that, in this part of Gloucestershire, tradesmen's delivery vans were extremely rare. Otherwise these sporting ascents might have been marred by some disconcerting confrontations.

Early in 1937 I learnt that Prescott House was empty and that the estate had been bought as a speculation by the Gloucestershire Dairy Company of Cheltenham. This seemed to bring the prospect of acquiring Prescott for a speed hill-climb within the bounds of possibility, so one fine Sunday morning after the May Shelsley meeting I led a small party thither which included Forrest Lycett, Sam Clutton and Tim Carson. After they had driven up the hill in their several cars, they pronounced it distinctly promising provided it could be widened and resurfaced.

While Sam Clutton and Kent Karslake investigated the possibility of floating a company to acquire the property on behalf of the Club, I obtained an estimate for the necessary work on the road from a Mr Stokes of the Beaufort Quarries in Dean Forest with whom I had been put in touch by my friend Mark Newth. Mr Stokes was enthusiastic about the project and his estimate was extremely reasonable. So far, so good, but it was reluctantly though wisely decided that the scheme was too ambitious for a small and youthful club to undertake. It was Sam Clutton who saved the day. He knew that the wealthier and more established Bugatti Owners Club were as dissatisfied as we were with Aston Clinton and were looking for some other course to take its place. He proposed that he should divulge our Prescott scheme to Eric Giles of the B.O.C. on condition that, if his Club brought it to fruition, the V.S.C.C. would be permitted to hold one meeting a year on the new hill. This was agreed by the committee of the V.S.C.C., which used to meet in Forrest Lycett's house in London and of which I was then a member. Things now began to move fast. In August I received a letter from Eric Giles and put him in touch with Holborow of the Gloucestershire Dairy Company and with Stokes of the Beaufort Quarries. Eric Giles and his brother bought the estate on behalf of the B.O.C. and the Beaufort Quarry Company set to work on the hill to such purpose that by the following spring it was ready for racing. A small informal party was held to celebrate the opening of Prescott at which those present were each allowed to make a timed ascent of the hill. Many of the drivers and cars who took part in this celebration are now no more, but it is interesting that three drivers are still driving the same cars today that they drove then. They are Sam Clutton, Itala; Ronnie Symondson, Bugatti and myself in my 12/50 Alvis.

Meanwhile, John and I decided to build a special sprint car more worthy of the Phoenix Green Garage than my old G.N. Like all good 'special' builders at this time, we made no working drawings, though I did go so far as to produce a general outline of the proposed car on a drawing board, re-shaping it by eye until I judged that it 'looked right'. This 'Phoenix Special' consisted of the rear half of my G.N. married to the front half of a Bugatti. It was fitted with a 1½-litre Brescia Bugatti engine supercharged at 20 lbs p.s.i. by a large Roots blower and running on dope fuel. We took crude but effective precautions to prevent the cylinder block from being blown off the crankcase as a result of the excessive pressure generated within. We designed and built the car entirely ourselves, the only exception being the single-seater bodywork. We made the light metal framework for this but prevailed upon two professional panel beaters from Windovers to come and fill in the spaces with light aluminium sheeting. The way those craftsmen shaped the curving panels of the tail was a joy to watch. The finished article was no string-and-sealing-wax special but, for the period, a very business-like looking racing car. It was painted black and it bore on its front cowling our badge of the phoenix rising from the flames. Unfortunately, however, it did not fulfil the promise of its looks although it might have done so had not the war supervened. As it was, its racing career was extremely brief. Our garage was commandeered during the war and not surprisingly, by the time it was over, the Phoenix Special, which had been stored in the paint shop under lock and key, had disappeared without trace.

To have run such a car on the road at Hartley Wintney would have been too much even for the accommodating local constable, so it was completely untried when it made its début at Prescott. On my first practice run, I left the starting line in an exhilarating burst of acceleration and torrent of sound. But gratification soon turned to despair when, after covering a mere fifty yards, the engine suddenly cut out completely and there was a humiliating silence. The car was coasting to a standstill when my head was jerked back as the engine suddenly burst into full song once more. Then it fell silent again and so I proceeded up the hill in a series of fits and starts. The explanation was simple. Running on dope fuel, the car needed an excessively large main jet in the carburettor. This jet was actually larger than the aperture of the needle valve which admitted fuel to the carburettor float chamber. Consequently, the engine took one large gulp of fuel and then waited for the float chamber to fill up again, just as one waits impatiently for some tardy lavatory cistern to refill after it has been flushed. Testing the engine on the bench under a light throttle, this elementary fault had never manifested itself.

This defect was easily cured, but there were other troubles of a much more fundamental kind. The rear half of my old G.N. strongly resented the unprecedented amount of power it was asked by the front half to transmit. The back axle whipped alarmingly, particularly when getting away from the starting line, and this caused the driving chains to ride up on the sprockets with a most disquieting ticking sound. We fitted heavier and stronger chains, but in vain. What was really needed was a central bearing on the axle. Although we subsequently ran the car at Prescott as well as at Lewes and Poole, I don't think I ever crossed a finishing line without disgorging a broken chain somewhere on the course, thus depriving me of one or other vital gear ratio. Moreover, that ominous sound of protesting chains from the rear made me instinctively ease my foot from the throttle. Thus, from memory, the best time the car ever made at Prescott was in the region of 54 seconds, whereas the record for the hill was already well down into the forties. Nevertheless, despite this serious fault, which we could have overcome had time allowed, the Phoenix Special was immensely satisfying to drive. It was the first really potent car I had driven, it handled beautifully and, because we had designed and built it ourselves, it was the source of more satisfaction to me than any 'off the peg' racing car, however fierce, could ever have been. Nowadays, when Prescott Hill climb is as renowned as Shelsley Walsh and earnest young men in full racing fig drive up the hill at dizzy velocity with immense expertise, I look back with a certain nostalgia to those happy-go-lucky, regulation-free days before the war when one jumped into a car and drove up the hill without even bothering to put on a pair of goggles, let alone a crash helmet.

This account of life at the Phoenix Green Garage must

suggest that it was all play and very little work. This was very far from the case. The garage was open long hours for seven days of the week and at one time we tried the experiment of remaining open day and night. As we only employed one mechanic for most of the time, John and I could never leave the garage together but took it in turns to attend Vintage events and other spare-time activities. Though we did much work that was interesting, there was a lot of pretty dull routine work to be got through as well. For example, I took it upon myself to keep the books and send out the monthly accounts, a task I found most uncongenial and one calling for great self-discipline, particularly when there were interesting things going on in the yard outside the little office.

We learned a great deal about the seamier side of garage life. Very soon after we set up in business, a chauffeur-driven car belonging to an elderly local lady drew up at our petrol pumps. The chauffeur asked for four gallons, saying in a lordly fashion that he always got his petrol here and that when he asked for four gallons we should book six to his mistress and split the ill-gotten gain with him. When told in no uncertain terms that he had come to the wrong shop, he strode away in high dudgeon, vowing he would take his business elsewhere. Fortunately for us, however, he got the sack shortly afterwards and the business returned to us, though whether his employer had found him out we never knew for certain.

Getting in the accounts was another constant worry. The local farmers, I am sorry to say, were the worst payers. One of these offenders, when at last he did pay up, used to delight in knocking off the odd shillings and pence from the account. I must confess that if this customer's account amounted to— say— £12 18s. 6d. I would contrive to increase it by one pound. Thus he was given the pleasure of knocking off 18s. 6d, little knowing that he was making a payment that was slightly over the odds. Nevertheless, despite gruelling work and long hours, despite the fact that we failed to make money, our accountant warning us each year that we were under capitalised and were what he termed 'over trading', on the whole these were happy and memorable years. Best of all, they brought me many friendships which I have valued ever since.

Chapter 12

Anna

THE previous chapter may have given the impression that from the moment I first visited the Phoenix in the early spring of 1934 my mind became totally absorbed by motor cars. Although the Phoenix Green Garage and the V.S.C.C. activities that were closely associated with it certainly claimed the lion's share of my time, this was not so. Throughout my life I have admired people of catholic taste and liberal intellect and have felt a strange antipathy towards any specialist, even though he might be capable of doing some one thing superlatively well. Only the discovery that a specialist was what I may term a bridge-builder, that he took an intelligent interest in subjects or skills that appeared to be divorced from, or only remotely connected with, his specialism, could induce me wholeheartedly to admire his particular expertise. Such discoveries of unexpected diversity, either in people themselves or in their writings, have always been a particular source of delight to me. In short, I have always abhorred the one-track mind and have therefore instinctively resisted any tendency to become one-track minded myself. One of the few remembered books from my childhood, Robert Louis Stevenson's *A Child's Garden of Verses*, contains the little jingle:

> 'The world is so full of a number of things
> I'm sure we should all be as happy as kings'.

It has always stayed in my mind. I think these simple lines contain a truth which, later in my life, I was to find much more profoundly and eloquently expressed by Thomas Traherne in the *Centuries*. Traherne resolved to spend his life in search of happiness, but the modern world has changed the meaning of that word. What Stevenson and Traherne meant was a purposeful quest for felicity and not an aimless, hedonistic and, in the last analysis, fruitless pursuit of pleasure. The world is so filled with riches and life is so brief that to spend it locked away in one small compartment has always seemed to me criminal folly.

In a world of professionalism, a world that venerates specialists who know more and more about less and less, this is an unfashionable view. Consequently I am often regarded as a Jack-of-all-trades with the inevitable uncomplimentary corollary. Also, because I tend to veer away from any interest once I feel there is a risk of its becoming obsessive, or so demanding as to threaten the overthrow of my mental balance, I am sometimes thought a mere dilettante lacking purpose and tenacity. This has never worried me very much. For I believe that no worldly interest should gain such power over a man that he has not the strength of mind to break free from it. Such an inability is often egotistical. An undertaking begun out of a genuinely disinterested concern can all too easily become, by insensible degrees, a little dunghill on which we delight to crow and flap our wings. The individual identifies himself with the project and his unwillingness to step down in favour of others becomes no longer a matter of selfless concern, but is due to a reluctance to forgo the petty sense of power and authority which he feels he has acquired. Too often in this imperfect world, human organisations founded with the worthiest aims become little empires for frustrated egos.

Happily, as I stressed in the last chapter, the Vintage Sports Car Club has never taken this sorry course, perhaps because of the breadth of mind of its members. Nevertheless, most of those members did not live with motor cars to the extent that I did, so that I felt an urgent need for diversity to restore the balance.

In another way the impression created by the last chapter may be misleading. For, if the truth be told, I found the ambience of the Phoenix in some ways strangely disturbing. So close to London and bordering the great trunk road to the west of England, the immediate district was to my mind, neither true town nor true country but a mixture of both that I found wholly uncongenial. From the scrub oaks on the common land not a hundred yards from our garage, on still nights in early summer there would come the sound of a chorus of nightingales. Yet their voices had to compete against the fretful roar of cars and lorries. For already the A30 was carrying a volume of traffic that far exceeded its capacity, particularly at holiday times. At summer week-ends streams of cars would pour out of London nose to tail like so many lemmings racing for the sea. And because the road was too narrow and most of the cars were small modern saloons with chronic unroadworthiness built into them, there were all too many horrible accidents. Our old Rolls Royce would have to pull the ghastly wrecks apart, looking like crumpled and bloody sardine cans. And meanwhile there would be a hubbub of activity in the brightly lit bars of the Phoenix; a blue haze of cigarette smoke, laughter and the clink of glasses; the mingled voices of men and girls competing with the sound of the radiogram playing Louis Armstrong or Duke Ellington or the latest jazz hit, 'These Foolish Things' or 'Night and Day'. Then, through the open door would come the throaty exhaust note of some car engine starting up and the sickly-sweet smell of Castrol 'R' would come seeping in to mingle with the scarcely less cloying perfume of the women.

All this added up to something feverish and fretful, it had an ominous quality which used to fill me with foreboding. Such a hectic party must surely be followed by some dreadful morning after. For this was the period of the rise of the great dictators and although I never had the time or the inclination to read the newspapers, like everyone else, I could not fail to be conscious of the ominous thunder clouds that were gathering over Europe however much we tried to reassure ourselves that such a storm would never break. A verse of *1919*, one of my favourite poems by Yeats, used often to be running in my mind at this time:

> 'Now days are dragon-ridden, the nightmare
> Rides upon sleep: a drunken soldiery
> Can leave the mother, murdered at her door,
> To crawl in her own blood, and go scot-free;
> The night can sweat with terror as before
> We pieced our thoughts into philosophy,
> And planned to bring the world under a rule,
> Who are but weasels fighting in a hole.'

But it was not only in Europe that signs of coming storm were appearing. In reaction against a Conservative 'establishment' most of the intellectual young men of my generation held decidedly left-wing views. Several whom I knew went to Spain to join the International Brigade in its fight against

Franco and one of them never returned. On the other hand, the second mechanic whom we engaged latterly, a pleasant, open-faced farmer's son from Dorset, was a member of the British Union of Fascists. He had been lured by the B.U.F.'s specious agricultural policy, a hook baited to catch such honest but simple men as he, and he proudly wore his Union badge of an encircled lightning flash. In the lunch hour, we would find him sitting on the bench reading *Action* and occasionally, when he went off to London of an evening to police some B.U.F. meeting, we used to tease him unmercifully. 'Got your rubber truncheon?', we would ask and, as he drove off, we would shout 'Heil!', click our heels and give him the Fascist salute. His response to this light-hearted badinage was frightening. His normally placid and kindly face would harden and his eyes blaze with anger. It was indeed no laughing matter.

For my part, I had no time for politics, extreme or moderate, left or right. It was not that I was indifferent but rather that, to my way of thinking, the policies of both left and right appeared equally inadequate and misguided. For a brief period at Stoke-on-Trent I had held Socialist views, but experience had soon disabused my mind on that score. Now, whenever politicians spoke of 'the workers' or 'the working class' I would remember the fate of those men who had worked beside me at Kerr Stuarts. With the alarmingly rapid growth of big business—the motor industry was only one example—the increasingly impersonal and powerful commercial world of the 'right' was robbing such men of their only real asset and source of true satisfaction—their skill—by substituting machines for men in the interests of mass production. This, and many other changes which I deplored, the waste, the ugliness, the deterioration of standards, was coming about because the whole industrial system was increasingly dominated, not by people who understood the men who made its wheels go round, but by economists and accountants. Blinded by figures, they were unable to see that their financial logic made brutal nonsense in human and natural terms when translated into action.

So much for my view of the 'right'. For the apostles of the 'left' I had even less time. For they appeared to think that they had only to take over the commercial machine of the 'right' and operate it in the sacred name of the State and hey presto! all the ills of modern industrial society would disappear. This so-called solution appeared to me to be ridiculously naïve and simplistic and at the same time highly dangerous. I had learned to hate commercial power, but at least, so long as it was divorced from Government, there existed two opposing forces and in that balance of power there seemed to lie what little was left of individual freedom and hope. But let the two amalgamate and the result would be an all powerful State, a monster beyond any individual power to control, a prospect which I dreaded. For it seemed to me that such a State would possess, in a vastly magnified form, all the faults of the huge commercial empire and none of its few remaining virtues. The economist would not be de-throned and the working man would be worse off than before under such a State system. So when Socialists held forth to me about 'the workers', I was not impressed. Some were Oxbridge intellectuals whose heads were filled with abstract political theory and dogma yet were completely ignorant of the class they claimed to champion, having never dirtied their hands or eaten fish and chips out of a newspaper in their lives. Those who had a working class background seemed of that jumped-up sort such as my mates at Kerr Stuarts had despised. Claiming to be plain men speaking for their fellows, they were in fact insufferably arrogant in their dress of brief authority and greedy for power. My arch enemy was that 'funding system' which William Cobbett hated and my views at this time were a mixture of old-fashioned radicalism, distributism and social-credit.

I managed to do quite a lot of reading although the demands of the garage were such that most of it had to be done in bed at night. Among the books that impressed and influenced me were H. J. Massingham's *Shepherd's Country*, which my mother had given me, and Aldous Huxley's *Brave New World*. Massingham's book is an elegy on the traditional rural culture of the Cotswold country, then perishing under the brutal impact of an urban and industrial society and now quite dead. It so impressed me that I read all his subsequent books. Massingham, who was later to become my friend, was fair game for those who believed in a technological utopia because he was inclined to overstate his case. Yet he continued to make that case to the end of his life with passionate eloquence and conviction and, had he lived, he would have found that the present confirmed his gloomiest predictions. At least Massingham was in a class apart from those authors of cosy country books who wrote as though there had never been an Industrial Revolution and the English countryside was the same as it had always been. For this 'There'll always be an England' school I felt nothing but contempt. As for *Brave New World*, I thought it quite brilliant. It seemed to me to portray the kind of future to which I felt that industrial man was heading. Of all the prose writers of the period, it was Huxley who most appealed to me. He revealed in his writing precisely the type of wide-ranging liberal intellect that I most admired and which I felt that an over-specialised age so sorely needed. When his *Ends and Means* was published in 1938 I at once procured a copy and found it equally stimulating and thought-provoking. Unlike other artists and intellectuals, Huxley did not subscribe to any facile political dogma, nor did he run away from the crucial problems posed by the march of science and technology by pursuing art for art's sake. I was later to admire the work of Arthur Koestler for the same reason. The Severn novels of Francis Brett Young were the only works of fiction which I remember reading with great pleasure, partly because they were set in country that I knew well and emphasised the contrast between the Black Country and the familiar landscape of the Welsh Border. They were weak in characterisation, but I thought, and still think, that his descriptions of landscape, of weather and season are masterly evocations. Brett Young obviously had a deep love and understanding for the country he described, otherwise he could never have distilled its essential quality and beauty so faithfully. Because technology has now alienated us from a natural world whose beauty and diversity it is rapidly obliterating, regional writing of this order no longer exists because it is no longer possible. They cannot write about Eden who have never experienced it.

One of my ex-school friends, visiting the ballet for the first time and asked what he thought about it, replied: 'Oh it was just a lot of bloody pansy boys with gold tits prancing about.' I, too, was not untouched by this characteristically Philistine attitude to the arts which a public school education had engendered. All artistic activities were considered 'cissy' and to indulge in them was something almost as shameful as masturbation. Thus my own attitude to the arts at the time I went to the garage was a curious love-hate relationship, ambivalent and even hypocritical. I still delighted in poetry, but I read it secretly in my room at night and divulged this activity to no one. My partner John Passini was of mixed English and Austrian parentage and had spent his youth in Vienna. With this background, he had no such inhibitions and was a frank devotee of classical music, opera and ballet. He used to play classical records on the radiogram in our cottage of an evening. He particularly admired the music of Stravinsky and now that I fully share that admiration it seems extraordinary that his record of the *Firebird* should have seemed to me then no more than a discordant and incomprehensible noise. I suppose this was because I subconsciously resisted any attempt to understand or appreciate it. John often went to the opera at Covent Garden and when Colonel de Basil brought the Russian Ballet company to London it drew him as surely as a magnet and I was left in charge of the garage night after night. I did not resent this; let him indulge his odd whim, I thought, though now I bitterly regret a lost opportunity. But this inhibited resistance to the arts was soon to be broken down with far-reaching results. The agent of this change was a woman whom I will call Anna with whom I had an affair at this time.

Although my association with Anna was of comparatively brief duration, when I look back on the first thirty years of my life I can think of no single person other than Kyrle Willans who had a greater influence upon its course than she did. In many ways she was a most remarkable woman, unforgettable both in appearance and personality. Although she was small and slight she had that mysteriously magnetic quality which, for want of a better word, we call presence. She was not in any way ostentatious and yet one sensed the moment she entered some crowded room that everyone present, women as well as men, had become instantly aware of her. This quality was the more remarkable because, although she carried her head proudly, almost arrogantly, and all her movements were naturally graceful, she was not beautiful in any conventional sense. She had high and prominent cheekbones, her dark hair was Eton-cropped, which lent her a boyish appearance, and although she had fine eyes, dark and expressive, her mouth and chin were ugly. Yet somehow these defective features, by eliminating any suggestion of mere prettiness, added great character to her face. She possessed the most beautiful hands. Small and long-fingered but capable, they were more like miniature man's hands in the way they revealed their bone structure and their veining. Of this last attribute she was not unaware, for she never made the mistake of gilding the lily by loading her fingers or wrists with elaborate jewellery. There was no need for such artifice.

Anna was ten years older than I was and far more sophisticated and worldly-wise. It would be more truthful to say that it was she who had an affair with me rather than I with her, though precisely why she should have picked on me of all people is something that will always remain a mystery to me. I can say this without false modesty for at this time, to anyone of the opposite sex, I must have seemed a very uncouth, gauche, untidy and unattractive young man. By a kind of inverted snobbery with which I was then afflicted it had become almost a point of honour with me not to appear 'smart'; not to betray any sort of pride in my personal appearance. My finger-nails were in perpetual mourning and my hands in-grained as a result of delving in the innards of elderly motor cars. My grease-spotted flannel trousers hung perpetually at half-mast. Like many of the Vintage fraternity in those early days, my pride was reserved for my cars. Had I spared for myself a fraction of the care and attention I lavished on them, my appearance might have been more prepossessing. Moreover, although I had some sexual experience by this time, I was still very much a man's man who found the exclusive company of the opposite sex an almost totally inhibiting embarrassment. Women seemed to me to inhabit a different world in which I could find no area of common interest, and since I have never been capable of carrying on a polite conversation about triviali-ties, in their company I would soon lapse into morose silence. For this, as for my attitude towards the arts, I believe the ethics instilled into me at my public school were responsible.

No closed communities of monks and nuns could have been more strictly segregated than were the boys of Cheltenham College and the girls of the neighbouring ladies college in my day. In the 'pie-jaw' that all boys customarily received from their housemasters on the eve of their confirmation, we were led to believe that sex was something shameful, a purely male indulgence which no 'nice' girl could conceivably enjoy. We were told always to respect and honour such nice girls, remembering the pain and suffering which our own mothers had endured in bringing us into the world. The result was that I left school with the fixed idea that any girl of my own class with whom I might have formed a normal relationship based on common interest and friendship was strictly taboo and un-touchable. Consequently, I sought the company of working-class girls with whom, unlike their menfolk who were my workmates, I could find nothing whatever in common. In these circumstances, physical intimacy seemed just as self-indulgent and shameful as I had been led to suppose it would be and as, indeed, it was. Such encounters used to leave me riddled with guilt.

In my attitude to the arts and to sex, therefore, my school days had tied some pretty complicated and firm knots in my psyche and I am eternally grateful to Anna for the fact that she unravelled them with such complete success. She was bi-sexual and was thus equally attractive to members of either sex. She had a masculine cast of mind which was capable of regarding the foibles and flirtations of her own sex with amused and ironic objectivity. This was the reason, I now believe, why I, who had never felt truly at ease when alone with a woman before, now found her friendship so enriching and enjoyable. I never felt constrained by the so-called 'sex war' but was always perfectly contented and at ease. I was never in love with her nor she with me; it was the absence of this frequently agonising emotional tension that made our friendship so intimate and so free from constraint. Nor was there anything cold-hearted about our physical relationship. In this, apart from a completely uninhibited enjoyment, she was wholly feminine. That a friendship so close should express itself in such a passionate way seemed entirely natural and logical. Anna showed me that, when two people are completely *en rapport* as we were, there can never be any feeling that one partner is using the other merely to gratify an appetite. In this way any sense of shame or guilt I might have felt was effectually exorcised. She also taught me that, given infinite finesse and consideration on both sides, physical love can become itself a form of art and a most subtle means of self-expression and communication. I count myself extremely fortunate to have been taught such lessons by so able a mistress, for the tragedy is that they can so seldom be learnt without causing misery or heartache to others, often inflicting permanent psychological damage in the process.

What was more important in the light of my future, Anna very soon drew the psychological cork which had hitherto bottled up my artistic inclinations. She regarded with amused tolerance the peculiar motoring activities at the Phoenix, particularly the women who were to be found in the bar at week-ends. They had driven down from London with their men-folk in a manner less romantic than that portrayed by Sir Osbert Sitwell, suffering agonies of discomfort from a combination of hard suspension, buffeting wind, exhaust fumes and tearing noise, only to find themselves huddled in a corner of the Phoenix while the men clustered round the bar talking unintelligibly about blowers and compression ratios or laughing uproariously at some strange joke. Anna had little time for all this, though she did come away with me in the Alvis for a brief but memorable holiday one fine September. We stayed at Chipping Campden, motoring to and from Stratford-on-Avon to visit the Memorial Theatre.

School had not only implanted in me the notion that a liking for art was cissy, but had done its best to put me off Shakespeare for good and all. It did this not only by forcing me to learn long passages by heart before I was of an age to appreciate or even understand them but, like the rest of the school, by making me attend compulsory special matinees of Shakespeare at the Cheltenham Opera House. These performances were decidedly second-rate. On one occasion in *King Richard II*, owing to a sudden structural failure backstage during Act III, Scene iii, the unfortunate King, accompanied by the Bishop of Carlisle, abruptly vanished from view behind the plywood walls of Flint Castle with a resounding thud to the evident dismay of Bolingbroke and his retinue. On another, a performance of the *Dream*, the curtain rose to disclose a wood near Athens in which two elderly scene-shifters in shirtsleeves and braces were in the act of setting down, with great deliberation, a rustic bench. Not until the house became convulsed with laughter did they realise that they were discovered. Their reaction was then even more diverting. Such incidents might appeal to a schoolboy's sense of the ridiculous, but they were hardly calculated to encourage an appreciation of Shakespeare.

But now, on this pilgrimage to Stratford with Anna, it was quite otherwise. Apart from the handicap of education, where appreciation for the arts was concerned I was obviously a slow developer and must have reached just the right mental age to be swept away on the tide of the plays' magnificent language. From a pose of affected contempt, I swung to the opposite pole of uncritical admiration and in this euphoric state I was fortunate in my companion. For Anna's interests were centred in literature and the arts and of this world, which was only just opening to me, her knowledge and experience was considerable. This had given her a highly developed critical sense which supplied a wholesome corrective. For a lately converted philistine at large in a new-found world there could have been no more discerning guide. Her taste, reflected in her possessions, was impeccable and she could unerringly detect the second-rate, the meretricious, the sentimental or the banal and demolish all such 'kitsch' with forthright and devastating effect. The ironic mockery with which she punctured the merely pompous or bogus reminded me of Kyrle Willans.

I discovered that in art and literature, Anna always tended to prefer the small and exquisite to the mighty masterpiece; the private to the public voice; the miniature rather than the broad canvas. In literature it was the prose of Sir Thomas Overbury, in music the last quartets of Beethoven. Until I met her I had never heard the last quartets, while all that my school had told me about Sir Thomas was that he had the misfortune to be slowly poisoned in the Tower on the orders of Lady Essex. With such a taste it is not surprising that, much as she loved the plays, Anna should have considered the Sonnets Shakespeare's finest work. They were her favourite reading. She thought that the sonnet, though so seemingly simple, was the most difficult of all poetic forms and Shakespeare the one absolute master of it. Reading the Sonnets in the privacy of my room at Hartley Wintney at night was a revelation; I could understand the reason for Anna's preference. I had never read them before. At school we had only 'done' the history plays and had certainly never heard of the Sonnets—maybe the school authorities considered them improper. The theme that love, like all created things, is born to perish echoed and re-echoed through the poems. This made them seem infinitely poignant to me. What made them great was that Shakespeare never allowed himself to be defeated by such a tragic awareness of the human condition but pitted his art against it with superb, at times almost arrogant, assurance:

> 'And all in war with time for love of you,
> As he takes from you, I engraft you new.'

This seemed to me like a brave man who, before some last desperate and fore-doomed encounter, bids all the trumpets sound.

Another part of my education was to be given the freedom of Anna's small but fine library. Browsing here it was interesting to me (as it always is in other people's libraries) to discover which writers she admitted to her shelves. She collected first editions and I was intrigued to see uncut volumes with reading copies of the same titles arranged on the shelf beside them. No bibliophile myself, and thinking that the whole purpose of a book was to be read, this mystified me. One thing we could share from the very start of our relationship was our admiration for the poetry of W. B. Yeats—Anna herself was Irish born. The poems of his 'Celtic Twilight' period which I had so much admired now seemed too cloying for my taste, too preoccupied with the music of words rather than with their meaning. But as my taste matured, so Yeats' style developed and tautened until it attained a superb, muscular eloquence, a style from which the last ounce of superfluous verbal flesh had with the highest artistry been pared away till every word that remained supported a tremendous weight of meaning. I have on my library shelves the slim first editions of *A Full Moon in March* and *The Herne's Egg* which Anna gave to me at this time. They recall the excitement we both felt as the later poems and plays began to appear.

One reason why I found the company of Anna so intensely stimulating was that her keen sense of humour was combined with an astonishing gift of rapid repartee such as I have never heard equalled. My conversational gifts have always been limited. It is only when I recall a conversation that I think ruefully of some brilliant thing I *might* have said at the time. It is such slow-wittedness that makes us doubt the spontaneity of many of the sayings attributed to such renowned conversationalists as Oscar Wilde. One feels they must have thought them up beforehand and then waited for—or created—an opportunity to lob them into the table talk with suitably devastating effect. But having listened to Anna when she found some opponent worthy of her art, I doubt this. It was the verbal equivalent of watching a first class tennis match.

We used to frequent a certain variety theatre where it was our custom to join the artistes in the theatre bar after the performance. On one of these occasions the star performer was a famous comedian noted for his 'blue' jokes. By the standards of the 1930s, his act was certainly near the bone, but we both thought it both humourless and vulgar. When Anna crossed swords with him in the bar afterwards he was soon reduced to sulky speechlessness, proving that he had no natural wit but merely the ability to put over the lines fed to him. But when, shortly after this, Nervo and Knox visited the same theatre it was quite the reverse. Not only was their act so funny (it included an unforgettable parody of *Spectre de la Rose*) that it reduced us to helpless tears of laughter, but their cross-talk with Anna in the bar afterwards was a brilliant verbal firework display as witty as their act.

Although John and I frequently complained of the amount of traffic on the A30, outside rush-hour periods it was then still possible to cover the 37 miles to the West End in the hour, so Anna and I used to meet in London fairly frequently. She introduced me to an urban society that was then completely foreign to me. Being country-bred and having an ineradicable dislike of crowds, I had never enjoyed London. I felt oppressed by the vast size of it. To me it seemed a great desert, cutting me off from the natural world, and I could understand only too well why Falstaff had babbled of green fields as he lay dying at the Boar's Head in Eastcheap. But although I have never been able to accept Dr Johnson's famous saying that a man who is tired of London is tired of life, at least Anna made me understand what he meant by it.

One of these nights that I spent with Anna in London stands out in memory because that evening King Edward VIII announced his abdication. For those who did not experience it, it is difficult to convey the extraordinary effect which this news had upon the people of London. It made me realise that the monarchy, though shorn of its power, was nevertheless still a most potent force. No news of the unexpected fall of a government could have caused so universal a sense of bewilderment and loss. All London seemed conscious of the fact that the throne was empty and everyone seemed to be discussing the situation. Since we had arranged it beforehand, it was a strangely apposite coincidence that Anna and I should have gone that evening to the play *Charles the King* which dealt with the trial of Charles I. There was an extraordinary moment when the curtain came down. The audience rose to its feet expecting the National Anthem, standing in silence while an embarrassed, whispered colloquy took place between the conductor and the leader of the orchestra. Then the members of the orchestra began to pack up their instruments and the audience, realising that at that moment there was no King for God to save, filed silently out of the theatre.

Sympathy for the King seemed to be almost universal and feeling was running high. We took a taxi from the theatre to the Café Royal where the most extraordinary talk was circulating among the tables. Maybe it was because my head was still full of the play, but it seemed to me to be a Cavalier and Roundhead situation all over again and that it would take only a little more heady drink and even headier talk to set us all marching on Westminster chanting Royalist slogans.

Because Anna could always be sure of finding acquaintances there, we used often to go to the Café Royal. It was then in its original state, an elaborate stage set which had been designed to attract the writers and artists of the English Decadence by reminding them of their beloved Paris of *La Belle Époque*. To the end—and this was so nearly the end—it still retained something of the atmosphere of a raffish and Bohemian club. Although the people occupying the famous red plush seats below the encircling balcony looked very different, one was still reminded of the paintings of Degas, Manet and, above all, Toulouse-Lautrec. There were still one or two striking figures to be seen: Radcliffe Hall in her wide-brimmed Spanish hat; bearded Augustus John looking like a tramp who has been sleeping rough. Nevertheless, with rare exceptions, I realised that these habitués were but pale shadows of those who had frequented the restaurant in former years and I was at once fascinated and repelled by the glitter of this wholly artificial world, a world so foreign to my previous experience. My life at No. 439, London Road, Stoke-on-Trent, or at the Aldbourne foundry might have existed on a different planet; even my present life at the Phoenix seemed completely divorced and remote. I revelled in such diversity. I was not dazzled by this sophisticated London life—far from it—but I relished keenly the piquancy of the contrast it presented.

The companionship of Anna induced in me a sensation of living upon some higher plane of being where all one's faculties become sharpened and so more receptive to the apprehension of the beauty and richness of life. But I remained wary of this sensation as of a too-potent liquor. It was, I believe, such a sensation as Walter Pater had in mind when he wrote that: 'To burn always with this hard, gem-like flame, to maintain this ecstasy, is success in life.' Finding the new industrial society ugly and hostile, the artists of the Decadence, taking their cue from Huysmann, had accepted this delusive philosophy as though it were some sacred canon, seeking refuge, not in the natural world, but in a highly artificial environment where sensation was created to feed imagination. The result had been tragic for, in their vain efforts to keep Pater's 'hard, gem-like flame' alight, they had resorted to drink, to drugs and to sexual debauchery, a desperate course that can lead only to despair. In London in the 'thirties I saw for myself the pitifu end of this road. For most of those who frequented the Café Royal at that time, though highly intelligent, seemed to be either perverts, alcoholics or drug addicts. I used to find this state of affairs infinitely sad and depressing; it seemed such an appalling waste of life and talent. It was also evil.

The one thing that repelled and disturbed me about Anna's milieu was its all-pervading scent of *Fleurs du Mal*. A hint of debauchery may seem wickedly attractive when we encounter it in literature or art. It is present in the writings of Wilde and in the drawings of Beardsley, suggesting that they are old in experience, having tasted forbidden fruit. But debauchery experienced at first-hand is as nauseating as the scent of the Pyrenean lily. For although this flower, when growing en masse, can fill the distant air with sweetness, at close quarters its blossom exhales a sickly stench of rottenness. I used to wonder why Anna failed to notice such a scent until I realised that she could not detect it because she herself was touched by it. Not that she had succumbed to drink or drugs—she had too much natural zest for life for that—but she made no secret of her sexual promiscuity. I was aware that I was regarded with a certain critical interest by her acquaintances as her latest young and bemused capture, nor was I so conceited as to suppose that our relationship was in any way special or different where she was concerned. These things did not seriously trouble me. I was content in the knowledge that, so far as this particular liaison was concerned, I was at the receiving end. For I could give her very little in return for all she gave me in the way of knowledge, experience and, above all, in critical appreciation.

I used to think it sad that Anna did not apply her undoubted talent to some creative purpose. She was certainly working on a biography of Queen Caroline at this time. But 'Poor Queen Caroline is lying about in folders and she'll never get done, poor girl', she wrote, and, so far as I know, she never was. For I think that Anna preferred to expend her gifts, as some spend money, in the encouragement of talent in others and that when this produced results she was as pleased as though they were the product of her own creative effort. She as good as admitted this in a letter to me when she wrote: 'I am incurably experimental, and I like juggling about with other people's brains. Think of the kick I shall get out of it if anything does come of it.' In this case she was referring to my unfinished novel *Strange Vista*.

As though they contained the most outrageous pornography, I had kept the two dog-eared books in which this novel was written most securely hidden from every prying eye. Yet it was not long before Anna had read them. In showing them to her I felt as diffident as I had done when first we had stepped out of our clothes, for the book had not been aimed at the public but had been written under a compulsion to set down on paper my reactions to my experience at Stoke-on-Trent. This analogy between mental and physical intimacy is apt, because I knew my style to be so unpractised and clumsy that, as a means of expressing my feelings, it must surely have seemed to Anna woefully inadequate. In both situations, she must have sensed that the future of our relationship was balanced upon a psychological knife-edge; that I was too conscious of my own shortcomings not to detect the falsity of mere flattery; too serious-minded to accept even the most affectionate ridicule. The merest suspicion of either might have sent me bolting back into my private burrow, never to emerge again so far as she was concerned. So she paid me the sincere compliment of treating me seriously, with an eye to future promise rather than present performance.

Anna read my text thoroughly, making perceptive and constructive critical comments. I realise now that the most conscientious of publisher's readers could not have done the job better. Most of them would never have got beyond the first page. No matter how sharp the criticism may be, nothing can be more encouraging to an aspiring young writer than to find his 'prentice work taken seriously by someone whose opinions he has learned to respect. It must have been at least two years since I had last touched that book, and until now I had never seriously thought of writing for publication. But when, after reading *Strange Vista*, Anna wrote: 'the futility of your doing what you are when you should be writing would be enough to make one weep if one didn't see the necessity behind it', I was made to think again. But aspiring authorship did not mix with running a garage and, despite all Anna's encouragement, *Strange Vista* was eventually relegated to the lumber room. So she never got her kick out of it. But she had implanted in my mind the idea of becoming a writer and so unwittingly plotted my future course for me.

So immersed was I in this new and rewarding relationship that I was content to live from day to day and never paused to think how it would end. Had I been more experienced I would have realised that the end of such an affair is almost invariably anti-climactic and unhappy. Inevitably, friendship cools more rapidly upon one side than upon the other, usually resulting in recriminations so bitter that they can poison the memory of all that has gone before. Anna, older and wiser than I was, did not wait for this melancholy ebb but wrote an abrupt 'finis' to our affair while it was still in full flood. In recollection, it seems as though one day she was there and on the next she had vanished. I would only see her once again, ten years later, and then only very briefly.

I remember that at the time I felt hurt and bewildered that a friendship so intimate could be so summarily broken, but soon I realised how right she was. Shortly before the end, Anna sent me a sequence of four sonnets which she had written about our affair. No one had ever felt inspired to write poetry to me before and I was so absurdly flattered and dazzled by such a compliment that I failed to realise that this was her way of saying thank you and goodbye.

Chapter 13

Design for Living

Although my interest in railways and steam locomotives dwindled almost to vanishing point during the years I spent at the Phoenix Green Garage my interest in canals did not. Excepting only my experiences in Stoke-on-Trent, it was the memory of my voyages in *Cressy* that remained most vividly in my mind. On hot summer days when traffic surged endlessly past the garage and the air was full of the stench of petrol fumes and hot tarmac I would think of *Cressy* gliding along some narrow ribbon of still water between green fields as a traveller in the desert dreams of an oasis.

When my uncle sold *Cressy* after the Kerr Stuart débâcle, I optimistically wrote to Fortune, the Leicester reporter who had bought her, asking him to give me the first refusal should he ever decide to part with her. At that time it seemed highly unlikely that I could ever afford to buy her and equally improbable that her new owner would want to sell in the foreseeable future, since I knew he intended to live aboard with his new wife. However, I had not been at the garage more than eighteen months before I received a sad letter from Fortune. His young wife had died tragically and *Cressy* held so many poignant memories for him that the sooner he could get rid of her the better. Situated as I was, there was nothing I could do about this unexpected offer, but I promptly passed on the news to my uncle Kyrle. Since the Willans family were still living in the West Country far from any navigable waterway, I scarcely expected any action to result but, to my pleasure and surprise, my uncle promptly got in touch with Fortune and agreed to buy *Cressy* back from him. At the first opportunity he travelled up to Leicester accompanied by my cousin Bill and together they worked the boat southwards, leaving her in charge of Frank Nurser at Braunston Boatyard near the junction of the Grand Union and Oxford canals.

A reunion cruise was planned for the autumn and accordingly, in October 1936, Aubrey Birks and I motored from Hartley Wintney to Blisworth on the Grand Union Canal where we found *Cressy* moored with Bill in sole charge. His father had helped him work her down from Braunston but had had to leave, though he hoped to rejoin the boat later. This was the first time I had set eyes on *Cressy* since the steam plant had been taken out and I noticed a number of changes. Both her original bow and stern cabins had been removed. The fact that she was now flush-decked at the bow greatly improved visibility from the little well deck for'ard. One could now sit at ease there and enjoy an uninterrupted view of the canal ahead. To sit thus while the boat glided slowly along, swinging now this way, now that, as she followed the windings of the canal and the green, ever-changing landscape flowed slowly past, was one of the most delightful experiences I have ever known. From that graceful, curving bow ripples fanned out over the still water with only the faintest chuckling sound. Aft, the new cabinwork had been extended over what had once been the steam engine-room while the length at the stern once occupied by the old aft cabin had also been flush decked and was surrounded by a railing. In the middle of this new aft deck sat a Model T Ford engine, mounted in part of its original car chassis and driving the propeller shaft by double roller chains and sprockets. This unorthodox arrangement was a typical example of an ingenious Willans improvisation designed to make virtues out of a necessity. The necessity was to avoid altering the line of the propeller shaft and stern tube. This had been determined by the original steam engine and was too near the keelson to accept any petrol engine if it were mounted in the orthodox position. Its virtues were unfailing reliability and—unlike most marine installations—the complete accessibility of the engine both from the sides and from below. In addition it created ample covered storage space below deck. The famous Model T epicyclic gearbox, less its low gear band, formed a ready-made marine reverse unit. The one disadvantage of this new installation compared with the old steam plant—noise—was minimised by a water-cooled exhaust manifold, the circulating water discharging into the canal through the exhaust pipe.

Aubrey, Bill and I soon cast off and during the next few days we cruised south down the Grand Union Canal, turning aside down the Aylesbury Branch to spend a night at Aylesbury on the way. My uncle Kyrle joined us near Berkhamsted and we proceeded as far south as Cassio Bridge Wharf, Watford, then thronged with timber traffic, where we winded the boat and began our return journey. Aubrey and I disembarked at Blisworth, leaving my uncle and cousin to work *Cressy* back to Braunston. An experience so often recalled in memory and so keenly anticipated often proves disappointing when realised, but in this case there was no anti-climax. To me this slow journeying was just as magical as it had been on that first maiden voyage from Ellesmere that now seemed so long ago. We had left Aylesbury early to rejoin the main line and it was our gliding over the glass-smooth surface of the long, deserted level of the canal through the Vale of Aylesbury on a still and misty autumn morning that stands out in my memory. Apart from an occasional Harvey Taylor boat trading to Aylesbury with coal, there was little traffic on the branch and so remote and lonely did its waters seem that it was difficult to believe that we were in the populous home counties.

It was shortly after this voyage that my uncle decided that Banbury and not Braunston should be *Cressy*'s base. It was planned to move her thither over a week-end and I received a signal at the garage that my help would be welcome. We must have been late away from Braunston on the Saturday, for dusk soon fell and we worked up through the last three locks of the Napton flight in pitch darkness, mooring at the head of the locks resolved to make an early start next morning. We awoke to find a thick fog, but nevertheless we cast off as soon as it was light. This was my first acquaintance with the Oxford canal and I did not then know how incredibly tortuous were the eleven miles of its lonely summit level from the top of Napton locks to Claydon, where the canal begins its descent into the valley of the Cherwell. Even in clear weather, the voyager is apt to lose his sense of direction, so to navigate this wayward summit level for the first time in thick fog was an eerie experience. I felt as though we had lost ourselves in some watery maze and must surely finish where we began. We sounded our horn repeatedly, expecting on every sharp turn and beneath each narrow bridge to see the bluff bows of an oncoming boat looming out of the fog. But we met no other craft in all those eleven winding miles, a fact that increased our sense of complete isolation. However, we eventually reached Claydon, the fog clearing as we locked down the Claydon flight and, just as darkness was falling, we tied up at Tooley's Boatyard,

Banbury. Although I did not realise it at the time, I was to become very familiar with Tooley's Boatyard.

These two canal voyages added substance to an idea which I had been turning over in my mind for some time until it had become a kind of dream of ideal bliss. This was that I should live aboard a boat like *Cressy* and journey slowly about England at will, taking my home with me like a snail. I got busy with pencil and ruler and came to the conclusion that, although the beam of a narrow boat was indeed very narrow, its length of 70 ft. allowed sufficient room for civilised living. As with all such romantic notions, however, there was one very big snag—money. My supply of this was non-existent. How would I earn my living? It was in answer to this question that the seed that Anna had planted in my mind began to sprout. I would live on my boat and write for my living. I was not so naïve and optimistic as to suppose that this solution was as easy as it sounded. I was never taken in by those specious advertisements for correspondence courses promising that I, too, could earn money with my pen. But at least I should be living cheaply with no rent or rates to pay, while writing seemed to be the only occupation which could be reconciled with such a roving existence. It seemed to me to be worth a trial. I decided, wisely I think, that, despite all the help and encouragement which Anna had given me, my novel *Strange Vista* was far too ambitious a bow to draw at the outset of this venture. Instead, I tried my 'prentice hand by writing three short ghost stories, 'The Mine', 'The Cat Returns' and 'New Corner'. The first was based on recollections of a bygone visit to the Snailbeach lead mining district of Shropshire, the second was purely imaginary while 'New Corner' was a motoring variant on the theme of H. R. Wakefield's golfing ghost story 'The Seventeenth Hole at Duncaster'. It was based on Prescott Hill where, by coincidence, a new corner was actually built many years later as described in the story, though happily not with any such dire results. I sent these three tales to a pulp magazine called *Mystery Stories* whose editor rejected the first but accepted the other two, much to my surprise and pleasure. It was a very small beginning, but it gave me quite a thrill to see myself in print for the first time and it made me feel that my new design for living might not be so fanciful after all.

At this time, if the Vintage Sports Car Club attracted a new member it was not long before he or she made a pilgrimage to the Phoenix. Through the long window above our work-bench in the garage which overlooked the inn yard, John and I would inspect these new arrivals and their cars with critical interest. One morning in the late summer of 1937, we were intrigued to see a white Alfa Romeo sweep into the yard, driven by a young girl with blonde hair wearing a white polo-necked sweater. This was my first glimpse of my future wife, Angela. Such a combination of exotic motor-car and beautiful blonde may sound like something out of a James Bond adventure but, so far as the car was concerned, the truth was quite otherwise. For Angela, it appeared, had lately rescued it from the clutches of a well-known scrap dealer at Dorchester in Oxfordshire. It was in that condition which dealers euphemisti-cally describe as 'a runner', meaning that it was just capable of pulling itself off the premises. Anxious to get her new monster on to the road, Angela had carried out a very hurried and superficial face-lift which had included repainting it with what looked like whitewash. However, although it was a tired specimen of a not particularly good car, it was an authentic vintage sports car of the type known as the RLSS of 22/90 h.p. Behind an imposing Vee radiator with its twin Alfa Romeo badges there lurked a large six-cylinder engine with push-rod operated overhead valves, but behind this was a gearbox which was the Achilles heel of the car. The gear ratios were disastrously ill-chosen and it emitted groaning noises reminiscent of some superannuated tramcar ascending a steep gradient.

Although the attraction was mutual so that we saw a lot of each other from that first meeting onwards, I do not know what became of Angela's Alfa. In recollection, it seems as though, having affected our introduction, it discreetly dis-appeared from the scene. It was no great loss for we soon found a far more entertaining toy lying in a scrap yard at Stratton, near Swindon, which Angela purchased for a song. This was a racing Horstman, alleged to be one of the original four cars of that marque to be entered for the JCC 200-mile race at Brooklands in 1921. However, its specification does not seem to tally with descriptions of these four cars, nor with that of the replicas which were built in limited number for sale in 1922. It had a typical light Brooklands aluminium body of the period with a long, pointed, quickly detachable tail and exiguously narrow staggered seats for driver and mechanic. This was mounted on a chassis having ash side-members strengthened with steel flitch plates, cantilever springs all round, no front wheel brakes and cable-and-bobbin steering which was so direct that the lower half of the steering wheel had been dispensed with to provide the driver with a bit more belly room in the cockpit. Power was provided by a side-valve Anzani engine with alloy head and high-lift camshaft. We put the car on the weighbridge at Winchfield station and found it scaled 10½ cwt. with fuel and oil. Angela entered and drove this car in the 1938 Lewes Speed Trials where its performance was mediocre in the extreme despite its light weight. This was not surprising because the Horstman only had a three-speed gearbox, the ratios of which had obviously been chosen, not for sprints, but for circulating the outer circuit at Brooklands at maximum velocity.

I will not bore the reader with the endless minor troubles we experienced with this car, chiefly due to age and neglect. Suffice it to say that Angela and I, taking it in turns to drive, did manage one long trouble-free and unforgettable drive in the Horstman from the Phoenix to Prescott and back. Although, with such a specification it may sound improbable, that little car was an absolute delight to drive. The steering was light and precise, it held the road perfectly and, on the comparatively empty roads of those days we were able to cruise effortlessly at around 70 m.p.h. That this was well within the capability of the car is shown by the fact that the actual 200-mile race car, with a similar Anzani engine, finished fifth at an average speed 82·37 m.p.h.

Angela shared a mews flat in South Kensington with a girl friend named Margot and my visits there became increasingly frequent. In November she came as my passenger in the Brighton Run. This was the last occasion on which I would drive my Humber to Brighton and it was quite the most enjoyable. For once it was a perfect November day, clear and frosty with bright sunshine, and the old car, fully restored to health after its misbehaviour with Aubrey Birks in the previous year, never missed a beat.

In the following spring I mentioned somewhat diffidently to Angela my idea of living on a canal boat and, somewhat to my surprise, she welcomed it enthusiastically. Nevertheless, I felt that we should have a trial run, so to speak, during the coming summer in order to find out whether she liked the idea in practice as much as she did in theory. So I hired for a week a small two-berth cabin cruiser named *Miranda*—she was a converted ship's lifeboat—from her owner who kept her at a mooring on the Warwickshire Avon at the village of Wyre Piddle. This choice of the Avon may seem strange now, but it must be remembered that there were then practically no suitable small boats available for hire on the canals.

The navigation of the Avon between Tewkesbury and Evesham has now been fully restored by the Lower Avon Navigation Trust, but in 1938 it was still the property of the moribund Lower Avon Navigation Company. During that week we were to learn quite a lot about ancient and semi-derelict river navigations. Heading upstream from Wyre in the direction of Evesham, our first surprise came when we sighted Fladbury Navigation Weir[1] ahead. My experience having hitherto been mainly confined to canals, I had never encountered such a thing before. Nor did I realise that this ancient device for raising the level in a river to enable boats to proceed upstream was already a great rarity. The big timber gate set in the masonry weir stood invitingly open so we forged gaily through the gap only to run suddenly and very firmly aground in the middle of the river some thirty yards or so upstream. In this predicament we were wondering what we should do next when we were hailed from a cottage on the Cropthorne bank of the river. A man appeared, rowed across the river in a small boat, closed the weir gate by winding on an ancient, creaking winch, dropped the paddles in the gate and called to us: 'When she floats off, let her drop back and lay her alongside of the weir.' Sure enough, she soon did float off and I came astern as instructed until *Miranda* lay beside the masonry wall. 'Now,' said the man, pointing, 'just you stay where you are until you see the level come up to that bolt on the gate there. Then you'll know there's enough water to float you up to Fladbury Lock.' And, sure enough, he was quite right. Such was our initiation into the gentle—and very slow—art of working navigation weirs.

We passed through Fladbury Lock beside the beautiful mill but were unable to reach Evesham because there was a 'stoppage' at the last lock at Chadbury. Here men were at work patching up the rickety gates so we came about in the river by the tail of the lock and set off downstream to Tewkesbury. There we entered the broader Severn and headed upstream as

---

[1] This weir and its fellow at Pershore have now been removed by the Trust and the river bed deepened.

far as Stourport. It was when we were returning *Miranda* to her mooring at Wyre at the end of a most successful week that we had our second mildly comical adventure on the Avon when we were within sight of our destination. Wyre lock has a curiously wide diamond-shaped chamber. The water level must have dropped since we had passed through it a few days before, travelling downstream, for when we ran in between the open lower gates we went hard aground on the mud in the middle of the lock chamber. Try as we would, we could not get her off so, as there was nobody in sight to help us, there was only one thing for it. Angela, who was more aquatically-minded than I was, stripped and swam for the shore, closed the lower gates and lifted the top paddles. By the time we finally stepped ashore from *Miranda*, Angela was as enthusiastic as I was at the idea of living afloat.

In the December following this voyage in *Miranda*, my career as a garage proprietor came to an end as a result of a financial crisis in our business affairs. Throughout we had suffered from a shortage of working capital, but now the need for it had become imperative. So far we had run the business on an equal footing, but now, whereas John's family were prepared to put up the necessary money, I could not and I decided I would have to pull out. So I said goodbye to the Phoenix Green Garage in January 1939 and returned home. Very soon after, Tim Carson left the Phoenix Hotel to take over the Sarum Hill Garage in Basingstoke and those memorable Phoenix years were definitely over. In any case, they could not have lasted much longer for the days of peace were running out on us. Since the Munich crisis we had felt, like so many others, that we were living on borrowed time. In the event, John joined the Royal Naval Supply Services while his garage was commandeered. Tim joined the R.A.F. and his Sarum Hill Garage was closed for the duration. He had very kindly offered to store my Humber and Angela's Horstman at Sarum Hill, but although the Humber survived the war, the Horstman did not. Like the Phoenix Special, our Rolls Royce and the 25/70 Vauxhall, it vanished without trace as did many another interesting car during the war years.

So far as the Vintage Sports Car Club was concerned, my last activity was to set out for Wales with a friend and fellow Club member named John Swainson to determine a route for a proposed Welsh Rally and Trial to be held in the spring of 1939. We travelled in John's 3-litre Bentley and headed for the Presteigne district of Radnorshire which John knew intimately. It must have been early in the year, for I remember we had to dig the Bentley out of snowdrifts in the narrow Radnorshire lanes. However, we managed to plot a suitable course for a trial and the event was duly held in the spring. It was voted such a success that it was resumed after the war and has since taken place every year.

The Presteigne Rally is now looked upon as something of an institution, not only by the Club but by the people of that little Radnorshire town. The first Rally was notable for the extraordinary feat of John Seth-Smith who, alas, did not survive the war. He had become the proud owner of Kent Karslake's Sizaire-Naudin, which I described in a preceding chapter, and he drove this car single-handed 180 miles from Chelmsford to Presteigne and back again, coping successfully with a succession of dire mechanical derangements en route. Only one who had first-hand experience of this wayward and peculiar vehicle could fully appreciate what this epic drive entailed. It made the Brighton Run seem an easy Sunday potter. After this event I fell completely out of touch with matters motoring and it was not until the summer of 1949 that I became actively concerned in the Club once more and began to renew the friendships I had made in the old Phoenix days which, as a result of the war, by then seemed a world away.

In February or March 1939 I drove over to the Stroud valley to visit my uncle Kyrle who was then working for an engineering firm at Chalford. The purpose of my visit was a momentous one on which my future plans might depend. I knew that *Cressy* was still lying at Tooley's Boatyard, Banbury, and I had come to ask my uncle if he would sell her to me. After a brief discussion he agreed to part with her for £100. This seemed a large sum at the time because it was almost all I possessed, but few young men, contemplating matrimony, can have set up house on so little money. I could hardly believe that I was now the captain of the *Cressy* and that my long cherished plan could be put into execution at last. I drove home in a state of trance, my head buzzing with my plans for converting *Cressy* from a holiday boat into a comfortable permanent home for two people.

In April, I loaded up the boot of the Alvis with such scanty possessions and tools as I had and headed for Banbury, my intention being to camp on board while I carried out the necessary conversion work. Angela and I planned to get married in the summer so there was no time to be lost. I did all the interior conversion work myself, but relied on the willing co-operation of old George Tooley and his two sons, Herbert and George, for such work as had to be done on the hull. As I have written about my own work, the boatyard and the Tooley family very fully elsewhere,[1] it will suffice briefly to describe *Cressy's* accommodation by the time the job was finished, starting at the bow. First of all, opening on to the little foredeck, there was a small dining saloon which I had designed to be readily convertible into a spare two-berth sleeping cabin. Next came the galley with a sink on one side and a cooker on the other. This gave into a large sitting cabin occupying the whole of the midships portion of the boat; its floor was close carpeted and it was equipped with a coal-burning stove, easy chairs and, against the aft bulkhead, built-in bookshelves and a writing desk, this last a most important adjunct in the light of my future activities. This was followed by a double-berth 'state room' or owner's cabin with bedside table, a dressing table and a hanging cupboard. But it was the bathroom with its gleaming copper pipes which opened out of the state room aft that was my chief pride and joy. The bath was mounted high so that it would drain over the side, so I had boxed it in to provide cupboard space underneath it. A wash basin could be hinged down from the cabin side and then slid under the bath taps when required. Opposite the bath was a small independent heating boiler which could provide enough water for a bath in about an hour from lighting up. This installation was supplied with water from a large flat tank on the roof, so designed that it would clear low bridges. When we were at moorings, I used to fill this tank from the canal with a bucket on a line, but when *Cressy* was on the move this could be done from the main engine. For this purpose I had fitted a stop valve on the cooling water outlet. Whenever *Cressy* was passing through a pound where the water was particularly clear, from my position at the tiller I had only to close the valve to divert the water up into the tank. Finally, right aft there was a chemical closet and a small workshop with bench, vice and tool racks from which steps and a hatchway led on to the aft deck. Emptying the chemical closet was the one unpleasant chore and it sometimes posed awkward problems, but I thought then, and still think now,

[1] *Narrow Boat* (1944).

that to fit a yacht type closet discharging solid effluent into a still canal is a disgusting practice.

Apart from small auxiliary electric lights (supplied by the engine dynamo and battery) and the coal stove, all lighting and heating on the boat was by paraffin lamps and stoves. Paraffin is dirty and apt to smell, but I decided that these disadvantages were outweighed by the danger of using gas in the confined space of a boat cabin. The choice of paraffin was also influenced by the fact that one could then buy it in the most remote places, whereas calor gas was by no means so readily available. Such, then, was my design for living.

In my long-abandoned novel, I had attempted to point the contrast between the new urban and industrialised England and that older England whose beauty meant so much to me. It had expressed the conflict between the two sides of my own nature. At the time I wrote the book and for some years thereafter there still existed substantial pockets of rural England where beauty survived substantially unsullied and unpolluted by urban man and where the way of life that had contributed to its beauty, though visibly failing, still possessed sufficient tenacity and strength to give an eloquent meaning to the landscape. In other words, man was still playing his true creative role in the ecology that had produced the beauty. Such a landscape, undefiled by industry, had not yet become either a dormitory for tired city commuters, a pleasure park preserved in the rigor of death, or a wilderness. But what I had wrongly assumed at the time I wrote was that these two worlds, the new and the old, would continue to co-exist. Thus, when the new world came to that apocalyptic end which I had envisaged in my book, my hero and heroine were able to seek refuge in a Welsh Border country very like that with which I was familiar. By the late 1930s, however, such a view had already come to seem almost incredibly short-sighted. For it had become apparent that what I had taken for permanent peaceful co-existence was in fact only a temporary truce enforced by the great trade depression. Now that trade had revived and England was arming herself for war, a war of a less bloody but equally ruthless kind had been resumed against the landscape and the life of rural England.

When I looked back over the first twenty-nine years of my life I realised that the one thing that had solaced and sustained me through every difficulty and disappointment, every black night of the soul, was the loveliness of the English landscape, whether seen in actuality or recalled to the mind's eye. It would remind me of those intimations of beauty and order which had come to me as a child in the Black Mountains.

'Truly there are two worlds. One was made by God, the other by men. That made by God was great and beautiful. Before the Fall it was Adam's joy and the Temple of his Glory. That made by men is a Babel of Confusions: invented riches, pomps and vanities brought in by sin. . . . Leave the one that you may enjoy the other.'

At this time I had not read these words of Thomas Traherne or even heard his name; nor did I believe in God. None the less, I had resolved almost intuitively to obey Traherne's final injunction by enjoying as much of that other world as was left in England before it was finally sullied and destroyed. How to achieve this? My experiences on *Cressy* had seemed to me to supply the perfect answer. Roads could be ruled out at once. The craftsman-built cars in which I had delighted had spawned an ugly crop of mass-produced successors which had become one of the chief agents of destruction. Nor could my other love, the steam locomotive, supply a solution. Even if I would, I could hardly buy myself a steam locomotive and a saloon carriage and trundle round the railway byways of England, stopping where I would. But on the canals and rivers of England we could do just this. They seemed to me then so many secret ways leading into the heart of England, peopled by men who were themselves a part of the English tradition. And at the end of the day there would be no anti-climax, no closing of doors and waiting for the next day, for even in the night time the silence and the solitude would still be with us and we would feel ourselves a part of it. More importantly, perhaps, the canals resolved in an unique way the contradiction in my own nature which worried me increasingly. For they seemed to me the one work of engineering which, so far from con-flicting in any way with the beauties of the natural world, positively enhanced them. This was the thinking that inspired me to work on *Cressy* with almost demonic energy. Like the canals she would journey on, I wanted to make her a thing of beauty inside and out and not a mere aquatic caravan. When she was at last completed and painted I felt well satisfied for, like Cleopatra's barge, she seemed to burn upon the water. But time was running out, though just how fast I could not then know.

'Man proposes, God disposes.' To conceive what one thinks will prove a perfect design for living and to translate such a long dreamed-of conception into reality is itself a form of pride. On this account it is a perilous proceeding. It is tempting providence too far. I still believe in man's free will, but then I held this belief too arrogantly and passionately. One cannot order all things to one's mind. Life is not like that. Even while *Cressy* was building troubles were coming to cloud what I had fondly hoped would be—and might have been—the most idyllic period of my life.

First and foremost there was the growing threat of war. We both hoped against all hope that it would never come, yet knew in our secret hearts that it would. It threw a great question mark, like some dark shadow, over the whole future of our enterprise. The other trouble was the implacable hostility of Angela's father towards our marriage. Looking back on this sorry business, it seems incredible that such a thing could have happened at the end of the fourth decade of the twentieth century. Almost from the outset I had made my parents aware of my attachment to Angela, whereas she continued to keep our association a secret so far as her family were concerned. She loved her mother, but obviously went in terror of her father. I thought such fears exaggerated and was frankly incredulous, but I was soon to learn otherwise.

By 1939, when we had determined to marry during the coming summer, it had become no longer possible to withhold her 'guilty' secret from her parents so, taking her courage in both hands, she told them. The reaction was immediate. I was peremptorily summoned to London to attend a family conference which had been arranged for twelve noon in a private upstairs room at the International Sportsmen's Club. The memory of that dreadful interview remains vividly in my mind. I ascended those stairs with a certain trepidation as may be imagined, but I had too much faith in the goodness of my fellow men to anticipate exactly what lay in store. Angela had driven her mother round from her flat and I arrived to find them already waiting. Angela introduced me and I felt momentarily re-assured for on this, the first and only occasion on which I met her mother, she impressed me as both beautiful and charming. But where was the Great Man? The appointed hour struck and still he did not come. Our desultory conversation faltered and died. In the silence of tense expectancy that followed I noticed that Angela's mother seemed as nervous as we were, her hands restlessly fiddling with her gloves. After waiting in this state of apprehension for about a quarter of an hour (a delay deliberately calculated, I suspect) there was a sound of heavy footsteps approaching rapidly down the corridor, the door was flung open unceremoniously and there in the doorway stood himself, as the Irish would say, regarding the three of us with such a baleful stare that we might have been plotting some assassination or the overthrow of the British Empire. Without addressing a word to us, he turned his head and bawled down the corridor 'Waiter! A double brandy and soda—and quickly!' It is perhaps significant that while I can recall Angela's mother with clarity after all these years, of her father I can remember nothing. Despite his dramatic and unmannerly entry he has become a faceless man in my mind.

When an obsequious waiter had hurried in with his drink and had been dismissed with a curt wave of the hand, the gallant Major (for such he was) seated himself comfortably in a chair, took a deep swig of his brandy and soda and proceeded to berate Angela and myself impartially. What did she think she was doing, a daughter of his, to begin such a shameful liaison with a dirty garage mechanic? As for me, had I the infernal impudence to suppose that he would ever permit someone like myself to marry his daughter? And so on. I am ashamed to say that I came off second-best in this encounter for I was left speechless with amazement—not that speech would have been of any avail. But I reflected ruefully that it was just this sort of ill-mannered arrogance, which is commonly, but wrongly in my experience, attributed to members of the upper classes, that makes people Socialists. In fact, as was true in this case, it is far more commonly a trait of the wealthier middle classes. Angela's mother was far better born than her father. She was an aristocrat, but what she must have thought of such a display, which was as discourteous to her as it was to us, we never knew for she never divulged her true feelings. Like any Victorian wife, she subordinated herself utterly to the will of her husband as head of the household. Later, she paid secret visits to Angela in London and helped her to choose curtain materials for *Cressy*. Such a revelation of sympathy was at once pathetic and heartening, but that was as far as it went. Never, so far as I could discover, did she betray the loyalty she felt she owed to her husband by a single incautious word.

When my parents heard about this frightful interview my

father was furious, not so much on my account as because he felt that the Rolt family honour had been impugned. 'Never heard of the damn feller,' he said testily, 'who the hell does he think he is?' Had our two fathers ever met it would have been a case of Greek meeting Greek, but such a battle royal never took place. My father was over seventy by this time and practically confined to his chair with crippling arthritis which had developed following a fall in the River Usk while he was trout fishing. So my mother, who had not visited London for thirty years and loathed it, very gallantly set off to beard the dragon. This second interview was no better than the first. I never heard the details, but she returned furious, declaring that the Major was the most insufferable man she had ever met.

It was under this heavy cloud of parental disapproval that we went doggedly ahead with our plans. One night, when I was fast asleep on my temporary bunk after a long day's work on *Cressy*, I was awakened by a frantic hammering on the for'ard cabin doors. I stumbled out of bed, switched on a torch, saw that it was the small hours of the morning and, wondering who on earth it could be at such an hour, opened the doors. Angela almost fell into the boat. She was trembling from head to foot and on the edge of hysteria. Realising that we had not been deterred, her father had staged a monumental family row. He had shouted and sworn at her, calling her a whore and a strumpet and finally told her to get out of his house. It sounded exactly like a scene from some Victorian melodrama, except that in Angela's case there was no shameful bundle. But for us, at that time, it was no laughing matter. When she had been shown the door, Angela had jumped straight into her little Fiat and driven desperately through the night to Banbury. It had seemed the only place to go. I managed to console her somehow and she took off for her London flat next morning in somewhat better heart.

In July, we were married at a London registry office with only two people present to act as witnesses, John Swainson and Margot, the girl who had shared Angela's flat. Afterwards, the four of us lunched at the Berkeley before Angela and I set out to drive to Banbury. Inevitably, it all seemed rather furtive and hole-in-the-corner. Angela was scarcely a radiant bride. Her father had seen to that and throughout the years of our marriage he did not for one moment relax his hostility. There was never any possibility of reconciliation. With the wisdom of hindsight I can now see that the fact that our

LANDSCAPE WITH CANALS

Contents

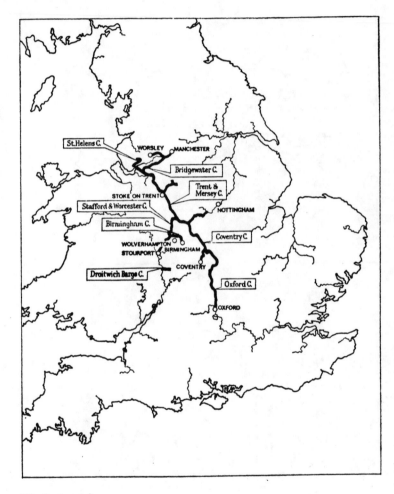

The first canals

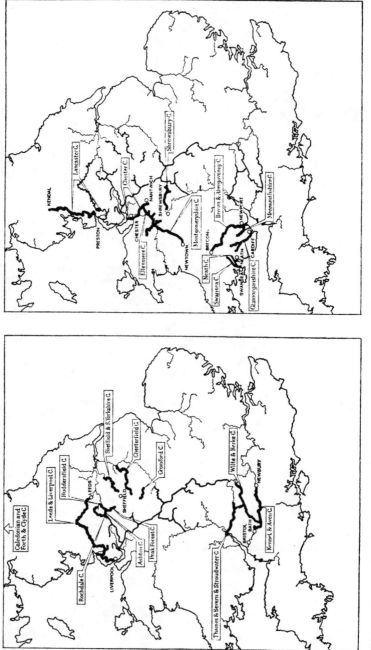

The coast to coast routes

The waterways of the west

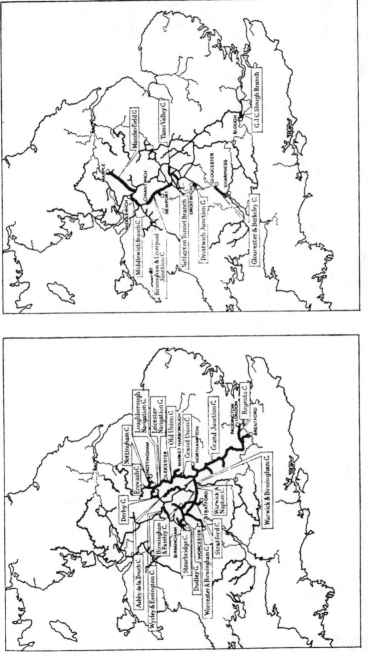

The Midlands network

The last canals

Chapter 1

An Interrupted Honeymoon

August is not the best month to choose for a honeymoon, especially as the year was 1939. Summer suddenly seemed to become over-blown. In the bleached fields, burdened trees stood motionless, their shapes of dark, lack-lustre green resembling those of the threatening cumulus clouds whose heavy froth hung high in the still air above them. The atmosphere was stagnant and oppressive; days had a sullen, brooding quality and the breathless nights, lit only by the flicker of summer lightning, brought no relief. Our minds became curiously disturbed so that we longed for something that would break an almost unbearable tension. Small wonder that it should be a season when accidents and great disasters happen and when wars break out.

Yet a design for living so long dreamed about and finally achieved after so many difficulties was not to be abandoned, no matter how threatening the portents might seem. Angela and I had married in July, and the beginning of August found us heading north up the Leicester section of the Grand Union Canal in our new floating home, the narrow boat *Cressy*. Our ultimate objective, we hoped, was Llangollen, for I planned to fulfil a long cherished ambition by piloting *Cressy* over Telford's great aqueduct of Pont Cysyllte.

It would be wrong to convey the impression that we did not enjoy ourselves, but our happiness was far from unalloyed and my memories of this first voyage are bitter-sweet. The implacable hostility of Angela's father towards our marriage and the growing menace of war were two subjects we never discussed but could not forget. Never to be dispelled, they seemed to

1

hang always, like those thunderclouds, on the horizon of consciousness.

The inland waterways of England are a little world of their own, a world which, in 1939, was but little known and still possessed its own indigenous population of working boatmen and their families, many of whom we had come to know and to admire. It had seemed to us that these narrow waters possessed some magic power to insulate both them and us from the feverish and fretful hurly-burly of the larger world around us. It was this feeling of detachment, so hard to define, which had drawn me to them in the first place and had made the idea of living on a canal boat so attractive for one who aspired to become a writer. But, on this first voyage, the world we had known proved hard to forget or forsake. Disturbing news kept breaking in. As we lay at moorings on the river Soar below Leicester we heard on the radio the news that W. B. Yeats, the poet who, above all others, I most admired, had died at Cap Martin. I could hardly bring myself to believe that he was dead. The very next day we bought a local paper in the village shop at Barrow-on-Soar and read that Sir John Bowen, a recent ex-boy-friend of Angela's who had taken our marriage very hard, had crashed his Maserati during a motor race at Donnington Park and had been killed instantly. Angela was deeply shocked and we both felt in some degree responsible for his death. The news of these two wholly unconnected events added to the growing sense of insecurity and fatality during that doom-laden month. Life had never seemed so disturbingly ephemeral.

It was as we were travelling up the Trent & Mersey Canal towards Burton that the sultry weather broke. Dark thunderclouds rolled steadily up the sky astern, birds ceased their singing and the evening became very still and tense as distant thunder growled and muttered over the Trent valley. We moored up hurriedly near the village of Findern about six o'clock as the first heavy rain drops began to pock the water. The storm raged for over four hours, the roar of the rain on our roof so loud that it almost drowned the crashes of thunder. Yet all this fury seemed to bring no release of tension, for the next morning was overcast and still sultry.

We were approaching Stoke-on-Trent and had stopped to take on some fuel at Trentham Bridge when the boatman at the tiller of an oncoming horse-boat gave us the news that Hitler had invaded Poland. War now seemed to be inevitable, but so long as the slenderest hope remained we could only go forward. That day we passed through the heart of the Potteries, through the pandemonium of the Shelton steelworks and so through the long darkness of the summit tunnel at Harecastle into Cheshire. We moored that night near a canal-side pub called the 'Red Bull' at Lawton and when, after dinner, we went along the towpath for a drink we were surprised to find it in darkness. It was our first experience of the black-out. Two days later we had descended the long flight of locks which leads down from the summit into the Cheshire Plain and were approaching Middlewich when we heard on our radio the solemn voice of Neville Chamberlain announce that Britain had declared war on Germany.

Now the worst that we had feared had happened, what next? After only a few brief weeks, all our hopes and carefully laid plans seemed to lie in ruins. A great question mark hung over our future. Angela burst into tears. I tried to console her by saying that the outbreak of war was not our personal misfortune but involved everyone in similarly agonizing situations, but this was cold comfort. She insisted that our situation was different and she foresaw a bleak future in which either *Cressy* would have to be abandoned or she would be left living alone on the boat, friendless in a strange district.

Our first reaction to such disastrous news as this was to assume that it would immediately cause the whole fabric of life to disintegrate; that every able-bodied man would instantly be called up; that all fuel supplies would dry up forthwith leaving the roads choked with useless cars; that trains would cease to run and even clocks might cease to tell the time as they did before. In fact we were to learn that even in the direst national emergency there is a certain inevitability of gradualness about the way our lives are changed by it. It is the sudden recognition that change must come, rather than change itself, which produces the initial shock. We spent most of the rest of that day somewhat miserably trying to adjust ourselves to a new situation and making plans to meet it. It was obvious that our original objective of Llangollen would have to be abandoned. It was equally obvious – though this was a bitter disappointment to me – that my ambition to become a writer which was part and parcel of our new life must also be abandoned and that I must return to engineering. War had no use for a putative writer, I argued, but every use for an engineer, particularly one who could move house so readily. But how could I remain mobile? Petrol rationing would surely come, and of petrol *Cressy's* engine consumed a gallon every three miles. Already we had travelled 190 miles from our base at Banbury. The only solution to this seemed to be to convert her Ford engine to burn paraffin, remaining moored in Cheshire until the necessary parts arrived. Meanwhile, where in the neighbourhood was I most likely to get myself a job? No sooner had I asked myself this question than I had the answer pat – at the Rolls Royce works at Crewe, where the famous twelve-cylinder Merlin engine which powered the Spitfire and the Hurricane was in production.

So we sailed on from Middlewich to Nantwich, whence I travelled by bus to the Rolls Royce works. As luck would have it, I had found among the few personal documents I had brought to the boat – little thinking I would so soon need them – the 'papers' which proved that I had served my five years' apprenticeship in the shops and testified to my experience and ability. After carefully scrutinizing these and asking me some searching questions, my interviewer at Rolls Royce told me I could start work as a fitter on the following Monday morning, but that I would have to join the Amalgamated Engineering Union. This was my first experience of a 'closed shop'. Instinctively I reacted against such coercion, but I had no option but to comply; and so, for the first and only time in my life, I became the holder of a Union card.

We had thought that the canal basin at Nantwich would be a strategically suitable mooring but we found that, try as we would, we could not get *Cressy* into it. The basin was disused commercially and the traffic on the main line of the Shropshire Union Canal, which at that time was quite considerable, had thrown up an impenetrable bar of mud across the entrance. So we had tied up at an inconvenient mooring out on the main line and now debated what we should do, poring over our ordnance map of the district. On our journey from Middlewich we had passed close by the little village of Church Minshull and had thought how attractive it looked. Now we saw from the map that it was only a short distance by by-roads from the Rolls Royce works. The only snag was that there was no bus service. We should have to be self-sufficient so far as transport was concerned. So I went into Nantwich, where I bought a second-hand bicycle for Angela and for myself an old square tank $2\frac{3}{4}$ h.p. A.J.S. motorcycle for a total outlay of £10. We laid the bicycle on the cabin top and I made a crude wooden cradle which supported the A.J.S. upright on the aft deck. Then, with our road transport safely stowed on board, we 'winded' *Cressy* with difficulty, turning her in the muddy mouth of the basin, and set off back to Church Minshull.

It was over eight years since I had last worked for a large engineering firm and although I realized that changes must have taken place during that time, I assumed that my new job would prove rewarding, so much did I revere the name of Rolls Royce. To me, it was synonymous with engineering craftsmanship. Remembering how I had built diesel engines during my time at R. A. Listers of Dursley, I now imagined myself fitting up Merlin engines from scratch in the same way, afterwards accompanying them to the test bed to ensure that they performed satisfactorily. I was to be sadly disillusioned when I left Church Minshull for Crewe on my elderly motorcycle early on the following Monday morning.

No daylight ever penetrated the big shop. For twenty-four hours a day, mercury vapour lamps blazed overhead. I had never encountered this type of lighting before. It made all my new workmates look as if they were suffering from serious heart or liver complaints; their complexions looked ghastly and their lips were blue. They were working a night-shift at Rolls Royce. Walking from the light and fresh air of an autumn morning into the unnatural glare of this shop, its atmosphere used to hit me like a blow in the face. Warm and stale, it reeked of a nauseating mixture of suds, stale cigarette smoke and sweaty, unwashed humanity. Instead of assembling engines as I had fondly imagined, I found myself tapping the holes for the cylinder-head studs in an endless succession of Merlin cylinder blocks which appeared before me. A jig was first clamped to the block through which the long shank of the tap passed, thus making it impossible to tap the holes crooked and so removing the last vestige of human skill from the work. It struck me as a job which an ape might have been trained to perform, and I reflected wryly on the care with which my credentials had been scrutinized and on the fact that I had been compelled to join a so-called 'craft union' before being assigned this mindless task. Nowadays, such a row of holes would be both drilled and tapped under a giant multi-spindle machine. In fact my monotonous task represented only a brief transitional stage in the process of 'building the skill into the tool', but to me it was a new and disturbing phenomenon. I despair of conveying the depths of boredom and apathy to which this job rapidly reduced me. I even found myself looking forward eagerly to my next visit to the urinal because it relieved the tedium. After such an experience, the strikes that have plagued the engineering industry since the war are no surprise to me. No amount of money can make such durance any less vile.

The contrast between my daytime occupation and the life of the canals to which I returned each evening at dusk was extreme. Then I would see *Cressy*, lying beside the graceful arc of the humped canal bridge, a long dark shape with chinks of golden light showing here and there through gaps in our improvised black-out arrangements. Once I had gained the refuge of this small island of warmth and stillness where the bindings of familiar books glowed in the mellow lamplight, my working days seemed like some bad dream. Not a nightmare exactly, but one of those disquieting dreams which continue to recur despite intervals of wakefulness. What made things so much worse was that we could foresee no end to it; no light at the end of the tunnel; the future could only grow darker.

But deliverance from this bondage arrived unexpectedly in the shape of a letter from my old employer at the village foundry at Aldbourne in Wiltshire where I had last worked in 1933. It had been forwarded to me by my parents. Owing to the wartime 'grow more food' campaign which was then just getting under way, his small business was extremely busy and he was desperately short-handed. Could I come down and help him out? The weekly wage he offered was less than half what I was getting at Rolls Royce, but the answer was an unhesitating Yes. So, after six weeks which had felt like six months, I 'asked for my cards' at Rolls Royce, keeping my Union card and my little RR lapel badge as souvenirs.

Meanwhile, the paraffin vaporizer I had ordered for *Cressy's* Model T Ford engine had arrived and it was a simple matter to fit it in place of the existing water-cooled manifold. Opposite the petrol tank against the aft-bulkhead there was already a twenty-five-gallon paraffin tank in which we stored fuel for lamps and stoves, so it was easy to run a second fuel line from this to the carburettor. We would still need a small amount of petrol for starting and warming up, but apart from this we should now be able to snap our fingers at petrol rationing. Normally, to keep *Cressy* at her stately cruising gait of 3 m.p.h., her engine ran at little more than a fast idling speed, and my one doubt was whether this would be sufficient to keep the manifold hot enough to vaporize the fuel.

We had to make a preliminary trip to Middlewich in order to 'wind' *Cressy* at the junction with the Trent & Mersey Canal below Wardle Lock, for I did not intend to head south by the roundabout route by which we had come. The engine ran perfectly on its new fuel; the exhaust was remarkably clean and a check showed that there was no dilution of the sump oil. In fact, it never gave any trouble throughout the lifetime of the boat, the only minor disadvantage being that, unless I turned over to petrol, the engine had to be kept running in locks.

On 15 November, with the bicycle and the A.J.S. on board, we set sail from Church Minshull, our ultimate destination being Hungerford on the Kennet & Avon Canal. Having served its immediate purpose we were in two minds whether or not to leave the motorcycle behind, but in the event it proved unexpectedly useful as a tender. For example, when we moored for the night at Norbury Junction on the Shropshire Union main line, I unshipped it and rode into Newport to do the week-end's shopping with Angela behind me on the pillion.

That late autumn voyage was wholly pleasurable. The weather was unusually fine for the time of the year, the tension and oppression we had both felt in August seemed to have vanished, and for my part I was delighted to be free once more after my brief spell of servitude. After long days spent at the tiller in the fresh air of autumn, how satisfying it was to tie up in some remote place, to go below, shut the hatches and settle down with a book in an easy chair beside the glowing fire. It was at such times that one savoured most keenly the contrast between the warmth and comfort of our cabin and the silence, the darkness and the loneliness of the world outside. For the long level pounds of the Shropshire Union command a great expanse of open country which rolls away westward to the distant Wrekin; even after darkness had fallen I remained very conscious of this landscape, so clearly was it registered by the mind's eye as the night wind stirred *Cressy* and set her bow nudging the bank.

The first week of December saw us back on the Oxford canal. Winter had set in early and on the last stage of her journey from Cropredy to Banbury, *Cressy* had to cleave a path for herself through the ice which had formed on the canal overnight. I planned to stay at Tooley's Boatyard at Banbury over Christmas while minor repairs were done to our boat; for we should be mooring for an indefinite period on a disused canal where there would be no repair facilities and where we should be far from any dry dock. But our stay at Banbury proved to be far more protracted than I expected. That first winter of the war was hard and bitter. For two months we lay locked fast in ice too thick for any ice-breaker boat to conquer and it was not until 1 March 1940 that we were able to slip our moorings and head south for Oxford and the Thames.

Cressy had never navigated the Thames before and neither had I. Due to the sudden thaw, we found the river was running fast and high, so that it was not without some apprehension that we locked out on to it through Isis Lock at Oxford. In time of flood, one always feels safer in a large and heavy boat when travelling upstream, for however slow one's progress may be as the boat battles against the current, at least it is fully under control because it always has steerage way. In order to maintain steerage way going downstream, however, the boat has to travel at a speed faster than the current. This meant that *Cressy* was soon sweeping down the Thames at a speed of 6 m.p.h. or more which, compared with her stately pace on the canals, seemed a positively dizzy velocity. It was also as alarming a sensation as driving a car without any brakes because I knew that even by putting her hard astern I could not hope to stop her. Fortunately, there were sufficient stretches of slack water at the heads of the lock cuts to enable me to get way off her in time to avoid crashing into the lock gates.

Our first 'moment' came at Abingdon that evening. We asked the lock keeper at Abingdon Lock if he knew of a suitable place to moor and he gave us singularly bad advice by suggesting a small pleasure garden just above Abingdon bridge. I put *Cressy* full astern and held her bow into the bank so that Angela could jump ashore with a line and make it fast to a convenient tree. But we realized too late that the current at this point was running like a mill race. The cotton line parted with a crack like a pistol shot, and *Cressy* swung across the stream until she was in imminent danger of crashing broadside into the piers of the bridge just below. Instantly I threw the reversing lever from full astern to full ahead, swung the rudder over and, a moment later, had shot safely through the arch to find myself sailing swiftly past the old waterfront of Abingdon, leaving Angela stranded on the bank. I doubted whether I would be able to stop the boat single-handed before reaching Culham Lock cut, but fortunately I spotted an individual who looked like a waterman standing on a little jetty close beside the river. I shouted to him, threw him my stern line which he deftly caught, and between us we managed to bring *Cressy* in to the bank. Presently, Angela appeared, walking down the opposite bank of the river, and was ferried across by an obliging boat-man. The moral of this little incident should be obvious to any tyro, but it had not appeared obvious to us I am ashamed to say. It is that when a heavy boat is moving with the current it should always be checked with the stern line and not by the bow.

Another alarming incident occurred next morning as we were sailing rapidly down the broad reach between Wallingford and Cleeve Lock. I suddenly saw to my horror a stout cable, secured to a stake on either bank, lying across the river. As it was almost awash, it had remained invisible until the last moment. *Cressy* stretched that cable like an arrow in a taut bowstring. Then both the stakes tore out of the ground, the cable sank and we floated over safely as I had meanwhile stopped our propeller. Later, when we complained bitterly to the lock keeper at Cleeve about this lethal obstruction, he explained that a Canadian contingent of the Royal Engineers had been practising building pontoon bridges and had obviously gone away without removing their cable. He promised to pass on our complaint to their C.O. It was the first war-time hazard we had encountered.

We reached Reading without any further incident and moored above Blake's Lock on the river Kennet just after noon on 6 March. Ahead of us lay the most difficult part of our long journey, a waterway disused and virtually derelict. The first eighteen miles of it to Newbury was the old Kennet Navigation, built in 1723 and consisting partly of the river Kennet and partly of artificial cuts. For the last lap of our journey, from Newbury to Hungerford, we should be on the Kennet & Avon Canal proper.

The Kennet, like the Thames, was running high, but now we were travelling upstream and there were times when we were only just able to make headway against the current with our engine flat out. Altogether, in those last 27½ miles to Hungerford I think we must have encountered every kind of hazard known to the inland navigator. In the first place, the reach of the Kennet through Reading between Blake's and County Locks was tricky in the extreme. Not only was the river very narrow and tortuous and the current swift, but to make matters worse, the brick walls of buildings rose sheer from the water on either side creating a kind of miniature man-made Grand Canyon. When we had ploughed our way up to County Lock, suffering no more than the odd bump or two, I asked the lock keeper there how on earth horse-drawn boats ever succeeded in making such a passage. 'Oh,' he replied. 'They used to float a long line down to 'em, see.' This is the kind of facile answer which one accepts at the time only to puzzle over later. It could not have been quite as easy as that. And how about travelling downstream? Did they just surrender themselves to the mercy of the current?

Armed with an extra long windlass for raising the rusty lock paddles, we headed for Newbury. I salute the memory of the bygone boatmen of the Kennet & Avon, for the Kennet Navigation might have been deliberately laid out to create the maximum amount of difficulty for the navigator. The downstream entrances to the lock cuts were so positioned that the river would very soon deposit a bar of silt across their mouths. And because most of the locks were sited at the head of these cuts instead of near their tails where they should have been, there was no hope of scouring these shoals away with a flush from the lower gate paddles. We just had to haul over them as best we could. From Burghfield onwards most of the lock chambers were the originals of 1723 with sloping turf sides instead of masonry walls. Guard rails, made from old G.W.R. broad gauge bridge rails, had been installed to prevent boats from settling on to these sloping sides, but this meant that it was very difficult to get on to or off the boat once it was in a chamber. These old locks must have been very slow to fill at the best of times, but now filling had become practically impossible because the amount of water leaking out through the rotten lower gates almost equalled that coming in through the top gate paddles. Fortunately there were plenty of reeds about. We gathered armfuls of them, sinking these bundles in the locks with our long shaft till they had staunched the worst of the leaks in the gates.

The many swing bridges across the waterway caused us even more difficulty than the locks. Some of these carried motor roads and, to prevent heavy traffic damaging the cast-iron ball bearings on which they swung, the left- and right-hand threaded buckles of their bracing rods had been slacked right off until the bridge deck rested solid on its brick abutments. In such cases, the bridge-swinging operation began with the tedious preliminary of tightening up these buckles with a tommy bar. Even when this had been done, however, our troubles were not over, for when the roadway had been resurfaced no attempt had been made to prevent the tarred chippings from fouling the slots between the bridge and its abutments. With half the able-bodied males of the village heaving on crow-bars under the direction of the red-faced landlord of the 'Row Barge' and with *Cressy* going full astern, her bow line fast to a bridge railing post, it took us three hours to open the bridge at Woolhampton.

However, all these obstacles were eventually overcome and at four o'clock on 12 March we tied up at the far end of Wooldridge's Wharf, just below the tail of Hungerford Lock and within striking distance of the foundry at Aldbourne. This pleasant, secluded and convenient mooring in crystal clear water was to be our home for just over twelve months. Beside our boat was an old weather-boarded shed with a tiled roof which contained a saw-pit. Assuming it to be disused, we made use of it as a convenient store shed. But to our surprise, on one occasion not long after we arrived, two men appeared, took the long pitsaw down from its hooks under the rafters, and proceeded to saw a log of timber into planks. Although we watched this operation with fascinated interest, we had no conception then that we were witnessing a spectacle that neither we nor, I suspect, anyone else would ever see again in England. For the last two wars changed all our lives, sweeping away into the limbo of memory a wealth of custom and traditional usages. This is why these wars appear to create rapids in the steady stream of time of a velocity out of all proportion to their actual duration. This has made the time we moored at Hungerford now seem an infinitely remote happening in a bygone age, and the scene of the two sawyers wielding their great saw as poignantly archaic as some medieval illumination.

Chapter 2

From Berkshire to Worcestershire

Before we left Banbury on our honeymoon cruise I had already decided on the subject for my first book – it would be the story of our voyage through the canals. Although I did no writing during the first weeks, with this book in mind I kept a very full log of each day's journey including details of our excursions ashore. All further thought of this project had been laid aside when I took the job at Rolls Royce, but as soon as we decided to move south my sense of relief was such that I took it up again eagerly. Besides keeping my log as fully as ever, I began writing the book itself during the long autumn evenings, sitting at the desk I had built in *Cressy's* cabin. The great spell of frost which immobilized us at Banbury had provided a heaven-sent opportunity for writing, with the result that by the time the thaw came and we could leave Banbury I had completed all but the last chapter or so. I finished it a few weeks after our arrival in Hungerford. There then began that deflating and depressing experience that is the common lot of aspiring authors. Over the next few months my precious manuscript, which I had entitled *A Painted Ship* from the well-known line in *The Ancient Mariner*, must have visited practically every publisher in London. It bounced back with unfailing regularity, sometimes with a polite note, but more usually with a printed rejection slip. Only two publishers, both with famous names, showed a flicker of interest. One undertook to publish the book at my expense, while the other offered me £75 outright for it. So poor was I at this time that the latter offer tempted me sorely, but I had read somewhere some cautionary words warning the tyro against the wicked ways of publishers and, very fortunately, refused. Had it not been for the war which had driven me back into engineering and thus given me another source of livelihood, I might well have accepted the tempting bait of that £75 down for the sake of getting my name into print. So, what may seem a disaster at the time can turn out to be for the best in the long run.

My final fling was to send my manuscript to that well-known literary agent, A. D. Peters. He returned it with a curt note declining to handle it. It was at this point that I gave up in bitter disappointment. For I argued that whereas a publisher's refusal was understandable because he had to back his faith in a book with hard cash, refusal on the part of an agent, who had nothing to lose and only his commission to gain, amounted to sentence of death. Sorrowfully, I put my literary creation back on the shelf and tried to forget about it. Those publishers who had troubled to reply had given as their reason for rejection the fact that, in their judgement, there was insufficient public interest in the subject of canals. Were they right, or was this their way of being tactful? Perhaps I should never find out.

Of my work at Aldbourne and of the foundry I need say little because I have already described my earlier experience there in the first volume of this autobiography, and now I found that there had been little change. The job was as varied and as interesting as it had been before, work in the little shop alternating with excursions to downland farms to deal with some ailing tractor, stationary engine or farm implement. Scarcely a day passed that did not bring some fresh challenge to one's ingenuity and skill, so that I could not help reflecting wryly that for this work I received half as much as I had earned in my mindless job at Rolls Royce. I realized then that wages were no longer related to skill but had become a form of compensation for its forfeiture and for all the drudgery and the wanton waste of life and talent which such deprivation involves. So I did not begrudge my meagre wage; it seemed a small price to pay for my release from bondage.

One thing I found saddening was that I no longer had old Mark Palmer as a work-mate. That rare character had now retired and was living in the village on his old age pension. Wearing a new trilby hat and a gabardine and looking unnaturally clean and tidy, he would often come pottering up the village street for a yarn with us. He must have wasted quite a lot of our time, but in a country workshop such interruptions are tolerated and no one ever questioned his right as an old and valued craftsman to come and go as he wished. Mark's eyes still twinkled with life behind his spectacles, and his tales were as richly humorous as ever.

As a result of the war, the downland landscape was beginning to change. For the first time in living memory its sheep-walks were coming under the plough. Already slopes that had seemed immemorially green were chequered with squares of brown arable, some already misted with the green of winter wheat, others bare and ready for the drill. It was the beginning of a transformation that would soon leave only a few of the steepest slopes untilled. I viewed this change with mixed feelings. After the agricultural depression and consequent rural dilapidation and neglect, any renewal of activity seemed welcome. On the other hand, the frantic speed with which this primeval landscape was being transformed into a huge mechanized ranch farm, ruthlessly exploiting its stored fertility, sickened and saddened me. It represented no change of heart towards the land, only a desperate reaction to an emergency. White patches like melting snow on the new-ploughed slopes revealed how desperately thin was the precious flesh of top-soil upon the bare bones of the chalk.

It was obvious that there was going to be the heaviest corn harvest that Wiltshire had ever known, and it was this prospect that had prompted the signal for help which had reached me in Cheshire. The combine harvester was as yet virtually unknown in England and the tool which would harvest this Wiltshire wheat crop was the power-driven reaper and binder, a machine driven, not by its landwheel as on the old horse-drawn binders, but by the tractor's power take-off. In May of 1940 I was instructed to go to Trafford Park where, I was told, the firm of Massey Harris had set up a 'binder school' for the instruction of those who would have to service their latest machines. So Angela and I drove northwards in an elderly 'chummy' Austin

Seven which I had borrowed and, on arrival, found lodgings in a depressing, blackened street on the outskirts of Manchester.

I soon discovered that the so-called 'binder school' was no more than a device for attracting a supply of cheap labour. For its pupils were immediately set to work assembling new machines from components which had arrived in crates from America via the Manchester Ship Canal. The one intricate portion of the machine about which I had hoped to learn more was the knotter mechanism which tied up each sheaf with binder twine. But as this device emerged from the crate in the form of a complete assembly which we merely had to bolt in its appropriate place, I was left none the wiser. In any case, our sojourn at Trafford Park was destined to be much briefer than I had supposed. For the months of 'the phoney war' were over; this was the time of the fall of France and the rescue of the British army from Dunkirk by the 'little ships'. No one knew what would happen next; there were rumours of invasion and, fearing that we might become stranded in the north, my employer sent a telegram bidding me return to Aldbourne immediately. So we headed south again, I knowing no more about power-driven binders than I had done when we set out.

Nevertheless, I found myself regarded from then on as the local binder expert, a wholly unmerited reputation I found hard to uphold when harvest time came round and I was sent out in answer to distress calls from farmers whose machines had gone wrong in the field. As I had feared, it was usually that infernal mechanism, the knotter, which gave trouble. Crudely executed yet as complex as a knitting machine, it was subject to subtle derangements that caused it to play the most infuriating tricks. Sometimes it seemed to suffer from constipation, finally ejecting with difficulty the most enormous sheaf. Sometimes the opposite would take place and it would proffer a pitiful bundle of four or five corn stalks loosely bound together with twine. At others, it would seemingly tire altogether of the task of endlessly tying knots and eject the sheaves unbound, carelessly throwing a short piece of twine after each one as though to say, 'Here, you do it for a change.' However, by a mixture of low cunning and perseverance I usually managed to get the better of this mechanical monstrosity in the end and so preserve my bogus reputation.

We had returned from Trafford Park to find unwonted activity on the Kennet & Avon Canal. In the War Office, some brass-hat who had probably never seen the canal in his life must have spotted its course from the Thames to the Bristol Avon on a map and decided that it was a ready-made defence line. So the old canal had emerged from nearly a century of neglect and obscurity to become the 'Blue Defence Line', an object of national strategic importance. Even at this most critical period of the war when we expected at any moment to hear the sound of church bells signalling Nazi invasion, there was something irresistibly comic about this decision and the action which followed it. In the light of our recent experience, one imagined villagers armed with crow-bars struggling to open the old wooden swing bridges in the face of advancing Panzer Divisions. In any event, the canal was no more than waist-deep in many places.

Now, concrete pill-boxes were built beside each lock, and since many of these sites were inaccessible by road, being islanded between river and canal, this was a work of considerable difficulty. In this emergency, one very old man, reputedly the last of the Kennet & Avon boatmen, who had been living in a ramshackle houseboat below Colthrop Mills, was dragged out of retirement and put in charge of a leaking maintenance boat which must have been nearly as old as himself. A broken-down horse, led by a dim-witted youth, provided the traction. Tipping lorries laden with aggregate roared on to Wooldridge's Wharf, depositing their burdens at the waterside for conveyance by water to Hungerford Marsh Lock. So we had the unique experience of seeing a working horse-boat on the Kennet & Avon. It did not last long, however. The weather was hot and the old boatman and his mate evidently found it thirsty work. Returning from a trip to Hungerford Marsh one evening, they tied up their empty boat at the wharf and adjourned to the pub opposite. Meanwhile, the men on the wharf, inspired by a greater sense of the urgency of the operation, proceeded to overload the boat before going home. By the time the crew returned from their protracted drinking session, only the diminutive cabin of their boat was still showing above water. Thus the Kennet & Avon's contribution to the war effort came to a premature end and how the remaining pill-boxes were completed remains a mystery.

When the contractors reached the summit level of the canal at Savernake, they were dismayed to see their Blue Defence Line disappearing underground. Not to be outdone, they dug a small ditch over the top of the tunnel. One feels it was providential that information about Britain's ground defences never penetrated to Hitler, otherwise he would surely have ordered his invasion fleet to sail forthwith. As it was, he inexplicably resorted to air attack with results that made history.

During those weeks of the Battle of Britain the whole bowl of the night sky reverberated like some huge deep-toned gong as the bomber fleets of the Luftwaffe passed high overhead en route for the industrial Midlands and then returned again having laid their deadly eggs. To our surprise the lady on the wharf from whom we obtained our milk complained bitterly of lack of sleep. In response to our solicitous inquiries she explained that nights spent under her kitchen table were the cause of her insomnia. Nor was she by any means the only one, we discovered, to adopt this ostrich-like policy, a fact which led us to conclude that our instinct for self-preservation must be underdeveloped. One night, indeed, *Cressy* shuddered from stem to stern as a stick of bombs fell nearby. The momentary glare from the open fire-door of a passing goods train on the nearby railway had attracted the attention of a stray bomber, but fortunately his load fell harmlessly, straddling the railway embankment immediately to the west of the little town. So far as I know, these were the only bombs to fall in the district.

Nevertheless, the Blitz had its effect on Hungerford. The town became a reception area for 'evacuees' from the East End of London, with disturbing results for all concerned. Respectable country folk could find no common ground with gaunt, loud-mouthed, feckless women whose domestic economy had been based on street-corner pubs and chip shops, while hordes of ragged children, many of them verminous, who did not even know that milk came from cows, provoked reactions of shock and horror. This was not simply a case of the rich and washed reacting against a sudden invasion of the poor and unwashed, as socialist theorists proclaimed at the time. For, as my own case proved, the level of wages in the country was far lower than in the big towns. For those who could read the lesson of this unexpected confrontation aright it revealed only too clearly the evils of industrialism: the degradation, the loss of responsibility and self-respect, the complete alienation from the natural world that it brought about. Of this state of affairs I had first been made forcibly aware fifteen years earlier by the annual invasion of the farm at Pitchill by 'the Dudleys' from the Black Country. Obviously there had since been no change for the better.

It was not only to East Enders that Hungerford gave refuge. Some old friends of mine who owned a small hotel in the High Street gave asylum to the paintings of a London art collector. It was an unusual and unrepeatable experience to sit drinking beer in the snug, contemplating works by Henri Matisse or Renoir instead of the more conventional, yellowed Cecil Aldin prints which they had temporarily displaced. Self-conscious art worship amid the distractions of a great public gallery can be no substitute for such peaceful and private acquaintance.

I now recognized a truth that should have become obvious to me long before. This was that for anyone who, like myself, possessed no inherited means or influence, it is impossible to lead a full life and at the same time to enjoy financial security. This may not always have been so, but in the modern world the two aims had become mutually exclusive. By relating them to 'higher productivity', wages had become a form of bribery – the more repetitive, monotonous and soul-destroying the work, the higher the wage – while in the upper echelons of the business world the single-minded pursuit of financial gain appeared to be the only secret of success. Between these upper and nether millstones of organized labour and big business, both wholly dedicated to the money in the till, the creative artist and craftsman seemed to me to be fated to be ground out of existence. Yet my own experience had convinced me that because the craftsman derived his satisfaction primarily from the work itself rather than from the reward it brought, he alone held the secret of the good life.

Nevertheless, money is something one cannot do without; and poverty, like the toothache, can play havoc with philosophers. Much as I was enjoying my work at Aldbourne, the harsh fact was that our finances were precarious in the extreme. All we had to supplement my slender weekly wage packet was the small allowance that Angela received, and such was her father's hostility towards us that we expected each month to find that he had cancelled this long-standing arrangement. These were the economic facts of life which persuaded me to abandon the foundry at Aldbourne and to become, of all things, a civil servant, albeit a temporary one.

The agent of this change was my old friend Harry Rose. From the day we left school together my friendship with Harry had been of that rare kind that is taken for granted by both sides and remains wholly unaffected by long absence. We never corresponded, yet, on the rare occasions when our paths happened to cross, our intimacy seemed to be easily and effortlessly re-established no matter how many months or even years might have elapsed since our last meeting. One of these rare occasions occurred in the spring of 1941 when I returned from work to find Harry comfortably ensconced on the boat, having introduced himself to Angela whom he had never met. I always took Harry's infrequent and unlikely appearances for granted, but presumably in this case he had learned of our whereabouts from my parents. Harry, who had served his engineering apprenticeship in the Trafford Park works of Metropolitan Vickers, was now, he told us, working for the Ministry of Supply in a Department known as TT3 which was concerned with the production of vehicle spares for the three services and for essential civilian use. It was at this time occupying temporary headquarters in Bromsgrove School, though it would soon move to Chilwell Ordnance Depot and finally to offices in nearby Nottingham where it remained for the duration. Why didn't I join him? he asked: it was an interesting job which entailed visiting engineering works all over the country, and the salary he mentioned was approximately three times my present wage. Despite this tempting bait of wealth that seemed to me beyond the dreams of avarice, the prospect at first thought appalled me. All my life I had been almost as allergic to bureaucrats as to policemen, so how could I now consent to become one without sacrificing all principle? But Harry explained to me that his Department was staffed entirely by engineers recruited from industry, men whose one concern it was to cut red tape rather than to spin it. In Ministry jargon, I would be a temporary civil servant, not on the establishment. This put the suggestion in a more favourable light, although what finally persuaded me to act upon it was the fact that – how, I do not know – Harry had already joined the Department. A more uncivil servant than he it would be difficult to imagine.

So, as a result of Harry Rose's visit, I shortly afterwards reported to Bromsgrove, where I was interviewed by an imposing individual in military uniform whose name I forget and was given the job. I was told to report for duty in ten days' time, which left us precious little breathing space in which to make our own arrangements. Because time was of importance, I at first thought of sailing to the Midlands by what was, on the map, the shortest water route: westwards through the Kennet & Avon Canal to Bath and Bristol and thence to Avonmouth and straight up the tidal Severn to Sharpness. In view of the state of dereliction into which the western part of the Kennet & Avon has now fallen, it is interesting to recall the argument then advanced by that canal's railway owners. They did not dispute my right of passage and, indeed, undertook to see me through, but they advised me that such a passage would be hazardous. The Luftwaffe were paying Avonmouth Docks some unwelcome attention at the time and I was warned that I might have to remain in that uncomfortable spot for some days awaiting suitable conditions of weather and tide for the passage up the estuary to Sharpness, itself a risky proceeding for a narrow boat. Apart from the possibility of being blown out of the water, this need to wait, perhaps for weeks, at Avonmouth put the idea out of court anyway. Even at that time it was hopelessly optimistic, and I strongly suspect that at the end of a week we should still have been battling our way through the mud towards Bath. Under the circumstances, this would have been an embarrassing predicament, so we decided to return by the way we had come with the familiar boatyard at Banbury as our first objective. Because it was within striking distance by road from the Midlands, I could make Banbury my temporary base while *Cressy* was docked for repairs, before we moved on to some mooring as yet undecided which would be more convenient for my field of operations.

Having with some difficulty 'winded' *Cressy* below Hungerford bridge on the previous evening, we left Wooldridge's Wharf, bound for Reading, on 28 April 1941. In one respect our passage was easier than before; all the old wooden swing bridges opened readily. This they had been made to do the better to dismay the advancing Aryan hordes. Nevertheless, this voyage down to Reading was not without its moments. The springs were up, as they say in the chalk country, and Kennet was flowing fast. I fear we anathematized the memory of John Hore who had engineered the navigation in 1724 and had presumably been responsible for siting his locks at the upstream instead of at the downstream end of his lock cuts. On our upward journey we had had to battle with shoals of mud and now we experienced the other consequence of this mistake. It is disconcerting for the steerer of a heavy craft, borne along by a swift current, on rounding a turn to be suddenly confronted with the choice between a weir on the one hand and a pair of closed lock gates on the other, the one inviting shipwreck and the other a violent collision. Ham Mills Lock, below Newbury, is a good example of this hazard and we soon came to the conclusion that the downstream navigation of the Kennet when a 'fresh' is running was no job for a tyro.

On the strength of his tales of derring-do on the high seas with which he had regaled us, we had shipped as crew as far as Reading an enthusiastic yachtsman whose acquaintance we had made at Hungerford. It soon became evident, however, that to him no perils on the sea could equal those of the Kennet and his presence therefore added not a little to our difficulties. On sighting any obstruction ahead he would ignore our pleas to jump ashore with a line, and take a stance on our foredeck with our long shaft outstretched before him like a lance in rest as though preparing to repel boarders. It required a practical demonstration to convince him of the futility of this exercise where such a heavy boat was concerned. *Cressy* was coming into a lock and, despite my shouted assurance that she was fully under control in the engine department, our friend assumed his customary threatening posture at the bow. So intent was he upon the lock gates ahead that he failed to notice that he was holding the shaft in such a position that it would inevitably be trapped between these gates and the for'ard bulkhead of the boat. Sure enough, the long shaft bowed beneath his arm, lifting him off his feet, and then broke with a resounding crack. We were not amused. However, despite this and other more or less alarming incidents, we succeeded in reaching Blake's Lock at Reading in three days as compared with our five days of hard slogging on the upward journey.

On the morning of May Day, I swung *Cressy* out on to the Thames and headed for Oxford. Navigating the Kennet against time had been a kind of aquatic obstacle race, and it felt very good to be out in broad clear waters once more. *Cressy* seemed to share our relief for she fairly galloped along, covering the forty miles to Oxford in two days with a night stop near Benson Lock. Thanks to this good progress we were able to tie up at Tooley's Boatyard at Banbury at midday on 6 May.

Before I could start my new job I needed a car and, because I had laid up my own 12/50 Alvis for the duration, my father, who had become too old and infirm to drive, agreed that I might borrow his. So I travelled home to Stanley Pontlarge by train to collect it, little knowing that this was the last time I would see him alive. Over the next four months that gallant old car must have covered a greater mileage than it had done in my father's hands in the previous four years. My Department was as yet ill-organized and under-staffed, with the result that I had to travel to places as far afield as Grantham, Chesterfield and Shrewsbury, seldom getting back to Banbury except at week-ends. The Alvis proved itself a good ambassador. It was not exactly the type of vehicle that engineers normally associate with 'the man from the Ministry' and on this account they were the more ready to be friendly and cooperative.

One day in June, Angela received the news by wire at Banbury that my father had had a stroke. She managed to get in touch with me through the Department and we drove over to Stanley Pontlarge immediately, but were too late. On our arrival, my mother, dry-eyed and apparently unmoved, told us simply that he was dead. Leaving Angela below with her, I went at once to the spare bedroom where they had laid him. It was a perfect midsummer evening and the late sunlight streamed in through the west window of this airy, white-walled room. From the garden there rose a chorus of birdsong and a recurrent shrill whistling as a bevy of swifts, hawking for flies, dived past the window in rapid, glancing flight. But inside, the room itself seemed strangely silent and still. A faint sickly-sweet smell hung in the air. I stood at the foot of the bed gazing down at my father. It was my first acquaintance with death. His complexion was yellow and ghastly, but the stroke had not distorted his features. He looked calm and peaceful enough, yet his face appeared shrunken because those who had laid him out had removed his false teeth. They had placed them on the table beside him along with his worn gold signet ring with its crest of a Wyvern and his gold watch which still ticked busily as its spring steadily released the stored energy put into it by his dead hands. Curiously enough I found the pathos of these few familiar objects, imperishable, yet now lying cold and forlorn, much more moving than the sight of the perishable body with which they had lately been so intimately connected. It was these things rather than the shell that lay on the bed that seemed to me to symbolize the chrysalis from which the spirit had so lately flown.

My father was in his seventy-sixth year. As I looked my last on him my feeling was not so much of grief as of remorse and self-reproach. I thought of the many times I had sided with my mother in family arguments; of the youthful intolerance with which I had so often cut short his interminable and oft-repeated stories; of his many enthusiasms which I had churlishly refused to share. And now it was too late to make amends. As though fearful of disturbing him, I closed the door noiselessly and tiptoed away.

As I had expected, my father left only an overdraft, raised on the security of the property, and a number of almost worthless rubber shares. I have an old-fashioned, almost medieval, dislike of usury, so in defiance of legal advice I sold the latter for what little they would fetch in order to pay off the former. At least the house would now be unencumbered and my mother would be able to go on living there, free of debt, on her own small income.

By the end of August, *Cressy* had been docked and refurbished so that we were free to move elsewhere. My Department was by now better organized and it was becoming clear that my work in the future would be increasingly confined to the area around Redditch, Birmingham and Wolverhampton. We were therefore concerned to find some place to moor which would be in pleasant country yet at the same time within easy striking distance of these industrial areas. After a great deal of pondering over ordnance maps we decided that Tardebigge on the Worcester & Birmingham Canal looked the most promising. Although neither of us had ever been there, we could not have made a better choice as things turned out.

In order to make this move, I took the week's leave that was due to me and on 30 August we cast off from Banbury, travelling north up the Oxford Canal as far as Napton Junction where we turned left on to the main line of the Grand Union Canal, heading for Warwick and Birmingham. We found the so-called 'new' wide locks on this canal by far the heaviest to work of any we had so far encountered. The gates seemed unnecessarily massive and the helical paddle gearing slow and tedious to operate. Nevertheless, the night of 1 September found us moored at the summit of the flight of twenty-one locks at Hatton which lift the canal out of the valley of the Avon at Warwick. The next morning, we continued through Shrewley Tunnel and along the Grand Union as far as Kingswood Junction.

At Kingswood, a short arm links the Grand Union with the Stratford-on-Avon Canal, the northern section of which runs directly to join the Worcester & Birmingham Canal at King's Norton. From the map it had seemed an obvious short cut, saving a number of miles and at the same time avoiding the necessity of passing through the centre of Birmingham. But it soon became evident that a route that had appeared obvious on paper was by no means so inviting in reality. For the Stratford Canal, like the Kennet & Avon, was then owned by the Great Western Railway Company and, like the latter, it was in a semi-derelict state. We had known that the canal at

Stratford was long disused, but for some reason we optimistically assumed that this northern section, being part of a through route, was still frequented by commercial traffic. We discovered just how wrong we were as we struggled up the flight of nineteen narrow locks at Lapworth. The short pounds between them were so densely packed with weed that *Cressy*'s propeller instantly became an ineffectual ball of green wool and we had to resort to bow-hauling. We speculated gloomily that if the eleven-mile level from the top of these locks to King's Norton was no better than this, we should either have to hire a horse or admit defeat and retire stern first down the locks. Greatly to our relief, however, the summit level appeared to be clear apart from a little duck-weed on the surface. There also proved to be quite a reasonable depth of water and we were able to travel another four miles before tying up for the night. For the greater part of its length, this long upper level of the Stratford lies in a cutting, its steep sides so thickly overgrown that occasionally the branches of leaning trees almost met over the ribbon of dark water. We had to bring the bicycle down from the deck and lower our stove chimney to prevent them being swept away. As we slid through this long tunnel of green shade, it was difficult to believe that we were so close to Birmingham, so remote from the world did it seem. From the look of it, the towpath appeared to be unfrequented even by the fishermen one usually encounters, particularly near large towns. Imagine then our surprise when, on entering King's Norton tunnel next morning, we saw lights glimmering in the darkness ahead. It was as eerie as discovering signs of activity in some long disused mine and it recalled legends of the 'knockers' or 'the old men'. It turned out to be a gang of maintenance men re-pointing the brickwork of the tunnel vault from a staging rigged on a maintenance boat, a sight which, though prosaic, was remarkable enough on a railway-owned canal. I think the gang were even more surprised to see us than we were to see them, and as we inched our way slowly past their boat in the gloom with precious little room to spare, our voices, as we exchanged greetings, raised sepulchral echoes. It was our first encounter with human kind since we had parted from the lock keeper at the head of the Lapworth locks the previous day.

We had now come within the outer suburban fringe of Birmingham, and between gaps in the neglected hedgerows we caught glimpses of new housing estates. The going had become steadily worse and even without such visual evidence we should have known we were back again in 'civilization' by the reefs of junk, old bicycle wheels and tyres, old perambulators, milk bottle crates and brick-bats, that lay in wait for us beneath every bridge. We had to drift through these bridges, otherwise our propeller would have become entangled in debris. Despite this precaution I had to spend some time hanging over *Cressy's* stern, knife in hand, hacking off the remains of an old car hood which had wrapped itself round our propeller blades.

Between the west end of the tunnel and the wooden Lifford drawbridge at King's Norton, which provided access to a new industrial estate, we were dragging and bumping over a litter-strewn bottom all the way and stirring up clouds of putrescent mud. It was the lunch hour and a little group of overalled men from a nearby factory were lounging on the drawbridge. Their presence was providential as we soon discovered. On sighting us, they obligingly pulled the bridge open and signalled us to come on. In doing so they must either have been optimistic or singularly unobservant, for the narrow channel beneath the bridge was thickly blocked with junk, as we soon found out when *Cressy* ground to a sudden stop. However, while two men continued to hold the bridge open, their fellows hauled manfully on bow and stern lines and managed to drag us over the obstruction. Beyond this, the canal was densely overgrown with weeds, but as we now had only three hundred yards to go to reach the stop lock, with its guillotine gates, which guarded the junction with the Worcester & Birmingham Canal, we ploughed on under our own power. By now our volunteer helpers, entering into the spirit of the thing, were accompanying us along the towpath with encouraging noises. It was as well that they did so for we needed their willing hands again when we stuck fast in the mouth of the stop lock.

Once inside the lock, I removed from our blades the Stratford Canal's final gift of two bicycle tyres and a length of old rope. Of the many miscellaneous objects that can become entangled in a propeller, tyres are the worst, as anyone who has ever tried cutting a tyre wire will readily appreciate. However, the job was done at last and the western guillotine gate opened like a camera shutter to reveal, framed in its aperture, a picture of the still, clear waters of the Worcester & Birmingham Canal. The sight was even more welcome than that of the Thames at Reading had been. To forge through disused canals may give one an exhilarating sense of pioneering achievement, but the constant risk of damaging the boat makes it an anxious business. Fortunately, with their two-inch oak planking and three-inch elm bottoms, wooden narrow boats are sturdy craft; but there are limits to the punishment they can take, particularly when they grow as old as *Cressy* was. A nightmare that haunted me during all the years I lived afloat was that I should one day knock a bottom up, causing the boat to sink with all our precious possessions on board. It was consequently a great relief to be heading *Cressy* south towards Tardebigge, knowing there was plenty of water under her bottom once more.

The uniformity later imposed by nationalization may be rational, but variety, however irrational it may appear, is nevertheless still the spice of life. The fact that our waterway system, like our railway system in pre-grouping days, was still owned by a multiplicity of old-established companies, each with its own by-laws, customs and traditions hallowed by time, added greatly to the charm and fascination of waterway travel. Canal boaters, too, were never the wandering 'water gypsies' of popular imagination but tended to stick to particular routes. Thus the boating families we had come to know best, the Hones, Humphreys, Harwoods, Wilsons, Skinners, Beauchamps, Townsends and Beecheys, had spent most of their lives on the Oxford Canal, boating coal from the Coventry area to Banbury or Oxford. Because the northern part of their respective 'runs' overlapped, these families were closely associated with – and in many cases related to – the much larger boating community that traded from the Midlands down the Grand Union Canal to London. So far as these boaters were concerned the Grand Union, Coventry and Oxford canals formed one parish in which everybody knew everybody else and where local news passed with astonishing speed from Sutton Stop to Sampson Road and from Bull's Bridge to Braunston. But now we had crossed the central watershed, and the canal we were entering was as unknown to this close-knit community as it was to us. I did not need the lettering 'W. & B. C.' on the cabin sides of moored maintenance boats or the heading 'Sharpness New Docks & Gloucester & Birmingham Navigation Company' on canal-side signs to remind me that I was now in the foreign waters of the Severn basin.

So, when the dark portal of the 2,750-yard West Hill tunnel loomed up ahead and I could discern no KEEP RIGHT sign such as I had become familiar with on the Grand Union system, I thought it would be prudent to discover what the native customs were in these parts before we ventured in. There was what I rightly took to be a canal lengthman's cottage perched on the hill directly over the tunnel's mouth, so we tied up while I climbed up to inquire. It was just as well that I did so. 'Keep left,' I was told. A possible subterranean collision accompanied by a great deal of profanity on both sides was thereby happily avoided.

While we passed through the long tunnel, Angela cooked our dinner by lamplight in the galley and the most appetizing smells wafted back to me through the open cabin doors. We emerged from the darkness into the golden light of a perfect late summer evening to find that we had left behind all traces of Birmingham's outer fringe. We ran past Hopwood and finally moored up beside Lower Bittall Reservoir. As we subsequently discovered, this large reservoir stretching away to the slopes of the Lickey Hills had to be built by the canal company as a condition of their Act in order to provide compensation water for the mill-owners on the little river Arrow whose headwaters the canal engineers proposed to tap. Not knowing this, we were mystified to find that the level of the reservoir was much lower than that of the canal. In fact, the canal embankment formed the reservoir dam so that from our mooring we could look out over a great glassy-smooth sheet of water. Through the thin mist that was already beginning to rise we could see that its mirror-like surface was speckled with hundreds of waterfowl: coot, moorhen, grebe and wild duck. Sometimes with sudden commotion a group of wild duck would take off to wheel against the sunset light, a small arrow-head, barbed with fast-beating wings. The evening air was still so warm that we dined in the open on *Cressy*'s foredeck. We stayed outside until the mist over the water had risen like a phantom tide to lap over the bank into the canal.

The following morning we were awakened by the familiar throbbing of a semi-diesel engine. We peered out eagerly, curious to see what strange 'foreign' craft this might be and who her owners. The mist over the canal was so thick that we could see nothing, but as the boat drew closer we could plainly hear above the noise of the engine two female voices conversing in the accents of Roedean or Westonbirt. Strange craft indeed! It could not be a working boat after all, we decided. Yet presently there glided into view the bluff bows of a narrow boat, low-laden in the water, and over the top of her side-cloths we could see a cargo of what looked like sacks of grain. What was stranger still, in her beautiful paintwork we recognized the unmistakable craftsmanship of our old friend Frank Nurser of Braunston Dock. We noticed her unfamiliar name, *Heather Bell*, before her unlikely crew had bid us good day and vanished once more into the mist.

Later, we came to know these two girls. The 'captain' was Daphne March whose brother had had *Heather Bell* built at Braunston just before the war with the intention of trading between his home town of Worcester and Birmingham. When, as a member of the R.N.V.R., he had gone on war service, Daphne had resolved to work the boat herself. Her companion was Kit Gayford, soon to achieve no small celebrity on the canals when she became responsible for training and supervising that intrepid band – so wrongly and rudely called the Idle Women – who volunteered to crew certain of the Grand Union Canal Carrying Co.'s fleet as their war service.

The sun soon dissolved the mist to shine down so brilliantly that we were able to eat our breakfast on deck. It was 4 September and our journey was almost over, for we knew that we had less than five miles of this beautiful summit level to cover in order to reach our destination. We sailed on into the dark tree-shaded mouth of Shortwood tunnel and were soon passing Tardebigge Old Wharf where we again plunged into the darkness of Tardebigge tunnel, cavern-like with its unlined walls of red sandstone. Emerging once more into the sunlight and rounding a bend, we saw before us for the first time our new home that was destined to become so familiar and so well-loved. It was exactly at noon that we put down our mooring lines at Tardebigge New Wharf. Apart from a couple of brief trips up to Bittall Reservoir and back with friends, *Cressy* would not move again for nearly five years.

Chapter 3

Eighteen Hundred Days in Tardebigge

In 1931, Miss Margaret Dickins, the daughter of a former vicar of Tardebigge who had held the living from 1855 to 1917, published *A Thousand Years in Tardebigge*, a book which, in its 180 pages, tells the story of the parish – it can scarcely be called a village – from the Saxon Taerdebicgan to the end of the Great War. Such a span of centuries made our brief sojourn in the parish shrink to an hour, meriting at most a single brief paragraph according to Miss Dickins's time-scale. Yet in spite of wartime difficulties and anxieties – and, indeed, to some extent because of them – these Tardebigge years turned out to be one of the most happy, full and fruitful periods of my life. It was for me a time of rapid spiritual and intellectual development. I nearly wrote 'maturity' instead of 'development' but realized that this would be an inappropriate word to describe someone who, intoxicated by his new powers and insights, felt confident that he held the key to all the world's ills, a key that could be used to build the new Jerusalem as soon as the war was over.

I marvel now that I could have accomplished so much and travelled so far (in a spiritual sense) in so short a time. Hence to write a coherent account of these years in one chapter entails as difficult a feat of compression as Miss Dickins achieved in her book. Let me first set the scene by describing the topography of Tardebigge and a little of what went on there. These things are important because I could never have lived there so contentedly had I not found the prospect so congenial. It was salutary to think that a landscape so near to Birmingham could remain so substantially unchanged, yet so it was.

The summit level of the Worcester & Birmingham Canal is 453 feet above sea level and extends for fourteen miles from Worcester Bar, Birmingham, to Tardebigge top lock. Because a considerable part of the Birmingham Canal Navigations (which the Worcester Canal joins) was constructed at the same height, this magical figure of 453 feet is usually referred to as the Birmingham Level. In the interests of water conservation and supply, the engineers of the new canal to Worcester (it was a comparative late-comer to the canal scene) were concerned to extend it southwards upon this level to the furthest feasible point. Tardebigge is that point. The southbound canal traveller gets no impression of the height of the Birmingham Level until he emerges dramatically from the darkness of Tardebigge Tunnel to find himself floating along the flank of a hill, a green promontory that juts southward into the blue sea of the vale. Three hundred yards from the mouth of the tunnel, the traveller comes to Tardebigge top lock, the first of that great flight of thirty locks by which the canal begins its descent to the Severn. It was a spot fifty yards from the head of this top lock that we selected for our mooring, so a landscape which the traveller only glimpses very briefly in passing, we were able to make a part of our lives, to be enjoyed in all weathers and all seasons.

To the right, a continuation of the low ridge called The Shaws that is pierced by the tunnel closed in the view to the north. Its cultivated slopes of red soil were patterned with a green corduroy of young fruit plantations, which whitened with blossom in springtime. Although this 'blowth' came markedly later here than in the vale below, these plantations escaped the pockets of deadly late frosts that in April, or even in May, are apt to fill the hollows of the vale with still pools of icy air, bringing despair to the fruit grower. To the west, the land fell steeply away from the very brink of the canal, the first focal point that the eye found to rest upon being the tall, crocketed red sandstone spire of Bromsgrove church about three miles away. The ugly, sprawling, brickish skirt about this old town was invisible thanks to the lie of the land and the many trees. That spire was the pivot of hills that often appeared so close to it yet were in fact far distant, being part

of that border country west of Severn: the dark slopes of the
Forest of Wyre by Bewdley; the Shropshire Clees; Wood-
bury Camp and the Abberley Hills above the valley of the
Teme. And sometimes, on evenings when the air became
crystal clear after rain, the remote shape of Black Mixen in
Radnor Forest would appear on the far horizon.

All this country that Housman and Brett Young knew and
loved lay spread before *Cressy's* windows. My fondness for
hill country in general and for the Welsh Border in particular
had not seemed to mix well with my love of canals. But I
had too easily assumed that they were mutually exclusive, for
here at Tardebigge the two were almost uniquely reconciled.
When we picked Tardebigge from the map, we had certainly
chosen better than we knew.

On the summit of the green ridge against the side of which
we lay was the village church, built by Francis Hiorne of
Warwick in 1777 out of the ruins of its predecessor following
the collapse of the tower. Hiorne, who usually worked in the
Gothic style, built here a classical tower topped by a spire of
great elegance and extreme slenderness which soon became a
familiar landmark. Seen from a distance it was difficult to believe that so delicate an object could be fashioned out of stone.
We literally lay within its shadow, for on sunny winter mornings the steeple's shadow would fall across our deck, its point
swinging like the style of a sundial over the meadows below.

The smooth green slope of the hill, and the particular
relationship of the slender spire to the shapes and contrasting
foliage of the surrounding trees made a composition so satisfying for the eye to rest upon and so perfectly complementary
to the blue of the distant prospect below that it might have been
contrived by Lancelot Brown or Humphrey Repton to gratify
some noble patron. Yet although the manor of Tardebigge
was owned by the Windsor family (later created Earls of
Plymouth) from the Dissolution until shortly before we left
the district, there is no evidence to suggest that this was so.
Fortuitously, architect and civil engineer had collaborated
with nature to provide for *Cressy* a landscape setting which
suited my taste to perfection. And just as the eighteenth-
century landscape architects would pander to the whims of

their noble patrons by throwing in a hermit's cell complete with hermit, so to crown all, I had for good measure the company of a little community of craftsmen which reminded me of those I had known at Pitchill and Aldbourne.

Between *Cressy's* stern and the mouth of the tunnel, on the New Wharf proper, was the principal maintenance depot for the Worcester & Birmingham Canal. It consisted of a huddle of workshops grouped around a dry dock, and a number of cottages built of local brick at widely different dates in the nineteenth century, yet all rubbing shoulders happily together. Here lived Mr Spiers, the Engineer of the canal, a shy, soft-spoken, gentle man with strange, frightened, restless eyes. In his youth, he had been a draughtsman with Belliss & Morcom, the famous firm of steam engine builders in Birmingham. A lonely man – he had lost his wife – Mr Spiers used often to visit us on the boat when we would talk engineering history by the hour. I remember once how he proudly showed me a beautiful coloured general arrangement drawing he had made of a Belliss vertical compound engine. Nominally, Mr Spiers was responsible for the management of workshops but in practice he seldom or never interfered with the four craftsmen, each a master in his own sphere, who between them ran the establishment. There was Mr Insull, the elderly blacksmith, portly and dignified; Percy Hawkins, the fitter and machinist who kept the nineteenth-century tools in the little machine shop so beautifully clean and oiled. It was only rarely that he had occasion to use them, but when he did so he often performed almost miraculous feats of improvisation and accuracy, such as boring a tapered hole in the boss of a new bronze propeller casting. Where I would have hesitated to undertake such a job on so ancient a lathe, Percy Hawkins set to work with complete assurance.

Then there was that short, thickset, jovial man, Tommy Hodges the boatbuilder, with his round red face glowing with exposure to winter weather in the open dock. He used to tell me that he could remember when twenty boatbuilders worked on the banks of this canal alone, yet now he was the sole survivor. But Tommy died before we left Tardebigge and we heard no more the regular thudding of his caulking mallet.

His last job was to replank an ice-breaker boat. As it lay in the dock, its curved oak ribs stripped of their rotten skin, it might have been the skeleton of some Viking ship. But it was George Bate, the fourth member of this quartet, whose skill I most admired. He was the lock-gate maker, and the wide doorway of his workshop opened on to a narrow quay so that a new-made lock-gate could be run out on a travelling pulley block and loaded directly into a maintenance boat. It did the heart good to watch George fashioning and assembling the massive oak principals of a frame gate: squaring the timbers, cutting tenon and mortise, drawing them together with powerful cramps and then finally bracing the whole with iron strap-work that had been made for him by Mr Insull. George was very proud of the fact that he was the latest representative of an unbroken succession of Bates who had worked on the Worcester & Birmingham ever since it was built. His shop was light and airy and always fragrant with the bitter tang of fresh hewn oak. It was also a very quiet and soothing place in which to linger, for George used no machines, even of a portable kind, after his timber had been squared in the saw-mill next door. Round its freshly whitewashed walls hung the tools of his trade, adze and shell-augur, not embalmed in some museum but, like that long pit-saw at Hungerford, still with the bloom of use upon them.

Bank Holiday week-ends, Easter, Whitsun and August, were the busiest times of the year for George Bate, for at such times a 'stoppage' on the canal would be announced so that new gates could be installed and any other necessary repair work to the locks carried out. At such times we would be awakened before dawn by the rumble of Worcestershire voices or the rattle of paddles at the top lock as there slid slowly past our cabin windows a maintenance boat laden with a new pair of gates and with all the paraphernalia necessary for installing them: sheer legs, pulley blocks, chains, coils of rope, a portable pumping set and lengths of hose for emptying a lock chamber somewhere on 'the thirty and twelve'.*

---

* So-called by George Bate and others because the famous Tardebigge flight of thirty locks was closely followed by twelve more between Stoke Prior and Dodderhill.

The only thing wrong with Tardebigge New Wharf was that it was teetotally dry. This had not always been so. The four-square Georgian brick building that was now the Plymouth Guesthouse, and whose windows overlooked the wharf, had once been known as the 'Plymouth Arms' until a bygone Earl of Plymouth, holding decided views on the evils of strong drink, caused its licence to be withdrawn. How many a boatman, having toiled to the summit of so prodigious a ladder of locks, must have cursed his lordship's scruples! But at least the boatmen were still able to slake their thirst at the 'Halfway House', so-called because it was situated beside the canal exactly half-way up the flight of thirty. This was our nearest pub and a pleasant walk it was down the towpath on a fine summer evening. The way led past Tardebigge Reservoir where, if you were lucky, you could watch great crested grebe performing their elaborate courtship ritual although they never appeared to breed. The reservoir was never used now and with its reedy, tree-bordered margins it more nearly resembled one of the Shropshire meres. It had been built by the canal company to store surplus storm water from the long summit level which was fed into the reservoir from just above the summit lock through a long culvert controlled by a paddle. In seasons of summer drought, water used to be pumped back to the summit from the reservoir by a beam pumping engine. Its engine house still stood near the reservoir though the engine had long ago been scrapped.

The 'Halfway' was a farm with a licence rather than an inn. This was just as well because on weekday evenings the takings must have been minimal; traffic on the canal had dwindled to a mere trickle and it was a true canal pub. It was clear that its original business had been with the towpath for it could only be reached with difficulty by the most narrow and tortuous of by-roads. Nevertheless, on Saturday evenings we could count upon finding a small but congenial company sitting round the scrubbed table in what had obviously once been the farm kitchen but was now the bar parlour. This company was made up of local farm labourers, smallholders and lengthmen or lock keepers from the canal with the addition of an occasional boatman or week-end fisherman. Most country pubs seem to favour some particular pastime or other; it may be darts, dominoes, table skittles, shove ha'penny or quoits, depending on what part of England you are in. On Saturday nights at the 'Halfway House', the favourite pastime was singing and a very jolly noise we made, sitting round by the light of a hanging paraffin lamp.

Master of ceremonies and star turn on these occasions was Jack Warner, a lock keeper whose cottage stood near the reservoir. A heavily built man of about seventy, his short legs were bowed and he walked with a rolling gait as though they were buckling beneath the weight of his body. With the heavy, sagging features of an ageing clown, Jack Warner was a 'natural'. He would get to his feet and treat the company to a rendering of some old music-hall song that included all the appropriate changes of expression, the graphic miming, the occasional dance steps and the inimitable way he could incite audience participation in the choruses. Though his repertoire was small, his audience never tired of it and the evening had seldom progressed very far before someone would call: 'Come on Jack, lad, gie us The Whitewash Brush,' and soon we would be roaring out the choruses which ended with the refrain:

> I put more whitewash on the old woman
> Than I put upon the parlour wall.

Jack Warner had a brother Joe who, though slightly the younger of the two, was much more staid and sober, perhaps because he was a married man whereas his brother was a widower. Joe Warner was our nearest neighbour as he and his wife lived in the cottage beside the top lock within fifty yards of our mooring. Though nominally the lock keeper, he also did labouring work at the New Wharf and each morning and evening he would clump past our boat in his heavy boots along the footpath that linked the lock with the wharf. Like his brother, Joe had a broad and musical Worcestershire dialect and his speech was peppered with unusual words and phrases. Thus he would always refer to wood pigeons as 'quice', an onomatopoeic word that I had never encountered before.

Thunder was always 'tempest': 'My word, tis 'ot,' he would exclaim, 'Reckon we shall ha' tempest afore night.'

The only new boatman friend we made while we were at Tardebigge was Charles Ballinger of Gloucester. To use the phraseology of the Oxford canal folk, he was the last of the 'west country boatmen', for as a young man helping his father he used to work through the Thames & Severn Canal and on to the upper Thames at Lechlade. On warm summer evenings when his low-laden boat was tied at the New Wharf, this long lean man with the worn and deeply tanned face used to hypnotize me with his stories of those far-off days until dusk deepened into darkness. He would shake his head over the chronic shortage of water on the summit of the Thames & Severn. So bad was it that, in the Canal's last days, the company provided what he called 'lightening boats' at each end of the great summit tunnel at Sapperton. He and his father used to offload part of their cargo into a lightening boat before setting out laboriously to 'leg' their way through the two-miles-long tunnel, towing the smaller boat behind them which, of course, had to be unloaded again into their own boat at the tunnel's end. But, as he pointed out, anything was better than being stuck on the bottom in those dark depths.

Charles Ballinger now owned four horse-boats, one of which he worked himself, all of them plying between his home port of Gloucester and the Midlands where they loaded coal. One of these was known as the 'match boat' because she carried 'England's Glory' matches from Gloucester to Birmingham on a regular contract. These boats were towed by tug between Gloucester Docks and Diglis, Worcester. At Diglis Basin, their captains picked up Company horses which hauled their boats to Tardebigge where the tunnel tug *Worcester* took over. This was a neat little craft with an outsize in Bollinder engines for which Percy Hawkins and his mate were responsible. When we first arrived at Tardebigge, there was a very beautiful steam tug, *Droitwich*, built by Abdela & Mitchell of Brimscombe, which was responsible for towage through West Hill tunnel, but eventually she needed re-tubing and this was never done as there was insufficient traffic to warrant two tugs. The single Tardebigge tug therefore had the task of towing through all three tunnels, after which the horses took over once more. This elaborate and costly arrangement of tugs and Company horses may have been all very well when dozens of horse-boats worked over the route, but now that their number had shrunk to four only it had obviously become hopelessly uneconomic. I used to reflect ruefully that it would have paid the Company handsomely to give Charles Ballinger an expensive 'golden handshake', although I was delighted that they never did so. All the rest of the traffic, such as it was, was self-propelled and, apart from the *Heather Bell*, which we have already encountered, it consisted entirely of single motor boats of the Severn & Canal Carrying Company's fleet: steel boats with drab paintwork of blue and white, some of the ugliest and clumsiest narrow boats ever built. They were crewed usually with pathetic incompetence by tatterdemalion families which the Company had obviously recruited from 'off the bank', as the boatmen say. It was sadly clear that this once flourishing carrying company was now nearing the end of its life.

So much for the small world to which I returned at evening. Of my work I need say little except that it provided me with instructive first-hand experience of the engineering industry of the Midlands, ranging from such large plants as Wolseley Motors at Ward End, Birmingham, or Guy Motors at Wolverhampton, to the smallest of back street press shops in Deritend or Aston. One interesting fact that I discovered at this time was how profoundly even the largest of works could be affected by the personality of the man in control. One could very quickly sense whether the atmosphere in a particular shop was happy or unhappy, while a few moments' conversation with the managing director almost invariably supplied the explanation.

I had no intention of wearing out my father's Alvis in the Government service so, soon after we arrived at Tardebigge, I bought a 1938 Austin 'Big Seven' saloon and returned the Alvis to its home garage for the duration. This meant that both Alvises were now in hibernation at Stanley Pontlarge awaiting better times. The Austin was such a terrible little car in every way that at first I felt ashamed to be seen driving it. It used to suffer from bouts of acute clutch slip due to the oil that found its way through the back main bearing. Carbon tetrachloride was the best palliative for this. I would head for the nearest branch of Woolworths, buy a bottle of Thawpit and pour it into the clutch housing. This effected a temporary cure and by such expedients I kept the car running until the end of the war when I could not wait to be rid of it. It is ironical to reflect that at this time the Austin was the most expensive single object I had ever purchased, *Cressy* herself not excepted.

By the Ministry I was known as an 'Isolated Technical Assistant'. My desk on *Cressy* was my 'office' although I also had the use, whenever I needed it, of a bare, ink-stained trestle table, a chair and a telephone in an office on the sixth floor of the C.M.L. building in Great Charles Street, Birmingham. Although I naturally became very familiar with the city during these years, it never endeared itself to me in any way. I used to feel oppressed by the thorough-going Philistinism of the place. It was so painfully evident that it was the creation of people who, for a hundred years or more, had pursued the making of money with completely single-minded devotion. Yet I admit this experience did later awaken in me a certain nostalgia for the older Birmingham, with its jewellery and gun quarters and its clanging trams reeling like galleons down narrow, setted streets or rounding impossibly sharp curves with a sudden shriek of protesting wheel flanges.

The most onerous and unproductive part of my desk work was the completion of a weekly claim form for travelling expenses and subsistence. This form had been devised by a mind exclusively concerned to circumvent the possibility of any falsification, accidental or deliberate, on the part of the applicant. The result was such a masterpiece of complexity that to fill it in honestly was impossible, short of adding pages of explanatory notes. Hence the form was always referred to by the irreverent 'temporaries' in my Department as the Swindle Sheet. It revealed the same careful, conscientious and humourless bureaucratic mentality that had not only caused every single sheet of the paper rolls in the lavatories at C.M.L. building to be rubber-stamped 'Government Property' but had placed a typed notice over each fitment which read:
PLEASE EXERCISE THE UTMOST ECONOMY IN THE USE

OF PAPER. To this, almost inevitably, some scatological wag had added: 'Please use both sides.'

The furthest afield that my work took me now was a fort-nightly visit to the Sentinel Waggon Works at Shrewsbury, with an occasional call in the Wellington neighbourhood on the way. As it was usually late by the time I left Sentinels and as I was due in Wolverhampton the following morning, it was obviously better on such occasions to spend a night in Shropshire instead of consuming precious petrol in returning to the boat. For this purpose I picked the 'Valley Hotel' at Coalbrookdale and was thus introduced to the Severn Gorge and the ancient industrial district of Shropshire. The first time I came to the 'Valley Hotel', having picked it with the aid of an ordnance map and an A.A. guide, it was late autumn and darkness had already fallen; yet I knew at once that I had hit upon a very special place, for as soon as I walked into the bar of the hotel my eye was caught and held by three large and handsome coloured engravings of local scenes which hung on the walls. As I subsequently discovered, these were three of a set of six, engraved from originals by George Robertson and published by the brothers Boydell in 1788. One was a romantic landscape featuring the slender arc of the famous first iron bridge against a towering background of hanging woods, while the subject of the second was John Wilkinson's Broseley Ironworks. Here the same romantic landscape of the Severn Gorge had been rudely invaded and blighted by the dragon of industrial revolution, breathing fire and foul smoke from furnace and stack. But it was the third picture that I thought the most striking. It was titled 'The Inside of a Smelting-house at Broseley'. It depicted a building which might have been a tithe barn were it not for the tall wooden pivoting crane in the centre of the picture, a triangle of timbers as massive as lock-gate balance beams. The main source of light in this building came from a rectangular open-ing to the right of the crane which resembled the mouth of hell, so fierce was the glare that issued from it. This was the fore-part of a blast furnace from which molten iron was being tapped. Three figures, one sharply lit, the other two seen in silhouette, directed the white-hot stream through the sand of the floor and into the runners of a pig-bed in the right fore-ground. In telling contrast to this fiery bedlam, an open archway to the extreme left of the picture revealed a tantalizing glimpse of a night landscape of calm serenity in which a full moon had just risen above a bank of white cloud.

It seemed to me a prophetic warning of the greater desolation to come that such crude but dramatic manifestations of the second Iron Age should appear in one of the most romantically beautiful landscapes in Britain. It is a pity that the originals of these engravings have disappeared, because George Robertson was one of the first artists to grasp the significance of this violent contrast and to give expression to it in paint. He was by no means the last. Many artists who appreciated the then unsullied beauty of the English landscape, but had hitherto taken it for granted as part of man's natural birthright, were drawn to the Severn Gorge and Coalbrookdale by a fearful fascination. They sought to express in paint and in words the strangely ambivalent feelings aroused by the dramatic contrast between the fuming, flaming clangour of the ironworks and their idyllic setting of wooded hills and streams.

In the course of subsequent visits when, in the long summer evenings, I explored 'the Dale' and the Ironbridge Gorge on foot, I came fully to share the feelings of those bygone artists. Although the famous iron bridge still spans the Severn and men still cast iron in the foundry at Coalbrookdale, the blast furnaces are dead; Wilkinson's Bedlam Furnace is no more than a cold ruin of crumbling, blackened brick beneath a kindly veil of creeper. Yet the whole area seemed to me to be haunted. Everywhere I was reminded of the fierce activity of former days, and every stick and stone of the place seemed to have absorbed something of its white hot violence. It was here that Abraham Darby the First succeeded in smelting iron with coke instead of charcoal; here that the first iron hull was made and launched, the first iron steam engine cylinders and the first iron rails were cast; here that the first steam locomotive was built to the design of Richard Trevithick. Yet I needed no such recital of historical facts to tell me that it was here that it had all begun. I could feel it on my pulses; and, if I needed any reminder, the great black semi-circle of Darby's iron bridge, springing over Severn, spoke to me more eloquently than any history book.

At that time there were still some astonishing survivals to be seen in this part of Shropshire. I once had occasion to visit the Horsehay Ironworks which stands high up under the Wrekin. In the open works yard I saw men busy making steel invasion barges in preparation for 'D' Day. This sight was remarkable enough in such an improbable situation, but to make it the more extraordinary these barge builders were kept supplied with materials by a horse-drawn plate tramway – waggons with flangeless wheels running on cast-iron flanged rails, or 'ginny rails' as they still call them in Shropshire. Nor was this all. When I left Horsehay, I took the road towards Coal-brookdale. Imagine my astonishment when I beheld, just to the left of the road, a scene which, though very familiar to me from early engravings, I never expected to see in actuality. It was a working 'ginny pit'. A horse, plodding round in a circle, was turning the wooden barrel of the gin to wind a corve of coal up the shaft of the pit. Some sceptical readers may think that on that particular day I was suffering from hallucinations but, improbable though it may seem, my recollection of this astonishing sight is perfectly clear.

Early one summer evening I was standing beneath the arch of the iron bridge admiring its construction when I was accosted by a most remarkable man. He was wearing buttoned cloth gaiters, a pair of cord breeches, a green cloth waistcoat trimmed with braid, a bright red neckerchief and a cap clapped flatly on the back of his head. His grey eyes were keen and deep-set, his face as weathered by exposure as a gypsy's and he had the proud profile of a Roman emperor. His name was Harry Rogers. No sooner had we introduced ourselves, it seemed, than we were on easy Christian name terms. Harry made coracles in a little wooden shed with a slip-way running down from it to the Severn within the shadow of the iron bridge. Officially, he was a rabbit catcher, but I suspect this was a cover. It did not explain those mysterious nocturnal expeditions when at nightfall he would slip away soundlessly downstream in his coracle, not to return until the small hours of the morning.

Harry's shed by the river was filled and festooned with a purposeful clutter of objects: coils of rope, bundles of netting, rabbit snares and other miscellanea less easily identifiable. There were also stocks of the materials from which he made his coracles: lengths of sawn ash lath, rolls of coarse canvas, pots of tar and pitch. Maybe a new coracle frame, looking rather like a huge scuttle or skep basket such as were then still made in the Forest of Wyre, was building upon the floor. Here, leaning against the workbench or sitting in the doorway in the westering sunlight, we used to talk away many a summer's evening. He spoke in an extremely broad and somewhat harsh-sounding dialect which surprised me at first; it was so utterly unlike the soft speech of western Shropshire with which I was familiar. It seemed to me more closely akin to Black Country dialect and led me to speculate whether, when that area succeeded Shropshire as the centre of the new iron age, the men of Coalbrookdale and district had migrated thither. We talked of many things. He told me that the secret of the iron hardness of old oak timbers was that the trees were never allowed to lie in the bark when felled but were stripped of that bark for the tanneries while they were still green. He told me why his cottage behind the shed was called 'The Victory'. The local Council had placed a demolition order on it and had crassly offered him a new council house at Madeley on the top of the Hill. 'I to'd 'em,' he said, 'that afore I'd leave Siven they'd 'ave t' carry me feet form'st.' So battle had been joined. Finally he and his son had set to work to rebuild their cottage completely, and its new name celebrated the defeat of local bureaucracy. He also told me the sad story of the last trading barge to be seen on the Severn north of Bewdley. She had loaded a cargo of earthenware pipes at Jackfield, but had come to grief at Bridgnorth where her cargo had to be taken off. She was then bought by a man in Shrewsbury for conversion into a stationary houseboat. Harry's father, with the assistance of his young son and a couple of horses, had then undertaken delivery to her new owner. Upstream to Shrewsbury, the river had long been disused for navigation, and Harry recalled with a wicked chuckle that the local landowners were not amused when they broke down their hedges to make a way for the horses, claiming the ancient right to navigate 'the King's high stream of Severn' without let or hindrance.

I liked best Harry's story of the would-be suicide. He was returning late at night in his coracle from some nefarious expedition when he saw, dimly outlined against the stars, a figure standing behind the high railings on top of the iron bridge. In a loud voice he was proclaiming his intention to do away with himself. Harry landed noiselessly at his slip, crept up behind the unsuspecting suicide and suddenly in a stern voice called out 'Hey, stop tha' 'ollerin', I'll gie thee a leg oop.' "Ee didn't arf run,' commented Harry. 'Reckon 'ee thought it was owd Nick 'isself as'd come fer 'im.'

While we talked, his keen eyes strayed constantly towards the river, ever on the look-out for a likely piece of flotsam. After a flood his slipway would be littered with the objects he had salvaged: a substantial tree trunk; a couple of stout fencing posts; part of a landing stage; an old punt. He used to boast that Severn supplied him with all his winter fuel. In a time of high flood, when the gorge brimmed with an angry torrent of swirling brown waters, I have watched admiringly as he manoeuvred his frail coracle with supremely confident skill to capture with a line a large floating log and bring it in to his slip. He was a man who had adapted himself to Severn as naturally and as perfectly as any otter or salmon.

I finally persuaded Harry to build a coracle for me and when it was finished, I bore it proudly home to Tardebigge on the roof of the Austin. On summer evenings in the still waters of the canal, I mastered the difficult art of propelling it with a single paddle in the direction in which I wanted to go instead of spinning round like a teetotum, providing the locals with much innocent entertainment in the process. Like riding a bicycle it was all a question of balance. Once you lost that balance, the coracle instantly turned turtle and its occupant found himself struggling in the water, his head trapped beneath it in the large bubble of air it held as in some dark diving bell. I still have that coracle. It is a constant reminder of Ironbridge and of one of the most remarkable characters I have ever been lucky enough to know. I cherish his memory dearly. For me, Harry Rogers seemed to incarnate the very spirit of Severn, a spirit infinitely more ancient than the ironworks that once flamed upon its banks.

I sometimes used to feel guilty about my work for the Ministry of Supply. It was the first 'white collar' job I had ever had and it was also the best paid. I was conscientious and knew that I was achieving as good results as most of my colleagues, and probably better than some. Yet after my experience on the shop floor it did seem to me to be what my workmates would have called a cushy job. There was no doubt in my mind that the work I had been doing at the Aldbourne Foundry, because it had called for a far greater expenditure of creative effort and skill, was the more intrinsically valuable. That it was so meagrely rewarded seemed contrary to common sense. Nevertheless, these years with the Ministry were not wasted; they yielded their quota of valuable experiences. I should never have visited Coalbrookdale and met Harry Rogers for one thing, for with petrol supplies restricted to essential purposes, I was luckier than most people in the extent to which I was able to travel about the Midland shires.

For all private and domestic journeys, of course, we had to depend on a public transport system that today no longer exists. My annual leaves we usually spent at Llanthony Abbey in the Black Mountains, and these recurring visits affected me so deeply that they were easily the most potent single influence upon my life during this period.

The first of them was in September 1940, while we were still at Hungerford. We were able then to travel by car, crossing the Severn by the Beachley–Aust ferry, but subsequent journeys from Tardebigge had to be made by rail to Llanvihangel Crucorney station and thence on foot for seven miles up the Vale of Ewyas with our belongings on our backs. This country, and in particular this valley of the Honddu, had made a deep impression upon me as a small boy. Moreover, with the passing of the years my childish memories of it had not faded but sharpened, so much so that when war broke out and the world seemed to come crashing about our ears I felt an irresistible urge to revisit this country of my childhood. On our first visit I had felt uneasy. Would I be disillusioned and disappointed? Might I not find that a magic which had worked so powerfully upon my childish imagination could no longer be received by my blunted adult senses? I need not have worried; experience soon proved that this homing instinct had been right.

As we walked beneath the arching hazels in the deep lanes of the valley floor or along the high ridges of the mountain walls that enclosed it; as we climbed the Gospel Pass, retracing that same green track by which I had first come to the valley by horse-drawn waggonette from Cusop as a small boy, I realized that remembered beauties were no figment of childish fancy. They were real and had not changed. To know that what had spoken to me as a child could speak just as eloquently to me now was a moving and exalting experience. But whereas in my childhood I had taken for granted that what I apprehended was eternal, now it appeared the more poignant and precious because, as a man, I had learned that my species alone possessed the power to disfigure or to destroy it utterly. Man could, if he willed it so, drown the landscape of this valley, these flowering meadows, those tall trees and small stone farms, fathoms deep beneath the waters of a reservoir, silencing forever the voices of its streams; he could mar the majestic profile of the mountains with a dark and deadening blanket of alien conifers leaving the barren earth beneath to leach away; or he could trample them under the arrogant steel feet of marching pylons.

Once we walked over the mountain ridge into the adjoining valley of Gwynne Fawr and saw with sinking hearts that its slopes had been planted with regimented ranks of conifers. The lines of the unclimbable wire fences that bordered these new plantations, so wantonly blocking ancient tracks and footpaths, had obviously been arbitrarily ruled by a hand utterly unmoved by any tenderness or reverence for the lovely natural folds and curves of the landscape. Within the confines of this vegetable concentration camp stood noble trees of native hardwood wearing their green leaves for the last time; for their bark had been ringed and they had been brutally left to die. The sight filled me with impotent rage.

For the rest, the landscape of the Black Mountains was still the same as it had been in my childhood; but the fate of Gwynne Fawr, as an example of man's arrogance, his folly and his greed, now made its beauties seem as ephemeral as a rose, and so the more keenly to be apprehended and treasured.

One occasion, especially, has stayed in my mind. I was looking out of a window of our candle-lit bedroom high in one of the south towers of the Abbey. This window looked across the roofless ruin of the Abbey church to where the high altar had once stood. The summer night was perfectly still and calm, and a full moon had just risen above the dark protective wall of Hatterall hill. The clipped turf below was lightly silvered with dew, and upon it the nave columns and arches cast shadows almost as dark and substantial as they themselves appeared. In this pattern of substance and shadow, the aspirations and the craftsmanship of long forgotten men, the loveliness of the landscape and the celestial beauty of the night seemed to become inseparable parts of one whole so majestical that no words of mine can describe it. I can only attempt to convey the effect it had upon me. It was no longer possible to believe, as does the materialist, that what I saw revealed no creative purpose but was merely the chance by-product of blind chaos. I became convinced that this was not so. Nor did the argument that all beauty is in the eye of the beholder shake this conviction. For even if it were true that what I saw before me was merely a pattern imposed upon a formless void by my own mind and senses, then from what mysterious source, I wondered, did such a vision spring? Reality or vision, the revelation remained. I am no mystic, yet I think I had come near to understanding what Henry Vaughan meant when he wrote:

> I saw Eternity the other night
> Like a great ring of pure and endless light,
> All calm, as it was bright . . .

In our long and often painful pilgrimage from birth to death, most of us set out with the notion that eventually we shall find a key to the mystery of life; surely there must be a wise man somewhere who, if only we can find him, knows all the answers? We eye our fellow pilgrims hopefully, wondering

from what source they derive the strength to stride so purposefully upon their way despite the tragedies and misfortunes
that are man's common lot. Failing to find this wise man in
the flesh, we then seek him at second-hand in the written
word. Often such a quest ends in the acceptance of a particular
credo which offers consoling, over-simplified solutions to every
problem, provided only that we suspend our own critical judgement and reject or ignore such of those lessons of experience
which conflict with that one true faith. I ran such a course,
but by this time in my life I had reached a point where I
realized that no one person and no one religion or philosophy
could claim a monopoly of truth; that truth was something to
be distilled from personal experience, to be felt along the
pulses but never to be purchased second-hand; the pursuit of
it a quest that must continue to my life's end. Deliberately to
choose such a hard road may sound proud and arrogant. In
fact I have never scorned or rejected the sayings or writings of
those older, wiser or more experienced than I am; and I have
known nothing more exciting and stimulating than to discover my own experience confirmed or enlarged in this way.
But for me, doctrine has always been accepted or rejected by the
touchstone of personal experience and not the other way round.

Now, as a fruit of experiences such as the one I have just
tried to describe, I conceived an idea of the natural world – or,
indeed, of the whole universe including man himself – as a vast
ordered system of interdependent parts. For someone like
myself, with an engineering cast of mind, I was tempted to
substitute the word 'mechanism' for 'system' although, as I
knew only too well, this was apt to be a misleading analogy.
For a so-called mechanistic view of the universe generally
implies materialism, whereas in my case this was very definitely
not so. For I found it impossible to conceive even the simplest
of mechanisms, let alone one so infinitely complex in operation
and so beautifully ordered, which had not been consciously
designed. It seemed to me that in this vast and elaborate
scheme of things, man occupied a position uniquely privileged,
and therefore responsible and hazardous. He alone was at
once inside and outside the system. On the one hand, as a
creature, he was a part of the mechanism and so ultimately

governed by its laws; on the other, as a man, he was uniquely equipped to comprehend it, to unravel and understand some, though not all, of the complex working principles by which it operated. It was knowledge so gained that gave man the power to tinker with the works, with consequences that could lead to total disaster.

Once conceived, this view of the universe seemed infinitely exciting; it influenced all my thought, gave to everything I read – and I now began to read much more – a new meaning. What was more important, it explained, to my own satisfaction at all events, the deep dichotomy in my own nature; why my consuming interest in things mechanical so often conflicted with my passionate feeling for the beauties of the natural world. This is why, as I wrote at the beginning of this chapter, I look back on the war years that I spent at Tardebigge as among the happiest and most fruitful of my life.

Through my friend Sam Clutton, we had acquired a small clavichord which was, I believe, the first instrument to be built by Alec Hodsdon of Lavenham who was later to become celebrated as a maker of harpsichords. It was the only type of keyboard instrument that would fit into the small compass of a canal boat cabin and I contrived a folding stand for it, so we could easily stow it away if need be. The clavichord's small and subtle voice which makes it unsuitable for public performance was perfectly suited to the confined space of our boat cabin. Of an evening, Angela would play some simple, plaintive little piece by William Byrd or John Bull while I would sit reading, or, preoccupied with my thoughts, gazing out of the deep windows of our cabin while the sun went down behind the Abberley Hills and shadows began to thicken in the vale below. After days spent in Birmingham or Wolverhampton, at such times *Cressy*'s cabin with its familiar bookshelves seemed mercifully isolated from the fretful fever of human affairs. Here, so it seemed to me, I could step aside from the world for a few hours and regard it objectively as though from some other planet. Illusory though this sense of detachment and isolation might be, it acted as a great spiritual and mental stimulus which I found immensely valuable.

My historical self-education had hitherto been confined to

the period of Britain's Industrial Revolution because this seemed to me to be the most significant and fateful movement in the history of man. Now, armed with new insights, I began to range much more widely in social history, and particularly in the histories of religion, philosophy and science, in an attempt to chart the currents of thought which had brought that Revolution about. In doing so I discovered to my surprise that my thinking was much more closely akin to medieval ideas about the cosmos and of man's place in it than to any subsequent scientific view of the universe. It seemed to me astonishing that men, so woefully ignorant of the laws by which 'the great machine' operated that they could believe that sun and planets revolved about a flat earth, should, none the less, have succeeded in arriving intuitively at an elaborate concept or model of universal order which rang prophetically true. Taken literally, the figures they employed to express and explain this concept of order, the chain of being, the correspondences, the music of the spheres and the cosmic dance, make so much scientific gibberish; yet, at the deeper level of poetic imagery and metaphor, such figures struck me as being profoundly meaningful. This conception of cosmic order was essentially moral because the medieval mind saw it as an ideal model for human society. It drew parallels between the natural order and man's social order, and judged the latter accordingly. It believed that, in so far as the lives of men, individually or collectively, were true to this analogy, goodness and harmony prevailed and, conversely, evil and chaos were the inevitable accompaniment of non-conformity.

It so happened that at this time (1943) the late Dr E. M. W. Tillyard's book *The Elizabethan World Picture* was first published. So far as I was concerned, its appearance could not have been more timely. In it Dr Tillyard shows how, despite the new currents of Renaissance thought which were beginning to flow in Elizabethan England, a 'world picture' of cosmic order inherited from the Middle Ages was still tacitly accepted and so continued to exercise a profound influence over the thought of the period. I owe a great deal to this book; not least, it enlarged my understanding of the plays of Shakespeare, making them seem immeasurably greater and more meaningful. Once one accepts the medieval concept of universal order, then the histories and the tragedies of Shakespeare become so many object-lessons on the consequences of violating that order, no matter whether it be through the sins of pride (Lear), ambition (Macbeth) or jealousy (Othello). *Macbeth* had long been my favourite play, but now it seemed to take on an entirely new dimension as I saw in Macbeth's undoing the image of modern man.

It is a measure of the greatness and universal quality of Shakespeare's art that, like life itself, it should be capable of bearing so many different interpretations. We look at his plays, as at life, through the polarized spectacles of our own 'world picture', seeing in them only what we expect to see. Thus current productions reflect the bleak existentialist view of man, and their weight of meaning is, in my view, immeasurably diminished thereby. Yet I take heart from the fact that although Dr Tillyard's book was not reprinted for twenty years, it has now been reprinted three times in paperback edition, a belated popularity which may reflect impending change.

Implicit in the notion of cosmic order was the belief that this world could become a paradise provided man recognized and obeyed the laws of that order and so steered clear of the seven deadly sins. Once I had grasped this, the story of Adam and Eve, which had previously seemed to me no more than a quaint and scientifically absurd fable, now suddenly assumed a new and tremendously significant weight of meaning: that paradise, where man had once walked naked and unashamed, was firmly rooted upon earth and was not in some remote and abstract hereafter in the skies. And ever since man's own follies had driven him out of this earthly paradise he had been haunted by ancient race memories, to remind him of the magnitude of that loss; by dreams, by intimations of beauty, or by that sense of sorrow, born of our inability to savour it sufficiently fully, to which the contemplation of natural beauty moves us. If, as has been said, such beauty does indeed reside solely in the eye of the beholder, then may not its apprehension be due to the mysterious working of some unbelievably ancient genetically inherited faculty, reminding us so poignantly of an Eden long lost?

Pursuing such lines of thought, it seemed to me that man's material progress had been accompanied by the gradual failure and loss of this ancient vision until, in the orthodox religious view, this world became merely a dreary battleground of sin, temptation and toil, its beauties and joys the seductions of the devil, in which man was abjured to 'fight the good fight' in the hope of earning his reward in a nebulous hereafter becoming, one must suppose, uncomfortably crowded. It was in the emergence of this bleak, puritanical view of the world as a kind of purgatory where each individual must strive for personal salvation against every kind of sensual temptation that I believed I had found the key to all that had followed, including the ultimate defeat of organized religion by scientific materialism. For to counsel the rejection of the world along with the flesh and the devil seemed to me a blasphemy which had completely changed man's 'world picture' and led inevitably to a fundamental change in the relationship between man and the natural world. Whereas before, the concept of human society modelled in a cosmic order implied a partnership between man and nature that was based on wonder and humility, man's attitude could now be summed up in the increasingly popular phrase 'the conquest of nature'. Humility was succeeded by *hubris*; the ancient vision of a lost paradise on earth faded and man declared total war upon his world. And because one of the first rules of war is to denigrate your enemy, the natural world was now seen to be merely the chance product of the interaction of blind forces. To win command over these forces and to harness them in the service of a campaign of wholesale rapine and rape thereafter became man's sole concern. There was no conflict here with the old puritanical religious concept of fighting the good fight through a vale of tears; only the desired goal had changed. The notion of individual reward in a mythical hereafter gave place to an unquestioning faith in material progress. In other words, ultimate victory in man's campaign against nature would spell Utopia on earth. As we are now very belatedly discovering, however, this vision of a man-made paradise is as illusory as that of the earlier hereafter which it superseded. Had we not been so beguiled by the scientific messiahs of material progress, forever promising jam tomorrow, we might have realized sooner that the only end product of total war is a scorched and pillaged earth, an uninhabitable desert.

I saw in the publication of Charles Darwin's *Origin of Species* the scientific shot which had finally scuppered the ship of organized religion. The notions of 'nature red in tooth and claw' and of 'the survival of the fittest' appeared fully to sanction man's conquest of nature, for by thus taking up arms against her, man was simply acting in accordance with these inexorable natural laws which had existed since time began. To prove himself the fittest to survive in a general free-for-all, with no holds barred, appeared to be man's natural role. To a religion which had lost its vision and clung doggedly to a literal interpretation of the scriptures, the Darwinian theory dealt a fatal blow from which it has never recovered.

I read of this century-old Darwinian controversy with absolute incredulity. Although science is dedicated to the pursuit of truth, scientific 'laws' invariably turn out either to be false or to be, at best, misleading half truths. The reason for this apparent paradox is that the pursuit of truth is an endless journey into undiscovered country. There is always more to be found round the next corner which is capable of altering our whole perspective of the road we have travelled. What had seemed to one generation of scientists an unalterable law is proved invalid by the next. So it is with Darwinism. The theory was correct, but the survival of the fittest is by no means the only law governing the evolutionary process, and we have since found that the genetic mechanisms governing evolution are infinitely more complex and subtle than Darwin supposed. But, even so, the formulation of a principle by which the mechanism of creative purpose operated should never have induced men to jump to the conclusion that because there was a mechanism there could not be any sentient agent of that purpose. This seemed to me a complete *non sequitur*. The only thing that Darwin's shot had sunk was the myth that the world had been created complete in seven days in a geologically recent past.

Of the religious writers that I discovered at this time it was the so-called Cambridge Platonists of the seventeenth century, especially Henry Vaughan and Thomas Traherne, who appealed to me most strongly, and it was with a shock of surprise that I found that both Vaughan and Traherne had known the Black Mountain country of my childhood and had obviously been influenced by it. Neither man subscribed to the gloomy, puritanical view of the world that became fashionable in their day. On the contrary they enjoyed its manifold beauties with wonder and humility as revelations of creative purpose. I felt that had they lived in the nineteenth century their vision and belief would not have been lost or shaken by any scientific discoveries of the methods by which that purpose operated. Traherne, in a passage which I quoted in the previous volume of this autobiography, specifically distinguishes between the world of men and the world of nature; 'leave the one that you may enjoy the other,' he exhorts. This is but a short step from the medieval doctrine that sought to bring the two worlds closer together by seeing the natural order as providing a set of rules for the guidance of man in shaping his social order.

It is easy to record outward happenings; it is far more difficult honestly to chart the spiritual progress that accompanies them, and which in part influences those events and is in part influenced by them. However, I have tried to summarize as faithfully as I can how far I travelled in the world of thought and imagination during the war years. It will, I think, help to explain future events and my reactions to them.

Chapter 4

Getting into Print

In my new-found philosophy I believed I had at last found the key to problems that had troubled me all my life. The effect that this discovery had upon me was intensely exhilarating, not to say intoxicating. Conundrums over which I had puzzled in vain were suddenly solved; what had appeared meaningless and chaotic fragments now became parts of an ordered pattern; the natural world had never seemed to me more beautiful. I cannot define and explain this euphoric state of mind better than by quoting a passage from Thomas Traherne's *Centuries of Meditations*:

> You never enjoy the world aright, till you so love the beauty of enjoying it, that you are covetous and earnest to persuade others to enjoy it. And so perfectly hate the abominable corruption of men in despising it, that you had rather suffer the flames of Hell than willingly be guilty of their error. There is so much blindness and ingratitude and damned folly in it. The world is a mirror of infinite beauty, yet no man sees it. It is a Temple of Majesty, yet no man regards it. It is a region of Light and Peace, did not men disquiet it. It is the Paradise of God. It is more to man since he is fallen than it was before. It is the place of Angels and the Gate of Heaven.

I, too, felt that I was enjoying the world aright and became covetous and earnest to persuade others to enjoy it with me. I was the more encouraged to do this by the interregnum of war and its effect upon society. When life is forced by desperate emergency out of its normal peacetime channels, when men and women are called upon to face common perils and hardships, their old rivalries and antagonisms tend to be forgotten and they become 'members one of another'. In such an atmosphere of goodwill it was easy to believe that 'the bad old days' of the nineteen-thirties would never return; that men had now surely seen the error of their ways and would start building a new and better world as soon as the war was over.

In this new mood of certitude and optimism I began furiously to write, oblivious of that rejected manuscript which lay forgotten in a suitcase beneath our bed. Considering that I could only write in my spare time, I marvel now that I accomplished so much in so short a space of time. Leafing through a scrap book of old and yellowing press cuttings, I am amazed that I ever had the temerity to write with such oracular assurance on so wide a variety of subjects. I aired my views in the 'little magazines', in *Horizon*, *Kingdom Come*, and *Voices*, and took part in many controversies in the correspondence columns of the weeklies. For *Horizon* I wrote an article which dealt with the tyranny of the machine over man and forecast that in the future a better educated generation would inevitably rebel against the stupifying monotony which it imposed; for *Kingdom Come*, 'Imagination and the Dramatic Art', a plea for an uncluttered stage and a more imaginative use of lighting in place of elaborate sets; for *Voices*, 'Letter to a Surrealist', a lengthy reply countering a series of articles expounding the surrealist philosophy. But the main object of my attack was the baneful effect of modern technology and economics on world ecology, particularly as applied to agriculture. In this battle I joined forces with Lord Portsmouth, Sir Albert Howard and H. J. Massingham.

My correspondence with H. J. Massingham began with a 'fan' letter from me and soon developed into a regular and frequent exchange of letters over a period of years in which we freely set down our views and ideas. I have never maintained such an intimate and lengthy correspondence either before or since and found it extraordinarily stimulating. Such a meeting of minds is a rare pleasure which has now been made almost impossible by the relentless pressures of modern life. Because they allow us no time to translate our thoughts on to paper, letter writing becomes merely a necessary and generally unwelcome chore, the result a brief and colourless short-hand of facts and banalities. One wonders how many of those bulky volumes of posthumous correspondence our generation will produce. Very few, I would guess.

In addition to all this ephemeral writing and correspondence I found time to set down my ideas on paper in a book which proclaimed that our machine civilization was heading for disaster unless it changed its course. I concluded that: 'the wastage of human and natural resources which an acquisitive society necessarily incurs, leads logically towards barbarism and the exhaustion of those resources'. While I explained how I thought this fatal course might be corrected, I came to the conclusion that such a correction could only be made by a generation which had received a more enlightened education. In other words, ambitious and precocious though it was, it offered no quick Utopian panacea. I took the book's title *High Horse Riderless*, from the closing lines of a poem by W. B. Yeats in which he laments the passing of an older and more stable society:

> But all is changed, that high horse riderless
> Though mounted in that saddle Homer rode
> Where the swan drifts upon a darkling flood.

A great, riderless horse; it made me think of the fabulous horses, the broken columns and the desolate and strangely menacing landscapes that I had seen in certain paintings by Chirico which I had admired on the walls of a friend's house near Hungerford. Though I could not fathom the precise meaning of Yeats's use of the image, it seemed to me an exactly appropriate one for a technological civilization which was nearing the end of its tether.

Like my first over-ambitious and unpublishable novel *Strange Vista* of ten years before, *High Horse Riderless* was written compulsively from the desire to clarify and codify my own ideas rather than with any thought of publication. When the book was finished it joined *A Painted Ship* in that suitcase under our bed – but not for long.

In one of his letters, Massingham asked why I did not write something about the canals. My reply, that I had already done so but that the result had gone the round of the publishing world in vain, brought a request to see the manuscript. So I dusted it off and dispatched it to him, though without any sense of expectation. A week later came a letter so enthusiastic that it made me realize how badly I had needed the tonic of encouragement. Could he, Massingham asked, send it on to his friend Douglas Jerrold of Eyre & Spottiswoode? Indeed he could, and soon I received an equally encouraging letter from Jerrold accepting the book. A contract followed in September 1943.

Only a fellow author can understand the jubilation a writer feels when his first book is accepted, particularly when that book has such a dreary record of hope deferred. I read through that contract over and over again to assure myself that it was really true. It was as though I had received an unexpected legacy from an unknown rich uncle. Yes, there was my name at the top (hereinafter called the Author) and, believe it or not, the Publishers did 'undertake to produce and publish a work at present entitled *A Painted Ship* at their own risk and expense'. Nor was there any attempt to take advantage of a 'prentice writer's natural desire to get into print. The terms were indeed extremely fair – very much fairer than many a contract I have had to haggle over since. There was only one disappointment. Eyre & Spottiswoode decided not to use the splendid set of photographs that Angela had taken especially to illustrate the book. They evidently classified *A Painted Ship* as a 'country book' and there was – and to some extent still is – a publishing convention that all books of this kind, if illustrated at all, should be illustrated in black-and-white by an artist. I think the theory must be that the cool objective eye of the camera is insufficiently 'romantic' to suit a hey-nonny-no, under-the-greenwood-tree type of text; if so, I think it was a pity to apply this to *A Painted Ship* which was not intended to be that kind of book at all. Its purpose was to make a personal record of the canals and their life which, in the words Massingham used in his Foreword, 'were perishing under the brutal impact of industrialism'. For this reason I wanted photographs to state unequivocally 'this was how it was'. All this must sound uncomplimentary to Denys Watkins-

Pitchford who was commissioned by the publishers to illustrate the book. His scraper-board pictures, most of which were based upon Angela's photographs, have been rightly praised but, however accurate and skilful they may be, it is impossible to rid this type of illustration from the suspicion of romanticism or 'artist's licence'.

I was somewhat mollified when the publishers accepted my suggestion that I should ask my friend Herbert Tooley of the Banbury Boat Dock, who had decorated *Cressy* with the traditional roses and castles so beloved of the boaters, to design a jacket for the book. The result, painted on a wooden panel, was one of the most original and beautiful designs ever to grace a book. It was a tragedy when eventually the block was broken and subsequent editions were no longer able to wear this brave and beautiful thing.

By the time I commissioned Herbert Tooley I had decided upon a change of title. There was something slightly arty-crafty about *A Painted Ship*, I felt. I had also come to the conclusion that a book's title should never be lifted from a poem unless the theme of that poem is relevant to the subject of the book. It certainly could not be said that the horrific story told by Coleridge's Ancient Mariner had anything whatever to do with the English canals, so I re-titled the book, very simply, *Narrow Boat*. The publishers accepted this change with some reluctance, arguing that the term would be meaningless because most people thought of all canal craft as barges.

Six months after *Narrow Boat* was contracted for, my morale received a second fillip. Massingham, for whose literary sponsorship I shall always be grateful, wrote to say that Robert Hale, the publisher, was planning a new series of books on the English counties and that he had recommended me as a likely contributor to his friend Brian Vesey-FitzGerald, who had been appointed general editor of the series. Almost immediately came a letter from Vesey-FitzGerald offering me a choice of three counties; one of them was Worcestershire which I chose without hesitation. Back came a contract from Robert Hale dated March 1944. I had won my first commission.

It was only later that I realized what a remarkable transaction this was. I was completely unknown and with only one book, as yet unpublished, to my credit. Yet I was not asked for any specimen chapter or even for a synopsis. Nor was there any preliminary meeting with editor or publisher. Brian Vesey-FitzGerald did not lay down any guide-lines whatever but gave me a completely free hand. Even the length of the book was elastic – anything from 70,000 to 120,000 words. Although I welcomed such a liberal attitude, I think it was the reason why, when the series eventually appeared, it was decidedly uneven in quality. Authors felt free to mount each his particular hobby horse and ride furiously away for chapter after chapter.

I was not a native of Worcestershire; in fact, I had never even lived in the county until we had moored *Cressy* at Tardebigge in 1941. But there were two reasons for my choice. The first was the purely practical one that, at a time when travel was still severely restricted, my work for the Ministry of Supply gave me a splendid opportunity to kill two birds with one stone by gathering material for the book while travelling round on my job. After all, as a result of such travelling, I already knew a great deal more about Worcestershire than I did when we had first sailed into it three years before. My second reason was that Worcestershire seemed, almost more than any other shire, to represent a microcosm of England both in its social history and in the variety of its topography. Extending northward to embrace Dudley in the Black Country, eastward to the foot of the Cotswold scarp and westward through the Teme valley gap almost to the Marches of Wales, its boundary embraced an immense and meaningful variety of landscape both natural and man-made.

I had always disliked those romanticized books about rural England designed to suppress ugly truths and to make their readers forget that there had ever been an Industrial Revolution or even any Enclosure Acts, by painting a false picture of a countryside unchanged since the Middle Ages, or certainly since the mid-eighteenth century. In this topographical dreamworld such facts of life as factories, housing estates, overhead power lines, railways, or even canals, did not exist. Such books are the literary equivalent of those photographs of olde worlde, picturesque villages taken early on a summer morning before any cars are parked around and from which the wirescape has been carefully touched out. Their writers make much play with the adjective 'unspoiled' without pausing to consider its significance, much less to ask themselves who has done the spoiling and why. I was determined that *Worcestershire* should not be a book of this genre but should present an honest portrait of the shire, warts and all, the black Worcestershire as well as the green. Having just finished *High Horse Riderless*, this commission seemed a heaven-sent opportunity to write a case-history illustrating the validity of the general arguments I had advanced in the earlier book. I would make two journeys through the shire, one through time and one through space; taken together, they would demonstrate the interdependence between man and nature by revealing man's influence, good and bad, upon the landscape and how, in turn, he had been influenced by it. So, in my introduction to *Worcestershire*, I wrote: 'If a topographer sets out to write about his chosen region something of more moment than a mere guidebook, or a record of a sentimental journey, he must approach and judge his subject from some particular standpoint. The standpoint I have chosen has been the ecological one.' But I very much doubt whether, at that time, more than one in a hundred readers knew what I meant by ecology.

Gathering material for this book was a fascinating and memorable experience. At the time I found it exciting and rewarding, such was the infinite variety and richness of the Worcestershire characters to whom it introduced me: Squire of Stourbridge making fireclay glass-pots by a method which pre-dated the invention of the potter's wheel; Weaver of Catshill, last of the Bromsgrove nailmasters, working the oliver in his back-yard nail forge; Birch of Bewdley, last of the Wyre Forest broom-squires making his besoms, whisks and skep baskets; Eddie Moore, the scythe-maker, plating scythe blades under his water-powered tilt hammer in a little forge at Bell End; a remarkable old man named George 'Aurelius' Marcuis, last of a long line of Bewdley river men and barge-masters; William Fowkes of Droitwich, silver-haired and soft-voiced, a master furniture maker if ever there was one. Fowkes, in particular, became a dear friend of mine. After a day spent in the offices and machine shops of large factories spewing out weapons of mechanized warfare, what a relief it was to climb the outside wooden stair to his loft workshop and, leaning against a corner of the bench, to talk to this gentle, wise and humble man while he worked, handling his simple tools with a precision marvellously deft. I saw such men as the last representatives of an older social order which, like the natural world, owed its stability to its diversity. In this it was the precise opposite of the society created by modern technology which, driven forward at headlong pace by false economics, is not only chronically unstable, but imposes the shoddy uniformity of the worthless and the second-rate, thus running counter to the needs of human nature and oversetting the delicate balance of the natural world – or the natural order, as I called it at this time.

One of my greatest sources of inspiration was the collection of Worcestershire 'by-gones' with which J. F. Parker and his wife had filled their house at Tickenhill, perched on a hilltop looking down on Bewdley. They had begun by collecting relics of the life and the manifold trades and crafts of that ancient river port, but had gradually expended their range until it covered the whole county. To visit Tickenhill and to take tea before the wood fire, which, in recollection, seemed to blaze perpetually in the open hearth of the great hall, surrounded by such treasure trove was a magical experience. It was utterly unlike any museum. Here were no dead objects, embalmed behind glass and self-consciously displayed; but a treasure house, an Aladdin's cave in which the infinitely varied riches of the past seemed to have acquired a strange new life through the knowledge, understanding and boundless enthusiasm of one elderly, white-haired couple. They proved a powerful source of inspiration where *Worcestershire* was concerned.

I sought out not only Worcestershire's individual craftsmen but also those industries peculiar to the region which had developed from older craft trades: Stourbridge glass workers, Redditch needle makers and the chain-makers of Cradley Heath.

In doing so I made some astonishing discoveries. I shall not forget my amazement on seeing in the barn of a farm near a fireclay mine outside Stourbridge, a small and elderly beam engine, supplied with steam by an old egg-ended boiler, driving a chaff cutter*. With the history of the canals and railways of the county I had long been familiar, but I spent a memorable morning on the footplate of No. 2290, the celebrated ten-wheels-coupled 'Lickey Banker', a labouring giant which spent a long lifetime pushing heavy trains up the 1 in 37 Lickey incline from Bromsgrove to Blackwell. How often of a night time as we lay in bed on *Cressy* did we hear the distant sound of her deep organ-pipe whistle speaking to the train engines, 'I am here and ready', a signal soon to be followed by the slow, syncopated rhythm of steam locomotives labouring heavily in full gear. At such times I would imagine I heard the clang and rattle of the fireman's shovels and see in the mind's eye the intermittent glare from opened fire doors, shining on steam and smoke.

In the first, historical, part of the book I paid tribute to the example of the monastic orders in Worcestershire, both as agriculturists and as founders of craft trades. It seemed to me that the history of these religious communities displayed an intuitive understanding of, and reverence for, the natural order which was summed up in the phrase *Laborare est orare*. Massingham shared this view. We both felt that, although they had been to some extent corrupted by their own worldly success, the dissolution of the monasteries was an almost unmitigated disaster for England. Consequently, because it was the modern custodian of the monastic principles which we so much admired, we both carried on at this time what I can only describe as an uneasy flirtation with the Roman Catholic church.

By what was surely a somewhat remarkable compromise, Massingham was eventually received into that church, but as a non-practising member; the liberal family tradition he inherited would never permit him to swallow the authoritarian dogma of papal infallibility. As he wrote in his autobiography *Remembrance*: 'The abrogation of private judgement is to me an impenetrable wall dividing me from the full Christian

* The engine is now in the Birmingham Museum of Science and Industry.

communion.' So whole-heartedly do I agree with this last statement that I do not think I could ever have struck even such an uneasy compromise. As it was, my flirtation with what my father always dismissed with a snort as 'popery' very soon cooled over the mundane but vital question of birth-control.

Birth-control seemed to me an unwarrantable interference with that 'natural order' whose virtues I proclaimed. Yet advances in medical science had already achieved a form of death-control by greatly prolonging man's expectation of life. Consequently, although at this time it was widely held that the population of England would decline after the war, I foresaw an inevitable population explosion which would subject the delicate balance of the natural order to such pressures that it must inevitably lead to a catastrophic breakdown. I had deliberately avoided mentioning this dilemma in *High Horse Riderless* because it seemed the one loose thread in an otherwise satisfactory fabric. I cudgelled my brains over it in vain for many months and finally resolved to write to a noted Jesuit apologist at Farm Street and find out what he had to say on the subject. He replied as follows:

> I think that the answer of the catholic non-technician must be that the end can't justify the means: that however useful a thing may be you can't do it if it's wrong in itself. But that of course isn't helpful. I should have thought that scientific agriculture etc might provide some sort of solution: I've read somewhere about ways of producing plants in tiers for instance, and that sort of thing . . . In fact of course I suppose we have to reckon with the effect of wars and other disasters if we take a factual view . . .

I found this reply so profoundly unhelpful and thought it revealed such shortsightedness, such vagueness and muddled thinking, that it effectually ended my brief flirtation with Catholicism. What struck me as bitterly ironical was that my correspondent should rely on wars and disasters, or on those modern high-priests, the scientists, who, by monoculture, poison sprays and machines, were destroying the natural order and laying waste the earth, to come to his rescue and solve the problem. It seemed to me that it would have been at once more honest and more logical if he had argued that men should not strive to prolong life. In other words, if you argued against birth-control you should take a similar stand against death-control too on the ground that both represented an unwarrantable interference with the natural order. This might seem to be an impossible *reductio ad absurdum*; yet was the suggestion that men should be left to die in their beds any more callous than the priest's own argument that millions might be massacred by modern methods of warfare?

I eventually reasoned that the answer lay in that same 'abrogation of private judgement' that had proved such a stumbling block to Massingham. For what was that abrogation if it was not a denial of man's unique and perilous gift of free-will? This gave to man alone of all species the choice of either recognizing and working with the natural order or flouting it at his peril. To say that men had been divinely ordered to breed like rabbits and then to rely hopefully on war, pestilence or famine to restore the ecological balance seemed to me to assume that man was no better than an animal. Expressed in religious terms, it was a blasphemous denial of a God-given gift. I therefore saw the principle of birth-control as part of man's conscious recognition of a natural order and his willingness to work for it. The alternative spelled chaos and disaster. So, to my own satisfaction at any rate, I solved this nagging problem but at the price of rejecting contemporary Catholic orthodoxy.

Soon after I had been commissioned to write the book on Worcestershire I received a letter from Henry Cornelius, a film producer from South Africa who had come over to this country to make a series of films for Ealing Studios of which the best-known was to be *Genevieve*. He was contemplating a film about the canals and asked whether I could advise him. How he had heard of me I cannot now remember. *Narrow Boat* had not been published, but I had written a number of articles about canals, advocating their greater use, and I can only assume that he must have come across one of these. The upshot of this correspondence was that Cornelius, accompanied by his director, Charles Crichton, came to visit us at Tardebigge, picking their way along the muddy path to the boat one cold day in earliest spring. 'Corney' was a fat and physically unprepossessing South African Jew, but I remember him with affection – he died in the 1950s. He was a strangely endearing and unconventional figure with a remarkably quick and astute mind. On reaching *Cressy* he climbed ponderously aboard, wrapped in an enormous overcoat, removed his pathetically sodden London shoes on the fore-deck, squeezed through the cabin doors and padded into the boat like some large bear. I can see him now as he filled one of our easy chairs before the open stove, twiddling his toes and still huddled in his overcoat. For he had not long arrived from Africa and disliked the English climate.

He was contemplating, he said, making a film about the English canals that would be partly fictional and partly a documentary. I think I must have told him the original title of my book, for he decided to call this film *Painted Boats* and the outcome of this first encounter was that I agreed to act as his technical adviser. I welcomed this opportunity, not because I was dazzled by the world of the movies – we hardly ever went to the cinema – but simply because it promised an entirely new and novel experience. He gave me an outline of the fictional part of the film and its requirements, which included a tunnel, and asked me to advise him as to the best location – preferably not too far from London. I suggested the stretch of the Grand Union canal between Stoke Bruerne and Braunston and this part of the picture was made there, although I was unable to see any of the shooting because my work for the Ministry of Supply prevented it. I introduced 'Corney' to Mr Patterson, the elderly managing director of the Samuel Barlow Coal Company of Birmingham, owners of the Braunston Boatyard, who agreed to the use of Barlow boats in the film. Because all Barlow boats were beautifully painted and turned out by my old friend Frank Nurser of Braunston, I judged that they would look splendid on film. They would have looked even better had the film been made in colour which, at this time, alas, was out of the question. For the purpose of the film, one Barlow butty boat was repainted and re-named *Sunny Valley*. Rather a stupid and uncharacteristic name, I thought privately, but the boat retained it to the end of her working life. Some time after

Sunny Valley's film career was over, Barbara Jones painted her picture as she lay in the covered dock at Braunston, and because I thought this the finest record ever made of a narrow boat in all her glory, I reproduced it subsequently on the jacket and as a frontispiece for my book *Inland Waterways of England*. A full-sized studio mock-up of the cabin and stern-end of *Sunny Valley* was made for the film and this is now displayed in the Waterways Museum at Stoke Bruerne.

I paid several visits to Ealing, first for script conferences and later to see the rushes, at a time when the V1s were droning over London like sinister maybugs. After the conferences were over I was free to wander round the mad, make-believe world of the studios where, with infinite pains, totally unreal simulations of reality were constructed, fit food for those who desired to escape from harsh reality for a while into a world of celluloid fantasy. In one studio they were filming some comedy set in ancient Rome and, lurking behind a seemingly substantial column of plywood and plaster to keep out of camera, I watched them filming over and over again one short sequence lasting not more than a minute and involving two lines of dialogue. I must have watched at least six takes before I became bored and tip-toed away. Those who hanker for the glamour of the movies and those rare mortals who act in them must realize in their saner moments what a tinsel world it is. But what they cannot know is the sheer tedium and frustration of film-making. This illusory reality is as fragile as a soap bubble; the smallest untoward incident, an uncontrollable sneeze, the fusing of a spot or the mechanical failure of a camera to traverse or pan at precisely the right moment and all must be set up again until the nerves of director, actors and camera crews become frayed to exasperation. On location the situation is even worse, for the natural world is seldom cooperative; clouds obscure the sun, rain falls, or a sudden playful wind ruffles the stars and booms in the microphones.

I thought the happiest and most placid man at Ealing Studios, and the only person I envied, was the model-maker. He lurked, like William Fowkes, in a little loft workshop reached by an outside stair. To meet the exacting demands of the film-makers called for boundless ingenuity and powers of invention. This

mild, middle-aged man showed me with pride a beautiful model
of a Spitfire he had just completed for some film about the
R.A.F. It did not have to fly, he had been told, but it had to
show flashes from its wing cannons. He showed me how he had
solved this problem: acetylene gas piped to the wings from a
cylinder in the fuselage. A small battery and electric motor,
also in the fuselage, actuated the gas valves and the ignition
system. But even he must have felt frustrated when the products
of so much thought and craftsmanship were soon cast aside,
assuming they had not been destroyed in the making of the
picture. I saw a large and beautiful model of a ship he had
earlier made for the film *San Demetrio, London* which had then
just been completed. This miniature *San Demetrio*, perfect in
every detail, had now been reduced to a burned and blackened
hulk, forlornly floating in the studio tank.

For the industrial documentary sequences of *Painted Boats* I
had selected five locations on the Birmingham Canals in the
Black Country. At that time the system was busy with horse-
drawn 'day-boats' as well as occasional long-distance pairs of
narrow boats, so there was no need to simulate the action. We
met at the 'Queens Hotel' in Birmingham early one chilly
October morning, Cornelius, Crichton, myself and Douglas
Slocombe, the cameraman. I had warned 'Corny' that bright
light in the Black Country in October was about as rare as
snow on the equator, but film producers seem to be incurably
optimistic. As it happened, we were fortunate, for as we drove
out of Birmingham towards Smethwick a pallid morning sun
was breaking through the mist and murk. But all day it played
a coy game of hide and seek with us, retreating behind some
infuriatingly slow-moving cloud whenever Slocombe was about
to shoot, but shining brightly while we were moving on to
another location. Tempers became frayed. Looking down from
a bridge high above the Tame Valley canal, a long straight
pound stretched away into the distance, its still water looking
like a strip of tarnished silver. Far below us a horse-drawn
day-boat was approaching, lazy ripples fanning out from her
bows. The black shapes of more boats could be seen in the
distance. 'Corney' stamped about on the bridge, shoulders
hunched and hands thrust deep in his overcoat pockets. 'For

Christ's sake shoot it man!' he exclaimed in sudden exasperation. But, shaking his head, Slocombe continued to peer at the
sun through his smoked glass and replied acidly, 'If these
pictures look as if they were taken through pea soup, it won't
be *you* who'll have to carry the can.' And so it went on. But, at
the end of a long day, all the shots had been taken and they
turned out to be an excellent record of still living waterways.

At 'Corney's' suggestion, I wrote the text of a commentary
to accompany the documentary sequences but, to my disappointment, it was rejected. Before film and sound-track had been
married together, the commentary was played over while the
film was shown in the studio cinema. I felt very dashed when,
as the lights came on, Cavalcanti, who was the great panjandrum
at Ealing in those days, threw up his hands and, exclaiming
'No, no, no! It will not do,' walked out. Louis MacNeice was
thereupon commissioned to write another commentary. I hesitate to criticize because it may sound like sour grapes and a
reflection on a dead poet whose work I greatly admire. Nevertheless, I found the result strangely unsatisfactory. It struck me
as too self-consciously 'arty' to fit a simple subject which asked
for equally simple and down-to-earth comment. Most of the
critics spoke well of MacNeice's commentary, but the film critic
of the *Observer* evidently agreed with me. Of the tunnel sequence
he wrote: 'It is always exciting to come out of close darkness
into strong sunlight, and if the moment is well photographed,
it does not require a snatch of modern verse in words of one
syllable to heighten the experience. "Must be, must be, must
be done" drones the sound track, as the prow of the painted
boat slides out into the open.'

At the end of September 1945, Angela and I, accompanied
by Patterson of Samuel Barlow's, attended the trade showing
of *Painted Boats* in a Birmingham cinema. We thought it pretty
good – at least our practised eyes could detect no glaring errors.
But I was somewhat chagrined to find that, after all my labours,
I had not been given a screen credit. It was probably my fault
for not insisting on it in the first place, but I was then totally
unfamiliar with the ways of the film world. In the foyer of the
cinema, Patterson introduced us to a strange dark-haired young
woman. She was wearing flat-heeled open sandals, a blue

peasant skirt of mid-calf length held up by a broad leather belt, and a tight bright yellow jersey. A copy of the *New Statesman* was tucked under her arm. Her name was Sonia South. She had been an actress before the war, whispered Patterson, but had come on to the canals as one of the 'Idle Women'. Now, he added, with a shake of the head, she was just about to marry one of his boatmen. I thought she looked a rather frightening left-wing blue-stocking, and if Patterson had added that this girl would one day become my second wife I would have thought he had taken leave of his senses.

By this time *Narrow Boat* had been published. It first burst upon the world in early December, 1944, and no one was more astonished than I by the reception it received. Not only were there long rave reviews in all the papers, but I was inundated with fan mail which went on arriving for months after publication. I had never expected anything like this. I realized that one of the many unpaid chores that the luckless author is expected to perform is replying to readers' letters. I remembered guiltily that I had never given this problem a thought when I had written to Massingham, but I learnt the lesson now that I was at the receiving end. In case this sounds ungracious let me say at once that some fan letters are charming, a delight to receive and a pleasure to answer. But the student who is writing a thesis and wants to pick my brains; the nigglers who delight to air their superior knowledge by picking on some point of detail ('I would point out that 21st January 1802 was not a Sunday but a Monday'); their letters are not so welcome. The frustrating thing was that the book rapidly went out of print and could not be reprinted because Eyre & Spottiswoode had exhausted their war-time paper quota. However, after an interval of a few months, it appeared again and it has remained in print ever since.

It is no false modesty to say that I cannot altogether account for the success of *Narrow Boat*. Turning back to it now after nearly thirty years I find it too self-consciously arcadian and picaresque. In this it was not strictly truthful. As the first chapter of this book reveals, owing to the outbreak of war, the journey it describes was not really roses, roses all the way. I find it all slightly embarrassing now, and believe its instantaneous popularity was due to the fact that it appeared at precisely the right moment. After four years of war it satisfied a thirst for what is called escapist literature.

It is a handicap to an author to score a success with his first book. After I had published several books, I found it discouraging, on being introduced to a stranger, still to be greeted with the remark, 'Ah! you're the man who wrote *Narrow Boat.*' Fortunately, I eventually succeeded in writing down *Narrow Boat,* and in an entirely different vein. For another disadvantage of a successful first book, I soon discovered, is that its author, if he is not careful, can become set in one groove. I began to receive flattering letters from publishers, many of whom had originally rejected *Narrow Boat,* all asking me for another canal book. But I decided that if, as I had planned, I was going to earn my living as a writer, I could never hope to do so by writing books about canals alone; it was far too narrow and specialized a row to hoe. I might return to the subject later, I thought, but meanwhile let me try something different. So I brought out the manuscript of *High Horse Riderless* from under our bed and sent it to Eyre & Spottiswoode. Although, curiously, their contract for *Narrow Boat* contained no option clause, I felt in honour bound to offer them my next book. They rejected it, which did not altogether surprise me. So I sent it to Philip Unwin of George Allen & Unwin who had been the first to write to me to suggest another canal book. He promptly accepted it as, I suspect, a sprat to catch a mackerel, for there *was* an option clause in his contract.

With those great Chirico white horses still in mind, I asked a friend of mine, Toni del Renzio, a surrealist painter and writer, if he would design a jacket for the book. The result was striking but the horse was quite unlike anything I had expected. In fact it was quite unlike a horse at all. It looked more like a unicorn, startled at having mislaid its horn. I felt I could not say anything to Toni without upsetting him and, after all, it was a symbolical horse and not a real one, so I sent the design to my publishers. It provoked a serious reply that I found highly diverting. The horse, they pointed out, was anatomically incorrect and, as Lady Wentworth's publishers, they were in a position to know. They went on to suggest that their artist should substitute another horse based on the Darley Arabian. They enclosed photographs of the jacket and of their artist's horse so that the latter could be superimposed. I found the Darley Arabian even less meaningful as a symbol than the original, so it was Toni's hornless unicorn that pranced before a bewildered public at a price of 10*s*. 6*d*. in the spring of 1947.

High Horse Riderless was surprisingly well and widely reviewed. Under the heading 'Freedom to Create', it earned a long three columns from Charles Morgan ('Menander') in the *Sunday Times*, something that would be unthinkable today, certainly for any book of this kind. But the review that pleased and encouraged me most was that in the *Listener* where it was noticed along with a book called *Science, Liberty and Peace* by Aldous Huxley. It began:

> Both Mr. Rolt and Mr. Huxley make precisely the same diagnosis of our ills, and both prescribe precisely the same immediate treatment. So closely, indeed, do they agree that on almost every page of Huxley's shorter essay you can find a passage which can be paralleled from Mr. Rolt's more detailed analysis.

The review went on to prove the point by a series of cross-quotations. Because for ten years Aldous Huxley had been my most admired of all living prose writers, it may be imagined how gratified and honoured I felt to find myself unexpectedly in such august company. It was as though some young and aspiring poet were suddenly to find his work compared with that of W. B. Yeats. The anonymous reviewer was unusually percipient for he wrote: 'Neither author mentions the population question. Surely we want to know how we are to decentralize a population of 766 persons per square mile, which was the figure for England in 1939.'* And he concluded sadly: 'We are not likely to change our ways under pressure of a threat which does not seem imminent.'

A dear and wise friend of mine in the publishing world once remarked to me: 'It's not column-inches of review space that sells books, nor advertising, it's personal recommendation.' In

---

* In fairness to the late Aldous Huxley, it should be said that he became deeply concerned with the population explosion long before such concern became general.

my literary career I have proved the truth of this over and over again. Books which have been virtually ignored by the popular press, and particularly by 'the Sundays', have sold widely and, what is much more important, have gone on selling. With *High Horse Riderless* it was the precise opposite. Its one small first edition slowly sold out and the book was never reprinted, although it did appear in Danish translation. Readers might have an avid appetite for what they regarded as an 'escapist' book about the canals, but the 'great questions', the uncomfortable and disturbing truths, they found unpalatable. The threat did not seem imminent, so they did not want to know.

High Horse Riderless was a pessimistic book written in an optimistic mood. When I wrote it I had felt so certain that there would be a change of heart after the war. But long before it was published the horrors of Belsen and Buchenwald had been revealed, and atomic bombs had been dropped on the cities of Hiroshima and Nagasaki. The news of these events turned my brief optimism to an extreme pessimism that came near to despair.

It was a gloriously warm and sunny day, I remember, and Angela and I had gone walking on the southern end of the Malvern Hills. We sat on the top of Chase End hill among the young bracken fronds and gazed out over the lovely landscape of the Severn vale below us, rimmed by the distant blue wall of the Cotswolds on the skyline. Peace had returned to Europe, the sun was shining out of a cloudless sky and it was good to be alive. It was when we returned in the evening that we heard on the wireless the news that the first atomic bomb had been loosed upon a defenceless city with such appalling results. In an essay which I wrote subsequently* I tried to describe the agony of mind and the sense of despairing impotence that I felt at that moment; it would be true to say that my outlook from that day to this has been profoundly affected by that event. It was as though the evils I had inveighed against in *High Horse Riderless* had suddenly materialized to reveal a hideous strength that exceeded my wildest imaginings. From that day I have never doubted that evil now possessed the power to commit the ultimate blasphemy of destroying all the life and beauty of the

* 'To Gain our Peace' in *The Clouded Mirror* (1955).

world: either by destroying the planet utterly or by transforming it into a poisoned desert peopled by deformed monsters.
From now on, all things seemed tragically ephemeral. To
typify the state of mind of those who could conceive and perpetrate such unbelievable horrors, in my essay I quoted Milton's
prince Lucifer:

> . . . To bow and sue for grace
> With suppliant knee, and deify his pow'r,
> Who from the terror of this arm so late
> Doubted his empire; that were low indeed.

In other words, it was better to reign in hell than serve in
heaven, even if that reign spelled ultimate self-destruction. This
was some years before the C.N.D. movement got under way and
I marvelled that few others appeared to feel as I did. Were they
too stunned by such appalling news to react to it? Or were they
unwilling to admit its dreadful implications to their conscious-
ness? Perhaps, as the reviewer had said, the threat still did not
seem imminent. However, no matter how grave the threat, it
was useless to give way to despair; one had to go on living.

With the ending of the war in Europe, my department of the
Ministry of Supply was rapidly running down. As I have said,
most of my colleagues were temporary civil servants recruited
from the engineering industry. Yet now they all began to
display a surprising eagerness 'to get on to the establishment'.
Perhaps they had learned to prefer the orderly, if dull and ill-
paid, routine of a Government department to the industrial
rat-race they had known before the war. I do not blame them.
I do not know whether they succeeded in their aim or not
because I was the first to resign. I was eager to resume the way
of life which had been so rudely interrupted by the war – to live
on my boat and write for my livelihood. Whether I should have
been quite so eager to throw up a secure job had it not been for
the unexpected success of *Narrow Boat* I cannot say. Some
Government departments, particularly, it seems, the Patent
Office, have provided many writers with financial security and
a peaceful haven. Yet my craving for freedom and independence
was so strong that I believe I would have come to the same
decision even if I had not had a word published. To hell with

security! As an earnest of my emancipation, I quickly sold my official means of transport, that terrible Austin, re-awakened my faithful old steed, the 1924 'duck's back' Alvis which had been slumbering in a shed at Stanley Pontlarge, and drove her triumphantly back to Tardebigge. What a rare pleasure it was to be at the wheel of a real motor car once more.

Angela had had a brilliant idea. This was that we should explore by boat the canals and rivers of Ireland – a country which neither of us had ever visited – and that I should then write a book about it, a kind of Irish equivalent of *Narrow Boat* in fact. Obviously *Cressy* could not cross the Irish Sea and we had some difficulty in locating a suitable craft in Ireland. Eventually we found *Le Coq*, a ship's lifeboat converted into a small cabin cruiser, which was lying on the Shannon at Athlone, and agreed to charter her for three months during the summer of 1946. I have chronicled this Irish adventure very fully in *Green and Silver** and it would be superfluous to tell that story again here. It is enough to say that three months of slow voyaging across the wide, dark bogs of Ireland's central plain, and over the broad lakes and reedy reaches of the Shannon, enabled us to get beneath the skin of that country as no visitor could ordinarily do. As a result, we fell in love with Ireland and the Irish people; and though I have been able to return all too seldom since, I shall always think of Ireland as a second home.

After more than four years lying idly at her moorings at Tardebigge, our good ship *Cressy* needed docking and repairs. We therefore planned to return to what we had come to regard as her home port, Tooley's Boatyard at Banbury, and leave her there in Herbert Tooley's care while we were away in Ireland. We hoped, optimistically as things turned out, that repairs would be completed by the time we returned. So, on 14 April 1946, we 'winded' her in the basin at the New Wharf and, as we waved farewell to our old friends in the canal workshops, *Cressy* slid into Tardebigge tunnel. A landscape that had become so familiar over four years was suddenly blotted out. As the darkness swallowed us up, it seemed to me as I stood aft, getting the feel of *Cressy*'s tiller once again, that it was as though a camera shutter had suddenly closed on a well-loved

* George Allen & Unwin, 1949.

77

Chapter 5

Canal Crusade

Before the war, when I first had the optimistic idea of trying to earn my living as a writer, I had thought of this new career simply as a source of creative satisfaction and as a means of achieving that complete independence and privacy which I had always craved. Strange though it may seem, it had never occurred to me that there was an inescapable corollary to this neat scheme which was the price of its success. Books need readers; I could not make a living by writing the kind of books I wanted to write without publicizing the things I loved and, incidentally, without publicizing myself. In the modern world, even the least dazzling beam of public limelight can prove as lethal as gamma rays, corroding the personality of the 'private man' with the most subtle of poisons. And, like so many poisons, this one is addictive; men seek it as desperately as any drug. It is also isolating, cutting men off from normal, unselfconscious relationships with all except a few most intimate friends. As for writing about well-loved things or places, in our overcrowded island this can be tantamount to giving them the kiss of death. It was the reception of *Narrow Boat* and the shoals of letters I received as a result that first made me realize that there were such unforeseen strings attached to my projected way of earning a living, although it would be hypocritical to say that I was not gratified. Yet I still had no inkling of – and, indeed, had never considered – the possible long-term effect of the book upon its subject, the English canals.

I had known the canals for fifteen years and lived on them for five, and in that time I had come to love them and their people. For me they represented the equivalent of some uncharted, arcadian island inhabited by simple, friendly and unselfconscious natives where I could free myself from all that I found so uncongenial in the modern world. It seems fantastic to me now that when I was writing *Narrow Boat* I did not realize that I was putting this island firmly on the chart. The book was described by one reviewer as 'an elegy of classic restraint'. If it was elegiac it was because I realized that this old and simple world of the canals was too fragile to resist for very long the relentless march of technology captained by modern economic theory. But I certainly never foresaw how very soon the natural life of that world would come to an end. Admittedly, on some canals such as the Worcester & Birmingham, commercial traffic was visibly failing; but on many other narrow canals of the Midlands traffic had increased substantially, so that I saw no reason to suppose that it would so rapidly decline into extinction in the post-war world.

Among the many letters I received following the publication of *Narrow Boat* was one suggesting the formation of a voluntary society ('something like the friends of Canterbury cathedral') to campaign for the greater use of canals and proposing a meeting to discuss the idea further. This letter came from an address in Bloomsbury and was signed Robert Fordyce Aickman. Such a notion had never occurred to me, but anything which might help the canal boaters could not, I thought, fail to be a good thing so I welcomed the idea enthusiastically. Had I not acted so impulsively I might have questioned whether it was such a good idea and so have avoided the storms which lay ahead. But at this time my experience of running voluntary organizations was extremely limited. It was exclusively confined to the Committee of the Vintage Sports Car Club before the war where there had been no clashes of temperament. On the contrary, the atmosphere there had been so harmonious that all the issues discussed were settled by mutual agreement and never had to be put to the vote. I assumed in my innocence that such a happy state of affairs was the rule rather than the exception, but I was to learn otherwise. The launching of the Inland Waterways Association, as we named it, and its promotion, was to become my major preoccupation for the first five years after the war. But although they were years of considerable achievement, some of them memorable, they led finally to a sense of growing frustration and ended in complete exasperation. Now that time has distanced these events I can see that they had their funny side, so that what appeared then to be a tragedy appears in retrospect a black comedy. There is certainly a ludicrous element about our foibles and frailties however infuriating they may be at the time; nevertheless, there can be no doubt that our infant Association would have had a much more healthy childhood had there not been so much bickering among its parents.

At a preliminary meeting in London at which Robert Aickman assumed the chair, my old friend Charles Hadfield and I were elected Vice-Chairman and Honorary Secretary respectively. Charles Hadfield has since become famous as a canal historian. He, also, had written to me as a result of *Narrow Boat* and I was responsible for drawing him in. After this first meeting I returned to *Cressy* filled with enthusiasm and bashed out on my typewriter a Constitution and Rules for the new Association, a booklet, to be illustrated with Angela's photographs, entitled *The Future of the Waterways* which set forth our aims, and a leaflet-cum-entry-form for distribution to likely members. These three efforts were approved at our next meeting, although the first two were subsequently destined to be much revised by another hand. Each of us compiled a list of names and addresses of possible members to whom the leaflet would be sent. Mine included all my *Narrow Boat* correspondents, for I had fortunately kept all their letters which made a formidable pile.

Because Angela and I had arranged our Irish canal trip before the new Association was first mooted, I was not in England but afloat on the Shannon when the new canal crusade was launched by the sending out of the leaflets in the late spring of 1946. I was told that subscriptions were coming in well; but coupled with this came the news that Charles Hadfield had resigned as Vice-Chairman. This was disturbing and saddening because I had taken an immediate liking to Charles who has been a very good friend of mine from that day to this. Remote from the centre of events, I could not then fathom the reason for his withdrawal, though I realized later that this was only the first ominous cloud in a sky presaging future storms. Charles had acutely sized up a situation that was still not clear to me.

We returned to England and Banbury in September to find that *Cressy* had still not been dry-docked but was lying at her moorings exactly as we had left her three months before. This was tiresome because it was not possible for us to live aboard while she was on the dock. We were forced to hire a caravan which we parked in the boatyard while the work was done, finding it very cramped and inconvenient after our boat. As autumn drew on we also realized that it was very much colder. We appreciated then as never before how effective an insulator water is, for although we turned on heat in that caravan until our heads were bursting, our legs remained obstinately numb from the knees down due to the cold that struck up through the floor. We were back on *Cressy* again by mid-November fortunately, because that winter of 1946–7 turned out to be the longest, coldest and hardest we had ever known. For weeks *Cressy* was locked in ice several inches thick, usually covered with a deep layer of snow, and it was early March before the weather broke with tremendous gales and floods. However, our boat was extremely warm and snug, and in this respect we were a great deal better off than most landsmen during that dismal winter of prolonged power cuts and fuel shortages. But it was a hard time for our friends the boaters, many of whom were frozen in beside us. Most of them found temporary employment with Banbury Corporation, clearing the snow from the streets. Even so, the 'Number Ones' – those who owned their own boats – were forced to draw upon their precious 'docking money', a sum set aside for the repair of their boats. Yet they managed to remain remarkably cheerful and many a pleasant evening we spent with them in the bars of 'The Leather Bottle' or 'The Struggler'; men and women – never together but always separately – dancing to the music of a melodeon that was passed from hand to hand among the boatmen.

'The Struggler' was a small and outwardly insignificant street-corner pub in a back-street which was much frequented by the boaters and also, at fair times, by gypsies and horse-dealers. It had the unusual sign of a globe with a man's legs protruding from one side of it and his head the other. It bore the legend: 'Oh Lord help me through this World'. This used to strike me as singularly appropriate for its roving, impoverished but undaunted customers, none of whom fitted into the neat, organized pattern of modern society. I once described a typical evening spent in 'The Struggler' so I will not do so again.* I did not then name either the pub or the place for obvious reasons. But now there is no further need for such reticence. Developers have destroyed 'The Struggler' and even if they had not, its bar would never again see such a company because the boaters and their boats are all gone. Most of the gypsies and horse-dealers have gone into limbo with them. In the tidy, aseptic world that we have made there is no place for them.

It was not only with the canal boaters and gypsies that I became acquainted during successive winters spent at moorings at Tooley's Yard. I never forgot my first love, railways, and got to know a G.W.R. relief signalman named Billy Bevington. A relief signalman must be prepared, often at short notice, to stand in for any signalman who may happen to be ill or on leave. This meant that Billy had an intimate knowledge of every box on the Paddington–Birmingham main line within cycling distance of Banbury. I used to receive cryptic messages from him such as 'Banbury Junction this week 2 till 10', which meant that he would be pleased to welcome me to that box at any time between those hours. Sometimes on such visits he would sit down in the home-made chair (essential in any signal box) by the stove and leave me to work the block instruments, set the road and 'pull the sticks off'. In this way I gained experience which would eventually become virtually unrepeatable, at any rate on a main line such as this, owing to the installation of modern electrical signalling systems. What impressed me was the strength of tradition on the railways, and also the comparative crudity of the old manual system on which railway safety depended. To illustrate the first point, Billy habitually referred to a stopping train that ran 'all stations' between Birmingham and Oxford as 'the Parly', a name going back to the early days of railways when a Parliamentary Act compelled reluctant

* *Inland Waterways of England* (1950), pp. 183–5.

companies such as the G.W.R. to cater for third-class passengers. As to crudity I vividly remember one Saturday afternoon at Banbury North Box when the signal wire of the down starter parted with a melodious twang as he was 'pulling his sticks off' for a 'runner' (a Paddington–Birmingham non-stop express). Knowing there was no hope of getting a linesman out at such short notice on a Saturday, Billy handed me an old pair of pliers and a coal hammer saying, 'Go down below and see what you can do about it, Tom.' Obediently I passed through the little door beneath the box stairway and threaded my way through a maze of point rods, signal wires, bell cranks and interlocking bars until I had found the broken wire. I never realized until then how extremely tough signal wire is, especially when one has to attack it with totally inadequate tools; the knowledge that time was not on my side did not help matters either. 'Look sharp' called a voice from above as I sweated and struggled. At last I managed to form the two broken ends into rough hooks which, by slacking off the wire adjuster, I managed to link together. 'Try it now,' I called up, 'but for God's sake take it easy.' Fortunately it was only a short pull and to my relief my extempore repair held, the lever swung over into the 'off' position and I emerged from the box to see for myself that the signal arm had obediently dropped. Hardly had I done so than the train, drawn by an immaculate 'Castle' class locomotive, flashed past me with a roar, a brief glimpse of thrashing coupling rods, the echo of a whistle just closed and the swift rhythm of bogie wheels over rail joints. I caught a momentary glimpse of passengers taking tea in the restaurant car and thought wryly that but for my pliers and coal hammer their train would have come to a grinding halt.

At Banbury Junction Box there existed a very curious device in the shape of a hand-cranked dynamo, the purpose of which was to provide power assistance for a set of points a very long way away from the box. The junction concerned was that between the G.W.R. main line and the Great Central Branch from Woodford and the point in question admitted freight trains from off this branch into Banbury hump marshalling yard. Whenever the lever controlling it needed pulling off, Billy would call, 'Wind away, Tom, go on – faster!' The whole operation reminded me of one of those children's toys that derives its motion from the energy stored in a heavy flywheel. The principle was exactly the same. But by far the most interesting and unusual signal box in the Banbury area stood close beside the Oxford canal just outside Fenny Compton station. It was islanded between the G.W.R. main line on the one hand and the single line of the S.M.J.,* now part of the L.M.S. system, on the other. It was a 'facing both ways' box with G.W.R. type block instruments and frame on one side and on the other a small L.M.S. frame with its accompanying tablet instruments to control the single line sections.

That bitter first winter at Banbury I was a member of a deputation, led by the late lamented A. P. Herbert (who had agreed to be the Association's President) which had been formed for the purpose of visiting the then Minister of Transport to urge upon him the greater use of canals in the post-war world. I recall this because our appointment was in the morning which meant our catching an early train from Banbury to Paddington. Woken by our alarum clock at a godless hour, we dressed by lamplight in unfamiliar and uncomfortable London clothes and then looked out to see, in the first pale light of dawn, that there had been a fresh and heavy fall of snow in the night which had covered the boat, the frozen canal and the stacks of seasoning oak planks in the boat-yard in a blanket of white eight inches deep. We floundered across the yard to the high wooden gate giving on to Factory Street to find it still padlocked. Instead of climbing it, how much easier, we thought, to walk across the frozen canal to the towpath. I led the way boldly and immediately my left leg went straight through the snow and ice into the canal up to the knee. As luck would have it I had picked the one place in the canal where the ice had been broken the evening before for the purpose of watering a horse. If we were to catch our train there was nothing for it but to press on, so we hurried through the snow to the station, my sodden trouser leg flapping against my shin and canal water squelching inside my shoe. Our hope of finding an empty

---

* S.M.J. stood officially for Stratford-upon-Avon & Midland Junction but unofficially for Slow, Mouldy & Jolting. The railway along with the box as I knew it has long ago disappeared.

compartment on the train was vain, and our travelling companions were somewhat disconcerted when I removed my shoe and sock and placed them against the radiator under the seat. But for their presence I would have removed my trousers as well. Fortunately there was just time to give them a hurried ironing and pressing before the deputation left for Berkeley Square House. It was all in a good cause, or so we hoped.

When a belated spring eventually arrived, we decided that the time had come to do some campaigning for the new Association by deed instead of merely by word. This was just before the canals were nationalized, and we decided that two of the railway-owned canals, the Stratford and the Welsh Section of the Shropshire Union, should be the targets for our attack. We had learned that the Lifford drawbridge at the northern end of the Stratford Canal, which we had passed under with difficulty on our way to Tardebigge in 1941, had since collapsed under heavy road traffic and that the G.W.R. had replaced it by a 'temporary' fixed steel structure which made the canal impassable by anything larger than a canoe. Unlike the southern end of this canal between its junction with the Grand Union at Kingswood and Stratford-upon-Avon which was then in an advanced state of decay, this northern section had been used in comparatively recent times by commercial traffic trading between London and the south of Birmingham. The trade in cocoa beans and chocolate 'crumb' from London docks to the Cadbury factory at Bournville had been a notable example of such movements, and I then saw no reason why such trade might not be resumed provided the canal could be opened up.

In challenging the might of the G.W.R. we had one trump card to play which has now, most unfortunately, been lost – a statutory right of navigation.* We therefore persuaded Lord

---

* This right was written into most, though not all, of the original canal Acts. The Act for the Derby Canal was one of the exceptions. This enabled the Derby Canal Company to defeat a plot, laid between Brigadier H. E. Hopthrow of I.C.I., Mr Mallender, Managing Director of the Derby Gas, Light & Coke Company and myself to bring a pair of boats laden with coal on to the eastern section of the canal. Somehow the canal company got wind of this scheme and foiled us by the simple expedient of chaining and padlocking the gates of the entrance lock at the junction with the Erewash Canal at Sandiacre. Shortly afterwards the Company applied for and obtained an abandonment order on the grounds that there had been no commercial traffic on their waterway for many years.

Methuen, who was a member of the new Association, to put down a question about Lifford bridge in the House of Lords. It is ironical that after nationalization such a question would have been brushed aside in the House as 'a matter for the day-to-day concern of the transport authority'. In 1947, however, it was quite a different story and it obviously caused quite a stir at Paddington. For the reply was that Lifford bridge would be lifted at any time on notice of an intended passage being given. So we duly gave notice of our intention to pass through the canal on 20 May.

Of this and subsequent voyages I have an accurate record because I continued to keep as complete a log of each day's journeying as I had done on our honeymoon voyage in 1939. I see from this that we slipped our moorings at Banbury on 14 May and moored in the basin at Kingswood on Saturday the 17th. We were surprised to see an empty motor narrow boat, *Bilster*, also moored in this deserted basin and discovered that the G.W.R. had chartered this craft from the Grand Union Canal Company's Hatton Maintenance Depot with the object of putting her through ahead of us to clear a passage and so avert the adverse publicity which might result if *Cressy* got hopelessly stuck or was damaged. The G.W.R. was obviously taking the affair seriously. Already the venture was attracting some attention and the next day's entry in my log reads briefly: 'Sunday, 18th May. Poured practically all day. Lay at Kingswood troubled by reporters and I.W.A. members.' This led me to reflect wryly on the contrast with our previous voyage in 1941 when we had slipped through the canal unnoticed and without any fuss. But I consoled myself with the thought that it was all in a good cause.

The next day dawned fine but cold and overcast. At 10 o'clock the *Bilster* set off up the Lapworth locks with G.W.R. and G.U.C. engineers on board. Knowing that even an empty boat of this type draws more at the stern end than did *Cressy*, from my previous experience of the canal I did not fancy her chances of getting through and my fear was that she might become hopelessly stuck in a bridge-hole and so block the canal for us. I decided to give her a good start, so we did not leave until 2 p.m. The state of the canal had certainly deteriorated since 1941, for although we climbed the nineteen locks without incident, the weed in the long summit pound was so thick that for about a mile in the neighbourhood of Hockley Heath we had to resort to bow-hauling from the overgrown towpath. Then conditions improved somewhat so that we were able to go forward slowly under our own power once more until we tied up for the night beside the junction of the canal feeder channel from Earlswood Lakes.

We had not travelled very far next morning before I saw ahead of us the sight I had most feared – the *Bilster* firmly wedged in a bridge-hole. A number of men were either pulling or shoving without result, and though we added our weight to theirs, still she would not budge, being obviously hard aground on a mound of debris. From the other side of the high towpath hedge came the unmistakable sound of a Fordson tractor at plough, and we succeeded in persuading its driver to unhitch it and drive it on to the towpath. Quite how this difficult manoeuvre was achieved I cannot now remember. For, as anyone familiar with canals will know, there are no gateways between fields and canal towpaths as local farmers and landowners had no desire to provide free pasturage for boatmen's horses. However, I have a press photograph to prove that this feat was achieved, whereupon the Fordson successfully pulled *Bilster* through the bridge. We then followed suit, man-handling *Cressy* as I was not going to risk a broken propeller.

We had hardly got fairly under way once more before, on rounding a bend, we saw *Bilster* once again, not stuck in a bridge-hole this time but aground in the middle of the canal. The only thing to be done was to try and edge *Cressy* past, and no one was more surprised than I was when this manoeuvre succeeded. Moreover, when alongside I was able to pass a line over *Bilster*'s fore-end stud and make it fast, which successfully pulled her off. I now had this official 'trail-blazer' in tow, a somewhat humiliating situation for her charterers though it proved to be short-lived. As we approached the next bridge-hole I stopped my propeller as a precaution and sure enough we grounded at the stern. Although we managed to haul her over the obstruction without much difficulty it was obvious that the *Bilster* would be in worse trouble here than ever before. Her captain had obviously weighed up the situation and had come to the same conclusion, for he signalled me to cast off the tow and leave him to his fate. What the end of his story was we never knew, for that was the last we saw of the *Bilster*.

We went ahead very slowly and cautiously. There was always in my mind the fear that *Cressy* might hit some under-water obstruction, 'knock a bottom up' and sink ignominiously and expensively in the middle of the canal. The thought of those muddy waters slowly rising over the floor of our carpeted saloon and up the spines of the lowest bookshelf was a nightmare prospect on which I did not care to dwell. Indeed this whole venture was rather like taking a long-cherished old family motor car on some tough, chassis-breaking reliability trial. But at last we reached King's Norton tunnel without untoward incident, and soon after we had emerged from its darkness the infamous Lifford 'drawbridge' appeared ahead. Unlike the previous occasion when we had passed this way, it presented an animated scene. The steel decking which had replaced the old wooden bridge had been jacked up on to wooden packing by a posse of overalled G.W.R. gangers who were standing by, and the towpath was lined with spectators, mostly press report-ers and photographers. The gang had evidently decided to do no more work on their jacks than was absolutely necessary, for there were only a couple of inches to spare over our roof tank as *Cressy* was slowly manhandled beneath the girders. I remem-bered the shoal beyond the bridge on which *Cressy* had grounded heavily on the previous occasion. It consisted of ashes ejected from the boiler house of a factory beside the towpath, and we soon found that it had grown in the five years that had since elapsed. But at least there was no lack of manpower this time. Normally, I dislike spectators when engaged upon exploits of this kind, but there are occasions when they can be useful and this was one of them. If the last hundred yards of canal to the junction stop lock had been completely dry, I think sheer enthusiasm would have dragged us there. Nevertheless, after the crowds and the questioning, it was a relief to plunge like a rabbit into a burrow into the dark depths of West Hill tunnel and so escape from it all. We were on our own again.

This episode was only the opening chapter in the saga of

Lifford bridge, for had we allowed matters to rest there is no doubt at all that the status quo would have remained undisturbed. Somehow, we had to ensure a series of repeat performances until it dawned on the canal owners (soon to be the British Transport Commission) that it might be cheaper to reconstruct the bridge than continually to send large gangs of men to jack it up. So we begged all members of our infant association to take their boats through the Stratford Canal, but unfortunately the number of members with suitable boats was in those days very small. One of this minority who had a go was Peter Scott. He had a narrow boat converted by a boatyard in Birmingham with the object that, when moored on the Gloucester & Berkeley Ship Canal, she would form a convenient hostel for students visiting his then newly formed Wildfowl Trust at Slimbridge. This boat, the *Beatrice*, followed the design of *Cressy* very closely, even to the paintwork and the fitting of a Model 'T' Ford engine. The only difference was that this engine drove a small propeller directly instead of copying Kyrle Willans's arrangement of reduction drive to a large propeller. This proved to be mistaken, for putting *Beatrice* full astern had no effect whatever on her forward progress, the little propeller being about as much use as an egg whisk.

When *Beatrice* was ready to make her maiden voyage from Birmingham to Slimbridge, instead of going by the direct route, Peter dutifully took her down to Kingswood and thence through the Stratford Canal. On this occasion I joined *Beatrice* on the Lapworth Locks and my voyage as 'pilot' was made ever memorable, not by any untoward occurrence on the Stratford Canal but by an episode in West Hill tunnel. We had just about reached the middle of this long tunnel when I heard the engine die, the ensuing silence broken only by an echoing exclamation from Peter who was at the tiller. I hurried aft and soon discovered the cause of the trouble. He had grossly underestimated *Beatrice*'s thirst for fuel. Her fuel tank was completely dry, nor had anyone thought to lay on any spare cans. There was nothing for it but to manhandle the boat out of the tunnel.

The Worcester & Birmingham Canal was, I think, unique among the old canal companies in possessing its own telephone system throughout. Although this had long ago fallen into disuse, the metal brackets that had carried the insulators still existed along the crown of the tunnel roof. By standing on the cabin, pushing against each bracket in turn while I walked aft and then running for'ard to wait for the next bracket to come up, I found I could keep the boat moving at about half its normal speed. By the time we finally emerged from the south end of the tunnel, dusk was falling and I was not only exhausted but black as a sweep from the accumulation of soot that the vanished steam tug *Droitwich* had left on the tunnel roof. It was noticeable that the other I.W.A. members present on this occasion took no part in these proceedings but remained below drinking tea, content to leave it to Peter and myself to extricate them from this predicament. I have never 'legged' a boat through a canal tunnel in the traditional manner, but this experience was the next best thing and gave me a very fair idea of the sheer physical effort involved despite the fact that *Beatrice* was only the equivalent of a half-empty boat.

My 1947 assault on the Stratford Canal was only the first stage of a much more ambitious and venturesome voyage. Ever since I had experienced her first steam trials on the Welsh Canal in 1929, I had determined that one day I would pilot *Cressy* over Telford's great aqueduct across the Vale of Llangollen at Pont Cysyllte. Ten years later I had been foiled in the attempt by the outbreak of war, and now I was going to try again. In the meantime, however, the outcome of this venture had become very much more uncertain. No boats had voyaged from Hurleston Junction to Llangollen since before the war and, what was more, in 1944 the L.M. & S.R. had obtained Parliamentary powers which enabled the company to abandon the entire canal. Boats were permitted to enter it on sufferance, but the 1944 Act had extinguished the right of navigation. This meant that if *Cressy* sank, became hopelessly stuck or encountered an obstruction like Lifford bridge, I could obtain no legal redress, nor could I invoke any aid from the company. Once past Hurleston Junction, where the canal joins the main line of the Shropshire Union Canal, it would literally become a case of sink or swim.

After a short stay in brilliantly fine weather on our old moorings at Tardebigge, we locked down the famous 'thirty and twelve' en route for Worcester and the river Severn. At Diglis, Worcester, we swung right-handed on to the river and headed upstream in the direction of Stourport. At that time some friends of ours were living at Shrawley Wood House which lies close beside the west bank of the Severn just below Stourport. They joined us at Worcester, the idea being that, after luncheon on board, they would travel with us as far as Shrawley where we would moor up for the night so that they could entertain us to dinner. This had seemed an excellent idea, but it proved singularly difficult to carry out as anyone familiar with the high and thickly overgrown banks of the Severn will appreciate. The tremendous wash created by the many tanker barges that were then using the river added to the hazards of such an uncongenial mooring. Nevertheless we contrived to moor eventually beside the mouth of the Dick brook, and in this way I discovered the mysterious ruins of the mason's lock chambers built by Andrew Yarranton when he made the brook navigable in 1652. The course of the brook is so narrow and tortuous, the lock (or half-lock?) chambers so large and massive, that the whole set-up was a profound puzzle to me then as it still puzzles industrial archaeologists today.

Happily no harm came to *Cressy* at her somewhat risky mooring, and next morning we were soon locking up through the two large locks at Stourport which link the Severn with the terminal basin of the Staffordshire & Worcestershire Canal. We now intended to follow this as far as its junction with the 'main line' of the Shropshire Union at Autherley. This particular length of canal carried a very heavy traffic that was almost entirely horse drawn, for the power station at Stourport then took the bulk of its coal by water from the Cannock coalfield. This traffic was worked exclusively by what the long distance canal boaters used to call, not without a certain disdain, 'Joey boat-men' – men who crewed the short-haul 'day-boats' peculiar to the canal system of the Black Country. More crudely built than the long distance craft, the diminutive cabins of these day-boats were never used as homes but only as shelters for the crew of two during the day. The 'turn' from Gailey to Stourport was the longest to be worked by such craft and it was organized in two shifts, one gang working the boats between Gailey and the

'Stewponey Inn' where they handed over a loaded boat to their mates for the remainder of the journey, picking up an empty boat for the return journey.

We also saw on this canal a very significant relic of the canal past. This was the *Symbol*, an old Shropshire Union Canal Carrying Company horse-drawn fly-boat. She was now drably painted and bore the letters 'L.M. & S.R.' on her cabin sides, but her graceful lines and the fact that her name was carved on her stern made her origin unmistakable. Worked by two men, she was carrying general cargo and assorted parcels – the sort of traffic that once travelled 'fly' – between an L.M.S. Canal depot in the Black Country and Stourport. The *Symbol* was thus an inexplicable survivor of the long defunct Shropshire Union Canal Carrying Company. With the coming of nationalization it quickly vanished; why such a traffic movement had survived for so long it is hard to say. Competition between rival railway companies is probably the answer.

Although it was obvious that the *Symbol* was an anachronism, the traffic in coal to Stourport power station seemed such a logical movement that we had no doubts about its future. Evidently the newly appointed Docks & Inland Waterways Executive had no doubts either, for one of its first acts after nationalization was to dredge the whole canal between Gailey and Stourport. Hardly had this costly exercise been completed when the National Coal Board and the Central Electricity Generating Board agreed between them that future supplies of coal to Stourport should go by rail or road, and the coal drops beside the canal at Gailey were promptly demolished. This was a typical example of the follies that so soon followed upon nationalization, and it explains why our experience in 1947 was so soon to become a part of history. To see a wide and dusty towing path trampled by the hoof prints of many horses, to smell horse dung and to see the 'eloquent grooves' worn in metal rubbing strips by innumerable tow lines still bright from constant use, such trifles, once so commonplace in the canals, were never to be experienced again. Next year, when we passed that way, the traffic had vanished; weeds were already encroaching on the disused towpath, and the bright rope grooves had grown dull.

Our journey up the main line of the Shropshire Union from Autherley Junction was uneventful and we arrived at Nantwich to find that the entrance to the basin had been dredged out since our previous visit; so, to our relief, we were able to find a good mooring in the basin. It was here we learnt that we were to have company on our voyage up the Welsh Canal: already moored in the basin was the small cabin cruiser *Heron* owned by the Grundy family of Liverpool. With the help of their two sons, Christopher and Martin, Mr and Mrs Grundy had decided to venture up the Welsh Canal and see how far they could get. As we had precisely the same intention we agreed there and then to set off together so that we could render each other assistance as necessary.

We had both heard a rumour that the wooden drawbridge over the canal at Wrenbury had been damaged and could not be lifted. On the previous day, however, we had moored at Hack Green Locks on the main line whence it was but a short walk over to Wrenbury to inspect the bridge. We found, much to our surprise, that repairs had been completed the previous day, so we were able to reassure the Grundys that at least one obstacle had been removed.

Anticipating difficulty, I had equipped us with new spare cotton lines and a set of pulley blocks which were soon to prove their worth. At first everything went deceptively smoothly; we climbed successfully up the locks at Hurleston and Swanley and found the travelling between them much better than we had expected. It was at Lock No. 9, Baddiley, that the first serious hitch occurred when *Cressy* stuck fast half-way into the empty chamber.

It is a weakness of the orthodox design of a masonry lock chamber that its side walls are apt to be forced inwards owing to the action of frost in the surrounding ground. That the disused Welsh Canal locks had been affected in this way by two very severe winters in the past six years was a contingency that I had failed to take into account. A narrow boat slides into a narrow lock chamber with only inches to spare at the best of times, so it does not need much deformation to create an impasse such as now occurred. Despite the efforts of helpful lengthmen, using extra lines and the pulley blocks, or alternately lifting and dropping the top gate paddles to create a 'flush', *Cressy* refused to budge. Fortunately, however, the lower pound was a short one and the Baddiley lock keeper finally suggested lowering its level by drawing off water at the lock below. It was a risky expedient, for either *Cressy* might fail to drop with the water level or, if too much water was released, she could come to rest on the bottom sill. Happily neither of these disasters occurred and the device worked; *Cressy* suddenly dropped free and floated easily into the lock. But as the lock was filled, how anxiously we watched to ensure that she continued to rise with the water!

As our boat slowly rose above the upper gate, our hearts sank at the prospect before us. The canal ahead appeared to contain more weed than water, so much so that it looked solid enough to walk on. Even by frequent reversals to unwind the weed from the propeller, it was impossible to make progress at more than a snail's pace; while *Heron*, with her small propeller, was an even worse case. We ended up with *Heron* in tow behind *Cressy* while every available hand bow-hauled both from the towpath, our engine giving what assistance it could. Matters were made more difficult by the fact that the trouble at the lock had undoubtedly lowered the water level quite considerably. We therefore soon agreed to call it a day in the hope that overnight the water would rise somewhat and so make the going a little easier.

At this point I should explain why, during the whole of this first voyage up the Welsh Canal, we were dogged by a persistent shortage of water. The canal draws its water supply from the river Dee at the so-called 'Horseshoe Falls', actually a diversion weir built by Thomas Telford, the engineer of the canal, at Llantisilio. The original Ellesmere Canal Act which authorized construction contained a clause which stipulated that this water was to be used for navigational purposes only, and eventually returned to the river at Chester. In the 1940s, however, the Dee Conservators discovered that the canal owners, the L.M. & S. Railway, were selling canal water in considerable volume to the Monsanto Chemical Company whose works now occupy the site of William Hazeldine's Plas Kynaston Ironworks where the iron trough of the Pont Cysyllte aqueduct was cast. Somewhat naturally the conservators decided that if anybody sold water to this large chemical plant it should be themselves, and they forthwith successfully challenged the railway company in the courts. As a result of this legal action, the canal intake was limited to a stipulated quantity per day; and to ensure that this was not exceeded, the railway company were to install a flow meter at Llantisilio. At the time we made this first voyage, this flow meter and the house which contained it were still under construction, and in the meantime water was being admitted to the canal in extremely meagre quantities through a temporary by-pass channel. Yet even if this supply had been more generous, it is doubtful if it would have helped us very much, for the canal was so choked with weeds that the water would not flow down. Consequently it could be running over the spill weirs at the Llangollen end while at New Martin locks, twelve miles downstream, it could be nine inches low. The Welsh Canal supplies a reservoir at Hurleston which, in turn, supplies the main line of the Shropshire Union between Hack Green, Chester and Ellesmere Port. So it was not only the Welsh Canal which suffered from this parlous water situation.

We awoke next morning to find that the water level in the canal had risen slightly and we were able to struggle on as far as the repaired drawbridge at Wrenbury. Here there was a turning place or 'winding hole' where, despite its disused and depressing appearance, we reckoned we might be able to turn *Cressy*. I have never been one who throws in the sponge lightly, so it is a measure of the appalling state of the canal that we seriously considered making a strategic retreat to Hurleston. Before making a final decision, however, I lifted down Angela's bicycle from the deck and cycled along the towpath to see what conditions were like ahead. There appeared to be more water and less weed so we decided to forge on.

Soon bow-hauling was no longer necessary, but a rising cross wind made progress increasingly difficult for *Cressy*, and at teatime we decided to moor up for the night above Marbury Lock, leaving *Heron* to go ahead as the Grundys were anxious to ascend the lock flight at Grindley Brook before nightfall.

We eventually reached Grindley Brook only to find that

1. *A muster of Rolt uncles and aunts at Chester,* c. *1902. Left to right: my father, Marjory, Wilfred, Harry, Gladys, 'Granny Garnett', Algernon, Vivian, Dorothy, Marjory's husband*

2. *With my mother at Cusop*

3. A picnic, Kilvert style, on Cusop Hill. Major Armstrong is seated (in uniform) with my mother behind him, and my tutor Thomas Southwick is standing on the left

4. First family transport: the Williamson Combination

5. On the footplate of the first Sentinel Ploughing Engine, Pitchill, 1926–7

6. Cressy under way, 1930

7. The engine room of Cressy

8. The G.N. and my Belsize at Stanley Pontlarge, 1933

9. *The G.N. as a single-seater at Bramshill, 1936*

10. *Design for living: an interior
view of* Cressy

11. Wartime mooring at Tardebigge, 1941–6

12. Cressy *at Lifford bridge, Stratford Canal*

13. Ambition achieved, 1949. Crossing Pont Cysyllte with Hugh and Gunde Griffith

14. Duke's Cut, July 1950. The Humphry family about to drop down the back water to Wolvercote Mill

15. The author steering Cressy *at Hawkesbury Stop, 1950*

16. Sonia Smith on Warwick *on the Grand Union Canal, 1950*

17. My own £10-worth of Alvis in Bryn Eglwys quarry

18. Talyllyn Railway 1951: Helping David Curwen (on footplate of Dolgoch) to marshal a train at Towyn Wharf Station

19. Centenary Celebrations, 1965. John Betjeman, first member of the Society, unveils a plaque to mark the completion of improvements to the Wharf Station

20. *International Rally 1963; the start of the Grand Parade at Goodwood that later got out of hand*

21. Talking to Maggie Dirane outside her cottage on Aranmore, 1963

22. Agricultural development at Stanley Pontlarge with the Norman church in the background

23. Stanley Pontlarge: the west front

24. *Portrait of the author*

25. The Great Steam Fair, Shottesbrooke, 1964: general view from the roof of the house

26. Driving the Alvis at the 35th Anniversary Meeting at Prescott, 1973

Cressy again stuck fast between the wing walls of the bottom lock. It was only after repeated 'flushing' from the top paddles that eventually, to our great relief, she came free and we were able to tie up to the bank below the lock. Here we held a council of war. Somehow or other we had to get *Cressy* up the Grindley Brook flight, for the prospect of retreat now did not bear thinking about; it would have meant stern-hauling our heavy boat back to that 'winding hole' at Wrenbury, and even there it was by no means certain that we could turn her. The day was Sunday, and we walked up to the lock house at the top of the flight where we explained our predicament to the lock keeper, Mr Howell, who promised to come down with an assistant to give us a hand next morning.

I spent most of the rest of the day planing obvious high spots off *Cressy's* wooden hull. I also greased her bow rubbing strakes, for I had resolved upon the desperate expedient of driving her at full speed towards the lock chamber. If she went in, well and good; if she did not, I realized that nothing would free her short of partly demolishing a lock wall as Brunel and Claxton had had to do in order to get the *Great Britain* out of Bristol Docks. There was another snag to this scheme: to be quite certain that she was well and truly in the lock chamber, I would have to keep her going full ahead so long that it would be extremely difficult to prevent her cannoning violently into the top gate sill. Such a disaster could only be averted if Angela checked her at the right moment with a 'stern strap' and at the same instant all the top gate paddles were raised.

When Mr Howell and his mate appeared next morning I explained my plan to him and, though he looked extremely dubious, as well he might, he agreed that it was the only thing to do under the circumstances. So, having secured everything on board that might be damaged by a possible impact, we moved *Cressy* astern for fifty yards or so and then, with a silent prayer, I gave her full ahead and approached the narrow chamber at what appeared to be an impossible speed. Everything worked perfectly. There was a creaking sound and I felt her check slightly as the side walls nipped her, but the next moment she was through. Angela had checked her with the stern line, Mr Howell had raised the top paddles, and a few seconds later the lower gates had slammed to behind me with a crash. I felt *Cressy* surge upwards. So far so good, but there were still five more locks to go, culminating in a triple lock staircase of awesome depth. It was so many years since a narrow boat had passed through the canal that Mr Howell was as much in the dark as we were as to the likely outcome of our venture. In the event, *Cressy* stuck again firmly coming out of the third lock and I had to use our pulley blocks to free her; yet, curiously enough, although the lock keeper had dire misgivings about the state of the staircase, she came through it without the slightest difficulty. It was with immense relief that we moored opposite Mr Howell's cottage at the top of the flight and caught a bus into Whitchurch to do our weekly shopping.

One could see from the weir beside the top lock that the canal level was at least six inches below normal; and in order to keep the lower part of the canal and Hurleston reservoir supplied, Mr Howell had the special by-pass paddle drawn. A very long level now lay ahead of us, so we could not expect any improvement but must make the best of it. As soon as we started off, it was obvious that the bottom was much too near the top. Happily, however, there was little or no weed and we were able to make slow but steady progress under our own power for a mile or two until we reached a point which, according to that canal traveller's bible, de Salis's *Guide*, was known as Blackoe Cottages. Here *Cressy* ran suddenly and firmly aground in mid-channel; so firmly, in fact, that her bows rose up out of the water. Investigation soon showed that a small stream flowed into the canal at this point and that over the years it had built up a bar of silt that extended from bank to bank.

Once again my pulley blocks and extra lines proved invaluable. Just above the mouth of the brook grew a stout tree whose bole made an ideal anchor for my double block, the single block being hooked on to *Cressy*'s fore-end stud. Then the free end of the cotton line was taken across the canal to the towpath where a long pull and a strong pull by Angela and myself, assisted by most of the astonished inhabitants of Blackoe Cottages, was sufficient to drive *Cressy* through the silt barrier. We then had lunch before continuing slowly on our way as far as the old wharf and bridge at Platt Lane where we found a party of gypsies encamped in a green road and stopped for a cup of tea to satisfy a mutual curiosity.

As recounted in the first volume of this autobiography, it was over this same Welsh canal that I had made my first voyage by inland waterway in 1930 at a time when *Cressy* was steam driven. The canal had seemed to me then to be so uniquely and magically beautiful that I was at once captivated by the idea of travelling by waterway. This narrow and winding ribbon of water conveyed such a strange sense of remoteness and seemed to pass through such an astonishing variety of scenery. Now, returning to the same canal in the same boat after the lapse of seventeen years I was interested to discover whether my first impressions had been correct, or whether I had been beguiled by distance and nostalgia. I could still recall vividly the enchantment of that first voyage, gliding through the glassy waters on that spring morning so long ago. I recalled ruefully that it had then been easy going and not a perpetual struggle with weed, lack of water and decaying lock chambers. Yet despite all the effort and anxiety, I decided as we left Platt Lane that it was worth it; the magic remained; it was no illusion.

At Platt Lane the Welsh Canal undergoes its first dramatic transformation. Up to this point we had been travelling through a typical Cheshire countryside of gently rolling pastures and large dairy farms of blackish red brick; a pleasant enough scene but somewhat tame. Now we suddenly found ourselves in a landscape that reminded us of our last year's journey across the great Bog of Allen on the Grand Canal of Ireland. Whixall Moss is indeed a replica of an Irish turf bog set down on the Shropshire/Cheshire borders, and the Welsh Canal cuts straight across it. For some reason, presumably connected with the nature of the peat, the canal becomes not only weed-free but both wider and deeper as soon as it enters upon the bog, so that from crawling along at snail's pace *Cressy* was suddenly able to travel as fast as upon some broad river. They had been cutting turf on the Moss, and the dark stacks of drying peats in the middle distance backed by the distant shapes of the Berwyns beyond, serenely blue and indistinct in the haze of the summer's day, made the resemblance to an Irish landscape complete.

We reached the end of Whixall Moss all too soon and once again the canal became narrow, shallow and winding, its banks lined with the yellow flowers of musk. But we were now in the wilder border country, quite unlike the broad pastures of Cheshire. Presently we reached the little village of Bettisfield where we decided to moor for the night. Politically, *Cressy* had now entered Wales for the first time since 1930, for Bettisfield is in 'Flintshire detached', that strange little Welsh island in Shropshire. Physically, however, those distant blue mountains marked the true Welsh border whither we were bound – or so I hoped.

After dinner that evening we strolled down the road into the village and had a drink at the 'Nag's Head'. The first thing I noticed as we entered the small tap room was a broken luggage rack bracket out of a railway coach reposing in a glass case on the wall. I had encountered some queer objects in pubs in my time, but nothing as odd as this. On inquiry, it transpired that this was a relic of the Welshampton railway disaster which took place on the main line of the old Cambrian Railway that runs parallel with the canal at this point. Apart from the better known – and worse – accident at Abermule, Welshampton was the only serious disaster that the Cambrian suffered.

A little distance beyond Bettisfield, the Welsh Canal springs a second surprise, comparable in beauty to Whixall Moss though of an entirely different character. It passes through the heart of what is sometimes called the Shropshire Lake District, a number of shallow, tree-fringed meres in the neighbourhood of the little town of Ellesmere. The water of these meres normally appears dark and peaty, especially under the shade of the encircling trees, but once a year a brief phenomenon, known locally as the 'break', occurs when a species of algae rises to the surface to turn the water an opaque green. Ellesmere itself, the largest of these meres, is also the most open and the most frequented, being the nearest to the town. By contrast, Colemere (pronounced 'Coomer' by the locals) and Blake Mere are tree-surrounded and secluded, the haunt of many wild-fowl. The canal passes close beside them and I remembered the impression they had made upon me when I had first seen them from *Cressy*'s deck in the grey stillness of an early spring dawn.

Now under the clear light of the summer sun I found they had lost nothing of their earlier enchantment. We moored up under the shade of the trees beside the narrow bank that divides the canal from Colemere and had a very protracted picnic lunch, interrupted only by the intermittent clucking and splashing of the coot and moorhen which alone flawed the mirror of the water. We felt it was a fitting reward for all the effort and anxieties involved in forcing a passage through waters which, in the course of recent years, had become virtually uncharted. Yet how many times, I reflected, must *Cressy* have passed this way in the course of her working life when she was one of the Shropshire Union Canal Carrying Company's fleet or, later, when she belonged to the owners of a mill at Maesbury.

Although the going had been slow since we left Whixall Moss, the canal had been pleasantly free from weed; but after lunch, as we passed through the very short Ellesmere tunnel, we saw that the canal ahead was choked with a dense blanket of green. So thick was it that it was only with the help of bow-hauling from the towpath that we covered the brief remaining distance to the junction of the short Ellesmere branch canal. At this point, the main line of canal curves sharply southward, rounding Beech House, once the headquarters of the old Ellesmere Canal Company, and the extensive canal workshops.* As at Wrenbury, we decided once again that discretion was the better part of valour and that it would be better to explore what lay ahead on foot before passing so convenient a turning point for *Cressy*. What we saw ahead could scarcely have been more discouraging; the canal was choked with dense weed as far as the eye could see. Moreover, we were told at the canal workshops that this state of things prevailed at least as far as New Marton locks and that even if we fought our way through this Sargasso Sea of weed, we could go no further than Chirk because a slip in the deep cutting to the north of Chirk tunnel had made the canal quite impassable.

So, once again, despite all our efforts, my ambition to take *Cressy* over Pont Cysyllte had been defeated; the way into Wales was closed to us, and it then seemed most unlikely that

---

* Although situated on a disused canal, in 1947 these workshops were still very active, making lock-gates for the whole of the Shropshire Union Canal system.

it would ever reopen. Sadly, we swung *Cressy* about in the mouth of the junction and tied her up alongside the towpath by Beech House. Although this was convenient for the town it was by no means ideal in other respects; so, as we had planned to stay in the area for several summer weeks, we determined to retrace our steps for three and a half miles to a disused wharf at Hampton Bank which had looked both inviting and convenient when we had passed it by.

Hampton Bank Wharf did indeed prove to be an almost ideal mooring. It lay just off the road from Ellesmere to Wem which then carried little traffic and from which the wharf was readily accessible. Although the wharf was grass-grown it provided a good hard standing for a car. A solitary cottage – obviously built for a wharfinger – was still occupied by a kindly country couple who gladly supplied us with drinking water and kept an eye on the boat when we were away. Here I left Angela in charge of *Cressy* while I travelled by train to Banbury for the purpose of collecting my Alvis.

During these summer weeks at Hampton Bank, despite having the Alvis, we made good use of the local railway system – in this case part of what had once been the old Cambrian Railway – for the sheer pleasure of sampling rural branch lines. It was a hobby which combined well with living afloat. We used that part of the Cambrian main line which keeps the canal company most of the way between Whitchurch, Ellesmere and Oswestry. We also travelled to Wrexham by the branch line from Ellesmere and, best of all, trundled up the Tanat Valley branch from Oswestry to Llanrhaiadr y Mochnant in a diminutive train of Cambrian four-wheelers, now smartly painted in G.W.R. livery; it was drawn by a little tank engine, the *Lady Margaret*, which had originally seen service on the Liskeard & Looe Railway in faraway Cornwall but had now come north to work out her last days in this remote Welsh valley.

From mid-July to mid-August, while *Cressy* lay at Hampton Bank, the weather was exceptionally fine and warm. Pleasant though it was, this four-week spell of heat and unbroken drought began to affect the canal. At first it was only a matter of an inch or two, but then the level suddenly began to fall alarmingly. Inquiries elicited the gloomy information that there had been a burst in the canal bank in the neighbourhood of Chirk and that in consequence the temporary feed from the Dee at Llantisilio had been shut off pending repairs. We had entered this abandoned canal at our own risk and peril and had no rights whatever; *Cressy* could sit on the mud at Hampton Bank until doomsday for all the L.M.S. railway cared, so it was up to us to do something quickly. For a while, business was brisk in the telephone kiosk at Hampton Bank. It was obvious that so long as Mr Howell, the lock keeper at Grindley Brook, continued to draw water down through his by-pass culvert into the canal below the locks, the situation would worsen rapidly. On the telephone he sounded most anxious to help, but said he dared not shut off supplies to Hurleston reservoir without authority from Crewe. So, in response to an S.O.S. message to Crewe, a remote official in the L.M.S. finally agreed somewhat grudgingly that Howell could drop his by-pass paddle for twenty-four hours and no longer. All this took place on a Sunday (17 August), and by the time we had got confirmation from Howell that he had complied with instructions it was 6 p.m. We got under way without more ado, travelling in close company with *Heron*. We were dragging the bottom as far as Bettisfield, but after this the going improved somewhat and by 9 p.m. we had reached Platt Lane Wharf, where we decided to lie for the night.

Remembering our experience on the upward journey, it was obvious that the toughest part of this race against the clock was still to come, but fortunately help was at hand in the person of one of the early members of the I.W.A. and his wife. He was a sterling character named Livock, an ex-R.A.F. Squadron Leader who, before the war, had pioneered the flying-boat route to Singapore. Precisely how we got in touch with each other at this providential moment I cannot now remember and my log is silent on the subject. Suffice it to say that Livock and his wife drove on to Platt Lane Wharf in a large estate car promptly at 9 a.m. the next morning. We then proceeded to discharge from *Cressy*'s aft hold everything that could be spared – five gallon drums of spare fuel, off-cuts of locomotive frame-plates from Kerr Stuart which had been serving as ballast ever since those far-off days at Stoke-on-Trent when *Cressy* had been steam-driven. All this was loaded into the back of the estate car. It settled down on its back springs rather like a broody hen, but at the same time *Cressy*'s stern rose out of the water nearly two inches. At a time when every inch counted, this was probably crucial. The transfer completed, Mrs Livock then set off in the car with instructions to keep in touch so far as possible until – we hoped – we were able to switch cargoes again at Basin End, Nantwich. Her husband remained with us to supply the extra muscle power which we would certainly need. *Cressy* then set off, towing *Heron* astern and with Angela, Livock and Christopher Grundy bow-hauling from the towpath. Their efforts were only occasionally needed until we reached Blackoe Cottages where, remembering the trouble we had previously had with the shoal across the canal, I thought we would most probably meet our Waterloo. Once more I rigged our blocks and tackle, but this time it was a much tougher proposition. For a long time, strain as we would, *Cressy* refused to budge until finally a team of nine, the combined crews of both boats, plus Livock, plus three able-bodied recruits from the Cottages, were mustered together on the towpath. Digging in our heels and heaving like a tug-o'-war team, we suddenly felt the line give in our hands and, with mutual cries of encouragement, we fought our way backward foot by foot as we watched *Cressy* drive partly through and partly over the obstruction. It was an immense relief to see her floating once more and on the 'home' side of the barrier. We celebrated victory by calling a brief halt for a lunch that consisted mainly of very welcome liquor.

Lack of water had worsened the weed problem, and when we continued after lunch we several times had to resort to bow-hauling for this reason. But now that our main concern was to stay afloat, weeds seemed a relatively minor worry. So, partly under power and partly bow-hauled, our boats arrived at Grindley Brook, with a very tired and sweaty crew in attendance, at 4 p.m. or just two hours inside our twenty-four-hour time limit. Mr Howell was delighted to see us. He had expected to see *Heron* but confessed that he had had grave doubts whether *Cressy* would be able to make it. Now, with her bows nudging the top gate of the triple staircase lock while we brewed a cup of tea, I no longer had any fear that we might be stranded. Once on the other side of that gate, there was no doubt at all in my mind that Mr Howell would let down enough water to float us back to Hurleston even if it meant emptying the entire upper portion of the canal. And so it proved. Looking down, we could see that the short pound between the bottom of the staircase and Lock No. 16 was completely dry, and both our boats had to lie in the chambers of the staircase while water was passed down to fill it. The bottom lock at Grindley Brook, where we had stuck so fast on the upward journey, did not delay us this time. With all the top paddles up and her engine going full ahead, *Cressy* shot out of that lock chamber like a cork from a champagne bottle. But not far, for the canal below the flight looked so low that we decided to tie up for the night to allow the pound to make up. After all, we were no longer working to a deadline and time was now on our side.

Our progress next day was very slow but sure, for now we were literally bringing with us the precious water we needed. This meant that there had to be lengthy pauses at each lock while we ran the water down from the pound above to the pound below. Apart from this there is little to say about the last stage of our adventurous foray up the Welsh Section. We spent the next night at the head of Baddiley top lock, and at 6 p.m. on the evening of the day following we moored in Nantwich Basin where we were able to relieve Mrs Livock of her car load of fuel and ballast. We celebrated victory that night with a protracted and memorable dinner at the 'Crown Hotel' in Nantwich. Everyone was in high good humour, for there is nothing to equal the power of an episode of this kind as a generator of friendship and fellow-feeling.

Next day we parted company, *Heron* sailing north towards Chester, while *Cressy* swung her bows southward. Our destination was Gayton Arm End, where the Northampton Branch of the Grand Union Canal joins the main line of that canal near Blisworth. We travelled via the Staffordshire & Worcestershire and the Trent & Mersey canals, and the rivers Trent and Soar to Leicester, where we joined the Leicester Section of the Grand Union. This whole journey of 203 miles from Hampton Bank Wharf on the Welsh Marches to Northamptonshire took sixteen days and I recorded the fact that throughout this time we enjoyed unbroken sunshine.

There was a particular reason why we had made Gayton and not Banbury our immediate objective. During our stay at Hampton Bank I had been pondering over possible ways of attracting new members to our Association and publicizing its canal crusade, and had hit on the notion of staging a canal exhibition in London. The great question was *where*, for the infant I.W.A. certainly could not afford to hire any gallery in central London. Then I thought of Anthony Heal whom I had known since the earliest days of the Vintage Sports Car Club at the Phoenix. Anthony received my idea enthusiastically, and readily agreed that we might use the Mansard Gallery outside the restaurant on the top floor of the Heal family's famous shop in Tottenham Court Road. With this satisfactorily settled it became a question of collecting suitable material for exhibition, and we had agreed that Gayton was the most convenient base from which to pursue this quest. Not only was it conveniently near the main line to Euston, but the Grand Union carried a much larger floating population than did the Oxford Canal. There was a third reason also. At Gayton Junction were situated the canal workshops for the district, and the home and offices of the district engineer, C. N. Hadlow. Charles Hadlow was a friend of mine and a canal engineer of wide experience with a deep interest in the canal past. So much so that, on his retirement, he played a great part in the setting up of the present Waterways Museum at Stoke Bruerne of which he became honorary curator. I guessed – rightly as things turned out – that he would be the best person to assist us in locating suitable material for display. It so happened that he had lately discovered, in an old loft over one of the canal buildings at Gayton, a pile of old glass-plate negatives, all showing early canal scenes, which had been taken by his predecessors. To examine this treasure-trove in his office, holding them up to the light and deciding which ones to print up, was a fascinating exercise. Charles Hadlow was able to lend us a pair of the brass armlets which were issued by the old Grand Junction Canal Company to the professional 'leggers' who had once been responsible for propelling the boats through Blisworth tunnel at 1*s.* 6*d.* a time. This was only one of the many two- and three-dimensional objects – boat furniture, traditional boaters' clothing, model boats, some made by professionals and others by the boatmen themselves – which we managed to collect in a surprisingly short space of time, for we had arrived at Gayton on 4 September and the Exhibition was due to open on 25 October. The find which most pleased me was a splendid diorama showing a pair of horse-drawn narrow boats entering the top lock at Stoke Bruerne. I cannot remember how we got to know of the existence of this, but I remember collecting it from its owner's garage in the suburbs of Leighton Buzzard. He explained that, with other dioramas, it had been made by his father many years before.

Angela and I spent several days arranging all this material in Heals' Mansard Gallery, an unfamiliar and satisfying task which we thoroughly enjoyed and which we were able to complete on time despite frequent interruptions. We walked in fear of one formidable lady of middle age who was in charge of the gallery and very evidently disapproved of our amateurish goings-on. She seemed to lurk perpetually in a little office in a corner of the gallery from which she would dart out at us from time to time whenever she observed us in the act of committing some dire offence such as sticking drawing pins into the woodwork. Altogether more encouraging and enjoyable were the visits of Anthony's father, old Sir Ambrose Heal, who took a lively and intelligent interest in our enterprise.

This 'Inland Waterways Exhibition' proved a great success. It attracted so much attention from press and public that I succeeded in persuading some commercial firm (I forget the name) to pack up the exhibition when it closed at Heals after a month and take it on a tour of provincial art galleries at no cost to the Association. One tragi-comic result of this was that the firm's packers, who were experts at this class of work, discovered that our precious Stoke Bruerne diorama was riddled with woodworm. The discovery that someone was suffering from bubonic plague could scarely have created a greater furore. The unfortunate model was at once isolated and subjected to such a barrage of poisonous sprays that it finally disintegrated and was never heard of again so far as I can remember. Its

radiated a tranquillity that was soon to be lost and never to be known again. On the Mythe meadow, corncrakes called to each other repeatedly as the sun went down behind the Malverns and a thick mist began to rise over the wide expanse of grass. The harsh call of this strangely elusive bird, sounding now here, now there, reminds me of the whirring of grasshoppers vastly amplified. It always brings back my childhood, for I often heard it in the small, summer hayfields of the Welsh Border; but now mechanical reapers have almost banished it and, although I have heard the corncrake since in Ireland, this was its last performance in England so far as I am concerned.

There was thick mist over the Mythe next morning presaging another glorious day. The sun was warm on our backs and our decks hot to the touch by the time we passed through Tewkesbury Lock and set off down the river towards Gloucester at a fine pace, passing fishermen, out in their black Severn punts, netting for salmon in the reach between Deerhurst and Apperley. At all seasons of the year, Severn flows faster than Thames because it is much less heavily locked. In this 28½ miles of river, from the tail of Diglis Locks at Worcester to the entrance to Gloucester Docks, there is but the one solitary lock at Upper Lode, Tewkesbury. Compared with the translucent reaches of the Thames, still as a lake except in times of heavy flood, Severn is a powerful river, a great body of dark water eternally flowing swiftly and silently down to the sea. We speak of 'Father Thames' and think of him as a jolly old soul, whereas Severn is feminine. Those who know this river speak of Severn, never 'the Severn', and usually refer to the river as 'she'. Sabrina may be fair, but if she is indeed feminine then hers is a sombre and subtle Celtic beauty, menacing and not to be slighted. Yet for the men who know her most intimately, as did Harry Rogers of Ironbridge, she holds a fascination that is almost hypnotic. Although my first-hand knowledge of Severn was brief, it was long enough for me to realize that she was not to be trifled with – especially when one is piloting a large and under-powered boat. The Model T Ford might be an ideal engine for propelling a 70-foot narrow boat in the still waters of the canals, but it was immediately obvious that on Severn it was woefully inadequate. Astern it was generally impossible to hold *Cressy* against the current, while travelling upstream between Gloucester and Worcester was, as we were later to find, a painfully slow and tedious business.

For craft travelling downstream as we were, the approach to Gloucester is particularly tricky, for above the city, at Upper Parting, the river splits into two streams; on the right is the old Maisemore Channel with its single lock. This is the old line of navigation. It communicates with the tidal river and was used before the Gloucester & Berkeley Ship Canal was opened in 1827. It was still used for many years after this by masters of Severn trows who preferred the hazards and uncertainties of the estuary rather than pay the toll charges on the canal. This old channel is now quite disused and all downstream traffic takes the left-hand channel that leads to Gloucester Lock and so into Gloucester Docks. This is half the width of the river above, the current runs swiftly and it is extremely tortuous. In 1948 we faced an additional hazard in the shape of the large petrol tanker barges trading between Avonmouth and oil depots at Worcester and Stourport. This traffic was then considerable and the tankers as large as Severn could handle. A laden tanker could only just round these tight turns on the Gloucester channel and needed all its width to do so. Therefore, owing to our inability to stop, to have encountered one in such a situation would have meant an almost certain collision. As we remembered, the narrow boat *Heather Bell*, which I mentioned earlier in this book, was coming up the Gloucester & Berkeley Canal one morning in thick fog with a cargo of grain from Sharpness when she was in collision with an empty tanker whose high bows suddenly loomed out of the fog ahead. She sank instantly. Fortunately, for craft heading downstream as we were, it was possible to predict fairly accurately when and where laden tanker barges would be encountered because they could only enter Sharpness Docks from the river at high water, and their running time up the canal to Gloucester was remarkably consistent. We had therefore armed ourselves with a local tide table and so were able to enter the Gloucester channel at a time when the risk of our encountering another large craft was minimal.

If, as was the case with us, Gloucester Lock is not set for

downstream craft, the entry to Gloucester Docks is decidedly
tricky because the river channel sweeps past the tail of the lock
and then almost directly over Gloucester weir en route for the
Lower Parting. Moreover, there is no towing path hereabouts,
only a high quay wall on our left. A signal indicated to us the
state of the lock, but by the time we sighted this we had to act
quickly. Fortunately, in our haste we did not forget the lesson
we had learned on the Thames eight years before – to hold her
by the stern. Angela jumped nimbly from the bow to the quay
stairs and I then threw her up a stern line. After that it was all
plain sailing; we found a quiet berth beside an old brick ware-
house in the docks where we lay until the next morning.

The Gloucester & Berkeley Canal does not go to Berkeley
although it has borne that name ever since it was first conceived
in 1793. With its swift currents, its shifting sand bars and its
tremendous tides (spring tides can rise thirty-four feet), not to
mention its famous bore, the Severn estuary is as dangerous a
piece of water as any in the world, and it was the purpose of
the canal to by-pass its upper portion from Berkeley Pill to
Gloucester. It was conceived from the first as a ship canal,
seventy feet wide and fifteen feet deep. These were ambitious
figures in eighteenth-century England; indeed they were over-
ambitious, for the project soon ran into such dire physical and
financial difficulties that it was not completed until April 1827.
By that time the original engineer, Robert Mylne, and several
successors, had come and gone and it was Thomas Telford who
finally completed it. In 1818, it was decided to increase the
depth of the canal to eighteen feet but to make Sharpness Point
the site of the junction with the river, so reducing its length by
one and a half miles.

To travel from Gloucester to Sharpness was a novel experience, for *Cressy* had never known a canal of this character before.
There are no locks but many swing bridges, manned by
bridge-keepers who, we found, lived in delightful little cottages
which, with their classical, pillared porticos, would not have
looked out of place as lodges on some great estate. At the
Gloucester end of the canal these swing bridges were sufficiently high to allow *Cressy* to pass beneath them without
disturbing their keepers, but after this they became lower so

that we had to alert their attendants by sounding the regulation two blasts on our air horn. With such a wide, deep and lock-free channel, with bridges opening before us at our bidding, there was nothing whatever for me to do except to lean upon the tiller. As soon as the sun had dissolved the morning haze it became very hot and I am ashamed to say that I must have fallen into a kind of daze or day-dream, lulled by the steady throb of the engine. From this I was rudely disturbed by the loud blast of a ship's siren behind me. It was as though someone had suddenly sounded a loud raspberry on a trombone just behind my ear. I nearly jumped out of my skin and looked round to see the grey bows of a steamer looming up just astern. It was only the very small coaster *Monkton Combe* of Bristol which we had earlier seen unloading at Gloucester; but, being empty, her bows rose high out of the water so that from my lowly vantage it looked as if we were about to be run down by the *Queen Mary*. Needless to say I lost no time in drawing into the side and slowing down to let this monster past. This was a manoeuvre that gave me some anxious moments for, in so narrow a channel, even with light draught and her engine going slow ahead, the *Monkton Combe*'s passing exercised considerable 'draw' on us so that it was not easy to avoid a side-long collision. Hardly had the ship vanished round a bend ahead than there appeared coming towards us the steam tug *Speedwell* with a train of barges in tow. In contrast to the deep-noted drumming of the *Monkton Combe*'s diesel, the *Speedwell* slid past us in silent dignity; the metronomic rhythm of her compound engine running slow ahead was only just audible, and a wisp of black smoke curled lazily from her funnel. Travelling by ship canal was more eventful than we had thought.

As we had all the time in the world and these were new waters to us, we decided to stay for two nights at Saul Junction, almost exactly half-way between Gloucester and Sharpness. Here the ship canal cuts across the old Stroudwater canal which, until the Thames & Severn canal became impassable, was a link in the through route between the two rivers. Now the Stroudwater had also become derelict and we moored on the only fragment of it that was still navigable – a length of three hundred yards east of the junction which was used as a leat, feeding water into the ship canal from the river Frome. The two miles of the Stroudwater between the junction and the estuary has been derelict for a very long time, for little traffic can have passed that way since the ship canal was opened.* After we had had tea, we walked the towpath of this long disused section of canal, past the 'Junction Inn', until we came to the old tidal entrance lock at Framilode and looked out across the estuary, watching the strong tide making and submerging the sand flats with astonishing speed.

Although I would not care to live in such a place myself, there is a strange fascination about the flat lands bordering the estuary of a great river, particularly when, as in this case, navigation is hazardous and the channel is too wide to be easily bridged. Such a natural barrier creates on its banks unfrequented hinterlands where roads lead nowhere or peter out in the rotting timber stagings of forgotten ferries, forlorn amid mud-banks where waders walk delicately. The main roads from Gloucester to Bristol and South Wales seem to draw the boundaries of modern urban civilization, and in the littoral between them lies an empty quarter where old trades and old ways still persist – or they did in 1948. For example, at Saul there was a dry dock that looked as though it pre-dated the ship canal and on its stocks lay the Severn trow *Water Witch* undergoing repairs; she had long since lost her mast and was working as a dumb barge carrying Dean coal between Lydney harbour and Bristol, but there was no mistaking her lineage.

We spent twenty-four hours exploring the Saul neighbourhood before setting off to cover the last eight miles of our voyage to Sharpness. The most dramatic moment of that voyage came just after we had passed through the little village of Purton. Hereabouts the ship canal makes a sweeping S-bend and then, for the last mile and a quarter, runs parallel with the shore line of the estuary with only a sea wall separating the two. The tide was out and from our deck we looked out over a great expanse of sand to the foothills of Dean Forest rising from the further shore. Ahead, the many lattice-girder spans of the Severn railway bridge emphasized the breadth of the

---

* There was possibly a little traffic in Dean coal from Bullo Pill on the opposite side of Severn to Stroud and wharves on the Thames & Severn.

estuary. The bridge was silhouetted against the westering sunlight and beyond it rose Sharpness Point and the docks.

The junction of the ship canal with the estuary was originally made on the upstream side of the red sandstone cliff of the Point, so that the entrance lock and the berths above it were sheltered to some extent from the force of the incoming tides and from the prevailing south-westerlies. In November, 1874, however, the New Docks were opened on the inland side of the point with a new and much larger entrance lock further downstream. This development was a result of the increase in the tonnage of shipping. If ships were too big to travel up the canal to Gloucester, at least they might be lured upriver away from Avonmouth either to discharge their cargoes or tranship them into barges or narrow boats in the new docks. The effect of this change was that Sharpness Point became an island, accessible only by swing bridges, and that the old entrance fell derelict.

Because I have always been fascinated by docks, I had paid several visits to Sharpness Docks long ago when I was working as an engineering apprentice at Dursley. It made a sad spectacle in those days of the great slump. The new docks had become a berth for rusting, idle shipping, while the old entrance lock and channel were derelict and choked with weeds. So, although I was familiar with the dock layout, returning after so many years I did not know what to expect but hoped it might be possible to moor in the old channel so as to be out of the way of traffic. Great was my surprise when we reached the junction to see a perfectly clear channel stretching away to my right and terminating in a very smart and obviously completely restored entrance lock. As I soon discovered, this work had been carried out as a war-time precaution in case the new entrance lock was damaged by enemy bombs. As soon as we made this pleasant discovery we put *Cressy* about at the junction, and came stern first into the old canal to find a perfect mooring alongside the disused towpath and the sea wall.

Here we lay for a memorable month of summer, from mid-June to mid-July and here, as was customary, I brought my 12/50 Alvis to serve as land transport. I had to park her on Sharpness Point near the top of a disused coal-drop immediately opposite our moorings, for to reach *Cressy* it was necessary to cross the old canal by the lock-gates. But this inconvenience was a small price to pay for our seclusion and for our splendid view over the estuary. One can never get to know a place or learn to savour its particularity without living in it. It was in this that our way of life proved so triumphantly successful. As now at Sharpness, *Cressy* would slide unobtrusively into some quiet mooring and at once we would feel at home and under the skin of the place. It was a pleasure which never palled. The fact that it is unknown to those who park caravans is something to do with the particular quality of boats and water. A boat is of necessity in her natural element whereas a caravan in a field is an intruder.

We certainly fell under Severn's spell during our stay at Sharpness. When we lay a-bed and heard the sound of the night tide rushing up the river or, on awakening, the crying of gulls and the piping of waders from beyond the sea-wall, it was easy to imagine we had put to sea. Between *Cressy*'s stern and the lock there loomed the bows of the merchant navy training ship *Invicatrix*. Sometimes, when we were breakfasting, we would hear the rhythmical creak of rowlocks and look out to see a party of cadets at rowing practice in a ship's lifeboat. Neither they nor anyone else dared interfere with our boat while we were away, for we had the most zealous of watch-dogs in the person of old Mr Smith down at the lock-house.

Mr Smith was a retired Bristol Channel Pilot who was appointed lock keeper when the old canal entrance was restored. Happily his job was a sinecure because the Luftwaffe never visited Sharpness. A man who had spent a long lifetime in sailing ships could not have found a more appropriate shore berth. His lock-house stood on a breakwater that projected beyond the tip of the Point to protect the mouth of the lock from the force of the ebb tide. The windows of his living-room looked right and left up and down the estuary. When we were greatly privileged to be invited to supper there, I thought it one of the most remarkable rooms I had ever been in. It was like being on the bridge of a ship and hard to believe that we were not afloat – indeed the water running so swiftly past the windows created in the house an illusion of movement. But the old man would move no more. On the shore beneath the red cliff of the point lay the bare ribs of his Pilot Cutter, looking like the rib-cage of some huge stranded sea monster. Had she been mine I do not think I could have endured such a sight, but her captain was more philosophical. He was the most authentic old salt I have ever encountered. He would potter along to *Cressy* of an evening and, sitting at his ease in our cabin, tell us tales, wondrous tales, of manning the yards to shorten sail with the reeling ship tearing through the water as 'she ran her easting down' – a lovely phrase. He had harrowing stories of hard tack, of maggoty pork and weevily biscuits, of a ship becalmed and food running low: '. . . and when we opened that last barrel of flour it was half-full of rats' turds'. We listened spell-bound; if he had claimed to have shot the albatross I think we would have believed him.

When he finally left the mercantile marine and joined the Bristol Channel Pilots, life was only slightly less hard for the service was then highly competitive. To seek and claim a Channel-bound ship, the pilots in their sailing cutters would range far out to sea like so many predatory pirates. According to this old man, it was no uncommon thing to sail as far as the Bay of Biscay before they found a ship to bring in. This meant that to do his job and pay his way the pilot needed a sailing craft that would carry him fast and far and in every sort of weather; through some of the most dangerous waters in the world, with their huge tides, their short, steep seas and their prevailing on-shore winds. The result was the Bristol Channel Pilot Cutter. Although it has a hull so beamy that it looks like a tub, it is surprisingly fast and has been described as probably the finest sea-keeping boat ever evolved for British waters.

There seemed always to be something to see at Sharpness. Distant trains moving swiftly under plumes of steam along the far shore-line of the estuary as they headed for South Wales, or crawling slowly (for there was a severe speed restriction) and with rhythmical rumbling, across the Severn Bridge. Except for a unique push-and-pull train consisting of compartment stock which shuttled between Berkeley Road, Sharpness and Lydney, there was little traffic over the bridge except on Sundays when the Severn tunnel was closed and freight traffic diverted over the bridge. These Sundays-only goods trains were hauled by the ubiquitous G.W.R. 2–6–0 Moguls, as these were the heaviest locomotives allowed over the bridge. Then there was the traffic on the ship canal to watch. The barge traffic – mostly diesel-powered tankers – soon ceased to attract our attention, but in the case of the coastal shipping that occasionally traded to Gloucester it was quite otherwise, and we were always given an audible warning when such a ship was approaching. There are three swing bridges of varying height at Sharpness, two road bridges over the inland entrance to the new docks, and the railway bridge which, by a handsome margin, was the highest. It was the practice for captains to sound one, two or three toots on their sirens depending on how many bridges needed to be raised, so that three blasts was our signal that something big was coming down the canal – although once it proved to be only a small yacht with an exceptionally tall mast. The best thing about a ship canal is that it provides the unique experience of seeing a large sea-going ship gliding slowly and serenely along through green fields, a spectacle which always strikes me as bizarre as that of a locomotive puffing along a country road or a flying motor car.

Often we would walk down to the new entrance lock to watch traffic coming into the lock from the Channel and to admire the tremendous expertise displayed in this operation. Anyone who doubts the power of Severn's tide should stand, as we did, on the wooden jetty that projects beyond the wing-walls of Sharpness lock when the tide is making. There is such an immensely powerful and irresistible onrush of tidal current beneath one's feet, making the whole stout timber jetty tremble with its violence, that the wonder is that the Severn Bore does not become a tidal wave as all-powerful and terrifying as Lear's cataracts, drowning the cocks on all the steeples of the Severn Vale. Traffic bound upriver comes up on the tide from Avonmouth, and a signal at Sharpness, hoisted shortly before high water, indicates that craft may enter. The ideal aimed for, of course, is to arrive off Sharpness as soon as this signal is hoisted and so proceed straight into the lock, but conditions of wind, tide and traffic are so variable that this is seldom achieved even by the wiliest old hands. Boats either arrive too early or too late, in which case the lock is already fully occupied. In both cases they have to wait in the tidal channel, and with a tide running at anything up to six knots this means coming about and heading into it and then coming about once more when the time comes to enter the lock. Standing on the end of the jetty, we saw this manoeuvre performed many times and could appreciate how tricky and hazardous it was. We could understand how, on a foggy night in the autumn of 1939, a towing hawser had parted and several dumb barges were swept up the river with tragic loss of life.

Through the good offices of my friend Billy Bevington of Banbury, I had become something of a 'collector' of signal boxes and could appreciate the oddity of the swinging cabin above the canal on the Severn bridge, and it was not long before I had invited myself inside.

Such was the scale of the bridge that from our moorings the cabin above the swinging span looked very small. The first time, however, that I laboriously scaled the iron steps and entered it I was amazed to find it was big enough to house the two sets of horizontal steam engines and boilers (one in service and one standby) that supplied the power to semi-rotate the bridge upon its massive central pier of masonry. The keeper of the bridge doubled the roles of engine man and signalman; besides the controls for the two steam engines, he had under his hand a small lever frame of orthodox railway type. In this, one lever released the bridge locks and was controlled by the block system for the section between Sharpness and Severn Bridge station on the further side of the river. This precaution meant that the bridge could not be opened without the sanction of the signalman at each end of the section. Another lever worked an orthodox railway semaphore signal mounted above the roof of the cabin: when pulled 'off' it indicated to approaching ships that the bridge was about to swing. The two remaining levers operated railway stop signals in each direction; because there could obviously be no direct connection between these and the frame, they were worked through push rods and rocking levers. Herein lay a further safeguard, for when the bridge was swung the push rods ceased to connect with the rockers and the signals would rise to danger by the weight of their levers even if the levers in the frame were 'off'.

We crossed the bridge in the Lydney 'push-and-pull' several times during our stay for explorations in the Forest of Dean. Strangely enough, although so much of my life had been spent within easy range of it, I had visited the Forest on only one occasion and then only briefly. Our most memorable excursion was the perfect summer day when we went to Cinderford by train (this involved two changes, at Lydney and Awre Junction) and then walked the long-forsaken roadbed of the old Forest of Dean Central Railway through the heart of the Forest and thence via a still used mineral line back to Lydney and a train home. There turned out to be quite a long tunnel on the latter and we had brought no torch. After the dazzling sunlight the darkness of the tunnel was Stygian. I was walking in the four-foot, trying to measure my stride to suit the invisible sleeper spacing while Angela followed behind me when suddenly some *thing* rose up from beneath my feet and made off into the darkness. I had recently written a ghost story about a tunnel and now it seemed to be coming true. To say we were startled would be an understatement. Not until we neared the farther portal did we discover that it was a sheep which had evidently gone into the tunnel to shelter from the heat.

We found the Victorian pubs of Sharpness rather depressing. They called themselves hotels and had large unwelcoming bars smelling of a mixture of floor polish and stale beer which appeared to anticipate a volume of trade which had never materialized. Entire ships' crews? Charabanc parties? Entrants. in fishing competitions? So whenever we felt like an evening stroll and a drink we headed along the canal towpath towards the small village pub at Purton which we found very much more congenial. Judging from the company usually to be found in the bar, the male inhabitants were all either salmon fishermen or bargemen or both, people who made Purton as organic a part of the great river as an otter's holt. Often when the tide was out we would see from our moorings, far out across the estuary, these Purton salmon fishermen with their lave nets at the ready. The net was outspread between the slender ash arms or 'rimes' of a Y-shaped framework so that, as the men bore it forward, they looked like strange black insects with long antennae, crawling and questing across that waste of sand. Like Harry Rogers, many miles upstream, these men had drunk Severn water with their mother's milk; no stranger would venture so far out on these treacherous sands which the tides overwhelm with terrifying stealth and swiftness.

On the other side of the river they seemed to prefer a variant of lave net fishing. In this, the 'rimes' that spread the net were crossed over the gunwale of a boat held offshore by a steel cable and a ground anchor. We could see two of these 'stopping boats', as they are called, at work in Wellhouse Bay where the railway ran along the shore line immediately opposite our mooring. This method of fishing called for as much skill and judgement as the other, for a stopping boat with its heavy net can easily be overwhelmed by a strong flood tide. It was obvious to us that, like the putcheon weirs, these traditional methods of netting salmon were doomed to disappear. All the fishermen we met were elderly men and it was obvious that they were the last of countless generations. All complained of a dwindling salmon population which they put down to the untreated filth spewed out by Gloucester's sewers. Because of the length of the estuary, this could not escape readily but was washed to and fro by successive tides, forming a lethal barrier which the salmon could not pass. A few got through, but many more perished with the result that fewer and fewer fish came up the river to spawn. Upriver, as I knew, other hazards lay in wait for them. Harry Rogers had told me how, at times when the river was very low, dozens of dead fish would come to the surface of Severn in the neighbourhood of Ironbridge. Harry believed, correctly I think, that at such times the hot condensate from Buildwas power station raised the temperature in the river to a point at which the fish were suffocated.

During this month at Sharpness we welcomed other visitors on board besides our ancient mariner. One of these was my cousin Bill Willans who had been recently demobbed from the Navy. As readers of the first volume of this autobiography will remember, he had played a large part in my earlier life, but it was twelve years since I had last seen him. Then there was Peter Scott, recently installed in the farmhouse at the nearby New Grounds which was to be the headquarters of his Wild Fowl Trust. Finally, there was the late Brian Waters from

Cirencester to whom I had written, inviting him to come over. If Angela had not given me his book *Severn Tide* as a Christmas present it is unlikely that we should have taken *Cressy* to Sharpness at all. I am glad I was able to extend hospitality to this gentle, modest, soft-spoken man and to thank him personally for having written such a splendid book. Though its author died untimely, *Severn Tide* still stands as the best book ever written – or likely to be written – about the tidal Severn and the country beside it. To read it is to understand how it captivated us and why the month we passed at Sharpness fled by all too soon. The visit had no motive so far as the I.W.A. was concerned, and in this sense it was a pure holiday. But now it was otherwise and so, regretfully, we slipped our moorings and headed northwards, our ultimate destination being Stone on the Trent & Mersey canal in Staffordshire.

I had no first-hand experience of the canals of northern England, nor had anyone else in the I.W.A. at that time, so Robert Aickman and I decided to embark upon a joint cruise over these unknown waters. It was, however, out of the question to use *Cressy* because she would be too long for the locks. On the 'Keel canals' of Yorkshire, for example, the locks are only 57ft 6in. long, which means that it is impossible to design a 'go-anywhere' craft without sacrificing a considerable amount of living space. So we decided to charter, although at that time suitable craft were not exactly thick on the water. Before the war there had only been one boat hirer on the entire narrow canal system and now there were two. The newcomer was R. H. Wyatt who, with his son, had set up in business at the old wharf and dock at Stone. When he was first fired with this idea, Wyatt had come to see me at Tardebigge and I remember being somewhat torn – and by no means for the last time – between my desire to find traffic of any kind that would help to keep the canals alive and my conscience in encouraging a man to take what I knew to be an extremely risky step. Even if Wyatt could find enough customers, and that was problematical, it was even more doubtful if he could find enough boats, while he lacked both the capital and the experience to design and build his own fleet.

There were then very few boats suitable for cruising on the

canals. The most popular form of pleasure boat on the inland waterways was a converted ship's lifeboat such as the *Miranda* which Angela and I had hired on the Lower Avon before the war. But almost invariably such craft were too beamy to pass through the locks of narrow canals. Nevertheless, Wyatt did succeed in acquiring a motley and dubious collection of boats which always seemed to be either breaking down or sinking. Their condition soon became so bad that they were unfit to hire and he asked me in desperation what he could do. I suggested that he should buy two old butty boats from S. E. Barlow, a canal carrier friend of mine at Tamworth who had a boat dock, and ask him to cut them in half and convert them into four canal cruisers. When these four craft came into service Wyatt's boat troubles were over, but in 1948 they were still in the future and we had agreed to charter from him for our northern voyage the *Ailsa Craig* which was by repute the best of his original bad lot. I think her hull had once been an exceptionally slim ship's lifeboat, but that must have been a long time ago because it was very rotten. Over the details of her engine room memory has drawn a decent veil; but I do recall that I, as the engineer of the party, was plagued with mechanical troubles of one kind or another. Altogether I marvel now that we were able to complete so ambitious an itinerary. This was to travel from Stone to Ashton-under-Lyne via the Trent & Mersey, Macclesfield, Peak Forest and Ashton Canals and then climb from Ashton over the Pennines by the Huddersfield Narrow Canal. As all these waterways except the first were disused and in a pretty deplorable state, our eventual arrival in Huddersfield was in doubt to say the least; but assuming we did so, we then planned to aim for Leeds via the Calder & Hebble and Aire & Calder Navigations, and then to re-cross the Pennines to Wigan and Leigh by the Leeds & Liverpool Canal. The final leg which completed the circuit would be the historic Bridgewater Canal from Leigh to Preston Brook, and thence back to Stone by the Trent & Mersey.

This venture was to be essayed by a crew of four, and because of the limited space on *Ailsa Craig* we decided to put on board a small tent and two sleeping bags, the idea being that we should take it in turns to sleep afloat or ashore. By the time

Cressy, reached R. H. Wyatt's wharf at Stone on 11 August, *Ailsa Craig* had already left with a full complement on board, the idea being that when they reached the summit level of the Huddersfield Narrow Canal at Diggle, on the Lancashire side of the Pennines, they would send us a signal whereupon we would travel by rail to Diggle station. I was determined not to miss what might be the last opportunity to travel through Britain's longest canal tunnel, over three miles long from Diggle to Marsden, on the highest summit level – 644ft 9in. above sea level to be exact. The couple we were replacing were likewise determined not to miss this unique experience, so it was agreed that they would leave from Marsden station beside the Yorkshire mouth of the tunnel. This meant that for her subterranean passage under the Pennines, *Ailsa Craig* would have a crew of six which, as things turned out, was just as well.

We lay at Stone Wharf for twelve days before the long awaited signal came and we set off for Diggle. The reason for this delay was that, despite *Ailsa Craig's* shallow draught, for most of the way the bottom was too near the top, particularly on the Ashton Canal where the bottom consisted mainly of scrap metal which had been tipped into the canal over the years. Her crew had had the most frightful trouble hereabouts, but they had survived it and had climbed the long ladder of locks leading to the summit so that as our train ran into Diggle station we could see *Ailsa Craig* moored just outside the mouth of the tunnel.

Many canal tunnels appear to have been driven without sufficient reason as though, like the builder of some model garden railway, the engineer had said, 'Let's have a tunnel'. The explanation is that the early canal engineers would rather tunnel than excavate a deep cutting because the amount of spoil to be handled was less. But here it was quite otherwise. Straight ahead of us rose the sooty-green flank of Standedge quartered with blackened dry stone walls. Beneath it; the black hole of the canal tunnel looked no bigger than a mouse-hole in a wainscot. Our passage through it was one of the most eerie and sensational experiences of my life. Begun in the last years of the eighteenth century, the driving of the tunnel took twelve years. It was a seemingly endless battle between man and stubborn rock fought by dim candle light in the bowels of the Pennines. One reason why it took so long was that the height above was so great that few working shafts were driven; even so, one of these, left open for ventilation, is 600ft deep. The tunnellers did have one bonus, however – the rock was so hard and free from faults that there was no need for any lining. Hence it resembled a natural cavern rather than a man-made tunnel. This resemblance was heightened by the great variations in the diameter of the bore. It appeared to me that whenever the miners had encountered rock of soft or doubtful quality they had cut it back until they found a safe roof; it was difficult otherwise to account for the fact that a tunnel of the minimum width of 7ft 6in. (officially) and only 8ft 6in. above water level would, every now and again, open out to such cavernous proportions. There was, of course, no towing path and such great variations in size must have made it extremely difficult to propel the boats through the tunnel. Traffic was operated on the 'one-way' principle and, according to de Salis in his famous *Guide*, boats were 'legged' through. In that case, I came to the conclusion, the boatmen of those days must have had telescopic legs.

The passage of the tunnel must have taken us at least two hours for we took it extremely slowly. The jagged rocks on either side looked peculiarly menacing and I was only too well aware that, instead of *Cressy*'s two-inch oak planking, there was only half an inch of rotten wood in our hull. In the narrow places, contact with the rock was unavoidable and in one of these *Ailsa Craig* stuck fast. As we had just about reached the middle of the tunnel by this time, it was not a situation calculated to appeal to sufferers from claustrophobia. The trouble was that *Ailsa Craig*'s hull was the wrong shape for the job. Instead of being almost straight-sided like a narrow boat and with cabin sides tumbling home from the gunwales, her hull flared outwards from the water and this line had been continued through to the top corners of her cabin work. It was true that her beam nowhere exceeded 7 feet, but 7 feet at a height of about 4ft 6in. above water level was too much for the low arch of the roof. I was reminded of the situation the previous year when *Cressy* had stuck in the lock at Grindley Brook and it seemed to call for equally drastic measures. It was fortunate that there were six of us on board, for not only had this brought the boat lower in the water but it spelled that much more man-power, which might well be needed in a situation such as this. Fortunately, too, the jagged walls of the tunnel provided plenty of purchase in our efforts to free the boat. These efforts were not helped by the atmosphere which was as thick and sulphurous as the infernal regions due to the presence of cross-galleries at intervals connecting the canal tunnel to the parallel railway tunnels on each side. These galleries had been driven by the railway engineers in lieu of working shafts. From their point of view the canal engineers may have laboured in vain, but they certainly made things much easier for their successors. As we struggled in the choking darkness to free *Ailsa Craig* an occasional thunderous reverberation followed by a fresh blast of smoke signified the passage of a train.

At length our boat floated freely astern. There was only room to crawl between the roof of the cabin and the low vault of the tunnel, but by lying on our stomachs we contrived to prise off the wooden rubbing strake which extended along each side at cabin roof level. Had the boat not been so rotten, this would have been a much more difficult and brutal operation. As it was, it was soon done and gained us about an inch and a half overall which, in the event, made the vital difference between go and no go. Having got the strakes off, the only course was to drive *Ailsa Craig* full ahead into the narrow place in the hope that she would go through -- which, with a certain amount of creaking protest, she did. Fortunately, we encountered no further similar obstacle until eventually we glimpsed, through the murky darkness ahead, the wan arc of daylight that marked the Marsden or Yorkshire end of the tunnel. Slowly the light ahead grew larger and brighter until at last we emerged, blinking, into the late afternoon sunlight.

Ailsa Craig was not the last boat to pass through Standedge Tunnel. Some years after the closure of the canal, British Waterways continued to run special trips through it for societies and parties interested in such things. But I think we may well have been the last boat to travel through the whole twenty miles of waterway from Ashton to Huddersfield, and it would be true to say that by this time the canal was only just navigable, the chief trouble being at the locks. When a canal falls into disuse, the locks are left empty so that, in the case of most narrow canals, it is not the small single upper gates of the locks but the deeper double lower gates which are the first to fail. As the months and years pass with no water against them, they dry out, shrink, crack and finally rot. In this case there were no less than seventy-four pairs of lower gates that needed replacing, for the Huddersfield Narrow Canal is little more than a ladder of locks, its summit, most of it in tunnel, being the longest level pound. And at each of these locks it was a matter of anxious concern whether the water entering the lock chamber through the upper paddles could overcome the amount that was leaking out through the lower gates. It was like trying to fill a bath with the plug out. The most critical moment came shortly after we left the east end of Standedge Tunnel and began the long descent to Huddersfield. A friendly and helpful lengthman from Marsden went ahead along the towpath to fill the locks ready for us. He had filled one of these locks when a sizeable portion of one of the lower gates blew out under the pressure of water. He had previously opened the top gate ready to admit us. Fortunately *Ailsa Craig* was already inside the chamber and we had begun to swing the top gate shut behind her when it happened, otherwise we might have had to beat an ignominious retreat. As it was, the top gate swung shut with a resounding crash by which time the water level had already dropped a foot. I have never seen a boat sink more swiftly in a lock chamber. I doubt if that lock gate was ever made good, for not long after our passage concrete weirs replaced the top gates at every lock so that never again would anyone travel in our wake.

Angela and I spent that night in the tent. It was for us a novel experience and we both resolved that, when this trip was over, it was one which neither of us would ever repeat. I write 'spent' rather than 'slept' advisedly. It was one of those small tents that you enter on all fours like a dog going into a kennel. We pitched it, not without difficulty, in a meadow that sloped down to the north bank of the canal midway between Marsden and Huddersfield. To anyone interested in the history of industrial England, the narrow valleys of the Pennines have tremendous character and atmosphere, but at the same time they make bleak and forbidding camp sites. This valley was no exception. Opposite, across the canal, a high straight-topped ridge of moorland enclosed it, and against this background there marched a succession of mill chimneys, each breathing a gentle fume of smoke from boiler fires banked against the morrow. About the feet of these tall spires consecrated to industry were the mill buildings and the little communities of mill workers: Slaithwaite, Linthwaite and Golcar. There were also some small scattered farms, their houses and buildings so low-browed that they seemed to crouch against the bitter east winds that funnelled up the valley. And everything, walls, factories and farms alike, was built of stone that looked as if it had been blackened by centuries of smoke. It must have been a wild and primitive country before the mills came. Now it was neither town nor country; yet, so far from civilizing it, the presence of the mills with their gaunt stacks seemed to make it more savage.

Although it had been a sunny day, by nightfall it had clouded over and this made the prospect of a night under canvas in such surroundings even less inviting. With great difficulty we undressed, insinuated ourselves into the narrow camp beds and then turned out the portable gas light. Hardly had we done so when rain began to patter on the canvas just above our heads, making sleep impossible. The tent began to stir uneasily in the wind that came with the rain, and then to sway more vigorously. There were unmistakable sounds from outside which indicated that a herd of bullocks was examining closely and curiously the alien object which had appeared in its pasture. I was well aware of the rule against pitching tents in fields with livestock in them and before dark I had satisfied myself, as I thought, that there were no such animals. I can only suppose I had failed to spot that our field was open to another from which they had now come to plague us. They blundered into the guy ropes and it was soon obvious that if they were not chased away we should be enveloped in the damp canvas ruin of our tent. Torch in hand, bare feet thrust into shoes and with a mackintosh over my pyjamas I crawled out into the night and

put the invaders to flight. It was pouring with rain, not vertically but horizontally, and I had to spend some time squelching
about retrieving uprooted tent pegs, driving them in again
with a mallet and replacing and adjusting guy ropes. All night
long the rain teemed down and ever and anon I had to make
further forays outside to stampede the cattle. Our tent was
unlined and one piece of camping lore I had picked up was that
if you pressed against wet canvas from the inside the rain would
come through at that point. Since no one who was not a practised
contortionist could avoid doing this in our tent, it soon became
almost as wet inside as it was out, and little rivulets of water
trickled over our ground-sheet as they made their way down
the gentle slope. It was a most blessed relief when the rain
ceased at first light and the sun rose. We had many more
uncomfortable nights in that tent before the voyage was over,
but never again, I am thankful to say, quite such a baptism of
flood.

In theory, at least, *Cressy* could have carried us thus far but
little farther; at Huddersfield she would have had to return by
the way she had come. For Lancastrians and Yorkists had
different ideas about canal gauges, the former favouring narrow
boats and the latter Yorkshire keels which are short but broad
of beam. So it came about that at Huddersfield our canal made
an end-on junction with the Huddersfield Broad Canal which is
virtually a short branch of the Calder & Hebble Navigation and,
like the latter, has locks less than sixty feet long. Consequently
only minuscule boats that were both narrow and short could use
this waterway as a through route. This is one of the more crazy
results of the fact that the English waterway system, if such it
can be called, was the product of many local undertakings, each
considered in isolation at the time of construction.

When we had passed through Huddersfield and reached the
Calder & Hebble it was a relief to find ourselves in well
frequented waters once again. As we dropped down the locks
towards the junction of the Aire & Calder Navigation at Fall
Ing, near Wakefield, we passed a number of commercial craft,
mostly timber-built Yorkshire keels with diesel engines in
place of their original square sails. It would be the same now
for the rest of the journey so that, provided *Ailsa Craig* could be

kept going and did not sink, we should complete the circuit. Certain things seen on that journey have stayed in my memory, such as the unexpected sight of an ex-Leeds & Liverpool Canal Carrying Company steamer which we overhauled on the Aire & Calder as it was puffing energetically towards Castleford Junction with a cargo of coal.

The broad reaches of the Aire & Calder Navigation approaching Leeds were memorable because they were the most polluted waters I had ever seen. It was like boating through black ink. In such depths nothing could live and what, at a distance, looked like a heavy rise of fish proved to be great bubbles of foul gas rising from the bottom to break upon the surface. I remember the climb of the Leeds & Liverpool Canal up Airedale, culminating in the sensational 'five-rise' lock at Bingley; and then the long, winding level of seventeen miles through the Yorkshire countryside and the market town of Skipton to Gargrave bottom lock. Of the long descent into Lancashire from Foulridge summit tunnel, it is the crossing of the long and high embankment at Burnley that stays in my mind. The view it afforded over Burnley with its many smoking mill chimneys was surely one of the most remarkable industrial landscapes in Britain, and certainly not one you might expect to see from a boat. I have never been back to Burnley and I suspect that developers have now transformed its old, gritty, dramatic, nineteenth-century self into a featureless concrete jungle. Better a bad character than no character at all.

Back in narrow boat waters, I remember exploring that birthplace of the English canals, Worsley Basin, and my excitement at finding, still afloat there, one of the 'starvationers' – the small, slim craft that were used to navigate the underground canal system leading to the 'Canal Duke's' collieries. Shortly after this, as we approached the Barton Swing Aqueduct, a cargo steamer was coming up the Manchester Ship Canal which gave us a memorable opportunity of seeing at close quarters the hydraulic doors closed against us and then this most remarkable device begin to swing, water, towpath and all. From this point, one long level of the Bridgewater Canal took us to the junction of the Trent & Mersey Canal at Preston Brook, and so through many tunnels and by Middlewich and Stoke-on-Trent back to

Stone wharf where we arrived on the evening of 17 September.

Although it had been such a memorable experience, how glad we both were to be home again aboard *Cressy* after those cramped quarters on *Ailsa Craig*, not to mention that terrible tent! After a couple of days laying in stores we were under way once more, heading south again via Fradley and Hawkesbury Junctions to reach our winter quarters at Banbury on a fine and frosty evening at the beginning of October. Since she had left Banbury in April, *Cressy* had covered 346 miles. By modern motoring standards this is a trivial distance, but it is not so trivial when, snail-like, you are carrying your house around with you at a steady 3 m.p.h.

Chapter 7

Pont Cysyllte – An Ambition Achieved

In spite of our defeat in 1947, I had by no means abandoned my seventeen-year-old ambition to take *Cressy* over the Vale of Llangollen by the Pont Cysyllte Aqueduct. For the old boat it would be in the nature of a homecoming after who knows how many years of wandering, for it was in a dock beside the north end of this aqueduct that she had been built just before the First World War. From our previous experience it was obvious that it would be pointless to make a second attempt on the Welsh Canal until the new flowmeter installation at Llantisilio had been completed and a reliable water supply assured. This was one reason why we had made Sharpness our objective the previous summer. But, with the coming of spring, encouraging reports from Wales made us determine to try again; so 21 May 1949 found us heading north from Banbury once more. As on the previous occasion two years before, we travelled via the northern end of the Stratford Canal. The G.W.R. had been nationalized in the meantime and we thought it would be a good idea to remind the canal's new owners of their obligations. This time we experienced only minor difficulties and arrived at King's Norton to find the infamous Lifford bridge jacked up to ample height, while the shoal of ashes which had almost filled the canal beyond had been cleared away. At the junction with the Worcester & Birmingham Canal, instead of turning left for Tardebigge and the Severn as we had done on previous occasions, we turned north towards Birmingham because this time I was anxious to head for the Welsh Border as quickly as possible and the shortest water route thither lay through the Black Country.

We moored that night beneath the trees a little to the south of the short Edgbaston tunnel, a remarkably secluded and peaceful place considering we were no more than a mile from the centre of the city. The only noise was made by the trains that passed by on the old Midland main line to the west which runs parallel with the canal hereabouts. Although the sound of motor traffic has lost me much sleep, trains have never disturbed me; in fact I love the sight and sound of them – particularly when they are steam-hauled as they were in 1949. I remember once about this period I deliberately moored *Cressy* for the night on the Oxford Canal at a point near Brinklow where it runs close beside the Euston–Crewe main line for the sheer pleasure of seeing the Night Scot and the Irish Mail come pounding past my windows at close range.

The route we had now chosen was not only much shorter but it saved us a great deal of lockage. In the fifteen miles of canal to Wolverhampton there were only three locks and I reckoned that if we made a fairly prompt start next day we should reach the Shropshire Union Canal main line before night fell. To anyone like myself over whom the early relics of England's industrial revolution exercised a curious fascination, part aesthetic, part dramatic and part horrific, travelling by canal through an urban and industrial area twenty-five years ago was an uniquely rewarding experience. I have mentioned the view of industrial Burnley from the Leeds & Liverpool Canal, and in *Narrow Boat* I described what it was like to travel by the Trent & Mersey Canal through the Potteries with their thickly smoking ovens, and through the heart of the Shelton Steelworks. To voyage through the Black Country by the main line of the Birmingham Canal Navigations was another rewarding and memorable experience. On either hand were visual reminders of that earliest industrial England which the canals had helped to create. Although it was ringed by areas of later growth brought about by rail and road transport, this old blackened core still survived and was, in many cases, still alive and still using the canal as its life-line. All this was particularly true of the Black Country and its complicated network of canals. The 'B.C.N.' was certainly very much alive the day that we passed through. Not only were there many long-distance motor boats and their butties, but also a great number of short-haul 'day-boats', some towed in trains by tugs but the majority horsedrawn.

Nevertheless, despite the fascination the Black Country then held for me, we decided not to spend a night in it but to press on through it if only because the waters of its canals were so grossly polluted. Such is the complexity of the Black Country canal network that this was the only occasion on the whole of my canal voyaging when I almost took a wrong turning. Shortly after we had locked up to the Wolverhampton level at Tipton and were approaching Bloomfield Junction, my sense of direction played me false and we should have sailed off down what is called the Wednesbury Oak Loop Line had not a friendly local character on the towpath set me right by shouting and pointing in the direction of Coseley tunnel. Had we taken this wrong turning we should eventually have rejoined our route at the expense of four extra, winding miles of canal, for this so-called loop line, like other similar diversions, was a part of the original tortuous main line of canal between Birmingham and Wolverhampton. The completion of Coseley tunnel in 1837 had led to the disuse of the loop by through traffic. Although it is only 360 yards long, we had never been through a canal tunnel of such princely proportions. Coseley's height above water level is over fifteen feet, while its overall width of nearly twenty-five feet is sufficient to allow for a towing path on each side. These dimensions were only later surpassed by the nearby Netherton Tunnel, the last to be built in England.

At Coseley we were only three miles from Wolverhampton and evening found us descending the flight of twenty-one locks that brings the Birmingham Canal down to the level of the Staffordshire & Worcestershire Canal at Aldersley Junction, a mere half mile away from Autherley where the Shropshire Union Canal begins. Some people think this canal from Wolverhampton to Nantwich boring because its course is so straight compared with the windings of the older contour canals. I never found it so. I admired the boldness of its engineering and the sense of spaciousness that this boldness imparted. I loved the wide pastoral landscapes that unfolded as one's boat slid out from the green shades of some deep cutting on to a lofty embankment. Here the only enemy was the wind; on the embankments it could be so strong that a boat drawing little water and carrying much 'top' was no longer able to go forward. In the attempt to counter such a cross-wind I would put *Cressy* full ahead and bring her bows into the wind. This meant that we progressed in a crab-wise fashion until the stern was on the mud on one side of the canal and the bows in the bank on the other. When this happened there was nothing to be done but shut our engine off and call it a day. On this occasion, however, we enjoyed calm weather and, despite stops for supplies and to pick up a visitor at Market Drayton and Nantwich, on the morning of Sunday 5 June we swung on to the Welsh Canal once more at Hurleston Junction.

With vivid memories of the many difficulties we had encountered on the previous occasion, we now went ahead with caution mingled with some trepidation, wondering especially what would happen when we came to that tight lock chamber at Grindley Brook. We need not have worried, for the improvement that had taken place in two years was quite remarkable, considering that the canal had been officially abandoned and no one was under compulsion to do anything to assist navigation. There was more water, less weed and fewer scours of mud from tributary streams. The villainous one at Blackoe Cottages, which had caused us so much trouble before, seemed to have disappeared. Most miraculous of all, work must have been done on the masonry of the lock sides and wing-walls, for we sailed up the flight at Grindley Brook with no trouble at all.

When the railway-owned canals were transferred to the Docks & Inland Waterways Executive, generally speaking the new masters proved very little better than the old, and they were certainly less accountable to Parliament for their actions. But in the case of the Welsh Canal the good fairy was Christopher Marsh, engineer for the North-Western Division and the only member of the senior staff of the new Executive who had canal water in his veins. At this time, the greatest threat to this waterway was that the highway overbridges would be lowered. Since the canal had been abandoned for navigation, the county highway authorities were no longer under any legal obligation to maintain navigable headroom. This threat took formidable shape about this time when the proposal was made to remove the awkward dog-leg bridge carrying the A539 Ruabon–Llangollen road over the canal at Brynmelyn and replace it by a culverted embankment. It was pleasant indeed to find Christopher Marsh on our side in the battle over this bridge, arguing that the waterway could only be maintained in a safe condition by water, and therefore there must be sufficient headroom for his maintenance boats to pass.

It was thanks to this change in the official attitude towards the Welsh Canal that our voyage to Ellesmere and beyond was so enjoyable, and so uneventful compared with the previous occasion. Nevertheless it was only by luck that this third attempt to reach Pont Cysyllte was not again frustrated. A chance visit to the pub at Bettisfield where we had moored for the night, followed by a conversation with a local farmer, gave us the information that a new water pipeline from Vrynwy reservoir was shortly to be laid across the canal at the village of Hindford, which meant that it would be blocked by a coffer dam for an indefinite period. I was determined not to be beaten a third time, even if it meant spending the winter in Wales, so we decided to press on and get *Cressy* past the point of obstruction before work started.

We only paused at Ellesmere for shopping followed by a brief picnic lunch before entering waters which had been unnavigable before but which were now almost weed-free. Soon we passed the junction with the derelict Montgomeryshire Canal and in another two miles came to the site of the new pipeline works just before the canal entered the village of Hindford, where we moored up about 6 p.m. It was over this length of canal that *Cressy* had run her first steam trial after conversion at Mr Beech's dock beside the locks at Frankton just twenty years before, and now she was revisiting it for the first time. In the interval, both the boatyard and the locks beside it had fallen to ruin. Just before the war, a burst in the canal bank near Lockgate Bridge, a little distance below Frankton Locks, had provided the L.M. & S.R. with a welcome pretext to abandon the thirty-five miles of canal that followed the Severn down the Welsh Border to Newtown. His occupation gone, Beech the boatbuilder went to work as a carpenter on a new

R.A.F. airfield near Oswestry; how I heard that he was now retired and living in Hindford I do not remember, but we sought him out and invited the old man and his wife on board for a drink and a talk. He took a wholly unfeigned and unself-conscious delight in seeing so unexpectedly this past product of his craftsmanship. To see this old boatbuilder seated in one of our armchairs, his gnarled hands grasped in his lap and beaming with pleasure, was alone worth the trip.

Next morning as we left Hindford and passed through the two locks at New Marton – the only locks west of Grindley Brook – it soon became apparent that no craft of *Cressy*'s size and draught had penetrated so far for many years. Progress became very slow. Numerous small scours from incoming streams had built up over the years, so that once again I had to put our pulley blocks to use to force a way through them. But these were only minor troubles and not to be compared with those we had experienced two years before. This is rather a dull stretch of canal. It winds through a somewhat flat and nondescript landscape and St Martins is unashamedly a colliery village, an untidy brick sprawl which might have been translated from Durham and dumped amid the green fields of Shropshire. But at Chirk Bank the Welsh Canal springs yet another of its landscape surprises. Closely accompanied by Telford's Holyhead Road, Telford's canal takes a sudden swing to the westward and soon we found ourselves looking down into the valley of the Ceiriog which here forms the boundary between England and Wales. Whereas the road swoops down to the valley bottom to cross the Ceiriog at low level, the canal clings to the contour high above until it turns north once more to stride across the river and its valley on Telford's splendid aqueduct of stone. With its ten spans and a maximum height of seventy feet, Chirk aqueduct is one of the major canal engineering works in England, and it would be more celebrated were it not for the proximity of its greater neighbour at Pont Cysyllte. As *Cressy* glided across the aqueduct, standing at the tiller I looked westward between the arches of the parallel railway viaduct at the green floor of the valley beneath the hanging woods of Chirk Castle park and thought nostalgically of childhood visits to Plas y Garth at Glynceiriog, rattling up the valley by a Glyn

Valley Tramway that had now vanished without trace. How much of my life had been associated in one way or another with the Welsh Marches and how powerful had been their effect upon me. *Cressy* herself had been built there and now, under my hand, she was being attracted back as the needle of a compass is attracted to the north.

The river Ceiriog hereabouts forms the boundary between Shropshire and Denbighshire and I know of no more dramatic entry to Wales than by Telford's Chirk aqueduct and the tunnel that immediately follows it. Because the hills of the north, or Welsh, side of the Vale of Ceiriog are higher than those to the south, there is only room for a basin at the north end of the aqueduct before the canal dives underground. It was in this basin, poised between hill and vale, that we moored for the night, feeling that now, for the first time, we really were in Wales – that brief excursion into 'Flintshire detached' seemed a political accident which did not really count.

Chirk Tunnel is just over a quarter of a mile long and was one of the first to be constructed with a towpath through it. Telford was a humane man who considered that the practice of 'legging' boats through tunnels degraded man to a mere beast of burden whereas his predecessors and contemporaries had no such scruples. The price of the towpath at Chirk is that it is a 'one way' tunnel, but we slipped into it next morning with no anxiety whatever, for on this pioneering voyage there was not the slightest prospect of meeting traffic coming the other way. The Shrewsbury to Chester line of the old G.W.R. crosses over Chirk Tunnel so that although the railway viaduct had been on our left hand as we crossed the aqueduct, when we emerged from the tunnel into a long tree-shaded cutting, Chirk Station lay to the right of us. We took this cutting extremely slowly and warily, for its waters were exceptionally shallow, and beneath the surface we glimpsed water-logged tree-branches here and there. Our progress was made slower by the fact that there was a perceptible current in the canal due to its function as a feeder to Hurleston reservoir. This became particularly noticeable in such shallow places where *Cressy's* hull virtually became a moving barrage.

On the right hand at the end of the cutting is Black Park

basin, now choked with reeds and mud but once a scene of great activity during the heyday of the Shropshire Union Canal Carrying Company. Here coal was brought from neighbouring collieries to be loaded into boats, and here also an extension of the Glyn Valley Tramway from Chirk Station brought for transhipment slate and granite roadstone from quarries at Glynceiriog and on the road to Llanarmon near the headwaters of the Ceiriog. A mile beyond Black Park we passed beneath Telford's Holyhead road by the second and much shorter tunnel called Whitehouses or Whitehurst. The next bridge beyond the tunnel is called Irish Bridge and so probably perpetuates the memory of the many Irish labourers who helped to build the canal, tramping across Wales from Holyhead. Here the canal again swings sharply to the west and crosses the line of Offa's Dyke to enter the Vale of Llangollen. As we approached the village of Vron Cysyllte we could see away to our right the tall stone piers of the aqueduct that carries the canal across the Dee.

We could have crossed the aqueduct that day, but instead we tied up at what had once been the village wharf at 'the Vron', as the locals call it, but is now disused and grass-grown. The canal widens into a small basin at this point for it was once its temporary terminus while the great aqueduct was still building. We decided to stop at Vron Wharf for two reasons, first because Angela was due in London on the morrow and secondly to await the coming of Hugh Griffith, the Welsh actor, and his wife Gunde who were coming to stay with us for a week and were anxious to share with us the experience of crossing Pont Cysyllte by boat.

My career as a writer has brought me too many correspondents and a number of acquaintances but few lasting friendships. Of the latter I can think of only four whom I would never have otherwise met. One of these was Charles Hadfield and another was Hugh Griffith. Charles had written to me when *Narrow Boat* was first published but Hugh, curiously enough, was attracted by *High Horse Riderless*. Hugh and Gunde were staying with friends in the village of Sibford Gower near Banbury early in 1949 when Hugh discovered quite by chance through a mutual acquaintance that I was then living at Tooley's Boatyard.

As a result, Angela and I motored out to Sibford to meet them. From that moment our friendship grew rapidly and over the next ten years Hugh and I saw a great deal of each other. Hugh is an Anglesey man and what I most admired in him was his intensely localized Welshness, his deep feeling for his native place, which has never been diminished or spoiled by his success. I think that what had drawn his interest in the first place was the chapter in *High Horse Riderless* in which I argued the case for the devolution of the powers of central government as one of the essential conditions for the more vigorous and self-sufficient regional society which I advocated. Although when I wrote this chapter it was with no particular district or country in mind, it was seized upon by Hugh in particular and by the Welsh Nationalist Party in general. It was with an odd mixture of gratification and embarrassment that I found myself quoted *in extenso* in the party's pamphlet arguing the case for self-government. Because it seemed to me to be trying to practise what I had preached, I felt that I could scarely do other than become a Welsh Nationalist myself. This was the only time I have joined a political party and I suppose that by doing so I became in the technical sense a traitor to my own country, but I fear it was not long before I allowed my subscription to lapse. My love has always been for that Border Country that is neither wholly English nor wholly Welsh but seems to me to combine the best of both. I was soon to become somewhat disillusioned about Welsh Wales.

It was while I was alone on *Cressy* at Vron Wharf awaiting the return of Angela and the arrival of our guests that I had an experience which, though it had a perfectly rational explanation then unknown to me, seemed so strangely dream-like and unreal at the time that the whole episode comes vividly to the mind's eye to this day. Just astern of *Cressy* was a typical Shropshire Union drawbridge of that graceful kind with overhead balance beams and dependent chains which is found in Holland and in the paintings of Van Gogh. A steep lane led down from the village to this bridge which provided access to the towpath and to the green pastures beyond, sloping down towards the Dee. It was a golden June evening and I was preparing my supper in the galley when, hearing a strange hubbub compounded of music and many voices, I ran towards the aft deck and saw to my amazement a scene that blended Van Gogh with Goya and our own Richard Wilson. Coming down the steep lane towards me was a company of Spanish dancers in full fig, followed by musicians and what looked like the entire population of Vron Cysyllte. The Spanish girls were the first to cross the wooden drawbridge; they moved with that particularly graceful swing of the hips which I had only seen before in certain young gypsy women. Their long full skirts swayed as they walked, and their lace mantillas swept back from the tall tortoiseshell combs in their dark hair. They were followed by their partners in short, black bolero jackets and tight trousers. So unlikely a sight in such surroundings it would have been difficult to conceive. If a sea serpent had suddenly swum into my ken along the canal I could scarcely have regarded it with greater incredulity than this colourful spectacle of old Castille crossing a drawbridge not thirty yards away. When the whole procession had crossed the bridge, the villagers formed a circle on the one piece of smooth and level turf in the meadow below. Then, on this impromptu stage, with a strumming of guitars and a clicking of castanets, the Spaniards began to dance. I quickly joined the spectators. It was as though a flock of dowdy sparrows had gathered to watch with envy the courtship rituals of some exotic, dazzling species of tropical bird. The explanation, of course, was simple. I was not aware that the Llangollen International Eisteddfod was taking place the following week; nor that it had become the custom to board the foreign teams in the villages round about. Vron Cysyllte, it appeared, habitually played host to the Spaniards who, in return for this hospitality, gave the villagers a special preview of their Eisteddfod performance. Yet no such prosaic explanation could erase from recollection the impression made upon my mind by the first vivid glimpse of that extraordinary procession trooping down the hill towards me.

When Angela returned, and Hugh and Gunde had arrived, we cast off from Vron Wharf to complete the last brief but highly dramatic section of our voyage. Pont Cysyllte aqueduct is approached by an embankment which is itself an unique feat of engineering, being no less than ninety-seven feet high at its tip. With the possible exception of the prehistoric Silbury Hill, no greater earthwork so far as I know had ever been raised in Britain by that date. Its slopes are now thickly clothed with trees which conceal its height and shut off the view of the valley below. All one can see ahead as one rounds a gentle bend between this shady avenue of trees is the long, straight perspective of the iron trough. These masking trees, however, do provide an effect of dramatic surprise, as I realized when *Cressy* slid out from their shade straight on to the towering aqueduct. On the east side is the towpath with its elegant iron railing, but on the west there is only the rim of the trough standing about six inches above water level, so that from my position at the tiller I had an uninterrupted view up the Vale of Llangollen towards the ancient Welsh fortress of Castell Dynas Bran that guards the little town. On this brilliant, cloudless June day, the valley floor was most richly green while the more distant hills basked in a shimmering blue haze of heat. In the foreground a game of cricket was in progress on the smooth, carefully tended turf of the local sports field, and I found myself looking directly down at the little, white, foreshortened figures as they crouched tense or, at a distant cry of 'Come on!', scuttled between the wickets.

This panorama, thus suddenly disclosed, was breathtaking, particularly when combined with the slow, gliding motion of a boat which one automatically associates with lush and level water-meadows, willow trees and browsing cattle. No wonder the romantic writers and artists of the early nineteenth century were united in their praise of the engineer:

> TELFORD who o'er the vale of Cambrian Dee
> Aloft in air at giddy height upborne
> Carried his Navigable road . . .

wrote Robert Southey. For engineering was then rightly considered by artist and engineer alike as an art rather than a science, and Pont Cysyllte aqueduct provided precisely that dramatic contrast between the art of man and natural beauty that they most admired, using such adjectives as 'awful' or 'sublime'. As, with *Cressy*'s engine slowed to a tick-over, we crept out on to the aqueduct, I found myself in complete sympathy with their ardour. It was an experience well worth the years of waiting and the repeated frustrations before we had been able, at last, to win through. I think we were one of the first boats, and certainly the first narrow boat, to cross Pont Cysyllte for at least ten years and I wished there had been somebody with a camera down below amongst the cricketers to record the event. But players and spectators alike were too absorbed in their game even to notice *Cressy*'s slow passing high overhead. Perhaps they had assumed too readily that such boats would come that way no more.

Since there was no one below to record this historic occasion – historic for me anyway – Angela stepped out on to the towpath with her camera. As *Cressy* was almost as wide as the trough, there was really no need for me to steer so, leaving the engine running slow ahead, I went forward to join the others on the foredeck while *Cressy* drifted slowly along on to the highest portion of the aqueduct where, as I sat on the gunwale, there was nothing below me but the waters of the Dee hurrying over rapids 127 feet below.

People often ask why such prodigious engineering works were ever undertaken merely to bring water transport to the small Welsh town of Llangollen. On the face of it, it certainly seems excessively optimistic even for the brief 'canal mania' years of the 1790s. The answer is that the canal was intended to run due north from Pont Cysyllte, climbing by locks to a summit level not far from the famous John Wilkinson's flourishing ironworks and Brymbo and Bersham, thus tapping the traffic of the Wrexham coal and iron district before descending by the valley of the little river Alyn to Chester and so on to Ellesmere Port. As a result of the changed conditions brought about by the Napoleonic War, the fortunes of the Ellesmere Canal Company withered and this part of its projected main line was never built; and because of this, the rest of the canal was deprived of its intended summit water supply. It was to remedy this deficiency that the canal from Pont Cysyllte to Llangollen and Llantisilio was built in the form of a navigable feeder. It is terraced along the northern slopes of the Vale of Llangollen and joins what was to have been the main line at right angles almost immediately after the end of the aqueduct.

Because of the difficult terrain, and since its primary function was to act as a feeder, this section of the canal is unusually narrow. At the time of which I am writing, its effective width was made even narrower by the amount of clay puddle which had been heaped against the bank on the valley side to prevent any tendency for the water to percolate through and so undermine it. The reason for this precaution was that a few years previously a sensational burst had occurred at a point known as Sun Bank where the Ruabon–Llangollen railway runs directly below. During the night a substantial portion of the canal bank had given way to produce a cascade of such force and volume that both tracks of the line were undermined, causing the derailment of the unsuspecting early morning 'local'.

I judged that these heaps of puddle had so reduced the width of the channel as to make this part of the canal impassable for a flat-bottomed boat drawing 2 feet, and only navigable by a small cruiser. And even if we did succeed in struggling up to Llangollen, the 'winding' place just beyond the wharf there looked far too choked with the mud of years to enable a 70-foot narrow boat to swing. The prospect of having to stern-haul *Cressy* for the four miles back to the aqueduct was not attractive; so, having accomplished our main objective we decided to call it a day. At the end of the aqueduct we manoeuvred *Cressy* until her stern was under the bridge over the mouth of the Llangollen canal. Then, while Angela and Gunde guided her with shafts, Hugh and I stern-hauled her up the canal for about 200 yards before we moored her up. Thanks to our temporary crew, we now had her pointing in the right direction when the time came to depart; also, the big windows of our sitting cabin looked straight out over the valley and so acute was the bend in the canal that this view included in the middle distance the aqueduct we had so lately crossed. On the opposite side of us and astern was a park-like landscape of heavy trees and greensward. A screen of trees and a steep bank sheltered us from the north and between them and the canal bank was a narrow strip of turf. A more perfect mooring it would be difficult to imagine.

There was one very curious feature of this mooring which may still be seen and which I leave to some enterprising local industrial archaeologist to unravel. This was a single enormous lump of what was undoubtedly tap-cinder from a blast furnace. This stood between our mooring and the bank; at least four feet in diameter, it looked like a strange meteorite, detached as it was from any other vestige of industrial activity. The iron trough of Pont Cysyllte is said to have been cast by Telford's friend William Hazeldine at Plas Kynaston – on a site now built over by the Monsanto Chemical Works – and conveyed by inclined tramway to the aqueduct. But the discovery of this enormous clinker made me wonder whether Hazeldine may have erected a special temporary furnace near the site from which to cast the trough sections. If this was the case, I felt that something must have gone terribly wrong with this operation in order to produce a single mass of clinker of such proportions.

We stayed at this mooring for the best part of three months of perfect summer weather, during which time we entertained on board both old friends who came to stay and new friends whom we made locally. Among the latter was Dorothy Hartley, an elderly spinster who lived with a friend in a cottage at the Vron. The couple reminded us of latter-day Ladies of Llangollen. They had not spotted us when we passed through the Vron, but their curiosity had been aroused by the strange bright blue and scarlet object on the opposite side of the valley so Dorothy Hartley had walked across the aqueduct to investigate, and introduced herself, somewhat diffidently, from the towing path opposite. I am usually embarrassingly bad at connecting names with faces or authors with the right books, but on this occasion the memory bank worked perfectly and I replied as I should: 'Not the author of *Made in England*!' She was visibly delighted to be recognized in this way, displaying a humility which I thought as disarming as it was unjustified, because *Made in England* was perhaps the best book which has ever been written about the English country crafts. Lavishly illustrated by the author's own drawings and photographs, its descriptions are strictly practical and workmanlike and it is refreshingly free from nostalgia and either artfulness or craftyness. It was first published in 1939 and so, like other good books of the period, was swept into oblivion by the war. Already the statement in her preface that the book recorded only living crafts had become almost impossible to believe.

During our stay at Pont Cysyllte, Dorothy Hartley could not have been kinder. Whenever we were away she became *Cressy*'s self-appointed guardian, crossing the aqueduct twice a day to ensure that all was well. She also insisted on pressing upon us the products of her cottage garden and kitchen – and delicious they were for, as one would expect of such an author, she practised what she preached and was highly skilled both as a gardener and as a cook. Needless to say we had a great deal in common and were both sad when the time came for us to sail away. We did not meet again. *Cressy*, too, soon met an old friend. She had not been at her new mooring many hours before a Welsh voice hailed her from the towpath opposite. It turned out to be an elderly local man who had helped to build her in dry dock only a few hundred yards away during the First World War. Truly she had come home.

When we grumble now at the appalling weather of the so-called English summer, it seems that in past summers the sun was always shining. This is partly because, by a kindly dispensation, it is only pleasant features that tend to linger in memory; the grey and sodden days are mercifully forgotten. Partly, though by no means wholly, true, for it is an indisputable fact that the summers during the decade of the sixties were consistently cold, wet and cheerless compared with those we enjoyed during these years on *Cressy*. This statement does not depend on fallible memory but is endorsed by my log in which I made a note of the weather each day. I realize now that this was not because I fancied myself some sea captain in the days of sail to whom the state of the weather was all important and could mean life or death, but simply because, living on a boat, we were far more acutely conscious of, and responsive to, the weather and to our natural environment generally than are those who today spend most of their existence in centrally heated houses, offices or factories, or in heated capsules in transit between them. Not that we led a life of spartan hardship. In times of rough weather we could batten ourselves down snugly enough; it was just that at such times one was ever reminded of the world outside by the sound of the rain pattering on the deck above or by the gentle rocking and nudging of our boat under the buffets of the wind that rattled our windows.

Under such conditions, grey days of ceaseless rain could be extremely depressing; but to such a degree have we now alienated ourselves from the natural world, that few can appreciate that great lifting of the spirits, that mood of exaltation which we experienced when at last the grey clouds dispersed and the sun burst out upon a fresh and glistening world. Our ancestors down to the nineteenth century were similarly deeply affected by the elemental realities of weather and season simply because they lacked the technology that enables us so effectually to insulate ourselves from their effects, greatly to our material comfort but at immeasurable spiritual loss. The still beauty of autumn evenings no longer speaks sadly to us of the mutability of all living things; the freshness of a fine spring morning no longer holds for us the promise of perpetual renewal and rebirth. Just as primitive man celebrated the passing seasons with appropriate ritual, so most great prose and poetry of the past reflects an elemental influence more self-conscious and sophisticated but no less profound.*

My log fully substantiates my recollection that both our pioneering voyages up the Welsh Canal were blessed by unusually perfect summer weather, and I have now attempted to explain how deeply we were able to appreciate it. We were lucky that on both occasions it continued unbroken into September, for August is generally a wet month, particularly in the Welsh mountains. But now there was none of that oppressive atmosphere that had marked the fateful summer when *Cressy* had first sailed out from Banbury ten years before. In 1947 the dry weather had been one factor responsible for an alarming water shortage, but now that the works at Llantisilio had been completed we no longer had any fears on this score. In the narrow channel beside our boat the water flowed past swiftly, deep and crystal, for its seven-mile course along the mountain sides from the Horseshoe Falls had left it quite unpolluted and during the hot days we bathed frequently. By this time we had, I regret to say, substituted an ex-R.A.F. rubber dinghy for Harry Rogers's coracle. Although the ash frame and tarred

* One of the very few modern writers to appreciate this is Winifred Gérin. See her *The Effects of Environment on the Brontë Writings*, a lecture read before the Royal Society of Literature in February 1969.

canvas of a Severn coracle was much more appropriate to *Cressy*'s hull of tarred oak planking, it was far too vulnerable in the only place where it could be conveniently carried – on our cabin top, where it was liable to be crushed like an egg-shell by the first arched bridge. Practically, the rubber dinghy was a far better substitute because it could so readily be deflated and stowed. In this craft it took only a few minutes to paddle down from *Cressy*'s mooring and on to the aqueduct and this became a popular experience for our visitors, always provided they had a good head for heights. For if, on looking down from the highest part, the swiftly moving waters of the Dee below suddenly appeared to stand still and, instead, the aqueduct seemed to be toppling, then it was high time that the visitor was back on terra firma.

I remember one warm and still summer night of such beauty that, reluctant to close our cabin doors and go to bed, I decided on a sudden impulse to take this rubber dinghy and paddle it alone on to the great aqueduct. When I reached the middle I shipped my paddle and sat quietly, one hand keeping the dinghy motionless by grasping the edge of the iron trough. It was after midnight and few lights pricked the darkness of the valley slopes, but a great golden harvest moon, looking almost as large and colourful as those we see in Samuel Palmer's visionary and paradisal landscapes, hung low in the sky over the rim of the southern slopes. There was not a breath of wind and the only sound was the soothing and ceaseless whispering and chuckling of the river as it rippled over its boulder-strewn bed far below. Of all the experiences of that summer, I think this was the most memorable, although I find it hard to explain now why this was so. As in an earlier chapter I attempted inadequately to express the essence of a similar experience at Llanthony, I will make no second attempt but will only remark upon certain similarities in the circumstances and surroundings that evoked them. I think it significant that both should occur at a late hour on a still and moonlit night. I believe it was no accident that so many of the pictures Palmer painted during his great but all too brief visionary period at Shoreham depict the tranquillity of such a still and silent hour as though he were,

as he said, 'preparing a rest for the people of God'.*
The poems of the Silurist, Henry Vaughan, are also, to me,
reminiscent of moonlight stillness as I wrote in a book I shall
have occasion to mention later.† But for me there had to be
another essential ingredient in the scene in order to make
possible a brief escape from the temporal into an eternal world
(for such I take these experiences to be). This was the presence
of a significant work of man's hands. At Llanthony it had been
the nave arcades of a ruined priory church which I had surveyed
from the height of one of its western towers. Like the great
cathedrals, those arches were the masterwork of humble men
who recognized, but had not yet learned to bend to their
purpose, the wonders of the natural world and believed there
was no greater purpose in life than to build to the glory of
their supreme author. Now I was again looking down at a dark
valley from a lofty vantage, but this time afloat in the air high
above it, buoyed up by Thomas Telford's towering stone piers
and cradled in iron that had once bubbled white hot in 'Merlin'
Hazeldine's furnaces at Plas Kynaston. At the time of its completion, Pont Cysyllte was unique, the grandest embodiment of
man's new confidence in his ability to master his environment,
of man's faith in his own, rather than in any external, powers.
Directly beneath me, fixed to the base of the pier on the southern bank of the river, is a cast-iron plaque bearing a long and
flowery inscription celebrating the opening of the aqueduct on
26 November 1805. Much more appropriate, I felt, would be
a single brief quotation from a poem by Yeats:

Measurement began our Might.

Maybe it will one day be clear to us that it also began our
downfall.

Hugh and Gunde had arrived in the little two-seater open M.G.
which he then owned, and although it was a nice little car it

* Quoted by W. B. Yeats in his last valedictory poem.
† *The Clouded Mirror*, Bodley Head, 1955. 'The white radiance of Vaughan's
greatest poems is of a quality no longer of this world. One thinks of moonlight
reflected in some cold, clear pool not flawed by any stir and fret of wind or current,
and for such unearthly tranquillity his poetry is the natural medium.'

was somewhat unsociable. Fortunately, however, my father's sports four-seater Alvis was acting as *Cressy's* 'land tender' at Pont Cysyllte. I had brought the car into commission for the first time since before the war because my own Alvis was undergoing a protracted engine overhaul at Banbury. In this larger car the four of us were able to make a number of expeditions together through the little mountain roads in the vicinity of the valleys of the Dee, the Ceiriog and the Rhaiadr, the latter with its magnificent waterfall. In perfect summer weather such as we were enjoying there can be no pleasanter vehicle than an open vintage touring car. Cars of this era really are full four-seaters in that they provide ample room for four people to sit in comfort and stretch their legs. Also, because one sits higher than in a modern vehicle, one can fully appreciate all the sights, scents and sounds of summer. It adds up to an almost forgotten form of transport.

As the guests of the Griffiths, we also motored farther afield to the Lleyn Peninsula where we visited Bardsey Island, 'the island of the saints'. After experiencing the passage through Bardsey Sound I can appreciate why, in the Middle Ages, two pilgrimages to Bardsey were worth one to faraway Rome, for it would be difficult to find a trickier piece of water anywhere round the coast of the British Isles. On the day we crossed, a heavy swell was heaving with hollow thunder against the inhospitable rock shelves that wall its shores. Yet, out in the sound, there were circular patches which looked from a distance to be perfectly calm and smooth water. This appearance was wickedly deceptive for, in fact, they were whirlpools or tide rips caused by converging tidal currents, and when we approached them more nearly we could see that they seethed like water in a saucepan just before it boils. The two elderly Welsh fishermen whom we had persuaded to ferry us over from Aberdaron obviously had infinite faith – certainly much more than I possessed – in the mechanical marvels of the modern world. Their open boat was equipped with neither oars nor sail, and they relied entirely on the efforts of an ancient and extremely rusty two-cylinder 'Handy Billy' Thornycroft engine. The two sparking plugs looked as though they were as old as the engine and had never been removed in its lifetime. No wonder the engine sometimes suffered from hiccups. Yet the two old men puffed imperturbably at their foul-smelling pipes as we chuffed slowly through the turbulent waters of the sound, an occasional seal popping a curious head out of the water in our wake to gaze after us with large, dark, wondering eyes. What action would have followed if that engine had suddenly expired it was impossible to imagine, and I did my best to dismiss such speculations from my mind. Our two elderly navigators had obviously done so years before and had so far survived successfully. They knew these treacherous waters like the backs of their hands, for on the return voyage we did not pass again through that alarming sound but, because they judged that wind and tide were unfavourable, went eastabout from the island landing place so that we had circumnavigated Bardsey by the time we landed at Aberdaron in the evening. On the island itself, thanks to Hugh's Anglesey Welsh (the purest Welsh spoken in the Principality, he insisted), the natives were certainly friendly, and if we had been shipwrecked mariners they could not have been kinder or more hospitable. The wife of an island farmer insisted on taking us to her kitchen where she gave us an unforgettable tea of crisp-crusted freshly baked bread and delicious butter of her own churning. I fear that farmhouse may be standing empty and ruinous by now. Even then, I remember, our hostess was worried by the fact that the island children had lately lost their school teacher, and a replacement had not so far been found. Like all island communities, although geographically so near the mainland, Bardsey is isolated by its dangerous seas, sometimes for weeks on end; the problem of providing educational and health services often becomes insuperable, and eventually brings about a sad exodus and desertion.

There is a lighthouse on Bardsey. It stands on the fist of an out-thrusting headland that has nearly become an island, for the sea's rage has almost bitten away the forearm connecting it to the mainland. It consists of a causeway of green turf which, from memory, is not more than ten yards wide at its narrowest point. While the others lay in the sun, I strolled off to look at the lighthouse, and Gunde's little corgi bitch came scampering after me. We had reached the midpoint of the isthmus when the dog suddenly stopped dead in her tracks; all her hackles went up and she began a low, continuous growling such as I had never heard before. I tried to coax her on, but she remained motionless; it was obvious from her eyes that she feared something which no human eye could see. So I went forward alone while she scuttled back to her mistress with such little tail as she had between her legs. This episode convinced me that even if Bardsey is deserted by human kind, the island will not be tenantless.

It would be misleading to give an impression that this summer in Wales was one long golden afternoon of leisure and pleasure. There was work to be done. I had to spend hours at my desk on the boat, some of it lucratively and some unprofitably on correspondence concerned with my Hon. Secretaryship of the I.W.A. And while Hugh Griffith was staying with us he spent much time lying on one of the bunks in our forecabin or outside in the sun studying the part of King Lear which he had undertaken to play in a production at Swansea that autumn as part of an Arts Festival. Hugh had convinced himself, and easily convinced me, that since Lear was an ancient British king and therefore Celtic, there was no occasion, in playing him, to disguise his own Welshness. On the contrary, he had decided that it could be turned to advantage. For example, in the famous scene on the heath when Lear at once invokes and defies the storm in the speech beginning: 'Blow, winds, and crack your cheeks! rage! blow!', he proposed to use the Welsh *hwyl*, an indescribable kind of incantatory intonation that was used by certain Welsh preachers when they felt themselves inspired with the gift of tongues. This interpretation of the part and the manner of its playing – determined so appropriately almost within the shadow of the hill-top castle of Dinas Bran that could have been the ruins of Lear's palace – certainly worked. We made the long journey to Swansea that autumn specially to see the result, and were rewarded by a memorable theatrical experience. It was certainly the finest and the most moving performance of the proud, distracted King that I have ever seen, either before or since. In playing Lear, even the finest English actors appear too intellectual and civilized to my way of thinking. They cannot bring to the part that mysterious quality, 'fire in the belly', which only the Celtic people, certainly among northern races, appear to possess.

At last a glorious summer drew to an end and it was time to be gone. *Cressy*'s engine throbbed again after long idleness; sadly we took in and coiled our mooring lines. After so much sunshine, the weather was still fine but now overcast, and although it was quite windless there was a first chill breath of autumn in the air as we passed once more on to the great aqueduct and headed southwards. Our destination was Gayton 'Arm End', near Northampton. It will be remembered that we had lain at Gayton temporarily after our first voyage to the Welsh Canal, but this time we decided to desert Banbury for once and make Gayton our winter quarters.

Chapter 8

The End of the Cut

Something about the Welsh Canal seemed to foster ideas so far as I was concerned. On our first visit there I had conceived a Canal Exhibition in London and now, on this second occasion, the thought suddenly struck me – why not organize a rally of boats? I had in mind a kind of aquatic version of the Vintage Sports Car Club's Rally to Presteigne which I had first helped to organize just before the war and which had proved so popular that it had since become an annual event. In the Presteigne Rally we had an award for the car coming the greatest distance, competitors sending telegrams from various towns en route as proof that they had been there. A prize was also awarded for the best maintained car and so on. It seemed to me that precisely the same sort of system could be applied to the inland water-ways. It would be fun for the competitors and at the same time be an object lesson to the lay public, who were at that time woefully ignorant on the subject. It would show them what improbably lengthy journeys could be made by using the canals and rivers of England.

This idea of a rally of boats having germinated, the next question to be decided was where to hold it, and here the range of choice was naturally much more limited than in the case of the vintage car rally where the choice of Presteigne, popular though it proved, was purely fortuitous. There were a number of conditions that the site had to meet. Because there was then considerable commercial traffic over most of the system, the rally would have to be held somewhere off the main routes where such an assemblage of boats would not cause an obstruc-

154

tion. Also, the site should not be on the narrow canal system where it would be inaccessible by broad-beamed river craft, a fact which, in these early days, would mean a seriously restricted entry. Finally, I felt that I should seek a place somewhere in central England, equally accessible from the four quarters of the compass. Pondering this, I looked hard and long at the large map of the canal system which almost covered one wall panel of *Cressy*'s sitting cabin. This map had originally been published by the old Grand Union Canal Company, and, although it marked all the inland waterways, the G.U.C. system was shown as a heavy blue line extending from London to Birmingham with a long secondary main line thrusting up into the east Midlands through Leicester and Loughborough to terminate at Langley Mill, near Nottingham. These primary routes threw off branches to Slough, to Aylesbury, to Northampton and to Market Harborough. I considered the merits of each of these in turn and came down overwhelmingly in favour of the last named.

The branch canal to Market Harborough from the bottom of the locks at Foxton on the 'Leicester Line' is just under six miles long and I was familiar with it because I had made Market Harborough a port of call, as described in *Narrow Boat*, on our first voyage just before the war. It was then still occasionally used by boats carrying imported soft wood from Brentford which was off-loaded at a timber yard beside the capacious basin at Market Harborough. But it had since become completely disused although, when we had last passed that way in 1947, travelling south from the Welsh Canal towards Gayton, it had still looked readily navigable apart from a certain amount of weed on the surface – and there were no locks on the branch to fall into disrepair. In fact, in origin it was not a branch at all, but part of the Leicester & Northamptonshire Union Canal, an abortive project for a broad canal which was intended to link the river Soar at Leicester with the Nene at Northampton but expired at Market Harborough when the money ran out. It was the later construction of the original Grand Union Canal from Norton Junction to Foxton that finally supplied the missing link between the east Midlands and the south, but only by narrow canal. However, it would be possible for wide-beam boats to reach Market Harborough from the river Trent and its associated waterways.

It was thus settled that the Association's first rally of boats should be organized at Market Harborough in the following summer and this was one reason why we chose Gayton instead of Banbury as a winter mooring; so far as the organization of the event was concerned it was strategically placed about half-way between Market Harborough and London. There was another good reason why we had chosen Gayton. I had just been commissioned by Harry Batsford to write a book about the Thames to accompany a set of engravings, paintings and colour prints which he had collected. I had accepted this invitation with alacrity because I saw in it a means of achieving another ambition, which was to navigate the whole course of the non-tidal Thames. My only previous experience of the river had been our two wartime journeys between Oxford and Reading, when the Conservancy had waived the licence fee because I was only using the river 'in the course of a through journey between one waterway and another'. But now that the Thames & Severn Canal had long lain derelict, there could be no such excuse for navigating the river up to Lechlade, and for a craft of maximum size – which was what *Cressy* was in the eyes of the Conservators – the cost of an annual licence, plus the total dues on forty-six locks, added up to much more than my shallow pocket could afford. But now, because I was writing a book on their river, the Conservators had very generously waived their charges and presented *Cressy* with a free licence plate and myself with a free lock pass. So, as soon as the spring came, we planned to sail straight down the main line of the Grand Union Canal towards London and enter the Thames at Brentford.

It must have been some time in October or early November that Robert Aickman, myself and our respective wives paid a joint visit to Market Harborough to look at the suitability of the canal there and to broach the project to the Town Council who swallowed the idea enthusiastically and, in the event, cooperated splendidly. This was the last occasion on which the first Chairman and the first Honorary Secretary of the Inland Waterways Association cooperated together, for it was not long before I wrote in to the I.W.A. office in Gower Street and tendered my resignation.

This was not a step I had lightly taken as a result of some passing mood of pique or exasperation, but the result of a difficult decision which I had only reached after much careful thought and long discussion with Angela. It was made for a variety of reasons, one of which was quite simply that I could not afford to continue. The success of my 'design for living' depended on my earning my living by writing, and the cold fact was that since I had cheerfully thrown up my wartime job and resumed my original pre-war plan I had not been paying my way. Indeed, without Angela's slender allowance (which was never assured anyway) we should have been on the financial rocks already. As a result of the success of my first book, I had allowed myself to become involved in a canal campaign which entailed far more unpaid work than I could properly afford. I reflected that if I had had to hold down a job over the three and a half years that had passed since the I.W.A. had been launched, I would have been quite unable to undertake the amount of active campaigning which I had done. I was discovering that a free-lance is always under pressure from others who assume that his time is his own, and it requires great self-discipline to resist such blandishments. He can easily find himself caught up in a plethora of unrewarding – and often thankless – 'honorary' tasks. Added to this was the fact that we both realized I was forfeiting the freedom which I had gone to the canals to seek. As the Association grew rapidly in stature and influence, this had become the more apparent. We no longer felt ourselves to be free agents; *Cressy* and her crew had become, by almost imperceptible degrees, the tool of the Gower Street office. Angela had been the first to realize this, and had been urging me for some time to be quit of the Association. I was less perceptive, and was also keener perhaps that a crusade to which I had set my hands should succeed. For this reason I tended to turn a blind eye to what was happening or pretend that it did not exist. The brutal truth was now becoming only too clear, it was becoming a band-wagon, as good causes, often started with the best of intentions, are apt to do, such being the frailty of human nature. We, who had originally sought refuge on the canals to escape from all we disliked in the modern world, deeply resented what we felt to be our exploitation for such purposes by others. The moment of truth so far as I was concerned occurred one morning at Gayton when there arrived a letter telling me to attend a meeting at Newbury in three days' time, couched in terms which I would have hesitated to use to anyone. Needless to add, I did not go.

Two other considerations played their part in a decision which was destined to have far-reaching consequences. One was the knowledge that the Association was by now so firmly established that it was certainly strong enough to survive the loss of any single individual connected with it, be he never so active in its affairs. The other was that I found myself increasingly out of sympathy with the Association's declared aim to restore to navigable order 'every navigable waterway'. With our limited resources of money and manpower this aim, it seemed to me, had inevitably led to too great a concentration of effort upon reviving the dead branches of a shrinking system at the expense of those parts of the tree which were still more or less precariously alive. What chiefly appealed to me about the canal system was its indigenous working life. On the narrow canals this meant the working narrow boats and their crews which were so essential a part of them. These working boaters, so many of whom I knew and admired, unconsciously supplied that subtle traditional patina of constant use – the worn and dusty towpath, the polish that generations of 'uphill or downhill straps' had given to the bollards of cast-iron or grainy oak at the locks; it was an essential part of that blend of utility and beauty which used to compound the particular magic of canals. This was something which some members in the I.W.A. could never fully appreciate. They could value canals aesthetically as an important contribution to landscape beauty, but they could not assess to how great an extent utility was responsible for this. In just the same way, urban man can never appreciate to what extent the changing methods of agriculture affect the beauty of the rural landscape. For this reason I felt we had been devoting far too great a proportion of our effort to the 'fringe' waterways at the expense of canals such as the Trent & Mersey or the southern part of the Oxford

Canal which were still alive. On these latter canals and on many others, trade still persisted stubbornly in the face of manifold discouragements. The captain of a pair of working narrow boats was paid for each particular trip at a rate of so much per ton carried. Considering that such payments covered the unpaid labour of his wife and family, as well as that of the captain himself, they amounted to little more than a starvation wage. For this inadequate return there were a number of reasons: the undredged state of the canals which both slowed the boats down and prevented them loading to their full capacity; the lack of any serious coordinated attempt to obtain back-loads which meant that boat captains spent far too high a proportion of their time travelling light for which they were paid only a low flat rate. Again, no attempt had been made over the years to reduce turn-round time by improving methods of loading and, particularly, of discharging boats. How often had I watched men take all day to unload twenty-five tons of coal from a narrow boat at Banbury Wharf using shovels and barrows, and reflected that the use of even the simplest form of mechanical elevator would have saved a great deal of back-breaking toil and reduced turn-round time by at least a half. Finally, the future of the family boat was also seriously threatened at this time, as it had been in the past, by reformers who would take the children off the boats, thus destroying the traditional family life of the boaters in the name of the sacred cow of education.

During these first years of the Association, I and a small minority who shared my point of view, such as those women who had served on the canals during the war and so become acquainted with the life of the canals, did what we could to campaign for more favourable conditions for the boaters. It has since become obvious that, if one accepts modern economic doctrines, the canal narrow boat was doomed to extinction by its small pay-load. Nevertheless, had all the reforms and improvements we pressed for in 1948–9 been carried out, I sincerely believe that the life of the working narrow boat might have been prolonged by at least ten years. One of the reforms we advocated was that the antiquated and complex system of toll charges based on tonnage should be swept away and replaced by a simple system of annual licence fees per boat. This sensible suggestion was ultimately adopted, but only many years later, by which time traffic on the narrow canal system had dwindled almost to vanishing point and no such transfusion could revivify the dying patient.

Although our campaign to ease the lot of the working boatmen received token support from some members, it never attracted the amount of publicity, attention and time that was devoted, for example, to the Kennet & Avon. This canal was of singular beauty and character as I knew very well, being the only person in the I.W.A. who at that time had actually navigated it. But since I had done so in 1940 the K. & A. had become virtually derelict, and the prospect of reviving commercial traffic on it was extremely remote. I was by no means guiltless in this matter myself because, largely for sentimental reasons of my own, I had devoted too much time to the Welsh Canal, another waterway whose commercial prospects were practically nil. It was because, I now think, of this failure to get our priorities right at the outset that the Association suddenly awoke to the unpleasant fact that traffic over the whole system of narrow waterways had ceased, and that as a result, canals which had hitherto received scant attention were suddenly at risk.

So, for all these associated reasons I dispatched my letter of resignation to Gower Street. I explained that the post of Honorary Secretary had become too onerous but that I hoped to remain as an ordinary member of the committee and would continue to help the Association in any way that I could. It is difficult to credit the almost hysterical reaction aroused by my resignation. It had been a case of 'united we stand, divided we fall', and by my sudden defection I had dealt the cause a traitorous and near fatal blow. If I persisted in my folly I could expect no further toleration. I was momentarily winded by this response as though someone had hit me in the solar plexus. No one could care more about the canals than I did, but this struck me as pitching things too high. It was as though I had committed heresy and high treason at one and the same time, and from that day forward *Cressy* and her crew found themselves increasingly ostracized by part of the membership.

We were both members of the committee responsible for organizing the Market Harborough Rally, until we learned that some members of that committee were organizing a play during the rally in which they had the leading roles. I felt it was their job to organize a rally rather than spend time on a venture which I thought was of no conceivable use or relevance so far as the waterways were concerned. For expressing this point of view, Angela and I were both made to feel that our continuing presence on the rally committee could not be tolerated.

Had my resignation not provoked so violent and hostile a reaction, the whole affair might have passed over peacefully enough; but as it was, it developed into a major row which split the Association from top to bottom. Our position inevitably attracted sympathizers, with the result that I found myself landed willy-nilly at the centre of a very vocal 'splinter group' claiming to champion the cause of the working boatmen and, quite as importantly, advocating a more democratic I.W.A. As happens in politics when similar situations develop, one side or the other sooner or later resorts to unfortunate tactics whereupon, human nature being what it is, the other side retaliates in kind so that the outsider can be forgiven for saying 'a plague on both your houses'. So it was in this case. Although I can now see it merely as a storm in a teacup, it then seemed a serious affair.

One small but humorous episode is sufficient to reveal the tenor of events in the canal world during 1950. When I had first launched my proposal for a rally of boats at Market Harborough, I had suggested that cups should be presented to the winning boats as was customary at the vintage car rally at Presteigne. This idea was accepted; it was proposed that each member of the committee should present a cup for a specific object (mine, I remember, was for the best kept engine-room) and we all trooped along to the Silver Vaults to select our respective trophies having agreed to pool the expense between us, leaving it to the Gower Street office to arrange for the engraving. Because we hoped that the rally would become an annual event, we all assumed that these would become perpetual challenge trophies to be competed for each year, the winner being awarded a small replica as is usual in events of this kind. Not until the rally programme appeared did we discover to our astonishment that we were most generously giving away our costly trophies and that only one of them was perpetual.

In the light of the strained situation it was a great relief when a long winter came to an end and we could be under way again, heading south down the Grand Union Canal. It was over ten years (1938) since I had last taken *Cressy* over this part of the canal, and then it had only been as far as Watford. Now we were to follow it to its end – or beginning – at Brentford. We locked down through the entrance locks at Brentford with the incoming tide, choosing our moment to slip out into the broad tideway of London River before the tugs, towing their barges high laden with esparto grass bound for the paper mills of Apsley and Croxley, arrived off the entrance. This one-and-only excursion into tidal waters was very brief indeed. Borne swiftly upstream by the last of the flood, *Cressy* swept through the open half-tidal lock at Richmond and was soon approaching Teddington Lock, the first under the jurisdiction of the Thames Conservancy and the entrance to the non-tidal Thames.

Although it has long been out of print, I have described *Cressy*'s Thames journey from Teddington to Lechlade so fully in *The Thames from Mouth to Source* that I will not do so again. The more perceptive readers of that book may notice that there is a certain sad, elegiac quality about the writing in some places. As *Cressy* made her slow way westwards up the great river in the golden weather of early June, I think I secretly knew in my heart of hearts that, so far as our design for living was concerned, this was to be the last summer.

There could be no greater contrast than that between the two largest of English rivers, Severn and Thames. Although the greater part of Severn's course is in England and it flows through the capital cities of three English shires, to call it an English river seems a misnomer because it retains to a remarkable degree the quality of the land of its birth. It is essentially a Celtic river of a character that has never been tamed. By contrast, the Thames seemed as thoroughly domesticated and placid as a lake created by Capability Brown in some nobleman's park. Whereas it was not until the 40s and 50s of last century that Severn's primitive violence was partially tamed in its lower reaches by the construction of the present infrequent locks, Thames has been domesticated by man for centuries past and its many locks are the successors of ancient flash locks whose origins go back to the Middle Ages. Consequently Thames seems to have long forgotten its native wildness, and the reaches between the locks appeared to us to resemble a string of lakes rather than a great river. Even its floods lack the headstrong violence of the swift Severn spates, Thames waters rising with slow and silent stealth to creep almost apologetically round the willow boles and out over the wide water-meadows.

The part of the river that we liked the best is also sometimes called the Isis, in other words it consists of the upper reaches west of Oxford. It was, and maybe still is, less frequented than that below Oxford, because Osney Bridge with its restricted headway excludes the large Thames cruisers. This upper river was the last to be improved by the substitution of pound locks for the ancient navigation weirs. From Medley to Godstow Lock beside Port Meadow is the last of the broad, lake-like reaches. Once through Godstow we found ourselves in a river of much smaller scale and more natural and unpretentious character than the lower Thames, a river that reminded us of the Warwickshire Avon above Tewkesbury except that its broad valley lacked the bold focal point of Bredon Hill. Instead, upon our left hand across a wide expanse of willow-bordered water-meadows, there was only the misty blue outline of that long, undulating ridge of high ground that stretches from the wooded Cumnor Hills by Oxford into Wiltshire through Faringdon and Highworth. In 1950, this upper river seemed lost and almost incredibly remote considering the populous countryside through which it passes. Whereas the lower reaches had been busy with every sort of pleasure craft from punts and skiffs at one end of the scale to Salters' steamers at the other, I cannot recall that we passed a single boat on the move between Oxford and Lechlade. Perhaps this was just as well because, particularly in its uppermost reaches, the river becomes so narrow and tortuous that it was only with difficulty that I was able to swing *Cressy's* seventy-foot length through the bends and, in the process, took up the whole width of the channel; for any craft approaching downstream a collision would have been almost impossible to avoid.

Having reached our journey's end, we winded *Cressy* just above the single stone arch of Halfpenny bridge at Lechlade before tying up in the shade of the willows at the foot of the town meadow below the bridge. It was early June, roses were everywhere blooming in profusion against walls of grey stone and the hay had not yet been cut. It was also the first occasion that we had tied up in Gloucestershire since we had moored at Sharpness two years before.

From bills posted in the square of the little town we learned that on the morrow John Betjeman was to open a village fête in the grounds of Buscot Rectory. I determined to go and, if possible, make his acquaintance. The fact that I had long admired his poetry was not, in itself, a sufficiently good reason for such a resolve. Because writers and artists put the best of themselves into their work, it necessarily follows that they cannot themselves be better than their work and indeed often appear distinctly inferior. In fact, with rare exceptions, the greater the art the lesser its creator appears by comparison. It is for this very simple and obvious reason that 'fans' are all doomed to disillusion. They expect to find a soul-mate or a super human being and instead find themselves in an embarrassing confrontation with a very ordinary individual who looks abstracted if not positively distracted as he mumbles some platitude or scratches his ear with a glazed look in his eye. Yet it was not as a fan but for a purely practical reason that I was anxious to meet John Betjeman.

One of the most looked-forward-to objectives of this voyage was a visit to Kelmscott Manor. My admiration for William Morris had made this house which he had loved an object of pilgrimage, and I felt that my book about the Thames would be incomplete if I failed to record in it my impressions of Kelmscott. Behind a screen of sheltering elms, we had caught a brief glimpse of its stone chimneys and gables as *Cressy* swung round the bends beyond Eaton Hastings; but when we reached Lechlade we discovered to our dismay that the Manor was locked and empty, the tenants who leased it from its Oxford Collegiate owners having recently departed. This was a great disappointment, but our spirits rose when we learned that John Betjeman had taken up the lease of Kelmscott, not because he had any intention of living there but from the purely altruistic motive of safeguarding it. For, incredible though it may now seem, the future of Kelmscott was at that time in some doubt.

We walked over St John's bridge to Buscot to find the usual tables piled with cast-off clothing and Women's Institute jams, the bran tub and the bowling-for-the-pig, laid out on the rectory lawn. John Betjeman had obviously been lunching with the rector for, accompanied by his host, he eventually appeared in the doorway of the Georgian house. I remember thinking that, in his straw boater and suit of clerical grey, he looked much more like the popular image of a country parson than the rector himself. Soon we got into conversation and I was gratified to discover that my name as a writer was not unknown to him. He at once linked my name with my book about the Irish canals, *Green and Silver*, which had been published the previous year, and this pleased me particularly. *Narrow Boat* had proved almost too successful. I had grown sick of being greeted or introduced as 'the man who wrote *Narrow Boat*'.

As for visiting Kelmscott, that was easily arranged. The next evening we were hailed from the water and looked out of *Cressy*'s windows to see John Betjeman punting Osbert Lancaster downstream towards us. As both were wearing straw boaters, they might have punted straight out of Edwardian England. If we cared to meet John at Kelmscott on the following afternoon, he would open the house up for us. I duly recorded my impressions of that visit in my book and, reading them again at this distance of time, I feel sure that if I were to revisit Kelmscott today my reactions would be very different. With youthful arrogance, I then considered both the Pre-Raphaelite and the Art and Craft movements, between which Morris was the linking figure, to be totally inadequate kicks against the pricks of the new industrial machine society which had already come to birth. I dismissed too arbitrarily, as ephemeral and self-conscious, the relics of Morris and Rossetti's occupation of Kelmscott, compared with the timeless tradition of Cotswold building which the house itself exemplified. But it must be remembered that Kelmscott was then standing empty following a long occupation by tenants who, it was obvious, had not been over-conscientious. This gave to the whole property a forlorn, neglected air very different, I imagine, from its appearance today. To add a lighter note which I did not touch upon in my Thames book, my attention was struck by an elegant little stone pavilion in one corner of the overgrown garden. This, as John disclosed to us, in fact housed a 'three holer' and he went on to explain how, in gratitude for his action in saving Kelmscott, Osbert Lancaster had recently presented him with a drawing of Janey Morris enthroned on the central seat with Morris and Rossetti on either side.

So idyllic was this mooring at Lechlade, so secluded and yet so conveniently close to the little town, that we seriously considered giving the Market Harborough Rally in August a miss and staying put until the autumn as we had done at Pont Cysyllte the previous year. We were undoubtedly swayed towards such a course by the change in our relations with the I.W.A. which had occurred since I had given up the secretaryship. Then two letters arrived which caused us to change our minds.

The contents of the first letter were so surprising that they made me gasp and stretch my eyes. It was suggested that nothing but harm could result from our bringing *Cressy* to Market Harborough and in strongest terms requested a withdrawal of our entry. Although I felt nothing but contempt for a childish prohibition that could not be enforced, how much pleasanter it would be, I argued, to lie here instead of journeying half across England in order to push *Cressy*'s bows into a hornet's nest. But Angela thought very differently. Her reaction to the letter was much more tigerish and belligerent. The rally had been my idea in the first place and the canals were free for all on payment of tolls, so who the hell presumed to stop *Cressy*?

That I eventually allowed Angela's argument to prevail over my own judgement was due to the contents of the second letter, which came from Philip Unwin of George Allen & Unwin. It was he who had published *Green and Silver*, and this year he was to publish my *Inland Waterways of England*, a purely factual and practical book about the canals and rivers for which I felt there was a need. Publication date for this new book happened to coincide with the rally week, but this was purely coincidental because to use such an occasion as a vehicle for personal publicity had simply never occurred to me and I had left my publishers in ignorance of the rally date. A bewildered Philip Unwin wrote to say that he now understood from the Association that there was strong opposition to any publicity for myself or the book at the rally. This was the last straw. My reaction was not to indulge in lengthy explanations but simply to tell him to ignore the whole episode. For the truth was that such an unwarrantable interference with my private literary affairs at first made me so hopping mad that for the only time in my life I contemplated litigation. Thank goodness I had cooled off and begun to see the absurd side of the whole affair before rushing into an action of uncertain outcome but certain great expense.

Although I soon dropped any idea of litigation, this second letter did make me angry enough to swing round to Angela's point of view, and from that moment it was a case of 'to hell or Market Harborough' where *Cressy* was concerned. These two actions that then seemed so provoking have, with the passage of time, come to appear trivial and even ludicrous. But for this, my publishers would never have heard of Market Harborough, and Philip Unwin would certainly not have visited the rally himself as he did. But for this we might never have left that so pleasant mooring at Lechlade.

The day after leaving Lechlade we were passing through 'the Duke's Cut' on our way to the Oxford Canal. This was a short canal built in 1789 by the Duke of Marlborough to provide a link between the canal and the Wolvercote backwater of the Upper Thames. Until Isis Lock was opened at Oxford in 1796 it was the only connection between canal and river, and, even after Isis was opened, the Duke's Cut continued to be used by boats passing between the Upper Thames and the canal. Considerable narrow boat traffic had used this route within the memory of boaters then still living. James Harwood of *Searchlight*, one of my Oxford Canal boater friends, had told me many a yarn of how he used to work 'up the west country' as a young man, including the frightening way his boat had to be winched up through the old navigation weirs which then still existed on this part of the river. But by 1950 such traffic was no more than a memory and the only commercial craft using the Duke's Cut was an occasional pair of boats carrying a load of coal to Wolvercote Mill. This was a paper mill owned by the Oxford University Press whose speciality was making India paper, famous for the way it combined extreme thinness with opacity. As luck would have it, we encountered our friends the Humphries with their beautiful pair of boats making one of their rare trips to Wolvercote Mill. He was a burly, powerfully built man who it would have been comforting to have on one's side in a rough house. His wife, a striking blonde, wore her hair in coiled plaits about her ears. When we had first got to know them, the family lived on a horse-boat, the *Captain Cook*, but although this was one of the few on the canal that still boasted a fore-cabin, it eventually became totally inadequate for their lengthening string of blond children, so they had graduated to a motor and butty. We met them at the junction of the cut with the backwater where they were performing the complicated manoeuvre of winding both boats and then 'breasting up' (tying up the pair side by side) before dropping astern down the backwater to the mill. They were the first working narrow boats we had seen since we had left Brentford two months before, and it was like coming home to one's native parish. We slowed down and exchanged shouted greetings and news before forging ahead into the narrow, willow-bordered cut that led beneath the railway and so into the Oxford canal where we swung north.

I think this was the only occasion when we passed our familiar moorings at Tooley's Yard, Banbury, without stopping. For we were in a hurry, and felt that by stopping we should all too easily be beguiled by old friends into lingering too long, especially as this had been the first occasion when we had not wintered there. So we lay for the night in the solitude of the disused Twyford Wharf just to the south of the town and slipped unobtrusively through Banbury in the early hours of the following morning. We were at Braunston by nightfall and the next day saw us on the long summit level of 'the Leicester Line' and within striking distance of our objective.

As we approached Market Harborough I was astounded by

the number of boats which had come to the rally. Moored stem to stern, they must have stretched for more than half a mile along the towpath. When I had first conceived the rally I had no idea it would prove so popular; indeed I had not realized that there were so many craft in England capable of navigating the narrow canal system – for it emerged that the majority of the entrants had come from the south through the narrow locks at Watford and Foxton. As *Cressy* drifted slowly past the long line of moored craft we received many a wave and friendly greeting from people we had encountered on earlier voyages, but when we entered the terminal basin we had a very different reception. I had decided to wind *Cressy* in the basin before returning to our mooring so as to be pointing in the right direction when the time came to move off. *Beatrice* was acting as the official headquarters of the rally and so this replica of *Cressy* occupied the most prominent position in the basin. Although we tried to appear totally unconcerned, we were well aware of hostile eyes peering at us through the window curtains. I felt sure that had *Beatrice* been equipped with torpedo tubes, *Cressy* would have gone straight to the bottom. It suddenly seemed very important to put up a bravura performance in the face of this antagonism so we winded *Cressy* without touching a shaft or putting a line ashore but using only rudder and propeller. Alas, this was pride before a fall. A few minutes later, when Angela was standing on our cabin top and bringing *Cressy* broadside into her mooring with our long shaft, the tip of the shaft unexpectedly lost purchase and Angela took a beautiful header into the canal. Fortunately, by this time we were out of sight of the basin and back among friends who could regard such a mishap totally without malice.

The rally was voted a great success, for I suppose only a small minority realized the absurdity of the two rival factions at the centre of things, circling each other warily like predatory tomcats. I think dear old Sir Alan Herbert, the Association's President, realized that there was some breach in the ranks and attempted to mend it by asking if he might visit *Cressy*. It was a most pleasant occasion and we spent a long while drinking and yarning, but I fear it did more harm than good. Things had by now reached such a pass that our opponents could not do other than impute evil intentions to our every action. I think they firmly believed we had inveigled A.P.H. aboard, plied him with liquor and then vilified themselves, whereas it would never have occurred to us to ruin a happy evening by thinking of such things, let alone indulging in deliberate denigration which would assuredly have recoiled upon us.

Although the unpleasant atmosphere clung about *Cressy* like a miasma, so that I could not forget it and often secretly regretted that we had ever left Lechlade, it would be too much to say that we did not enjoy the occasion. The weather was perfect throughout and we thoroughly enjoyed entertaining, and being entertained by, the many old friends we met there. There were working boats at the rally as well as pleasure boats, something that can no longer happen today, more's the pity. A resplendent pair of 'Ovaltine boats'* lay in the basin and won the prize for the best kept pair of working boats. Another pair, the motor *Cairo* and the butty *Warwick* from the Samuel Barlow Coal Company, had benches in their holds and ran regular trips for visitors between the basin and the junction. The Market Harborough Council played their part by arranging a truly splendid display of fireworks to round off the proceedings on the last night.

From Market Harborough we returned by easy stages to our familiar moorings at Banbury for the winter. It was to be the most unhappy winter and early spring of my life. The prime cause of this was that my relationship with Angela had been deteriorating ever since our summer at Pont Cysyllte. I will not attempt to explain why this was. There are some things which a biographer, writing in the future, may nose out if he can, thereby shedding fresh light on his chosen character, but such things are not to be set down in an autobiography. An account of a broken relationship between two people must, if written by one of them even after the passage of years and with the utmost magnanimity, inevitably present a partial view of such a painful event. As I wrote in the first volume of this autobiography, I believe that the extraordinary, implacable hostility of Angela's parents towards her marriage, by cutting

* The firm of A. Wander & Co., the makers of Ovaltine, then owned their own boats to supply their canal-side factory with coal from the Midlands.

themselves off from her for good, placed an intolerable psychological burden upon her which I did not fully appreciate at the time. Let us leave it at that. Two other factors combined to complicate and aggravate this domestic crisis. One was the state of *Cressy* and the other was our deteriorating relations with the I.W.A.

It is easy to be wise after the event, but a fatal error had been made when *Cressy* had first been converted into a houseboat twenty years before. This was a failure to provide through ventilation under the floorings. These floorings fit flush with, and on either side of, the oak keelson. This means that there is a space beneath the floorings and the elm bottoms of the boat equal to the thickness of the keelson – usually not more than six inches. On a working narrow boat it was usual to take up these floorings when the hold was cleaned out after each trip; but on a houseboat, provision for lifting the floorings is seldom or never made with the consequence that, unless there is some special arrangement for through ventilation, the space beneath becomes an ideal breeding ground for dry and wet rot. In the case of *Cressy* this was aggravated by the fact that all the rainwater falling on the little open deck for'ard had to pass through this under-floor space to collect in the bilges aft where it was pumped out – the boat being trimmed to be down by the stern to ensure that the twenty-two-inch propeller was under water. I had been fighting rot on *Cressy* for years before I realized the source of the trouble, and now it was too late. Although to an undiscerning eye she looked as bright and as beautiful as ever, only I knew that she was like some elephant stricken with a mortal disease and, as old elephants and old boats do, she had to find a place to die; to rot away in some old, abandoned winding hole or wharf, her bare ribs hidden by the kindly reeds. I had set so much store by my idea of living afloat on the canals, had pondered it so long before it was finally achieved, that to bring it to such a sad end was something I could not contemplate coldly. Over the years I had come to love *Cressy*. It was an affection that was more than house-pride. I can only explain it as a combination of love for a home which one has created oneself with the kind of affection one feels for an old and trusty vintage car that has carried one staunchly through the years over countless thousands of miles. Yet an end had now become inevitable. To restore *Cressy* to perfect order would mean virtually a new boat in which nothing would be left of the original but the iron knees. Even if everything else had been right in my life, I could not possibly have afforded such a costly rebuild.

I realized now that I had been so enamoured of my design for living that I had never clearly envisaged what my next step would be when, as all things must, it came to an end. Three factors now combined to make me feel disillusioned with the English canals: the present Association unpleasantness; the visible decline in commercial canal carrying; and, lastly and ironically, the fact that, largely as a result of my own efforts as a publicist, what had been a secret world was now obviously in process of becoming a fashionable playground for frustrated urban man. The question was: what next? On this, Angela and I flatly disagreed.

Curiously enough, although it was I who had suggested our present way of living in the first place, I discovered that her wanderlust was much stronger and more deep-rooted than my own. To Angela the answer to the question seemed obvious – a bigger and better version of *Cressy*, a converted sailing barge of some kind in which we could cross the narrow seas and so explore the continental canal network. I could not see how we could possibly afford such a craft, but in any event I did not relish the idea. I have never been drawn to the sea and the prospect of continental travel, even by canal, did not appeal to me. With all their faults it was the British Isles that had prior claim on my affections, and there was so much of them still to see that I doubted whether even the longest lifetime would allow me time enough.

For this and other reasons it had become clear by Christmas that our life on *Cressy* was fast running out and, as if this alone were not hard enough to bear, that winter was bedevilled by more unpleasantness in the Inland Waterways Association. The immediate cause of this was that the opposing faction put forward a new constitution which rapidly spread alarm and despondency among a small, but extremely active and influential group of long-standing members who constituted themselves an opposition party with R. H. Wyatt of Stone acting as a kind of liaison officer and coordinator.

I remember one dark winter night at Banbury when, like some gunpowder-plot conspirator, Wyatt came to visit me unexpectedly on *Cressy* and we agreed to circulate the whole I.W.A. membership with a statement over our several names. This statement not only called attention to the dangers in the proposed changes in the constitution but it also stressed that the I.W.A. must in future do more to help the working boatmen, including more attention to that part of the narrow canal system which was still in commercial use. Wyatt undertook to duplicate this document and to send it to all members. I still wonder whether I was right to put my name to this statement and so, inevitably, to be regarded by the membership as the spearhead of a dissident movement and, by the opposition, as a deadly rival struggling for power. Under all the circumstances I had never felt less in the mood for a power struggle; on the contrary, I only wished to have done with the whole silly business. But then I reflected that, had it not been for me, most of those who signed this heretical document would never have joined the Association, and so would never have become embroiled in such a squalid affair. For this reason I decided, rightly or wrongly, that I could not let them down and so added my name to theirs. The result of all this was that the date of a special general meeting was fixed in Birmingham in the early spring at which the issue would be finally decided.

This was the spring of 1951 when life on *Cressy* was drawing to its expected end. For the sum of £10 Angela bought herself a 'flat-nose' Morris Oxford two-seater coupé. It both looked and sounded pretty down-at-heel, but after suitable treatment by me it became reasonably reliable. When she had stowed her belongings in the dickey, I watched from *Cressy*'s deck as she drove away over the wooden drawbridge at the end of Factory Street. I then went below into a boat that suddenly seemed to have become very silent. Twenty years were to pass before I saw Angela again, and for her they were to be years of wandering, beginning with a long spell of travelling with Billy Smart's circus. As for myself, I soon took *Cressy* away from Tooley's Boatyard and, with the help of a good friend, Melville Russell-Cooke, worked her northwards to Stone where R. H. Wyatt had told me he had a customer eager to buy her. But one cannot leave the past behind as easily as that; every yard of the canal was haunted by memories of past voyages. The presence of 'Mel' undoubtedly helped to make this gloomy last voyage bearable. She had never been on a canal before, and it was a new and rich experience which she relished hugely and to which she often referred in later years. Although no longer in her first youth she scorned my offer of the sprung berth in the stateroom, electing to sleep on the hard spare berth in the fore-cabin so that she could be up betimes to cook the breakfast. For a tyro she was also surprisingly efficient as a lock-wheeler; her only serious error was to drop one of my windlasses into a lock chamber. A perfectionist in everything she undertook, Mel never forgot this incident. At Great Haywood, she had to leave to catch a train at Stafford and this meant that I had to journey on alone to Stone Wharf. The last ten miles and nine locks were into the low sunlight of a perfect spring evening. To say that I felt sad would be a gross understatement, and yet it struck me as only fitting that *Cressy* and I, who had voyaged together through so many years, should now complete our last journey alone.

When eventually I pulled in to Stone Wharf just as dusk was falling, Wyatt was waiting to greet me accompanied by a lady who was literally waving her cheque book in my direction. She was all set to write a cheque for the extremely modest sum I was asking; what she wanted was a static houseboat for herself and her elderly father. I had a clear conscience about such a sale because I knew that despite *Cressy*'s inward rottenness she was perfectly capable of staying afloat for years. But when Wyatt insisted on a hull survey in the dry dock at Stone before any money passed, I knew at once that this amounted to sentence of death. Sure enough, a boatbuilder from the Anderton Company unhesitatingly condemned her. I spent a few more melancholy days on board sorting out and packing my portable belongings to be sent home. Most of *Cressy*'s equipment consisted of fixtures that were still as sound and serviceable as on the day they were made, yet were doomed to die with her. I thought of all the satisfaction, the energy and the optimism that

I had put into their designing and making just twelve years before. Mel, who had volunteered to drive me back to my mother's house in Gloucestershire, drove on to the Wharf. I heard the crunching sound of the tyres and knew that the moment had come. I glanced around; at the bunches of bright painted roses on the wall panels of our stateroom and on both sets of cabin doors; at the painted castle in the forecabin, at the scratch-comb graining and at the brave chequerwork of the leg of our folding dining table. Then I shut the cabin doors behind me and turned my back on her for the last time. I did not look back as we drove away. From now on I should be living 'on the bank' as the canal boaters put it.

I understand that *Cressy* lay at Stone Wharf for some weeks, if not months, before they towed her away to some backwater of the Trent & Mersey where they left her to sink and rot. I have never inquired the precise whereabouts of this watery grave because I did not want to see her again. Yet for over twenty years, from her birth as a houseboat on the Welsh Border to her death at Stone, the old boat had exercised far too important an influence over my life to be banished from my mind. There could be no forgetting, and for years after I used frequently to dream that I was back on board. Often it was in circumstances of dire emergency like drifting out of control towards a weir on a rapid current. Maybe this was the psychological price to be paid for the many hazards I had managed to avoid either by luck or judgement during my boating years.

Not since the failure of Kerr Stuarts in 1930, which I described in the first volume of this autobiography, had I felt so disorientated, not to say disenchanted, as I did during the few weeks I spent with my mother at Stanley Pontlarge after abandoning *Cressy*. Once again I had built around myself what I believed to be a stable world but now the whole fabric seemed to have crumbled about my ears; my marriage had broken, my home was gone and the canal crusade to which I had devoted so much energy, time and enthusiasm had ended in futile and degrading bickering. In short, I felt very sorry for myself at this moment. Even the fact that six books of mine had been published since the appearance of *Narrow Boat* seemed small consolation. For although these books received good notices and, in fact, two of them, like *Narrow Boat*, are still in print today, in my gloomy mood I had become convinced that so far as the reading public was concerned I was a 'one-book' author.

However, the support of staunch friends was something I had not had at the previous débâcle in my life. I shall always remember Gunde Griffith's vigorous refutation when, wallowing in an ecstasy of self-pity, I declared that the whole of my twelve years with Angela on *Cressy* had been a disastrous and unproductive failure. This, she replied tartly, was utter nonsense and I should know better. The present cannot undo the past, she pointed out. Nothing which had endured for twelve years could conceivably be judged a failure, and in fact the whole long episode of living afloat had been an immensely rewarding and creative experience for us both. Now, like all good things, it had come to an end. Instead of bewailing and belittling what had gone, I should have the grace to be thankful for past favours and the courage to turn the page and begin another chapter. Fortunately, and quite fortuitously, the means were at hand to enable me to do just this.

Over the special meeting of the I.W.A. in Birmingham which broke my last link with the canals, it were best to draw a kindly veil. Squabbles of this kind which seem so momentous when they take place, stand revealed by the passage of time as the trivial things they really are. They bring out all that is worst in human nature, and this goes for both sides and does not exclude myself. Suffice it to say that the 'heretics' lost the day by a narrow margin, leaving the opposing caucus triumphant in the stricken field. I left the hall with a decidedly unpleasant taste in my mouth and, by one of those strange coincidences which sometimes occur in life, walked into another and much pleasanter meeting held in a small office in Waterloo Street, Birmingham, a mere three hundred yards away. This was one of the first – if not the first – committee meetings of the recently formed Talyllyn Railway Preservation Society. But how this swift transition from canal to rail came about is another story.

LANDSCAPE WITH FIGURES

Contents

For
Sonia, Richard and Timothy

Introduction

This is the third part of the autobiography of which the first two volumes have remained in print in one form or another since they were first published. Why has this volume been so long in joining the others, particularly as there has been pressure over the years from readers who want to know the end of the story?

There is very little to say by way of explanation other than that, to the writer's family, after an initial flutter of indecision, it seemed best to let time go by. Better we felt to let time pass while we settled down to this, to us, most personal of testaments: one in which the retrospective summing up of a life was attempted by its protagonist.

It is now nearly two decades since the death of the author and the events described, the old passions and feelings and their outcome in action have slipped imperceptibly into history.

We have not changed the viewpoint of the book except to add a necessary note where needed. Therefore a subject which was felt so deeply by a professional author, such as Public Lending Right, is left to appear as it did to him. It was introduced a matter of weeks after his death although, as it was not based on copyright, of no direct benefit to him or his heirs. Many of the enterprises inspired by the campaigns described here have consolidated and given inspiration to yet others in a way that clearly could not have been foreseen by him.

I am glad the gentle but persistent pressure from the present publisher, and the encouragement from the author's old friend and reader, has resulted in letting the story of one man's account of the things he cared for, and the struggles and campaigns of the time, to ensure that some of them survived, be completed.

SONIA ROLT, 1992

Preservation cannot be a one-sided affair of people vaguely wishing that 'developers' or 'they' wouldn't pull things down. Only by the example of each individual patiently living out a faith in his cultural roots by inhabiting – say – the most beautiful old building he can find in the locality, can we hope to turn the tide of such destruction.

Alison Smithson, *The Euston Arch*, 1968

Foreword

This book, like its two predecessors, is mainly concerned with the English landscape and with the machines – say rather those manifestations of the Industrial Revolution – which have captivated me throughout my life. Yet I think the reader will find that, as I have grown older and acquired a philosophy of life and a greater understanding of the Industrial Revolution, the conflict between these two loves – between the two halves of my own nature, if you like – has become less divisive and bewildering. Very briefly, I have learned that, where the machines are concerned, it is the quality that counts.

As in the earlier volumes, with the exception of the final chapter of this book, I have attempted so far as possible to deal with events as they occurred and with my reactions to them at that time no matter how jejune they may now appear to be. In other words, I have attempted to evoke the past without benefit either of hindsight or foresight; to avoid the temptation to nudge the reader into looking 'now on this picture, now on that'. This can blur the truth besides being tiresome for the reader. Not that I possess the gift of total recall; I have had the benefit of my writings at different periods which provide a guide to what I was thinking and of my reactions to events at any particular time.

The last chapter of this book has been written wholly from the standpoint of the present. As it took three chapters of the first book to describe the events of a mere two years of my adolescence, it may surprise the reader to find that this chapter deals with some events that happened as long as fifteen years ago. I accounted for those three early chapters by advancing the theory that the stream of time does not flow past us at a constant rate, but appears to flow faster as we grow older because, metaphorically speaking, our hearts beat slower. That certain events of the last fifteen years should appear to me as 'now' as I write these words, therefore seems as logical as that two years should become a whole epoch when I was young.

Writing an autobiography is an act of self-indulgence which I did not think I would ever perpetrate. As a biographer I take for granted the reader's interest in such great men as I choose to write about, but why should I assume a like interest in my own small doings? My only excuse is that some of my activities have not been without influence on present and future events. This being so it may prove to have been worth-while historically to put them on the record.

L.T.C.R., April 1974

1
Narrow Canals to
Narrow Rails

Cradled in the mountains of Merioneth the Talyllyn was the 'Sleeping Beauty' of Britain's railways. The concern fell into a trance very soon after its birth in 1866 and it continued so until 1950. Nothing changed except that the course of the line came to resemble some disused country lane rather than a railway. Down this overgrown way, on the original rails, hidden, yet at the same time held to gauge by the thick grass, there reeled at very infrequent intervals an original tall-chimneyed locomotive hauling an equally original train of Victorian four-wheelers. Owing to the state of the permanent way – if such it could be called – this Talyllyn train made a curious and totally unrhythmical clattering noise, while it proceeded with a strange undulating and swaying motion as though the coaches were a string of towed boats surmounting a succession of small waves. Seen in its setting of mountains, this lost railway had a certain magical quality about it which makes me wonder sometimes whether we did right to disturb it. Yet, had we not done so when we did, it is certain that its sleep would very soon have become the sleep of death. One could not perpetuate so deep and precarious a state of trance.

Although there is no documentary evidence to prove it, I am now convinced that the Talyllyn Railway owes its existence to the belief that there was gold to be found in the vicinity of the remote Bryn Eglwys slate quarry, perched high in a cleft of the mountains surrounding Cader Idris. Since 1847 slate had been worked here on a small scale by John Pughe and his descendants, the slate being carried by pack-horse over the mountains to Aberdovey for shipment by sea. In 1863, however, the Pughe family sold the quarry to a group of Manchester business men headed by the brothers William and Thomas McConnel, owners of the largest cotton-spinning business in Manchester. At this time the cotton trade was badly hit by the effects of the American Civil War and the McConnel brothers were looking eagerly for some promising alternative investment, or, in modern parlance, they were seeking to diversify their business. In order to acquire and develop Bryn Eglwys, the brothers formed the Aberdovey Slate Company in January 1864 with a capital of £75,000. In the following year capital was increased to £112,500 of which £15,000 was allocated to the construction of the Talyllyn Railway to provide a rail link between the quarry and the Welsh coast. It was the first narrow gauge railway in the world to be constructed at the outset for steam traction.

Although there was good slate to be found at Bryn Eglwys, extraction by underground methods was difficult and costly and, like other quarries in the area, production would always remain small scale compared with the mammoth quarries further to the north at Penrhyn and Dinorwic. It is hard to see why these astute Lancashire business men were prepared to stake this very considerable capital sum on the future of this small quarrying concern. The answer is that gold-lust is a disease that can infect even the keenest of brains. The Pughe family are said to have held the firm belief that there was gold to be found at Bryn Eglwys, but one feels that this may have been expressed tongue-in-cheek for the benefit of would-be English purchasers. Certainly, in the vicinity, occasional veins or outcrops of white quartz occur containing little golden flecks of pyrites or 'fool's gold'. Such quartz veins often indicate the presence of gold, though there is no evidence that gold has been found anywhere in the area. Yet the McConnel brothers would have been encouraged to believe the Pughes' story by an extraordinarily rich strike at the Clogau Mine between Dolgelley and Barmouth. This Clogau Mine had originally been sunk in an abortive search for copper, but in 1860 it became a gold mine when the vein of gold was discovered. Within three years gold to the value of £43,783 had been produced from this one small working and by 1865 the mine was paying out £22,575 per annum in dividends. Nor was this a mere flash in the pan. As late as 1904 Clogau produced 18,417 ounces of gold from 14,384 tons of ore. So the McConnel brothers' expectation of finding gold at Bryn Eglwys was not so fanciful as one might suppose. Yet, not only was there no gold, but even the slate-quarrying venture failed to come up to expectations and, in 1883, the Abergynolwyn Slate Company, as it was then called, went into voluntary liquidation. Thereafter the quarry was worked upon a much more modest scale by William's son, W.H. McConnel, until 1911 when he sold out to Henry (later Sir) Haydn Jones.

With this background of commercial failure, it is easy to see why the Talyllyn Railway became a sleeping beauty. What is much more difficult to understand is why it was endowed at the outset with the dignity of a statutory railway company intended for public passenger traffic. It could so easily have been built as a mineral line by way-leave agreement like the railways which served the Penrhyn and Dinorwic quarries, but for some reason this did not suit the McConnels. They went through the whole costly and time-consuming ritual of promoting an Act of Parliament, a proceeding that subsequently entailed an inspection of the line by the Board of Trade, prior to opening, to ensure the safety of the travelling public. One can only think that in the first flush of enthusiasm for their new venture only the best was good enough. They had to have a real railway which had been blessed by parliament or none at all.

I first became acquainted with the Talyllyn Railway in the summer of 1943 when Angela and I decided not to spend my annual leave at Llanthony as usual but to seek pastures new. After much brooding over maps we agreed that the vicinity of Cader Idris and Talyllyn Lake in Merioneth looked intriguingly wild and mountainous and we succeeded in booking rooms at a small farm called Minfford near the head of the lake. We reached this retreat from Tardebigge by taking the train to Dolgelley and thence by taxi.

I did not – and do not – consider that the mountain landscapes of Wales, beautiful though they are, can rank with those of the Welsh border. By comparison with the latter, the mountains, though they may be much higher and wilder, seem to lack that majesty that comes from outline and symmetry. Similarly, the valleys seem never so rich as in the border country; the trees have a stunted look; the pastures, though green enough, look poorer and there is never an arable field to be seen. Consequently, there is lacking that striking contrast between wild highland and rich lowland which makes the landscape of the border so uniquely beautiful. Again, by comparison with such border towns as Hay, Presteigne, Clun or Bishops Castle, the small towns of real Welsh Wales seem bleak and dreary. To walk, as we did, down the single long main street of Towyn when a storm of wind and rain was funnelling through it off the sea, made me feel homesick for England. There were few people about, and those that there were stood huddled in shop doorways watching despondently as the curtains of rain drove past. This all-pervading moisture darkened still further the funereal hues of the dour nineteenth-century houses, all purple slate and dark, rough-dressed stone. This was our first impression of Towyn. We had come in from Minfford by bus with the idea of travelling back to Abergynolwyn on the train, but when we finally reached the Wharf station it was to find a rain-smudged hand-written notice pinned to the board by the entrance proclaiming NO TRAIN TODAY. It subsequently transpired that the only serviceable locomotive had broken down and, as the return bus had left by this time, there was nothing for it but a long walk home.

We walked back along the line and very soon it stopped raining although the mountain ridges were still lost in swirling mists. In this way we learnt more about the Talyllyn Railway than we would have done had we been able to travel over it. So alarming was the state of the track that I marvelled that any train could possibly run without becoming derailed, not once but several times, on the journey between Towyn and Abergynolwyn. It was made the more alarming by the fact that as the line climbed up the valley, clinging to a narrow mountain ledge, there was an almost sheer drop on the valley side of the rails. When we finally reached Abergynolwyn station, nearly seven miles from Towyn, it was growing late and we were faced with a further five miles of hard slogging along the road home to Minfford. In those petrol-less days, Welsh roads were deserted and there seemed little prospect of a lift. We were lucky, however, for no sooner had we reached the road than a car stopped and picked us up. It turned out to be a friendly district nurse bound for one of the farms near Minfford.

I must not paint too black a picture of this Welsh holiday. Although it is true that it left us with no desire to repeat it, nevertheless the weather on the whole treated us kindly and we had some memorable mountain walks. One day I recall particularly. We had taken the morning bus over the pass into the Corris valley. This set us down opposite the little railway station at Corris and no sooner had we alighted than I glimpsed a plume of steam coming up the valley towards us. This turned out to be Corris Railway locomotive No.3* hauling a few empty wagons with a diminutive brake-van coupled in rear. So apposite was this arrival that it might have been specially staged for our benefit. Ever since I had first travelled on the Glyn Valley Tramway as a boy, narrow gauge railways held a peculiar fascination for me, partly, I think, because they were small and individualistic, not to say idiosyncratic, and partly because, almost invariably, they were to be found in mountainous or remote settings, difficult country which only the narrow gauge could penetrate economically. As I admired this brave and unexpected sight, I little thought

---

* An 0–4–2 tank locomotive built for the railway in 1878 by the Hughes Engine Co. of Loughborough, later the Falcon Engine & Car Works and now later of the Brash Company.

that in a few years the Corris Railway would cease to exist and that, through my agency, this entire train, locomotive, wagons, brake-van and all, would enjoy a fresh lease of life on the Talyllyn Railway.

We walked back from the Corris valley over the mountains by Bryn Eglwys to Abergynolwyn. I recall that at the summit of the pass we came upon a remote mountain farm that had obviously only lately been abandoned. The door hung open and within we found the pathetic remnants left behind after long occupancy. There were Victorian dresses and a whole series of black-bordered memorial cards commemorating members of the family who had 'passed on', each bearing a photograph and an appropriate text. The house stood open to the four winds and even on this fine day a mountain breeze sighed about its walls and rattled a loose casement upstairs as we looked through these dour reminders of mortality. The effect upon us was indescribably melancholy and we were glad to be out in the sunlight and on our way once more. Curiously enough, although I recall most vividly this eerie, empty house, the Bryn Eglwys quarries failed to leave any impression at all on my mind although they must have been working at this time, albeit in a very desultory fashion owing to the war. I clearly remember skirting the margin of the small reservoir which supplied the quarry with waterpower*, but after this my mind is like an unexposed negative.

Though the quarry failed to register, the Talyllyn Railway certainly did. Five years later a mental picture of that grass-grown, wavering track sprang most vividly to mind as I sat in the Inland Waterways Association office in Gower Street and leafed through the pages of the Bill which was to nationalize Britain's transport. The IWA had procured a copy of the Bill to see how it was going to affect the canal system, but I soon found myself turning to the section dealing with

---

* The reservoir supplied Pelton wheels which drove the slate saws and, via a wooden launder, an overshot waterwheel which drove an air compressor to supply power to the underground workings.

railways where I came upon a list of the companies, additional to the 'big four', which would be taken over if the Bill became law. The list was extremely comprehensive, indeed I could think of only one statutory railway company – the Talyllyn – which had been omitted. It was by no means the first time in railway history that this obscure railway had been overlooked.*

A few days before this, I had been listening to a party political broadcast during which a labour party spokesman had assured me how wonderful it would be when I, as one of the citizens of Great Britain, owned the railway system instead of a bunch of acquisitive capitalists. How different it would be, when railways were run for the benefit of all! Because I was old enough to remember the pride and efficiency of the old pre-grouping companies, the spit-and-polish of their loco-motives and rolling-stock which spoke so eloquently of that tremendous *esprit de corps* that existed throughout the railway service, I doubted the truth of this socialist dogma. Instead of 'our railways' it seemed to me that they were far more likely to become nobody's railways under nationalization. They would fall into neglect and decay just because they had become political pawns about which nobody felt responsible and nobody cared. It was with such gloomy thoughts in mind that I reflected what a fine thing it would be if at least one independent railway could survive to perpetuate, if only upon a small scale, the pride and the glory of the old companies. Why not the Talyllyn? Why not indeed? But then I thought of that seven miles of worn out track . . . As a romantic it seemed a brave notion, but as a practical engineer it seemed madness to attempt to re-animate a railway so run down that it had become so much scrap metal. Then a compromise occurred to me for which there was a good precedent in the north of England.

* For example, it was the only public railway which ignored the Board of Trade's instruction to install continuous brakes on its trains following the Armagh disaster. I imagine the management did not deliberately disobey the order but either failed to read it or forgot about it.

The first event ever organized for IWA members was an excursion in 1947 on a 'trip boat' on the Lancaster Canal ending at the bottom of the Tewitfield Locks near Carnforth. I seized this opportunity to pay my first visit to the neighbouring Ravenglass & Eskdale Railway in Cumberland. This had been built and opened in 1875 with the backing of the Whitehaven Iron Mines Ltd as a 3 ft gauge line for the purpose of carrying iron ore and granite from mines and quarries in Eskdale. This staple iron ore traffic soon failed but, by dint of carrying an increasing amount of holiday passenger traffic during summer seasons, 'Ratty', as the railway was known affectionately by the locals, struggled along until 1913 when it finally closed down. The closure of the granite quarry the previous year had proved to be the last straw. In 1915, however, the derelict railway was leased for a trial period of three years to a concern called Narrow Gauge Railways Ltd. This company operated miniature railways at seaside resorts and one of its directors was W.J. Bassett Lowke, a name revered by every railway-minded school-boy*. Using most of the original permanent way materials, the gauge of the railway was then reduced to fifteen inches and the line worked by miniature locomotives designed by Henry Greenly. These *Greenly* locomotives were of 'main line' type correctly scaled down to 15 inch gauge, and while they charmed the children at Rhyl or elsewhere, they were scarcely man enough for the seven steeply-graded miles of line in Eskdale. Consequently, since 1924, when the shipowners Sir Aubrey Brocklebank and Henry Lithgow took over the company, there was a tendency to increase the size of locomotives and stock to 'over-scale' proportions as advocated by that Victorian engineer, Sir Arthur Heywood who held that 15 inches was the smallest practicable gauge and who had designed and built the Eaton Hall Railway for the Duke of Wesminster. (It was at Eaton

---

* I had been privileged to welcome the idol of my schooldays, W.J. Bassett Lowke, with his wife, aboard *Cressy* on one occasion. They took tea with us while *Cressy* was lying at Gayton Arm End, Blisworth.

Hall that I had glimpsed, as a very small boy, Heywood's *Katie* and was captivated immediately.) Under this new regime the Beckfoot granite quarry had been re-opened and special high capacity bogie vehicles were introduced to convey the stone down to a new crushing plant which was built at Murthwaite, $2\frac{1}{2}$ miles from the lower terminus at Ravenglass. To obviate the transhipment of crushed stone at Ravenglass, this $2\frac{1}{2}$ miles of line was 'gauntleted' by standard gauge track. It was to handle traffic over this section that Kerr Stuart of Stoke-on-Trent built an 0–6–0 standard gauge diesel-mechanical locomotive of 90 hp in 1930.*

The early history of the Ravenglass & Eskdale was so like that of the Talyllyn that I saw no reason why the parallel should not be carried still further. Conversion to a miniature gauge might prove to be a cheaper, quicker and more economical solution than any attempt to restore the worn out railway to its original state. The old track could be sold for scrap and replaced by new rail of a lesser weight per yard, laid to a gauge of only $10\frac{1}{4}$ inches. I reckoned that scaled-down versions of narrow gauge locomotives running on this slim gauge should be capable of hauling as many passengers as the original Talyllyn locomotives had done in their prime. For example, I had in mind a 2–8–2 locomotive which Kerr Stuart had once built for the 2 ft gauge Gwalior Light Railway of India. This had a tractive effort of 15,206 lbs; suppose a scaled down version of such a prototype on the $10\frac{1}{4}$ in gauge . . .

I did not envisage scrapping the original Talyllyn loco-motives and coaches. They could form the nucleus of a narrow gauge railway museum at Towyn and become 'operable relics', running over a length of original track laid between the two

---

* This locomotive, one of the first of its type, was designed by my uncle, Kyrle Willans and, as a young apprentice, I drove it on test before despatch to Ravenglass. I stood on the footplate of this locomotive once more in 1973 after an interval of forty-three years; it is now working for a firm near Lichfield and is still giving good service.

stations at Towyn. The whole project would be manned by volunteers recruited from the ranks of railway enthusiasts. I argued that, unlike the members of the Vintage Sports Car Club, railway enthusiasts had, hitherto, been denied any practical creative outlet other than model-making and would, therefore, be only too glad of the opportunity to assist in the construction, maintenance and day-to-day running of a public railway; the more so as most of them were condemned by the age to wholly uncreative jobs in normal life.

The more I thought about this scheme the more promising it seemed and, during the winter of 1947/8, I discussed it at some length with two railway-minded friends of mine at Banbury, Bill Trinder and Jim Russell. Bill Trinder ran a radio shop in the town and I had first met him just before the war when I had bought a portable radio from him for *Cressy*. It was Bill who introduced me to Jim Russell, an ex-GWR employee who had since become a professional photographer. They were quite excited by the idea and at their suggestion we consulted Messrs Fuller and Franklin of Basset Lowke Ltd of Northampton as to who was the best person to advise us about the feasibility and cost of converting the line. They told us that an engineer named David Curwen was the best person in England to help us, so we drove down to Baydon, the next village to Aldbourne in the Wiltshire Downs and reputedly the highest village in the county, where we found David building miniature steam locomotives in a small workshop down a rough track near the village. He estimated that conversion would cost around £10,000 which seemed a very large sum at that time but was probably only a fraction of the expense of restoring the existing line to perfect order. I was at once very impressed with David both as an engineer and as a person. I think we took an immediate mutual liking to each other and he proved to be one of the very few intimate friends I made as a result of this railway venture. Our friendship was later cemented when, although I played no part in bringing them together, David married my cousin Barbara Willans.

An outcome of this visit to Wiltshire was that in 1949 David came north and spent a couple of nights with me aboard *Cressy* at Pont Cysyllte while Angela was on holiday in Venice. We got up at first light on the morning after his arrival and, in perfect late summer weather, had a splendid run into Wales in my Alvis. Our object was to catch the morning train back to Towyn from Abergynolwyn, but though we arrived in time and waited patiently in the little station shelter, the train never appeared. As we eventually discovered, *Dolgoch*, the only workable locomotive, had broken her frame, putting an end to the train service for a week or more. So we spent an afternoon exploring the abandoned 'ghost town' of Bryn Eglwys before returning to *Cressy*.

Over the next two years Bill, Jim and I paid several visits to Towyn in the course of which we talked to old Sir Henry Haydn Jones, who had owned both the quarry and the railway since 1911 and was now aged eighty-five, trying in vain to interest him in our project. He intended to keep the railway running so long as he lived, he said, but he was not prepared to spend any money on it. It was abundantly clear that there was nothing further we could do but watch the situation until Sir Haydn died, for it was certain that when he did so his executors would be forced to sell the railway for scrap.

In September 1949, to my surprise, a nostalgic article on the Talyllyn Railway appeared in the *Birmingham Post*. The anonymous writer extolled the beauties of a railway which, he said, was obviously on its last legs and ended with a plea to the government or British Railways to do something about it. This seemed much too good an opportunity to miss, so I replied with a letter in which I said: 'Surely it is a sorry symptom of the decline of individual initiative at the present time that we so often grumble and say: "Why don't they do something about it?" and so seldom pause to consider whether we might not be doing something about it ourselves.' Then, without going into details, I went on to say that a scheme was afoot to ensure the future of the railway and would anyone interested please write to me. I promised to keep them informed of developments, including the date of a possible future meeting in Birmingham. As a result, I received a surprising number of letters which I filed as a possible 'bank' of future members. They would serve precisely the same purpose as my *Narrow Boat* 'fan' letters had done when the IWA was launched.

As it happened, these letters did not lie in the file for very long. But in the meantime, Jim Russell, who was more closely in touch with Birmingham railway enthusiasts than either Bill Trinder or myself, told us that it was their considered opinion that the idea of the conversion of the railway was most unlikely to attract support and that only a plan to preserve the existing railway would prove sufficiently popular. Against my own judgement I allowed myself to be persuaded by this argument, though no one knew better than I did what an immense gamble we were taking. In the event, it would take seven years to re-lay the whole of the old line and not until then could it be said with confidence that the future of the railway was assured.

I was working *Cressy* through one of the locks on the Oxford Canal on my way north to Market Harborough in 1950, when I received verbally the news that Sir Henry Haydn Jones was dead. It was now or never. As soon as we moored that evening at Twyford Wharf, just south of Banbury, I typed a letter to Mr Arthur of Machynlleth, the solicitor to the Haydn Jones estate, outlining our new proposals for the Talyllyn Railway which were: that a society should be formed to preserve the railway; that the executors should allow the railway to be run by this society for a trial period of three years and that the railway company should be administered by a joint board consisting of directors nominated by the society and by the executors. I urged that the executors should come to no irrevocable decision before I had had time to organize a meeting in Birmingham to discuss the formation of such a society. While I was at Market Harborough I received a very satisfactory reply to my letter confirming that no decision would be made pending the outcome of the Birmingham meeting.

Such ready acquiescence was entirely due to the advice given by our friend, Edward Thomas. Having first joined the

Talyllyn Railway in 1897 as a seventeen-year-old assistant clerk to his father, Hugh, who was then manager, Edward Thomas, in effect if not in name, succeeded his father after the railway had been acquired by Sir Henry Haydn Jones. To anticipate, he subsequently became one of the two representatives of the executors on the Board (the other being Sir Haydn's widow), a post which he relinquished owing to advancing years in 1967 having notched up a record seventy years in the service of the railway company. When he died in 1972 at the age of ninety-two I mourned his passing for, where this railway project was concerned, I could have had no more loyal ally. From my first visit with Bill Trinder and Jim Russell in 1948, it became clear to us that, in our efforts to save the railway, Edward Thomas was wholeheartedly on our side. So, when it came to winning over Lady Haydn and her solicitor to what must have seemed to them – as it did to many others – a completely crack-brained idea, his advocacy proved far more effective than any Englishman's could conceivably have been.

The fateful Birmingham meeting was fixed for 11 October 1950 at the Imperial Hotel. I sent a circular letter to all those who had responded to my earlier letter in the *Birmingham Post*; what is more, that paper announced the meeting on its front page, for in 1951 the concept of volunteers preserving and running a railway made news because it was then wholly novel. As a result we had a full house. Bill Trinder chaired the meeting very ably and was supported on the platform by Jim Russell, myself and Edward Thomas. We were surprised and delighted by his response to our suggestion that he should attend, for already Edward Thomas had reached his seventieth year and never left his native Towyn if he could possibly avoid it. Yet he needed no second bidding to make the long journey to Birmingham where his eloquent speech on behalf of the railway undoubtedly influenced the decision to form a Talyllyn Railway Preservation Society, there and then, by inviting volunteers from the floor to join with the 'three musketeers' from Banbury in setting up a committee.

20th September, 1950

Dear ....

TAL-Y-LLYN RAILWAY

As you are no doubt aware, the Tal-y-Llyn Railway is the last surviving independent Statutory Railway Company in Britain. It is also the last of the once numerous independent Welsh narrow gauge lines still carrying passenger traffic. Built in 1865 and retaining its original locomotives and rolling stock, the railway is of great historical interest, is within measurable distance of achieving its centenary and traverses some of the finest scenery in Wales

Owing to the recent death of the owner and Manager of the railway, Sir Haydn Jones, it is extremely unlikely that the railway will re-open for traffic in 1951 unless some practical and financial help is forthcoming. This despite the fact that its popularity with holiday makers is such that demand frequently exceeds present carrying capacity.

It is felt that all who are in any way interested in railways will endorse the view that it would be deplorable if the year 1951 should be marked by the permanent closure of this unique and historic railway. For this reason a meeting has been arranged at which it is hoped to found an organised body which will ensure that the railway shall continue as a going concern. This meeting will be held at the Imperial Hotel, Temple Street, Birmingham at 7-0p.m. on Wednesday, 11th October, 1950. The organisers cordially invite you to this meeting and hope you will make every effort to attend.

Lady Haydn Jones has graciously expressed her willingness to consider any practicable proposals which may be put forward at this meeting, and it is hoped that her legal representative will be present.

Yours Truly,

Original circular letter advising correspondents to attend the meeting at which the first Railway Preservation Society was founded

To cut a long story short, following this Birmingham meeting, Bill Trinder, Pat Garland and myself met Lady Haydn Jones and Edward Thomas in Arthur's office at Machynlleth where an arrangement, very similar to that suggested in my letter to Arthur, was agreed upon. However, one vital addition was suggested by Pat Garland, a Birmingham accountant who acted as Hon. Treasurer to the venture for many years. This was the setting up of a private limited company known as Talyllyn Holdings Ltd, to hold the shares in the Talyllyn Railway Company. But for this device, in order to legalize the new joint administration which I had proposed, it would have been necessary to amend the Talyllyn Railway Act of 1865, a very costly and tedious legal proceeding. Not having a legal mind and knowing nothing of the intricacies of company law, this was a difficulty I had never envisaged. Its ingenious solution meant that the railway could still boast that it operated under its original 1865 Act of Incorporation.

While the Talyllyn Railway had been struggling towards rebirth, its neighbour the Corris Railway had practically disappeared from the face of the earth. In the early spring of 1947, exceptional floods on the Dovey had undermined the piers of the bridge by which the railway crossed that river in order to gain access to Machynlleth station, its point of traffic interchange with the ex-Cambrian. The line had been sold to a local scrap-dealer who soon tore it up, but not before the rolling-stock and the two surviving locomotives had been moved down the valley and over the weakened bridge into Machynlleth station yard. One of these locomotives was No. 3, which I had seen on my first visit to Corris during the war; the other, No. 4, was a standard type built by Kerr Stuart in 1921. This type, known to the works as a 'Tattoo' had become very familiar to me during my apprenticeship with that firm. Because the Corris was of the same uncommon gauge as the Talyllyn, it seemed to me absolutely vital that we should acquire these two locomotives and so solve our motive power problem. Not only were they close at hand but we should thereby avoid the costly task of re-gauging. This was the last job which we, the trio from Banbury, undertook to negotiate before handing over to the committee, two of whom had sportingly agreed to put up the purchase price of the engines provided we could get them for a reasonable figure. There was no time to be lost, for it was remarkable that they had survived the demise of the railway for so long before being sold for scrap. Accompanied by David Curwen we paid a hurried visit of inspection to Machynlleth yard. Partially covered by old wagon sheets and with all the cab spectacles and gauge glasses shattered by vandals, the two locomotives looked very neglected and forlorn. It was clear that they needed considerable repair, particularly No. 4 which looked as though she had been out of use for a long time. Nevertheless, we decided they were well worth having.

The Corris Railway having become the concern of the Western Region, there followed, hard on this inspection, an excursion from Banbury to Swindon Works where we found the engineers responsible so sympathetic that I believe, had they still been representatives of the GWR, they would have given us the locomotives. But now that the company had been nationalized their freedom of action was as cabined and confined as that of civil servants, a state of affairs they obviously deeply resented. However, after some discussion among themselves, they informed us that they had decided they could safely write them off their books at £25 a piece. No matter how bad their condition was, we felt we could not go far wrong at that, so we accepted on the spot and drove back to Banbury in high good humour. Both locomotives are still giving good service and run on the Talyllyn under the names of *Sir Haydn* and *Edward Thomas* respectively.

From all this it will have become clear how I was able to walk out of the last disastrous meeting of the IWA in Birmingham, straight into a meeting of the new committee of the TRPS in Pat Garland's office in Waterloo Street. The idea of this railway venture had first occurred to me in the early days of the IWA when I had no notion of the storm that lay ahead. Even when I had resigned as Hon. Secretary in 1949, Sir Henry Haydn Jones was still alive and, as there was still no indication when the project might mature, it had not entered into my calculations. Not until I was heading for Market Harborough and it had become clear that my association with the IWA was drawing to an end did the Talyllyn Railway scheme, suddenly and providentially, come alive to provide an alternative outlet for my energies just at the very moment when it was most needed. In retrospect, this sequence of events seems almost miraculously providential.

At that meeting of the TRPS committee, someone asked the question: who was going to be in charge of the railway during the critical summer season of 1951? Strangely enough, this was a problem which had never occurred to me. Clearly, at this early stage in the proceedings we could not possibly afford to advertise for a salaried manager. The members of the committee first eyed each other round the table and then every eye finally came to rest on me and I realized that I was the only one present who was what is called a self-employed person with no ties. I nodded, 'Alright', I said, 'I'll do it, provided the Society can make some contribution towards my expenses', whereupon the amount of £30 per month was agreed upon – scarcely a princely sum, but I hoped it would serve to keep the wolf from the door until the autumn when I could resume my writing.

It was little more than eighteen months since I had resigned as Hon. Secretary of the IWA, largely because it was taking up more of my time than I could afford; so on the face of it, it seemed crazy to commit myself to five months of full-time work for a pittance. Crazy from a monetary, materialistic point of view, perhaps, and yet in the circumstances in which I found myself at that time, I could not have made a better move. The IWA débâcle, coinciding as it did with the breakdown of my marriage and the loss of *Cressy*, had left me feeling completely alone and disorientated, and, filled with self-pity. For this disease, some totally absorbing occupation that filled every day from dawn till dusk in an entirely new environment was without doubt the best cure. For me it was the equivalent of the traditional palliative of going out on safari in darkest Africa.

I have written in detail of my experiences during that first crucial 1951 season in my book *Railway Adventure* and it would therefore be superfluous to repeat it here. So those who have not read that book must take my word for it, that from May to the end of September the task of keeping the trains running against every kind of odds, both human and mechanical, totally absorbed all my thought and energy. That the railway staggered through the season successfully was entirely due to the unfailing support and good advice I received from my predecessor, Edward Thomas, plus the labours of a small and dedicated team of friends and members who stood by me loyally throughout the season. These were David Curwen, my cousin Barbara his wife, and a young man named John Snell who had volunteered to work for nothing on the railway after leaving school at Bryanston and before going up to Oxford. David acted as Chief Mechanical Engineer in charge of the running shed and repair shop at Towyn Pendre with John as his assistant while Barbara frequently helped me out at the Wharf terminus. All four of us stayed together in lodgings at Dolgoch, half way up the line, throughout that ever-memorable summer. In addition two volunteer members of the Society, Bill Oliver and 'Maggie' Maguire assisted by other volunteers performed wonders as permanent way men by holding the worn out track together against all the laws of probability.

In addition to this band of stalwarts, we inherited from the old regime the Welsh permanent staff, but in the event they only provided the human problem, the last straw that almost broke the camel's back. When I first arrived they had seemed to me pleasant and willing enough so that I was surprised when Edward Thomas warned me that I would find them: 'Very difficult people, you know, yes indeed!' I reflected gloomily that if he, a fellow Welshman who had known them all their lives, had found them difficult, what hope had I.

What hope, indeed! Within weeks both walked out on me without any warning whatever. David, John and I arrived at Towyn from Dolgoch one morning to find the locomotive that was to haul the morning train cold and without a driver. David Curwen, instead of working in the shop, was compelled to act as driver while he trained his fireman, John Snell, to succeed him.

It later became obvious that these 'difficult people' bitterly resented our new regime and thought that by letting us down without warning they would make the Society's failure certain. But when the reaction of the stubborn Englishmen was merely to close ranks and, by a prodigious feat of improvisation, to carry on as though they had never been, their resentment seemed to know no bounds. One of them, who lived in a cottage beside the railway, made a jolly practice of pouncing, like some old man of the sea, upon new and unsuspecting volunteers who had come down to work on the railway and informing them that I was mad, that my crazy attempt to run a railway which was obviously unsafe was bound to end in disaster, and the sooner they dissociated themselves from the railway and returned whence they had come the better. Looking rather white about the gills, one volunteer turned up at the Wharf station office one evening and reported to me an encounter of this kind. It had been a frightening tirade, he said, so venomous that he feared the man might do the railway some serious mischief. I succeeded in calming him down, told him of Edward Thomas's warning to me, and assured him that no wild talk of that kind was going to prevent the trains from running so long as I was in charge.

In 1951 I was much too fully occupied with practical problems to concern myself with the more unpleasant quirks of human nature, though I was also not unaware of a certain jealousy in the ranks of railway enthusiasts. They were saying in effect: 'Rolt, Rolt, he's a canal man, isn't he? What's he doing muscling in on our pitch and what does he know about railways, anyway?' For the same reason I was also impervious to the final purge of the heretics following the hard-won victory of the IWA establishment. I had intended continuing to pay my IWA subscription even though I had no intention of playing any further active part in the organization, but it was not to be. One day, while I was busy issuing tickets to passengers for the morning train, a letter arrived from the Bloomsbury office of the IWA. This solemnly informed me that by decision of the Council I had been expelled from the Association. I read this hastily, then tossed it aside and went on date-stamping tickets, reflecting that a year ago such a letter would have infuriated me in view of the efforts I had made to get the IWA off the ground. Yet now, so remote and so ludicrous did the whole canal quarrel seem that it had become 'a tale told by an idiot, full of sound and fury, signifying nothing'. I subsequently learned that, with one exception, all the signatories to that heretical manifesto had been similarly excommunicated. The exception was the Earl of Lucan.* Apparently Bloomsbury, inveterately snobbish, could not summon sufficient courage to expel a belted earl, thus creating an anomalous situation which Pat Lucan promptly and honourably remedied by resigning.

My unfortunate experience in the IWA had one definite effect upon the TRPS which was somewhat ironical because,

---

* Pat Lucan was the kindest and most courteous of men who became my friend and one of my most loyal supporters. As Lord Bingham he had joined the IWA in its earliest days and soon joined the committee. Soon afterwards he succeeded to the Earldom. He acquired an old and rather tired looking ex-Grand Union motor boat and with this he became quite the most intrepid of the early IWA 'trail-blazers'. My exploits on the Stratford and Welsh Canals fall into insignificance beside Pat Lucan's epic east-west voyage through the Kennet & Avon culminating in a journey up the Severn estuary from Avonmouth to Sharpness, or his voyage across the Wash from the Nene to the Great Ouse. It must be said, however, that whereas *Cressy* was a floating home with all our precious possessions on board, *Hesperus*, as she was ominously called, was a holiday boat and was not even converted. While Pat and his wife occupied the motor cabin, their family camped under canvas in the hold. When under way they looked the scruffiest crew imaginable.

as a direct result of it, as the years went by and I eventually became Chairman of the Railway Company and the Preservation Society, I found myself fettered by my own rules. It came about in this way. After that historic meeting in Birmingham when it had been decided to form the TRPS, I had hurried home and, there and then, had drafted out a publicity leaflet and a set of Rules and Constitution for the Society for approval at the first meeting of the newly formed committee – or council as it was later called. As I did so, I recalled wryly that it was only five years since I had undertaken precisely the same job for the nascent IWA. With this very much in mind, I devoted much thought to the Rules and Constitution of this latest venture in order to ensure that no single individual cock could ever succeed in imposing his will on the organization and so make the Talyllyn Railway his private dunghill. I produced a democratic document which I believed to be proof against such 'take-overs' and so it has proved. Of the many similar preservation societies which have since sprung up, the TRPS remains to this day by far the most democratic. The Society really does own and run the railway unlike many others which are little more than supporters' clubs with, at best, token minority representation on the managing body of the railway.

But as the railway and society flourished and grew over the years and the amount of business increased, so the defects of this democratic system I had devised became the more apparent. In order to satisfy Society members that their wishes were truly represented, we had to have a huge and unwieldy council and a plethora of sub-committees. As a result, decision-making became exasperatingly slow and difficult. Even so, when a decision was eventually reached, it was often bitterly contested by the membership who would claim that the council were out of touch and unrepresentative. Sometimes, things would reach such a farcical pitch that the impossible course of holding a plebiscite of the whole membership seemed the only way of reaching an acceptable decision. When I became Chairman I frequently used to chafe against this slow and infinitely laborious method of policy-making. Too often it meant that the decision, when at last it was reached, was but an emasculated version of the original proposition. Representing the lowest, rather than the highest common denominator of the intelligence of all those present, it simply proved the truth of the old saying that a camel is a horse designed by a committee. So, ironically, I was ulti-mately hoist with my own petard as colleagues like Pat Garland and Pat Whitehouse, the Hon. Secretary, who had joined the venture at its beginning, jokingly pointed out. When I grew impatient of delay they would remind me that I had brought such a state of affairs upon myself since I had been the chief architect of the Constitution, including the manner in which the Society controlled the Railway Company.

Yet, when I look back on my eighteen years of active association with the Talyllyn Railway, despite the fact that they yielded more frustration and pain than reward where I was concerned, I would not have changed the set-up even if I could. For it seems to me that my experience of these two organizations, the IWA and the TRPS, typifies in microcosm the perennial, unsolved dilemma that besets all human government. Impatient of the inefficiencies, the compromises and delays inseparable from the cumbersome democratic machine, there is an understandable tendency to streamline and simplify that machine in an attempt to make its action speedier. The logical end of this road is to leave decision-making to some super-man regardless of the fact that, according to the inexorable law that absolute power corrupts absolutely, even the wisest of men in such circumstances soon begins to display symptoms of paranoia or megalomania.

In order to draw a moral, I have been anticipating the future and must now return to the events of 1951. It was a most significant year in my life. It had begun with the final dissolution of the way of life I had so long dreamed about and finally achieved just before the war; it ended in what was to prove to be the start of a new life immediately after the summer season on the Talyllyn Railway was over.

Whereas under the old regime trains had only run on three days of the week, we had succeeded, against all the laws of probability, in maintaining a five-days-a-week service from the beginning of June to the end of September. But it had all been pretty exhausting, and I heaved a mighty sigh of relief when the last train of the year appeared under the bridge and ground safely to a standstill at the Towyn terminus. I must say, too, that I felt very glad to be leaving Towyn behind me when, a few days later, I headed eastwards up the familiar valley through the mountains in my old 12/50 Alvis; my destination was Shrewsbury station where I had arranged to meet Sonia South off a train due in from Birmingham in the late afternoon.

2
Beginning a
New Life

Sonia South had been among the first to join the IWA and her unique position soon earned her a place on the committee. She had been a member of that early deputation, led by A.P. Herbert, which had visited the Minister of Transport during the bitter January of 1947. In my – largely unsuccessful – campaign to improve conditions for the working boaters she became my right hand, for the simple reason that she had first hand knowledge of those conditions such as no one else possessed outside the ranks of those who had been born in a boat cabin and who could seldom speak for themselves. I had thus grown to know Sonia well during my last IWA years and soon came to realize that, though she was highly intelligent and much better read than I was, she was by no means the rather frightening, left-wing blue-stocking I had supposed her to be at first sight in the foyer of that cinema in Birmingham towards the end of the war.

Sonia was an orphan. She had never known her father, while her mother had died just before the war in tragic circumstances which had affected her outlook on life profoundly. Trained for the stage by Michel St Denis at his London Theatre Studio, she had only a brief theatrical career – the London Village Players, the Players' Theatre, OUDS Shakespearean productions under the direction of Neville Coghill – before the war intervened. Lodging with an aunt in London, she had then got a job as an Aeronautical Inspection

Directorate inspector at the Hoover factory which was manufacturing components for the aircraft industry. This was her first experience of what life inside a modern factory was like and she hated it so much that she soon fled, as I had done from Rolls Royce, joining the ranks of the 'idle women' under the command of Kit Gayford, crewing pairs of Grand Union boats between London and Birmingham. Unlike me, therefore, her experience of canals and canal boaters was gained the hard way. Indeed, as I subsequently learned from her and from other members of that select sisterhood, *Cressy* and her bath (which they glimpsed through a window as they chugged past) became a fabled dream of luxury, to be regarded with that mixture of envy and scorn such as the muscled driver of the huge 'artic' reserves for the owner of the Rolls Royce as it sweeps silently past him on the motorway. It certainly did not escape us that by these amateur Amazons of the cut we were regarded as mere drones. And yet, despite the fact that her initiation was so much more rugged than mine, the canals and their nomadic population had the same fascination for her as for me. She certainly proved this, for whereas I was content to dabble my feet in the shallow margins of the canal, she had plunged straight into the deepest part of the channel by marrying a boater who could neither read nor write. By so doing she moved on from the ranks of the 'idle women' into the class of the real professionals. The cabin of the butty boat *Warwick**, drawn by the motor *Cairo*, became her home from then on. She and her husband worked this pair of boats two-handed between London and Birmingham or the Coventry coalfield, and, as anyone who has ever been on a canal even

---

* When *Warwick* had to be docked at Braunston her place was temporarily taken by *Sunny Valley*, the boat which was renamed and repainted for the Ealing film. At the time Barbara Jones painted the splendid picture which appears as a frontispiece to my book, *Inland Waterways of England*, Sonia was occupying *Sunny Valley* and the pot plant which appears beside the cabin chimney was hers. Boaters do not normally go in for pot plants!

for a brief holiday will appreciate, working a pair of boats two-handed on such a trip as this was the toughest possible form of professional boating. Not only was it extremely hard work, but it was also dangerous because keeping pace with more adequately-manned pairs (which were in the majority) involved taking unwarrantable risks at the locks. In these circumstances it is no wonder that the cabin on *Cairo* was always available to guests, particularly those with canal experience, and both Angela and I successively made a trip with them to experience at first hand what real boating involved. With such a third hand to lock-wheel (set the locks in advance) and generally help with the locks, most of the hazards and stress of working two-handed were obviated.

From this it will be understood why, during the first years of the IWA, Sonia's knowledge and experience was so uniquely valuable to anyone as concerned as I was to improve conditions for the working boaters. However, she, like me, was expelled as a heretic from the Association. The last canal assignment we undertook together before I left narrow canals for narrow rails was to arrange a meeting with some prominent official in the Transport & General Workers Union in Birmingham, whose name I now forget. Most of the boaters were members of the TGWU and we both felt that the union ought to be on our side in our efforts to improve working conditions on the canals so as to enable the boaters to earn a better livelihood. Sonia maintained that the union failed to help because its officials were completely out of touch with, and therefore did not understand, the peculiar working conditions obtaining on the waterways. She thought that this state of affairs might be remedied if the union could be persuaded to form a special 'Inland Waterways Branch' to deal with the boaters' problems. This was the reason for our meeting in Birmingham. Sonia, less disillusioned about trade unions than I, was optimistic but, alas, our mission was as completely abortive as I had feared it might be. I was left wondering why the TGWU had the nerve to go on collecting dues from impoverished boaters when this official made it abundantly clear to us that his organization just did not want to know about their problems. So far as he was concerned the canal community was an anachronism and, like the gipsy community, the sooner it could be tidied away the better. The fact was, of course, that the union was geared to cope with the never-ending demands of dissatisfied wage-earners for more money for less work; the needs of such a strongly individualistic community as the canal boaters were something entirely alien to its experience.

After this frustrating interview was over we had tea together in some squalid Birmingham café before we parted. It was during this simple meal that I looked up from my plate to find Sonia regarding me with the deepest compassion and tenderness. Although in all my thirty-nine years, no woman had looked at me in quite that way before, there could be no mistaking the meaning of that glance. I felt unworthy and deeply abashed. As I learned subsequently, she had only recently admitted this disturbing truth to herself; disturbing because she had determined, as a result of a bitter example, never to give all the heart for love. In other words, in any relationship with the opposite sex she had determined that her will should remain in control of events and that she would never permit herself to be swept away on a tide of emotion.

At the time this meeting took place I was still living on *Cressy* although it had already become clear that my marriage was breaking up and that *Cressy*'s days were numbered. In such a state of disorientation, this sudden and totally unexpected discovery had an effect on me which I can only liken to the sensation of one who comes out of a bitter-cold night into the comfort and warmth of a fire. Yet, at the same time, I found myself confronting a deeply bewildering and disturbing situation. So much so that I fear Sonia could read no answering comfort in my eyes but only trouble and dismay. It was in this unsatisfactory and turbulent state of mind, and with no more said, that we went our separate ways, she to New Street station, I to Snow Hill to return to *Cressy*.

I was alone on my boat at the time, so I had ample opportunity for self-questioning in an attempt to reach the right answer to what for me was an agonizing problem, so many were the pros and cons. Where Sonia and myself were concerned I now realized with hindsight that during our purely platonic association within the IWA, we had been totally unaware of the fact that, to coin a metaphor, the voltage between our two psychical poles had been steadily rising until, that evening in Birmingham, the current had suddenly sparked across with the alarming suddenness of a lightning flash out of a clear blue sky, disconcerting us both. Such an experience had never happened to either of us before, and for my part I questioned whether it was the real thing or whether it was merely an infatuation which was liable to end as suddenly as it had begun. Since I was experiencing the agonies of a broken marriage at the time, the prospect that the whole thing might happen all over again was something I could not bring myself to contemplate. There was also the thought that there were not two but four people involved in this dilemma and that to jeopardize the happiness of our respective partners for the sake of a mere infatuation would be unthinkable. Moreover, I was only too well aware that infatuation – call it the illusion of love if you like – is a chimera which is particularly prone to lead astray people in our situation. Precisely because they recognize each other as fellow victims of failed marriages, both are at once desperately seeking, and eager to give, solace.

I was not so worried about my marriage from this point of view because Angela had already made it clear by word and action that our relationship was drawing to a close. What caused Sonia and myself so much distress was the future of her husband, that simple, blameless man who could neither read nor write. She had willed their marriage in fulfilment of a consciously conceived romantic theory of which he had been the victim. This decision she had taken against the advice of all her friends, new and old, who could see nothing but disaster ahead for a marriage between two people having such a vast disparity of intellect and temperament. The boaters, too, had shaken their heads over the marriage but for a different reason. Naturally they could not evaluate Sonia's stature as a person although she was very popular with them, but they knew her as someone 'off the bank', as they termed it, and in their long experience mixed marriages between boaters and girls off the bank only very rarely proved lasting. Either the woman left the man, or the man concerned left the canals and, to please his wife, took a job ashore. The reason for this was very simple; no girl off the land could stand the conditions of life afloat; the close confines of a narrow boat cabin, the long hours of physical toil in every kind of weather which had to go on even when she was in an advanced state of pregnancy. To do this the boaters said, you had to be born in a boat cabin; only then did the work seem second nature which meant that you were able to appreciate its undoubted compensations including the sense of belonging to a close-knit community whose bonds were strengthened by shared rigour and stubborn independence. As one from 'off the bank', Sonia had performed manfully (literally), but now at last she had come to realize that her friends on the land and on the canal had both been right after all. She dared not contemplate the psychological and physical stresses and strains to which she would be subjected if she attempted to prolong her boating life much longer. This despite the fact that she had had no children. These made the burden of most boaters' wives very much heavier until they were old enough to become active members of the crew. But this knowledge caused her to grieve over the future of her husband who was immensely proud of her and who, if she left him, would become the innocent victim of an experiment in living that she had deliberately willed.

Yet the knowledge that she would have had to leave her husband, whether or not I had ever swum into her ken, could not lighten my load of guilt. For those contemplating such a step, the 'innocent party' is always a problem, particularly if he or she is a likeable person who has done no wrong to the other partner. In my case, however, it was more than ordinarily difficult, in fact the situation must have been almost unique. Few people can appreciate what a handicap illiteracy is in the modern world. When it came to knowledge of the natural world based on acute powers of observation exercised on many slow journeys, the canal boaters far surpassed modern urban man; yet on the other hand, Sonia's husband had great difficulty in finding his way across London by himself, owing to his inability to read destination boards and the multiplicity of direction signs. Where I was concerned, it was like a strong man taking unfair advantage of one seriously handicapped; I felt as one who had eaten of the Tree of Knowledge and was contemplating mortal injury to another who still walked the Garden in a state of innocence. This may sound a gross exaggeration, but it is the nearest I can get to expressing my feeling at that time. On top of this, I felt it must appear that I was dealing an underhand blow at that unique community I had so long admired. Further – though this I minded less – there was the thought that it must seem to my late associates in the IWA that my close collaboration with Sonia was simply a cover for a prolonged seduction aimed to entice a boater's wife away from him under pretence of helping his fellows.

Throughout the long summer of 1951 Sonia and I never met – we were far too fully occupied – though we exchanged long letters almost daily in which we debated the doubts and the problems which I have mentioned. Her letters were hastily scribbled in snatched moments of leisure in the small cabin of *Warwick* and subsequently posted at strategic points on the canal that I knew only too well; at Sutton Stop, Sampson Road, Warwick Two, Buckby, 'Maffers', Bulls Bridge or Limehouse Dock. To these I replied at length, writing by candlelight at night in the privacy of my bedroom at Dolgoch; candlelit because the house was lit by a small hydro-electric plant powered by a mountain stream. In summer the water supply to this plant ran out about 10.30 p.m., the light slowly fading away like some stage twilight effect. In September a letter arrived from Sonia telling me that, come what might, she had finally determined to leave the boats and to lodge with friends who lived in Braunston until she could decide what next to do. Physically, this would be a simple move because her personal possessions were very few – necessarily so. To this I replied with the question as to whether it would be possible for us to stay together for a week on neutral territory after the Talyllyn Railway season ended as this might surely help us to decide upon the future. Such vital questions could not be settled by correspondence and to this she agreed.

I cogitated long and earnestly, poring over maps, to decide where this trysting place should be. Llanthony I at once ruled out – it was too filled with old associations; there I would be continually reminded of times past. No, it must be somewhere entirely new to us both, an empty pitcher waiting to be filled with our own memories. After a great deal of thought I had decided upon the Anchor Inn which stands high on the Kerry Hills between Clun and Newtown on the westernmost extremity of the Shropshire March. In later years I often drove past this lonely inn as it lay on one of my alternative routes between Gloucestershire and Towyn, but in 1951 I had never set eyes on it so it was a shot in the dark. In reply to my letter of inquiry, Mrs Phoebe Moody, the mistress of the Anchor, wrote that she would be delighted to put us up for a week in early October, so this was how I came to be heading west towards Shrewsbury from Towyn on this fine autumn day.

Although Sonia's train arrived punctually at Shrewsbury in the late afternoon, the shadows were beginning to lengthen as we drove south down the Welsh border through that eerie lead-mining district of the Stiperstones and so on by Bishops Castle to Clun. There we turned westwards to follow the valley of the little Clun river across Offa's Dike until, climbing steadily, we came to the Anchor. By the time we reached the inn it was almost dark. We found that we were the only guests and that Mrs Moody had prepared for us a delicious dinner of jugged hare which we ate before the cheerful fire in the small dining room.

The Anchor Inn lies athwart the junction of the roads from Clun and Beguildy to Newtown. It presents only its northern gable end at first floor level to the Clun road, thus appearing to crouch beside that road in so insignificant a fashion that a traveller from England could hurry past without being aware that there was an inn there. It came into existence in the days when cattle in great number were exported from Wales to England 'on the hoof', for it stands upon what was once one of the great trunk drove roads between the two countries. Although the inn is in Shropshire, it is almost within a stone's throw of the Welsh border with the effect that it attracts many a thirsty Welshman on a Sunday. Why it was ever called the Anchor is unknown. Anything further removed from any maritime associations than the top of the Kerry Hills it would be difficult to find. Perhaps the name was adopted to suggest a safe harbour, for the inn certainly becomes a place of refuge amid these desolate hills in winter, especially when, as frequently happens, snowdrifts block the border roads. Seen from the lower, Beguildy, road it is apparent that the Anchor is much larger than it appears from other vantages. Extending round three sides of a courtyard, at the time of our visit it was equipped to withstand a long siege with ample covered stores of fuel, and a general store and grocery whose well-stocked shelves seemed primarily intended to meet the emergency needs of the inn itself rather than those of the few scattered farms in the vicinity.

That evening drive from Shrewsbury to the Anchor marked the beginning of the most memorable week of my life. I cannot explain precisely why this was so because there are times when even the most honest autobiographer must be reticent. I will only say that any lingering suspicion I might have harboured, that ours might be merely a brief infatuation, very soon blew away and by the end of the week I had become convinced that the foundations of a true and lasting relationship had been laid. I also discovered for the first time how such a relationship can miraculously sharpen one's five senses and so cause the magical doors of perception to open. Those who insist upon regarding the lover with sympathy or indulgence as one temporarily besotted, or as suffering from an acute mental illness whose symptoms are delusions and hallucinations are, in my view, mistaken. Why should people whose senses are trammelled by space and time into a grey prison belittle those who, temporarily at least, are privileged to perceive in all its rich colour, brilliance, and beauty, the transfigured world that exists in an eternal now beyond such arbitary confines? It is this world that children and mystics can see and it has been claimed that modern synthesized drugs have made it accessible to all. Although I have never tried them, I do not believe in such 'instant mysticism' drugs any more than I believe that a medium has the power to make the dead speak. For I am told that a uniquely significant thing about the strange and glittering world conjured up by drugs is its utter lack of humanity. It is essentially a world of things, colours and essences in which people do not exist, the creation of some supreme egotist designed to charm the self alone. This is not the world which the child, the mystic and the lover share; the visionary landscapes that Blake or Palmer depict are filled with life, be it human or superhuman. In Thomas Traherne's superb evocation of the child's timeless vision of the world where 'all things abided eternally as they were in their proper places', it was not only the green trees, when first seen, that transported and ravished him but the people also. 'I knew not', he says, 'that they were born or should die.'

So it was, certainly for me and I believe for us both, during that week. The weather was fine and our routine simple. Each day, with one exception, we set out with our packets of sandwiches to walk over the high, bare hills. Although the Kerry Hills afford some splendid prospects looking westward over Wales, they do not stand comparison with the landscape splendours of the Black Mountains further to the south. The Kerrys lack the superb symmetry and shape of the Black Mountains; they are a mere inchoate upheaval of the earth, most of which has become enclosed sheep walk while the highest, unenclosed portion is not true moorland but a bare expanse of bent grass. The Kerrys have also suffered severely from that inhuman monster the Forestry Commission.* Yet we asked no more; it was for us an enchanted landscape from which we were loth to retreat as dusk fell despite the lure of a warm fire and Mrs Phoebe Moody's superlative cooking. Only two incidents on these walks come to mind. One was the discovery of a grassy bank starred with the purple and gold blossoms of late flowering wild pansy, a flower which, although it is not described as rare, for some reason I had not seen before although I had walked much on the high pastures and waste places which are its natural habitat. The other memorable occasion was when we saw, nestling in a high fold of the hills far from any road, a small and apparently ruinous shepherd's or crofter's stone-built cottage. To anyone familiar with such remote districts the sad evidence of rural de-population and the decline of subsistence farming is a commonplace, but in this case our assumption was false. Whenever I pass such an empty or ruinous house curiosity gets the better of me, but as we were approaching this one we were startled to hear sounds of movement within accompanied by an unmistakable male cough. We stole silently away over the soft turf without inquiring further, leaving the identity of the occupier forever a mystery. I was reminded of Mr Tod's house at the top of Bull Banks or the cottage of the solitary of Llanbedr which Francis Kilvert describes so graphically in his diary.

The one exception to this daily walk was when we decided to drive down to Clun one morning, having taken a liking to the little town when we had passed through it on arrival. It seemed typical of that enchanted week that, all unknowing, we should have picked on the day of Clun's annual carnival. It might have been staged for our especial benefit; for we arrived

---

* Along the road to Newtown a plantation had just been clear felled. This had been so close planted that there was no ground cover beneath the trees with the inevitable result that the rain had already begun to leach the precious top soil away down the steep slope. The road in places was covered with silt that looked like brown drifts of snow, eloquent evidence of man's folly.

just as the procession was forming. We watched it pass over the ancient river bridge and up the short, steep pitch into the town. To the jaundiced eye, for all I know, it may have looked pretty tatty, but for us all the participants resembled the people described by Traherne: '. . . young men glittering and sparkling angels, and maids strange seraphic pieces of life and beauty.'

Our week together ended when I drove Sonia to the Low Level station at Wolverhampton, travelling through Much Wenlock and Ironbridge, and having done so, headed the Alvis southwards towards my home in Gloucestershire. The big question was, what now? Sonia was bound for her friends at Braunston where she was welcome to a bed whenever she needed it. As for myself, it looked as though I should be staying with my mother at Stanley Pontlarge for an indefinite period. There could be no question of our setting up house together even in the most modest fashion because we simply could not afford it. In April, before I went down to Towyn, my bank balance had looked fairly healthy but it had been plummeting downward ever since and, what was worse, there was no best-seller in the pipe-line to reverse this situation. Sonia, now that she had left the boats, had no income whatever.

It was my friend Melville Russell-Cooke who, bless her, rescued us from this dilemma. She and my cousin David, the painter, were going to spend the winter at Kilsalla, her house on the coast of County Mayo, near Westport. Would we, she asked, like to keep her house at Leafield warm while they were away? More than this, she made it clear that she had no objection to our using her house for that dreary charade that was then necessary to provide the required evidence for divorce. On the strength of this, one of my old VSCC friends nobly volunteered to play the part of witness and was invited down to Oxfordshire for the weekend, while I drove over to Braunston and collected Sonia.

Although it may sound a gross abuse of hospitality, that winter we spent together at Leafield turned out to be a strange, dream-like, and not by any means wholly pleasurable period in our lives. Not only did we have to learn to live with each other and to make the many small adjustments which this implies; not only did we both suffer acute pangs of remorse on account of our previous partners, but we had to act out these exacting parts on a stage that was completely foreign to us. From the cramped confines of a boat cabin and the austerity of my Welsh farm bedroom with its horse-hair mattress and uncertain light, we had suddenly been dropped, like a couple of poor church mice, into the lap of luxury. This world of central heating and constant hot water where even the bathroom had a fitted carpet was something outside our experience. Moreover, everything in that house reflected Mel's unerring good taste, and in this respect she reminded me of Anna whom I had known before the war. Furniture, china and glass all delighted the eye and the touch, while on the walls hung valuable pictures; here and there a sombre, stormy landscape by Vlaminck, a strikingly sinister portrait by the Australian artist, Sidney Nolan, who had then still to make his reputation; over the fireplace a small but exquisite Jack Yeats showing a train on the West Clare line running along the shore of the Shannon estuary between Kilrush and Kilkee at dusk. So alien were these trappings of what the media are pleased to call 'gracious living' that we felt as though we had suddenly been transported to another planet. Past struggles, Sonia with the recalcitrant locks and the mud banks of a badly maintained canal, and I with the manifold ills of a worn out railway, seemed to have been relegated to a region of remote fantasy. Only my ancient Alvis, slumbering in the unaccustomed luxury of the garage next door and incontinently dropping gobbets of black oil upon its pristine floor, served to remind us of the world we had so lately left. We went on shopping expeditions to Witney and, more rarely, to Oxford; we walked in the forest of Wychwood on a bitter, misty day in the dead of winter when all the world was rimed with frost, and in the evenings or in bad weather I tried to make up for time lost during the summer by writing a book which, in the event, was not conspicuously successful.

It was during this weird interregnum at Leafield that I was asked by the committee of the TRPS whether I would be prepared to take charge of the Talyllyn Railway again during the coming 1952 summer season. I considered this invitation long and carefully, not only on financial grounds but also because I knew I should no longer have the skilled and unfailingly willing and cheerful support of David Curwen in the loco shed and repair shop at Pendre. In association with a financial partner, David had bought himself a small general engineering business in Devizes and had told me he could not come to Towyn again. It was not that I doubted my ability to keep the locomotives steaming. No self-respecting Stuart apprentice could possibly admit to such a doubt. It was a simple matter of geography. I could not be in two places at once. From my experience last summer I knew that it would be quite impossible for me to be 'shedmaster' at Pendre and at the same time look after the passenger side of things by issuing tickets at Towyn Wharf station and acting as guard on the trains when, as often happened, no suitable volunteer offered himself for this duty. So far as I could see the railway would only become workable if Sonia was prepared to take charge at Wharf, leaving me free to keep mechanical matters under control at Pendre. This, Sonia was perfectly prepared to do, so it seemed an ideal and – from the point of view of the railway – most economical solution to the staff problem, always provided the puritanical Welsh made no objection to the CME and the Traffic Manager 'living in sin', for there was no prospect of our respective divorces being made absolute by the summer. Strangely enough, although this did prove a stumbling block, the objection came from certain English members of the TRPS committee and not from the Welsh. For many weeks this question made it very doubtful whether or not we should go to Towyn at all, though if we had not I do not know what would have become of the railway because the TRPS was then in no financial position to advertise the posts of two senior staff and pay them the rate for the job.

In 1951, the prospects for a successful season were very nearly ruined when, at the eleventh hour, the TRPS committee got cold feet and forbade me to re-open the line throughout to traffic despite the fact that I had already advertised the service. Then it had been Edward Thomas who had saved the day by remarking: 'If I had been told by Lady Haydn to run the railway this season, I should have done so without any of your assistance.' This forthright rejoinder instilled some Dutch courage into the doubters and I was given the signal to go ahead. Now, for the second time this indefatigable little Welshman proved himself my stout ally, although I like to think that it was the future of the Talyllyn Railway that was uppermost in his mind. It was the occasion of a Board meeting at Towyn at which both he and Lady Haydn were present. It was getting perilously near the start of summer services on the railway, but the Society representatives were still earnestly debating our scandalous situation until Edward Thomas, as he afterwards told me, spoke up saying that he thought the proposed staffing arrangement was an excellent one and that our private lives were nothing whatever to do with the Railway Company. Faced with such a forthright pronouncement from an elderly chapel-going Welshman, his fellow directors capitulated there and then and, without more ado, Sonia and I found ourselves in charge at Wharf and Pendre stations respectively. For reasons of economy we did not stay in digs as I had done the previous season but hired a caravan and obtained permission to park it in a field at Dolgoch. Here we lived pretty well except that Sonia found shopping for food difficult owing to sheer lack of time. We rarely found time even to speak to each other during the five working days except when I called for her at the Wharf station to take her out for a hurried lunch at a small café in the town.

Those who want to read a full account of this 1952 summer season on the railway will find it in the last chapter of *Railway Adventure*. After so long a spell of boating on the canals, it must have been a strange experience for Sonia suddenly to find herself issuing tickets and acting the part of a passenger guard on a train. The latter was rather a unique role for, unlike all other passenger brake-vans, that on the Talyllyn was equipped with a minute ticket office from which tickets were issued at all intermediate stations. To withdraw the right ticket, date stamp it and deal with change in a dark little cubby-hole, perhaps while the train was in motion, causing the van to rock and plunge like a ship in a seaway, called for considerable presence of mind combined with sheer physical agility. Yet I was able to spend most of my time in the little loco shed and workshop at Pendre, secure in the knowledge that the traffic department was in capable hands.

A great deal had been done on the railway since the previous winter to make my life easier. The track layout at the Wharf terminus had been re-designed in a way that made working much safer.* A private telephone line had been installed between the Wharf and Pendre which meant that, in the event of difficulty or emergency, Sonia and I could now communicate with each other. No longer was it necessary to drive pell-mell through the streets of Towyn with howling tyres or, failing a car, send a volunteer hot-foot along the track as David and I had had to do in the past. John Alcock, Chairman of Hunslets of Leeds, the locomotive builders who had taken over Kerr Stuart's goodwill and manufacturing rights in 1931, had most generously undertaken to overhaul the ex-Corris Kerr Stuart locomotive No. 4 at his works and deliver it back in time for the start of the season. This meant that I no longer had to rely upon one 86-year-old-locomotive (*Dolgoch*) to maintain the service. Yet in spite of these improvements, there

---

* There was no means of running the engine round its train in 1951. Instead, the only means of getting the engine to the head of the train was as follows: the engine propelled the stock up the incline out of the station where the latter was then held on the brakes while the locomotive retired into a siding. Then the train was allowed to run back by gravity into the platform road. If no one was on hand to apply the guard's brake at the right moment the entire train would have leapt over the end of the Wharf to block British Rail's Cambrian Coast Line.

were still many unexpected vicissitudes to cope with and in one respect – the state of the permanent way – my anxieties were greater than in the previous season. For the need to run more trains in order to earn more revenue for rehabilitation was taking more out of the track in terms of wear and tear than we could possibly put into it. By a superhuman effort we had managed to re-lay so far approximately half-a-mile of track, leaving over five and a half miles in a worse state than ever before despite crude 'first-aid' cobbling measures. This appalling track was racking the locomotives and stock to pieces and there was a constant and growing risk of derailment. Derailments, in fact, did occur during both seasons though fortunately they caused no serious injury, human or mechanical. Yet it was only too clear that we were fighting a losing battle against wear and tear and for the life of me I could not see how this vicious circle was ever to be broken. It called for a massive re-laying programme which was quite beyond the Society's resources.

Despite the hazards of an appalling track, we won through once again, more by luck than judgement, to the end of the summer season on 30 September, by which time the number of passenger journeys stood at 22,866, an increase of 7,238 over the previous year.* But despite this successful result and the fact that at one stage we had seriously thought of finding a house near the railway, we finally decided for various reasons, notably the financial one, that I should announce forthwith that I was giving up the job of Railway Manager so as to allow the Society the maximum of time to find a successor. I remained a member of the committee and acquired the honorary title of 'Superintendent of the Line'.

As in the previous year, the end of the season was marked by the Annual General Meeting of the Society at Towyn. In

---

* When these figures are compared with that of 5,235 passenger journeys for 1950, the last year of the old regime, the reason for the increased wear and tear can be better appreciated. It is also enlightening to compare these figures with that of the 170,690 passenger journeys for 1972.

1951 it had struck me that this occasion had fallen pretty flat. The platform party seemed to be so busy congratulating each other on the conclusion of a successful season that they had not spared a thought for, or even a cursory mention of, those who had born the burden and heat of the day. In this I was not thinking of myself but of my friend David Curwen. Knowing as I did then that it was only due to the almost miraculous feats of mechanical improvisation he had performed at Pendre which had kept the trains moving, I thought it disgraceful when his name did not receive a mention from those who, at the beginning of the season, had doubted whether the railway should be re-opened at all. So I was determined that this AGM weekend should not fall flat where we were concerned; at least we would make it the occasion for a little private celebration, so I invited down Hugh and Gunde Griffith and my friend John Morley, of pre-war Vintage Sports Car Club days, who had presented the railway with two of his firm's electric ballast tampers. They stayed at the Tyn y Cornel hotel beside Talyllyn Lake, where we joined them. By these participants, this occasion has gone down in history as the 'lost weekend'. At one stage in the proceedings I am told that Hugh and I were to be seen in a stationary boat in the middle of the lake, each rowing hard in opposite directions and both singing lustily some traditional Welsh air, though not using the orthodox words.

We stayed on for a week or so in our caravan at Dolgoch, partly to recover from the party and partly to explore the area which we had not the time to do during the season. We travelled on the Snowdon Mountain Railway, visited the Dinorwic slate quarries and the Gwynffynydd gold mine. Visiting the latter was a very strange experience. The gold mine is in a remote situation in a deep and narrow valley near the headwaters of the river Mawddach some hundreds of feet below the road from Dolgelly to Trwsfynydd. When I stopped and switched off my engine at the head of the rough track that follows the floor of the valley towards the mine, silence seemed to fall like a heavy blanket. This was broken by the barking of a dog and presently a man emerged from a solitary cottage that we had assumed to be empty and approached the car. 'Have you been sent by Mr Roberts?' he inquired eagerly, and when I shook my head he was visibly downcast. He then explained that the mine was on the point of re-opening; it only awaited the arrival of a particular part which the mysterious Mr Roberts had ordered from America before work would be in full swing again. As I had done my homework and knew that the mine had lain derelict since 1929, I must have looked a little sceptical for he waved his arm in a dramatic gesture towards the mountain ahead, declaiming passionately: 'I can take you in there and show you visible gold'. He lowered his voice and repeated the words 'visible gold' with extraordinary emphasis and awe as though he were describing some holy presence made manifest. It was obvious to us both that the man's wits were crazed and I pondered why it was that a near-useless metal should have been capable of wielding such power over the minds of men since the beginning of time. After all, but for gold-lust there might have been no Talyllyn Railway. We shook off our crazy friend somehow and walked past the burnt out ruins of the ore-crushing mill up to the mouth of the adit. Beside it stood the old Dolgelly lock-up which had been rebuilt up here to serve as a strong room for the gold. We noticed the recent footprints left on the muddy floor of the adit, presumably by those hypnotized by the prospect of 'visible gold'. The massive iron door of the gaol was bolted and barred, but someone under the influence of the same lure had actually quarried a hole through its immensely thick wall, presumably in the fond belief that some gold might have been left behind when the mine closed.

By mid-October our hired caravan at Dolgoch was becoming distinctly chilly, especially as the sun only cleared the rim of the mountain for a couple of hours either side of noon. Soon Dolgoch would lose the sun altogether. So we returned the caravan to its owner and became nomads again, poorer than when we had come down to Wales in the spring. This time it was an aunt of Sonia's who came to our rescue. A sterling character she had acted *in loco parentis* towards Sonia since the death of her mother and now she invited us to stay over the winter in her house at Roehampton. It was here, in January 1953, that our elder son Richard first saw the light.

It was during this winter in London that the President of the TRPS, David Northesk, and I were between us able to solve the problem of the rapidly deteriorating permanent way. I discussed this with David, explaining that only massive aid could save the day, and he had the brilliant idea that a contingent of TA Royal Engineers from Longmoor might come down to Towyn and re-lay track for us as a training exercise. An ex-Guardsman himself, David knew all the right doors to knock on, but he wanted me beside him to explain the position in some detail and to emphasize just how vital to the railway's future the job was. I remember talking long and earnestly to some high-up in the War Office, but this was the first time I had ever tiptoed timidly along the so-called 'corridors of power' and I was somewhat bewildered by the ramifications of this strange old-boy network. However, our ploy was successful and it was agreed that a Longmoor detachment would visit the railway next summer although, owing to a most absurd hitch, this very nearly failed to come about. The man responsible for this hitch was none other than Vic Feather, that doughty champion of the trade-union movement. How he got to hear of our scheme I do not know; but like some Don Quixote clad in rusty nineteenth-century armour, he came thundering down upon our pathetic little Talyllyn windmill shouting: 'Unfair to railway workers'. But soon the forces of reaction, led by David Northesk, became locked in combat and eventually Vic Feather and his TUC cohorts beat a retreat. Perhaps it dawned upon them that they were making themselves more than usually ridiculous.

TA contingents from Longmoor paid three visits to the Talyllyn Railway: in the summer of 1953, during the winter of 1953/54 and again during the 1954 summer season. Unfortunately they could not completely re-lay the line because we could not afford enough replacement rail at that time, but most of the trouble and danger was due, not to the fact that the rails were badly worn, but that all the sleepers were rotten so that there was virtually nothing to hold the rails to gauge but the thick grass that had spread itself all over the formation. We were able to provide plenty of sleepers which we bought second-hand from British Railways and then sawed in half so that one sleeper made two for the narrow gauge. At the loss of some revenue in fares, the army were given total occupation on both their summer visits. They tore out the old track, ran a bulldozer along the formation to remove the grass and level it off and then laid out the replacement sleepers, spiked the old rails firmly to them and re-ballasted. Altogether, the army re-laid two miles of track during these three visits of which a quarter of a mile was re-railed as well as re-sleepered. At the end of 1954 there were still substantial lengths of track sorely needing attention, while the railway as a whole still left a lot to be desired. Yet this massive help from the army undoubtedly broke the vicious circle and, to mix metaphors, turned the tide in our favour.

As spring came in, some good friends of Sonia's offered us the use, as a flat, of the upper floor of their house at Aller Park on the north Devon coast, on the Cornish border near Morwenstow. Feeling we had already leant too heavily on her aunt's kindness, we accepted gladly and set off one March morning from Roehampton bound for Devon feeling like some tinker family on the move with all our worldly possessions on board plus a two months old baby. My car was even then twenty-nine years old, but never in its history can it, or any other 12/50 Alvis duck's back for that matter, have borne such a burden. The boot in the pointed tail (which has a greater capacity than one might suppose) was stuffed with belongings including a basket for the baby; bulging suitcases were strapped onto each running board. Sonia sat beside me with Richard in her lap. So far as I can remember he never complained throughout the long journey. Perhaps he was already displaying a taste for vintage cars; certainly he soon showed his distaste for modern ones by turning a bright shade of green within five miles and then being violently sick. My old car would have to perform two more similar moving operations before our nomadic existence finally came to an end.

Aller Park was set four-square to the winds on the top of a treeless headland, one of a series of promontories with deep valleys between that north Devon and Cornwall thrust out, like so many aggressive knuckles, to meet the challenge of the Atlantic. The saw 'From Padstow Point to Lundy Light is a watery grave by day or night' is not a time-honoured local adage but an invention of the celebrated Parson Hawker of Morwenstow, but it is none the less true for that. The west window of our upstairs sitting room looked down upon one of the most savage stretches of coast in all Britain. On all but the calmest days we lived within sound of the ceaseless warfare waged between stubborn rock and great Atlantic roller, an unending thunder of battle.

In addition to our sitting room, I had the use of a little writing room with a desk set beneath a window that faced south. Whenever, momentarily stuck for the right word, I looked up, I found the prospect from this window very satisfying. Down below was the deep valley of the Marsland stream, the boundary between Devon and Cornwall. Its lower slopes were covered by dense wood of scrub oaks whose tops were so evenly brushed and combed by strong winds off the sea funnelling up the valley that it had the appearance of a green fleece, recently clipped. On the bare slopes above this wood and therefore directly on a level with my eye a man was at plough with a tractor, slowly transforming the smooth green slope of this first Cornish headland into a corduroy of red earth, a white scatter of gulls wheeling at his back. I used to reflect that if I had had the sea instead of mountains in my genetic back-ground, I would doubtless find this majestic landscape as spell-binding as the Black Mountains. Yet although I admired its quality, it failed to move me and sometimes its air of desolation and savagery oppressed me.

After we had stayed for a while at Aller Park, we came to the conclusion that the time had come when we could batten upon the kindness of Sonia's friends and relations no longer. We decided that, money or no money, we should try to find a home of our own somewhere along the Welsh border. To this end, I made a lightning foray from Aller Park up the border as far as Ludlow, where I learnt from a house agent that Laurel Cottage at Clun was to be let furnished for a very modest rental. At least this would be a very convenient base from which to look for something more permanent that we could make our own; also Clun was a place of very pleasant memories for us so I took Laurel Cottage on the spot without consulting Sonia.

So earliest summer saw our Alvis caravan once more upon the move, this time bound north from the west country for Clun. Laurel Cottage was a simple, square stone house of indeterminate date but probably Regency. It was on the eastern edge of the town facing a narrow lane which had not been built up on the opposite side with the effect that it had an uninterrupted view to the east over green fields. Later, we had the chance to purchase Laurel Cottage, but after much thought we decided against it. Because the house was built into rising ground at the back, its rooms got no sun except in the early morning which would make it very gloomy in winter. Owing to this rising ground it was almost impossible to build a garage or even form a parking bay and the lane itself was far too narrow to admit parking. Finally there were persistent rumours of a new council estate to be built in the green field opposite. Nevertheless, despite these disadvantages, present or to come, it was a pleasant, comfortable, friendly little house in which we were very happy during our brief occupation.

Besides Laurel Cottage, we viewed and contemplated purchasing a number of houses in the border country, but either they were quite beyond our financial reach even with the aid of a mortgage or, if they were within our means, they invariably suffered from one or more serious snags. At this point the reader may well ask, if he has not asked long before, what about my family house at Stanley Pontlarge? What indeed!

Unlike Sonia's aunt, my mother had not proffered a helping hand. Nor would I have been particularly anxious to grasp it if she had, for I knew that the house was bitterly cold in winter. There was no electric light and no telephone. My mother had never used the latter instrument in her life and when one rang in her vicinity she would regard it as though it were a poisonous snake. In the long winter evenings the house was not only chill but in almost perpetual darkness as my mother groped her way around or sat and read, crouched over a small fire, by the light of a small wick paraffin lamp. She cooked on the same two wick paraffin stove which I remembered from boyhood. It was now blackened with age and fumed and smoked atrociously. Through the whole house the walls and ceilings were blackened by the paraffin fumes which could be smelt in every room.

My mother had been a source of great anxiety to me ever since my father died in 1941. It had never occurred to her to take a job and she had continued to live, on her miniscule and dwindling income from investments, in a house that was not only much too big for her, but which she could not afford to repair. Her sole interest and her great labour of love was the garden which she kept immaculately but in such a way that it demanded the maximum amount of hard work. So concentrated was her mind upon horticulture that she seemed blissfully unaware that the house was in an advanced state of dissolution. Through loss of the oak hanging-pegs or failure of the cleft laths, stone slates were slipping from the roofs; in winter, snow blew under the roof creating miniature snow-drifts in the attics which, melting, had brought down the plaster ceilings in the bedrooms beneath; owing to the failure of the flashing between the roof of one wing and the gable end of the other, whenever there was a storm from the north rain streamed down one wall of a bedroom and into the kitchen below. My mother seemed oblivious to these defects, which was perhaps just as well since she lacked the means to have them put right. Since 1941 this state of affairs had been a mounting anxiety to me, yet my mother would not entertain any suggestion of change in her way of life. So a large question mark hung, not only over our future but over that of my mother and the house in Gloucestershire. I realized that if we did succeed in finding a house of our own, this would do nothing to solve the problem of what was to be done about my mother. Could I ignore it until the roof of the house fell about her ears as it undoubtedly would do given a few more years?

At the eleventh hour I received an overture from my mother saying that she would like to see us and also her grandson whom she had not yet set eyes on. Accordingly we motored over from Clun and spent the day with her at Stanley Pontlarge. This visit marked the beginning of discussions between my mother and myself whereby she finally consented to make over the house to me by deed of gift while I, in return, agreed to build a small 'dower house' for her in our orchard about 100 yards distant from the old house. I drew a succession of ground plans of such a house until I arrived at something which suited her and then handed over the approved sketch to an architect. In the late autumn of 1953, my mother went to lodge with a friend in the neighbouring village while we moved into the old house and commenced to dig the foundations of the new with our own hands. The house was built (or rather the operation was directed) by an old Winchcombe builder who had always worked for my family. He was able, conscientious and cheap, but he was old and slow and undependable so that the house, though it was of the most modest description, seemed as though it would never be finished. After interminable, frustrating delays it was finally completed at the end of 1954 and my mother was able to move in. As can be imagined, this was a very difficult transition period for all concerned.

Years before, I think it must have been in 1943, I remembered discussing the problem of what I should do about my solitary mother and the decaying family home with H.J. Massingham. He had replied without hesitation; it was my heritage, and therefore a responsibility which I could not and should not evade. At the time I stowed this advice away in the back of my mind as one hiding away an unwelcome letter in the hope that it will disappear. For at the time my thoughts were all of *Cressy* and I could not see any future beyond her eventual end. And as for Angela, I already knew her to be such a restless mortal that I realized she would never be content to settle down to a conventional life 'on the bank', as the canal boaters say. Yet here was I, at the age of forty-four, and after years of peripatetic existence either in digs or on a canal boat, settling down to a conventional and static way of life 'on the bank'. At least I had salved my conscience by accepting at last Massingham's advice which had been niggling away at the back of my mind. I had accepted my responsibilities and returned like a homing pigeon to Stanley Pontlarge. But I would have my work cut out to restore and maintain my ancient heritage.

Wick paraffin lamps and paraffin stoves, although they had served me well on *Cressy*, are not the safest forms of lighting and heating where babies or small children are concerned, so it was a stroke of luck when the mains electricity at last came to Stanley Pontlarge very soon after we had moved in. An early Talyllyn volunteer named John Rapley, who at that time ran a one-man electrical business known as the Hydropower Company in the wilds of Cardiganshire, wired the house with me as mate. What unknown pitfalls lie in wait for those with the temerity to bring such new-fangled devices into medieval houses! One example will suffice. 'Good', said John, when we had rolled up the carpet on the first-floor landing and noticed that the floor-boards ran lengthwise along the corridor, 'We'll take a run along here'. But when we had, with difficulty, prised up a floor-board, it was only to find that there was a second set of boards below the first but running cross-wise. This, as we subsequently discovered from our old builder, was the practice known as 'casing'. It meant that when one set of floor-boards wore hollow, you simply nailed another set across them. We were also lucky enough to get a telephone pretty soon. With such mod cons as electric light and telephone my mother would have no truck; she moved into her new house with her old wick lamps and her old stove, both of which she was still using at the time of writing, with the effect that pristine walls and ceilings soon became appropriately blackened. But she had to have piped water and drainage. The former was no problem; it simply meant coupling her up to our supply which was spring water piped from a point sufficiently high on the hillside above to run into the roof tanks by gravity.

Providing the new house with a drainage system was a very different story. In theory it should have been an equally simple matter, for the line of the main sewer from the old house to a septic tank at the bottom of our orchard ran within twenty feet of the new one. Yet the orchard resembled the scene of some desperate search for treasure trove before we finally located that sewer pipe at a depth of eight feet. This, despite the efforts of Sonia (who fancied herself at the art) to locate the pipe by walking to and fro with her divining rod while we had every tap in the house running. We came eroniously to the conclusion that such rods don't respond to piped water.

Most of Sonia's belongings, including a large quantity of books, lay mouldering in a tiny condemned cottage which she had rented as a store at Buckby Wharf beside the Grand Union Canal in Northamptonshire. Most helpfully, John Rapley lent us his lorry to go and fetch these. When Sonia's books were added to mine they made a formidable pile even after the duplicates had been weeded out. New bookshelves were therefore a high priority, but the difficulty was that timber was still in short supply. Here again the ever re-sourceful John saved the day. Apparently, in the village with a long and unpronounceable name where he lived in darkest Cardigan, the bureaucratic writ concerning timber licences did not run, for one day he turned up from Wales with a load of planks from which I constructed the first of many sets of bookshelves. These first ones occupy the whole of one end wall of our drawing room. The other do-it-yourself job I did at this time was to create a small writing room-cum-business office on the first floor. This I did by partitioning off a small portion of the very large bedroom which my mother had used and which occupied the whole south end of the medieval part of the house. This bedroom had four windows, two facing south and the others east and west respectively. My new office took away an east and a south window and still left us with a large, light bedroom.

Much as I enjoyed working with my hands, all this do-it-yourself activity was undertaken because I could not afford to employ anyone else. For our coming to Stanley Pontlarge had coincided precisely with the moment when my financial affairs had touched rock bottom and when, for the first time, I began to entertain serious doubts of my ability to earn a living by writing. To the cumulative effect of the past two summers I had spent at Towyn with not a word written was added the unpalatable fact that the last two books I had produced had turned out financial failures. A third book, which I had completed while we were at Clun, was due to appear in the spring of 1954 and was to be the most monumental failure of my whole literary career. I shall expand upon these literary disasters later; the operative fact here is that by the time this final heavy blow fell in 1954, its effect upon me was mercifully cushioned because I had obtained another lucrative and interesting, albeit temporary, job through the good offices of my old pre-war friends in the Vintage Sports Car Club.

3
On Vintage Motoring

For obvious reasons, the VSCC had suspended its activities during the war years and I had dropped out of touch with all the friends I had made at Phoenix Green where the Club was born in the mid-1930s. When the war ended the Club was one of the first motoring organizations to become active again and its membership began to grow rapidly, as it has continued to do ever since. But although I continued to use one or other of my two 12/50 Alvises for every-day motoring and to pay my Club subscription, I was slow to pick up this particular thread in my many-stranded life owing to my almost total involvement in the affairs of the IWA. Indeed, so detached had I become from the world of motor cars, that when I received a letter from Alan Southon, my successor at the Phoenix Green Garage, saying that he had my 1903 Humber there and what should he do with it, I had instructed him without hesitation to get it into running order (it had been in store since 1939) and then sell it for what it would fetch. I reflected that as I had only paid two pounds for the old car and it had given me an immense amount of pleasure, it certainly did not owe me anything and I was therefore perfectly satisfied with Alan's cheque for £35 which was the net result of this correspondence.

Of my two vintage Alvises, the 1924 'duck's back' two-seater which I acquired in 1935 and the 1925 model four-seater which I inherited from my father, I greatly preferred the former, not merely because it had been in my ownership for so long but because I considered its handling qualities vastly superior to those of the later car. With its light, whippy chassis and brakes only on the rear wheels, with the exception of the engine it was virtually an Edwardian design, and cars of that epoch are always a delight to drive. They reveal how much was lost when chassis became stiffer, when tyres came to resemble doughnuts and when the first, not particularly effective front wheel brakes, added unsprung weight and ruined the precision of the steering. One drives a car of this Edwardian type through the seat of one's pants. In other words, it communicates knowledge of varying road conditions and of its own power of adhesion to the driver in the most subtle manner. As cars became gradually more sophisticated and refined, so this *rapport* between car and driver has been almost lost. It was for this reason that, while I lost no time in getting my own car onto the road again after the war, my father's old car continued to slumber in its garage at Stanley Pontlarge until 1949.

In the spring of that year my own car, XU 362, broke a connecting rod which came out through the side of the crankcase. This meant a major rebuild of the engine which could not be hurried and as I needed road transport I went over to Stanley Pontlarge with Jim Russell and Bill Trinder, got my father's car off its blocks, and towed it back to Banbury where I restored it to running condition. This is how it came about that during the summers of 1949 and 1950 it was the 4-seater Alvis that acted as tender car to *Cressy*. It was partly the fact that this car was running very well at the time and partly some sixth sense which knew that my life afloat was coming to an end that made me decide, in August 1949, while *Cressy* lay at Pont Cysyllte and Angela was in Italy, that I would enter for the Vintage Sports Car Club annual hill climb at Prescott. I was thus brought into personal contact again with many old friends of pre-war days who had thought me lost forever to the canals. This renewal of my links with the VSCC was to stand me in good stead later although I little realized it at the time.

During the winter of 1953/54, the British Travel & Holidays Association (BTHA), with the object of attracting American tourists to England, thought up the notion of holding a competitive car rally between equally-matched teams of American and English vintage cars. The Association thereupon approached the committee of the VSCC to ask if it considered the idea feasible and, if so, whether the Club would be prepared to organize such an event, to take place early in the following September. The Club committee thought it a splendid idea and, early in 1954, I was asked if I was prepared to organize it by acting both as Secretary of the Meeting and Clerk of the Course. On signifying my agreement in principle, I was bidden to a joint meeting of the Association and the Club in the former's offices in St James's where my appointment was officially blessed. It carried with it a handsome salary, plus all expenses, to be paid by the Association. Thus, thanks to the VSCC I had obtained, at one stroke, an assignment that promised a most rewarding experience and a welcome financial boost that could not have been more timely.

At first it was mainly a matter of desk-work for there were innumerable arrangements to be made and details to be settled between the VSCC, its opposite number, The Veteran Car Club of America; with the R.A.C.; with the police and with Shell-Mex & B.P., the latter company having agreed to give competing cars and those of travelling marshals free petrol at selected garages along the route. It had been suggested that this route should be from Edinburgh to Chichester where final tests might be carried out on the nearby Goodwood Circuit. The BTHA felt that for the benefit of the visiting team, the rally should pass through, and preferably stop at, as many historic towns as possible; also places of particular American historic interest such as Boston and Sulgrave Manor. But the route could not be finally fixed until hotel and meal arrangements had been made. Britain's hotel and catering industry had not then got into its post-war stride and it was no easy matter to find accommodation for sixty-five people and twenty-nine cars, figures that include reserves and travelling officials. Very fortunately for me, the BTHA undertook to deal with this problem and in the spring I set off to drive along the line of route with A.M. McNab, representing the BTHA. It was McNab's thankless task to arrange luncheon stops and book suitable overnight accommodation for this large party, sometimes spread over two or more adjoining hotels but preferably in one. To some extent his search was limited by my judgement as to the suitability of the route and the desirable length of each morning and afternoon stage; also on the availability of suitably supervised car-parking space at midday stops and covered garaging at night.

We headed north through Lancashire, for the Americans and their cars would be disembarking at Liverpool some days before the start of the event, and the idea was that I should meet them at the landing stage and subsequently pilot them by easy stages up to Edinburgh. For this preliminary canter we arranged a first night stop at Grange-over-Sands, followed by lunch in Keswick, so that our guests could see the Lake District, before going on to Carlisle for the second night. On the third day the drive would be from Carlisle to Edinburgh via Moffat and the Beeftub Pass. Because both teams would be arriving in Edinburgh during Festival Week, hotel reservations there were particularly important. In Scotland, however, McNab's writ did not run; protocol demanded that the Scottish Tourist Board should be responsible for the Edinburgh bookings – with embarrassing results as things turned out.

With the Edinburgh arrangements in capable hands, or so we thought, we set out to plan the long rally route southwards. We considered the White Swan at Alnwick, our projected first night stop, and quite the best hotel on the entire programme, but unfortunately it was small and we were obliged to split the party by booking additional accommodation at an hotel at Alnmouth. We hoped to make our next night's stop at York, but this proved to be quite impossible and we had to make Harrogate our destination instead, visiting York the next morning. However, these were the only two cases where hotel problems enforced a change of plan. When I was able to finalize the route it read like this: (see page 56)

Day	Start	Time	Lunch Stop		Tea Stop	Finish	Time
1	Edinburgh Castle	10.00 a.m.	11.00–1.45	Dirleton	–	Alnwick Castle	4.45
2	Alnwick, White Swan	10.00 a.m.	12.30–1.45	Durham	–	Harrogate	5.40
3	Harrogate	10.15 a.m.	11.15–1.30	York	–	Boston, Lincs.	5.30
4	Boston	10.30 a.m.	12.30–3.00	Ely	–	Cambridge	5.00
5	Cambridge Backs	9.30 a.m.	12.20–1.30	Sulgrave	Oxford	Leamington	6.30
6	Leamington	10.00 a.m.	12.30–3.00	Stratford	Prescott Hill	Cheltenham	6.30
7	Cheltenham	10.00 a.m.	12.–1.45	Savernake	Winchester	Chichester	6.15
8	Chichester	10.00 a.m.	to Goodwood Circuit for final tests.				

There then followed much correspondence with both the competing Clubs about the selection of their teams. In each team there were to be five Edwardian cars (i.e. cars built before 1915) and five vintage cars built between 1915 and 1926. I have to admit that I brought a lot of pressure to bear on the American Club to include a Stanley steam car in their team. This they very sportingly agreed to do, but although the steamer created more public interest than any other competing car, it lost the Americans a great many points in the competition. The moguls of Shell seemed quite foxed by the news that a steam car was coming over and asked me what fuel it would require. But when I replied 'lamp oil', from my experience of a Stanley at Evesham many years before, Shell at once put me in my place by saying that surely I must mean TVO. I did not argue further; after all they should know.

When the two teams had been picked they consisted of the following: (see pages 58–9). The American Team was also allowed two reserves which would accompany it throughout the event. These were a 1916 Stutz 'Bearcat' driven by Tony Koveleski and McKelvie's 1929 Dusenberg roadster.

It is worth noticing that the American cars were older than ours but that their engines were of considerably larger capacity, thus reflecting that big car tradition in America which has persisted to this day. Besides these twenty competing cars and the two reserves, there were those of the members of the VSCC who would accompany them as stewards or marshals. These included Sam Clutton's 1908 Itala, Forrest Lycett's famous 8 litre Bentley, Kent Karslake in a Hispano Suiza, Laurence Pomeroy, most appropriately driving a 'Prince Henry' Vauxhall of his father's design, and Arthur Jeddere-Fisher in an Edwardian Lancia 'Theta' coupe. Finally, there were the two Alvises of John Morley and myself, his a 12/60 'beetle back' and mine the 1924 'duck's back' which had been back on the road again since 1951.

That summer, McNab and I had a second run over the course to ensure that everything was planned down to the last detail. The route had been arranged to enable the Americans

to see something of our historic towns and buildings, but although an allowance of seven days to cover a total of 768 miles may sound like a very leisurely tour, in fact it was quite a tough assignment for elderly motor cars. On each stage they were expected to average not less than 25 and not more than 30 mph. Each team was credited at the start with 2,500 marks and individual cars lost one mark for each minute's late arrival at the finishing controls. On the other hand, a competitor averaging more than 35 mph between controls would lose thirty marks for his team. Besides the final tests on the Goodwood Circuit, there were four special tests which I located at various points along the rally route: a slow-fast test on a straight and level stretch of bye-road near Cambridge; a starting test in which each driver had to start his car from cold against a stop watch – this was arranged at Leamington as the hotel there had a large garage and yard at the rear which was very suitable; a speed hill climb at Prescott where each competitor would be allowed one practice and two competitive runs; and finally, on the last stage of all, a stop and restart test on the steepest section of South Harting, a hill on the Chichester road out of the village of that name which is well known in motoring history as the scene of many hill climb meetings in the early days. Each car failing to restart in this test would cost his team forty marks.

So, with all the arrangements made, in the last week of August Sonia and I set off from Stanley Pontlarge with our small son in the Alvis, our destination being Sonia's aunt's house at Roehampton where we had arranged to leave Richard in charge of a nanny for the duration of the rally. After a night in Roehampton we headed for Liverpool where the American team was due to arrive the following morning. For the first thirty miles or so of that journey I remember feeling very uneasy, imagining I heard every kind of ominous sound from the engine. For although I had devoted such care and forethought to the motoring side of the whole event, only now did I realize with a dull thud that I had taken no account at all of what would happen in the ignominious event of my own car breaking down. Added to this realization was the fact that I had recently had to do some major work on the engine and therefore had reason to expect teething troubles. But as we left London behind and the roads became clearer I ceased to worry for the old Alvis was running like a watch – as indeed, it continued to do throughout the event which, for us, meant well over 1,000 miles of motoring during which I never had occasion to lift the front seat and get out my tool roll.

Soon we were diving through the Mersey Tunnel to arrive at the Adelphi Hotel garage where we were pleased and relieved to see the Lancia 'Theta' parked. We met Arthur Jeddere-Fisher and his wife Marcia in the hotel. Over the next four days they were towers of strength to us in the task of shepherding the American team up to Edinburgh and in making them feel at home. This social side of things became progressively easier as the event went on and we came to know the Americans better; also, on the rally itself, there were many more of us around to play host. Anyway, by the end of it all the fact that they had shared in such a large slice of experience acted as a bond between the two teams. It was a case of hands across the sea with a vengeance because we all became firm friends who might have known each other for years. However, our first encounter with the American team in Liverpool was somewhat embarrassing.

The ship, the small Cunarder *Media*, came alongside the landing stage and we duly greeted the Americans as they filed down the gangway. Then we all stood around talking while we awaited the unloading of their precious cars. Eventually the hatches were off and the ship's derricks were lowered into the holds. From the for'ard hold there presently emerged, not a motor car as we expected but an outsized and very expensive-looking refrigerator. This had been lifted fully and was in process of being swung overside towards the quayside when it suddenly slipped from its slings and fell, hitting the edge of the quay wall. It burst asunder on impact, releasing coils of pipe, wires and suchlike complex technological intestines, some of which remained behind on the quay to remind us of its passing after it had toppled into the opaque waters of the Mersey. Between those responsible this episode occasioned some profanity, though no more than would have occurred if one had accidentally nudged and spilt a drop of the other's pint of beer, but its effect upon the Americans was understandably traumatic. Putting a brave face on it, Arthur and I argued cheerfully that the fate of the refrigerator was bound to act as an Awful Warning and that their cars would be handled with extra care in consequence. And so it proved, although as each car was landed safely the sighs of relief were almost audible.

That evening our American guests and ourselves were entertained to dinner in the Town Hall by the Lord Mayor of Liverpool. This splendid late eighteenth-century building was originally built, to the designs of the Woods of Bath, as the Liverpool Exchange but was subsequently enlarged and the interior reconstructed, following a fire, by John Foster jun., a local architect and the son of the engineer of Liverpool's docks, acting in collaboration with James Wyatt. It would have been difficult to imagine any more suitable setting for the lustrous mahogany dining table, lit by candelabra and burdened by a dazzling display of the City's ceremonial silverware, than a great room that represented the apogee of the Age of Reason. This scene was the subject of mixed feelings on my part. Although my reason knew that it was all a charade, an elaborate piece of municipal flim-flummery staged at the request of the British Travel & Holidays Association in order to impress our visitors and so help to earn dollars for Britain, nevertheless I must confess to being impressed in spite of myself. I could not help feeling proud of the fact that the Americans, many of whom had never crossed the Atlantic before, were being given a welcome to this country which they were unlikely ever to forget. Before the rally was over it would be made an occasion of a number of municipal junketings of one kind or another, but for sheer stately magnificence none surpassed that staged by the City of Liverpool.

Next morning we were provided with a police escort as far

as the city boundary. This was a relief to Arthur and myself since neither of us could guarantee to find our way out of the Liverpool labyrinth without hesitation, and I could imagine nothing more humiliating than to lead our flock into some cul-de-sac. We had agreed that I should head the procession while Arthur followed in the Lancia to round up any stragglers and render assistance where necessary. Apart from some slight difficulty over parking at the lunch stop at Garstang, this first day's run went pretty smoothly so far as I was concerned. I turned into the drive of the hotel at Grange – a huge place dedicated to conferences – right on schedule and then counted nine American cars safely home, but of the tenth, the Stanley steamer, there was no sign. When Arthur eventually put in an appearance in the Lancia, I was as alarmed as he was surprised. He assured me that he had not seen the Stanley and had naturally assumed that all ten cars were ahead of him. He very nobly volunteered to go back over the route and look for the lost sheep and very soon returned again, accompanied, to my intense relief, by the Stanley, puffing as heartily as ever.

It transpired that the proud owner-driver of the Stanley, Paul Tusek, had only had the car two years and was as yet unversed in the vagaries of steamers. Knowing this, the American Club had nominated as his passenger/mechanic one Ed Battison who was reputed to be one of the foremost American authorities on the steam car. Ed was a tall, loose-limbed New Englander with a long face and a lantern jaw. His was a delightfully dry wit, there was a humorous twinkle in his eye and he was immensely knowledgeable, not only about steam cars but also on horology, and on archaeology generally, particularly that branch of it which is now termed industrial. We took an immediate liking to Ed but it soon became clear that all was not as it should be between him and the pilot of the Stanley. Paul's motto appeared to be 'don't talk to the man at the wheel' for he persistently ignored Ed's sage advice while driving, yet whenever he paid the penalty for this ignorance, he relied upon Ed to get him out of trouble. The chief cause of dissension was Paul's failure to stop in time to replenish his water tank. Because they exhaust freely to atmosphere, early Stanleys such as his have a far brisker performance than the later condensing models, such as I had known in my youth at Pitchill, where the engine has to fight against back-pressure on the exhaust side due to the inadequacy of the condenser. But this superior performance of the older cars is offset by the need to refill the water tank every 30 to 35 miles or so. Once at the wheel, however, Paul seemed to become so intoxicated by his car's effortless performance that he would ignore all his mechanic's entreaties to stop and take on more water. It was just as well that the crew were equipped with a generous supply of spare fusible plugs. On this first occasion, however, they had not actually 'dropped the plug' although the situation had become so desperate that Ed had eventually prevailed upon Paul to turn aside up a track to a farmhouse. What the stolid occupants of that farm thought of the sudden arrival of two Americans riding a strange machine trailing a cloud of steam behind it and crying 'Water! Water!' is not recorded.

I seldom sleep well during a first night in a strange bed especially when, as on this occasion, I feel tense and excited, my mind preoccupied with details of days past and to come. Perhaps I was too concerned that the event should prove a success, yet I could not escape the fact that success depended very heavily on me. Consequently I had missed out on a great deal of sleep by the time the rally came to an end. Somehow the recollection of this first night at Grange has remained vividly with me whereas so much else has gone beyond recall. I remember how I awoke very early in the morning and, finding further sleep impossible, crept stealthily out of bed so as not to disturb Sonia. The window was wide open at the bottom for the night had been balmy and still considering how far north we had come. I knelt behind the curtains with my elbows resting on the sill, chin propped on forearm, and watched the dawn break over Morecambe Bay. It was low tide and a great expanse of sand stretched southward down the Lancashire coast in the direction of Heysham. The still air was filled with the crying and piping of innumerable sea birds and, directly below my window, dozens of small waders were hurrying to and fro on delicate feet as though walking over perilously thin ice. Before the railway age, travellers on foot, and even by coach it is said, used to avoid the long detour between Lancashire and Furness by crossing these sands. This looked an improbably daring exercise to me and I am not surprised that there should be so many legends, probably exaggerated or apocryphal, of people sinking in quicksands or overwhelmed by the tide.

While we were lunching in Keswick next day, Ed Battison suddenly turned to me and announced that he did not want to leave the town without seeing the Castlerigge stone circle. I felt thoroughly ashamed to admit that I was unaware of what he assured me was the finest stone circle in England, Stonehenge apart. It was arranged there and then that while I took Ed up to Castlerigge in the Alvis, Sonia would accompany Paul on the Stanley to Carlisle. Castlerigge was certainly well worth seeing. The circle of stones is almost complete and, set as it is on the summit of a green knoll, it is surrounded by a magnificent panorama of the Cumberland Fells, looking over Derwentwater towards the jaws of Borrowdale. Nevertheless, I confess that at this moment machines took priority over landscape in my mind. How I envied Sonia her journey to Carlisle on the Stanley! The run from Keswick was just within the steamer's tank capacity so there were no more water crises and, according to her account, the Stanley fairly ate up the miles to Carlisle, bowling along with effortless ease and silence. As things turned out, I never did succeed in having a ride on that Stanley thus my jealousy has never been appeased.

What happened next morning on the stage from Carlisle to Tweedsmuir is best told by quoting from my account of the Liverpool–Edinburgh run which I wrote for the VSCC *Bulletin* when the scenes it describes were still fresh in my mind:

Two days on the road had revealed one oversight in our itinerary due to our native inability to cater adequately for the needs of long-distance motorists. Whereas our

womenfolk have become resigned to climbing field gates
and disappearing behind hedges in pouring rain, every
American 'Gas Station' worthy of the name provides what
is euphemistically called a 'Ladies' Powder Room'. Not
unnaturally, our lady visitors had expected to find the same
amenity provided at our filling stations and had suffered
considerable discomfort as a result. This being so, I had
made a tactful announcement that on this day's run the
cars would make a mid-morning stop in the square at
Moffat so that those who wished could take coffee at the
adjoining hotel. At the same time I had impressed upon
Paul Tusek that he must stop and fill the Stanley's water
tank at Moffat because he would find no water at all on the
long climb over the Tweedsmuir Hills to Tweedsmuir by
the Beeftub Pass.

We left Carlisle in pouring rain, but nine cars arrived in
good time at Moffat after an uneventful run. Needless to
add, the missing tenth was the Stanley. Arthur Jeddere-
Fisher arrived to report that the car had been seen leaving
Carlisle in the direction of Keswick, that it had been
retrieved and headed back with some difficulty, but had
since disappeared. Meanwhile I had sought local help in
laying on a convenient watering arrangement for the Stanley if it arrived. This consisted of a length of hose attached
to a tap inside the Public Lavatory. One by one the cars
moved off in the direction of the lunch stop at the Crook
Inn at Tweedsmuir, and soon I was left alone in the
rain-swept square. Where *was* the Stanley? Perhaps Paul
had missed the Moffat turning at Beattock and was well on
the way to Glasgow by now.

But no – suddenly above the roof of an approaching car I
caught sight of two cowled heads and a cloud of steam. But
relief turned instantly to dismay as Paul drove rapidly
through the square and vanished up the road.

Jumping into my car, I managed to head him off and
shepherd him back to the Public Lavatory where, before a
large audience, the tank-filling operation was smoothly and

swiftly carried out. For me this was the most memorable scene of the whole event and I bitterly regret that no pictorial record was made of it.

Fortunately the weather improved as the day went on and by the time we reached the Edinburgh city boundary, where we were met by a motorcycle police escort, it was quite dry though still overcast. At first it seemed to us that the Scottish Tourist Board had made their arrangements with great efficiency. The police led us to a single large garage where all the cars were to be parked until the start of the event on Saturday. On arrival, each competitor was handed a duplicated sheet indicating at which hotel in the city he and his passenger had been booked in. Furthermore, a row of taxis stood ready and waiting outside the garage to ferry us to these hotels. Within minutes of our arrival Sonia and I found ourselves in a comfortable bedroom at the very top of the North British Hotel. This room had curious little *Oeil-de-Boeuf* windows in the angles of the room which framed Waverley station and Princes Street as in a pair of vignettes. I could see to my delight, far below, Gresley Pacifics coasting majestically into the station or, southbound, vomiting clouds of smoke and steam as they pulled away with that characteristic three-cylinder beat that sounds so strange and syncopated to ears accustomed to the locomotives of the Great Western.

We were delighted with this accommodation, but, on glancing down the list, we were a little puzzled to know why we should be the only members of our cavalcade to be booked into this very large hotel. I also noticed that Arthur and Marcia Jeddere-Fisher had alone been booked into a hotel which, on referring to my AA book, I found was even more liberally endowed with stars than our own. I decided to ring Arthur and enquire after his welfare. 'Fine!', was the answer, 'This hotel couldn't be better, why don't you two come over and dine with us?' We thought this an admirable suggestion so we walked over and were rewarded by a meal which, coming so soon after post-war austerity, seemed quite outstanding. With the journey from Liverpool safely accomplished by all concerned, we were in a mood to celebrate and it was not until we were feeling thoroughly mellow after a second glass of port that we decided it might be a good and hospitable idea to visit our American guests and see how they were faring. A glance at our duplicated sheet had shown that most of them were quartered in the same hotel: obviously some large caravanserai designed to impress overseas visitors, we thought; but when the four of us had piled into Arthur's Lancia, it did strike us as a little odd that no one, from the doorman of Arthur's hotel to strolling policemen, appeared to have the faintest idea where this hotel was to be found. We spent a lot of time cruising round Edinburgh before we finally ran it to earth in one of those suburbs which have seen better days but which, by a superhuman effort, have contrived to remain precariously respectable. The hotel consisted of a number of terrace houses run together so that it possessed no depth but considerable length. The façade was not impressive, however. Through an uncurtained window, immediately to the right of the front door, we glimpsed a scene that instantly overwhelmed us with embarrassment. We found ourselves looking into what had obviously been in palmier days a 'front room' but had been thriftily converted into a bedroom by the insertion of two double beds which took up most of the floor space. There was, of course, no fitted wash basin let alone the private bath which most transatlantic visitors expect. Sitting or sprawling on the two beds were our American friends and their wives eating fish and chips out of paper bags by the light of a naked bulb overhead. They were delighted to see us and very cheerful under the circumstances, but we doubted if they would have been so forebearing had they known the standard of their hosts' accommodation. We gave the only explanation possible under the circumstances – difficulty of booking rooms during Festival Week – apologies for sub-standard temporary accommodation and an assurance that they would be moving to more appropriate quarters the next day.

If the worst came to the worst we were perfectly prepared to exchange rooms with our guests. That would at least have made two couples happy, but in the event this sacrifice proved unnecessary. By reading the riot act to the Scottish Tourist Board next morning, the individual responsible for the bookings contrived, heaven knows how, to move all the Americans to better hotels forthwith. Why in the first place he should have housed us in luxury while he relegated our American guests to what was virtually a doss-house is something I have never been able to fathom. Either he must have been preternaturally stupid or else he concealed a positive phobia about Americans. Anyway, he was responsible for the only really embarrassing few hours we experienced during the whole event.

A high proportion of the English team railed their cars up to Edinburgh and these arrived in covered vans ahead of their owners. I have pleasant recollections of driving the 'Prince Henry' Vauxhall through the streets of the city early one morning en route for the garage where the rival team was housed. It had a very brisk performance for a car of 1914, reminding me of its derivations, the famous 30/98 Vauxhall with which I had become so familiar in my days at the Phoenix Green Garage before the war.

The morning of the start was fine and sunny as the two teams lined up together for the first time on the Castle Esplanade at Edinburgh. The competitors were arranged in numerical order which meant that the oldest cars were at the front with Sam Clutton's Itala and my Alvis heading the columns as pilot cars. With polished brass and nickel plate twinkling in the morning sunlight, the two columns of cars made a brave sight as the Lord Provost officially started us on our way and into the first hazard. This consisted of driving between ranks of pipers who, dressed in full fig, piped us such a deafening farewell salute that it quite drowned the noise of our engines, which were not of the quietest.

I do not intend at this distance of time to give a blow-by-blow account of the days which followed, but only to mention certain incidents which spring vividly to mind whenever I recall this memorable event in my life. The first day's run was smooth and uneventful, but towards the end of Sunday's long stage from Alnwick to Harrogate it became obvious that all was not well in the American camp. First, we sighted the Stanley stopped beside the road amid a haze of smoke and a strong smell of burning paint, its crew standing regardant on the grass verge. The burner beneath the Stanley's boiler, which operates upon the primus principle, had suddenly ceased to vaporise with the effect that yellow flames and thick black smoke began to belch from every cranny of the car. Ed had promptly released the tank pressure so that by the time we arrived upon the scene the fire was out and Ed was regarding the car with calm amusement, particularly the yellow paint on top of the snub bonnet which had risen in one enormous blister. 'Looks like a mighty fine omelet', was Ed's laconic remark. Ed seemed satisfied that he could cope with the situation so we went on our way and soon overtook the Lozier limping slowly along emitting a horrible clanking noise from its nether regions.

At the Harrogate hotel, Sonia and I were allotted a most spacious and luxurious bedroom complete with private bath but, tantalizingly, I saw practically nothing of these creature comforts because I spent practically the whole night working on these two American lame ducks which had managed to crawl into the Harrogate garage. Because it was a Sunday evening, no mechanics were available, yet the cars must be ready for the road by the morning if it was humanly possible. The Stanley's trouble, which had made its burner increasingly temperamental ever since the car left Liverpool, proved to be that the vaporiser tube was almost blocked solid with carbon. So solid was it, in fact, that the in-situ steel wire 'pull-through' provided for cleaning the tube was so firmly embedded that it was impossible to extract it. The burner had to be removed and the offending tube drilled out. The reason for this excessive carbonization, the like of which Ed Battison had never seen before, was undoubtedly the use of TVO. For

shortly after this when, characteristically, Paul Tusek ran out
of fuel in a small village miles from anywhere, they were
obliged to refuel at a village shop which only stocked lamp oil.
There was no more trouble in the Stanley's steam-raising
department from then on, much to the delight of her crew. So
the boffins of Shell had been wrong in recommending TVO
and my hunch had been right after all. And while on this
subject of fuel, I fear that the Shell Company and their filling
station managers were somewhat downcast to discover members of both teams queuing up for the BP Commercial pump
and leaving the more exotic Shell brands severely alone. We
were not looking any gift horses in the mouth; it was simply
that, as our American friends knew as well as we did, modern
high octane fuels make an unsuitable diet for elderly, low
compression engines.

The trouble with the Lozier proved even more intractable
than the Stanley's choked vaporiser. Indeed the car had been
lucky to reach Harrogate at all for its front universal was in an
advanced stage of disintegration. At this stage I have to say
that, compared with English practice of equivalent date, the
American cars were archaic in design and crude in execution.
The side-valve L head engine of the 'Prince Henry' Vauxhall
might seem archaic by modern standards, but it was highly
efficient compared with the contemporary T head side-valve
American power unit as this rally revealed. The Lozier was
particularly agricultural in its engineering, the offending
universal being the most primitive type of Hooke joint. I spent
a long time flat on my back under the car dismantling it,
only to find that part of the joint needed welding and
re-machining before it could be assembled again. By this
time I was almost asleep on my feet, but I have dim
recollections of knocking up a general machinist, to whom I
had been recommended, in the early hours of the morning
and of holding converse with him as he leaned out of his
bedroom. I can't think why he did not throw a jug of water
over me and slam the window shut, but instead that stout
Yorkshireman dressed, opened up his little workshop and

did the job. Then I had to reassemble the car and it was broad daylight before it was ready for the road.

It was an overcast morning and although it remained fine during the prolonged midday stop in York, when the time came round for starting the long timed section to Boston it began to rain relentlessly and continued to do so all the way to Boston. Nevertheless, when I think of the rally it is this afternoon's run that I recall more clearly than any other. For some reason which I cannot now remember, having timed the competing cars away from York it was essential that I arrived at Boston in time to clock them in at the finish control. Although the cars were forbidden to exceed a 35 mph average on pain of penalty, to overtake all of them meant some pretty hard driving, particularly as it was wet and the greater part of the route consisted of narrow 'B' class roads through flat, fenny country where occasional long straights alternated with sharp corners and twisting sections dictated by the dikes and drains bordering the road. As a result of press and radio reporting we found that the rally was attracting an increasing amount of interest as we progressed. Undeterred by the rain, there seemed to be little groups of people gathered in each village and at most road intersections to watch the cars go by. To a man they were evidently convinced that they were watching a long distance road race and, because I was driving noticeably faster than the others, I found myself repeatedly greeted with cheers, wavings on and shouts of 'Come on England!' Obviously they were under the impression that, having been delayed in the earlier stages, I was, despite the bad conditions, making a determined bid for the lead. Although it was misplaced, I became infected by this enthusiasm and had a most enjoyable drive, arriving at the point I had selected for the finish control on the outskirts of Boston well before the first competitor came into sight. Granted that I had been indulging in a piece of exhibitionism, but nevertheless that afternoon I came neaerer to experiencing what it must have felt like to drive in one of the great trans-continental road races of the Edwardian era than I shall ever do again.

The next memorable event for me was the lengthy and leisurely lunch stop at Sulgrave Manor. Most of our previous stops had been in towns where crowds swarmed round the cars like wasps round a honey jar so that they had to be cordoned off and protected by the local police. But at Sulgrave there were no crowds and there was plenty of time to stroll about in the sunshine and examine each other's cars, something we had not had time to do before. Apart from the Stanley, which was in a class of its own, I thought the most covetable car in the American team was Ralph Buckley's magnificent 1914 Mercer 'Raceabout' and at Sulgrave I was privileged to take this rakish, splendidly restored open two-seater out for a short run with the owner in the passenger seat. My opinion of early American cars went up many points for I found it handled with beautiful sensitivity and accuracy, while with 5 litres of engine in a light chassis and a 2.5 to 1 top gear ratio, it displayed that kind of effortless performance only to be found in Edwardian cars of the highest class. No wonder this car ran perfectly throughout the event. Although otherwise starkly functional, the Mercer displayed one piece of typically American bravura in the guise of what was described as a 'monocle windshield' clipped to its long steering column. This left the mechanic to face the full rigours of the cold blast, deprived of even this minimal protection, yet Mary Buckley accompanied Ralph throughout the entire event apparently feeling, and certainly looking, none the worse for it.

It was on the afternoon's run from Sulgrave to Oxford that we sighted Ed Battison standing beside the road. There was no sign of the Stanley or its driver. Our hearts sank. Had there been some unimaginable disaster? If the Stanley had exploded leaving not a wrack behind, why was Ed still with us? It transpired that after a more than usually temper-trying argument, Ed had declared that he intended to wash his hands of the whole affair and demanded to be set down. Though we had no room for Ed, he was picked up by a more spacious following car and by the next day the crew of the Stanley were reunited, both having agreed to bury the hatchet.

At the start of the penultimate day's run from Leamington to Cheltenham via Prescott, disaster struck Elmer Bemis's beautiful 1906 six-cylinder Ford Model A, which shared with the Stanley the distinction of being the oldest car in the event. The Ford broke the driving pinion of its differential, yet, by some miracle, the local Ford agents managed to repair it and have the big white car on the road again within twenty-four hours so that it was able to rejoin us at Cheltenham next morning. This unlucky breakdown compelled the American team captain, Austin Clark, to call in his first reserve and so it was the Stutz 'Bearcat' which replaced the Ford on this day's run and at the hillclimb at Prescott.

In the latter event, each competitor was allowed two practice runs followed by two timed runs, the best time to count. Fastest time of the day went to Ronald Barker driving the 'Prince Henry' Vauxhall in 61.56 seconds but, considering they so seldom drive their veteran motor cars in anger in their own country, the American drivers performed very creditably indeed. Captain Clark did very well to get his immense Pierce-Arrow up the hill in 67.54 seconds considering that it was so long it could hardly get round one hairpin bend without a shunt. Another outstanding performer was Paul Tusek on the Stanley who ascended the hill in almost total silence to become the outright winner on handicap with a time of 72.04 seconds. From near the top of the hill, I watched the Stanley coming up swiftly towards me between the trees, buoyed up, it seemed, by its white cloud of exhaust steam. Passing closely by me as it accelerated away towards the top of the hill its exhaust sounded like the quick panting of some over-eager dog, a subdued and gentlemanly sound compared with the raucous hubbub and mechanical commotion of its successor. No wonder that steam engineers round about 1900 considered it engineering indecency to cause anything so violent as an explosion to take place in a closed cylinder for the purpose of propelling a piston. This was certainly the first time a steam car has made the ascent of Prescott and it is probably the last.

The performance of the Stanley at Prescott, coupled with

the happy solution of its vaporiser problems, seemed to have inspired in Paul Tusek an over-optimistic faith in the capacity of his car which ignored its advanced age, and this brought about the Stanley's sad downfall on the very last stage of the rally. After performing brilliantly in the stop and restart test on South Harting Hill, Paul Tusek turned his car round and returned to the foot of the hill to collect his passenger. Cars were allowed to shed their passengers for this test and arrangements had been made to ferry them to the top so this was quite unnecessary and was evidently undertaken, not out of consideration for Ed Battison but in order to impress the bystanders with the hill climbing powers of the Stanley by making a second climb, this time non-stop. Starting with a full head of steam and opening the throttle wide, he charged the hill at a fine pace until, when he was nearly at the top, the normal healthy panting sound of the Stanley's exhaust suddenly expired in a hissing sigh of steam as the car rolled to a stop. It was evident that the valve gear had become seriously deranged and the car had to be conveyed by lorry over the last few miles to the garage in Chichester where the cars were to be stabled prior to the final tests at Goodwood.

I felt it was vitally important that the Stanley should run at Goodwood on the morrow and so, immediately I arrived in Chichester, I telephoned my friend David Curwen at Devizes to invoke his aid. I knew that he had recently overhauled the only Doble steam car left in England and that if he could not put the Stanley to rights nobody could. Like the good friend that he was, David responded to this SOS immediately and together we laboured for most of the night in the Chichester garage. Having got the engine out of the Stanley chassis we could see that repair would be a comparatively simple operation provided we could remove a steam chest cover in order to get at the slide valve and its spindle. This was our undoing. This cover was not held on by studs as is the usual steam practice but was a large circular cast-iron plate threaded directly into the cylinder and steam-chest casting; a somewhat dubious piece of mechanical engineering design, we thought.

As we struggled to get this cover off, it became obvious that it had never been removed during the car's restoration; indeed from the look of the engine as a whole, David and I judged that this must have been no more than a superficial face-lift.

When at last we succeeded in getting the cover off, its threads proved to be so hopelessly rusted and corroded away that there was no hope of making the cover hold against full steam-chest pressure. So, tantalizingly, although the original defect could now easily be put right, our necessary surgery had immobilized the patient until a replacement part could be fitted. This would be difficult and quite impossible in the time available because the female threads in the steam-chest itself did not look too good either. There was nothing we could do but put the existing cover back as well as we could, using plenty of gasket 'goo' on the threads and to tell Paul that provided he used only a whisper of steam he might be able to coax the car to Goodwood and perhaps make a couple of slow demonstration laps of the circuit which, in the event, he just succeeded in doing.

Goodwood was, as was our intention, the climax of the rally and the owners of some 290 vintage and veteran cars had assembled at the circuit to welcome the two teams and to watch the final tests from the grandstand. By far the most spectacular of these was euphemistically called a 'Stamina Test' whereby, to avoid loss of marks, competitors had to complete a minimum of fifteen laps of the circuit in forty minutes. While the American team understandably decided to play it cool by concentrating on completing the fifteen laps in the specified time, the Englishmen who, it is apparent, do not treat their elderly machinery in the kid-glove fashion notable elsewhere, decided that the test was a glorious excuse for a final flat-out blind. Ronald Barker driving the 'Prince Henry' Vauxhall set the pace by lapping consistently at just over a mile-a-minute which is not bad going for a 1914 motor car. Also impressively fast was Anthony Heal's 3 litre Sunbeam despite the fact that, unknown to the driver, its hood had become unfurled and was billowing out behind like a parachute brake. Meanwhile Jimmy Skinner's Rolls-Royce and Francis Hutton-Stott in his Lanchester 'forty' continued to fight a relatively slow and silent yet grim and hotly contested battle from start to finish, their two stately carriages exchanging the lead on almost every lap, the Lanchester keeling over on its cantilever springs on the corners in a most unstately manner. Everyone completed the required number of laps except the unfortunate Tony Koveleski's Stutz 'Bearcat' which developed undisclosed engine maladies. Having at last been given a chance to show his car's paces by the failure of the Stanley, this was a bitter disappointment for Tony and a sad blow for the prospects of the American team.

By way of a grand finale and 'goodbye' to our friends from America, I had planned that all 290 of the attending vintage and veteran cars should debouch from their parks onto the circuit and process round for two laps in line ahead before dispersing. As anyone with any experience of organizing such events will know, where the number of cars is so great such an apparently simple exercise is easily ordered but difficult to perform successfully. It was greatly to the credit of the Vintage Sports Car Club's team of marshals that this final event went off splendidly so that, as the last car left the circuit, I was able to breathe a final deep sigh of relief, not unmixed with sadness. It was all over now except for the announcement of the results at a final party at Goodwood House where it transpired that the English team had won by the embarrassingly large margin of 1,333 marks and Tim Carson, our team captain, was presented with a trophy of appropriate size by the Duke of Richmond and Gordon. In fact, of course, the visiting team is always at a grave disadvantage in an event such as this as the Americans were to prove when they turned the tables on us in a return match in America two years later to make the score one all. There has yet to be a decider. The award for the best overall performance of any car in the rally went, to my surprise and delight, to John Clarke's 12/50 Alvis, the touring equivalent of my father's car. What also pleased me was the fact that the three Alvises which had been round the rally course, John Clarke's, John Morley's and my own, had each performed faultlessly throughout although their combined ages added up to eighty-one years.

Now that one of the most memorable events in my life was suddenly all over my feelings were a curious blend of sadness and relief; sadness because that unique feeling of camaraderie that had possessed us all while the rally was on now instantly dissolved leaving only an empty feeling of anti-climax behind it; relief at the thought that now there was nothing that could go wrong and with the realization that there was nothing left to worry about came a great relaxation. I felt as though I could sleep for a week.

The success of this first Anglo-American rally led to two jobs of a similar kind though nothing like so onerous, the first being exactly a year later – the twenty-first birthday party of the Vintage Sports Car Club which was celebrated at Goodwood on 10 September 1955. In spite of the gulf of the war years, to one who remembered so vividly the Club's small beginnings at Phoenix Green it was difficult to believe that so many years had passed, and I felt suitably honoured when I was asked if I would organize the motoring side of the celebrations. Someone had had the happy notion of inviting, as guests of the Club, those whose names had become famous in motoring history either as drivers or designers or both. After being entertained to luncheon by the Club in a marquee, these distinguished visitors emerged, each to make a *tour d'honneur* of the Goodwood Circuit in a motor car appropriate to his achievements. In most cases this motor car was provided by a member of the Club, but a notable exception was H.R. Godfrey (the 'G' of G.N.) who drove down to Goodwood from London with his wife in his own beautifully-preserved 1922 G.N. in which he duly lapped the circuit. As readers of the first part of this autobiography will know, my first two cars were G.N.'s, while I knew that when Godfrey and Nash were building their first car before the Great War, both were young apprentices at the Willans Works at Rugby. So I was not going to let this occasion pass without making the acquaintance of this particular celebrity, and as he is now no longer with us I am extremely glad that I did so. I found him a humorous, charming and completely natural and unassuming individual; in fact I was soon swapping jokes with him about our experiences of the car's foibles, roaring with laughter at the recollection of bygone mechanical misfortunes and entirely forgetful of the fact that he had designed it. Had my duties as Clerk of the Course permitted, I could have talked to him all the afternoon. It was what might be called a star-studded day. Sir Harry Ricardo had designed the engine of the 14/40 Vauxhall and, sure enough, there he was being driven round in a 14/40. Georges Roesch of Talbot fame was there and so was George Lanchester, then a lively octogenarian who drove a 36 hp Lanchester round the course. Of the drivers, there was H. Kensington-Moir at the wheel of a 4½ Bentley to represent 'the Bentley boys', Sir Francis Samuelson, who had won his first race at Brooklands in 1910, driving his own 3-litre TT Sunbeam, while our host, the Duke of Richmond, with Lord Essendon beside him, circulated in a 30/98 Vauxhall; both had been well known in motor racing circles before the war as the Earl of March and the Hon. Brian Lewis. But the personality who made the greatest impression upon me was that incorrigible old character Lord Brabazon of Tara.

'Brab' was down to drive the Austin which he had first driven in the French Grand Prix of 1908. Herbert Austin had built four of these cars for the race of that year of which three were driven in the event at Dieppe by Moore-Brabazon, Dario Resta and Wright. They were not conspicuously successful to put it mildly and 'Brab', in fifteenth place, was the first of the team to finish. For this he was presented with a special cup by a grateful Herbert Austin. No doubt he richly deserved it. Now, a survivor of these four cars, beautifully polished and prepared, had been brought down from Longbridge in a transporter attended by numerous white-overalled mechanics for his lordship to drive. In the process of unloading in the paddock, this equipage attracted the attention of an admiring crowd. At that moment 'Brab' arrived. He bounced into the

Clerk of the Course's office at the opposite end of the paddock exclaiming brusquely: 'Now then, where's this damned car I'm supposed to be driving?' I offered to lead him to it and we strode off up the paddock road together. At our approach the crowd parted respectfully and then stood hushed while the great man, legs apart, hands clasped behind his back, stood silently contemplating a car which in all probability he had not set eyes on since he had raced it in 1908. Finally he exclaimed in a loud voice 'Hmm! – it always was a bloody awful car', turned on his heel and walked away leaving mechanics and spectators dumbfounded. However, no matter what he might think of the car he certainly had not forgotten how to drive it. Indeed his verve as he propelled it out of the paddock was almost frightening, and what was even more alarming was that on reaching the course he turned left instead of right and roared round the circuit in the wrong direction completely ignoring the agitated signals of the marshals. 'Brab' was the kind of man who could get away with murder.

The day's celebrations ended with another 'Grand Parade' consisting this time of 250 vintage cars proceeding round the circuit headed by four Presidential cars: 'Prince Henry' Vauxhall, 8 litre Bentley, Hispano and, needless to say, the Itala. It was an impressive and appropriate finale and it sounds a fairly simple thing to organize. But ask anyone who has ever marshalled at a motoring event what it takes to extract drivers and cars out of paddock and car parks and formed up into an orderly queue and then, when it is all over, to disperse them again in an equally orderly manner.

This problem of dealing with numbers arose in the biggest possible way in the last motoring event which I was asked to organize – the 4th International Veteran & Vintage Car Rally at Brighton in May 1963. International interest in early cars grew so rapidly during the 1950s that an International Federation of Veteran Car Clubs was formed, its main object being to organize a rally in a member country each year. It was Britain's turn to be host to this rally and a joint committee consisting of members of the VSCC and the VCC was set up to organize it, Brighton being chosen as the starting point owing to its associations as the finishing point of the original 'emancipation day' run of 1896. In the autumn of 1962 I was asked if I would organize this event and act as Clerk of the Course. The rally was planned to last two days. On the first, the cars would start from the Madeira Drive at Brighton and take part in a road run, with a midday stop for lunch. In this the cars would have to maintain a certain average speed and there would be secret checks to ensure that they did so. On the following day competitors would converge on the Goodwood Circuit – with which I was by now becoming very familiar – where they would be called upon to carry out special driving tests against the watch. This sounded a simple enough programme until I was told that the committee was expecting 300 entries. In the event, there were 312 cars which meant that, allowing for the fact that some drivers might bring two or even three passengers and that there would be the crews of official cars in addition, there were likely to be over a thousand people to be bedded down and catered for.

Given sufficient notice, accommodation in Brighton the night before the event was relatively easy. But how were all these cars to be got away promptly from the Madeira Drive without causing, and being bogged down by, hopeless traffic congestion in the morning rush hour? Where could one halt such an army for lunch? Where could they park their cars together and sleep for two nights? Cars varied widely in date; car number one was a wheezing one-lunger of 1896, while at the opposite end of the scale were some of the fastest cars of 1930: a Speed-Six Bentley, a 38/250 supercharged Mercedes and a Type 43 blown Bugatti. To select one road course to suit everyone was obviously out of the question and I eventually decided to plan three routes each distinguished by colours on road signs and car numbers: a green route for veteran cars, a blue route for Edwardian cars and a red route for the vintage boys. Ideally, these would diverge at Brighton, converge for a communal lunch stop and then diverge once more to meet again at the night stop.

It was quite obvious that no hotel in Sussex could cope with such a lunchtime invasion, so I wrote to the National Trust asking if we might have the use of Petworth Park, and, somewhat to my surprise, the Trust agreed. It was arranged with a Brighton caterer that on arriving at Madeira Drive for the start, each driver and passenger would be handed a boxed picnic lunch while an enterprising local man at Petworth agreed to set up a small marquee in the Park from which he would dispense hot coffee and tea. As to the problem of night accommodation, the committee suggested that this would be solved by our taking over Butlin's Holiday Camp at Bognor for two nights, which was why the rally was timed to take place early in May just before the Camp was due to open and receive its first contingents of happy inmates. I had never been inside one of these camps in my life, but from what I had heard about them I confess I felt some misgivings about this part of the proceedings. Nevertheless, with ordnance maps of Sussex spread all over the drawing room carpet at Stanley Pontlarge, I began to plan my three routes between Brighton, Petworth and Bognor and was eventually able to work out what I believed to be a workable scheme.

Only the veteran cars would leave Brighton by the London road, turning left as soon as they had crossed the South Downs to pass through Poynings, Bramber, Steyning and Storrington to Petworth. The Edwardian and vintage cars would also make for Poynings, but by going straight along the sea front to Hove where they would turn righthanded and cross the Downs by the steep road that passes the Devil's Dyke. At Poynings the Edwardian and vintage cars would part company, the former following a zig-zag route through Partridge Green, Ashurst, Ashington and Wisborough Green, while the vintage cars travelled much further north, covering three sides of a square whose topmost corners were Staplefield and Loxwood.

After lunch at Petworth, the veteran cars would drive directly to Bognor, facing their biggest trial of the day in the inevitable climb over the South Downs. Many of them faced

this annually at Pycombe on the Brighton Run, but this time
they would have to tackle the Downs at Bury Hill which was
longer and steeper. The Edwardian and vintage cars would
take different routes which converged so that both could tackle
South Harting Hill. Then they diverged once more, the
Edwardians passing to the north of Chichester while the
vintage cars took a longer route to the south of that city, by
way of North Mundham. This meant that the cars would
approach Bognor from three different directions which, I
hoped, would ease congestion.

It was just as well that I was able to do so much advance
planning on our drawing room carpet because it may be
recalled that the winter of 1962/63 was the severest within
living memory. It began to snow heavily in Gloucestershire on
the afternoon of Christmas day, and frost and snow did not
relax their grip until mid-February. Our signpost, bearing the
legend 'Stanley Pontlarge No through road', almost disappeared from sight beneath a mountainous snow drift. But
thanks to the fact that we were running two vintage cars, both
with very good ground clearance, we were never quite snow-
bound. It was, of course, essential to verify the suitability of
the three rally routes I had planned, and to record times and
mileage, by driving round them, and I had arranged to do this
accompanied by two members of the rally committee on
28 January, but the weather made such an exercise quite out
of the question, so, hopefully, we put the date forward a
fortnight to 18 February. Even then, some of the minor
Sussex roads were only just passable and the bare Downs
roundabout Devil's Dyke seemed a very fair imitation of
Siberia. Nevertheless, we were able to confirm that, with only
very minor variations, the routes I had chosen would be
suitable and length and time about right. I was also able to
determine sites for six secret time checkpoints, two on each
route, and also note down certain traffic intersections where,
on the day of the event, control would be desirable either by
the police or by RAC patrols. But whether the event could be
held in May as planned seemed very doubtful, so severe was

the havoc wrought by the intense frost to the Sussex roads on many sections of the course. At the top of South Harting Hill, for example, the tarmac surface of the road looked as though it had been lifted by a scarifier. In the event, however, the West Sussex Highways Department did a splendid job and had all the rally routes repaired in time.

Very soon after this I paid a second trip to Sussex in the Alvis to confer with the local police, with the officials responsible for Goodwood Circuit and to pay a visit to Butlin's Camp at Bognor. By now the thaw had set in and all the roads were passable but there was still a great deal of snow lying around, the weather was overcast and the wind very 'peart', as country people say, particularly when confronted in an open motor car. Under such conditions, to look a holiday camp in the face is an experience calculated to daunt the stoutest heart. A monochrome setting of grey skies, melting snows and cold, grey seas made the crude primary colours in which the camp was tricked out seem more than usually tawdry and depressing. The high, unclimbable wire ring fence with which the camp was surrounded to ensure that its inmates had their good time at Butlin's and nowhere else, made me think of concentration camps and the Berlin Wall. 'Abandon hope all ye who enter here', I muttered gloomily as I swung the car in, drew up outside the camp offices and stated my business. I was shown in to the office of the Camp Commandant who, with a broken nose and a jutting jaw looked like everyone's idea of a heavyweight boxer. Perhaps this occupation was an essential qualification for the post, I speculated. What we were asking of Butlins was two nights bed and breakfast plus dinner after arrival on the Friday night plus, on the Saturday, a packed lunch to take to Goodwood and finally a buffet supper to accompany the presentation of the awards and the inevitable speechifying which marks such a farewell occasion. Because a number of guests were to be invited on this second evening, I estimated that the buffet would have to cater for at least 1,500 people and I doubted whether Butlins could cope with such a situation, bearing in mind that the taste of the guests would be somewhat more exacting than the average holiday camper. I voiced my doubt as tactfully as I could to the Commandant, whereupon he replied 'I'll send for my Catering Manager' and pressed a bell.

There presently shambled into the room an individual who looked as though he might have come straight from taking the money on the dodgem cars at an autumn mop fair. He was swarthy, hirsute and unshaven and he was wearing a dark overcoat that descended almost to his ankles. He held the lighted end of a cigarette cupped within the palm of his right hand and, every now and again, he would take a deep and sibilant drag from the yellow butt that protruded from between his fingers. At sight of him I had a sudden horrific vision of a long table groaning under the burden of golden mountains of fish and chips garnished with pink candy floss. 'Bert', said the Commandant, 'This is Mr Rolt who's organizing the car rally; he'd like to know what you're going to give them for the buffet supper on the Saturday night.' Bert looked at me speculatively for a moment before replying. Then with a shrug of his padded shoulders he replied; 'You can 'ave whatever yer wants guv – smoked salmon, the lot'. Despite my private doubts, there was nothing I could do but take his word for it and in the event Bert did not let me down. He produced the largest and most sumptuous cold buffet table I have ever seen at which white-hatted chefs deftly sliced up enough smoked salmon to stock a fair-sized river.

The only snag about Butlin's Camp was that there was nowhere to put the cars under cover during their owners' two nights stay. There was no security risk, but competitors might well complain bitterly if their precious cars had to be parked in the open on that exposed site near the sea. So at great expense and difficulty it was arranged between Butlins and a local tenting contractor that a series of huge marquees sufficient to house all the 312 motor cars should be erected on the camp site. All in vain. On the day of the event the wind blew so boisterously off the sea that the contractor was obliged to strike his marquees before they were struck for him.

Consequently, when the competitors arrived at Bognor it was to find no shelter for their cars but only grim-faced men engaged in desperate conflict with yards of wildly flapping canvas. But, much to my surprise and relief, there were no complaints.

Apart from this failure over the marquees, the event on the Friday passed off with a clockwork regularity which surprised me considering that the drivers included so many strangers from overseas. There were entrants from America, Belgium, Eire, Germany, Holland, Italy, New Zealand and Norway of whom only the Italian team of Alfa Romeos, led by Count Johnnie Lurani, lent a characteristic touch of light comedy to the proceedings by arriving at speed only just in time for the start to the accompaniment of much shouting and gesticulation. Like Paul Tusek and his steamer, these Italians were apt to cause consternation by making sudden appearances travelling rapidly in the wrong direction. Because the veterans taking the green route through Brighton were heavily outnumbered by the entrants in the Edwardian and vintage classes who would be going out through Hove, I made a last minute decision to make the number of cars using the two routes exactly equal by sending some of the older and smaller Edwardian and vintage cars out with the veterans as far as Poynings where they could rejoin their proper routes. This meant that the cars could be lined up for the start in two columns and despatched from the end of Madeira Drive in pairs, those in the right hand column turning right onto the London road. In this way the drive was cleared of all 312 cars in less than half an hour.

When the entry list was complete I had been surprised and pleased to see that they included four steam cars. These were: No. 2, the Soame 'Steam Cart', a one-off job of 1897 from Norfolk of such archaic form that it might have been thirty years older: No. 50, also from Norfolk, a Gardner Serpollet of 1904; No. 106, a 1911 non-condensing Stanley, and finally No. 215, a 1920 condensing Stanley, said to have been the demonstration car sent over to the English distributors by the Stanley brothers just after the Great War. Four steam cars in one event was something so unusual that, on the spur of the moment, I decided to offer a special award for the best performance by a steam car.

The somewhat complex arrangements at Petworth went almost miraculously to plan, the cars converging on the park by their several routes and then diverging once more after they had lunched. Some of the crews from overseas found time to visit the state rooms at Petworth House. As they were walking across the Park the 1911 Stanley panted quietly past them heading for the lake. Descending to the water's edge it extended a delicate copper-tipped proboscis into the lake and took a deep draught. Steam cars have an endearing animal quality about them such as no petrol car however characterful can ever display. In this case the Stanley's master showed a very proper concern for the thirst of his steed and was rewarded for his consideration by winning my award.

Competitors had a series of four driving tests ahead of them at Goodwood next morning and, as this would have been a very slow proceeding and difficult to organize if 312 cars had taken each test separately, the tests were laid out consecutively in front of the grandstand in such a way that, once he had been started, a competitor drove through all four tests, the average time taken to complete them being little over a minute so that we had got through them by early afternoon. I had looked forward to staging another 'Stamina Test', that thinly disguised long distance race that had provided such an appropriate conclusion to the Anglo-American Rally but, alas, it was not to be. Since 1954 the general competition regulations of the RAC had multiplied exceedingly and this 1963 International Rally was described on its RAC Permit as a 'Touring Assembly' at which racing of any kind was stricty *verboten*. Nevertheless, I did stage a series of two lap 'Demonstration Runs' by successive pairs of carefully selected cars whose performance was, in theory at least, strictly comparable. This produced some interesting results. One of these match events was between the two Stanleys, surely the only 'race' between steam cars to be staged in this country since the earliest years of this century. This proved to my satisfaction my belief in the superiority of the earlier, non-condensing car. By the time they had entered their second lap, all that the driver of the 1920 car could see of his rival was a little white cloud of steam in the distance.

It was at the conclusion of these interesting, if slightly irregular proceedings that I made my one serious error of judgement. Remembering how successful and impressive a finale it had been at the last two events I had organized at Goodwood, I decided to round off the day with another Grand Parade round the circuit. But, whereas previously 250 or so vintage cars had taken part, this time there were 312 cars of vastly wider date range and consequently variation in performance and, as I soon discovered to my cost, this was more than could be managed. To put the oldest cars in front seemed to be asking for trouble because no self-respecting Bentley or Bugatti could fairly be expected to adapt its gait to that of the Soame Steam Cart which could hardly have kept pace with a funeral procession. When assembled, the line of cars seemed to stretch almost half way round the circuit. From my position at the head of the procession I could just see over the roofs of the pits a thin column of smoke rising from the chimney of the Steam Cart half way down the Lavant straight. As we moved off I became acutely conscious of the powerful machinery that was impatiently breathing down the back of my neck, but I continued to crawl along in bottom gear hoping that in this way I could prevent the procession from eating its tail so that at least the spectators in the stand would see all the cars pass once in reverse number order even if chaos broke out later. But evidently those behind me failed to appreciate the reason for this slow motion exercise and were determined not to waste the opportunity by such snail-like progress. With a snarl a Bugatti tore past me in a fierce burst of acceleration closely followed by a Mercedes emitting an eldritch scream from its blower, and hotly pursued in its turn by three thunderous Bentleys. The floodgates had been unloosed and there was nothing whatever I could do about it. The surprised and startled owner of the Steam Cart had not even opened his regulator before he saw a melée of fast cars bearing down on him. Chaos ensued. I don't now what it looked like from the stands, but to me it seemed almost as hazardous as the notorious Paris–Madrid, an organizer's nightmare in fact. Providentially there was no accident and somehow the anxious marshals managed to slow the cars down and shepherd them off the circuit and on to the road for Bognor.

And so back to Butlins and Bert's fabulous buffet supper. I think any English competitor would say that our stay at Butlins was the most memorable feature of the event. I do not believe that anyone had seen the inside of a Holiday Camp before, so that to do so was a wholly novel and interesting experience. The beds in the chalets were comfortable, the appointments adequate and instead of the canned music or the cheerful 'Wakey, wakey!' over the public address system, which I had dreaded, there was only a discreet feminine voice informing us that it was 8 a.m. Altogether the service could not have been better or less obtrusive. Most of us spent the first evening wandering about the camp discovering, with fascinated interest, how the other half of the world spent its holidays. The Camp seemed to have a curious mixed ancestry, part show-biz, and part fairground. In one hall we looked through a glass wall into a swimming pool as though into some monstrous goldfish tank. In one of the many bars we were treated to a representation of a tropical thunderstorm every hour. We were fascinated, too, by the calculated efficiency with which the bars were run. As soon as the till takings in a bar fell below some pre-determined figure, when it was judged no longer economic to keep it open, out went the lights and the customers were forced to move on. As a result, by 11 p.m. all the bars had closed save one into which all the more hardened drinkers had perforce gravitated. I heard of only one disappointed customer, a lady passenger who, having come to the seaside, understandably wished to see the sea and even, perhaps, dabble her toes in it. She was disappointed and angry when she found herself barred from the sea by the Camp's perimeter fence. She did not appreciate that, unlike the amusements provided inside the Camp, the sea was for free and therefore represented unfair commercial compeititon.

These three events in 1954, 1955 and 1963 did a great deal to enliven and enrich, in both senses of the word, my early years as a father and a householder. After all, I might have 'gone on the bank', in other words 'settled down' at last, but I had no intention of becoming a vegetable. In his speech at the birthday party luncheon at Goodwood my friend, the late Laurence Pomeroy, pointed out that there was nothing common or mean about vintage cars and that in this way they resembled their designers and their drivers, for they continued to attract people of character and personality. This may sound snobbish but I have proved it to be true. Of the different worlds in which I had moved over the years, it is in this world of vintage motoring that I have found kindred spirits and most of those whom I regard as my truest and oldest friends ever ready to come to my rescue in time of trouble and difficulty.

4
Irish Interludes

My three months voyage over the Irish inland waterways in 1946 which I describe in *Green and Silver* enabled me, as it were, to get under the skin of Ireland in a way that I do not believe I could have achieved by any other means, not even by tramping the roads. For a boat seems to stimulate talk as no other vehicle can, especially when, as ours did, it puts in an unexpected appearance on such a disused waterway as the Royal Canal which pursues its lonely way through the midland bogs between Dublin and the Shannon. In the course of that voyage not only did I get under the skin of the country but the country got under mine, so much so that as the years passed I felt an increasing desire to go back. This magnetic attraction might be explained by the few genes I inherit from my Anglo-Irish great-grandfather in County Cork, yet I think it was due in much greater measure to the fact that in rural Ireland I was irresistibly reminded of the simpler, more natural world of my childhood on the Welsh border. The sheep and cattle fairs in the streets of the small towns with men leaning on sticks earnestly assessing quality or striking each other's palms to seal a bargain; the small, crowded bars and the individual shops where nothing was hygienically packaged; the paucity of motor vehicles and, in their place the creaking and click-clack of carts; here was the scent of turf fires instead of the wood smoke of Wales but the smells which mingled with it were the same; homely, natural smells of animals or of dust and dung upon the roads; above all perhaps the sheer luxury of breathing such soft, bland unpolluted country air, the blessed quiet of it all and the lack of feverish hurry. All these things brought memories of childhood welling up from a world that no longer existed on the other side of St George's Channel.

My first return to Ireland was only a flying visit to Dublin in 1949 where I had been invited to speak to the Royal Dublin Society on the subject of canals. My lecture was in the afternoon, and before it I was entertained (literally) to luncheon by members of the Society in an upstairs room in a certain famous Dublin Hotel that is frequented solely by Irishmen. I felt tremendously honoured and conversation scintillated as it always does on such occasions in Dublin. My immediate companion was a charming, witty, wizened, white-haired little man who, he told me, owned an old established photograhic and optician's business in Dame Street. But my day was made when I discovered to my delight that his name was none other than Thomas H. Mason, author of *The Islands of Ireland*, one of the select few books that I had carried around England in *Cressy's* bookshelves. I cannot at this distance recall one word of our conversation, but I know I found the talk of this delightful old man as spellbinding as his book which so perfectly distils the magic of the Irish islands. Not only did Thomas Mason write the book, but he also took the superb collection of photographs with which it is illus-trated. Both text and pictures are manifestly the product of a life-long love affair with the islands of Ireland and a deep understanding of their peoples. The author writes about them not coldly as an anthropologist or sociologist would do, but as his fellow countrymen and his friends. For this reason the book positively exudes that particular combination of beauty and sorrow, comedy and tragedy that is the very stuff of life in the islands of the west.

That day in Dublin has become memorable for another reason – it has gone down to history as the day on which my tongue was loosed. The great British public appears to assume, quite wrongly, that because a man succeeds in mastering the very private and solitary art of the written word he should also be master of the publicly spoken word as well.

This was another professional hazard which I failed to take into account when I decided to take up authorship, so when the first invitations to lecture came in, I was not only surprised but terrified by the prospect of having to speak in public. Consequently, the first few occasions when I was forced to do so are best forgotten, so acutely embarrassing were they. I totally lacked self-confidence and started with the fatal assumption that my audience knew far more than I did on the subject they had asked me to speak about. Yet on this particular afternoon in Dublin my Irish audience displayed such warmth and were so obviously sympathetic towards me, so eagerly responsive, that I found my tongue, and from that day to this I have never again found myself at a loss or been daunted by an audience.

My next visit to Ireland was in the early spring of 1952 and was of longer duration. The purpose this time was to gather material for the Irish chapter of a book called *Lines of Character* which was to describe a selection of the more characterful railways in England, Scotland, Wales and Ireland. In Ireland as elsewhere, most of the lines we travelled over have vanished without trace. So has the steam locomotive so far as commercial service is concerned, whereas in 1952 its continuing existence was taken for granted. As a consequence the book has become an historic document together with the pictures which were specially taken for it by Pat Whitehouse, the Hon. Secretary of the Talyllyn Railway Preservation Society.

On what was to be a sort of unofficial honeymoon, Sonia and I crossed by sea from Fishguard to Cork, about ten days before we were due at Towyn to take up our duties on the Talyllyn Railway. Our first objective was the Tralee & Dingle Light Railway in remote West Kerry. It was this craziest and most characterful of all narrow gauge railways which had determined the timetable of our expedition, for the line operated only on the occasion of the monthly cattle fairs in Dingle. I had obtained footplate passes for us and we aimed to board one of the empty cattle trains which left Tralee westbound on the Friday afternoon, and returned from Dingle with their freight on the following afternoon when the fair was over.

It was the first time I had made the Cork crossing and, as we steamed slowly up the lovely estuary of the Lee in the cold, clear light of that early spring morning, I thought there was no better way of approaching Ireland. Because we had arranged to stay in Cork that night, later in the day we went exploring along the north shore of the estuary having taken a train to a little station on the Cork–Youghal line. We discovered a long-ruined 'demesne', a sad relic of 'the troubles' no doubt, and walked in the pale sunshine through what had once been a large garden sloping down to the reedy margin of the Lee. It was a magical place that we had stumbled upon, reminding me of *The Secret Garden* which was one of my childhood's favourite books. For in this mild climate of southern-most Ireland, this forgotten garden had become a dense jungle which, even so early in the year, presented a spectacle of almost tropical splendour. Camellias had reached the stature of tall trees and their shapes of glossy green were starred with blossoms, crimson, pink and white. Curiously enough, I only discovered later that this ruined house may have been once the home of my Cork ancestors.

Next morning we changed trains at Mallow Junction and so commenced a slow journey into the west along that seemingly interminable single line that follows the Blackwater to its source and then strikes across the bogs to Killarney and so on to Tralee. I have seldom enjoyed a railway journey more. When we got to Mallow we had been surprised to discover that the train included a restaurant car, something one does not expect to see on a stopping branch line train, but then the English visitor is apt to forget that Irish branch lines can be so long and Irish country stations so few and far between. Unlike England where hundreds of stations have been closed and demolished, Irish stations have always been sparse, particu-larly in the west, simply because the population is so small and scattered. At this time, just before the railway systems of both countries began seriously to shrivel, branch line travel was a special pleasure but a totally different experience in Ireland. In England, the frequent wayside stations became the chief source of satisfaction and of a curiosity that increased the more deeply rural the stations became. As soon as my train had jerked to a standstill I would be on my feet and looking out of the window to see what the station building looked like and what manner of folk – if anyone – were leaving or boarding the train at such a remote spot; also to admire the stolid quality of the station staff, the rich country burr of their accents and their bright flowers – and even sometimes the topiary work – on the station platform. At each such stop one could capture something of the flavour of the place: its scents and sounds, the smell of new-mown hay or the church clock striking the hour; perhaps even a glimpse of a village street or of a spire rising above elm trees. But such scenes of cosy domesticity are much rarer in Ireland.

Almost alone in the dining car, we ate the usual Irish tea consisting of fresh soda bread, delicious butter and anonymous red jam while we chatted to the steward who, lacking company, was in a mood to talk. All the while the train trundled sedately along on its undulating way across the bogs and, through the wide windows on our left hand, there began to loom up the majestic blue shapes of Maccgillycuddys Reeks beyond Killarney, their peaks outlined against the westering sun. There was little sign of habitation beyond the occasional white-washed cabin on the green rim of the tawny bogland and the only sign of life we saw was when the train ran over one of the rare ungated level crossings and we would catch a glimpse, brief as the opening of a camera shutter, down the perspective of one of those long, white, and dusty roads that are laid straight as a ruler over the plains of Ireland. Here we would see for an instant, dwarfed to the size of insects by the scale of the landscape, tiny, crawling black figures: two women with shawls over their heads perhaps, a boy trotting on an ass with panniers, or a man carting turf. A slender spiral of blue smoke, rising far away, probably showed where the turf cutters were brewing up a dish of tea. I thought to myself then that branch line travel in Ireland is much more closely akin to a slow sea voyage or a journey by desert caravan. The infrequent stations are the small ports or the welcome oases. This simile is made the more apt by the inhabitants who, in the more remote parts of the west, line the platform of their local station simply for the pleasure of seeing the train come in, just as on some remote island of the Pacific, the quay is crowded to greet the monthly mail boat.

We were feeling a bit gummy-eyed and the worse for wear as we hurried through the streets of Tralee next morning on our way to what had once been the passenger station of the Tralee & Dingle Light Railway: for we had had little sleep. When we arrived in Tralee the previous evening we saw form the bill-boards that a grand Ceilidh was to be held that night in a local hall so we resolved to go. We were dazzled and enchanted, wondering what other town of equivalent size could produce such an array of talent. The only trouble with the show was that it was far too long. It was nearly midnight when we got back to our hotel only to find that the extensive re-construction of the interior, in readiness for the forth-coming summer season, was still in full swing. The hammer-ing, or what sounded like the sudden dropping of heavy planks from a great height, went on all night long. Who says the Irish are a lazy and shiftless race?

Dingle is the northern-most of the five peninsulas, two in Kerry and three in Cork, that southern Ireland thrusts out into the Atlantic. It is a wild and savage coast. Each of these five fingers is mailed with rock and cliff and engaged in a perpetual combat with the Atlantic surges. Each has a high backbone which, in the case of the three northern-most, achieves the stature of mountains. It is because the land between the mountains and the sea is of particularly good quality that the Dingle peninsula has become celebrated as a cattle raising district, while it was thanks to this richness that it weathered the great famine much better than other areas of the west. It is rare to see a ruined farm on Dingle, whereas if you follow the south-west coast of Cork from Skibbereen to Mizen Head, the fact that three out of four farms are ruined still bears grim witness to the famine. I find no romance in such ruins but prefer a prosperous countryside which is why I prefer Dingle.

The Tralee & Dingle Railway ran (for alas I am compelled to write of it in the past tense) for three-quarters of the length of the peninsula. Having perambulated half way round the town of Tralee it headed west along the shore of Tralee Bay as far as Castlegregory Junction where, having thrown off a branch to the town of that name, the main line swung inland and set out to climb the mountainous spine of the peninsula to reach the south coast. Dingle is on this south coast, but even if it were not, it would have been impracticable to carry the railway much further along the north side because the formidable massif of Brandon juts out into the Atlantic to form an almost impassable barrier. One of the peaks of Brandon, Masatiompan, sweeps steeply down to the sea from a height of 2,500 ft to make an obstacle daunting even to the optimistic engineer of the Tralee & Dingle. He, therefore, chose to scale the central ridge by way of the Glenagalt pass, the railway clinging to the side of the Glen and clawing its way upward on a seemingly interminable gradient of 1 in 29. No wonder the train of empty cattle wagons that awaited us at Tralee was double-headed. Behind us there was to follow a second and much shorter train hauled by the third surviving example of the railway's motive power.

I mounted the footplate of the pilot engine and Sonia that of the train engine, the guard squeezed into what little space was left to him in a bogie brake-van largely given over to cattle-carrying, and we were off. I wrote a full account of this journey by rail to Dingle in *Lines of Character*, so I will not repeat it here. What I did not record in that book, however, was the much more eventful journey back, loaded with cattle, to Tralee on the following day. The shape of the book decreed that I leave this out. Although we subsequently journeyed northwards from Tralee, first to Sligo and then into Donegal, travelling on other odd lines which are now no more, such as the Sligo, Leitrim & Northern Counties, the County Donegal and the Londonderry & Lough Swilly, I decided to describe these at the beginning of the book and to end with our arrival at Dingle. As Dingle has the distinction of being the most westerly town in Europe, Dingle station with its monthly train service had become a kind of railway ultima Thule and the artistic appropriateness of ending the story there made anti-climactic any account of the journey back to Tralee the following day.

The monthly cattle fair at Dingle was over by noon and by one o'clock or soon after, we pulled out with a train packed from end to end with cattle. As on the outward journey, a second, shorter train was due to follow us. All went well until we were pounding up a steep bank between Anascaul and Emalough. We had reached a point where the line had climbed out of Gleann an Scail, where Cuchulainn is supposed to have fought one of his legendary battles, and were crossing a desolate stretch of bogland on the high flank of a mountain known as Brickany, when I happened to glance back from the footplate at the long train snaking along behind us and noticed that the roof of one of the wagons in the centre of the train was heaving up and down and rocking from side to side in a most alarming manner. 'Hey!' I shouted above the tumult of the labouring locomotive, 'We've got one off.' The driver leaned over my shoulder, 'The devil we have!' he confirmed. He whistled and gesticulated to the driver of the train engine, snapped his regulator shut and then cautiously applied the vacuum brake.

We all climbed down for the inquest: the two drivers and their firemen, the guard and ourselves. The cattle wagon was certainly well and truly off the road with all four wheels and the wonder of it was that it had not made matters worse by turning over. At that time there were only three plate-layers employed on the thirty-one miles of line so a mishap of this kind was not surprising. It had been sunny when we left Dingle but now clouds had rolled up the sky driven by a north-east wind and there were occasional scuds of hail or sleet. It was bitterly cold out there on the open mountain and I felt very small indeed in that vast, sombre landscape of mountains and hurrying clouds as I listened to the animated debate between the five Irishmen as to how best to deal with the situation. First, two urgent telephone calls had to be made; one to Tralee to summon a breakdown gang to come out by road, the other to Anascaul to hold the following train and to ask the driver to detach his locomotive, come forward to pick up the rear portion of the train and return with it to Anascaul. Meanwhile our two locomotives would take the front portion of the train over the pass and down to Castlegregory Junction where the pilot would be detached and come back to Anascaul to assist the now heavier second train. It was hoped that by this time the breakdown gang would have got the derailed vehicle onto the road again so that the pilot engine could propel it to Anascaul.

So we went forward once more and when we eventually came to a grinding halt at Castlegregory we were given the choice of continuing with the train engine to Tralee or going back over Glenagalt with the pilot. Because this was certainly the last opportunity we would ever have to travel on this remarkable railway it was a case of in for a penny, in for a pound, so we were soon clanking over the pass once more, our light engine making easy work of the gradient. As we descended the far side we could see across the open bog that the breakdown gang had played their part. The wagon was back on the rails; we could also see a little knot of men sheltering from the wind in its lee and their lorry standing on the road nearby. We were taking all this in when we were momentarily startled out of our wits by the sudden loud explosion of detonators under our wheels. Although the errant wagon had been visible at least half a mile before we reached it, it was awesome to think that the writ of the railway rule book ran even on this semi-derelict outpost of the furthest west.

We propelled the re-railed wagon before us back to Anascaul where a certain amount of shunting was necessary before a long train of cattle wagons with two engines at their head was once more ready to depart. Two chimneys vomited steam and black smoke and for the second time that day we began the climb to Emalough. As we approached the scene of the derailment we saw that the breakdown gang had remained behind to watch us pass. It was just as well that they had done so, for, right in front of their noses, a wagon in the middle of the train jumped the rails in precisely the same fashion as before. We began to wonder if we should ever see our hotel beds in Tralee that night. And what of the unfortunate cattle, crammed for hours into those small vans? However, the gang with their re-railing equipment to aid them soon had the train under way once more. But there was one more hazard ahead of us, a hazard of an improbable kind such as one could only encounter in Ireland. It was nearly dark when we stopped for water at the crane at Castlegregory. Our driver looked at his turnip watch by the light from the firehole, shook his head and muttered with dire foreboding that he feared the 'tide would be makin''. We failed to see the relevance of this remark until he patiently explained the situation to us. The banks of the estuary of the river Lee which empties into the head of Tralee Bay have been raised in time past to prevent flooding, but these flood-banks fell into neglect and have now been breached in many places. One effect of this neglect is that high spring tides flood over the track of the Tralee & Dingle as it approaches Tralee, to a sufficient depth to extinguish the fires of the locomotives, or so we were told. At any rate our drivers evidently believed it, for the two locomotives, shooting sparks into the night air, their flailing side-rods clanking like a runaway steam roller, fairly ate up the remaining level miles to Dingle, the long train of cattle wagons snaking crazily behind them. I never thought I should find myself on a train racing to beat the tide and I found it a truly dream-like experience – like much else that can happen to one in Ireland.

In the event, all was well. We found the tide just lapping the tracks; it was over the sleepers but not over the rails so the train passed and, whistling madly at each unprotected crossing, circled round the outskirts of the town and drew to a final stop in the station from which we had departed – could it only have been yesterday morning? It seemed half a lifetime ago. We bade farewell to our engine crews while a number of drovers, who had been waiting for us for hours, set about unloading their beasts. Then we made all speed to our hotel, for we were madly hungry, and were soon consuming an enormous Irish 'tea' consisting of steak and chips upon a vast scale followed by the inevitable soda bread, butter and red jam.* We realized then that we had seen the last of the Tralee & Dingle Railway – even in Ireland it obviously had no future – but Dingle itself had cast a spell over us and we knew that one day we should return.

We did go back to Dingle, travelling by the same route and staying in the same hotels, but only after nine years had gone by and it was May 1961. There was no dining car any more on the train from Mallow to Tralee and of the Tralee & Dingle Railway there was practically no trace at all. A stranger to Dingle would have been surprised to hear that there had ever been a railway; but there were forlorn and dilapidated remains to be seen if, as we did, you knew where to look. Otherwise, little had changed in the space of nine years. In fact, so little of note had happened in these nine years that we were welcomed back to Dingle as 'those two English people who were on the little train the day they had the derailment'. It is this relatively slow pace of change which, for us, made a visit to Ireland such a solace.

In Ireland I found I could relax and recover from an overdose of rebuilding, redevelopment, re-structuring, re-organizing, reorientation and rationalization. We booked a

---

* At this time a few provincial Irish hotels offered 'Dinner' as a concession to English tourists which we soon learnt to avoid. For twice the price of 'Irish Tea' one got the same steak and chips but with tinned soup and tinned fruit salad instead of the unlimited and delicious fresh soda bread with jam and butter.

room in Dingle for a week and hired two bicycles from a shop just round the corner. Each morning we were awakened by the sound of creaking carts as their owners queued up in the street outside while waiting to deliver their churns of milk to the dairy. After their turn had come and gone they would disappear into an adjacent bar to fortify themselves for the return journey with pints of porter, leaving their horses or asses standing outside, heads a-droop, with long-accustomed patience. Bearing in mind the amount of time consumed in travelling to and fro, it seemed a very tedious and costly way of delivering a few gallons of milk each morning. Would not collection by dairy lorry from the farm be much more economical? But at this point I reminded myself that this was Ireland where no one asked such coldly logical and calculating questions simply because other considerations, tradition, custom, old habits, the imponderable things that make up the quality of life and give it savour even for the poorest, properly took priority over mere efficiency.

On our first day out from Dingle we had an easy but spectacular ride along the deserted coast road that rounds Slea Head, the furthest tip of the peninsula. For most of the way the road clings to a ledge cut in the lower slopes of Mount Eagle which here stoop steeply down to the sea. On this wild western rim of the old world, craggy, treeless and storm-swept, where one is very much alone and there are no sounds other than the thunder of breakers, the booming of the wind and the cries of sea birds gliding and swooping on up-currents of air, the sense of the force of an ancient and elemental world is overwhelming. It is a very salutary experience because it cuts a man down to size. One is also made aware that very slowly but none the less surely, stubborn rock is losing the battle with the sea, for the advance guards have already been overwhelmed. Like so many armed knights, cut off but still fighting on against desperate odds, the western islands began to come into view as we rounded Slea Head, rocks ringed about with white water: Inishtooskert, Beginish, the Great Blasket, Inishnabro, Inishvickillane and, in the furthest west, invisible behind the bulk of the Great Blasket, the drowned peak of Tearaght. There were once oratories of the Celtic church on Inishtooskert and Inishvickillane, the former credited to St Brendan, although how such holy men managed to subsist at all in such wild places is past knowing. Within the memory of man, these and other smaller islands have been uninhabited or only used for summer pasturage by the people of the Great Blasket where the island village was inhabited until 1953 when its dwindling population moved with reluctance to the mainland. Such remote islands and their inhabitants are capable of casting a spell upon certain people 'from over the water' as strong as any enchantment of Prospero's making. The name of Robin Flower has become as inseparably associated with the Great Blasket as has that of J.M. Synge with the Aran Islands.

Robin Flower visited the island frequently from Cambridge over a period of twenty years beginning in 1910. He became an Irish speaker and was beloved of the islanders who called him 'Blaheen', the Little Flower. In his book, Thomas Mason describes how Flower was responsible for introducing him to the island and its people. 'Blaheen' also became a great friend of the island patriarch, Tomas O'Crohan, and he was responsible for translating into English and publishing under the title of the island patriarch, Tomas O'Crohan, and he was responsible for translating into English and publishing under the title Blasket in 1856 and had lived there all his life. He was much loved and respected in Ireland as a Gaelic scholar. Robin Flower, too, paid tribute to the island and its inhabitants in *The Western Island*, first published in 1944. In the last paragraph of this book there occur the prophetic words: 'Here, too, they will be gone in a few short years', but in fact he is referring here to the fairies who lived on only in the minds of a few old people. The book betrays no inkling that the island community he knew and loved for so many years would so soon cease to exist. Happily, he did not live to see the islanders leave.

Although, as its name denotes, the Great Blasket is by far

the largest of the group, it is little more hospitable than the smaller islands. It consists of the top of the drowned mountain of Slievedonagh whose long, narrow ridge runs from south-west to north-east and for the most part falls steeply to the sea. It is only at the north-eastern end that the slope become more gentle so that pasture and tillage become possible. There is actually one patch of near-level ground on the northern-most tip of the island and here the people would play their games, or the young folk dance to the music of a fiddle. As we approached Dunquin, the point of departure for the Blasket, this north-east face of Slievedonagh began to open up so that we could see the whitewashed cabins of the deserted village scattered down the lower slopes above the cliffs. From a distance one might think them still inhabited.

Like the island of Bardsey, the Great Blasket is a great deal less accessible than it appears at first sight. For both are separated from the mainland by a narrow but very treacherous strait, in this case Blasket Sound. It is beset on every side by cliffs and jagged rocks and its waters, even on the calmest day, seem always restless. To make the passage between the island and the mainland more difficult, the so-called harbour below the cliffs of Dunquin is exposed to the south-west, while the entrance through the rocks to the island landing place is so narrow that it is extremely difficult to make with safety when there is a strong sea running.

It was in this Blasket Sound that *Our Lady of the Rosary*, one of the finest and largest ships of Spain's Armada met her end. According to tradition, either by luck or by superb navigation, this great ship weighing 1,000 tons had success-fully passed through the narrow, rock-strewn channel between Beginish and the Great Blasket to anchor safely in the sound. With her elaborately painted and gilded upper works, one can see her riding there like some bird of exotic tropical plumage that has been blown off course into this alien and menacing world of monochrome. But this spectacle did not endure for long. As the light began to fail a south-westerly gale blew up, *Our Lady of the Rosary* began to drag her anchor and was dashed to pieces with the loss of all hands against the cliffs about Dunquin.

This particular visit to Ireland was made especially memorable because I achieved at one stroke two ambitions: to land on the Great Blasket and to ride in an Irish curragh. As the owner of one of Harry Rogers' Severn coracles, I was naturally very interested in the various forms of curragh which we saw in the course of our journeyings in the west. What was most fascinating to me was the discovery that from an ancient, wattle-framed original covered in cow hide, both Severn coracle and Irish curragh had developed on precisely the same lines as regards the materials used and the methods of construction employed, although it seems highly improbable that there has been any connection between the two for centuries. Both use sawn ash laths for the frame and cover it with white cotton duck coated with tar. They even appear to paint the inside of the ash frame with the identical shade of green paint!

The story of the curragh in Ireland goes back to those legendary days of the Celtic church when St Brendan and other holy men set out in their skin-covered craft in search of Hy Brasil, that island of the blest which, men said, could occasionally be seen from the cliffs of western Ireland as a shadowy shape in the path of the setting sun. Brendan is said to have sailed as far as the Everglades of Florida in quest of this holy land of lost Atlantis. Such sea-going curraghs were considerably larger than anything known today. The modern forms of the curragh still to be found along the west coast of Ireland are intensely localized. Their construction and use appears to have spread very slowly southward down the coast from the primitive little tub – no more than a slightly elongated coracle – used by the Tory islanders off the coast of Donegal to the latest and finest flowering of the curragh-maker's art – the Kerry or Dingle curragh which, it is said, did not exist before 1850. Moreover, Tomas O'Crohan in his autobiography says that in his youth on the Great Blasket all the islanders used wooden boats until two of them went off to

Dingle Fair and purchased a curragh or 'canoe' as the islanders called it. When they proudly appeared in Blasket Sound with their purchase, their craft looked so frail compared with the wooden boats that the island women, anticipating their imminent demise, began keening. Nevertheless, the islanders soon became wedded to the Dingle curragh.

This is how James Hornell, in his fundamental and definitive study of this subject*, describes the Dingle curragh:

> The curraghs that go fishing from the many little harbours in this district are the largest, the most elegant, the most beautifully proportioned and the most carefully made of all surviving types. Every part harmonises; they ride the water more lightly than the sea-fowl yet are strong enough to battle successfully with the wild Atlantic gales that torment this coast in winter.

It took something very special to make this otherwise sober researcher wax almost poetic. The nearest relative to the Dingle curragh is the type used – perhaps for centuries – by the Aran islanders; it is certainly the nearest to it in size and lines. Most Irish curraghs have a bow sheer so pronounced that when lightly laden the bows ride high above the water. In the case of the Aran curragh, as on other types, this is achieved by an ugly angular break in the line of the gunwale which gives the impression that the otherwise straight gunwale has been bent upward as an afterthought. On the Dingle curragh there is not only a smooth sheer on the bow but on the stern also, the gunwale describing one supremely graceful arc from stem to delicately in-curving and up-tilted stern. No wonder the Blasket islanders called their curraghs canoes. They were 25 ft long with a maximum beam of 4 ft 6 in and they were fitted with four rowing thwarts although three oarsmen were the

* 'The Curraghs of Ireland' from *The Mariner's Mirror*, the Quarterly Journal of the Society for Nautical Research, Vols XXIII, XXIV, 1937–8.

usual complement. They were also equipped with a fifth thwart right for'ard in which a small mast for a lug sail could be stepped. There are plenty of references to these Dingle curraghs sailing, but it is not a sight I have seen myself. When Hornell was in the area in 1936 he reckoned tht Michael FitzGerald of Ballydavid on the northern rim of Smerwick Harbour, which lies to the north of the Blaskets, was Kerry's, and therefore Ireland's master curragh-maker.

The balance of probability is that the curragh in which I voyaged to the Great Blasket was one of FitzGerald's making, but I could not be certain of this because of difficulties of communication. For the three islandmen who rowed us over to the Blasket were all Gaelic speakers and had not a word of English between them. We had met one of them in the little bar at Dunquin and, although we could only communicate with him through a bilingual third party, we thought we had managed to establish a satisfactory relationship with him and to secure an undertaking that he would row us out to the Great Blasket next Sunday at noon. We had made it clear that there would then be four of us because on the Saturday two of our vintage car friends, John and Paul, would be flying out to join us for the whole of the following week. What we did not realize as we pedalled our way back to Dingle by another route was that the intermediary concerned was mistrusted by the islanders and that our friend had taken our expressed desire to visit the Blasket with a very large pinch of salt. So, when Sunday came round, it was Sonia who had to seek out our 'captain' and, without the aid of words, so convince him of our bona fides that he relented, summoned two of his fellows and beckoned us to follow him down the steep cliff path to the harbour where, upon the narrow shore above the tides, several curraghs lay bottom up looking like small stranded whales. The selected whale soon resembled some strange six-legged monster as the three dark-suited men lifted it over their heads and then bore it aloft down to a grey but silver-shining sea. As it rode lightly as a leaf beside the little quay it seemed absurdly fragile. How could such a cockle-shell possibly bear its crew of three plus four passengers? The question answered itself as we stepped gingerly on board and I found myself balancing as I used to do in my coracle. I remembered an Irishwoman referring to the clumsy clinker-built rowing boat we had towed around with us on our *Green & Silver* expedition as 'a very giddy boat'. I wondered what she would think of this one.

As an engineer, I found myself thinking of similar structures in which all superfluous material must be pared away to leave a sparse rib-cage, where each member is precisely suited to its purpose so that the whole achieves the goal of supreme lightness and great strength. I thought first of the frame of a big rigid airship and then, becoming more up to date, of the space-frame of a modern racing car. But then I realized that these were objects of scientific calculation and therefore not analogous with FitzGerald's beautiful curragh frame because the latter was perfected by intuition and not by calculation; by that mysterious gift which inspires the hand of the craftsman. The mud-wattled nest of a bird seemed a more fitting analogy than a space-frame.

The three islanders took their places on the thwarts, pushed off, and then struck out to a lovely rhythm with their long, thin-bladed oars. No doubt it was calm to them, but to us the Sound seemed decidedly choppy, its surface corrugated by short steep little seas. Now I understood why, in the last century, the Blasket islanders had been so speedily converted from their wooden boats. Seated in the bow as I was, I should very soon have been drenched under such conditions had this been a wooden boat, burying her nose into each wave. But like a practised steeplechaser to a jump, this curragh lifted lightly and effortlessly to whatever obstacle the sea cast in her path so that throughout our entire trip, out and home, she never shipped a drop of water. She was like some wild thing, reacting instinctively to her element and, in this this respect, totally unlike any form of boat which I have experienced either before or since. It was all most exhilarating.

By contrast, the island was a sad place. The once obviously well-used track that led from the landing place and climbed up between the terraced cabins now wore a neglected air, being obviously only rarely used. The reason why the village looked so deceptively habitable from the mainland was now made plain – the dilapidation of their old homes was being held in check by these men. They frequently visited the island to shoot rabbits, or in the course of fishing expeditions, and used their cabins for shelter or storage. The captain of our curragh kept chickens on his little holding and we found a hen sitting on a clutch of eggs. It became clear to us that although Dunquin was only the breadth of a narrow sound away it represented exile to these men as surely as would the antipodes. Hence the chickens and the brave attempts to check the effects of wind and weather on their island homes which I found extremely moving. It made me realize that the spell cast by islands cannot be dismissed as a mere modern romantic dream of the simple life; of getting away from it all. God knows these men knew all there was to be known about the hardships of life on this speck of land on the wild westernmost rim of Europe, yet the Great Blasket still had them by the heart and would do so till their dying day. I not only felt moved but also embarrassed. These men would have been justified if they had refused a passage to four English people to whom a deserted island was merely an object of curiosity to wile away a Sunday afternoon. I felt like some stranger who comes to a wake merely for the morbid pleasure of staring at the corpse. So, while the men busied themselves in the village and caught rabbits, we strolled on the slopes above until they signalled us that it was time to return to the landing place.

The other highlight of this week's stay in Dingle, and certainly our most energetic day, was our ascent of Brandon Mountain, at 3,127 ft the second highest peak in Ireland. We set off on our bicycles, following the road that cuts due north from Dingle across the peninsula until it ends at the little fishing harbour of Brandon Creek. It was hard slogging. The long straight road led us continuously upward, alternately riding and walking. On either hand our way was lined by great bushes of fuchsias in full crimson blossom which were growing on top of the typical celtic hedge-banks. To this austere and treeless landscape the fuchsias that grow in such profusion not only bring welcome colour but a certain tropical luxuriance that seems almost bizarre in such a context. A native of the rainforests of Central and South America, the fuchsia was not brought to England until 1788, to presumably we have 'the old ascendancy' to thank for its introduction to western Ireland.

Our immediate objective was a farm named Ballybrack that lay up a steep little lane to our right just before the gradient eased and the road began to drop towards Brandon Creek. Ballybrack had seemed, from my inch-to-the-mile map, to be the best starting point for the ascent because a path marked 'The Saint's Road' appeared to lead thence directly to the summit. What I had failed to notice was that the map, which I had ordered specially from the Irish Ordnance Survey Office, had last been revised in 1899. When afterwards I checked this against a more modern half-inch map I found that the ominous words (site of) appeared below the Saint's Road. I should have realized from my previous experience of climbing Ben Gower, one of the Twelve Pins of Connemara, that the ascent of Brandon might be difficult. It is not that Irish mountains call for rock climbing or any do-or-die expertise of that kind, but they do have a habit of surrounding themselves with treacherous wet bogs in which he who was so foolish as to plod on would presumably gradually disappear from sight. And where there is not wet bog, the mountain flanks are fleeced so luxuriantly with tough-rooted ling or gorse that walking is at best extremely arduous, and at its worst impossible. Beneath such a dense miniature jungle there was no trace whatever of the Saint's Road. Nor was there even a sheep track to help us through the undergrowth, for the good reason that sheep seem to be a rarity on such Irish mountains as I have seen, presumably owing to the bogs and the sheer lack of nutritious bite. Nevertheless, we struggled on towards the summit, consoling ourselves with the thought at at least the weather was favouring us. For in this mild and humid maritime climate, Brandon Mountain, like Snae Fell in the Isle of Man, is lost in mists and cloud more often than not. But today it was clear and sunny and we could see the peak plainly before us.

By two o'clock we had reached the fragmented ruin on the summit which is presumably all that remains of St Brendan's oratory. The view was breath-taking. The mountain is the highest point of a ridge that extends from Brandon Peak in the south to the northern coast where Masatiompan sweeps superbly to the sea. To the west we could see far below the little inlet of Brandon Creek, while to the east we looked down the valley of the Owennafeana river to the waters of Brandon Bay and beyond to that strange little archipelago, the Seven Hogs or Magharee Islands that lie off Rough Point on the further side of the bay. But we were only just in time to see this wild landscape in all its splendour, for we had not finished our sandwiches before the sun, which had been blazing down out of a clear sky, suddenly lost its power. No clouds were to be seen but, on jumping up, we noticed that the sea, which had hitherto been visible to the horizon, had now become shadowy and indistinct, veiled by mist like the waters of some inland lake in an autumn dawn. Although we did not fear rain, we plunged back down the mountain, not wishing to be lost in the mist. We eventually reached Ballybrack without mishap and looking back, saw that Brandon had already withdrawn itself from sight.

At intervals during this rigorous day we had thought how delightfully refreshing was the prospect of a six-mile free-wheel back to Dingle as soon as we regained the hard road. Alas, it was not to be. I was leading and we had only gone a hundred yards or so when I heard behind me a sharp report like the crack of a .22 rifle. No, we had not been ambushed by wild Kerrymen; it was the sound of Sonia's back tyre exploding. Sonia was stoically prepared to face a six-mile tramp back to Dingle, but I would have none of it and set off free-wheeling in search of rescue with her useless bicycle, clasped by its steering head, towing alongside. It was characteristic of

Irish hospitality and friendliness that, on hearing of our plight, the proprietress of our hotel in Dingle, without a moment's hesitation, offered me the use of her small Austin car. So, thanks to her we were spared a wearisome anti-climax to what had been another memorable day.

On the Monday after our voyage to the Great Blasket we left Dingle with Paul and John to explore by road the so-called 'ring of Kerry' and the south coast of Cork from Skibbereen to Mizen Head. This was all new country to us and it was, therefore, a most enjoyable experience though we thought none of it the equal of Dingle. The first night we spent at Glenbeigh and after dinner walked down a bosky private drive that linked our hotel with Glenbeigh station on the broad gauge Valentia branch. From the look of things, the station might have been a private one built to serve the hotel only. But we were saddened to see a demolition train slumbering in the platform. Eastwards the metals were still intact, stretching away to their junction with the Tralee-Mallow line at Farranfore, but westwards the train had left behind it only a vacant road-bed, a thin layer of ballast which bramble and briar would very soon penetrate. It had been a spectacular railway and expensive to build, but now Cahersiveen will never again hear the sound of a railway train.

I think it was on the next day that the small but memorable episode of the ford occurred. I do not recall the precise wherabouts, but all four of us lay sprawled on a little grassy knoll, a ruined castle to the left and, running from left to right in front of us, a narrow tidal creek. Between us and the castle a white road led down to a ford across this creek. Came a crunch of cart wheels and we saw, coming down this road towards us, a typical Irish two-wheeled cart drawn by an elderly and tired looking horse. Its driver looked equally tired as he lolled, swaying slightly, a-top of a miniature mountain of sacks piled on the flat platform of the cart. We were thinking how typical the whole scene was of rural Ireland – it could have made an Irish Tourist Board photograph – until the cart rolled down to the ford and the scene became quite untypical. Without slackening pace or any sign of animation on the part of its conductor, the whole equipage went deeper and deeper into the water until nothing whatever remained visible except the horse's head and the driver. We got to our feet, expecting in our innocence to see the horse begin to struggle and plunge or the whole outfit begin to float away. Not at all. At the same pace the horse and cart emerged from the ford, ascended the slope opposite and presently disappeared. At least we understood the reason for that pile of sacks.

In 1963 I paid my latest visit to Ireland. We resisted a strong pull from Dingle and decided to break new ground by exploring Donegal, making our base at Killybegs. That small fishing port was the western-most terminus of the County Donegal narrow gauge railway system so that we had spent an hour or so in the town during our rail tour in 1952 and to go back there, after the lapse of over a decade, was a railway experience as sad as our return to Dingle. Killybegs is one of the most thriving fishing ports on the whole west coast, but its rail connection, like Dingle's, has disappeared almost without trace. I recognized the shed where the fish crates were loaded into railway wagons, but now it stood silent and shuttered at the head of the quay, a couple of rusting rail-ends protruding from beneath its bolted doors.

I shall remember the week we spent in Donegal for two things: Slieve League and the little deserted village and harbour of Port. Slieve League is a mountain almost 2,000 ft high which rears itself from the very brink of the sea. To climb it from inland as we did and, on reaching the summit, suddenly to see beneath one's feet the waves crawling far, far below over a steely grey sea like a shimmer of shot silk, or a fishing boat reduced to the size of a water boatman, was a breath-taking experience. On the landward side the mountain falls away equally steeply to a small lough, held like a drop of dew in a green hollow between its knees. Consequently, the summit of Slieve League consists simply of a straight and narrow ridge that appears razor sharp from a distance yet, in fact, contains just room enough for a narrow path known as the 'One Man's Pass'. The seaward flank is claimed by some to be the highest cliff in Europe, but whether this stands or not depends on your definiton of a cliff. To be truthful, Slieve League's fall to the sea is not vertical except for the last few hundred feet. Nevertheless, I am glad it was a fine, calm day when we walked the One Man's Pass, for the slopes are extremely steep and I would certainly fight shy of such a place in a high wind.

Port is on the west coast, north of Glencolumbkille and it is sheltered from the north by a great cliff called Port Hill. We reached it from Meenacross by one of those seemingly endless bog roads. This one swooped away westward, following the gentle lift and fall of the bog, until it could go no further and there was Port, a little huddle of empty cabins under the lee of the headland to our right, the small, disused quay straight ahead. The cliffs of the headland and the vertiginous stacks which had broken away from them were all pink-capped with sea thrift, among which hundreds of tern and kittywakes, were either nesting or resting. There was no sound but the slump and fret of the waves against the cliffs, the roar of wind in one's ears and, of course, the crying of seabirds. It seemed to me that until the last trump sounded these elemental voices alone would be heard here, for I thought Port one of the loneliest places I have ever visited, the deserted village on the Blasket not excepted. Lonely and sad, but not in the least awe-inspiring, sinister or frightening. It was sad because here was yet another point of intimate contact with the natural world that man had forsaken and each such withdrawal can only be made at the price of spiritual loss.

This visit was the reverse of our previous one in that our friends, John and Paul, joined us for this first week in Donegal, but then had to fly home leaving us with a second week on our own. We had come out without any clear idea what we should do with ourselves, but I now decided with Sonia's agreement that we would do our best to visit the Aran islands and so fulfil another long-standing ambition of mine. So I booked us a hotel room in Galway and our friends agreed to drop us off there before heading east to Dublin. We stopped once en route from Killybegs to Galway – to pay homage to Yeats in Drumcliff churchyard. They had not brought the poet back to Ireland when first I visited Drumcliff in 1946. I had known the epitaph he had composed for himself for years:

> Cast a cold eye
> On life, on death.
> Horseman, pass by!

Read off the page the words compose a tyically proud and gnomic Yeatsian utterance, but to read them from the graven stone in this wild place with majestic Ben Bulben towering above the little churchyard was a very different experience. It made the hair on my head stir, as the poet no doubt intended it should, as I saw in imagination a rider on a great white horse sweeping past on the road to Sligo.

As a preliminary to our 1946 voyage, we had visited Galway and I described in *Green and Silver* how we watched the Aran steamer, the *Dun Aengus*, come into the harbour and how the islandmen wore suits of home-spun 'bawneen' which were held up at the waist with gaily coloured belts (*crios*) which I had likened to the 'spider-web' belts once worn by the boatmen of the English canals. Circumstanced as we were then, a visit to the islands which had been made real for me by the writings of J.M. Synge was not possible, but now it seemed that the moment had come at last.

We learned in Galway that the island steamer, now the *Naomh Eanna*, was due to dock on the evening of our arrival so, after an early dinner at our hotel, we walked down to the harbour to watch her come in. Asking where we could stay on Aran, a friendly member of her crew gave us an address and telephone number at Kilmurvy on Aranmore and we took action accordingly. After the long sea passage and the times of sailing had been allowed for, we reckoned we could only spare two nights on Aranmore and would have no opportunity to visit the other two islands where landing is more difficult,

Aranmore possessing the only deep-water quay. But at least we should have seen Aran with our own eyes.

Aranmore is by far the largest of the three islands; it spreads its length of eight miles west to east in the approaches to Galway Bay. It is never more than two miles wide and in section it is wedge-shaped, the formidable cliffs of its southern shore tapering down to golden strands divided by little broken rock promontories on the northern coast that looks toward Connemara and the Twelve Pins. For seven of these eight miles the island's one main road wanders along this northern coast. It runs from Killeany, through the island capital of Killronan where the steamer calls, to the tiny hamlet of Bungowla near the western tip of the land. At intervals along this road one comes upon strange rectangular pillars of stone topped by crosses and bearing inscribed entablatures. They are memorials to bygone generations of islanders, but when I first saw them I speculated whether their bones might not be immured within the pillars, for Aran is a place where anything is believable.

The house where we stayed at Kilmurvy lay toward the western end of this road. It was not actually on the road, but a little to the south of it, sheltering under the lee of the rising ground from the prevailing south-westerlies. Behind the house the rocky ground rises to the terrific climax of Dun Aengus, the mightiest pre-historic stronghold I have ever seen or am likely to see. The central citadel was originally protected from the north (the direction from which we approached it) by four successive stone ramparts, semi-circular in plan. The outer two have been almost quarried away, but the inner pair still stand almost unbelievably intact in all their forbidding grandeur, 18 ft high and 13 ft thick with an inner platform for the patrolling defenders, themselves protected by a menacing *chevaux de frise* of jagged stones which would effectually prevent any mass assault. Each of these surviving lines of fortification is pierced by a single low and tunnel-like sally port, the one offset from the other. Doubtless the outer fortifications were similarly equipped.

Some believe that the fortress was originally circular and that the southern half has been washed away by the sea. I do not think that this is so because the inner citadel is protected on the seaward side by cliffs which here form the most formidable natural barrier that man could conceive. Although of puny height in comparison with towering Slieve League, these cliffs are infinitely more vertiginous and awe-inspiring for they have actually been undercut by the sea. I crawled forward on all fours to a cliff verge, as sharp as the edge of a wall, and found myself gazing directly down 300 ft to a swirling confusion of dark waters marbled with veins of foam. In such situations the Aran islander would sit line fishing by the hour, legs nonchalantly dangling in space, the line descending between his thighs or fixed to his toe. I have a fairly good head for heights, but such feats are not for me; I withdrew my head and crawled slowly backward from that dreadful edge. Dun Aengus certainly needed no man-made defences on its seaward side.

Throughout the history of Western Europe the flow of successive colonizations has always been from east to west. Newcomers have always pushed the older race before them until, on the rocky coasts of the Atlantic, they could go no further but could only stand and turn to meet their adversaries. Sometimes there was no adversary because in much of the west the land was too poor to be covetable, but in the case of the Belgic Celts, the Firbolgs, the Tuatha de Danaan, or whoever were responsible for Dun Aengus they must have had some peculiarly relentless foe to force them to build so impregnably here on the rocky rim of the known world.

Our brief visit to Aran was favoured by quite exceptionally fine weather and it was a wonderful evening, calm and still, with the Twelve Pins standing up roseate in the distance across Galway Bay, as we set out to stroll westwards along the island road as far as the hamlet of Onaght where I had noticed the words 'Seven Churches' marked on my map. Presumably the number seven held some mystical significance for the saints and scholars of the celtic church, for in Ireland they are

always number seven, no more and no less, the most famous
being the seven churches of Clonmacnoise beside the Shannon. Here on Aranmore the seven were on a much more
modest scale being each no larger than an oratory intended for
private prayer. Whereas the white-washed cabins of the
hamlet were at the roadside, these little ruined holy places lay
huddled below road level and midway between it and the
strand. Dusk was beginning to fall by now and so intent were
we in tracing the walls of the churches that we did not notice a
woman come out from the cabin opposite and stroll towards us
until she accosted us in her soft Irish voice. It was not long
before she had introduced herself. She was Maggie Dirrane,
star of that great Flaherty film *Man of Aran* which I had seen
many years before and never forgotten. She was no longer the
slip of a girl she was when that film was made in the early
1930s, but her calm, unlined face was still beautiful and her
voice would have soothed an insomniac to slumber. When we
told her we had both seen the film she was delighted and
talked on into the deepening dusk about it and how she had
come to London for the première. It was clear that this
episode had been the one great event of her life, but she was
content to treasure the memory of a now almost incredible
happening as an astronaut might recall a past landing on the
moon. Unlike so many others, she had remained untouched
by the tinsel glitter of an urban world but had returned to her
island birthplace with no unsatisfied cravings. When we told
her we intended to walk to the western-most tip of the island
next day she invited us to call in at her cabin as we were
passing. We did so and stepped into an interior of stone flags
and gleaming white walls that was scrupulously clean and
spotless. But the seven churches below could not have displayed a healthier disregard for material comforts or possessions than did Maggie Dirrane's cottage.

On no island but Aranmore have I been given so strong a
feeling that I had come to the end, or the beginning, of the
world and this sense of elemental simplicity and austerity is
particularly strong as one reaches its western end at Bungowla.

It is not only that the islanders lack all those main services which we now consider essential to civilized living, for they share this deprivation with many other island communities. What makes Aran unique is that there is no fuel on the islands* and precious little soil either. The only element which is present in abundance and of which one is made ever conscious is stone. Wherever naked rocks will permit, the whole surface of Aranmore is parcelled into minute plots of 'gardens' by an intricate network of stone walls, not the neat dry walls to which we are accustomed but merely boulder piled precariously upon boulder so that when seen against the sky they frequently appear translucent like a pile of cannon-balls. There are no gates because there is no timber. When an Aran man puts a beast out to pasture he takes the wall down to let it in and builds it up again behind it. But many of these tiny walled enclosures contain no soil at all, only huge flat plates of fissured limestone. When we were on Aran in June, the only natural feature to soften the harsh, almost sinister, face of this stoney landscape were the brilliant wild flowers growing in profusion in the fissures of the limestone.

It is in these small stone fields that the potatoes are grown. First the fissures in the rock are plugged as well as may be with small stones; then a series of broad ridges consisting of alternate layers of sand and seaweed are built upon the rock and in these the potatoes are planted. In *Man of Aran* we are shown Maggie Dirrane cutting seaweed on the strand and then carrying it up to the fields in a pannier on her back. We saw Maggie Dirrane's successor coming up from the sea with her harvest of seaweed, the only difference being that she carried her pannier on donkey-back. Life does not change much on Aran. Yet change there is, none the less. Despite lavish financial aid from the Irish Government, the population of Aran continues to dwindle. It is increasingly a population of the old and the very young; the able-bodied have emigrated to

* Turf has to be imported by sea from Connemara as there are no bogs on the islands.

England or to America. The fish, they will tell you, no longer come to the shores of the island so that one of Aran's traditional trades and staple foods has gone. I suppose the growth of tourism to some extent compensates for the loss, but this is a humiliating trade. It seemed to me that the shabby men, who brought their side-cars down the pier at Kilronan to meet the steamer and jostled each other for the custom of the few tourists who landed, looked very different from those figures in homespun clothing and bright belts I had seen coming ashore from the old *Dun Aengus* in Galway only seventeen years before.

Yet the most remarkable thing about Aran is that a small country, so arid and inhospitable to life despite its beauty, should have supported through so many centuries a self-sufficient community whose rich life could be an inspiration to an artist like J.M. Synge. This ancient life continued here generation after generation undisturbed for the very simple reason, I imagine, that the land, if such it can be called, was much too poor to attract absentee landlords. Naked rock is not a marketable commodity. If the sad day should come when Aran, like the Great Blasket, is depopulated, then future visitors to this lonely bastion of rock in Galway Bay will surely marvel that man was ever able to wrest a living from such a desert. That he did so and brought to fruit so fine a human flowering gives food for thought. I am glad I was able to visit Aran when I did; it is a salutary example to over-civilized man.

5
The Truth about Authorship

Beyond retailing how my initial debut as a writer came about, earlier chapters of these volumes have had so little to say about my life as a writer that the reader could be forgiven for suspecting that the new career which I had embraced so enthusiastically in 1939 soon began to pall. Or, to put it in another way, that forcing a passage up some derelict canal, injecting new life into a moribund railway or organizing a rally for vintage cars were all much more exciting occupations than sitting at a desk. It is certainly true that it was only after I had made the decision to become a writer that I realized that I was a man of action and not a contemplative or an intellectual. Although I have always enjoyed writing, I soon discovered that the writer's study could too easily become a place of retreat, a convenient escape from the harsh world outside into a smaller, cosier world of the writer's own ordering or creation. A writer may delude himself that by thinking great thoughts onto paper he is thereby enlarging himself, yet by so confining himself to his study he is diminishing his wholeness as a person as surely as if he were to spend all his daylight hours hewing coal underground. For this reason I have never made writing a nine to five job. Self discipline, yes, but rigid routine, no. Moreover, no matter how pressed I have been financially I have never dropped my outside interests. In any event I am sure it would have been a mistake so to do, so closely were these interests identified with my writing.

Nevertheless, when all this has been said, a great and increasing slice of my life, particularly in the years after I settled in Gloucestershire, has been devoted to writing. That this does not emerge from the preceding pages is due to the simple fact that outside interests are likely to be more interesting to read about. There is not much to be written about the hours one has spent in the study, although in my case they were absolutely vital because I possessed no other source of income. It is true that my salary as a car rally organizer helped me out at a particularly difficult period, but this was exceptional. That I have succeeded in keeping a wife, bringing up and privately educating two sons, assisting an impoverished mother and maintaining an ancient Gloucester-shire house, all solely upon my literary earnings is a source of pardonable pride to me. It was not an easy achievement. It involved great self-discipline and long hours of work seven days a week.

In the palmy days before the last war, successful and lifelong 'marriages' between author and publisher were the rule rather than the exception. Then as now, most publishers' contracts contained an 'option clause' giving them first refusal of the author's next book. Provided the author was sufficiently eminent and the quality and subject matter of his output predictable, then there was very little reason why either side should wish to break this option clause. If a writer did appear under a number of different imprints, it was generally held in the trade to indicate that he was a difficult character. I estimate that my books have appeared under no less than fifteen different imprints, a figure which excluded paperbacks and foreign editions, so by the standards of yesterday I would be judged a very awkward customer indeed. But times have changed. The rewards are relatively lower and the pace hotter; so much so that it is no longer possible, as it was in more spacious days, for a successful author to earn a living from one publisher. Hence, when a publisher has offered to commission me to write a book on a certain subject, the holder of the option on my future work has raised no objection.

Two other factors tend to militate against long or exclusive author/publisher relations and one is the conservatism of publishers. Though they would have you believe that they are past masters at spotting new talent or exploiting new literary pastures, their bias is always in favour of the known talent working in a familiar field. Hence the tendency of writers to become as type-cast as actors. Thus the author of a definitive history of lightships who follows it up with a study of the uses of sealing wax or a complete natural history of the cabbage is unlikely to have his option clause invoked. From the publisher's point of view such an attitude is understandable for, having decided to accept a book his great problem is to decide how many copies to print of the first edition. This decision is much more easily made if there is some safe precedent to guide him. From the point of view of the professional author (by which I mean full-time) this pressure from publishers for 'the mixture as before' may prove disastrous in the long term when he suddenly realizes that he has run out of mixture. It was the realization of this danger at an early stage, coupled with an innate dislike of specialism, that led me to ring the changes on subject with the result that I found myself fluttering from publisher to publisher. As I have said, because Eyre & Spottiswoode published my first book, I felt in honour bound to offer them my next, yet they were obviously disconcerted when *High Horse Riderless** fell upon their desk for they declined it. In the light of subsequent events, I think they were mistaken, for George Allen & Unwin, who accepted the book as a sprat to catch a mackerel, landed as a result *Green and Silver* and *Inland Waterways of England* both of which were successful, the latter extremely so, and are still in print at the time of writing.

Why then did I not remain an Allen & Unwin author? I should have liked to do so. I got along famously with Philip Unwin and I have always thought that *Green and Silver* and *Inland Waterways of England* were the most handsomely

---

* [*High Horse Riderless* was re-issued by Green Books in 1988.]

produced of any books of mine. But, alas, this marriage was soon dissolved. Philip Unwin was keenly interested in railways, and this was reflected in the firm's list. So naturally I offered them my next book *Lines of Character*. However, unlike the two previous titles where the illustrative material had been supplied gratis by Angela, this new railway book was illustrated by Pat Whitehouse who, not unnaturally, expected his fair share of the proceeds. But the policy of that dynamic little man, Sir Stanley Unwin,* who ruled the firm, was to take care of the pence and to leave the pounds to look after themselves. He considered that Pat Whitehouse's fair share was too much and the book was rejected. So, for the sake of a trivial sum my relationship with Allen & Unwin was broken to our mutual loss.

Lines of Character was subsequently offered to and accepted by Constable who published it with conspicuous lack of success. And this brings me to the third and final reason why a writer tends to change publishers. It is that for some mysterious and unfathomable reason certain author/publisher relationships tend to be unfruitful. Although my relations with Michael Sadleir and Ralph Arnold of Constable were very happy and they appeared to be prepared to publish any book I was prepared to give them the big snag was that they could not sell them. My association with the firm began when my agent (the same who attempted to interfere with the publication of *Inland Waterways of England*) placed with them my little book of ghost stories, *Sleep No More*, which could be held to represent my earliest literary effort since it included the three stories I had written for magazine publication before the war.† Michael Sadleir's reception of this modest collection of stories was so extravagant that it quite went to my head. He hailed me as the successor to M. R. James,

---

* Author of *The Truth about Publishing* from which the title of this chapter is unashamedly derived.

† See *Landscape with Machines*, p. 218.

whose *Ghost Stories of an Antiquary* I first read at the age of
eight and at five-yearly intervals ever since. He further insisted
that we find an illustrator for *Sleep No More* of the calibre of
the artist who was responsible for so splendidly illustrating
James's first collection of stories before his untimely death.
Somehow, I cannot now remember in what way, a young
artist named Joanna Dowling was discovered and proceeded to
produce some really excellent illustrations for my stories. Poor
Joanna, she looked upon this commission as her big break-
through, yet for some reason that was never really clear to me,
Constable, having commissioned her, decided in the end to
use only one of her pictures, and that the least satisfactory, as a
jacket illustration. It was a little slim mouse of a book that
eventually appeared in 1950, a book whose inferior paper soon
yellowed. It was never reprinted although some of the stories
were subsequently anthologized and others read over the
radio.* So ended my only venture into fiction.

Had not my hopes been raised by Michael Sadleir, I should
have expected little from *Sleep No More*, but I confess I
expected a great deal from *Horseless Carriage*, my first literary
expression of my vintage car enthusiasm, which was likewise
published by Constable. I sensed that interest in this subject
was expanding rapidly and hoped that this would be reflected
in sales, but I was disappointed. The book when it appeared in
1950 was unattractive; it wore an unfortunate jacket and the
publishing style was stolid but uninspiring. Although it won
good notices, particularly in the motoring press, sales wholly
failed to come up to my expectations. It was left to my old
friend Sam Clutton to prove beyond dispute that my hunch
was correct when, in collaboration with John Stanford, he
published from Batsford *The Vintage Motor-car* in 1954. This
book was an immediate best seller and it went on selling for
years, being the undoubted precursor of the spate of motoring

---

*   [*Sleep No More* was reprinted by Harvester Press, 1975 and the ghost
      stories continue to appear in anthologies, most recently in the *Oxford
      Book of English Ghost Stories*.]

books that marked the later fifties and sixties. There is no sour grapes about this because I would be the first to acknowledge that *The Vintage Motor-car* is a vastly better and more entertaining book than *Horseless Carriage*. Nevertheless, the success of the former makes me certain that in other hands my own book could have sold a great deal better than it did.

The failure of *Horseless Carriage* was only the first of a series of progressively heavier blows whose cumulative effect, apart from being financially disastrous, made me, for the first time, doubt my capacity as a writer. First, *Lines of Character* appeared in 1952 and straightaway sank without trace beneath an incoming flood-tide of railway books. Next came *Railway Adventure*, the story of my experience of running the Talyllyn Railway in 1951 and 1952. I set great store by this book. I saw it as the railway equivalent of *Narrow Boat* and felt confident that it would retrieve my fallen fortunes. I even designed a jacket for it which would make clear its affinity with *Narrow Boat* and persuaded John Betjeman to write a foreword for the book. All to no purpose. When it was published in 1953 the hush that greeted it was positively deafening and soon the book had sunk like its immediate predecessors – or so I thought at the time. However, *Railway Adventure* was subsequently successfully revived by David & Charles in hardback and by Pan Books in paperback, thus proving the moral of this sad tale.*

There was to be one final crowning disaster. While Sonia and I were living in Laurel Cottage, the little furnished house we took at Clun, I conceived the idea of concentrating a number of actual historical happenings in the English Midlands upon one imaginary industrial town. The book would present the story of the growth of this archetypal town and the fortunes of its chief families from the days of the first monastic mill on the river to the present day when the presence of an atomic research establishment on the outskirts of a huge blackened town struck a new apocalpytic note. The book

* [It has continued in print and in 1992 is about to be re-issued again.]

ended with the bewilderment of the town's 'labour' inhabitants on finding that, despite the fact that their elected representatives had nationalized the basic industries, the gap between wages and prices had continued to widen until the prospect of starvation became very real.

It had always struck me that, despite its overwhelming importance in the story of mankind, far too little attention had been paid to the Industrial Revolution in the worlds of literature and art. I was resolved, in my small way, to remedy this deficiency, my object being, not to glorify but to explain and to awaken understanding. It seemed to me that with this book I had hit upon an ideal vehicle to give the whole course of the Revolution a concise and dramatic shape. I called my imaginary town, and the book about it, Winterstoke. I invented the name because I felt it had a suitably dour and foredoomed ring to it; it was only subsequently that I discovered there was a real Winterstoke in Somerset, near Taunton, but no matter. I began by drawing two maps (which eventually appeared as endpapers) of Winterstoke, one c. 1790 and the other modern. I lived with those maps for six months and during that time Winterstoke, which was in fact an amalgam of Stoke-on-Trent and Coalbrookdale with bits of Wolverhampton and Derby thrown in, became intensely real to me. I walked its shabby streets, the towpaths of its blackened canals or the bank of its stinking river, the Wendle. I smelt its acrid polluted air, I knew its pretentious Victorian buildings and statuary, and was equally familiar with its every colliery, ironworks and factory. I hoped I could make my readers share this knowledge with me and see Winterstoke for the terrifying urban monster it was, typifying what English history over the past three hundred years had all been about. But such hopes proved vain. For although I thought, and still think, that the book rang wholly true and that what I wanted to say could not have been said in any other way, the fact remains that it fell between every kind of stool, being neither fact nor fiction. As the reviewer in the *Daily Telegraph* justly observed:

> Fictionalised history is ninety-nine times out of a hundred productive of fallacy; either by the subordination of fact to the requirements of the plot, or by over-simplification, or by gross partisanship on the side of the hero. But *Winterstoke*, by L.T.C. Rolt, is the hundredth case.

This was very nicely put, but unfortunately the hundredth case only went to prove the rule. I had not any great expectations, for although I knew that *Winterstoke* was one of the best things I would ever write, I also knew that it would be a difficult book to sell. But I was unprepared for the catastrophic result. Sales were so minimal that they did not even cover the paltry £100 advance on royalties which I had received. I do not believe that the book was even remaindered; I think it was mercifully pulped into oblivion, a kindlier fate for an author's brain-child in such circumstances. I was later told that the book had been short-listed for a well-known literary award but a miss is as good as a mile and this was cold comfort. The happiest outcome of this melancholy publishing episode was that *Winterstoke* brought me my best friend in the world of publishing, John Guest of Longmans. John wrote me a genuine fan letter when he had read the book, suggesting a meeting in London. I write 'genuine' advisedly and with emphasis because letters from publishers' readers are often designed, by flattery or otherwise, to attract new authors to their publisher's list. In John's case this was not so, although he had cast bread upon promising waters, for it would not be long before I should beat a path to Longmans' door.

Winterstoke was published in 1954, the year of the Anglo-American Car Rally, so the providential nature of the latter assignment can now be more fully appreciated. In retrospect, the remarkable thing about this unfortunate period in my literary career is that Constable, in spite of repeated failures, should have continued eagerly to accept any book I cared to offer them. Indeed, in the end it was I and not they who was forced to break their option on my future books. It is the only time I have done such a thing. I received an extremely pained

letter from Ralph Arnold to which I replied that the break was
due to no personal reason whatsoever but was purely financial,
in other words if I continued our association any longer I
should be stoney broke. I confess that at this nadir of my
fortunes I began to question my future as a writer. After all,
over the past four years Constable had published no less than
five of my books covering a very wide range of subject but had
failed to make a success of any of them. But was this their fault
or mine? Very fortunately I was soon to be reassured on this
point because my luck was about to turn.

By no means all ideas for books originate with their authors.
It frequently happens that a publisher or his reader may have a
promising idea for a new book, think of the most suitable
author to tackle it, and approach him with their scheme even
though they may have had no dealings with him before. If the
author likes the idea too, the result is a commissioned book.
My next three books, *Red for Danger*, *A Picture History of
Motoring* and my biography of Brunel, all originated in this
way although the last book, in the event, was not commissioned by its originator.

It was *Red for Danger* that first revived both my morale and
my sagging bank balance. The idea for a book about railway
accidents was put up to me by Richard Hough, who was at
that time with the Bodley Head in Little Russell Street, and it
immediately struck me as an extremely promising one. I
realized also that I was unusually well placed to write such a
book because my two summers on the Talyllyn Railway had
brought me into contact with the Railways Inspectorate, the
government department responsible for investigating all railway accidents. The then Chief Inspecting Officer, Colonel
G.R.S. Wilson, not only gave me the freedom of all their
records and reports but placed a room at my disposal so that I
could study them undisturbed. This was the first book I had
tackled which entailed research and I soon found myself
suffering from too much source material rather than too little.
Moreover, the evidence of eye-witnesses at the accident
inquiries, the patient efforts to establish the true cause and to

ensure that such a thing could never happen again, all this was intensely dramatic, and I felt I should be a poor hack indeed if I could not use such material to good account. But the sheer volume of it alarmed me. It covered a period of more than one hundred years and most of the accidents reported upon were of a very minor kind. What I really needed were some kind of guide-lines on which to work. Then I remembered that an old copy of the *Railway Year Book* which I had on my shelves included a table of major railway accidents in chronological order. This gave brief details of the cause in a final column headed 'Remarks'. It was from this list that I was able to make my preliminary choice of accidents to be described in the book and, thanks to that last column, I was able to group them into categories for chapter purposes. Armed with this 'scenario' I was able to attack the reports in a much more purposeful manner. The fascination of these reports in most cases fully justified my selection, though occasionally my studies in London uncovered some unexpected nugget which I either substituted or added. I am aware that some of the drier (or should I saw more classical?) railways writers condemn *Red for Danger* as over-dramatic and sensational. To this I would reply that they must level the same criticism at the transcript of the inquiries, for it is all there and is not my invention.

When *Red for Danger* was published by the Bodley Head in 1955 I would not allow myself any expectation of success, for my hopes had been dashed too often. Nevertheless, it soon became clear that this book, at any rate, was going to sell. It quite quickly went through two Bodley Head impressions and was also published by Pan Books, my first title to appear in paperback format. This brings me to one of the mysteries of the trade which still eludes me: What governs a publisher's decision to let a title go out of print or 'o.p.'? I eventually began to receive letters from my readers complaining that *Red for Danger* was unobtainable, so I wrote to the Bodley Head asking if it was their intention to reprint. No, it was not, they replied, and would I like all rights to revert to me? To this question they received a very prompt 'yes please' for, knowing that publishers move in a mysterious way, I was already negotiating with David & Charles to produce another edition of the book with an additional chapter at the end to bring it more up to date. What I never anticipated was that there would be another Pan edition. In my ignorance of paperback publishing I regarded paperbacks as almost as ephemeral as magazines, so that after one large edition had been sold out a title would be forgotten. Yet not more than a fortnight after my acquisition of the rights, the Bodley Head forwarded to me a letter to them from Pan Books in which the latter announced their desire to print a further edition.

At this point I should explain that one of the most contentious clauses in the hardback publisher's 'standard' form of contract is that whereby he lays claim to no less than 50 per cent of the proceeds of a paperback edition. He justifies this by arguing that whereas he incurs a considerable financial risk in undertaking first publication of a title, by picking the plums from his list the paperback publisher is betting on a certainty. His 50 per cent share of the proceeds therefore represents a fair return for this risk. To this the writer replies that although this argument may be valid in the case of a first novel, it certainly should not apply to the work of an established author. Under such a clause, half the proceeds of the first Pan edition of *Red for Danger* had gone to the Bodley Head, but their renunciation of rights meant that the whole of the proceeds of the second edition would come to me. At this time I badly needed such a stroke of good fortune. In the event, the new hardback and paperback editions of *Red for Danger* were published simultaneously and, mysteriously, neither seemed to inhibit the other for both have gone on selling briskly through further impressions. But why, oh why, one wonders, did the original publishers, whose idea it was in the first place, decide to drop the book?

One unexpected side-effect of *Red for Danger* was that I succeeded in persuading the Bodley Head to accept a little book consisting of four inter-related essays called *The Clouded Mirror*. This book, like *High Horse Riderless*, was an expression of the spiritual side of my nature; a self engaged upon a different journey through life than the physical and temporal self who chiefly holds the stage in this autobiography. These two selves, the one introverted, inquiring, humble, contemplative, sustained and sometimes moved to ecstasy by mysterious intimations of ineffable bliss, and the other extrovert, outgoing, restless and impatient, ever seeking some new field to explore with passionate enthusiasm; these two went their separate ways through life yet influenced each other at many points. This first self was a shy and reticent creature reluctant to set pen to paper except under the influence of some strange, over-mastering compulsion which was fortunately of rare occurrence because his writings proved virtually unsaleable. *The Clouded Mirror* was a case in point. The theme or themes of the book are complex, so I will not attempt to describe it, but it was triggered off in the first place, by my reaction to the atomic bomb and atomic power generally, something that had not existed when *High Horse Riderless* was written. The book was written very quickly and at high pressure during the early spring of 1953. It was begun in Roehampton and finished in that little writing room I have described at Aller Park in North Devon where, as from some low-flying aircraft, I looked straight down into that deep valley where gulls wheeled in a deep void of ocean air. Even Constable turned down the result, so I count myself very lucky to have persuaded Richard Hough to publish it. *The Clouded Mirror* also appeared in 1955 and sank without trace.

The second successful book I mentioned, *A Picture History of Motoring* needs only a brief mention. It was one of a series planned by Edward Hulton, at a time when his magazine empire was still at its zenith, with the idea of making use of the big Picture Post Library of Photographs* which he had established off Fleet Street. It was published by the Hulton

---

* It was subseqently taken over by the BBC and was moved to Marylebone where it is known as the Radio Times Hulton Picture Library. [Now The Hulton Picture Company.]

Press, did well in this country and was extremely popular in America. In case this should conjure up visions of showers of golden dollars falling into my lucky lap, I should explain that in a transaction of this sort, particularly where such lavishly illustrated books are concerned, the American publisher buys the sheets of the book from England which he then has cut and bound in America. Such a deal is the subject of very hard bargaining, which usually results in the American publisher getting the sheets at a knock-down price, and all the unfortunate author receives is a small percentage of this price.

It was David Cape who first conceived the notion of a biography of the Victorian engineer, Isambard Kingdom Brunel. Like all brilliant ideas it seemed obvious. Why had I not thought of it before? I had been a lifelong admirer of the Great Western Railway and its famous engineer whose powerful and extraordinary personality made him a plum subject for a biography. Yet no biography of him had been written since 1870. I suppose the idea did not occur to me simply because I had never thought of trying my hand at biography. Yet I intended to try now and try with a vengeance for here was a book which could scarcely fail. In the event, however, few books can have had a stormier passage before it was eventually published.

David Cape had recently come out of the army and joined his father's firm. He mentioned his idea to Frank Rudman, a mutual friend in the publishing world who very kindly suggested me as the only possible author. Frank then wrote to me with the effect that, one lunch-time, the three of us met together in a London pub to discuss the project. It transpired that David had not yet broached the idea to his father and he appeared to be rather shy about taking this hurdle for a reason with which I was later able fully to sympathize. However, now that he had found his author he said he would certainly do so and that I might expect a letter from his father within the next few weeks.

Sure enough I did receive a letter from Jonathan Cape suggesting an appointment and in due time I visited No. 30,

Bedford Square and was ushered into the sanctum of this doyen of publishers with his impressive mane of white hair. I have never had a less satisfactory interview with any publisher. So far from being at pains to put me at my ease, he seemed more concerned to impress me with his own eminence. It was clear that David's idea had not raised a spark of enthusiasm; also that old Jonathan had never previously heard of Brunel. He obviously looked upon me as a complete novice whom his son had picked up somewhere, for he talked of the submission of a synopsis and a specimen chapter for approval prior to signature of contract. Although I am not a vain man, this surprised me because I had always assumed that on occasions such as this an astute publisher would make it his business to find out something of the background of the author he was going to interview. In my case this would have involved Jonathan in the minimum of trouble for I noticed there was the inevitable volume of *Who's Who* in the bookshelf behind his head. However, he finally said grudgingly that he would send me a contract. I left.

I wish now that I had kept and framed that contract instead of sending it straight back accompanied by a stiff note saying exactly what I thought of it. It was quite the worst contract I have ever seen. It contained every clause that the tyro author is warned to beware of when dealing with the big bad wolves of the publishing world. At the same time I wrote a personal letter to David Cape explaining why I had had to turn the contract down, how sad I was about it and that, as the idea of the books was his, I wanted him to feel free to pursue it elsewhere. To this David replied that he made me a gift of the idea because he was sure I was the man to write the book and that he intended to give me what help he could to find another publisher. Shortly after, David left the family business. To what an extent this row over the book was responsible I never discovered.

David strongly recommended me to place matters in the hands of a good literary agent and offered to introduce me to one of his acquaintance. My past experience of agents made me feel extremely doubtful about the wisdom of this course but, under the circumstances, it would have been most churlish of me to reject, out of hand, David's counsel and offer. So I was introduced to an agent of the greatest eminence and repute who, having heard our story, unhesitatingly recommended Collins. If we wished he would do his best to interest them in the project. This he certainly succeeded in doing, for he came back to me with a very fair contract which included an advance against royalties larger than anything I had been offered before. On the strength of this I began work on the book in very good heart.

My knowledge of Brunel at this time had been largely gleaned from E.T. MacDermot's masterly *History of the Great Western Railway* which I had acquired when it was first published between 1927 and 1931, so it was obvious that if my biography was to stake any claim to be definitive there was a great deal of research to be done. I had never embarked upon such a piece of detective work before, searching here and there for clues and stray facts until, like the pieces of some scattered jig-saw puzzle, they fitted together and a picture began to emerge. That picture was a portrait of Brunel and, unlike most heroes of one's childhood, as I added fact to fact so he was not diminished but rather grew in stature. Not literally, for Brunel was a small man, but in the sheer overwhelming magnetism and force of personality. From his granddaughter's house in Royal Crescent at Bath with its furniture and pictures rescued from the sale of his vanished house in Westminster; from the coffin-like box of original documents, including all his exquisite sketch books, in the library of the University of Bristol; to Walwick Hall, the home of his great-grandson, Sir Humphrey Noble, high on the line of the Roman Wall in Northumberland, I followed him, and to evoke his shade I stood before the great sulphureous southern portal of Box Tunnel, on the dizzy height of the Clifton suspension bridge and, at midnight, in the dark depths of the Thames Tunnel, the silence there so profound that the churning of the screws of passing river craft could be heard overhead. Just as Brunel's handwriting became more easily decipherable the longer I studied it, so the man himself seemed to become more substantial. I could almost smell the smoke of his cigars.

The happiest outcome of this particular quest was my friendship with Sir Humphrey Noble and his wife Celia. Sir Humphrey was enthusiastic about my project and invited me to stay at Walwick while I studied such original material as he had there. I found that this consisted of copy letter books, original diaries of Brunel's father, Sir Marc Brunel, dating from the Thames Tunnel period and, greatest prize of all, two volumes of a journal kept by Brunel between 1830 and 1834 with occasional entries to 1840. These last I was permitted to bear away with me so that I might have them at my elbow as I wrote the book and they proved to be the richest treasure trove, making me feel closer to the man himself than anything else. No research could have been carried out in more congenial surroundings and never was researcher more hospitably entertained. For life at Walwick was lived in a style that reminded me of the Edwardian days of my remote childhood and which I had thought quite extinct.

The house stood precisely on the line of the Roman Wall at the point where, coming from the west, it begins to sweep steeply down in order to cross the valley of the North Tyne. By lifting a trap door in the polished floor of Sir Humphrey's library, one could descend a short vertical ladder and actually stand on the Roman paving below. The drive gates opened onto that splendid Roman road that parallels the Wall on its southern side, arrow straight for most of its course, but lifting and falling continuously as it cuts across the rolling green waves of the Northumbrian uplands. Apart from occasional journeys either by rail or road through Newcastle by the east coast route, I knew Northumberland not at all and I was at once struck, by the spaciousness and the heroic scale of the landscape. These views over miles of moorland, forest and fell conveyed a sense of freedom by contrast with which the small hills of a typical southern landscape seemed miniscule and claustrophobic. To a visitor from the south there seemed far less people about and far less traffic on the roads.

From the terrace at Walwick, in clear weather, one could look across the valley of the South Tyne and over the upland miles of Alston Moor to the dark heights of Cross Fell and Milburn Forest sharp against the skyline. Somehow the fact that it stood alone and that it commanded such a wild sweep of landscape made me appreciate the comforts of Walwick the more. The range of outbuildings that enclosed a courtyard had been converted into comfortable self-contained flats which housed the domestic staff whose sole function it was to maintain the rhythm of country house life with smooth and unobtrusive efficiency. There consistently came into my mind when staying at Walwick that saying of the aesthetic Villiers de l'Isle Adam which Yeats was fond of quoting: 'As for living, our servants will do that for us.' From morning till night there was nothing whatever to do except to obey the discreet signals of the deep-toned gong summoning one to luncheon or warning one that it was time to take a bath and dress for dinner. The elderly butler, Tod, would double the role of valet when any male guest was staying in the house, unpacking the luggage and laying out whichever clothes he considered suitable. Personally, I hated this last service. I felt self-conscious about my clothes, imagining Tod curling his lip at a darned sock or a shirt cuff just beginning to fray. When unpacking it seemed to me that the old man took a perverse pleasure in stowing things in the most unlikely places, for it often entailed a most protracted search to discover their whereabouts. In return, I took an equally perverse pleasure in asserting my independence by not wearing what Tod had decreed I should wear, changing a green tie for a red, or putting on the other pair of trousers.

The popularity of spas and their cures before the First World War was, in great measure, due to the fact that the Edwardian rich ate too much and, in this respect also, Walwick maintained the true Edwardian tradition. It was a diet that even an agricultural labourer would have found more than adequate, so it made me, who was doing only sedentary work poring over papers in the library, feel like a Strasbourg goose. This daily marathon began with breakfast which was a purely male affair; ladies took breakfast in their rooms and were not expected on the scene until mid-morning at the earliest. Often only Sir Humphrey and myself appeared for this meal. We would together confront an array of silver covers standing upon the largest hot plate I have ever seen and concealing beneath them every variation upon the theme of breakfast that the mind could conceive. Even had we been tramping the high fells since dawn, the two of us could have made little impression upon such a prodigal mountain of food and I used to wonder what became of it all. Were the servants gathered in the servants' hall waiting impatiently until we had finished? To a zealous research worker, time passes swiftly, so that it seemed that I was constantly interrupted by some fresh assault on my digestive tract. Hardly had I got breakfast below my belt before dry sherry and salt biscuits appeared in the library as a warning that the luncheon gong would sound in half an hour's time. When it came it was no light meal but one which, in ordinary circumstances, would have set me up for the rest of the day. And, of course, it was followed by the time-consuming ritual of coffee, taken either in the drawing room or the library. It seemed as though the taste of that coffee had scarcely left my tongue before a delicious tea was served before the fire in the library. If one lingered over this as I was tempted to do, the next thing one knew was that the first warning dressing gong was sounding from the hall.

Dinner at Walwick was more than a meal, it was a ritual and a very protracted one at that. My host and hostess invariably dressed for the occasion no matter whether there were guests or no. Whereas at luncheon the wines were the responsibility of Tod, before dressing for dinner it was Sir Humphrey's custom to descend to his cellar to select the wines himself. To the right of his chair at dinner stood a small revolving dumb-waiter upon which, among other things, resposed his wine book, a diary of successive dinners in which he would note down all particulars of the wines drunk and then, pencil poised, invite the comments of his guests upon them. My knowledge of wine was practically nil. Before the war I had never been able to afford to drink it, while during the war it had been unobtainable. So my embarrassment may be imagined when my host turned inquiringly towards me, notebook in hand, and asked for my considered judgement on the claret. Dinner ended with the retirement of the ladies to the drawing room while the men resumed their seats at the dining table and a cut glass decanter of port was circulated, its contents glowing in the light from the branched candelabra. It was at this stage of the ritual that I once committed a most tremendous gaffe by lighting up a cigar. In the more depraved circles in which I normally moved, cigars went with port as naturally as Guinness with oysters or chips with fish, but not so at Walwick. My rashness earned me a stern whispered reproof from my host which did not escape the fellow guests who had been invited to dinner to meet me. Wishing the ground would open and swallow me up, I somehow managed to stub out the thing and surreptitiously replace it in my cigar case. It was an inflexible rule of the household that so long as the port decanter was circulating there would be no smoking and, as Sir Humphrey was apt to linger long over his port, and as I was at this period a compulsive smoker, I found this the one deprivation of life at Walwick. When, after taking coffee in the drawing room, I finally tottered up to bed it was to find a large plate of fruit and a tin full of assorted biscuits on my bedside table, just in case I should suffer an attack of night starvation, presumably.

If the Noble family sound unusual descendants for a Victorian engineer to have, I should perhaps explain that Isambard Brunel, unlike some of his contemporaries, was no horny-handed, self-made and self-taught prodigy but a man of taste and sensibility who would have fitted effortlessly into the *milieu* of Walwick Hall – except that, knowing his forceful personality, I very much doubt whether even his great-grandson could have dissuaded him from lighting up one of his favourite cigars after dinner. Here, as elsewhere the impress of that strong, perfectionist personality made itself manifest. In the hall hung the superb regulator clock which had once swung its slow pendulum in the engineer's office at 18 Duke Street and which still kept perfect time. Treasured in the library were a beautiful set of ivory-mounted drawing instruments and a great leather-covered cigar case, with a separate cedar wood compartment for each cigar, which Isambard used to carry with him on his interminable journeys of inspection. Sir Humphrey showed me these and other things with intense pleasure and pride, not only because they were relics of his ancestor but also because he shared with him the same discriminating taste and love of well-made things. They also shared a certain physical resemblance. Both were small in stature with the same dark eyes and heavy brows. Sir Humphrey's hair was white, but had Brunel lived into his sixties and himself become white-haired, the resemblance might have been even more striking.

I was interested to discover that Sir Humphrey was linked to engineering history through both sides of his family. His grandfather, Sir Andrew, held a commission in the army and became a ballistics expert of considerable repute who was sent to Newcastle by the War Office to test Sir William Armstrong's new breach-loading gun. Armstrong formed so high an opinion of Andrew Noble's ability that he persuaded him to become his partner. There is one curious sidelight on this story which I did not discover until much later. Sir Andrew Noble brought to the north with him, as tutor for his sons, a certain Oxford scholar, a palaeographer and student of liturgies named John Meade Falkner (1858–1932). This strange man, who seemed predestined for an academic career, became, first secretary and then Managing Director of Armstrong Whitworth & Company, travelling widely and negotiating contracts with foreign governments. He then retired from business life and returned to Durham where he became Librarian to the Dean and Chapter of the Cathedral and the chief authority on its rites and music. He is best remembered today for his three works of fiction: *The Lost Stradivarius**, *Moonfleet*, and that strange novel, *The Nebuly Coat*. Those who have read *The Nebuly Coat* can scarcely fail to deplore the fact that a man of such remarkable literary talent allowed himself to be persuaded, presumably by Sir Andrew Noble, into the world of business. Nevertheless, that he was such a success in that world surely reveals his unusual, many-sided character. Falkner is a man whose biography I would like to write, but unfortunately the books I would most enjoy writing are seldom those that bring the money into the till.

I am often asked how much work a particular book involved. This is a difficult question to answer because I am usually finishing one book at the same time as I am doing research for the next. Nevertheless, I would estimate that the research and the writing of my Brunel biography took me eighteen months. If this does not seem much for a book of 120,000 words containing much original material, I would only reply that authors cannot afford to work a forty-hour week. Also, that I have learnt by experience that the whole art of research is knowing when to stop. As the work of adding fact to fact goes on, so the writer must constantly sift the inchoate mass of material so acquired until a pattern of order either emerges or is by him imposed upon it. It is at this juncture, when the shape of the book becomes clear in his mind, that the author can afford to stop research and start writing. Without this vision of order, research into any subject can easily become obsessional, the pursuit of facts never ending, and the projected master work either never written or unreadable. Because my work has never been assisted by any

---

*   My attention was first drawn to Meade Falkner by a friend of mine who pointed out that the last ghost story in *Sleep No More*, 'Music hath Charms' (I think it the best story I have written), was but a variation on the theme of *The Lost Stradivarius*. Never having heard of the latter and feeling rather piqued, I went straight off and bought No. 545 in the Oxford World Classics Series which contains the story in question and also *The Nebuly Coat*.

kind of research grant, academic or otherwise, I could not in any case afford to carry on in such a fashion.

'What book are you working on now, if I may ask?'
'A book about Brunel.'
'Brunel? Who's he?'

Interchanges of this kind had occurred with depressing frequency during the past eighteen months so that when I submitted the finished typescript to George Hardinge at Collins, although I was confident that I had made a good job of it, I did not feel so optimistic about the book's future. Biographies of little-known characters are usually foredoomed to failure; in my enthusiasm I had assumed that Brunel's name was a household word and was discouraged to find that this was by no means the case.

However, George Hardinge was enthusiastic about the book and all seemed set fair when I received a mysterious message from Collins to the effect that Mr Milton Waldman wished to see me and would I please arrange an early appointment. Mr Waldman, it transpired, had but lately returned to the Collins fold from America where he had acquired some ideas about publishing. When I was shown into his office he was seated at a table leafing through my Brunel typescript. He slapped the palm of his hand down on the book and pronounced: 'We've got the makings of a best-seller here' and then went on to tell me just how this desirable goal could be achieved. It was a simple recipe which consisted of lifting the more dramatic incidents out of the book like so many plums out of a pie, stringing them together and throwing the rest away. This, I realized, was American publishing philosophy which holds that no book is incapable of improvement and employs a team of editors to do the improving, grooming books for best-sellerdom as Hollywood starlets used to be groomed for stardom. As these editors have to justify their salaries few books, unless they are by some acknowledged master, escape their attention, the end product being almost as mediocre and lacking in individuality as that American horror, the abridged or condensed novel. I explained that it was the object of my exercise to write a definitive biography of Brunel, not to produce a hypothetical best-seller. Even if it failed to sell widely, at least the former would possess a certain permanent value, whereas a failed best-seller is a worthless thing. In any case it was never my ambition to write a runaway best-seller as such a thing can be a financial embarrassment to an author, earning him far too much money in too short a period with the result that he falls prey to the tax inspector.*

It was obvious that our meeting had reached a complete impasse since we both held fast to our respective opinions. One side or the other had to make a token submission so I concluded our uncomfortable session by agreeing to take the typescript home with me and mull the idea over. I was a very worried man when I got home that night. It is a bold author who backs his own judgement against that of an experienced publisher if only because it is difficult to assess the merits of his own brain-child coolly and objectively. And yet I felt in my bones that I was right and that it would be madness to tamper with the text in the way that had been proposed. Suddenly I made up my mind – I would send off the text to my friend John Guest of Longmans first thing in the morning. John received the book on a Friday and, as he told me afterwards, he spent the whole weekend reading it because a decision was obviously of some urgency. That decision was quickly made and gratified me exceedingly; Longmans would publish the book as it stood and would repay Collins the amount of the advance they had already paid me. So, after many vicissitudes my Brunel biography was finally 'put to bed'. It was published in 1956. A month or two after these events I walked into

---

*   To mitigate this injustice a meagre tax concession was made whereby an author is allowed to 'spread back' his earnings on a book over the previous three years. I once tried this. By the time claims for back tax had been settled and my accountants' extra charges paid (for additional correspondence) I found I was exactly £15 to the good.

Longmans offices in Clifford Street and was very surprised to see George Hardinge; he had moved over with Brunel.

Longmans netted from Collins not one book but three. I had become so enthralled with Brunel that long before I had finished his biography I began to see myself as a kind of latter-day Samuel Smiles, producing a whole series of engineer biographies. The considerations governing the choice of subject were that they should be well-known names about whom there was something new to be said, for there is no point in writing a serious biography unless it can shed some fresh light on its subject. James Brindley, Thomas Telford and the two Stephensons were the characters I originally selected but I eventually decided to drop Brindley because there seemed to be insufficient material to add to what Smiles had already written about him.

Research and field work on Telford and the Stephensons naturally took me to the north again. In the case of Telford, whose major engineering works seem invariably to be set against some of the most spectacular landscape backgrounds in Britain, I decided to combine business with pleasure. Sonia and I had a most delightful run to the north along the backbone of England by way of Buxton, Chapel-en-le-Frith, Holme Moss, Huddersfield, Halifax, Skipton, Richmond, Barnard Castle and Stanhope to Hexham. We stayed a few days with the Nobles at Walwick before leaving the Alvis and going on into Scotland by rail. We caught a train at Humshaugh station on that long-vanished branch line of the old North British that winds up the valley of the North Tyne and through the wilds of Kielder Forest. This eventually landed us at Riccarton Junction, one of those strange, completely isolated railway enclaves set in the midst of a desolate moor. Here we caught a train by the old Waverley route to Edinburgh, then north again to Inverness where I had arranged to spend some time going through the records of the Caledonian Canal in the canal offices at Clachnaharry. On completing my work there, we were lucky enough to obtain a passage through the canal in a brand new inshore fishing boat from Lossiemouth which was making her maiden voyage to the west coast fishing grounds. Her crew were kindness itself plying us with mugs of hot cocoa and the most enormous Abernethy biscuits I have ever seen.

Unless one travels through the Caledonian Canal with a knowledgeable eye, it is apt to be dwarfed by the sheer scale and grandeur of the landscape of the Great Glen. This is a false impression, for the truth, as I now discovered, is a tremendous work of civil engineering, especially bearing in mind its early date and the wild and almost trackless state of the Highlands at that time. Had such feats of engineering been carried out in England (as they later were by the railway builders) they would have been hailed as the wonder of the age, but in the Highlands of Scotland they were largely unsung except by personal friends of Telford, like the poet Robert Southey. This emphasizes the truth of one of my golden rules which is never to write about anything of which one has not had first-hand experience.

From Fort William we travelled by rail to Mallaig, by steamer to the Kyle, and so back to Inverness whence we returned to Northumberland. Picking up the Alvis, we next motored westward into Dumfries in order to visit Telford's birthplace and the country in which he grew to manhood in the neighbourhood of the village of Westerkirk and the little town of Langholm in Eskdale. Here a particularly satisfying piece of detective work was the discovery of what I am confident were the ruins of the shepherd's cottage in which Telford was born. This was done by comparing the actual lie of the land with the somewhat romanticized steel engraving of the birthplace in Smiles' *Life of Telford*. The ruins appeared just where we expected them to be, but as this was in the midst of a new Forestry Commission plantation, by now either they will be hidden beneath funereal spruce or they will have been digested by some monstrous stone-crushing machine such as the commission use to provide road material.

Before *Brunel* was published, an advance copy was sent to the panel of literary experts who select the Book Society choices and also award 'recommends' to the also-rans. *Brunel* was not even among these also-rans, a fact which was not in the least surprising, for how could a book about an engineer possibly qualify as literature? In other words I was a victim of Sir Charles Snow's 'two cultures'. So I was surprised to see, when *Telford* was published, that it bore the legend 'Recommended by the Book Society' on the jacket. When I asked Longmans for some explanation of this, they advanced the theory that the Book Society panel had been so surprised by the success of *Brunel* that they had decided to play safe by bestowing a cautious laurel leaf on *Telford*. In fact, although *Telford* went on selling, it was at a lower rate than the two other volumes in this trilogy. I am sure this is because Telford the dour, reticent, solitary and single-minded Scot, is a far more difficult character to bring alive than the others. Hence there is a certain lack of human interest in the book, although to some extent this is compensated for by the magical, fairy-tale quality of Telford's great engineering works and the romantic landscapes in which they were invariably set.

In quest of the two Stephensons I again motored north, this time alone in the duck's back Alvis.* I stayed for the inside of a week at Walwick while I made pilgrimages to Wylam, Willingdon Quay, Killingworth and other sites associated with George or Robert Stephenson and then, bidding farewell to the hospitable Nobles, moved to a hotel in Darlington so that I could explore, by foot and by car, the line of the old Stockton & Darlington Railway. I was surprised to find how much evidence – stone-block sleepers, bridges, the ruins of winding-engine houses – remained to be seen.

It was on the long drive back from Darlington to Stanley Pontlarge that an amusing, in retrospect almost surrealist, incident occurred. I had just driven through Leek and I was

---

* By this date we were regularly using both Alvises, the four-seater as a family car, usually driven by Sonia and used for shopping, ferrying our two young sons to and fro to school and so on. While the duck's back, as always, remained my personal transport.

brooding sadly over the fact that on this whole long journey
out and home I had so far encountered only one fellow vintage
motorist in the shape of a rather tatty 3-litre Bentley when I
saw ahead of me an almost unbelievable sight. It was the rear
of a large blue touring car of, it appeared, late Edwardian date
with a smart brown cape-cart hood erected which prevented
me from seeing the driver or his passengers, if any. But the
most remarkable thing was that this vehicle was emitting
indubitable puffs of steam. A steam car, by heavens! Aside
from the rallies I mentioned in an earlier chapter, this was the
first and last time I have seen a steam car being driven on an
English road in the ordinary way of business. We were still in
the outskirts of Leek, so I decided to pass the steam car,
driving on until I came to a suitable stretch of road in open
country where I could park the Alvis on the verge to await the
steamer's arrival. I argued that an enthusiast would surely stop
on seeing my car. At length the steamer appeared, proceeding
at a slow and stately pace. As it approached I saw that it was
being driven with intense seriousness and concentration by a
tall, gaunt old man who looked to be at least eighty years of
age. There was no other occupant. Standing beside my car, I
beamed at him and waved, but if he saw me he did not betray
the fact, keeping his gaze fixed on the road ahead. My
curiosity now thoroughly aroused, I determined to follow him
to see whither this strange old gentleman was bound. This
meant for me a third gear crawl, but it did not last long. A
gloved hand was punctiliously extended from the steamer to
indicate that its driver was about to turn right. Automatically,
I made a similar signal, thinking we were approaching a road
junction, but then hesitated on seeing that the steamer was in
fact turning into a private drive. I pulled into the left and
slowed to a crawl. On one of the gateposts was fixed a board
bearing the legend CHEDDLETON MENTAL HOSPITAL. At
this point I considered it prudent to abandon the chase and
drive on, but I am still curious about that car and its elderly
conductor. I think the car was an Edwardian Stanley somewhat rebuilt and modified, but I cannot be certain.

With the publication of my three engineer biographies between 1956 and 1960 I found to my profound relief that the ghost of *Narrow Boat* no longer hung round my neck like an albatross. Although that first book is still in print and still selling, it has been quite eclipsed by my biographies. I was no longer introduced as 'the man who wrote *Narrow Boat*' but as the man who wrote *Brunel* or, more commonly, as the engineering historian. This did my morale an immense amount of good, banishing once and for all that gloomy notion that I might, after all, be only a one-book man. *Brunel* and its immediate successors made me a new reputation and this is why I think it is unnecessary to pursue this book-by-book account of the vicissitudes of my literary career any further. Instead I shall end this chapter with some reflections and opinions based on experience. But in case I should sound sour and embittered, I would say at once that if I could have those thirty years over again I would not do other than I have done. This is because all the hazards, the financial worries, the disappointments and frustrations have been well worth enduring for the sake of the blessed freedom I have enjoyed. Ever since 1945, when I left the Ministry of Supply, I have been my own master, free to come and to go as I please. In the modern world this is a pearl beyond price as I well know.

I have heard many an author praising his agent as though he were some kind of miracle man. This has not been my experience. Perhaps I do not write the kind of books an agent is accustomed to handle. Perhaps I am not the right kind of author. The eminent agent to whom David Cape introduced me proved no more satisfactory than his predecessors. When I transferred *Brunel* to Longmans, the contract he had won from Collins became null and void but, by an act of inconceivable stupidity, instead of using this opportunity to get away. I passively allowed him to draw up contracts with Longmans for *Brunel* and for the other two biographies. He obtained no better terms than I could have got myself, yet for this I have had to pay dearly ever since by parting with his percentage pound of flesh on every penny these three books have earned.

The reason why I finally decided that I must get rid of this agent was simple. I was commissioned to write a short text for a new educational series aimed at teenagers. Its title was *Transport and Communications* and it was tailor-made to the editor's wishes. I had just completed and submitted this book when the firm concerned sold their publishing division to Ward Lock, who said they did not intend to proceed with the new series. I obtained meagre conpensation plus the right to publish the book elsewhere. A tailor-made book of this kind is not easy to place and I had not the time to flog it around. This, I thought, is what my agent is for, so I promptly sent it off to him. After six months, nothing had happened although he assured me he was doing his best. So I asked him to return the typescript to me and within a week I had placed it with Methuen Children's Books who produced it very well and subsequently published a revised second edition.

Not surprisingly, after this experience I decided once and for all that I would have no further truck with agents. What about handling foreign rights? A question that is often asked at this point. The answer is that any publisher worth his salt can handle such rights as well as, or more efficiently than, any agent, at least that is my experience, while the author pays less away in commission because a publisher exacts his share of foreign rights whether or no the author has an agent. Conversely, the fact that the publisher has placed the foreign rights does not stop the agent drawing his commission on the proceeds from them. In my view the answer to the deficiencies of the literary agent is a simple one of £.s.d. Compared with an actor's agent, the literary agent's commission on the average author's earnings is miniscule so it is a case of the old saying: 'yer gets what yer pays for'.

To anyone engaged in any other business the accounting methods of publishers seem unbelievable. Authors' royalty accounts are made up at half-yearly, or sometimes yearly, intervals. Moreover they are not actually issued and paid until at least two months after the end of the period concerned. It is an accounting practice handed down from days when rows of clerks before stand-up desks wrote out the statements with quill pens, and it has become completely anachronistic in days when it would be perfectly feasible to settle accounts quarterly. But, of course, it does mean that the publisher has the author's money to play around with, interest free, for quite a while. The author must needs take the publisher's royalty statements entirely on trust. If he has a suspicious mind he could instruct his accountant to inspect his publisher's books, but apart from ruining author/publisher relations, few authors could afford such a course, his accountant's time being far more costly than his own. In any case such an exercise would normally be fruitless because the great majority of publishers are strictly honourable.

The injustice of the tax system where authors are concerned is not widely appreciated. For example, the copyright in my books is my capital and my royalty payments represent the annual interest on that capital. Yet if I fall into such dire financial straits that I am forced to sell the copyright in some of my books, the sum realized is taxable as income. Another example: the inland revenue cannot be made to understand why, in a period of galloping inflation, my income, along with that of other authors, is slowly but surely falling. Such a reversal of the norm simply cannot be. Consequently, 'allow-ing', as he puts it, 'for normal growth' my tax inspector makes regularly an absurdly high assessment of my next year's income so that I am forced to go through the annually expensive ritual of appealing against it.

Besides his never-ending running battle with the inland revenue, the unfortunate author has to tolerate, with as much patience as he may, many other difficulties or frustrations peculiar to his profession. He continually receives letters from his readers complaining that a particular title of his is out of print and asking how can they obtain a copy. This particular query recurs with such depressing frequency that I have sometimes thought it would be time-saving to have a duplicated reply to it which would read: 'the book you mention is not out of print. If you would patronise an honest bookseller instead of a chain-store, he would order you a copy.' Unfortunately, good, honest booksellers grow fewer and further between, while chain-stores, selling fewer and fewer books and more and more worthless bric-à-brac, proliferate. If it is not on their shelves, the latter simply cannot be bothered to go through the motions of ordering a single copy and so come up with the facile lie that the book is out of print. So the author has to tolerate a retail trade the majority of whom refuse to sell his books despite the fact that they get a 'cut' of 33⅓ per cent compared with his own meagre royalty of 10 or 12 per cent.

Despite all the efforts that authors have made in recent years to enlighten it, the great general public remains extraordinarily – one might almost say obstinately – ill-informed about the rewards of authorship. They are unable to comprehend the fact that, alone of the professions, an author can earn a national reputation yet still remain as poor as a church mouse. My name first featured in *Who's Who* in 1953 at a time when I was sailing perilously close to the financial rocks.* From then until now the number of circular begging-letters I have received from innumerable deserving causes would fill a large cart. If those responsible for these campaigns realized that authors are in no position to dispense alms, they would save a great deal in printing and postage. But no, it is assumed that because an author has graduated to the 'establishment' he is naturally affluent. Fifty years ago, this might have been a correct inference to draw, but it is certainly not true today.

Then there is the fallacious argument that because an author's royalty is calculated on the selling price of his books, in these days of high book prices he must be sitting pretty. The law of diminishing returns begins to operate. It also disregards the fact that, owing to these high prices, the author

---

* As my name was not particularly well known in 1953, I wondered then, and still wonder now, by what means the publishers of this unique work decide who shall be numbered among the elect.

is subjected to increasing pressure from publishers to accept a lower percentage royalty. After all, such as printers and book-binders, are tightly organized in trade unions so there is only one person left to squeeze, the primary producer, the unfortunate, unorganized author.

The greatest social injustice from which the author suffers in this country is that, through the public library system, it has been taken for granted by the citizens of the Welfare State that he exists to provide them with free entertainment. If the tax man is the author's enemy number one, I would name the public librarian as enemy number two for his implacable opposition to PLR. Even when a scheme is devised which does not commit him to any extra work, his attitude does not change. What I find peculiarly odious is that the librarian likes to pose as the author's chief patron. Without library sales, his argument runs, most authors could not exist, ergo, by campaigning for public lending rights, the author is biting the hand that feeds him. Such an argument betrays a wilful ignorance of the economics of authorship. It would have been economically impossible for me to have earned my living for thirty years on the fruits of library sales alone. In fact, the boot is on the other foot and all librarians are, in the last analysis, dependent, like everyone else concerned with books, on the work of the author. Had PLR been instituted at the time I began my literary career I should by now be able to retire. As it is, I must go on working until I drop and the relief of PLR, though there are signs that it may come soon, may come too late to help me.

In preparing my annual accounts I group my sources of income under the following four headings: Royalties; Advances and Other Payments; Articles and Reviews, BBC etc.; Lectures. The phrase 'Other Payments' I shall explain later, suffice it to say here that these first two items represent my income from writing books which far outstrips the figures under the other two headings. The latter represent the odd jobs that come my way because I am known as a writer of books. As it is, I suppose I turn down about 50 per cent of the total number of requests I receive. There are several reasons for this. First, it is distracting when one is in the middle of writing a book to have to break off and bend one's mind to a magazine article or review. Secondly, there is the knowledge that one is devoting precious time to something essentially ephemeral, whereas no book can be so described. Even if a book appears to be a ghastly failure at the time of publication it has a stubborn survival value. It continues to live on the shelves and in the minds of the discerning few until suddenly, perhaps many years later, its merit is recognized and it is reprinted. Thirdly, there is the simple fact that, with rare exceptions, ephemeral writings are seldom worthwhile financially. For example, if a reviewer is conscientious, as I try to be, and actually reads the book he is sent to review, then the paltry fee he receives is an insult to his intelligence. The most I can say for reviewing is that it is a way of building up a modern library on one's subject.

I include the BBC and its independent rival in the category of unrewarding ephemera. That this should be so is certainly true. Broadcasting and television rates are so low that one is forced to conclude that they are based on the assumption that no author will be able to resist the publicity value of microphone or television camera. I find such an assumption so distasteful that, having no thirst for the kind of publicity that 'the media' purveys, I became stubborn and uncooperative at the mere mention of a possible appearance on 'the box'. The usual tactic is for the producer or his secretary to ring up and ask very deferentially if he could possibly run down to Gloucestershire to consult me about a new programme on some historical engineering topic. After wasting the whole of an afternoon of my time picking my brains, the possibility of my participating in some way in his programme is tentatively raised. To my natural question about fees he makes the routine reply that that must be left to the Contracts Department. The inference is that he is an artist and that I, like him, should be above such financial haggling. This is an invariable gambit and unless the victim is forewarned it usually pays off:

he may even find himself in the studio and taking part in a programme without having received any contract, as I very foolishly did on one occasion. The only rule is to insist upon a fee being agreed before allowing them to waste your time.

I blame the influence of television for that 'personality cult' which has invaded the press and, with rare and honourable exceptions, has pushed serious reviewing into the background. When I leaf through my old press-cutting books, the obvious shrinkage of review space and the decline in the quality of reviewing during my writing lifetime is saddening. In the place of reviewing we have interviews with writers in which the reader is regaled with their views on this and that, a pen portrait of their wife or mistress, what their literary ambitions are, their taste in food and drink and their 'life style' generally. Authors presumably endure such inquisitions, like television appearances, for the sake of the publicity, but no writer would consider a column of such trivial gossip a fair substitute for a serious and honest attempt to assess the merits or demerits of his latest book.

This is not to say that I consider that column inches of reviews are of vital importance to an author any more than I think publicity efforts on the part of the publisher are vital. Many a new author feels aggrieved when he finds, not only that his precious book is not reviewed in the 'Sundays' but that it has not been included in his publisher's advertisements either. He should not worry. No amount of rave reviews and no amount of publicity will sell a bad book, whereas a good book sells primarily on personal recommendation passed on from reader to reader. From experience, I am sure that this is true because I do not think that any author can have achieved so large a reputation and sales as I have over the years to the accompaniment of less publicity or so meagre a ration of review space. The reason is, of course, that to literary editors, the kind of subjects I write about are technical and therefore unsuitable matter for Literature (with a capital L) which should be concerned with art and not with science or technology.

Lecturing makes another very small item on my annual

balance sheet because the paltry fees offered again illustrate the popular fallacy that an established author must necessarily be well-heeled. I receive letters from innumerable local societies, or branches of national ones, inviting me to lecture at some remote town which may be in England, Scotland, or Wales. They invariably offer to reimburse my expenses but only very rarely is there any mention of a fee. So, instead of presenting me with a straight offer to be accepted or rejected, they put me to the trouble of replying and stating my fee, an invidious chore which I dislike. This disclosure of my fee is frequently the end of the matter, for these enthusiastic lecture organizers will never realize that an author's lecture fee must cover, not only the lecture itself but the time he consumes – usually the best part of two days – in travelling to and fro between his home and Leeds, Liverpool or Norwich as the case may be. If the fee does not cover this loss of time, then it means that I can earn more by sitting at my desk at home. University Extra-Mural Departments, who should know better, are among the worst offenders in this respect, offering insultingly low fees for their lecture courses.

I have found that lecturing is like acting in one respect in that one's performance is dependent on the responsiveness of the audience. I can tell in the first few minutes whether they are 'with me' or not. Strangely enough, I have found that the quality of the audience in this respect varies from county to county and town to town. I have found my most responsive audience in Leicester and my least in my local town of Cheltenham, a judgement that is based not upon one but on several experiences in each town. But my least responsive audiences of all consisted of members of the Historical Association to whom I had been asked to speak on the subject of Thomas Telford at Attingham Park in Shropshire. Their average age must have been about seventy and before returning to Attingham for dinner they had had a very long day's sight-seeing. Consequently, when they adjourned to the library for my after-dinner talk, the entire audience fell asleep as though they had been pole-axed. I talked on against a background of deep breathing and gentle snores, observing in the reflected light from the screen the rows of closed eyes and open mouths.

The other unnecessary hazard to which a lecturer is subjected arises from the inability of organizers to provide the correct equipment with which to project the slides or film strips used for illustration. This, despite the fact that I always spell out my requirements in words of one syllable. I arrive to find either the wrong projector or no projector at all, whereupon members of the audience volunteer to set out upon a frantic combing of the town in an attempt to track down the correct machine, often returning flushed and breathless after a fruitless quest. Alternatively, they have the correct projector but either the lead is not long enough to reach the nearest power point, or the plug does not suit and no alternative plug or adaptor can be found. Sometimes incidents of a more dramatic kind occur. I was about to address a packed audience in a large hall in Llandudno and as soon as I called for the projector and it was switched on, every light in the hall went out, plunging us into total darkness. I groped my way back into the little room behind the platform, felt for a chair and left them to sort it out, listening to the muffled sounds of confusion, the calls for torches and matches, from without. As no one appeared to know where the main fuses were, it was some time before order was restored.

My most memorable experience as a lecturer occurred at a large technical college in a Lancashire town not many miles from Manchester where I had been invited to deliver the annual Ramsbottom Lecture.* As he was driving me to the college after meeting me at Manchester Piccadilly station, I thought the college lecturer seemed rather ill at ease. Finally, he swallowed and said nervously that he hoped I would not be disappointed in my audience. To the question: 'Why should I be?' he explained rather lamely that, owing to a stupid oversight, a rival lecture had been arranged for the same night.

* The name is fictitious.

Proceedings began according to custom with dinner in a nearby hotel given by the current representatives of the Ramsbottom family to the lecturer and the Principal of the College. This over, we all progressed across the street to the imposing portico of the college where, in the entrance hall through the glass doors I found myself confronted by these notices:

SMALL LECTURE THEATRE: L.T.C. ROLT

LARGE LECTURE THEATRE: Dr. J. BRONOWSKI

The Principal and I turned left and walked onto the platform of the small theatre together. I was gratified to see that the auditorium was packed and that the porters were carrying in extra chairs which they were setting out in the aisles. The Principal stopped in his tracks 'Good gracious me!' he exclaimed, 'There must be some mistake.' He banged on the table for silence and announced in a loud clear voice 'This is NOT Dr Bronowski's lecture. Will those who think it is move as quickly as possible to the large theatre across the hall.' No one stirred. 'Extraordinary', he muttered, before repeating his announcement in a still louder voice. This time it provoked some faint, ironical cheers from the audience, but still no one moved. There was then nothing for the Principal to do but to introduce me, which he did perfunctorily and with a just perceptible shrug of the shoulders as if to say there is no accounting for human nature. Lancastrians are not the most tactful of men and I can well understand why they have a reputation for calling a spade a bloody shovel.

6
Writing for Industry

The 'other payments' mentioned in the last chapter represent the fees I receive for writing books for industry, usually to mark a particular company's centenary. This is a source of income I had never considered when I decided to make writing a career, yet it adds up to a very substantial sum over the years. Usually such books are produced for private publication and distribution in which case I receive an agreed outright fee payable in instalments, but occasionally a company history may be made available for sale as well as for private distribution so that I then get a small royalty additional to my fee.

Looking back over the years, I think my survival as a writer would have been far more difficult, if not impossible, had it not been for this lucrative side line. It has led me into some embarrassing situations but it has also produced some very interesting experiences which I would not on any account have missed.

This particular story began when I was at Towyn in 1951, running the Talyllyn Railway. One morning I received out of the blue a letter from a firm of publishers, whose name I had not heard of before, who described themselves as 'publishers to industry'. They asked permission to add my name to their 'panel of authors' and since there appeared to be no strings attached, I naturally consented. Months and years slipped by and I had forgotten all about the matter when, in the winter of 1954/55 I received a letter from this firm inquiring whether I would be interested in writing a centenary history for Samuel Williams & Co. of Dagenham Dock. Although I had never heard of this firm, it sounded an interesting assignment so I accepted and, in the light of after events, I am very glad that I did so.

Old Samuel Williams, the founder of the company, was a working lighterman on London River who prospered until he owned a modest fleet of lighters. By 1855 there was only one small part of the lands bordering the Thames between London and the sea which must have looked substantially the same as it had done in the days of the Roman occupation. This was the site where the celebrated Dagenham Breach had occurred in the seventeenth century. This was a serious failure of part of the embankment which protected the neighbouring flat lands from being overwhelmed by the tides. To close this breach posed an almost insuperable problem to seventeenth-century engineers and when, after years of effort, it was finally closed by the redoubtable Captain Perry, a large lake and a great area of salt marsh remained behind. Samuel Williams had the wit to realize the potential value of this marshland and he bought it for a song. He next secured a contract to dispose of all the spoil produced during the building of London's Metropolitan and District railways. This he lightered down the river and dumped on Dagenham Marsh, thus gradually reclaiming it. It is now the site of the company's busy Dagenham Docks and it is also, incidentally, the site of the Ford Factory which Samuel Williams & Co. sold to Fords, also carrying out all the preparatory works including a great deal of pioneer concrete piling.

I found this Dagenham job most interesting and enjoyable, while it was also directly responsible for providing me with a new and novel experience – an ocean voyage in a cargo ship. Although I am not particularly attracted to the sea, I had always felt a desire to make a long sea voyage just to see what it was like. But I was determined not to travel as a cossetted passenger in one of those ships designed to make her customers forget they are at sea by providing the illusion of a luxury hotel. Instead, I wanted to travel the ocean the hard way by a merchantman in which I hoped I might have the run of the ship from bridge to engine-room so that I could experience at first hand what a modern 'life on the ocean wave' was really like. Now, at Dagenham, precisely this opportunity offered itself.

One of the company's principal activities was the traditional one of shipping 'sea coal' coastwise from Tyne to Thames. This traffic was handled by a subsidiary known as the Hudson Shipping Company and shortly before I came onto the scene the decision had been taken to expand this company's activities. No longer would they be confined to coastal trade; they would also go deep-sea. To this end two new bulk carriers were ordered from Readhead's yard on the Tyne – this at a time before the bulk carrier became as popular as it is today. Considering what traffic these two new ships might profitably engage upon, the company decided that the West Indian sugar trade appeared the most promising. The raw sugar had, up to now, been carried in bags so that carriage in bulk offered substantial economies, as was quickly appreciated by Tate & Lyle who chartered both ships.

The first of these ships, the *Hudson Deep*, was commissioned while I was still working at Dagenham. The second, the *Hudson Point* was not completed until after I had finished my history of the firm, but I received an invitation to a cocktail party on board her as she lay in Dagenham Dock prior to setting out on her maiden voyage to the West Indies. While the rest of the company present seemed intent on serious drinking, the Managing Director, John Carmichael, and I set out on a tour of exploration. The *Hudson Point* had the usual layout of a bulk carrier with engine-room, crew's quarters and dining saloon right aft and bridge-house for'ard, a series of enormous cargo hatches occupying the space between. We were investigating the bridge-house where I found that directly below the Captain's cabin there was a second cabin, as large as a bedroom in a house, having twin sleeping berths and its own bathroom, shower and loo. Over the doorway to this palatial apartment were carved the words: OWNER'S CABIN. 'Does the Owner ever travel?' I asked Carmichael, half enviously and half in jest. 'No', he replied, 'I shouldn't think so', and then he added as an after-thought, 'Why, would you like to?' So it came about that January 1958 saw Sonia and myself embarking on the *Hudson Point* for a voyage to the West Indies.

Having left our two sons, Richard and Timothy, at Stanley Pontlarge in charge of a nanny, we joined our ship at Readhead's yard on the Tyne whither she had gone for her first re-fit. This was the first time I had seen a shipyard at close quarters and I was astounded by the primitive and dangerous working conditions, the dirt and the apparent disorder and muddle that appeared to prevail. Most of the dock was unprotected from the weather and the ground was covered by a slippery mixture of thin mud and suspended oil. On this surface electric arc welding cables snaked about everywhere for the unwary to trip over, perhaps to fall into the unprotected depths of a large dry dock. We went aboard the *Hudson Point* to find that the ship's fitters had finished their work but had left an indescribable mess everywhere. New paintwork was covered with oily fingermarks, the decks were strewn with balls of filthy cotton waste and there were heaps of metal and wood shavings in corners. The crew appeared to take this state of affairs quite philosophically. Apparently it was usual because the shipyard worker argues that once the ship puts to sea her crew will have all the time in the world to clean up after him.

We met the Master, Captain Platt, a genial Tynesider who had graduated from the coastal coal trade, and the young Shetland Islander who was Chief Engineer. It was explained to us that as the ship did not officially carry passengers we would have to sign on as steward and stewardess. In the afternoon, the *Hudson Point* moved to the bunkering berth and then, at 11 p.m., finally cast off, moving slowly towards the mouth of the river where she was swung to adjust compasses. This done we set course down the east coast but caught no glimpse of land the following day owing to bad visibility.

When, at 11.30 p.m. that night, we rounded the North Foreland and entered the English Channel, I was up on the bridge gazing in absolute fascination at the radar screen. It was my first acquaintance with radar in action and I could not have chosen a better moment. There, outlined in white on the sides of the screen were the familiar outlines of the channel coasts, while over the black void between there moved like so many luminous water-boatmen, numerous points of light from each of which small arrowheads of wake fanned out. I had no idea that these narrow seas carried so much traffic and to my inexperienced eye it all looked very fraught, imminent collisions appearing inevitable. But the radar screen, like a map, is on a small scale and in this respect conveys an alarmist impression to those unfamiliar with it. In fact, we scarcely glimpsed the lights of another ship in our passage down channel.

When the reluctant January daylight came there was a thick mist over the land and distant foghorns were groaning and grunting. Once a corridor opened in the mist to starboard to reveal some vicious fangs of rock which we were told were the Casquets. Distantly, we could hear the melancholy clangour of a bell buoy. This was the last sight and sound we had of Europe.

As soon as we got out into the open Atlantic we ran into heavy weather which lasted for four days and nights and was made worse by the fact that we were travelling light ship with only water ballast to steady her. It seemed to me extremely rough, though the crew assured me that it was nothing unusual for the North Atlantic in January. The weather proved too much for Sonia who had to retire to her berth. So long as she remained in a horizontal position she felt alright, but as soon as she got up she began to feel sea-sick. Fortunately I am a good sailor and was quite unaffected. At first I thought it was all rather exciting, but after four days of it I had grown heartily sick of rough weather. I found the sheer physical strain of keeping my balance extraordinarily tiring and by the end of the day felt as stiff as after a twenty mile walk. Again, sleep, for me at any rate, became almost impossible. Because the ship was both rolling and pitching it made little difference whether one lay fore and aft or transversely. The berths in our cabin (they were virtually twin beds) were disposed fore and aft which meant that every time the ship rose to a wave I found myself sliding down in the bed, while as she descended into a trough I found my head pressed firmly against the bedhead.

I spent quite a lot of this stormy time up on the bridge. The outlook forward through the whirling spinners was hypnotic as a succession of great waves attacked the port bow of the *Hudson Point*, causing the whole ship to tremble under their impact and sending a pother of white water creaming over the bows only to pour from the scuppers as she recovered from the blow. We were travelling on a set course by automatic pilot and although I have an ineradicable mistrust of such gadgetry, particularly on ships, I could not help admiring the way this device held the ship to her proper course under such conditions. The effect of the wind and the battering seas was that the ship kept on tending to veer away to starboard. Each time this happened there was a rapid whirring, clicking sound as of the striking train of a large clock starting up as the pilot, or 'Iron Man' as the crew nicknamed it, took instant corrective action and the wheel spun as though turned by a phantom helmsman. Yet no human hand upon the wheel could have reacted so accurately or with such unfailing promptitude.

It was at this time I discovered that life in the exclusive bridge-house was not without certain disadvantages. The prostrate Sonia's needs were supplied by a devoted steward, but Captain Platt and I must needs battle our way aft to the dining saloon along the length of the open deck, clinging to the lee rail and trying to dodge the clouds of flying spray. In the dining saloon, which was right aft, a new phenomenon was manifest as the ship pitched which I found very alarming the first time I experienced it. The whole saloon would suddenly seem to fall by several feet, not all at once but in a series of shuddering jolts, a foot at a time. At this the crew would remark jocularly that 'the old girl's falling down stairs' which, in fact, was exactly what it felt like. It was due, they explained, to the whip in the empty steel hull.

My only regret, as an enthusiast, was that the *Hudson Point* was not a steamer. She was propelled by an eight-cylinder Doxford opposed piston diesel engine which was coupled to an exhaust heat boiler to provide deck steam for winches etc. I grudgingly had to give this engine full marks for its relative silence and lack of vibration as it kept slogging away through fair weather and foul. One of my vintage car friends owned an Edwardian Gobron-Brillié car with an opposed piston engine, and, except for the difference in scale, it was interesting to see how closely the layout of the modern Doxford followed this pioneer design.* Only one feature of this Doxford alarmed me at first sight. The upper pistons were water-cooled. As the stroke of these pistons was quite considerable this water was supplied to them through rubber pipes, each between two and three feet long. On entering the engine room at deck level, standing on the iron staircase and looking down upon the main engine, the first thing to catch the eye were these eight rubber pipes, snaking away like so many captive writhing serpents at each stroke of the engine. I felt they could not possibly withstand such an ordeal for very long, but I evidently underestimated the properties of modern synthetic rubbers for, in reply to my question, the Chief said he had never known one fail although they were changed as a precautionary measure after each round voyage.

At length we left the winter storms behind, emerging into calm and sunlit blue waters. Soon we were able to sit out in the

---

* In an engine of this type the explosion takes place in the middle of the cylinder between two pistons which are thus driven apart. The upper pistons drive a common crankshaft by means of piston rods, crossheads and connecting rods. In a large marine diesel, one of the great advantages of this layout is that the explosion forces are equalized by the two pistons. There is thus no tendency, as there is on an orthodox engine, for the explosion to lift the cylinder head and block off the crankcase. Hence the latter can be made much lighter.

sun in deck chairs in the lee of the bridgehouse watching the flying fishes flutter from wave-crest to wave-crest. It was at this time that we sighted our first ship since leaving the English Channel. This was another surprise, for the phrase 'the North Atlantic shipping lanes' had given me the naïve impression that we should be encountering a constant stream of fellow-voyagers. Now I was learning the truth that, despite all man's trafficking, an ocean remains a very wide and lonely place.

When the *Hudson Point* was passing down channel she had still to receive her loading orders and the crew had speculated whether their destination might be Cuba, a prospect which, from previous experience, they regarded with disfavour as that country was still under the Batista regime. So it was a relief when orders came through that we were to make for the port of Barahona in San Domingo not far from the border of Haiti. Eventually – and almost miraculously it seemed to me – the little town and port, crouched beneath high and densely wooded hills loomed up dead ahead. Captain Platt moved the telegraph from full to slow ahead and, for the first time for many days, the familiar rhythm of the Doxford slowed and the ship's wake died. We continued to drift ahead while the Captain and I studied the harbour through binoculars – for this was the ship's first visit. We watched two dark figures, who had been reclining at their ease on the sun-drenched quay, suddenly awakened to frantic activity as the bray of our siren echoed among the surrounding hills. They ran down some steps and piled into a small white launch, one madly cranking the engine while the other frantically fumbled with mooring lines. The Barahona harbour pilot had been alerted and was on his way.

Although the *Hudson Point* was a very small ship as modern bulk carriers go, being a mere 10,000 tons burden, her arrival caused something of a sensation in Barahona as she was said to be the largest ship ever to enter the port. We discovered that the principle of bulk carriage had not yet been accepted by the West Indians. Not only did it spell formidable labour problems but the installation of new and costly mechanical handling equipment. So every day an elderly Baldwin metre gauge wood-burning steam locomotive, with a tall balloon stack, shuttled to and fro between the quay and Barahona's one sugar mill freighted with stacks of bagged sugar. These sugar sacks were swung aboard four at a time by the ship's derricks. On board, the enormous hatch covers were only opened to the extent of about eighteen inches, just sufficient to allow a grating to be inserted in the gap. Two native loaders received the sacks from the derrick and, while one withdrew the draw-string from the neck of each sack, the other up-ended it over the grating so that its contents fell into the cavernous hold beneath. The whole operation looked as tedious as trying to fill a large bath with a teaspoon, but it suited us for, as was proved on our return to Dagenham, had the right equipment been available we should scarcely have had time to put a foot ashore.

When we realized how long the loading was going to take, we had the optimistic notion that we might visit the ruined palace of the black emperor Christophe in the interior of Haiti, but when we learned that we should have to hire mules and that the journey would take at least two days, we reluctantly abandoned the idea and confined ourselves to things nearer to hand. With Captain Platt we were the guests of the local Rotarians who held a dinner for us in a Barahona restaurant. It was here that we tasted the local coffee for the first time and fully endorsed our hosts' claim that it was the finest in the world. So enamoured were we of this discovery that Sonia determined to take a bag of the green beans back with us so that they could be freshly roasted at home. We combed the open market and every provision shop in the town in vain. The fact that we could not speak Spanish did not make this quest any easier, but finally we were directed towards an ironmonger's shop. Here, surprisingly, we found our quarry, for in these unlikely surroundings there reposed a great sack full of green coffee beans. At dusk we liked to sit in the small town square under the palm trees, watching with amusement the nightly parade of the youth of Barahona, the boys circulating in one direction and the girls, graceful and beautifully dressed, in the other. Apart from an occasional shy interchange of glances, there appeared to be no communication whatever between the two sexes.

We were befriended by the Spanish manager of the sugar mill who showed us over his mill and also arranged a footplate trip for us on a Baldwin diesel locomotive up into the sugar plantations. I was surprised both by the extent of the plantations and by the size and complexity of the railway system which served them. Our friend also introduced us to Mrs Grant, the only English resident of Barahona. This very remarkable old lady lived alone in a bungalow overlooking the harbour. The widow of a former sugar plantation owner, she was a survivor of the days when the greater part of the sugar industry of the West Indies was owned either by the English or by the Americans. She received us most graciously but with a surprising degree of detachment considering we were probably the first people of her own blood she had seen for months. We sat chatting and sipping cups of china tea for all the world as though we were near neighbours making a polite call. Her bungalow translated us into Edwardian England, or rather the Ewardian Empire's version of England. It was obvious that she stood very high in the estimation of our Spanish friend and that she was still a force to be reckoned with in Barahona. But we speculated long on the considerations that had induced her, after her husband's death, to go on living entirely alone in this alien community.

Just before our ship sailed for home we had an opportunity to see the capital of San Domingo, then known as Cuidad Trujillo after the reigning dictator. We visited the city's two historic buildings to survive the hurricanes, the cathedral and the palace of Diego Columbus, both built in coral limestone of a most ravishing colour. That evening, after darkness fell, we also visited the new city which dictator Trujillo had caused to be built on the outskirts of the old. This was a weird experience. It consisted of a grid pattern of almost absurdly wide avenues with groups of modern statuary on islands at each intersection. These avenues were flanked by modern high-rise buildings. Not only were the roads brilliantly lit, but every window of the buildings which flanked them blazed with light. The air was filled with the sound of sickly canned music issuing from invisible loudspeakers. What made this modern city so very odd was that there was not a single solitary soul to be seen in it; no cars on the avenues, no people on the pavements or framed in those blazing windows. It might have been a city of the dead. We agreed that it was more than odd, it was decidedly sinister and we could not get away from the place quickly enough.

The voyage home was uneventful and, where Sonia was concerned, much more comfortable as the *Hudson Point*, now that she was fully freighted with sugar, behaved in a much more decorous manner. It was now March so we hoped that we had avoided the worst of the winter, but our hopes were dashed when we passed up channel through a raging blizzard. We docked at Dagenham at about 10.30 p.m. and by 11.30 a.m. next morning, when we bade farewell to Captain Platt and left the ship, her cargo had been three-parts discharged by the dock's 12-ton grabbing cranes loading into an endless string of lighters. The whole voyage had been a most interesting and worthwhile experience but one which I have no desire to repeat. For it taught me something of the deadly monotony of life in the merchant navy, a monotony that is made worse by the characteristics of modern shipping, by all those technical aids to navigation and by that ever increasing speed of turn-round upon which modern economics insists.

As I had previously had nothing whatever to do with the shipping industry, it was something of a coincidence that the very next commission I obtained was to write a centenary history for a well-known firm of ship store dealers named Burnyeat Ltd. The Burnyeats are a very old Cumberland family whose name can be traced back to the sixteenth century and the founder of the firm was William Burnyeat who opened his ship store business in the then flourishing Cumbrian port of Whitehaven. This William served his time at sea until he was twenty-one when he took over a butchery business in the vanished Georges Market at Whitehaven from his widowed mother in 1840. Precisely when he started in the ship store trade was uncertain at the time I undertook the assignment. The firm's letter heading and its considerable fleet of vans proudly announced 'Established 1861' yet I could find no shred of evidence to support such a claim in the firm's archives, a circumstance I found somewhat embarrassing as I had been commissioned on the assumption that 1961 would be their centenary year. I have never undertaken such a history where there was less documentary evidence to work upon. All that was known about William Burnyeat was that at the time he started his ship store business he was already a man of considerable substance. He owned land on which he reared his own stock for the butchery; he had a considerable investment in local mining companies and, above all, in shipping. At that time, when a new ship was laid down, it was customary to divide her estimated capital cost into sixty-four shares and William Burnyeat eventually became known in shipping circles as 'the greatest sixty-fourther of them all'. In addition to these considerable shareholdings, William Burnyeat was known to have owned and worked at least two ships, the barque *Sarah Burnyeat*, and the brigantine *Emily Burnyeat*, named after his wife and daughter respectively.

There was so much hearsay and so little hard evidence about William Burnyeat's career in Whitehaven that there seemed to be nothing for it but an investigation on the spot so, having bespoken a room in Whitehaven's only listed hotel, one day in the early autumn of 1957 I headed the Alvis north for Cumberland. I was able to kill three birds with one stone on this one northern trip for, when my work at Whitehaven was done, I went on to stay with the Nobles at Walwick Hall where I was able, not only to do some research for my Stephenson biography as I have already mentioned, but also some work on the history of Burnyeat Ltd's branch depot and offices on the Newcastle quays.

One amusing little incident occurred as I was driving into Cumberland. I had unwisely allowed the level of petrol in the scuttle tank of the Alvis to fall extremely low with the inevitable result that, half way up a long hill on the approach to Millom, petrol failed to reach the carburettor and the car came to an ignominious halt. As there was no sign of a petrol pump, in these circumstances there was nothing to be done but to free-wheel back to the foot of the hill, turn the car round, and then ascend backwards. I was making a rapid ascent in reverse gear (for the Alvis has a high ratio reverse) when I was overhauled, but not passed, by a baker's delivery van. The baker and I found ourselves regarding each other, eye-ball to eye-ball over our respective steering wheels, he with an expression of mingled fear and bewilderment that was comical to behold. He was obviously not accustomed to the spectacle of men in strange looking motor cars going up hills backwards and when I smiled and waved to reassure him that everything was under control it appeared to have the opposite effect from that intended. The hill ended in an abrupt summit where there was a view of a long descent with, in the distance, an undoubted filling station on the outskirts of Millom. There was also a convenient side turning at the top for me to reverse into, waving the van past. When I passed the baker at a rate of knots on the long, straight descent he must have been more than ever convinced that I was a lunatic. He probably had drinks on the story for weeks afterwards.

I had never been to Whitehaven before and found it precisely the sort of place to appeal to me. I have always been strangely fascinated and moved by places of bygone industrial activity. It is as though they remain forever haunted by that tide of fierce and often terrifying energy which had created them and then passed on. It was this quality which had first attracted me to Ironbridge during the war and which now attracted me to Whitehaven. The port had begun to grow in the latter part of the eighteenth century until it became one of the first six in the kingdom, flourishing exceedingly as a consequence of the exploitation of neighbouring resources of coal and haematite ore. Whitehaven coal mines, extending under the sea, were one of the wonders of the early industrial revolution period. At the time of which I write, one of these pits was still working, its gaunt stack and winding gear dramatically crowning a headland jutting out into the sea on the south side of the harbour. Wagons of coal were lowered from it down to harbour level by a perilous-looking, sharply curved and graded cable-operated incline. On the opposite side of the harbour was a second colliery which had been closed and its workings sealed following a terrible disaster.

Such was the prosperity of Whitehaven that eventually no less than seven massive stone piers were built – one of them by Sir John Rennie – to contain and shelter its growing volume of shipping. On these piers there stand charming little stone lighthouses. It was the rapid rise to wealth and fame of the port of Liverpool that sealed the fate of Whitehaven. The writing was on the wall when the two uncrowned kings of the port, the brothers Thomas and Jonathan Brocklebank, ship-owners and shipbuilders, removed their business to Liverpool. The astute William Burnyeat was not long in following them and Liverpool has remained to this day the headquarters of the company he founded.

My hotel was close to the waterfront and after I had dined I set out on foot in the deep dusk of an autumn evening to explore the harbour. The walls of the row of eighteenth- and early nineteenth-century houses that overlooked the basin of the inner harbour supported gas lanterns whose mantles flared and flickered in the breeze blowing off the sea. Except that the capacious basins contained only two small steam cargo ships, it was a scene that can have changed very little since the heyday of Whitehaven. I determined to walk out to the distant extremity of the southern piers and from that vantage look back at the town. It was quite a way, and as I walked on I soon passed out of range of the last gaslamp and it became quite dark although I could just see the colliery and its headgear looming against the night sky on the headland to my left. I stopped to look up at the colliery and as I did so I heard, for a moment only, the sound of footsteps behind me. It was as though I had caught an echo of my own footfalls except that this sound was the unmistakable dot-and-carry-one of a man with a wooden leg. When I moved forward, the sound began again, yet whenever I stopped it stopped. It was a strange experience to be followed in this way on a walk which I knew, and as my pursuer must have known, would end at the pier head. At such a time of night the piers were completely deserted and I confess that I experienced a slight *frisson* of fear.

About a hundred yards from the pierhead I found some stone steps on my left which led to a narrow walkway at a higher level on the pier wall leading to a lookout over the open sea beyond. I swiftly turned aside up these steps and ran on tip-toe to the lookout. Short of jumping into the sea I could go no further. I listened and for a moment there was nothing but the sound of the sea breeze in my ears, but then I heard the clear sound of the one-legged man laboriously ascending those stone stairs. As is usual in the case of true stories of this kind, the ending was anticlimactic in the extreme. My pursuer turned out to be no sinister character out of *Treasure Island* but an old Whitehaven salt in a heavy blue seaman's jersey whose wits were fuddled either by age or alcohol so that he had seen fit to follow me thus far, like the ancient mariner, until I became literally a captive audience for his yarns. I was so relieved that I have not remembered one word of what he said.

Next morning my insatiable urge to explore the port of Whitehaven led me to make an extraordinarily lucky chance discovery. I was peering through the cobweb-blurred panes of a window of an old and ramshackle wooden hut on the quay. To my amazement I saw, standing out from the rusting and mouldering junk within like a rose among nettles, the beautiful, freshly painted figure-head of a woman. Three old men were seated on a bench nearby gazing ruminatively out over the empty harbour, so I asked them who owned the hut. Mr Keenagh, an old ships' rigger, I was told. He had retired from business now, but if I cared to wait around he would most likely be down before long. Sure enough, an ancient bent figure presently appeared and proceeded to unlock the door of his hut.

Asking him to forgive my curiosity, I explained how the figure-head had attracted my attention and asked him if he could tell me anything of its history. The old man chuckled, 'Ain't she lovely?' he asked rhetorically, 'you don't know who she is so I'll tell you – that's Emily Burnyeat that is.' I could hardly believe my ears, but old Mr Keenagh went on to assure me that this was indeed the figure-head of William Burnyeat's brigantine. For years it had lain gathering dust in the sail loft of the Keenagh family business, but when the loft was either sold up or pulled down, he had rescued it, removing it to his hut where, with loving care, he had restored the figure to its former glory. It became clear that the old man had fallen in love with the effigy and was terrified lest someone should take her away from him and 'put her in some museum'. I had to assure him that I had no such intention and he finally allowed his darling to be taken out of his hut, perched on the edge of the quay wall and photographed in colour for the cover of *Mariners' Market*, as my Burnyeat history was called.

I still had to find out where and when William Burnyeat had started his ship store business. In an investigation of this kind the public librarian is usually helpful and Mr Hay of the Whitehaven Library was no exception. At his suggestion I was soon looking through piles of dusty bound volumes of the local newspaper, *The Cumberland Pacquet and Ware's Whitehaven Advertiser*, searching the announcements on the front pages. I do not know what made me go back earlier than 1861, but it was fortunate that I did so, for before very long – eureka! – there was the vital clue, an advertisement inserted by William Burnyeat announcing the opening of new and commodious premises at 23 King Street, Whitehaven. This was dated December 1851, so the firm was just ten years older than had been assumed.

It remained to find the whereabouts of 23 King Street and then see whether any traces of William Burnyeat's occupancy were still to be found. King Street was, and still is, the main shopping street of the town and Mr Hay, who was by now as hot and keen upon the scent as I was, explained that, although the street had long ago been re-numbered, we had only to go along to the Lowther Estate Office and ask to see an estate map of the right date in order to pinpoint No. 23. The Lowthers own the whole of Whitehaven and, sure enough, their Estate Office produced a superb map of the town, *c.* 1860, on which every property was identified. By cross referencing to a modern street map it was easy to establish the whereabouts of No. 23.

When we walked down King Street to discover that the premises were now occupied by a cheap multiple clothier, all plywood panelling and plate glass, our spirits sank. Had this ever been a butcher's shop? We asked the startled youth in the winkle-picker shoes behind the counter. Not that he knew of; the business had not been there very long and had succeeded a tobacconist and confectioner. But, he added, we could take a look round the back if we liked. As he spoke he opened a door behind the counter to reveal an enormous whitewashed slaughter house, its ceiling supported by cast-iron columns, still carrying the large hooks from which William Burnyeat had suspended his carcasses. It became clear to us now that the modern clothier's shop only occupied a fraction of the original premises and that there were buildings at the back, most of them now falling derelict, sufficient to house not only the butchery business from Georges Market but that stock of provisions and chandlery which an expanding ship store business would require. I was particularly intrigued by a curious building in the yard outside the slaughter house. This consisted of a row of what appeared to be single, self-contained rooms, three in number, each with a front door opening onto a balcony equipped with a cast-iron balustrade and approached by a short flight of steps. The youth followed my gaze 'The older folk what comes in here', he volunteered, 'call them "the Captain's Flats".' So, this had all been a part of the service. For a consideration William Burnyeat would provide his captain, cronies and customers with a room ashore while their ships were in port without attracting unwelcome attention. Such a man deserved his success. Unfortunately 'the Captains' Flats' were derelict when I saw them so they have doubtless been demolished long since.

Although I was trained as a mechanical engineer, the commissions I found most enjoyable and interesting were those concerned with some big new civil engineering project. These usually consisted of writing the text of an illustrated booklet, published to coincide with the official opening by HM The Queen or some other grandee and commissioned either by the main contractors, by the consulting engineers or, in some cases, by the committee responsible to local government for the project. I preferred such assignments because any work of civil engineering is necessarily unique; it is a one-off job whether it be a great bridge, a towering masonry dam or a tunnel beneath a river. Although the modern civil engineer can call to his aid equipment and plant such as his nineteenth-century predecessor never dreamed of, because he is dealing with natural things, earth, rock, air and water, his work remains subject to imponderable hazards which often cannot be foreseen and which, when they arise, he must wrestle with as best he may. For this reason, although great civil engineering works seldom excite the admiration and public acclaim that they did in the nineteenth century, there is usually an element of the heroic in the story of their successful completion.

My first commission of this kind was to write the story of the building of Britain's first motorway, the M1, for the main contractors, John Laing & Sons. When this new road was put out to tender in 1957 it was divided into four contracts of approximately equal length because it was felt that a single contract for the whole 52½ miles of road would be beyond competitive reach. However, Laings tendered for the four contracts and, greatly to their surprise, won all of them. It was one of the biggest civil engineering jobs ever to be awarded to a single British contractor. Laings established site offices at Chalton, Newport Pagnell, Collingtree and Walton on each of the four contracts, that at Newport Pagnell also serving as the headquarters and nerve centre for the whole gigantic operation. It was to be a fight against time for, England being a late starter where motorways were concerned, it had evidently been decided to make up for lost time and completion date was only nineteen months from 24 March 1958 when the Minister of Transport inaugurated the work.

So far as I was concerned the job could not have started at a more apposite time, for I had then just completed my researches into the construction of Robert Stephenson's London & Birmingham Railway and the opportunity to study a very similar example of modern construction being carried out on a closely parallel route would be most instructive. The two ceremonies inaugurating construction symbolized the difference between the two undertakings. Whereas the customary ceremonial barrow and spade was used on Stephenson's railway in 1834, work on the M1 began when the Minister of Transport pressed a button, sounding a horn which summoned the bulldozers into action. Although the new motorway was only half the length of the railway, the formation width was more than double so that the two are strictly comparable. A total of 25,000 men, the equivalent of 225 per route mile, toiled for four years on the 112 miles of railway. By contrast, the maximum number engaged on the $52\frac{1}{2}$ miles of motorway never exceeded 4,700 and the work was completed on time. The explanation, of course, is the use of mechanical power. Plant totalling 80,000 hp was used on the M1 which meant that each man employed wielded approximately 20 hp.

Laings broke down their four contract lengths of road into 'sub-projects' of four miles each as they considered this the maximum which could be effectively supervised by one man. The four main contract site offices and the small sub-project offices were, of course, linked by telephone, while a helicopter, on charter from BEA, was used to provide rapid physical communication between these offices. Robert Stephenson had likewise divided the London & Birmingham into four divisions, each in charge of an engineer. Each of these divisions was in turn divided into two districts over which there presided an assistant engineer with a staff of three sub-assistants under him. The administration of both these great works of civil engineering, separated though they were by nearly 125 years, was thus strikingly similar. But what amazed me, having seen the M1 under construction, was how such a system could possibly have functioned at a time when there was no method of communication faster than a man on horseback. It is this fact that makes the achievement of the railway builders seem almost miraculous.

I flew over the line of the road twice by helicopter which was a novel experience for me as I had never travelled in this type of vehicle before. On the first occasion it was in a small machine with only three passenger seats powered by an Alvis Leonides engine. I thoroughly enjoyed this flight, the only drawback being the fearful mechanical commotion. So high was the noise level that conversation was only made possible by headphones and throat microphones. My second flight was far less pleasurable. On a very hot June day and after a heavy lunch, we took off from Laings' sportsfield at Elstree in a very much larger helicopter bearing a dozen or so VIPs. The passenger cabin, like a fat seed-pod hanging below the rotor, swung continuously to and fro like a pendulum and its interior was almost unbearably stuffy. I found the motion so uncongenial that I came nearer to being sick than I have ever been at sea.

The consulting engineer for the M1 was Sir Owen Williams, one of the very few living men (if any) who, like Telford and other pioneers, combined the roles of civil engineer and architect. He was also a great character with an impish sense of humour. I had several long conversations with him including a luncheon at the house he had rented for the duration of the contract in the Northamptonshire village of Milton Melzor which I had known very well as a boy.* He claimed to have been responsible for the design and construction of more new bridges in Scotland than any engineer since Telford and he delighted to tell the story of the occasion when, accompanied by his faithful dog, he had gone to examine a suspension bridge over the river Garry at the western end of the Great Glen. As he walked onto the bridge, his dog positively refused to accompany him but lay on its belly in the approach roadway whining piteously. 'And when I examined the bridge', said Sir Owen, 'By God the dog was right!' This story must have got around locally, for when Sir Owen's new replacement bridge was formally opened by Cameron of Lochiel escorted by a detachment of pipers, in his formal speech Lochiel said how delighted he was that Sir Owen had been able to be present and then added drily that he noticed the engineer had wisely left his dog at home.

I like to think that my old duck's-back Alvis was the first car to travel the length of the M1 from Slip End, near Luton, to the junction between the so-called 'Birmingham Spur' and the existing A45 trunk road at Dunchurch. There was certainly plenty of contractor's traffic in Land Rovers to be seen on the road by this time, but for obvious reasons this was mostly short distance. I wanted to see the progress of the work at close quarters, also to visit the four site offices, and it struck me that an open vintage car with good ground clearance would be an ideal vehicle for such a tour of inspection. By keeping a good look out for distant obstructions and switching from one carriage way to another as occasion demanded, I got along famously, sometimes travelling on the levelled earth formation, sometimes on the sub-base of lean concrete and sometimes rolling smoothly along on a short stretch of completed road. It was when I neared the village of Milton that I thought I had met my Waterloo. For the plate girder bridge carrying the Roade–Northampton railway line over the motorway had only been rolled into position the previous week-end

* See *Landscape with Machines*, p. 63.

and the 'dumpling' of old embankment beneath it had still to be removed. I had drawn to a disconsolate standstill when a bronzed and muscled giant in a singlet, the modern successor of Stephenson's railway navvies, gave me a reassuring wave and clambered up into an enormous bulldozer. With a cloud of black smoke and a thunderous roar he started this machine whereupon, signalling me to follow him, he headed full-tilt at the bank ahead. Feeling like a small launch in the wake of an Atlantic liner, I did as I was bidden. The seemingly so solid earth parted as miraculously as the waters of the Red Sea and in a few moments we were through. With a creak and screech of tracks my friend in need swung his great machine abruptly to one side and waved me enthusiastically forward. The road was clear ahead and I was on my way.

When I stopped at Walton, the most northerly of the four site offices, situated near the Watford Gap where the Birmingham Spur and the M1 proper divide, I was particularly curious to know how work had progressed in an area notorious in civil engineering history. Here the contractors for Crick Tunnel on the old Grand Union Canal had been compelled to adopt a different line when one of their preliminary shafts had struck a water-bearing quicksand. Robert Stephenson knew of this and, hoping to avoid such a hazard, selected a line for his railway tunnel at Kilsby, further to the south. As is well known, this tactic proved vain and Stephenson's great battle against the Kilsby quicksand has become one of the epics of railway history.

Almost covering one wall of the Welton site office was a large scale map of the division. While I was chatting to the engineer in charge, I noticed that the line of the Birmingham Spur passed over the top of Kilsby Tunnel* and this prompted me to ask whether he had experienced any particular trouble on that stretch of road. He looked at me sharply. 'What makes you ask that?' he asked, and then went on, 'I'll

---

* One of the great brick ventilation shafts of the railway tunnel may be seen close beside the road at this point.

say we have, in fact we call that "tiger country" up there.' The road is in shallow cutting thereabouts and he went on to explain to me how, when they had excavated this almost down to formation level, they had suddenly struck a totally unexpected quicksand. This had involved pumping, drainage, further excavation and finally the importation of hundreds of tons of fill to restore the correct level. This is an illustration of the strange fact that civil engineers are so often taken unawares through their failure to benefit from the experience of their forerunners. This engineer had never heard the story of Kilsby Tunnel until I told him. In just the same way, although he knew about Crick Tunnel, even the great Robert Stephenson had evidently never heard of William Jessop's long battle against rotten, water-bearing oolite when he was driving the Grand Junction Canal Tunnel under Blisworth Hill. Otherwise Stephenson would not have been taken by surprise when he encountered the same difficult conditions in driving the Blisworth railway cutting nearby. Apart from Kilsby, this cutting was the biggest trouble spot on the London & Birmingham. Bourne's engraving of the cutting shows rocks supported by timber props, and eventually most of the cutting sides had to be held back by massive retaining walls.

I had passed through 'tiger country' and was almost within sight of my goal at Dunchurch when I had to stop because both carriageways ahead appeared to be completely blocked either with heaps of road surfacing material or machinery of one kind or another, rollers, pavers and graders. I was sitting on the back of the Alvis with my feet on the seat, peering ahead over the top of the screen and pondering what I should do, when I observed an individual who looked like the district engineer advancing purposefully in my direction. I was quite prepared for him to ask me brusquely what the hell I thought I was doing there; instead he remarked, in a delightful Irish brogue, 'I'm afraid we're not open yet', for all the world as though he were a polite landlord and I a member of the public who had strayed into his bar during closing hours. Having delivered himself of this blinding glimpse of the obvious, and when I had explained the purpose of my journey, this charming Irishman proceeded, with miraculous efficiency, to clear a path for the Alvis through the chaos of machines ahead, shooing them aside like so many cumbersome elephants. In a very few minutes I was on the A45, had turned to the left and was heading home to Gloucestershire down the lonely miles of the Roman Fosse Way.

After the M1 was finished, I subsequently wrote the text of booklets to celebrate the completion of the new Severn Bridge, the Tyne Tunnel and, much more recently, the first of the new twin road tunnels under the Mersey between Wallasey and Liverpool. Following so soon after my work on those pioneers of the suspension bridge Thomas Telford and I.K. Brunel, I naturally found the Severn Bridge assignment particularly interesting.

In the second half of the nineteenth century, the initiative in the design of long span suspension bridges passed from England to the United States thanks to the American A.W. Roebling, inventor of the modern system of cable suspension and builder of the Brooklyn Bridge. Hence when the first modern suspension bridge in Britain was built across the Forth, British engineers played safe by adopting American methods using a deep lattice girder deck which had to be laboriously assembled piecemeal across the Forth. But for an accident, the new Severn Bridge would have been similar to the Forth. A model of that design had been sent down to the National Physical Laboratory for wind tunnel tests but, when Sir Gilbert Roberts of Freeman, Fox & Partners inquired as to the results of these tests he was dismayed to learn that due to an insecure anchorage the model had been blown out of the wind tunnel and completely destroyed. This was a major set-back, for to make another model would take time whereas the wind tunnel had been 'booked' only for a brief period. It was at this juncture that Sir Gilbert conceived the idea of substituting, for the conventional lattice girder construction, a deck made up of a series of prefabricated steel box sections which could be welded together *in situ* and which in cross section would resemble an aerofoil and so offer minimal resistance to cross winds. To make a series of simple wooden models of such box sections for testing in the wind tunnel in order to arrive at the best form was very quickly done. So the design of the Severn Bridge, which won back for Britain the decisive leadership in this field, was determined.

The actual deck sections were fabricated in Fairfield's yard at Chepstow, where, long ago, the ironwork for Brunel's Chepstow Bridge had been wrought, and these were then launched into the Wye and towed by tugs to the bridge site. There, each in turn was hoisted aloft, attached to the suspension cables, and then welded to its neighbour. To ascend to the very summit of the tall steel suspension towers as I did and watch this operation going on far below was an ever-memorable experience.

The Severn Bridge is a great, original feat of engineering. It is most unfortunate that it was so soon followed by other bridges of prefabricated and box-girder structure but of most unsatisfactory design. This was shown by two cases of failure, in this country and Australia, where the use of calculators and computers alone in their design led to disaster. Had they been subjected to practical tests such as those applied by Stephenson, Hodgkinson and Fairbairn to a model of the Menai Bridge box girder in 1846, so disastrous and ignominious a series of failures might never have occurred.

Sonia and I were invited to attend the ceremonial opening of the Severn Bridge by the Queen at Aust, following which she drove over the bridge to perform an exactly similar ceremony on the other side and so propitiate the Welsh. When she had returned to the English side, loudspeakers announced that we were free to walk onto the bridge if we wished. From each bank a dense crowd surged onto the bridge to meet and mingle in the centre. The effect of this unusual load upon the bridge was most remarkable. One could feel the movement of the deck which was set up and both feel and see the fact that every suspension cable was quivering like harp string with a curious high frequency vibration. Such an experience made it easy to understand why an early, and admittedly defective, chain suspension bridge had collapsed beneath the measured tread of an army platoon, thus leading to the 'break step' rule. What would have been the effect, I wondered, if this huge crowd had all been walking in step?

It was not very long after this that I was in Newcastle having a brief introductory talk to the secretary of the joint committee, consisting of representatives of the counties of Northumberland and Durham, which was responsible for the administration of the new Tyne Tunnel works. He was telling me of the arrangements that were being made for the opening by the Queen, whereupon, remembering the Severn Bridge affair, I remarked that at least on this occasion she would not have to perform twice over. 'Don't you believe it!', he retorted, and in the event she had to do just that in order to satisfy both Durham and Northumberland. I had not reckoned upon the strength of county loyalties, particularly in the north of England.

Of these three great civil engineering projects, the latest was the driving of the first of two new twin tunnels under the Mersey. In the novel methods used and in the unexpected and daunting difficulties encountered and triumphantly overcome, it was this work which, in my opinion, could most worthily be compared with those of the heroic age of engineering when any major project was a venture into the unknown.

A pilot tunnel, which was first driven by conventional means beneath the Mersey, revealed the fact that, apart from a short section of boulder clay at the Liverpool end, the entire tunnel would be cut through soft red Bunter sandstone. Bearing this in mind, when the contract was put out to tender, the consulting engineers, Messrs Mott, Hay & Anderson, specified that the tunnel should be driven by mechanical means. No subaqueous tunnel on such a scale (7,000 ft long, 33 ft 2 in unlined diameter) had ever been driven by mechanical means before. The contract was won by a British firm of contractors who specialized in tunnel work and who, in order to carry out this job, had formed a partnership with an American firm who owned the world's largest tunnel boring machine. This had previously successfully driven five tunnels, each 1,500 ft long, in connection with the huge Mangla Dam project in Pakistan, and for this reason it became known as the Mangla Mole. It weighed 350 tons, was 45 foot long and, under favourable conditions, it was capable of cutting at the rate of four feet per hour. It presented to the rock face a cutting head resembling a giant lathe face plate on which were mounted radially a series of conical steel cutters. This face plate was originally solid, but one of the modifications carried out after it had been shipped to England was the insertion of a central hole through which it was possible to crawl into the pilot tunnel ahead. By this means the machine could be kept on its true course by directing a laser beam from the pilot tunnel through this central hole. In the case of the Mangla tunnels there had been no pilot bore so there was no necessity for such a provision. Hydraulic rams were capable of exerting a thrust of 500 tons on the cutting head which was rotated by ten electric motors of 100 horsepower each. Besides the propelling rams, the rear part of the machine included hydraulic arms for placing the tunnel lining segments in position and the endless bucket conveyor used to remove spoil from the working face directly to waiting trucks behind the machine.

From this brief description it may be judged how exciting it was when, clad in unfamiliar protective clothing and feeling rather like Charlie Chaplin trapped amid the cog wheels in *Modern Times*, I threaded my way through the intricacies of this huge machine and finally crawled through the hole in the cutting head to find myself in the dripping cavern of the pilot tunnel beneath the Mersey. I have never encountered working conditions so unpleasant or so potentially dangerous; it was very wet, very muddy, claustrophobic and dark despite the bright electric lights, and one seemed to be menaced on every side by angular and potentially lethal pieces of machinery.

Whereas the Mangla tunnels had been dry, the Bunter sandstone under the Mersey was fissured and faulty, admitting water in considerable quantity and it was this fact which nearly spelled disaster. Despite all efforts to prevent it, so long as it was working the Mole was constantly drenched with an abrasive slurry of water and sand. This proved to be too much for the protective seals to exclude and the giant machine had reached the midpoint of its drive under the river when the bearing behind the cutting head failed. This was a massive roller thrust bearing, 15 ft in diameter and weighing six tons. The pessimists, who were in the majority, shook their heads sadly. The breakdown had occurred at the end of a 2,500 ft tunnel no larger than the machine itself. Of the two alternatives, to replace the bearing on the spot or to dismantle the machine completely and withdraw it piecemeal by the way it had come, both seemed at first thought Herculean and almost impossible. Nevertheless, the brave decision was made to attempt to replace the bearing despite the fact that it was a shrink fit on its shaft having a negative tolerance of five thousandths of an inch. Naturally this demanded fitting conditions of almost clinical cleanliness and accuracy.

A cavern was first excavated round the Mole and a protective roof of corrugated iron and polythene sheeting attached to a series of steel arch ribs to protect the machine from water and grit. When this roof was completed there was six feet clearance over the top of the Mole. It was vital to the success of the whole operation that the cutting head should be held in an absolutely vertical position before its support was retracted. To this end it was welded to two steel beams securely concreted into the rock. A spare bearing had accompanied the Mole from Pakistan, but when it was unwrapped it was found that a number of rollers were badly corroded due to the failure of the protective grease and no less than forty new rollers had to be made to replace them. The six-ton bearing was then manoeuvred horizontally over the top of the Mole and finally lowered to the necessary vertical position by means of chain hoists moving on steel runway beams welded to the centre of the arch ribs. In this fashion was the bearing successfully fitted and the Mole duly completed its drive beneath the Mersey. This breakdown occurred on 20 February 1970 and yet the Mole was able to complete its drive on the 4 March following. This was a feat worthy to be compared with Sir Marc Brunel's struggles against adversity in his Thames Tunnel and that old engineer would surely have admired the energy and resources with which the emergency was met.

As a result of my writing for industry I sometimes found myself in somewhat unusual situations. For instance, when I was writing a history for a well known London-based firm of civil engineering contractors, they were insistent that I should interview their erstwhile chief civil engineer who had recently retired and bought a farm near Perth. So I travelled by night sleeper from Euston, taking a taxi from Perth station to the farm which lay on the fertile levels of Strath Earne against a magnificent backdrop of mountains. It was a brilliantly sunny morning in the early autumn with an invigorating nip in the air and those outlying peaks of the Highlands, Ben Chonzia and Ben Vorlich showed up blue and majestic in the distance. I had never seen a 'strong' Scottish farm before and admired its great ranges of substantial stone-built covered yards and buildings, the latter including a circular one which had originally housed a horse-engine for driving the barn machinery.

Although I was hospitably received, the engineer was obviously too pre-occupied with farming matters to discuss his past career. When an agitated stockman arrived to inform him that one of his pedigree Aberdeen Angus cows was just about to calve, he hurried out of the house, saying to me over his shoulder 'Come on, you may be able to help.' Before I knew where I was I found myself hauling with all my might on a rope attached to the emergent legs of a half-born calf while the engineer and the stockman assisted the cow more directly. I had never taken part in such an exercise before and it all seemed so brutal that I felt certain the little creature would be born dead. Yet having eventually fallen onto the deep layer of straw in the byre, it was staggering onto its spindly legs in a surprisingly short space of time and the engineer, now in high good humour, was leading me back to the house where he soon became expansively reminiscent.

Among other things he described to me how he had dismantled the old Chelsea suspension bridge prior to erecting the present one which was completed in 1937. Having removed the deck of the bridge piecemeal, the problem was how to dismantle the massive suspension chains with the minimum disruption to river traffic. To do this he slung cables across the river beneath the chains and on these placed a timber staging. He then tautened these cables until the staging had taken the weight of the chains so that their link pins could readily be removed. He was obviously pleased with his ingenuity and was a little dashed when I told him that more than a century ago Thomas Telford had used precisely the same procedure, but in reverse, in order to assemble the chains of his Conway suspension bridge. This was yet another example of the failure of engineers to proft from their own history.

When I wrote at the beginning of this chapter that writing for industry had led me into some embarrassing situations, it was not of delivering calves that I was thinking. Such embarrassments were invariably caused by conflicts between the need to meet the wishes of my client and my own conscience as a writer and historian. It is significant that in the case of the smaller companies such a conflict never arose. They would be well satisfied by an honest history of their company, warts and all, whereas the executives of a large group of companies would commission me to write a history whereas what, in fact, they wanted was an unreal exercise in public relations in which nothing to the company's discredit had ever occurred. A commercial enterprise, like the individuals of which it is composed, has its ups and downs, its faults and its failures as well as its successes, and any history that pretends otherwise not only must ring false but also makes very dull reading. It is the equivalent of the worst kind of Victorian biography in which the subject is portrayed as an inhuman paragon of all the virtues. The directors of one large group even went to the length of asking me to suppress my account of a disastrous factory explosion even though it had occurred during the Great War, long before the company concerned had become a memeber of the group. In this particular case I had been commissioned to write a text of about 60,000 words which was none too long in view of the size of the company, controlling as it did many plants both in this country and overseas. Yet when presented with the result after a year's hard work, the Board could not agree to its publication and suggested it should be cut to 10,000 words. It was at this point that I withdrew, suggesting that such a short text would be better done by their own Public Relations Department. Exactly the same thing had happened earlier in the case of another large, nationally known company; the Board could not agree to publication so my typescript lies gathering dust on some forgotten shelf.

In both these cases my handsome fee was paid in full, yet an author naturally feels that he has wasted precious time if the result of his labours never sees the light. The root of the trouble with such large companies is that the unfortunate author they commission suffers acutely from too many cooks. Copies of his typescript are circulated, sometimes to every member of the Board and sometimes to every managing director of however many subsidiary companies there may be. Each of these individuals feels compelled to justify his existence by making some criticisms and, as these often contradict each other, the wretched author becomes distracted to the point of despair.

Nevertheless, I have found writing for industry an interesting and worthwhile exercise, and I do not mean this solely in the monetary sense. By providing me with valuable knowledge of what was going on in the engineering world of today, such experience has helped me to see the engineering past in more correct perspective than would be the case if I were to become wholly pre-occupied with that past. Moreover, like my wartime job with the Ministry of Supply, it gave me a first-hand knowledge of industrial conditions while remaining myself independent and detached. I became aware, for example, of the folly of the modern fallacy that the bigger the business the more efficient it becomes. This is the outcome of the 'economy of scale' argument advanced by economist and accountant. They may be able to prove that it is much cheaper to produce 5,000 tonkle valves a week than 500, but what their figures can never show is the catastrophic result in human terms, the wastage of creative talent either in repetitive or unproductive administrative tasks, the lack of a sense of responsibility due to the breakdown of communications between employer and employee. No 'Personnel Department' however efficient can ever compensate for the latter failure. Above all, comparing this experience with my earlier one, I was dismayed to find to what an extent the accountant had usurped the place of the engineer in the conduct of large industries. When interviewing such new men of power in the Boardroom, I must confess I found them uniformly cold, unsympathetic and often more than a little sinister.

7

The Fight for Stanley Pontlarge

When I lived afloat I was always fearful that my boat might suddenly spring a leak and sink under me. There was a terrible occasion one winter while we were moored at Banbury when I stepped out of bed on a dark morning into water. I thought the end had come but it turned out that I had neglected to shut the sea-cock and that frost had split the pipe connecting this cock to the circulating pump. Shivering in pyjamas and dressing gown, I manned the bilge pump and soon disposed of the water which fortunately had not risen high enough to cover the carpet in our sitting cabin.

Again, because *Cressy* was old I was kept constantly at work with paint and putty or tar to prevent rainwater invading our cabins from sides or roof. For these reasons I have to admit that there were times when I found myself secretly envying the householder, protected by more durable materials than wood and surely based on firm ground. When we moved into Stanley Pontlarge, however, I very soon learned that a house can be as big a source of anxiety as a boat, particularly if it is an ancient one in a state of disrepair.

The antique plumbing gave cause for anxiety. One Saturday morning the galvanized steel cold water storage tank in a cupboard in the bathroom began to drip ominously from the bottom, from which it was evident that it must be paper thin. The old builder who had worked for my parents had retired, so we had to telephone for a strange builder from

Winchcombe. He arrived, accompanied by his plumber and, on being shown the drip, before anyone could stop him he had pushed his first finger straight through the bottom of the tank. 'You shouldn't 'a done that' remarked his plumber reproachfully as torrents of water gushed everywhere. 'Well, what do we do now?' I asked, exasperated. The precious pair shook their heads sadly, saying in unison 'Sat'day arternoon; can't do nothin' till Monday mornin'.' I was left to make a temporary repair by sticking a large patch cut from an old inner tube on the inside of the tank bottom. This lasted until a more efficient plumber installed a new tank on the following Monday.

But our chief worry was whether we should continue to have a roof over our heads. I should not like to guess how long it had been since any substantial repair work had been carried out on the roof. Many of the old cleft laths had broken, the inside plastering had fallen away and, as I mentioned earlier, most of the oak pegs by which the stone tiles were hung upon the laths had fallen out. The roof over the later, eighteenth-century, wing of the house was of 45° pitch and not ceiled on the inside in any way with the result that snow blew under the slates in quantity every winter. Many years before, my parents had appealed to their old builder to do something about this, whereupon he had 'torched' the slates upon the outside, a cheap and simple, but unsightly and injudicious remedy. In any case, much of this torching had since cracked and fallen away with the result that the snow trouble was now almost as bad as before. The older, medieval wing had a much more steeply pitched roof and we would sometimes be alarmed to hear a sound like a miniature landslip as one, or sometimes a whole patch, of stone slates slipped off the roof to crash either onto the garden side of the house or, more seriously, into the lane which ran close beside the back of the house. If anyone happened to be passing at the time we should have been liable for a serious claim for damages, but most fortunately this never happened.

After a particularly bad fall on the older part of the roof I summoned a Winchcombe builder to repair it. Obviously there could be no way of making a sound and permanent repair. All he could do was to push the peg-less slates back as best he could and apply some mortar to hold them there. When he had done this he came down his ladders white and shaking saying he had never seen a roof in such bad condition and that it was only by the mercy of providence that he had not brought half the roof down with him. It was obvious that something would have to be done so I asked whether the slates could be re-hung. The builder shook his head and assured me that the existing slates were all too rotten to be re-used and that to remake the roof with new stone slates would be prohibitively expensive if not impossible. He strongly advised me to re-roof with concrete tiles. Poor though I was, I refused to contemplate such a course which seemed to me as serious a crime as to chromium plate the nickel radiator on a vintage car.

It was Sam Clutton who pointed the way out of this dilemma when he advised me to seek the aid of the Society for the Protection of Ancient Buildings whose response was to send down one of their consultant architects. The choice of architect could not have been more appropriate for he arrived in a modern 3-litre Alvis and was, it transpired, a lifelong Alvis enthusiast, so this common interest put us on the best of terms immediately. On seeing the timbering of the roof he expressed the greatest surprise and appreciation, attributing it to the fourteenth century if not earlier. When asked on what grounds he dated it so early, he pointed to the massive size of the ridge piece or 'roof tree', explaining that it was only the earlier medieval builders who had yet to learn the fact that such stout ridge pieces were not necessary as they carried no more load than the weight of the ridge tiles. He would, he said, make the strongest recommendation to the society that they should endorse an application from me for a grant from the Historic Buildings Council.

The next development was that I received a most un-bureaucratic letter from an inspector in what was then the Ancient Monuments Department of the Ministry of Works.

He proposed a visit, explained that it was his job to evaluate the historic and architectural merit of a building and that he proposed to bring with him a colleague who would estimate the amount of work involved and its cost. He finished his letter by saying he was a fellow member of the VSCC and that he had long hoped for an opportunity of meeting me. On the occasion of his visit we spent a great deal of time closeted in my study discussing the merits and demerits of different makes of steam car while his colleague stumped up and down impatiently in the corridor outside. In fairness I should add that he did look at our roof and was as impressed as the SPAB architect had been, with the result that we were duly awarded a grant. This was an immense stroke of good fortune, for although I was just able to afford my share of the cost, I certainly could not have afforded the whole sum but would have been forced to adopt some cheap and unsightly expedient if the house were not to become uninhabitable.

On the recommendation of the SPAB architect, two brothers from Tyrley, a small village near Haw Bridge on the Severn, were contracted to do the work. They had lately re-slated the roof of the Ashleworth Tithe Barn for the National Trust and ours was a small job by comparison. When I told them what the Winchcombe builder had said on the subject of the slates being rotten and unusuable, they smiled and explained that had I accepted his offer to re-roof with concrete tiles he would undoubtedly have removed the originals 'to get them out of the way' and then sold them for a high price. By trimming some of them down to a smaller size if necessary, they estimated that they would be able to re-lay at least 90 per cent of the original slates, a forecast which proved suprisingly accurate. They were superlative craftsmen, so neat, precise and orderly that it was a delight to watch them at work. As most people are aware, in traditional Cotswold roofing the slate courses diminish in size from eaves to ridge, a fact which contributes greatly to the beauty of the finished roof. Our builders had a name for each size of slate and when, in 1957, they had reached the ridge on the second side and they had laid the last and smallest course (known as the 'Farewells' because they represented the end of the job) we broached a bottle of wine with them in celebration.

I had feared that when the roof was stripped it would be seen that some of the medieval timbering needed replacement, but in the event it was only necessary to renew one rafter. The builders did find, however, that the timber supporting the single dormer window in the roof, which was inserted in the seventeenth century, was rotten. But instead of pulling long faces as do most of their kind on making such an unexpected discovery, these craftsmen took it in their stride and in no time at all, it seemed, they had supported the weight of the dormer on jacks and packing and replaced the timber.

Over the next ten years the roof of the eighteenth-century wing deteriorated far faster than we had anticipated. Finally, it became the object of a second Historic Buildings Council grant and was reconstructed by the same builders. Because of that injudicious external torching, I had feared that a much higher porportion of slates would have to be replaced than had been the case on the older roof. However, in the event, the mortar flaked away from the slates very readily so that the proportion re-used was as high as before.

With a sound roof over our heads which will probably last for another two generations, we have been able to carry through, as our means have allowed, a long overdue programme of internal improvement, restoration and redecoration which the old house richly deserved. When I remember the words of H.J. Massingham's injunction to me on the subject so many years ago, at least I now feel I have honoured them to the full.

In return for the public money which had been expended on the house, we are under obligation to admit interested visitors by prior appointment during the summer months and are somewhat embarrassed when they naturally ask us what is the history of the medieval portion. The answer is that nobody knows for certain so that we can only conjecture. It is very unusual to find so early and so small a house built in what, in those days, must have been the grand manner. The interior is surprisingly spacious and the ceiling heights generous. Unlike the eighteenth-century wing which is built of rubble stone, the walls are of dressed stone laid in courses, albeit rather irregular ones. Sometimes a large squared block of stone may appear which extends over the height of two, or even three, courses. Again much of this stone is of a most attractive and unusual colour for this district, so that we speculate whether it may not have come from Caen in Normandy to be shipped up the Severn as was the stone of which Tewkesbury Abbey was built.

The manor belonged successively to the Abbeys of Winchcombe and Hayles, and my father always maintained that it had been built by one or other of these monasteries to house the priest who served the small Norman chapel of ease nearby. Built into the fabric of the free-standing chimney at the south end of the house is a small, carved niche, which obviously once contained an image, also a stone with a mass dial inscribed upon it. My father used to point to these as proof positive of his theory, whereas they are nothing of the kind. This area is littered with carved fragments dated from the time when Winchcombe Abbey was dissolved and its fabric became a convenient quarry.

We have come to the conclusion that a much more plausible theory is that it was originally a Court House where the manorial courts were held. The words 'Court House' certainly appear here on the earliest maps of the district, while one old document refers to 'that Stanley where the Court House is'. Since Sonia and I have lived here we have discovered traces of a blocked up arched entrance at first-floor level in the north gable end which had been rendered invisible externally by the building of the eighteenth-century cottage against it. The timberwork of the ceilings on the first floor are clearly of seventeenth-century date and the single west-facing dormer in the roof was added at the same time to afford extra light. Our theory is, therefore, that there was originally one large hall, open to the splendid roof, on the first floor reached by a tallet or outside stair, probably of stone, at the north end. Here, presumably, the manorial courts were held. On the ground floor there was originally one large room of the same floor area as the hall above and with a great open fireplace in the south gable. This is now divided into hall and drawing room by a partition wall of brick, presumably built at the time the building was converted into a cottage and an interior staircase put in, perhaps in the 1780s when we think the second cottage was built. Originally, however, we believe it was used as a single living room by whoever was responsible for looking after the Court House.

This manor was originally awarded by William the Conqueror to one of his henchmen Robert de Pont l'Arch, hence the curious name. Pont l'Arch is a town on the Seine near Rouen and boasts a railway station so called. Curiously enough, I was shown a photograh of a stone-built farmhouse in Normandy with a stone outside stairway which bears an almost uncanny resemblance to this house. The only major difference is that the roof is of thatch, but judging by the unusual height of the gable-end capstones above the line of the present stone slate roof, I speculate whether, when first built, our roof may not have also been thatched.

As a family we are devoted to this ancient house. But for its unique quality and its associations with my boyhood I would have found abandoning *Cressy* and going 'on the bank' very much harder than I did. But I confess that there have been many times when I have wished that, like *Cressy*, I could move it away to some more congenial surroundings. For the changes that have taken place in the surrounding countryside since the Rolt family moved into this house have been greater than any its windows have seen over the past five centuries with the possible sole exception of those brought about by the enclosure movement. And most of them have not been for the better where the vigour of English rural life and the beauty of the landscape is concerned. I do not pretend that they are unique, however. Unfortunately they are only a typical example of the revolution that has taken place in the English

countryside as a whole, with the exception of a few of the more
remote and favoured areas where the same process of change
has not yet become noticeable.

In the first volume of this autobiography I gave some
description of this part of Gloucestershire as it was when my
parents first moved into this house and their friends and
relatives thought them crazy to bury themselves in such
remote country. No one could describe it as remote today,
even though we do, at least, have the good fortune to live up a
dead-end road and so are spared the ceaseless, distracting
noise of passing motor traffic. But the road to Cheltenham
with which our lane connects is no longer a narrow and dusty
one but a widened tarmac highway carrying buses and an ever
increasing volume of motor cars, most of them commuters.

It was during the last war that this drastic process of change
really began. There were two principal factors involved. First,
there was the growth of the aircraft industry in the vicinity of
Gloucester, Cheltenham and Tewkesbury. The grid system
made this possible and the fact that Gloucestershire was
considered a safe area where bombing was concerned made it
desirable. Secondly, the need to produce more food from our
own land without increasing manpower began that process of
mechanizing agriculture which has now effectually depopulated the fields.

There is in the Cheltenham Art Gallery a rare picture, said
to have been painted in the early eighteenth century, which
shows the villagers at work in their common fields lying
between our Cotswold slopes and Bredon Hill. This shows
that in those pre-enclosure days they were, as Langland would
have said, 'fair fields full of folk'. There is even a company of
morris dancers performing in the foreground. The fact that
they are still known as Gretton Fields and Alderton Fields
presumably commemorates the days when they were owned in
common by these villages, but mechanization has completed
the process which enclosure began and the fields are now
emptied of life. They reflect this in their unkempt hedgerows
and generally neglected appearance, such as the empty plastic

fertilizer bags which litter the choked ditches. For unlike the equipment of the industrial machine shop, agricultural machines, although they may be faster and more economical, seldom do the job better than the older method they have superceded, in this case the man and the horse. For example, one man with a tractor equipped with an efficient modern hydraulically-controlled hedge-cutting machine can, in a few hours 'brush' a length of hedgerow that would take the same man as many days to trim by hand, but no machine has yet been devised which can lay a hedge and as this manual skill is rapidly dying out, hedges soon thin out and begin to look 'woody' and unsightly. Also, whereas the man could recognize and spare young saplings such as elm or holly, the machine cannot, so we can look forward to a day when there will be no more hedgerow timber and may realize when it is too late what a contribution this made to the beauty of the English landscape.

Despite the effects of enclosure, fifty years ago the population of the neighbouring villages was all directly employed in agriculture or else in some ancillary trade or craft which either served the local people, like the cobbler or the thatcher, or the local farming community, like the blacksmith, the wheelwright or the saddler. This common interest gave the village an organic link with the countryside around it besides welding it into a community. Now, in this area at least, this common interest has gone and our neighbouring villages, Bishops Cleeve, Gotherington, Gretton, Alderton, bloated with new building, have no links with the countryside and, because they have become mere dormitories for commuters, little communal life and only a nominal identity.

Because of mis-application of the well-intentioned Slum Clearance Act by a zealous Medical Officer of Health, most of the old village cottages I knew were condemned on grounds of their low ceilings, or lack of through ventilation. Even with the aid of the available local authority grants, their occupants could not afford alterations which would conform with local regulations. Consequently, such houses have been acquired by those who could afford reconstruction, executives or retired business men, with the result that they have been 'prettified' beyond recognition and embellished with such things as bogus wrought iron work of welded steel strip, carriage lanterns or wooden wheelbarrows filled with flowers. Meanwhile such old village families as have survived this upheaval live in council houses on the village outskirts from whence they are collected and delivered daily by special coaches which take them to work in the nearby factories.

By that process known as 'judicious infilling' whereby every available orchard or paddock in or around the village has been built upon, these raddled relics of the old villages I used to know are now surrounded upon every side by new houses. In the mistaken belief that they will thereby conform to the traiditonal style, most of these buildings are built in what I call pre-digested stone (blocks made from cement with an aggregate of pulverized Cotswold stone) or from sawn blocks of the genuine article. Apart from the fact that the former never appears to weather but retains indefinitely its raw yellow colour, the effect of both is equally unpleasing, especially when it is associated, as it usually is, with modern standard steel-framed windows and concrete roofing tiles. Although the blocks are produced in different lengths so that the coursing may be varied, a variation so produced naturally looks too regular and contrived while the surface texture is unpleasantly smooth. Presumably in an unsuccessful attempt to obviate this visual defect, some of these new houses are built from blocks whose external faces are rusticated so that their joints are slightly recessed. If anything the effect produced is even less pleasant than that of smooth blocks, especially as these roughened blocks are usually laid in cement mortar of a darker colour. The beautiful old Cotswold town of Winchcombe is now beset on three sides by a great area of new housing estates and, because site values and buildng costs have soared, in the more recently built houses all attempt at aping the regional vernacular has been abandoned. After so much ghastly good taste it is almost a relief to see such unashamed jerry building.

When a village has been 'infilled' in this way, it is the turn of the local council to step in by installing concrete lamp posts, side-walks with tarmac surfaces and high concrete kerbs, and conventional road name-boards for what were once quiet country lanes. Thus the whole village loses its rural identity to become a detached satellite suburb.

Except at weekends, these erstwhile villages and newly built suburbs are never fully populated. Weekends appear to be devoted to gardening, the ritual washing of cars or to watching the telly and the only vestige of communal life the customary foregathering in the village pub on Saturday nights or, more particularly, on Sunday noons.

I have described in *Landscape with Machines* how, as a boy, it was my delight in summer to ensconce myself in a seat I had made in one of the apple trees in our orchard and to watch the trains go by on the Cheltenham–Honeybourne line of the GWR which passes our house. The story of the decline and fall of this railway since nationalization reads like a tale told by an idiot although, I suppose, it could be paralleled in many parts of the country. In addition to expresses between Birmingham and the West Country or South Wales there was a regular local service of 'push-and-pull' trains which served all stations and halts between Cheltenham and Honeybourne. These trains were well patronized, particularly by housewives and school children, because they not only offered a quick service to Cheltenham but also to Gloucester by means of convenient connections at Cheltenham Malvern Road. To my certain knowledge many children used to travel daily to school in Gloucester from Gretton Halt and many adults from the village used to visit Gloucester market every week by this means. One could even travel to Paddington from Gretton Halt without too much inconvenience. I remember doing this on several occasions during our earliest years as a family at Stanley Pontlarge when, for one reason or another, it was inconvenient to take a car for the day, either to London or to be parked at a main line station. One left Gretton at 8 a.m., changing to a through train at Evesham and, in the reverse direction, off an evening express at Moreton-in-Marsh. But all this came to an abrupt end when in 1955 or '56, the Western Region decided to put in hand major civil engineering works.

When the line was built between 1900 and 1906 the contractors, Messrs Walter Scott & Middleton, made two fatal mistakes; they failed to ensure effective drainage of the cuttings and they did not remove from them at formation level the sticky clay which is found all along the base of the north Cotswold escarpment which the railway follows. Water-logged clay makes a chronically unstable base for permanent way and despite constant re-ballasting and tamping there had been endless trouble with sleepers 'pumping' or working, a slurry of clay and water spurting up as a train passed over them. It was also as a result of this treacherous clay that there had been much trouble with cutting slopes slipping. Now at last the Western Region decided to take the bull by the horns and put an end to these troubles by laying improved drains, by building retaining walls where necessary, and by the costly process known as 'track blanketing' which consists of removing the offending clay and replacing it by more suitable material. As a result of all this work, as Mark Smith, the then chief civil engineer, admitted to me, more money per mile was spent on the Cheltenham–Honeybourne line than on any other section of the Western Region over the period that had elapsed since the last war.

But – and it is a very large but – whereas if the GWR had tackled such an operation they would undoubtedly have planned it in such a way that single line working was maintained, the engineers of the Western Region had total occupation of the line for months. Meanwhile, through goods and passenger traffic was diverted over the old Midland route between Cheltenham and Birmingham, while our local train service was simply suspended until further notice. Now, if you suddenly decide to shut up your shop for six months or so, when you do decide to unlock the door again you cannot expect to see your faithful customers standing in a queue outside. Yet it was precisely this that the Western Region did appear to expect and were surprised to find that they had lost the local traffic to double-decker buses plying on an unclassified and totally inadequate road and taking nearly twice as long over the journey to Cheltenham.

While the civil engineering works were in progress, the 'push-and-pull' trains, which had worked the local service for years, were scrapped. They had been popular with the locals and, because of their ability to run in either direction at will, they were peculiarly suited to this particular service which entailed a reversal at Cheltenham Malvern Road so that trains could start and terminate at Cheltenham St James. When services were at last resumed, the unit used consisted of two standard GWR non-corridor thirds hauled by a 2-6-2 tank locomotive.

With this combination of a more expensive vehicle and fewer passengers the next move became inevitable – an application to withdraw local services and close all intermediate stations. This became the subject of a Transport Users Consultative Committee inquiry which I attended. From the outset it was clear that the result was a foregone conclusion. We were kept waiting in a cold and dreary room near Gloucester station until long after the inquiry was due before the members of the committee and the local officials of the Western Region came in together, laughing and joking among themselves. It struck me then that we were wasting our time; that while we had been sitting shivering, they had been settling the whole matter on an 'old boy' basis next door. To our questions they returned, with completely straight faces, replies so asinine in their illogicality that they insulted our intelligence. For instance, when asked why they did not replace the costly steam train with a small diesel rail-car such as they were running at that time on the Tetbury branch, we received the *Alice-in-Wonderland* reply that such a car would be insufficient to carry the traffic at present offering at peak periods. So we lost our local train service and all the stations and halts were demolished with almost indecent haste. Through passenger traffic lasted longer and my two sons were born just soon enough to see and to appreciate as I had done the sight of a steam-hauled Penzance express ('The Cornishman') thundering past our orchard. It was hauled by a *Castle* class locomotive now instead of the four-coupled *County* class engines of my own youth. But this proved to be only a brief interregnum before all passenger trains were switched to the Midland route and this late-built and most costly of railways was relegated to 'freight only' status. At the time of writing the big diesel locomotives still go grumbling by, though they have become invisible such is the wilderness of bramble bushes and sapling trees that has grown up on the railway banks which the local gang once scythed and made into hay each year. These diesels draw their trains of antique freight vehicles at far too fast a rate, and as there is only one surviving signal box in the twenty miles between Honeybourne and Cheltenham, there are no eagle-eyed signalmen to give early warning of a hot box. Consequently this malady is chronic and we recently had one of such magnitude that not only did the axle box disintegrate entirely, but the spring then cut through the axle causing major derailment and much damage to the track. The damage was eventually made good, but there are regular rumours of closure.

Meanwhile, so many of the villagers, now even the council house dwellers, have motor cars that our local bus service, like the train service before it, is running at a loss. Many people blame the private car for the decline in rural public services whereas the boot is often on the other foot; certainly in this area. I can think of many local people who would never have invested in a car, which they could ill afford, had it not been for the fact that a speedy and efficient train service was cut off at a single stroke. An aggravating factor here was the closure of Cheltenham's central railway station. What is now the only station, Cheltenham Lansdown, is an impossible distance away from the central local bus station, and as its rail services to Gloucester are now infrequent, it is virtually useless to the commuter. Dr Beeching and his ilk have a great deal to answer for.

So far I have described some of the changes that have taken place in the country round about. Where Stanley Pontlarge itself is concerned, the threat so far has not been from new housing development, but from the new mechanized agriculture and factory farming, the effects of which on the landscape have been as dire as that of the new housing estates in pre-digested stone. To some extent, of course, we sacrifice the landscape to our own comfort and convenience. I am reminded of this with an acute sense of guilt every time I look from my windows at the cat's cradle of poles and wires with which Stanley Pontlarge has been disfigured as the price of mains electricity and the telephone. But the so-called agricultural disfigurement has been far worse. In the previous volume of this autobiography, *Landscape with Canals*, I described how our neighbour Mr Bowl of Manor Farm could be seen leading his sheep down the lane wearing a smock and carrying a crook. Alas, under modern conditions traditional mixed farming, as he used to practice it, has become no longer economic, particularly on this belt of heavy clay land at the foot of the north Cotswold escarpment. It was to compensate for this natural handicap that some of the local farmers, including, unfortunately, at Stanley Pontlarge, took up factory farming.

When we first came to this house fifty-two years ago, our only neighbours, apart from the Bowl family at Manor Farm, were a Mr and Mrs Johnson who owned a small farm then known as the Close which was virtually no bigger than a small-holding. Sadly, the Johnsons lost both their sons in the Great War as a wall tablet in the little Norman church testifies. Consequently, there being no one to succeed him, Mr Johnson sold his farm to a man who, although of local extraction, had previously run a greengrocer's business in the Birmingham area and it was he who began factory farming. Our eastern windows look directly over the lane onto a green meadow where, in Mr Johnson's day, his Jersey cows had grazed. Now, under the new regime, there grew up in this once attractive meadow a hideous conurbation of Nissen huts and other ex-army portable buildings while what was left of the field gradually became a wilderness of nettles and thistles. For many years these buildings were used as battery chicken houses. During this period Stanley Pontlarge after dark resembled some large factory on night shift, to be seen from afar across the vale, the buildings blazing with light so that the wretched birds, imprisoned in their wire cages, would be persuaded by the illusion of daylight to continue laying throughout the twenty-four hours. When eventually battery chickens ceased to pay, the buildings were converted into intensive pig fattening units. At least this put an end to the lights at night, but the smell and the swarms of flies which we had to suffer each summer were worse than before. Apart from the fact that their muck was periodically spread on the surrounding fields, (a highly malodorous proceeding) neither chickens nor pigs had any organic relationship with the surrounding countryside whatsoever so that their 'concentration camps' might equally well have been situated in a town except that no townsman would tolerate so great a nuisance. Neither were ever allowed to see the light of day and their feeding stuffs were imported in ever larger lorries which came grinding up the hill past our house. The pigs arriving for fattening and those departing for slaughter travelled by the same means in huge cattle transporters.

Most of our visitors would mistake this example of the new farming for a derelict army camp and sympathize with us accordingly. The County Planning Officer, when appealed to on the matter, viewed it from my windows and, having admitted that he had seen nothing worse in the entire county, shook his head quite sadly and said that as they were agricultural buildings he was quite unable to help us. But there was an ironical twist to this as he went on to explain. He did have a measure of control over agricultural buildings erected within a certain distance of a classified road. In other words, if the road past our house had been a major highway howling with traffic we might have been spared this eyesore, but because it was a quiet country lane leading nowhere we had to learn to live with our affliction.

At about the same time we had another example of the curious philosopy that this planning policy reveals. This was a dispute over the route of a new 'super grid' overhead line from Melksham to Hams Hall. The issue was whether, in descending from the Cotswold escarpment into the vale, the line should run on the east or the west side of Langley Hill. While the easterly route would pass near new housing estates on the outskirts of Winchcombe, the westerly course meant that the huge pylons would march through a wild and lovely valley known as Frogalls Bottom, then pass between us and Dixton Hill before striding off across the vale in the direction of Bredon. At the public inquiry at Winchcombe, those of us who opposed the westerly route argued that it was surely better to carry the line through country already encroached on by new housing development than to impose it on a virgin and beautiful countryside. But we lost the day, the argument being that if the pylons took the easterly route, far more people would see them from their windows.

If the planning philosophy exemplified by our 'concentration camp' and by the pylons was to be applied on a nationwide scale it would surely mean that, with the sole exception of our National Parks, the whole of our English landscape would eventually be defaced by a thin coating of undesirable 'things in fields' instead of confining such things, so far as possible, to areas of existing industrial and urban development. Apart from this general consideration, I have always felt strongly that the immediate surroundings of any historic building such as ours on which public money has been spent should be subject to special planning protection. This view, which I have constantly pressed on the SPAB, was not prompted in the first place by the selfish considerations of my own case, but by the sight, many years ago, of a large and unsightly caravan site established cheek by jowl with the ruins of Valle Crucis Abbey in North Wales which the then Ancient Monuments Department of the Ministry of Works had lately restored. This was a flagrant example, but many other ancient buildings still suffer in this way.

Our local factory farmer flourished as the green bay tree and eventually acquired part of the lands and all the farm buildings of the Manor Farm in addition. He then initiated a series of actions which I could not do other than oppose with the consequence that we soon found ourselves in the thick of that most unpleasant of all situations – a bitter feud between neighbours.

When my father had bought his Alvis in 1925, because there was no suitable land near the house,* he asked his neighbour, Farmer Bowl, whether he might put up a wooden garage on a small patch of waste land in front of the Manor Farm buildings. Permission was freely granted and the existence of our garage was accepted by successive tenants and owners until our factory farmer came upon the scene. Then, without a direct word spoken, I received a letter from his solicitor instructing me, either to remove the garage within seven days or pay his client an exorbitant rental. In such circumstances I could not do other than consult my London solicitor, an old friend of my IWA days. On being told how long the garage had stood there, he pointed out that I had established a squatter's right to the garage. In reply to increasingly lengthy and threatening letters from my opponent's solicitor, he would reply very briefly: 'I shall require evidence of title' or, 'I still await evidence of title' until the farmer finally gave up the struggle. Naturally this contest did nothing to improve the atmosphere at Stanley Pontlarge.

Things got to such a pitch that if Sonia and I went away for a holiday we used to dread what fresh horror we might find when we returned. On one such occasion we got back to find the farmer and his son digging a trench in the lane beside our little church so as to lay a high concrete kerb. He had obviously acquired a job lot of these kerbs somewhere. I was

---

*   I have since been able to put up an inconspicuous two-car garage on a
     strip of additional land I have purchased and added to the property.

appalled. Apart from the fact that I loathed the prospect of our lane being given the semblance of a suburban street, I felt he had no right to tamper with a public highway. So I asked him to stop and, on being met with a refusal, rang up the local road surveyor who came over at once and ordered the work to stop. Finally, in consultation with the vicar and the local authority, a compromise was reached whereby a line of inclined and inconspicuous granite setts was laid by the local roadmen to form an edging to the strip of mown grass outside the church.

The effect of these two defeats on our opponent was that his bitterness towards us knew no bounds, so much so that, believe it or not, we thought our house might very probably burn down. Despite the warnings of the local fire prevention officer, on two successive Guy Fawkes' nights he built an enormous bonfire, as high as a two storey house, in his ruined field in a position only a dozen yards away from my house. On the first occasion we had arranged to be away and could only hope that the wind would be in our favour. In fact it was not and my mother was so terrified by the showers of sparks that flew over our roof-top that she sought the aid of our friendly neighbour from the Manor Farm house who very nobly patrolled my property until the fire died down. On the second occasion we were at home and again there was a strong east wind which blew sparks onto and over our roof in such a flowing river and with such violence that there was a very real risk that they would set fire to the roof timbers. In these circumstances I felt I had no option but to call the Winchcombe fire brigade. They arrived very promptly and, while some of the firemen went up into our roof, others quickly and calmly extinguished the bonfire with their hoses, ignoring the fire-crackers and the abuse hurled at them by the fire-raisers who seemed by this time to be almost demented. It was a most unpleasant situation.

One of our neighbour's least endearing characteristics from my point of view was his propensity for cutting down trees. He persuaded British Railways Estate Department to fell a fine row of trees that stood on railway property opposite our orchard on the pretext that they were shadowing his wheat-field. In this case I lost the day. I only knew of his intention when I heard the deadly sound of the chain saws buzzing, though I did my utmost to bring about an eleventh hour reprieve.

If there is anything calculated to raise my blood pressure it is the maiming or hacking down of trees, and here local philistines are not the only culprits. From my study window one day I noticed an officious-looking individual strolling about in the orchard belonging to my neighbour at the Manor Farmhouse. He was also peering in a suspicious manner over the drystone wall that divides the orchard from my garden. Always acutely mistrustful of such official snoopers, it was not many seconds before I was inquiring about his business. It appeared that he was an official of the Midlands Electricity Board and he calmly announced that he was proposing to fell – at the Board's expense, of course – three large old perry pear trees, two in my neighbour's orchard and a third, a particu-larly beautiful tree, that shades the lawn at the end of our garden. He explained that there had been so many cases of accidents caused to people gathering fruit for Showerings of Shepton Mallet through their aluminium ladders making contact with overhead power lines that his Board had ruled that all large fruit trees in the proximity of power lines should be felled. Now although the fruit of these trees is rarely used now, they are objects of delight at all seasons, while in spring, when they are covered with clots of white blossom, they take on a beauty that would have ravished Samuel Palmer. So I informed this official that, while I could not speak for my neighbour, he would cut down my tree only over my dead body, a reply whose vehemence evidently surprised him exceedingly. It was clear that he thought me eccentric to say the least. This particular story has a happy ending, for my neighbour supported me as I thought he would and, at the price of adding an extra pole to our wirescape, the cables in the vicinity were insulated and the trees spared.

I am aware that the foregoing account of what has befallen

this particular part of the Gloucestershire countryside makes sad reading. In this case time has not given but has taken away its rural character. Yet no one who has loved the landscape of England as I have could honestly fail to put on record the sweeping changes that have come about in the last thirty years, particularly as they are but a microcosm of what has occurred, or is in the process of occurring, in England as a whole. I console myself with the fact that I am old enough to remember the older, rural Gloucestershire that has been temporarily submerged. These memories, once given by time, time is powerless to erase. I write 'temporarily submerged' because, unlike the older Gloucestershire, the urban tide that has swept over it represents a society so unstable that it will ebb away as quickly as it came. I give it three generations at the most.

So far as Stanley Pontlarge itself is concerned, this chapter has a happier ending. Our local factory farmer has retired and his land and buildings have been acquired by a more amenable neighbour. Thanks to the munificence of the Landmark Trust*, it seems very likely at the time of writing that our view will soon be greatly improved, that the unsightly huddle of sheds in the fields opposite will disappear so that it will once again become a green pasture and that the present cat's cradle of poles and wires will be banished underground. Even if I should not live to see such a transformation completed, it is good to know that Stanley Pontlarge will once again look much as it did when first I saw it as a boy over fifty years ago.

---

* See next chapter for a full account of this Trust's activities.

8
Reflections

From Marlborough's eyes the streams of dotage flow,
And Swift expires a driv'ller and a show

Samuel Johnson

If his subject expires at the height of his powers when life is still
at full flood it is very much easier for a biographer or
autobiographer to shape his book into a satisfactory artistic
unity. Would our perennial interest in those romantic figures,
Byron and Shelley, be so great had they not both died young
and on a foreign shore at Missolonghi and at Spezzia? Despite
the unquestionable brilliance of the Brontës, would we find that
ill-fated family quite so fascinating had its early-flowering
genius lived on into old age? To bring this question within the
orbit of my own work, I do not think that my biography of
Brunel would have been so successful a piece of literature had it
not been rounded off by its subject's dramatic death while still
at the height of his powers, coinciding as it did with the first sea
trial of his most ambitious but ill-starred achievement, the
Great Eastern. Conversely, I found my biography of Telford a
far more difficult book to bring to a satisfactory conclusion
simply because its subject continued to live and to practise into
old age. His design for a Clifton suspension bridge, so correctly
scorned by the young and up-and-coming Brunel, was surely
the equivalent of the work of painter, poet or novelist whose
talents fail with advancing years. Whether they are aware of
such failure or not, the situation is equally tragic. But this is the
common tragedy of the human condition and one that it is not

easy for the biographer to turn to dramatic account. Men such as W.B. Yeats, whose poetry continued to change and develop into old age, are the exception rather than the rule.

It is in childhood and youth that an author's readers take delight, not second childhood. As we grow older we naturally tend to become more conservative and less venturesome when it comes to setting our hands to some new work. We tend to talk more and to do less and, for the readers of biography or autobiography, the doing is always more interesting than the talking. It would seem that the older people grow the more the committees they are invited to serve upon. This activity gives them the illusion of 'doing' without the physical effort. Such invitations assume that the recipient is a wise man, but unfortunately your habitual committee man all too often suffers from what I can only describe as a 'corridors of power' complex. He cherishes the belief, that when he comes to the committee room he is influencing the course of history by shaping events and the destinies of men. Yet the committee minutes seldom support such illusions of consequence but make dull reading.

Since 1956 or so I have been, as I still am, a member of many committees, mainly devoted to some aspect or other of what is generally called 'the amenity world', in other words that small minority concerned to fight against the philistines and the destroyers with the object of preserving what is left of the English landscape and those infinitely varied and meaningful man-made things associated with that landscape which represent the English tradition. To say that my part in these activities would make dull reading is not to imply that such bodies do not do a good job. They most certainly do.

Only three of these committees deserve mention here because they are, or were, connected with personal interests of long standing. These are The Inland Waterways Redevelopment Committee, The Council for British Archaeology's Industrial Archaeology Research Committee and, lastly, the Science Museum Advisory Council.

I served on the Inland Waterways Redevelopment Committee from 1959 until 1962. It was appointed by the then

Minister of Transport, Mr Ernest Marples, to advise him what was best to be done about certain derelict, or at least moribund, sections of the canal system. Our periodic tours of inspection, which took us all over the country from Kendal in West-moreland to Taunton in Somerset, were most enjoyable and instructive. Enjoyable, because my colleagues were all such interesting, intelligent and likeable men, especially our chairman, Admiral Parham, who personified everything I expected a retired Admiral of the Royal Navy to be like. He used to come out with the most delightful nautical phrases. It was interesting because it made me intimately acquainted from the towpath with precisely those waterways which *Cressy* had been unable to visit, and so greatly increased my first-hand knowledge of England's canal system. The so-called redevelopment schemes were mostly concerned with eliminating canals by infilling and the majority were prepared by the Inland Waterways Executive, although two came from local authorities. Those put to us by the former included figures showing profit and loss, the latter always featuring an item headed 'Head Office Expenses, Proportion'. This increased steadily from year to year, indicating to me that, while the waterway system contracted, the administrative machinery responsible for it did not, and I speculated whether our shrunken railway system was burdened in the same way. If it was, then the process of creeping paralysis initiated by Dr Beeching becomes easier to understand.

A proposal to infill the Ashton Canal came from Manchester Corporation and a similar scheme for the Pocklington Canal from the city fathers of Sheffield. Both were remarkable for their ineptitude, a fact I found saddening because, in principle, I am all in favour of the decentralization of government. The city engineer of Manchester described his scheme for the Ashton Canal, which consisted of constructing a series of concrete basins, or 'lagoons' as he called them, to supply the various canal-side mills which depended on the canal for water. These were to be connected to each other by lengths of buried pipeline, but this was where he had failed to do his homework. The canal is (or it was at that date) in the vicinity of an active colliery and we had therefore ascertained beforehand from the NCB the subsidence anticipated in the area over the next twenty years and learned that it was considerable. I forget the actual figures now, but it was something of the order of six feet. When we asked the engineer whether his pipes could withstand that amount of settlement without fracture, the corporation's scheme collapsed like a house of cards.

Sheffield Corporation proposed to use the Pocklington Canal as a convenient dump for semi-liquid slurry from their nearby water-softening plant on the Derwent. The engineer responsible for this scheme explained how he proposed to lay a porous pipe in the bed of the canal before dumping began. This would allow the moisture in the slurry to drain away, leaving a solid residue to be covered with a layer of earth so that the site of the canal could gradually be restored to agriculture. At this point a representative of the local drainage board rose and asked the engineer if he was aware that a substantial portion of the canal was regularly flooded in winter. Once again the engineer was completely confounded and another 'redevelopment' scheme collapsed in ruins.

In these two cases, as in most of those for infilling advanced by the Inland Waterways Executive, we rejected the schemes as either impracticable or too costly, recommending restoration in whole or in part as a cheaper and more desirable alternative on the grounds of multiple use – land drainage, water supply and amenity. We also supported two out of three positive restoration proposals submitted to us by the Stratford Canal Society, the Kennet & Avon Canal Trust and the Derby Canal Society. The lower part of the Stratford Canal was subsequently restored and is now owned by the National Trust.* The Kennet & Avon is a much bigger and tougher proposition. We recommended that restoration work should begin at both ends with the idea that the canal could start earning revenue from pleasure traffic as soon as possible and although this has been adopted there are still some years to go before the two sundered

---

* [Later returned to British Waterways.]

ends are joined.* Only in the case of the Derby Canal did we come to the regretful conclusion that the canal was too far gone to make restoration a practical proposition.

It was towards the end of this committee's life that a conservative government abolished the British Transport Commission as transport overlord and replaced the old executive by a newly appointed and autonomous British Waterways Board whose members, including as they did Admiral Parham and my old friend Charles Hadfield, pursued a far more positive policy than their predecessors. It was to this new Board that our committee's recommendations were passed and as many of them have since been acted upon, I feel that we really did achieve something worthwhile.

The Council for British Archaeology is a government-assisted body whose object it is to encourage, promote and co-ordinate research and field work into sites of every period from the remotely prehistoric onwards. It is also concerned with the recording of threatened sites and with their preservation where possible. To this end it works closely with government representatives of those departments concerned with the preservation of historic monuments. In December 1959 the CBA organized an Industrial Archaeology Conference at which it was decided to add to its various 'period' committees an Industrial Archaeology Research Committee. To this committee I naturally gravitated, for it was recruited on an *ad hoc* basis from anyone who seemed likely to make a useful contribution. I had been interested in this subject long before it acquired its present cumbersome but aposite title. For although my primary interests had been vintage cars, canals and railways, these had soon widened to include all the visual three-dimensional evidence of the industrial revolution in Britain. If I were asked what single event had been responsible for firing this wider enthusiasm, I think I would say that it was my first visit to the Ironbridge area during the last war.

The present and growing popularity of industrial

* [The canal was re-opened by the Queen in 1989.]

archaeology may be said to stem from the setting up of this committee. One of its first objectives was to persuade the government of the day to finance a national survey of industrial monuments. To this end I spoke about the significance of these monuments to the Conservative Arts & Amenities Committee at the House of Commons in March 1962. Exactly a year later, at the instigation of Pat Lucan, I addressed the Labour Party equivalent to the same tune. It was a consequence of such campaigning that the national survey was authorized with my friend Rex Wailes as survey officer. It was remarkable how, as he travelled the length and breadth of the country carrying out his survey, local societies seemed to spring up in his wake wherever he went so that what had been a minority interest, in the passage of very few years, became a popular nationwide pursuit engaging people from every walk of life. I had only one personal experience of the way in which this movement snowballed when I joined Rex Wailes in addressing a meeting at Stroud where a Gloucestershire Society for Industrial Archaeology was founded there and then.

How to account for this sudden popularity? Many reasons have been given: that because the industrial revolution – surely the most significant revolution in man's history – began in this country, we possess industrial monuments of unique significance. Also, that the process of change and the forces of destruction have gained such momentum that these monuments are very much at risk and that unless forces could be mobilized to defend them, all too frequently it was a case of here today but gone tomorrow. This is all true, but speaking for myself I would say that what has all along attracted me to industrial monuments, be they beam engines or buildings, is their quality. Their social consequences may have been disastrous; they may have been built by grossly underpaid labour, working overlong hours and living under appalling conditions, yet they reveal the most superb and painstaking craftsmanship. Work of such quality is almost poetic in its significance, especially bearing in mind the conditions under which it was done. Such workmanship surely reveals that even the humble artisan shared the conviction that he was helping to build a new and better world. It is bitterly ironical that, in fact, the world they helped to create would have no time for the craftsman and little appreciation for his handiwork. It is a world which, just at this time (1962) wantonly destroyed the Euston Arch. This great arch was the supreme industrial monument because it was a memorial to the craftsmanship and the aspirations of all those thousands who, captained by Robert Stephenson, had laboured to build Britain's first main line. On the part of the philistines who connived at its destruction it was a compulsive, ritual act of repudiation of all those values which the arch stood for. But their vandalism has recoiled on their own heads for, by revealing the magnitude of the threat, the destruction of the Euston Arch has mobilized the opposition forces with the effect that such a thing would not happen today.

Because the steam railway was the one form of transport that we indisputably pioneered in England, I have for a long while been convinced that Britain of all countries ought to possess a National Railway Museum that would worthily represent a national heritage that changed the world. The existing set-up whereby such a museum became the responsibility of our nationalized railway system was entirely due to Lord Hurcomb, the first Chairman of the Transport Commission, who displayed a great respect for the railway past, a quality in which his successors have shown themselves sadly lacking. Because they are so manifestly inferior to their great predecessors who created our railways, is, I believe, the psychological reason for their almost pathological concern to destroy all evidence of that past. In what other way is it possible to account for the needless destruction of the Euston Arch, that supreme symbol of past greatness, and of much else besides? They justify such acts with jargon about the need to create a new and progressive public image. Yet what image, one might ask, has their mean work succeeded in creating? It struck me as sheer folly to entrust to such men the great heritage of the railway past, especially when they declared quite openly that it was their job to run a railway and not to run a museum, a statement in which there is, at least, a certain logic.

After years of indecision and argument over a site for a new railway museum, the BTC finally offered its unfortunate Curator of Relics a disused bus garage at Clapham as a man flings a dog a bone. A less suitable place for a railway museum it would be difficult to conceive. Lacking any form of rail access, it was impossible to move any large object into or out of the museum except at vast expense, with the result that all the steam locomotives and rolling stock became frozen like so many ships in bottles. For the same reason it was impossible to make Clapham a live steam museum despite the fact that some of the locomotive exhibits there were in steamable condition. Nevertheless, the Clapham scheme went ahead but, even when it had been set out as well as it could be, it remained closed to the public for some months because the then chairman, Sir Brian Robertson, sensible of British Railways' heavy deficit, felt that the public might see the new museum as a piece of needless extravagance.

These briefly were the reasons why I decided to make the creation of a National Railway Museum the object of my latest, and probably my last, campaign. The opportunity to fire an opening shot occurred in 1960 when I read the Conservative government's Bill abolishing the British Transport Commission and setting up autonomous Boards in its place. Now the Relics and Records Departments had hitherto been administered directly by the BTC, as was only natural since they were originally intended to cover all forms of transport. Yet there was no mention of them in the new Bill, nor any clue as to who would be responsible for them in the future. It was obvious to me that the drafters had been unaware of their existence. On consulting an MP friend of mine as to what would be the best course to take, he explained that such questions, as to who should be responsible for what, were usually decided by the Prime Minister personally and he went on to suggest that if I would draft a suitable letter, he would send it over with his signature to Mr Harold Macmillan. This I duly did, pointing out the omission and suggesting that the opportunity should be taken to transfer the relics to the then Ministry of Education, now the Department of Education and Science (DES). It was evident from his reply that the PM did not accept this proposition though he promised action of some unspecified kind. In the event this took a most unsatisfactory form. He made the new Railways Board temporarily responsible for the relics and charged them to prepare a scheme for their long term future and submit it for approval to the Ministry of Transport by a specified date. Many people besides myself felt that this was a wrong decision and that such a scheme should have been directed to the Ministry of Education and not to the Transport Ministry which was not in the least interested in the future of museum collections.

This was the state of play when, by the greatest piece of good fortune, I was invited to join the Science Museum Advisory Council which gave me a unique opportunity to press my view of a National Railway Museum as an 'out station' of the Science Museum. At the same time I was able to lobby sympathetic MPs on the Conservative Arts and Amenities Committee whom I had met earlier in connection with the Industrial Monuments Survey. The latter effort culminated when a party of MPs were taken by bus from the House to Clapham to view the collection. As a result of this visit, they said they were prepared to back such a scheme provided it could be shown that it was workable. The then Director of the Science Museum, Sir David Follett, also favoured the scheme and was able to begin exploratory talks with Mr John Scholes who was responsible for the Clapham Museum. All this activity was just as well because the so-called 'scheme' submitted to the Ministry of Transport proved to be little more than an application for a mandate to disperse the Clapham Collection. Of the other two collections for which the Railways Board was temporarily responsible, the new Great Western Museum at Swindon and the original Railways Museum at York, responsibility for the former passed to Swindon Corporation, but the future of the latter remained doubtful.

Negotiations were still going on when a general election took place and a Labour Government took office. To my great satisfaction, however, the Transport Bill introduced by this new government contained clauses authorizing the transfer of the Clapham and York collections to the Science Museum and

their removal to a new museum building sited in York. With the
choice of York as a site for the new National Railway Museum I
had nothing to do except to endorse it as a member of the
Advisory council. It was a part of the bargain between the
government and British Railways that, in return for being
relieved of their responsibility for the collection, they should
provide a new museum building on a suitable site, financing the
operation by the sale of the Clapham property. A reconstruction of the existing steam motive power depot at York was
proposed by British Railways and approved by the Science
Museum. Personally I had no strong feelings as to where the
new museum should be. A much more important thing to my
mind was that the building should be suited to the display of
large locomotives and that it should have good access to some
railway that was most unlikely to be closed, thus enabling the
exhibits to be moved around or got out of the museum and put
into steam. None of the three existing museums possessed these
essential attributes whereas the new museum building at York,
with its two turntables and radiating tracks, certainly did. What
was equally important was that it offered the possibility of
future expansion which the old sites did not. Unless a museum
has room to expand its collection, eventually it becomes
fossilized and dead.

So far all appeared to be going well, but the powers that be
were soon to learn what I had already learned by bitter
experience – that whatever you may do you cannot please the
railway enthusiasts. They contain more wrong-headed cranks
per thousand than any other body of men I have ever
encountered. As soon as the York proposal became known a
babel of confused protest broke out from their ranks. Some, for
reasons best known to themselves, began a 'save Clapham'
campaign; others argued that the new museum should not be
confined to railways but should represent all forms of transport.
Apart from the fact that such a museum, if truly representative,
would have to be of huge and bewildering size, it ignored the
fact that other forms of transport were already adequately
catered for by existing specialist museums at Stoke Bruerne

(canals), Beaulieu (cars), Crich (trams) and Hendon (aircraft). Almost the only aspect not catered for was the theme of urban transport, but these protestors ignored the fact that the Science Museum Advisory Council had already agreed that the London Transport exhibits at Clapham should remain in store in London with a view to their eventual display in a museum of just this character sited in the London area. In fact, most of them are already on display at Osterley. Yet another body of enthusiasts maintained that the new museum must be in the London area and, despite the fact that it was up to British Railways to provide the site, gratuitously advocated alternatives.

Most unfortunately, when the Labour Government's Transport Bill was in debate, the guillotine put an end to it before the clauses concerned with the setting up of the York Museum had been considered. Yet another change of government gave the dissidents their opportunity and they appealed to the ombudsman on the ground that the issue had never been discussed. By this time work on the new museum building had already begun, but owing to this ill-judged intervention, it was now suspended while, so that justice should be seen to be done, Lord Eccles, the new minister responsible, weighed the York scheme against the rival proposals. It was the York scheme which ultimately prevailed. When work was eventually resumed, the target date for completion was 1975, the 150th anniversary of the opening of the Stockton & Darlington Railway. Owing to the current recession, it now seems unlikely that this target will be achieved.*

One of the sad things about growing old is the loss of friends. In recent years I have suffered a number of such casualties. Two of them were Harry Rose and Mark Newth, the only surviving friends of my school-days, the others representative of my varied interests: Laurence Pomeroy of the VSCC, Pat Lucan, a friend from the early days of the IWA, and from the railway world that delightful character Tommy Salt, railway enthusiast, veteran car-owner and champion of the Welshpool

---

* [The York Railway Museum was opened by The Duke of Edinburgh in September 1975.]

& Llanfair Light Railway, David Northesk, Edward Thomas, that old and staunch ally, and George Tibbitts, the Warwick solicitor, a most endearing character who for many years acted as honorary solicitor to the Talyllyn Railway Company. Dear old George wrestled indefatigably on behalf of the company, most notably over the acquisition of land for the extension of the railway to Nant Gwernol and it is sad that he did not live to see his work completed and the extension actually under construction as it is now. The latest loss has been Sir Arthur Elton from the world of industrial archaeology. He was best known for his work in the film industry, but what I most valued in him was his rare appreciation for the art of the industrial revolution, an appreciation which I share but in which I have benefited immensely from his tremendous enthusiasm for, and knowledge of, this neglected but fascinating aspect of the subject.

Yet I count myself fortunate that in my case I have made new friends to redress such losses. I think of two particularly whose friendship has proved especially valuable and life-enhancing, Doctor Richard Harper of Barnstaple and J.L.E. Smith. To call them new friends is misleading, for on leafing through past diaries to discover when it was that I first met them, I find with a shock that it will soon be twenty years since they came into my life with such rewarding results.

I met Dick Harper at Llanthony Abbey in 1956. It was on the occasion when I first introduced Sonia to a place that had exercised so great an influence on me, both in my childhood and on my return thither which I have described earlier. Ten years had then elapsed since my last visit, and as we drove down in the Alvis on a perfect June day, I recall a growing feeling of trepidation as to what changes might have occurred since my last visit. I need not have worried. Nothing had changed. The old tranquillity and the old magic still invested the place.* I

---

* Alas, this is not longer altogether true today. As a result of the making of a road over the Gospel Pass, where there was previously only a grassy track, the valley has been invaded by an increasing volume of people and motor cars at holiday times and summer weekends, a trend that has

usually looked forward to meeting congenial company there, but our meeting Dick Harper and his wife was an unexpected bonus and proved the beginning of a most valued and enduring friendship.

Dick Harper, it appeared, was a regular visitor although we had never coincided before. It became clear that he had been drawn to the place in the same fashion as I had been, and this common attachment was the starting point of our friendship. He had for years been a great student of evolutionary theory so that his heroes were Darwin and Mendel and, like a good evolutionist, he professed no religious belief. Although I have never subscribed to any particular religious creed, I consider my own philosophy to be fundamentally religious and anti-materialistic, and as that philosophy had largely grown out of my love for the Black Mountains and Llanthony, the fact that he and I should find so much common ground may seem unlikely. Yet it might surprise Dick to know that I consider him one of the wisest and most saintly men. I found in him a great reverence for life in all its forms and that basic humility that recognizes the limitations of man's knowledge and his power. While professing no religion, he has the keenest awareness of the mystery of life and it was here that we found common ground. He has a long-cherished theory, still not accepted by the medical world, of the influence of evolutionary vestiges upon illness. Many modern diseases including cancer are, he believes, due to ancient evolutionary mechanisms in the human body which, having long lost their original purpose, are triggered off under modern conditions of stress to operate in a harmful manner. Although I have little knowledge either of evolution or of medicine, we have had long discussions on this subject which I find utterly fascinating and convincing. I am quite certain that although Dick's theories may not win acceptance in his lifetime, they will eventually revolutionize our

---

become more marked since the Severn Bridge was opened. At such times the valley and the abbey have become a place to be avoided, although one can still easily find solitude on the mountains.

knowledge of the origins of many diseases and thus profoundly change methods of treatment.

The recollections of our discussions as we strolled together in the high-banked lanes around Llanthony after dinner, when the sun was setting behind the mountains and the summer dusk was falling, are now among my most cherished memories, for owing to advancing years and ill-health Dick Harper can no longer travel so far afield from his native Devon. Yet we still keep in touch both by telephone and letter. Although they are very different characters, this exchange of correspondence reminds me of that earlier exchange of letters with the late H.J. Massingham which I found so stimulating during the last war.

It must have been shortly after I first met Dick Harper that my old friend Sam Clutton expressed a wish to see Eddie Moore 'plating' scythe blades under his water-powered tilt hammer at Middle Mill, near Belbroughton. I had first met Eddie Moore of Middle Mill during the war and knew that he was about to retire and that with his retirement the mill would close, so it was a question of now or never for anyone who wished to see this ancient process in action. So it was arranged that Sam would drive up from London and meet us for lunch at the Bell Inn at Bell End, between Bromsgrove and Stourbridge. Later, he telephoned to ask if he might bring an interested friend with him. This friend turned out to be John Smith. We found we shared so many interests that it was a case of friendship at first sight. When I look back over the years that have since passed, no single individual has done more to enrich and enhance them. To say any more than this would be to embarrass him.

At the end of his entry in *Who's Who*, John names his favourite recreation as 'Improving the View' and this is not just a humorous quirk but is quite literally true. So far as my experience goes he has contributed more towards the preservation of the English landscape and its buildings, including its industrial monuments, than any man living, though so unobtrusively that few people are aware of the fact. If other rich men applied their wealth to such good purpose, England would be transformed. He is extremely perceptive, and possesses an insatiable appetite for the individualistic, the eccentric and the bizarre both in people and things, for all, in short, that adds a spice to life. For this reason he has given his support to a great variety of unusual enthusiasms and causes. At the time I first met him, John was playing an extremely active part in the National Trust and, as a member of the IWA, was also deeply interested in canals. He served with me on the Inland Waterways Redevelopment Committee, and it was he who was responsible for persuading the National Trust to become responsible for the Stratford Canal.

In 1963, John became disenchanted with the National Trust and though after a while he returned to this particular fold, there was an interim when his abundant energies lacked an outlet. He has often allowed me to stay at his London house in Smith Square when my business in town required me to stay overnight. It was sometime during this year that I arrived there to find him poring over the columns of *World's Fair* and, on inquiring the reason, he told me that he was planning to organize a Great Steam Fair in the grounds of his house, Shottesbrooke Park, at White Waltham, near Maidenhead. It was to be a once-only event the like of which had never before been seen, certainly not in the period following the last war. To this end he went to immense time and trouble to track down the best examples of such traditional fairground 'rides' as still survived, gallopers, a scenic railway, steam yachts, a helter-skelter, a big wheel and so forth. This painstaking quest also included appropriate side-shows and, in this department, he succeeded in discovering rarities such as a flea circus which few people would have believed still to exist. He even contrived a 'bioscope', the fairground parent of the cinema, actually showing short early films to the accompaniment of appropriate piano music provided by an elderly man who was one of the last survivors of the days of the small-town silent screen. To power this bioscope, which was complete with high-kicking dancing girls and a bowler-hatted barker with a big drum, an enthusiast lent and manned an authentic example of the type of steam generating set which was originally used for such shows.

For supplying power to the big rides, such as the gallopers, or the scenic railway, John had to rely upon the amateur owners of showman's engines as, although these rides were traditional, their professional owners had long ceased to rely on steam power to travel and to power them. The ubiquitous diesel had taken over. The amateurs responded magnificently to the idea, but the professionals, naturally, were much more cautious, especially as many of them had to make long journeys far from their accustomed circuit in order to appear at Shottesbrooke. They would not do so to satisfy what they regarded as a rich man's whim unless they were guaranteed against loss. This meant that if the Great Steam Fair proved a failure due to public apathy, bad weather or a combination of both, John stood to lose a very substantial sum of money.

The Great Steam Fair was finally scheduled to open on the last weekend in August 1964, opening on Friday 28 August and closing on the following Sunday evening. On the preceding Thursday afternoon, Sonia, myself and our two boys motored down to Shottesbrooke from Stanley Pontlarge to render such help as we could. It was an absolutely unforgettable occasion. The weather was perfect throughout, while it became evident from the moment of opening that the fair was going to prove overwhelmingly popular. So much so that at times the roads round about became blocked by traffic queues and it was just as well that there was almost unlimited car-parking space available in the park. The fair itself was laid out in the space immediately in front of the house and included attractions such as Harry Lee's Steam Yachts which a younger generation of southerners had never seen. For Harry Lee had hitherto confined himself to travelling in Yorkshire and had never come south before. Incidentally, his steam yachts really were what they claimed to be, being the only major ride to be steam-powered, The other rides drew their power from a ring main supplied by an impressive row of gleaming showman's engines, Fowlers and Burrells, drawn up in front of the stable block.

It was over this supply of power that the only real hitch occurred in the arrangements, although only a very few of the public realized the fact. As the enthusiastic owners of these engines very soon discovered, it was one thing to take their engines to a traction engine rally and display them quietly turning over or slowly perambulating a parade ground; to be asked to work them hard and continuously from noon until well after dark proved a very different proposition. With one significant exception, these amateur enginemen proved unequal to the task, and although they managed to keep their glittering monsters ticking over to the admiration of the crowds, the amount of current they were able to pump into the ring main was quite inadequate. Fortunately, one of the professional showmen, perhaps a pessimist, had brought along a powerful diesel generator and this, discreetly concealed from the public eye in a nearby shrubbery, made good the deficiency. Most owners of the showman's engines blamed the coal for their shortcomings. John had asked my advice on what coal to provide, and from my past steam experience I had recommended Welsh Steam which was supplied to all engines throughout the duration of the fair by a small Garrett steam tractor and trailer. It was soon apparent that most owners were unaccustomed to the use of such fuel and kept up too thick a fire with the effect that they complained bitterly of burnt firebars. Had they applied the rule of 'little and often' they would have had little trouble. If any of these owners should happen to read this and feel aggrieved by my remarks, I can only point to the exception, the engine belonging to my old friend, the late Tommy Hunt of the Griffin Foundry, Oldbury.

Tommy Hunt was a splendid Black Country character with whom I had first become acquainted through our mutual interest in the Talyllyn Railway. In that connection he had proved a tower of strength, promptly supplying anything the railway might need in the way of castings from his foundry at no cost. When John was planning his fair, I had told him that Tommy was a 'must' and the latter had responded by bringing down his magnificent Gavioli fairground organ with a small Burrell showman's engine to draw it and power it. In addition to this outfit, Tommy also brought down his Foster showman's engine. This stood apart from its fellows and, because it was less showily finished than they, it attracted less public attention. Only the knowledgeable could appreciate the fact that whereas the other engines was merely turning over most of the time, the Foster, as could be heard from its exhaust beats, was working hard, pumping its full quota of current into the main. As Tommy remarked to me in his broad Black Country accent, it was just a question of knowing how.

Both Sonia and I were kept busy, usually by relieving other volunteer helpers so that they could have a break. Sonia assisted with the ox roasting, while I found myself performing several unusual roles such as taking a turn in the paybox on the bioscope. Little did I think I should ever find myself working beside a vociferous barker and two high-kicking dancing girls. From my position beside the entrance I could hear the piano tinkling away inside so I was amazed when the old accompanist suddenly emerged and, with a broad wink at me, sloped off in the direction of the nearest beer tent. Suffering as he did from an unslakeable thirst, he had had the forethought to provide a tape recording of himself and the necessary reproduction equipment so that he could gratify his periodic craving without ostensibly interrupting his performance.

Our work for the fair was enough to give us the satisfaction of feeling we were active participants, but not so exacting that we could not enjoy the fair to the full. Walking around, it was astonishing how many friends and acquaintances I met. They were representatives of all my varied interests, vintage cars, railways, canals and even the world of publishing. It seemed that they all found common ground in the fascination of this fair. It was for them as for me a never to be forgotten occasion, a kind of feast of Crispian where those absentees, hearing accounts of it afterwards, would 'think themselves accurs'd they were not here'. For John had no intention of making it an annual event and most people realized they were experiencing an unrepeatable occasion. Nevertheless, its success had an important long term effect. With the sole exception of the Travelling Circus, which alone might have done better had the weather not been so perfect, John did not have to pay out any guarantee money to the professionals and the money they had earned over the three days made them realize the value of traditional 'rides' as nothing else could. Potential organizers and amateur owners of suitable fairground equipment were also suitably impressed, with the effect that 'Old Time Steam Fairs' have ever since been popular annual fixtures in many parts of the country and showmen like Harry Lee no long confine the appearance of their rides to a particular district. Yet, in the minds of participants and spectators alike, there will always be one one Great Steam Fair. One night, accompanied by the Smith family, we climbed up to the roof of the house after dusk had fallen to look down at the panoramic view of the fair spread out below, the rides and side-shows outlined with multi-coloured lights and the bright glare of arc lamps lighting up the shifting crowd and the smoke and steam of the engines that drifted overhead. It was this picture that I carried away.

It was in the year following this unique event that John and his wife Christian started the Landmark Trust 'for preserving small buildings, structures or sites of historic interest, architectural merit, or amenity value, and where possible finding new uses for them; and for protecting and promoting the enjoyment of places of historic interest or natural beauty'. This is financed by a more general charitable trust which they had founded a few years earlier. This Landmark Trust was not intended to compete with the National Trust in which John has again become active. On the contrary, the Landmark acts as a kind of safety net by saving those small properties which, for lack of any endowment or for some other reason, the National Trust is unable to assist. In this way the two Trusts frequently act in concert. In the case of most of the properties which the Landmark has acquired since 1965, they are funished either wholly or in part and so made available for short term letting. This gives practical expression to the word 'enjoyment' in the Trust's aims for, as John has so rightly written 'to appreciate a place properly it is not enough to see it briefly by day; it is essential to go to sleep there and wake up there and be there in all lights and weathers.' He adds that many of those who stay in a Landmark 'just for a holiday return with an interest in "conservation" which will last them all their lives and greatly benefit us all.'

I have mentioned the Landmark Trust in some detail because, since 1965, it has become very much a part of our lives. For soon after the Trust was founded Sonia was asked if she would be responsible for furnishing its properties and this proved a most fascinating and exacting job in which I have naturally taken a close and often active interest, just as she has done in my own activities. With the needs of different properties in mind, she buys furniture at local auctions, has it renovated where necessary, and arranges for its delivery to what was once the laundry of Sudeley Castle, near Winchcombe, which the Trust rents as a store. Here, when the collection of furniture for a particular property is complete, it is loaded for delivery to Cornwall, North Wales or East Anglia as the case may be. Where a large property is involved, the delivery is done by professional removers, but usually the amount of furniture needed is not too great and in such cases she has hired a self-drive van, and, having loaded up, we have set off together for our destination, sharing the driving between us.

I have said that this job is exacting and challenging because Landmark properties vary so widely in character and period. Also, because the bulk of the Trust's resources must necessarily be devoted to restoring its properties, coupled with the fact that they are destined to be occupied by a long succession of tenants, to furnish a place with pieces wholly 'in period' is out of the question, particularly at present day prices. Consequently, to furnish appropriately places so varied in character as a medieval tower on the walls of Caernarvon, a gothic temple at Stowe, the eighteenth-century Luttrell's folly tower on the shore of Southampton Water, the engine house of the old Danescombe Mine near Calstock, the Egyptian House at Penzance, an eighteenth-century cotton mill in Edale, or the stationmaster's house at Alton station requires considerable thought, ingenuity and discernment. It has frequently happened that, having set out the furniture in such places, Sonia and I have camped for the night in them before starting on the long journey home. In this way we have become the first to occupy them and the first to appreciate their unique quality. It has been for us both a most rewarding exercise. It has been, as John puts it, equivalent 'to making a new home half a dozen times a year'. This comment stresses the laborious part of the job; its satisfaction comes in seeing a bare room suddenly come to life and acquire a character so right and so natural that it might have been there from the beginning. I have said that John is unusually perceptive, but why he chose Sonia for this particular job is a mystery because I do not myself know from what source this talent springs and neither does she. I have speculated that it may come from her past theatrical experience, but she denies this. I have often helped to load into a van what struck my untutored eye as a depressing load of assorted junk, yet when furniture and pictures are unloaded and put in their intended places, they are mysteriously transformed.

The Landmark Trust also assists by donation other worthy causes to an extent that is not widely realized. The extension to our Narrow Gauge Railway Museum at Towyn; the restoration and removal to Penrhyn Castle of an ancient locomotive *Fire Queen* from Dinorwic; the rescue of the cruiser *Belfast* and her removal to a permanent mooring on London River opposite the Tower; the transfer of the two Beam Blowing engines from the Lilleshall Ironworks to the Blists Hill site of the Ironbridge Gorge Museum. But the most important donation of all, in my opinion, was the very large contribution made by the Landmark towards the repair of Abraham Darby's famous iron bridge, the first in the world, at Coalbrookdale.

The state of the iron bridge, the most important industrial monument in Britain, had been the cause of great concern for many years. The Ironbridge Gorge is geologically unstable and, as a result, the massive stone abutment on the Ironbridge side of the river was slowly but remorselessly moving inwards, bringing increasing pressure to bear upon the bridge causing some of the cast-iron arch ribs to crack. For years the bridge had been scheduled as an ancient monument, but this failed to mend matters. Rescue was obviously going to be a very expensive operation and for years the Shropshire County Council and the Ancient Monuments Department were locked in fruitless argument as to which should bear the brunt of the cost. The department argued that as the responsible authority for highways and bridges in the area, the county council should assume prime responsibility. To this the county council replied that it was not prepared to spend a great deal of ratepayers' money on a bridge that had been closed to vehicular traffic for many years. On the contrary, as the bridge was scheduled as an ancient monument it was clearly up to the department to initiate repair work. This stalemate dragged on for so long that many of us feared that the bridge would lie in fragments at the bottom of the river by the time it was resolved. It was the Landmark Trust's donation which was really responsible for setting in motion the present costly rescue operation which includes the construction of an inverted reinforced concrete arch beneath the river to hold back the abutment.

Another recent event which has given me immense pleasure and satisfaction has been the dramatic salvage of Brunel's *Great Britain* from the Falkland Islands and her voyage home to her native Bristol where she now lies in the dock where she was built and where she is now being restored to the condition in which she was launched. I confess I was lukewarm about this project when it was first mooted, arguing that so much money was needed to save industrial monuments at home, most notably the iron bridge, that we could ill afford such an extremely costly salvage operation. However, when the munificent Jack Hayward came forward with his offer to meet the entire cost of bringing the ship home, the whole situation was completely transformed where I was concerned and the *Great Britain* Project now has no more loyal and enthusiastic supporter.

In my biography of Brunel I told how, after being damaged by a storm when rounding the Horn in 1886, the gallant old ship managed to limp back to the Falkland Islands where she was condemned and converted by the Falkland Islands Company into a hulk, a floating store for wool and coal. I also told how, following an unsuccessful attempt to raise funds on the part of the then governor of the islands, in 1937 she was towed away to nearby Sparrow Cove where she was holed, beached and left at the mercy of the sea. There, I wrote, 'the indestructible hull of Brunel's splendid ship may still be seen'. But what I did not realize when I wrote these words was just how indestructible she was and envisaged a rusting skeleton of bare ribs. It was not until 1964 that I realized just how complete her hull still was when I was sent a set of photographs of her taken recently by the Admiralty fishery protection vessel, HMS *Protector*. Yet it was apparent to me from these pictures that she could not last much longer. For a close examination of the photographs revealed that the hull had been seriously weakened when the ship had been converted into a storage hulk by the cutting of an access door in her starboard side amidships, and she was beginning to 'hog' and must eventually break her back. The reason for this · became apparent when the hull was inspected on the spot by Dr Ewan Corlett, the naval architect, a man who has since become the technical brain behind the project and who knows more about the history of the *Great Britain* and her construction than any man now living. The ship had been run into the cove in such a way that her bow was hard aground. Meanwhile the action of the tides over a period of nearly thirty years had been to scour away the shingle aft with the effect that the ship's stern was hanging in deep water. By the time of his visit, the hogging had become much worse than it was in the 1964 photograhs and a large and sinister crack had appeared in the vicinity of the access door. So the rescue operation, like that of the iron bridge, came only just in time.

Although they had been unable to save the ship, the islanders were proud of her – she was the only object of historical interest they had to show visitors. Also, they were extremely sceptical of the outcome of the salvage operation and some were not a little chagrined to see their one show-piece disappearing. Yet any hard feelings of this kind were very soon dissipated for, on behalf of the islanders, the governor presented to the project the ship's bell which had been brought ashore for safekeeping. It is now exhibited in Bristol where it has since acquired a fitting companion.

Only a short while ago I received a letter from a correspondent informing me that the bell of Brunel's first ship, the *Great Western*, was hanging in the hall of a large country house which had become the headquarters of the South Eastern Gas Board. How on earth had it got there and why had its presence passed without remark for so long? The story sounded so improbable that, as my correspondent had not seen the bell himself, I wrote back asking whether he could confirm by the evidence of his own eyes. Having received such confirmation, I passed the news on to Ewan Corlett with the result that the bell will shortly hang beside that of the *Great Britain*. I understand that the project has since tracked down the whereabouts of, not one but two *Great Eastern* bells, so that tangible reminders of all three of Brunel's great ships may soon be hanging side by side at Bristol.

It was in connection with the *Great Britain* that, by a curious coincidence, I made a discovery which carried me back to pre-war days. I had been invited to join the *Great Britain* Restoration Committee and drove down to Bath to attend its first meeting at Lord Strathcona's house in Lansdowne Crescent. Lord Strathcona was a leading member of the project and one of the lucky few who had gone out to the Falkland Islands at the time of the salvage operation. When I walked into the room in which the meeting was to be held in the company of my host, my eyes were at once drawn to an oil painting on the wall. This depicted, in side view, a 1903 Humberette which looked remarkably like the car I used to own and which I drove regularly in the Brighton Run in the thirties.* It was even painted in the same shade of green which I have used for all my vintage and veteran cars from my first G.N. onwards. I remarked on this similarity to Lord Strathcona whereupon he asked me if I could remember what the registration number

---

* See *Landscape with Machines*, plate 21.

was. 'FH 12', I replied promptly. 'Then that's the very same car', he assured me, nodding in the direction of the picture, and adding 'I'm the owner now.' Unfortunately, I could not see the car itself because it was at that time garaged in Birmingham and although I was promised a run in it for old times' sake, for one reason or another this has never been achieved. I had lost track of the old car completely and, although I have not seen it in the flesh, it was nice to know that it was still in running order and in good hands.

> Of dying man
> His living mind
> By writing deeds
> His children find.

I noticed, and noted down, this inscription over a cottage doorway at Welcombe during the brief period that Sonia and I spent at Aller Park in the spring of 1953. The lines now seem prophetic although, not having the gift of prophecy, I cannot think what made me use them to preface the first volume of this autobigraphy. Any writer likes to console himself with the reflection that his written words will long outlive him, that 'he being dead yet speaketh'. But at the time I wrote that book I had been lucky enough to pass the age of sixty without ever having had any serious illness or seen the inside of a hospital. Some racing driver has written, I think it may have been Charles Jarrott in his classic book *Ten Years of Motor Racing*, that the longer his car went on running perfectly the more convinced he became that some dire mechanical disintegration was due, the more disastrous for being so long postponed. Perhaps subconsciously I harboured some such pessimistic notion about my own health. If so it certainly proved to be correct. For nine months after *Landscape with Machines* was published in the summer of 1971 I had to go into hospital for what proved to be only the first of a series of five major operations which, separated by brief intervals when a return to normal health seemed likely and I was able to lead a normal life, have been spread over the past two years. During my second and third operations, which followed closely upon one another in the early autumn of 1972 I literally 'diced with death', to use a motor racing cliché. Now, in February 1974, sixteen months and two operations later, it has become clear that, although I won that particularly hard-fought game, I have not won the match and that my expectation of life may be measured in months rather than years. It is, after all, a match that we must all lose eventually, some to be hurried out of life suddenly and unexpectedly and others to await their end as philosophically as may be. As Dr Johnson said, the latter situation certainly 'concentrates the mind wonderfully'.

To undergo such an experience naturally raises the question whether the pain and discomfort suffered by the patient on the one hand, and on the other the skill of his surgeon aided by all the costly equipment and know-how of a modern hospital, are really worthwhile. To this my own answer is an unhesitating 'yes'. For one thing, but for this reprieve I could not have produced this book, much of which was written in hospital and all of it since my health broke down. More important than this, however, has been my intense enjoyment of life during the all too brief periods of reprieve. The reason for this is difficult to explain. Although I may have believed at such times that I was on the road to full recovery, I yet felt in some strange way like a *revenant*. It was as though the bonds attaching me to this world had already been loosed so that I possessed no longer any natural right to be alive. I found that I had lost my fear of death, and this I suppose is natural because it is not 'easeful death' itself which we fear but the pain and suffering associated with it and I have had my fill of that already. But because I no longer fear death does not mean that I have grown tired of life – far from it. Each day and its events, some of them quite trivial, has become infinitely precious to me. I have maintained all my varied interests, so far as this has been possible, with even greater enthusiasm. Above all, I have learned to value and appreciate my friends more than ever before. I must admit that I have always been more interested in things than in people and the fact that I now feel quite otherwise is by no means wholly due to the way they have rallied round Sonia and myself during this time of adversity. Of this I will quote but one example. Following my major operations in 1972, I reached the stage of convalescence just as we were entering the dead of winter. Quite unknown to us, a number of old friends in the VSCC had clubbed together and offered us a three-week holiday in the Algarve in southern Portugal, with a house and a car at our disposal, something which we could not possibly have afforded. As a consequence, we flew out of a grey England flecked with patches of snow into a June climate where the sun shone from cloudless skies. Not only did I return feeling twice the man I was when I left England, but it was a shared experience of rare pleasure which made all the darkness that had preceded it seem worthwhile.

But the most important result of this shared adversity has been its effect on the relationship between Sonia and myself. It is impossible to describe this, for to say adversity has brought us closer together, or that our relationship has been deepened and mysteriously enriched, implies that it was in some way lacking in depth before, which would be wholly untrue. On the contrary, when I look back over the past twenty-three years I realize the full extent of my good fortune in having such a partner. They could never have been so happy and so fruitful had they not been shared with her. So much so that I marvel now that at the outset I could ever have harboured doubts as to the strength and lasting quality of our relationship. Our only regret now is that we did not meet sooner so that we could have shared a greater part of our lives together. Looking back on our lives before we met, I can see how we both made the same mistake of consciously willing our former marriages. In a sense, we both married the canals. Although it is true that I was deeply attracted to Angela, the decisive factor was *Cressy* and the fact that Angela took to a life afloat as a duck takes to water really determined the outcome. Ironically, however, that she took to the life as readily as she did, was a symptom of her incurable wanderlust which was one of the many reasons why our marriage finally broke down. As for Sonia, she married the canals in an even more literal sense by marrying a man who, as a canal boater himself, personified that way of life. This, for reasons even more obvious, was a marriage doomed to failure. The lesson we have learned from the past twenty-three years is that the strength and durability of a relationship between two people rests on the depth of that relationship and not on any preconceived notions, however romantic, as to how life should be lived. I know that for my part I became so obsessed with my 'design for living' on *Cressy* that I could not see beyond it, with the result that it ultimately ended in unhappiness. On the other hand, I began my life with Sonia under most inauspicious circumstances when we had no idea how the future would work out. That it has worked out so well, so fruitfully and so completely happily has been entirely due to the strength of our relationship.

If there is any truth in Dr Johnson's dictum which I quoted earlier, then this book is perhaps the better for having been written under such adverse circumstances. For it is natural at such a time to look back dispassionately over one's past life, to assess the gains and the losses and to ask oneself whether at any stage one should have acted otherwise. Reviewing my varied interests and the activities associated with them which I have pursued, although these have sometimes developed in ways that I could not possibly have foreseen and which, in some cases I do not now think wholly desirable, nevertheless I do not regret my part in them because I consider the gains to be much greater than the losses.

To take such causes in chronological order, they begin with the founding of the VSCC and the inauguration of Prescott. Where the VSCC is concerned it is somewhat ironical that it began as a very small club for poor men and is now a very large club for very rich men, at least so far as its most active members are concerned. This is no fault of the club but is simply due to changes in the society in which we live. In a world of mass production in which money steadily diminishes in value, a vintage car like any other surviving example of craftsmanship and quality, has come to be regarded as a gold-chip investment commanding a phenomenal price. Hence, such cars are frequently bought by investors who are not enthusiasts and who store the car where it can never be seen by the public and would not dream of driving it in anger. But, apart from this sad fact, the mere knowledge that their cars carry such an extravagant price tag must necessarily affect the thinking of even the most enthusiastic club members and unless they are very well-heeled it makes them hesitate to hazard their expensive properties by competing regularly in club events. It was quite otherwise in days when one could buy a good 30/98 Vauxhall for £50 or less.

As for Prescott Hill Climb,* it continues to give pleasure to thousands of motor racing enthusiasts each season. In the 1950s the course was extended by the construction of a new loop in the belief that it would make the hill more attractive for spectators. Personally, I doubt whether it has achieved this objective and I secretly regret it because the sense of continuity has been lost, records made today being no longer comparable with those set up earlier over the old course. By virtue of the gentleman's agreement made before the war, the VSCC still has the use of the hill for one meeting a year and it is significant that the club prefers to use the older and shorter course. In 1973, a special meeting was organized by the Bugatti Owners' Club over this short course to celebrate the 35th anniversary of the opening meeting. I was very glad that ill health did not prevent me from competing in this event by driving my faithful Alvis up the hill, just as I had done at that opening of the hill thirty-five years earlier. This car will be fifty years old this year (1974), and since the passing of *Cressy* it has become my oldest and best-loved material possession. Except during the war years, it has never been off the road except for periodic overhauls and, as the preceding chapters reveal, in all my activities it has been my faithful companion. To those who argue today that in order to conserve precious resources we should build our cars to last longer it has surely become an object lesson.

---

* See *Landscape with Machines*, p. 194.

Turning now to the canals, who could have envisaged the tremendous enthusiasm the IWA has now generated and the influence it now wields? Such activity is no longer confined to boating but to navvying; gangs of volunteers, often knee deep in mud, are to be found hard at work restoring derelict canals. What would have surprised us even more in 1947, such works now enjoys the blessing, and often the active cooperation of, British Waterways and local government. Nevertheless, one of the things I most regret when I recall the canals as I knew them is the passing of the working narrow boat. I realize now that even if our early effort to improve conditions for the boaters had been more successful, given the present economic climate, they could only have postponed by a few years the inevitable end of the narrow canals as a way of life. It was the fact that these canals were the territory of a colourful and unique community that made my years aboard *Cressy* so memorable. That is why the present 'cruiseway' system with its ever growing population of pleasure boats seems a poor thing compared with the canals I was fortunate to know. The moral is that you can preserve material objects, but you cannot preserve a way of life. Yet I console myself with the thought that, but for our effort, much of our canal system would either have been filled in or become neglected ditches choked with weeks and rubbish. Instead, they have been given a new lease of life, albeit a different one, and give to thousands a pleasure which has brought to their lives a fresh dimension. In particular, the Welsh Canal, where *Cressy* was the first boat to venture soon after the war, has now become the most popular of cruising waterways. So, despite its unhappy ending, on balance I do not regret my years of canal crusading. Such an ending cannot, after all, take away the value and satisfaction of the achievement.

After the working narrow boat, the thing I most regret is the passing of the steam locomotive. In retrospect, it seems to have happened so swiftly. When we founded the TRPS in 1950, the passing of a machine which had been an object of awe, wonderment and delight to me since earliest childhood seemed inconceivable and did not enter into my calculations at all. Yet the disappearance of steam from British Railways has attracted to the steam-hauled Talyllyn Railway an ever increasing flow of passengers. The success of the Talyllyn has also sparked off a great railway preservation movement, not only in this country but world-wide. I remember that when a scheme to re-open the Festiniog Railway came to successful fruition a few years after we had taken over the Talyllyn, I entertained misgivings as to whether there was a sufficient reservoir of enthusiasm and money to support two railways. Surveying the railway scene today this now seems a comical misjudgement. And yet I cannot help wondering, with the passage of time, whether it may be shown that the results would have been better if efforts had been more concentrated and less diffused. But railway enthusiasts are a peculiar breed. Each has his or her own particular pet railway and the mere fact that so many railways appear to have been successfully preserved becomes sufficient reason for starting yet another preservation society.

A big question mark that hangs over the long term future of preserved railways, particularly those of standard gauge, concerns their steam motive power. Who will cope with the locomotives when they need a major overhaul and, in particular, a new boiler? The number of steam locomotives, in this country alone, which enthusiasts have preserved is truly remarkable, yet I cannot help feeling that the future of many of them is by no means certain. Some quite short preserved lines seem to have collected locomotives far in excess of their real needs and I speculate whether this may not solely be due to too much zeal but to ensure the long term working future of the railway by building up a reserve of motive power so that when one locomotive has been run into the ground it will be possible to replace it by another. If this is the case then it is the negation of preservation.

My experience on the Talyllyn Railway has convinced me that it is impossible to preserve the life of a steam railway just as it has proved impossible to preserve the life of the narrow canal system. Both were fated either to die or to change. Like the canals, the preserved railways now handle a prodigious volume of pleasure traffic which has necessitated physical changes in the railway itself to enable it to cope and so subtly transformed its character. I am aware that when we took over the Talyllyn it already relied primarily on holiday-makers, but it performed a small local function. In 1951/52, when I was running the railway, we still carried local passengers down to Towyn on market days, while local Towyn tradesmen still brought parcels and sacks of meal to the Wharf station for delivery to farms up the line. Although such traffic made an infinitesimal contribution to our revenue, I valued it greatly and enjoyed entering particulars in the weighty leather bound parcels book which Edward Thomas had so scrupulously kept.

I mourn the disappearance of the rural branch line just as I do that of the working narrow boat. As is evident from the first part of this book, we and our friends made great use of branch lines when *Cressy* was moored in deep country. I remember with particular affection the Midland & South Western Junction Railway which we used in the early years of the war for journeys between Hungerford and Cheltenham, or the old Cambrian line from Whitchurch through Ellesmere to Oswestry over which we made many journeys during our pioneering voyages up the Welsh Canal. For me no preserved line can ever make up for the loss of such railways as these any more than a 'cruiseway' can be an effective substitute for a working narrow canal. Yet, here again, half a loaf is better than no bread and I do not regret the part I have played in the railway preservation movement. As in the case of the canals, such railways have given, and will continue to give, pleasure to many thousands of people and there is great satisfaction in that knowledge.

In reviewing *Landscape with Machines* in a provincial daily, a very dear and loyal friend of mine called me the 'Patron Saint of leisure hobbies' and the words were used as a headline for the review. That such a form of beatitude surprised me does not imply false modesty or that I do not appreciate the intended compliment. 'Hobbies' is a word that has never occurred to me in describing my varied activities, and in order to explain why this is so brings me to the influence of my ideas upon my actions. Although ideas are the mainspring of action, the space I have devoted to them in this book stands in about the same proportion as do *High Horse Riderless*, *The Clouded Mirror* and *Winterstoke* to my total literary output. I believe with Eric Gill that the artist is not a special kind of person but that every man is a special kind of artist given, I would add, the opportunity. It has been my aim in life to create such opportunities in a civilization which denies them. There is much talk nowadays about the wastage of precious natural resources brought about by the economic concept of unlimited growth* in a finite world. Yet nothing at all is said about the equally disastrous wastage of man's creative potential to which the same concept has led. It has been my aim from first to last to find outlets for that potential and not merely to find new ways of occupying leisure time.

In 1965 we celebrated the centenary of the Talyllyn Railway, and of the many events which were held at Towyn in that year it was the service of thanksgiving in Towyn parish church that remains most clearly in my mind. Plate-layers' tools and a wagon were arranged in the crossing of the church and, most appropriately, the service was conducted by the Revd W. Awdry, celebrated as the author of the 'little engine' books for children. He asked me to read the lesson for which he had so aptly chosen the famous passage in praise of craftsmen from Ecclesiasticus, Chapter 38. After describing the work of different craftsmen, the ploughman, the smith and the potter, it concludes as follows:

All these put their trust in their hands; and each becometh wise in his own work. Without these shall not a city be inhabited, and men shall not sojourn nor walk up and down therein. They shall not be sought for in the council of the people, and in the assembly they shall not mount on high . . .

---

* This concept of unlimited growth is really another name for that assumption of automatic material progress which H.J. Massingham, myself and a few others denounced thirty years ago.

But they will maintain the fabric of the world; and in the handywork of their craft is their prayer.

So eloquently and in such magnificent language do these words express my own belief that I found myself profoundly moved; so much so that I could scarcely get the words out and nearly made a fool of myself in consequence.

It has been vastly encouraging to see such a multitude of volunteers from all walks of life happily engaged on so many different manual tasks. But projects of such magnitude cannot depend on the work of spare-time volunteers alone. More encouraging and significant to me have been the number of people who have given up well paid and promising careers in industry and come to work for one of these projects full-time, accepting a much lower salary and insecurity for the sake of the creative satisfaction that such work brings.

In *High Horse Riderless* I emphasized the importance of education in bringing about the changes I advocated and among the conclusions in which I summarized the book's argument was this one:

That the conflict developing between a generation so educated and conditions of life and work becoming increasingly stultifying may lie the foundation of a renaissance.

The outcome of my own activities is not the only sign that this is happening. An increasing number of the younger generation seem determined 'to do their own thing' despite the carrots dangled enticingly before them by the world of commerce and industrialism. At the moment, many of them fail to find their bearing and become mere aimless drifters, despised by the majority. Yet I cannot help feeling that these signs of revolt may prove in the long term to be a good thing. For, again, as I wrote in *High Horse Riderless*, 'we are witnessing, not the laborious construction of a new world, but the ruin of a civilization which, like a tower built upon a quicksand, sinks faster than we can add brick to brick.' This ruin appears to be coming about far more quickly than I could ever have believed. When it comes it can only be succeeded by some more self-sufficient form of society designed to make the fullest and best use of natural resources and human ability. It is in such a society that I believe those who have opted out will find their niches. It is certain to be a slow and painful process of transition, but less painful for those who have already contracted out than for those who still cling to the tenets of our consumer society where, in the words of Wordsworth, 'Getting and spending we lay waste our powers'. In order to produce more we must consume more and we are all urged along this fatal course by a vast advertising machine designed to make today's luxuries become tomorrow's necessities. Nor can we look to either of the main political parties to break this vicious circle because both are chiefly concerned in trying to win a bigger slice of a diminishing cake for their respective supporters. And yet an awareness of the necessity for fundamental change has become more speedily apparent than I had dreamed possible. For example, the word 'ecology', from being virtually meaningless to the majority thirty years ago, has now become almost an over-used cliché. But it is an easy matter to pay lip-service to inexorable ecological rules; to practise them, as we must, is a far harder and more difficult matter.

There was a time when I used to wonder what attracted me so powerfully about such old and traditional features of the English landscape as men and horses at plough, or innumerable watermills and windmills. Was it merely nostalgia, a yearning for the 'good old times' which never existed in fact? I now know that it was much more than this; that what attracted me about such things was their eternal quality. They did not depend, as our civilization depends, on the depletion of the world's limited resources of capital. If we are to survive as a species, it is to this simpler, harder and more realistic world that we must ultimately return.

To sum up, looking back over my life, I consider I have been singularly blessed. I have known the true meaning of love and I have been able to live a varied life of intense creativity. The thought that such creativity has brought pleasure to so many people is a great source of satisfaction and consolation to me at this moment. But this, so to say, has been a spin-off, for the source of my greatest satisfaction has been the creative work itself, quite apart from its results or rewards or such little celebrity as it may have won for me. I have had many good friends and made, to the best of my knowledge, very few enemies. I have not consciously wronged anyone and I have no regrets for opportunities lost or for what might have been. Hence when the end comes I think I shall experience a sense of sorrow such as one feels when a long and supremely happy holiday draws to a close, but certainly there can be no sense of bitterness, no remorse or regret. Certainly I have never succeeded in making much money, but money and true happiness seldom go together. Though it may be thought presumptuous of me to do so, I shall end this book by echoing the words of that great engineer, Richard Trevithick, as he lay dying at Dartford: 'However much I may be straitened in pecuniary circumstances, the great honour of being a useful subject can never be taken from me, which to me far exceeds riches.'